Roger B.

AF693144

Mini/Microcomputer Hardware Design

George D. Kraft
Wing N. Toy

Bell Telephone Laboratories, Incorporated

Prentice-Hall, Inc., Englewood Cliffs, New Jersey 07632

Library of Congress Cataloging in Publication Data

KRAFT, GEORGE D (date)
Mini/microcomputer hardware design.

Includes bibliographical references and index.
1. Minicomputers—Design and construction.
2. Microcomputers—Design and construction. I. TOY, WING N., (date) joint author. II. Title.
TK7888.3.K7 621.3819'58 78-13605
ISBM 0-13-583807-X

To our families—
Peggy, Stephen, Mark, and Michael Kraft
and Romayne, Liane, Arthur, and Sue-Lin Toy

Editorial/production supervision and interior design by Marianne Thomma Baltzell
Cover design by Edsal Enterprises
Manufacturing buyer: Gordon Osbourne

© 1979 by Bell Telephone Laboratories, Incorporated

All rights reserved. No part of this book may be reproduced in any form or by any means without permission in writing from the publisher.

Printed in the United States of America

10 9 8 7 6 5 4 3 2

PRENTICE-HALL INTERNATIONAL, INC., *London*
PRENTICE-HALL OF AUSTRALIA PTY. LIMITED, *Sydney*
PRENTICE-HALL OF CANADA, LTD., *Toronto*
PRENTICE-HALL OF INDIA PRIVATE LIMITED, *New Delhi*
PRENTICE-HALL OF JAPAN, INC., *Tokyo*
PRENTICE-HALL OF SOUTHEAST ASIA PTE. LTD., *Singapore*
WHITEHALL BOOKS LIMITED, *Wellington, New Zealand*

Contents

2

DIGITAL LOGIC CIRCUITRY *68*

4

THE ORGANIZATION OF MEMORY *175*

5

MEMORY REFERENCING TECHNIQUES *214*

6

THE ELEMENTS OF AN INSTRUCTION SET *266*

7

CONVENTIONAL AND PLA CONTROL *306*

8

PROGRAM CONTROLLED INPUT/OUTPUT OPERATIONS *364*

9

CHANNEL-ORIENTED INPUT/OUTPUT OPERATIONS *427*

Preface

Originally, this book was meant to be a text on the use of minicomputers. It evolved, during its writing, into a presentation of the hardware design of small-scale processors (the term *processor* and *computer* are used interchangeably). The book attempts to address the techniques for designing and using a small computer. A decision had to be made early in the development of the manuscript as to what emphasis would be placed on software. Since both of us work on a day-to-day basis with software considerations *as well as* hardware design techniques, our natural tendency, at first, was to include detailed aspects of software development. However, we both believed, and still believe, that software techniques for the mini/microcomputer require a separate text entirely. Therefore, the approach taken in this manuscript has been to address the hardware and systems aspects of using small-scale computers.

In particular, every attempt has been made to treat these computers as *computing components*, to be distributed in an application environment in a cost-effective manner so that everyday maintenance is simplified and the overall system reliability is improved. Because of this approach, we have addressed, both in the text and in the end-of-chapter Problems, the control aspects of small computers that are embedded in applications from a *philosophical* point of view. *Flowcharts* are emphasized as opposed to the coding of individual programs designed to run on a specific mini or microcomputer. Detailed software definitions and concepts have been relegated to an appendix. We believe that this approach makes the hardware interconnection of the various components used to interface with an application more obvious. In addition, the detailed control considerations can be generalized instead of being closely associated with a specific small machine.

With the veritable explosion in LSI technology, writing a book on mini/microcomputers is analogous to trying to describe the exact position of a moving target. Consequently, we have tried to present fundamental concepts, definitions, and well-established design techniques in each chapter. We have attempted to use the Problems at the end of each chapter as a vehicle to introduce state-of-the-art concepts. The Problems have been deliberately designed to be *difficult*. In many cases, there is no one correct answer but, instead, a family of solutions which the reader must first identify and then attempt to optimize. The book has been designed with the college junior, senior, and first-year graduate student in mind. It can also serve as a reference for the practicing electrical engineer and/or computer scientist who has a need to work with mini/microcomputers. The text is neither definitive nor exhaustive in terms of its description of hardware control techniques used at the mini and microcomputer level. It is an exposition of ideas and philosophies that we believe are directly relevant to the direction in which the new LSI technologies are taking the whole field of computing—namely, *distributed processing*.

Chapter 1 deals with the historical evolution of the small computer from the ENIAC and the Mark I down to the latest mini/microcomputers designed around microprocessors used as central processing elements. The Problems at the end of this chapter specifically address the practical aspects of acquiring a mini/microcomputer system and what, exactly, is distributed processing.

Chapter 2 covers the digital logic circuitry used to configure a small computer. Included in this discussion are the types of various storage elements, a description of integrated circuit technology, and the details of such LSI devices as ROM, PROM, EPROM, PLA, and RAM. Some of the Problems at the end of this chapter apply these devices to *unconventional* situations.

Chapter 3 addresses the basic architectural features of a generalized computer. Data transfer circuitry and busing systems are treated as *fundamental* design components of any digital machine. The concept of a computer family is introduced; how this concept has been observed by both the mini and microcomputer manufacturers is discussed. The Problems at the end of this chapter develop these ideas further.

Chapter 4 considers the organization of internal storage and deals with such concepts as the working register set, a read/write register array, and the usage of a last-in-first-out (LIFO) buffer or push-down stack. The Problems associated with this chapter address the practical hardware realization of various memory structures.

Chapter 5 deals with the development of a useful word length for a specific processor and the possible instruction formats that may be employed. The various techniques used by a central processor to reference an operand in main storage are developed in detail. These addressing techniques are discussed in terms of their actual hardware implementation. The Problems apply these addressing modes to various central processor structures.

Chapter 6 defines the instruction repertoire of a digital machine and gives one approach to classifying its command elements. Some consideration is given to optimizing instruction set design in terms of the needs of a given application.

Chapter 7 covers the conventional design of the control section of a small computer and an alternative implementation of the control logic using a programmed logic array. A practical design example is considered and then expanded in the associated Problems at the end of the chapter.

Chapter 8 explains the details of program-controlled I/O operations at both the mini and microcomputer level. Included in this section are discussions on polling techniques, interjection, and interrupt structures.

Chapter 9 considers the overall concept of a channel and what constitutes a direct-memory-access operation. In addition, the use of a serial communication channel is explored from the points of view of implementation and reliability.

Five appendices offer the reader detailed information on: (a) MOS technology, (b) bipolar technology, (c) the characteristics of software, (d) the Bell System's MAC-8 microprocessor, and (e) the Tandem 16, a high-reliability commercial minicomputer.

This manuscript was developed over a period of five years as part of the In-Hours Continuing Education Program (INCEP) at Bell Laboratories. Portions of this material were also developed in courses taught at the University of California at Berkeley and at the Illinois Institute of Technology in Chicago.

Acknowledgments

Many people, have contributed to the completion of this manuscript. Four individuals, in particular, were instrumental in our undertaking the writing of this book: John R. Sheehan, formerly of Bell Telephone Laboratories and now with Western Electric, and E. Pierce Felch III, W. A. Depp, and E. A. Irland, all with Bell Laboratories. Without the personal support and encouragement offered by *each* of these men, this manuscript would not have been initiated.

A deep sense of appreciation is felt for the Bell Labs Education Center and Norman F. Foster, who took on the partial support of our effort under the Bell Laboratories In-Hours Continuing Education Program (INCEP). That support never wavered during the years it took to complete the manuscript. Special thanks are extended to Professor E. S. Kuh and Professor T. E. Everhart of the University of California at Berkeley. They made it possible for Wing N. Toy to spend the 1973–74 academic year at Berkeley, during which portions of the text material were first developed.

We are indebted to Ms. Kareen K. Hagopian, of the Bell Labs Indian Hill Technical Documentation Department, for her very effective assistance in the preparation of the manuscript.

No individual contributed more to the final form of the manuscript, both in terms of its writing as well as its physical appearance, than Patrick Loprete, Jr., also of Bell Labs Indian Hill Technical Documentation Department. Mr. Loprete functioned as the virtual *alter ego* of both authors over a 2-year period.

For the cooperation of the Technical Dodumentation Department at Indian Hill, under the guidance of Ralph A. Meacham, Jr., we are very grateful.

Finally, without the full support of Bell Laboratories and the use of its associated facilities, this work could never have been produced in its present form.

GEORGE D. KRAFT
WING N. TOY

Naperville, Illinois

1

The Evolution of a Philosophy of Computing

1.1 INTRODUCTION

The philosophy embodied by the emerging computer industry from the late 1940's and well into the 1950's was characterized by the concentration of computing power in centralized, physically large processing units with limited input/output facilities, and by the processing of jobs in a sequential batch mode. The vacuum tubes used in the early machines required large amounts of power and were responsible for the large size of the machines. Reliability was poor, and the available memories ranged from only a few hundred to a few thousand words of main storage. In addition, the cycle time of main memory typically ran from several hundred microseconds to tens of milliseconds. This period, the era of the vacuum-tube digital computer, has come to be regarded as the *first generation of computing technology*. This first generation spanned the years 1945 to approximately 1958. During this period, the cost of a computer installation was prohibitive; only the largest organizations could afford one.

The transistor, developed at Bell Laboratories in 1948, evolved into a commercially feasible circuit component during 1957 and 1958. Its incorporation into the digital computers of that time began the *second generation of computing technology*, also known as the *era of the transistorized digital computer*. This era spanned the years from 1958 to approximately 1964. The transistor permitted designers to build digital machines that were more reliable, had higher processing speeds, and cost less. The power dissipation of a transistorized digital computer was considerably less than its vacuum-tube counterpart. With the corresponding development of core memory technology, the instruction cycle time dropped from several hundred microseconds to tens of microseconds. Since the cost of such computing systems was still extremely high, centralization remained a fundamental concept. Main memory size expanded during the second generation to several hundred thousand words of core storage.

The launching of the Russian Sputnik catapulted U.S. computer technology into an accelerated evolutionary mode. The need for extremely reliable, small, sophisticated computers for navigation and control aboard U.S. space vechicles led to a reorganization in the philosophy of centralized computing. The idea that levels of computing power—or "intelligence"—could be distributed away from the central processing core gradually emerged. The central facility could still interact meaningfully with this distributed intelligence, but decision making would have a hierarchical structure, beginning with a local control facility that might communicate with the remote central processor through several levels of preprocessing. The concept of local control was probably fostered by the various military projects of the late 1950's that required decision making to be made in flight by guided missiles and other projectiles. The control facility did not require a large, sophisticated, digital computer; a smaller, specialized computing structure was more cost-effective and easier to package. Such small-scale computers offered the user actual "hands-on" processing capability, which helped remove the mystique surrounding the large digital machines of the late 1950's. Hands-on processing also stimulated applications engineers to think of using these small-scale computers for local control applications far removed from large number-crunching.

The accelerated development of integrated circuit technology, culminating in the implementation of several logic functions on a single chip, ushered in the *third generation of computing technology*. This era is generally considered to span the years from 1964 to mid-1970. During this period, the capability of placing 12 or more gates on a single chip was developed into a well-defined technology of *small-scale integration* (*SSI*). In 1970, this technology was refined to a point where 100 or more gates could be placed on a chip and incorporated as a functional logic block in an overall system. This technology was termed *medium-scale integration* (*MSI*) and began what many technologists call the "*third-and-one-half*" *generation of computing* [1]. The result was an intense pressure on the semiconductor manufacturers to provide greater densities of gates on a single *integrated circuit* (*IC*) chip. This pressure, generated by the electronics marketplace, motivated manufacturers to increase production and develop more complex chips, with the ultimate goal of obtaining a central processor on a single chip with its higher reliability, lower power dissipation, and substantially reduced size. It was during the third-and-one-half generation that component densities of 1000 to 10,000 gates on a single chip became a reality. The former technology consisting of 1000 gates per chip, termed *large-scale integration* (*LSI*), started to become commercially viable in 1975. The latter technology consisting of upward of 10,000 gates per chip is referred to as *very large scale integration* (*VLSI*) or *grand-scale integration* (*GSI*). This appeared to be the upper boundary of the third-and-one-half generation.

It was during the late 1960's and early 1970's that the small-scale computer became the "minicomputer" and its areas of application began to be defined. MSI permitted the minicomputer to incorporate many of the architectural features of the large-scale processors, but at a fraction of the cost. During this period, software supplied by the minicomputer manufacturers became quite sophisticated, freeing the user from having to develop application programs and system software. By late 1972, the minicomputer had become a system component that could be placed where needed in a given application environment, provided that its usage could be shown to be cost-effective. The economics of minicomputer usage rapidly caused them to be incorporated in a wide variety of areas, including process control, data communications, and business data processing. Functioning as a system component, multiple minicomputer configurations were used to distribute computational capability, obtain higher overall system reliability, and provide easier maintenance through simple replacement of the entire central processor.

Concurrent with the evolution of sophisticated computing in the middle 1960's, the development of fault-tolerant and ultra-reliable computing techniques took on greater importance. The U.S. space program provided the impetus for the design of digital machines that could continue to operate even after one or more faults had occurred in their associated control circuitry. Techniques evolved, applicable either to space-borne computers or to commercial machines such as the IBM System/360, that permitted a variety of digital faults to be detected. Diagnostic programming techniques were developed to identify the detected faults and provide information leading to the speedy repair of the faulty device. Redundancy of system components and even the entire processor itself was one approach taken to compensate for potential machine faults. Redundancy found wide acceptance in establishing an ultra-reliable system environment for space-borne computers.

The Bell System used a dual-processor redundancy approach for the No. 1 and No. 2 *Electronic Switching Systems* (*ESS*). These configurations consisted of two processors operating in a step-by-step match mode. The selected processor outputs were matched against each other to determine if both machines agreed to the machine state and the results of the operation. No real time was expended in this process. If a mismatch occurred, a fault detection program was used to identify the erring processor. The system could then run "simplex" (with only one processor on-line and operational) until the faulty machine was repaired. The failing machine was automatically switched out of the matching mode by fault identification logic. The Bell System, in addition, pioneered the application of self-checking and high-resolution diagnostics to isolate faults to within a group of several replaceable circuit packs. Each of these systems was designed to meet the Bell System's reliability objective of 2 hours downtime in 40 years.

The commercial minicomputer manufacturers flirted with the concept of machine reliability by associating a parity bit with each word in main memory and performing a cyclic redundancy character check on information stored on magnetic tape. Until the fall of 1974, no minicomputer manufacturer had gone beyond the implementation of these basic checking schemes, since it was not financially attractive to incorporate such features as self-checking, error detection and correction, and high-resolution diagnostics. These features represented additional hardware and software packages that the typical user of a minicomputer neither needed nor was willing to spend extra dollars for.

Late in the fall of 1974, Data General announced its Eclipse series of minicomputers. An optional feature of the Eclipse series was error detection and correction on its interleaved core and semiconductor memory modules. This feature allowed critical applications to continue functioning in spite of a fault condition in the main memory. Although Texas Instruments had been the first manufacturer to incorporate this feature, Data General adopted the technique and expanded on it. This implementation represented the first strong commitment on the part of the minicomputer industry to recognize machine reliability as a major area of concern to the commercial user. Hewlett Packard also employed error-correcting code units with semiconductor memory modules for the HP21MX and the HP3000 systems. Prior to this time, the area of ultra-reliable computing had largely been the private domain of the Navy, the space program, the Bell System, and large mainframe manufacturers such as IBM.

In late 1972, at a time when the industry itself was overwhelmed with the potential applications of the minicomputer, the first microprocessors using the emerging LSI technology were introduced. The microprocessor, apparently, was a secondary result of the memory development work carried on by the Intel Corporation in the late 1960's [2,3,4]. Its acceptance, which was immediate and explosive, influenced the entire area of computer technology. A range of applications beginning with the hand-held calculator and including special-purpose controllers that could not be economically implemented with a dedicated minicomputer became financially viable when a microprocessor was used.

Concurrent with the development of the microprocessor, substantial advances were taking place in memory technology. The cycle time of core memories was cut almost in half, and semiconductor memory devices began to be incorporated as sections of main computer memory by several major manufacturers. The microprocessor structures were used in conjunction with these semiconductor memories to provide low-cost, distributed computing power.

The appearance of the microprocessor ushered in a revolutionary computing era in which the building blocks of digital systems became not electronic components but functional units that included memory, interactive terminals, and *central processing units* (*CPU's*). The technology that spawned the microprocessor used advanced MSI designs that eliminated the hierarchical structure of distinct logic, memory, and interface boards by relocating all these functions on a few semiconductor chips. The microprocessor manufacturers added new features to the existing MSI CPU's by increasing the functional complexity of the semiconductor chips. This complexity forced the development of true LSI circuits that could function as system components. This increase in complexity resulted in a phenomenal drop in cost. Sophisticated computing structures became available at a price well under $1000. These inexpensive, powerful LSI computing structures moved the field of computing rapidly toward its *fourth generation*. The Diebold Group [1] has called this generation "the user's generation." It was visualized that in such a technology environment, computing would be distributed where it was needed in a cost-effective and efficient manner [5, 6]. Extensive use would be made of LSI and GSI, and clusters of processors or aggregates would be used to do the job that a single large machine had done before. These clustered processors would generally be low-cost, highly refined microprocessor structures. It was generally conceded that the fourth generation would be fully developed by 1978. Table 1-1 provides a summary of the four generations of computing technology and their characteristics.

Manufacturers conservatively estimated that by the early 1980's a single-chip *random-access memory* (*RAM*) would contain 256 K bits of memory and bipolar logic

TABLE 1-1 Evolution of the Four Generations of Computing

First	Second	Third	Third-and-One-Half	Fourth
1945—ENIAC, first commercial machine available in 1951	1958	1964	1970	1978–1980
Special purpose	General purpose	Compatible families, centralized control multiprocessors	Same as third plus minicomputers	Polyprocessor networks forming distributed control
Business and scientific computation	Data processing	Information processing	Information processing	On-line problem solving
Vacuum tubes	Transistors	Integrated circuits	Medium-scale integration	Large-scale integration
Electrical components	Logic gates	Multiple circuits	Registers, decoders, adders, I/O devices	Processors, memories, terminals
Simple, few	Complex, few	Complex, many	Programmable	Dynamically variable
10,000(s) inst/sec	100,000(s) inst/sec	Million(s) inst/sec	Million(s) inst/sec	10 million(s) inst/sec
Machine language Subroutines Utility routines Libraries Symbolic assemblers	Higher-level languages (COBOL, FORTRAN) Monitors Macro assemblers Executives	Operating systems Many languages Multiprogramming Packaged programs Simulation languages	Extendable languages Meta-compilers Subprograms in hardware Conversational systems	User- and application-oriented higher languages Systems software microcoded or in hardware

Reprinted from *Computer Decisions* (Jan. 1975, p. D6), copyright Hayden Publishing Co.

would permit the manufacture of single chips consisting of more than 10,000 gates. They also estimated that the implementation of this super-chip technology would provide a further revolution in the features available at the mini/microcomputer level.

The full implications of low-cost, extremely sophisticated computational capability available at the personal (or local) control level have not been well understood by the modern computer applications specialist. One way to attempt to clarify the applications area is through the use of historical perspective, that is, an examination of the development of the philosophies that led to the appearance of the minicomputer and the microprocessor. The remainder of Chapter 1 will discuss the evolution of the computing field in terms of user needs and the features developed to meet those needs. This discussion, which is not intended to be exhaustive, will highlight the philosophical development of the mini/microcomputer.

1.2 THE EARLY COMPUTING MACHINES

1.2.1 The First Practical Innovators

The concept of the digital computer did not spring full-blown from the mind of one individual. Instead, it evolved from the work of a small group of practical thinkers over a 13-year period beginning in 1937. This small group was profoundly influenced by the initial work of three men, who, essentially, laid the groundwork for the development of the stored-program digital computer. In a paper presented before the First Symposium on Large-Scale Digital Calculating Machinery at Harvard University in January 1947 [7], John W. Mauchly outlined the fundamental differences that he visualized existed between the EDVAC machine being developed at the University of Pennsylvania and the four other computing machines in existence at that time (the Bell Laboratories relay computer, the Mark I, the Mark II, and the ENIAC). In identifying these machines, Mauchly also identified for posterity the three men who led the way in the development of the digital computer. These three men are so intimately associated with the evolution of computing machines, it is worthwhile examining each of their contributions.

In 1937, George R. Stibitz of Bell Laboratories amused himself at home by assembling a simple binary adder using several relays, a few flashlight batteries, and some bulbs. Henry Tropp, in an excellent history of the precomputer era, has pointed out that this appears to have been the first time that anyone successfully adopted the binary numbering system for use in mechanical computation [8]. Shortly thereafter, Stibitz was encouraged by a colleague to apply these concepts to the development of an electromechanical calculator that would manipulate complex numbers. Such a machine, which was made operational in 1939, used the Excess-3 code developed by Stibitz to identify a malfunctioning relay. This complex number calculator was designed with built-in teletypewriter features so that it could be operated remotely. Stibitz successfully demonstrated the first remote operation of a calculating machine using these features at a meeting of the American Mathematical Society in the summer of

1940. This meeting was held in the auditorium of Dartmouth College. Ordinary telephone lines were used to link a keyboard and associated printer in the auditorium with the relay calculator located at the New York City facilities of Bell Laboratories. Among those in attendance was a little-known college professor, John W. Mauchly [9].* The demonstration was both successful and impressive.

The press of the war years drew Stibitz into the development of a relay interpolator and a ballistic computer. The relay calculator was used by the Aberdeen Proving Grounds for computational problems arising in the ballistics of antiaircraft fire control. Ultimately, five relay computers were built by Bell Laboratories incorporating the telephone industry's requirements for high reliability in an environment of heavy utilization.

Howard Aiken had first been confronted with the problems of involved, tedious hand calculations while working on his doctoral dissertation at Harvard University in 1935. Keenly perceptive, Aiken recognized the advantages that a high-speed, automatic calculator offered in terms of the increasing calculation requirements of the physical sciences of that day. After receiving his doctorate, Aiken developed an elaborate description of a relay computer that would accept control information from 24-column-paper-tape data from IBM cards; a bank of sixty 10-pole dial switches functioned as constants. Output was provided by either punched cards or teletypewriter. Aiken first proposed the development of such a machine to the Monroe Calculating Machine Company in 1937, but his proposal was turned down. Encouraged by several colleagues, Aiken approached Thomas Watson, Sr., and his business associates at IBM and convinced them that a relay-based structure was practical and could be built from the technology available. In 1939, IBM in conjunction with the U.S. Navy provided financial support for Aiken's work. IBM also provided a team of four engineers.

In April 1944, the IBM Automatic Sequence Controlled Calculator began full-scale operation (24 hours a day, 7 days a week) at Harvard University. Also known as the Mark I, it ran continuously until it was shut down for relocation purposes in the fall of 1947. This machine, which was almost identical to the one Aiken proposed in 1937, completely vindicated his technical insight and optimism. Data were entered into the Mark I from either punched cards or manual switch settings. Control was obtained by sequentially reading one instruction after another from 24-column paper tape into the machine. This arrangement, which completely isolated instructions from data in the storage facility of the computer, is referred to as a *Harvard machine structure*. Aiken used the Mark I to evolve some of the earliest concepts of programming. These ideas were later developed by Grace Murray Hopper into the first formal language structures and associated compiler concepts. The Mark I was so successful that Aiken developed three successors, each built on the experience gained by implementing the previous machine. The Mark II, also a relay computer, was much faster and larger than the Mark I. It processed data internally as 10-digit decimal numbers.

---

*Rosenberg, Jerry M., *The Computer Prophets* (chap. 8), New York: Macmillan Publishing Co., Inc., 1969.

The Mark III incorporated electronic components and explored the use of a magnetic drum as a storage medium. Figure 1-1 is a photograph of the Mark I as it appeared in 1946.

1-1 Photograph of the Mark I circa 1946 [Smithsonian Institution photo no. 62971]

Even though Aiken was personally responsible for introducing IBM to the embryonic computer field, Tropp has suggested that his greatest contribution appears to be the influence he had on the wide range of people with whom he interacted. Aiken had a forceful and attractive personality that drew outstanding people into his organization at Harvard University. He freely disseminated information about his work and his thoughts on the future of automatic calculation. He coordinated several symposia on calculating machines, exchanged ideas with such researchers as Stibitz, and provided an atmosphere in which the early computing thinkers could easily correspond.

John Mauchly, like Howard Aiken, was drawn into involved, hand-computational techniques because of his work on a doctoral thesis. After becoming intrigued with the procedures involved in performing these calculations, Mauchly began a serious study of computation. While at Ursinus College in the late 1930's, he became interested in statistics and data gathering, including data processing using punched cards. Always an experimenter, he apparently implemented several decimal counters in this period and considered how such electronic devices might be built. In 1940, he joined the Moore School of Electrical Engineering at the University of Pennsylvania and became involved in the development of firing range tables for the Aberdeen Proving Grounds. Mauchly proposed a means of automating this entire process using several workers to perform the calculation function. In 1942, he wrote a proposal describing how the computations of these ballistics tables could be completely automated using an electronic calculating machine, but the proposal was turned down by the federal government [10]. In the same year, Mauchly became acquainted with Herman H. Goldstine, who was associated with the Aberdeen Proving Grounds. Mauchly communicated his ideas of an automatic computation machine to Goldstine and J. Presper Eckert, then a graduate student in the Moore School. Goldstine, who was considerably impressed with Mauchly's ideas, encouraged Mauchly and Eckert in the spring of 1943 to submit their proposal to the Ordinance Department of the U.S. Army. Work commenced on the proposed machine on May 31, 1943. The machine was called the *ENIAC* (*Electronic Numerical Integrator And Computer*), and its development began the formal evolution of the digital computer, which ultimately led to the appearance of the small-scale computer.

1.2.2 The Atanasoff–Mauchly Litigation

In October 1973, Judge Earl R. Larson of Minneapolis, Minnesota, handed down a momentous decision in a $200 million suit brought by Sperry Rand charging Honeywell, Incorporated, with patent infringement in the invention of the electronic digital computer [11]. Since 1950, John Mauchly and J. Presper Eckert had shared the original computer patent rights based on their development of the ENIAC. In the 135-day trial, Judge Larson ruled that John Vincent Atanasoff should rightfully be credited with the invention of the digital computer and declared the Eckert-Mauchly patent to be invalid.

It is interesting to note that no technical details were published of Atanasoff's work, aside from two brief newspaper articles that appeared in early 1942. Assisted by graduate student Clifford Berry, Atanasoff began work in the fall of 1939 at Iowa State College in Ames, Iowa. His objective was to build a special-purpose computer that would solve up to 30 simultaneous equations with 30 unknowns. Although the Atanasoff–Berry computer was designed to accept input from IBM cards in a decimal format, it used the binary number system for all its internal calculations. The concept of an internal store, or memory, was implemented by a drum (9 inches in diameter and 11 inches in length) in which there were mounted 1632 capacitors in 32 tracks, each track having 51 capacitors. A binary 1 or 0 was represented by the polarity of the charge on a capacitor. The electronic part of the computer was fully functional in the spring of 1942, but the card reader was not completely operational when World War II brought the work to a halt. The project was not continued after the war's end.

Atanasoff met John Mauchly at a meeting of the American Association for the Advancement of Science in Philadelphia, Pennsylvania, in December of 1940 and disclosed to Mauchly his efforts at Iowa State. The following summer, Mauchly visited Atanasoff in Ames and reviewed, but did not copy, Atanasoff's copious notes describing his invention.

1.2.3 A Genealogy: From the ENIAC to the UNIVAC

Eckert and Mauchly completed their work on the ENIAC in 1946 at the University of Pennsylvania. The ENIAC, which was the first electronic digital computer to be used extensively, consisted of about 18,000 vacuum tubes [12]. It was capable of performing either 5000 additions or subtractions per second. Its storage capacity was only twenty 10-decimal digit numbers. Programming was achieved through an elaborate mechanical setup procedure that consisted of about 6000 multiposition switches and the use of plug wires to interconnect selected control sections for program sequencing. Figure 1-2 is a photograph of the ENIAC as it appeared in 1946. The frustrations of this early mechanical programming forced the crystallization of the "stored-program" concept that appeared in the proposal for the *EDVAC* (*Electronic Discrete Variable Automatic Computer*) in 1945. This was the next machine to be developed at the University of Pennsylvania. John von Neumann was primarily influential in recognizing that the ENIAC switch settings and plug-wire interconnections simply represented digital information that could be placed in main storage

1-2 Photograph of the ENIAC circa 1946 [Smithsonian Institution photo no. 53192]

in the same manner as the data administered by the program. In addition to employing the stored-program concept, the EDVAC used the binary number system for all of its internal calculations instead of the decimal system used by the ENIAC. However, the very first operational stored-program machine was implemented at Cambridge University by Maurice V. Wilkes. The motivation for creating this machine, called the *EDSAC* (*Electronic Delay Storage Automatic Calculator*), was the work done at the University of Pennsylvania. The EDSAC became operational in May 1949. It was a single-address machine that received input from punched paper tape and sent output to a teletypewriter. Like the EDVAC, it used the binary number system for its internal calculations. The main storage of the EDSAC consisted of a set of mercury delay lines. In addition, the EDSAC permitted instruction modification through the use of arithmetic operations.

A remarkable refinement in computer technology was achieved during the period 1946 through 1951. In 1946, Eckert and Mauchly left the University of Pennsylvania to form the Electronic Control Company in Philadelphia. Their initial project was the development of a mercury delay line machine that incorporated much of the design philosophy of the EDSAC. This machine, called the *BINAC* (*Binary Automatic Computer*), was developed for the Northrop Aircraft Company. Although this machine was less expensive and faster than either the ENIAC or the EDVAC, only one was ever built. However, it was during this project that Eckert and Mauchly explored the use of magnetic tape as a storage medium for digital computers. About the same time, Eckert and Mauchly reorganized their partnership to form the Eckert-Mauchly Corporation. Their corporation was eventually absorbed by the Remington–Rand Corporation, with Eckert being made vice-president of the computer division. Eckert and Mauchly were then put in charge of developing the UNIVAC (*Universal Automatic Computer*) for the National Bureau of Standards. During this development, the groundwork laid by the BINAC project was expanded upon, and the use of magnetic tape was demonstrated as a feasible auxiliary storage medium.

In a private conversation with one of the authors (George D. Kraft) on May 4, 1975, Captain Grace Murray Hopper of the U.S. Navy elaborated on the early days of computing.* After her association with Howard Aiken at Harvard, she joined the Eckert-Mauchly Corporation in the late 1940's and helped to program the BINAC. When asked how she viewed the major contributions of these two pioneers of the computing industry, she replied that:

1. Mauchly has not been properly appreciated historically. It was Mauchly who provided the basis in electronic technology to demonstrate that a "high-speed" computing machine would work.
2. Howard Aiken produced the first true programming techniques for a program-controlled machine with his development of the Mark I computer.

As an interesting aside, Captain Hopper remarked that she regarded the UNIVAC as the first minicomputer but thought that the ENIAC could be put in the same category

*Cited with permission of Captain Grace Murray Hopper, USNR, 1978.

as well. She based her remarks primarily on the limited processing capability of the two machines and the physical accessibility required by each machine of its users.

1.2.4 The IAS Computer and Beyond

In 1946, von Neuman left his informal association with the Moore School of Engineering at the University of Pennsylvania to return to Princeton University.* Herman Goldstine joined him in the move to Princeton's *Institute for Advanced Studies* (*IAS*). Goldstine and von Neumann, while working at the Moore School, spent the war years consulting at Los Alamos and the Aberdeen Proving Grounds. The two proposed and directed the development of an experimental digital machine known as the *IAS computer*. This machine employed the stored-program concept first described by von Neumann in the 1945 EDVAC report. The machine architecture permitted instructions and data to share main memory. This architecture is now called a *von Neumann* or *Princeton-type machine*.

The IAS computer was a parallel binary machine with a main memory capacity of 1024 words. It used a 20-bit instruction word and a single-address instruction format. The distribution of information concerning this machine was widespread, greatly influencing the direction of the computer industry. By late 1950, it was apparent to many of the individuals engaged in digital computer development that these machines could be used in a myriad of applications beyond the confines of the academic communities engaged in scientific research.

Von Neumann was an intellectual giant whose varied gifts included linguistics (he was a master of many languages, including Greek and Latin), history, the physical sciences, and mathematics. He possessed total recall of any information he read, saw, or heard over a vast array of subjects. This statement is apparently no exaggeration, since Goldstine has discussed [13] witnessing several incredible feats of total encyclopedic recall in such diverse subject areas as literature, the history of the Byzantine empire, and abstract mathematics. In a striking tribute, Goldstine has described von Neumann as the greatest intellectual figure to appear during the Austrian–Hungarian renaissance after World War I. (Theodore von Kárman and Sigmund Freud were two other members of this same group of intellectuals.) Goldstine apparently did not meet von Neumann until the summer of 1944, when he encountered the brilliant mathematician on a railroad platform in Aberdeen, Maryland. Goldstine introduced himself and immediately struck up a conversation. During this exchange, he told von Neumann that he was engaged in the development of an electronic computer. Von Neumann, who immediately perceived the possibilities of such an automatic calculating machine, joined Goldstine on the ENIAC project shortly thereafter. They remained collaborators and close friends until von Neumann's death from cancer in February 1957.

---

*Von Neumann was involved at the Moore School following September 1944 with both the ENIAC and EDVAC projects. He was invited to join them and supervise the EDVAC project but declined and returned to the Institute for Advanced Studies. [Private communication from H. S. Tropp to George D. Kraft, Summer, 1978]

In 1951, the digital computer was put into true commercial use for the first time when the U.S. Bureau of Census accepted delivery of the UNIVAC I. This machine employed the mercury delay line storage pioneered in the EDSAC. By this time, the technology of computer development had absorbed the best features of the early machines and had evolved to the point where reliable, cost-effective machines could be supplied to business and industry.

1.3 THE DEVELOPMENT OF THE COMMERCIAL COMPUTER MARKETPLACE

IBM had been commercially active in business data processing since the introduction of its electrical tabulating machines in the early 1930's. Based on Aiken's success at Harvard with his Mark family of computers, IBM made a decision at the end of World War II to incorporate the features of the stored-program computer in their line of business machines. In 1948, IBM introduced the first commercial machine that could electronically alter its instructions. It was called the *Selective Sequence Electronic Calculator* (*SSEC*). Spurred on by the Korean War and the success of the UNIVAC I, IBM formally entered the commercial computer field with its introduction of the IBM 701 in April 1953. The 701 represented the first production model of a scientific computer. The UNIVAC I was intended for data processing applications and some scientific computing. Unfortunately, the marketing of the UNIVAC I was minimal, and the machine did not influence the commercial marketplace as did the IBM 700 series.

To the early commercial digital machine developers, it appeared that a major distinction existed on a functional basis between what came to be called *business computing* and *scientific computing* [14,15]. Scientific computing was characterized by large computing capability and little *input/output* (*I/O*) capacity. Into this category could be placed the IBM 700 scientific series, consisting of the 701, 704, 7090, 7040, 7044, and 7094, models 1 and 2. Business computing was characterized by extensive I/O capability, including the use of multiple magnetic tape transports and limited calculating capacity. Into this category could be placed the UNIVAC I (with its 10 magnetic tape units), the IBM 650, and the IBM 700 business series, consisting of the 702, 705, 708, and 7080. With its 709, IBM attempted to incorporate the highly flexible and extensive I/O facilities of its business computers into its scientific computers. The IBM 700 series for both business and scientific computing consisted of 36-bit instruction-word machines. Consequently, since IBM set the industry standards, the length of a byte or character in that period became 6 bits for most machines. Business computers were normally character-oriented machines, designed to manipulate text or variable-length strings of characters. The introduction of the IBM System/360 in the early 1960's, with its 32-bit instruction word, shifted the length of a byte from 6 bits to 8 bits. It also successfully combined the features of the character-oriented business data machines with the floating-point processing capability of the scientific computer.

It is significant that all of the large computing systems developed between 1951 and 1963 observed the *economies-of-scale theory* [16,17]. This theory states that it costs less to run many different jobs on a single facility than it does to dedicate that facility to a single user. Since the cost of a computational facility during this period was substantial, the per-user cost could be reduced as the number of users increased. Economy of scale required maximum utilization of the computational facility; underutilization could not be tolerated. Such a situation prevented the development of a personal or local computational environment.

During the formative years of computing in the late 1940's and early 1950's, H. R. J. Grosch observed that large economies of scale could be achieved by the machines of that period. He theorized that an empirical relationship existed between the speeds of two competitive machines and their respective costs. While Grosch apparently communicated this opinion *verbally* to several people in the computing field, he never had it formally published. Nonetheless, his opinion became widely circulated and entered the field's literature [18]. *Grosch's Law* asserts that the ratio of the speeds of two different computers is directly proportional to the square of their costs. In other words, a computer costing twice as much as another computer should be four times as fast as the less expensive machine. The formal expression of *Grosch's Law* is given by the relationship

$$\frac{S_2}{S_1} = \frac{C_2^2}{C_1^2}$$

where

S_1 = speed in instructions per second of machine 1

S_2 = speed in instructions per second of machine 2

C_1 = cost in thousands of dollars of machine 1

C_2 = cost in thousands of dollars of machine 2

Various individuals have examined the applicability of Grosch's Law to the early computing machines. Solomon [16], in particular, examined the IBM System/360 series and found close agreement with Grosch's Law for those machines on which scientific computation examples were used as a benchmark. Conversely, programs incorporating data processing features provided a poor fit. These conclusions appeared to hold across a large spectrum of computing machines.

Since Grosch's Law is just a restatement of the fact that the early computers possessed large economies of scale, it is worthwhile considering the actual cost and performance of some of the computers found in the 1950's and 1960's. Figure 1-3 illustrates the cost of several large computers between 1950 and 1968. Within certain broad bounds, Grosch's Law applied to several categories of large computers produced in the 1960's. If the consideration of performance was confined to different models in the same product line, such as the IBM System/360 series, a reasonable approximation

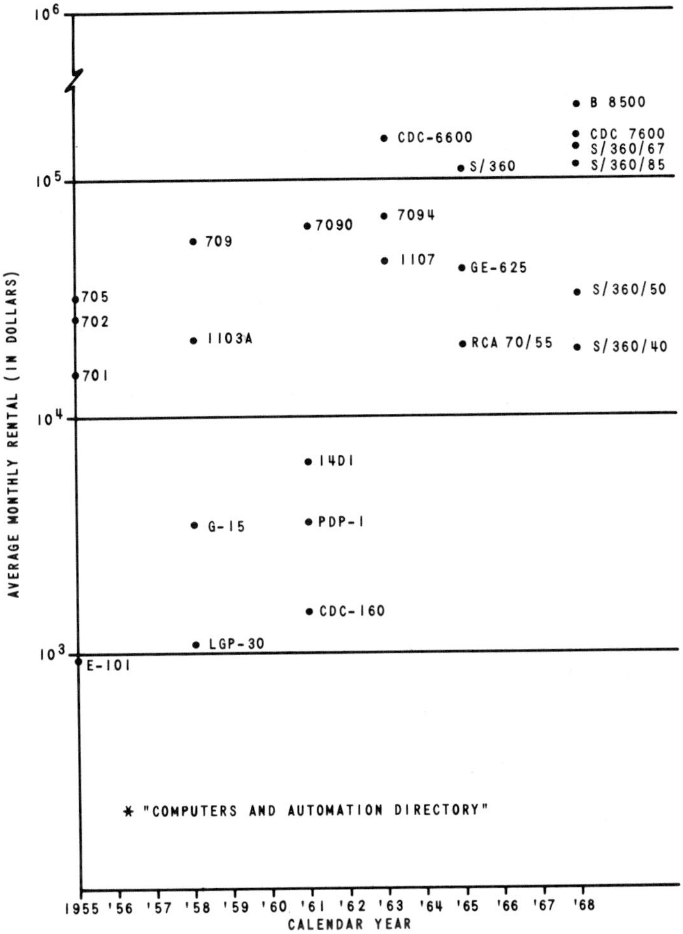

1-3 Cost of several large computers (1955–1968)

to Grosch's Law could be obtained for certain application problems. This was observed by Solomon. However, if machines from different product lines were compared, such as the CDC-6600 series and the System/360, the applicability of Grosch's Law was not apparent. In point of fact, the computing power of a given digital system is dictated by all of its various components and their interaction. Speed of computation can only give a gross measure of performance.

In the spring of 1975, Grosch took a new look at the law named for him [19]. He concluded that the law still held for either a desktop mini/microcomputer or a network of small machines. Grosch maintained that in order to do useful work in an expanding applications environment, peripherals that convert a simple machine into a computing system are required. It is the system, he felt, that continues to observe Grosch's Law—and would for some time to come.

1.4 THE EMERGENCE OF THE SMALL COMPUTER

1.4.1 The MIT Whirlwind

A remarkable digital machine became operational in 1951 at the Massachusetts Institute of Technology (MIT). The Whirlwind computer used a 16-bit word length and an electrostatic storage tube for memory. The 16-bit words were used to represent either data or an instruction. The Whirlwind was capable of 20,000 single-address instructions per second, and for several years it had the fastest execution time of any computer in the world. It was the first machine that could handle real-time applications. Figure 1-4 is a simplified block diagram of the computer.

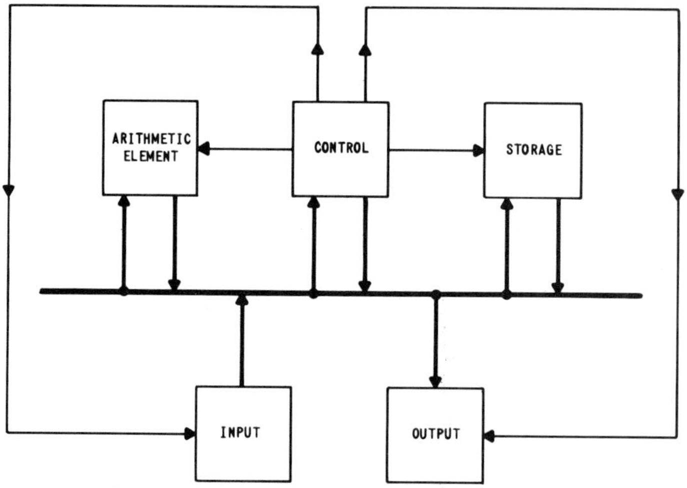

1-4 Simplified block diagram of the Whirlwind computer

In 1953, the Whirlwind became the first major computer to receive a magnetic core memory. The core plane consisted of 2048 16-bit words. The major significance of the Whirlwind was that a user could get his hands directly on it [20]. This approachability made users feel that the machine was easy to understand and use. The Whirlwind was a physically imposing machine, housed in several rows of racks, each measuring 10 feet high and 26 inches wide. Its small word length, limited instruction set, and small memory placed it in what is now called the *small computer category*. It was the first entry in the development of limited-scale computing facilities that eventually led to the appearance of the minicomputer in the mid-1960's.

1.4.2 The MTC, TX-0, TX-1, and TX-2

The main storage requirements of the Whirlwind led Lincoln Laboratories at MIT to design the *Memory Test Computer* (*MTC*), which was used to test the first coincident current core memory. Jay W. Forrester, designer of the core memory, incorporated his initial design into the MTC for evaluation prior to installing the core memory in the Whirlwind. The MTC, in turn, led to the development in 1953 of the TX-0 [21], an experimental computer also designed at Lincoln Laboratories. The TX-0 was built to test a 65,536-word magnetic core memory. This new machine employed an 18-bit instruction word. Two bits of the instruction word were used to specify the opcode, and the remaining 16 bits were used to address any of the $2^{16} = 65{,}536$ storage locations in memory. In addition, four internal registers were provided for use in arithmetic operations. In terms of approachability, small word length, and limited instruction set, the TX-0 could be classified as a small computer. The TX-0 and its successors, the TX-1 and TX-2, can be regarded as the first high-performance transistorized digital computers.

1.4.3 The E-101, G-15, and LGP-30

In 1955 and 1956, three machines became commercially available that underscored the approachability of the small computer. Each of these machines incorporated an additional factor in their marketing—low cost. All three were marketed for under $50,000. These three machines have been identified by Koudela [22] as the Burroughs E-101, the Bendix G-15, and the Librascope LGP-30. Each machine used the vacuum-tube technology of that period in its serial central processing unit. These machines had fixed configurations that permitted only a magnetic drum, keyboard printer, and paper tape reader–punch to be interfaced with the mainframe. Table 1-2 lists the

TABLE 1-2 Basic Characteristics of the LGP-30, E-101, and G-15

Characteristics	Librascope LGP-30	Burroughs E-101	Bendix G-15
Internal form of data processed	Binary	Decimal	Binary
Memory word length	30 bits	12 digits	29 bits
Memory capacity	4096	220	2176
Programming level	Assembly	Plugboard*	Microcode
Higher-level language	Interpreter	None	Interpreter

*The E-101 was programmed by the insertion of conducting programs into a matrix. Only data were placed on the drum.

characteristics of these machines. The philosophy behind their software may have influenced the development of the minicomputer. For example:

1. Assembly language programming was used. The merits of an interpretive language that was *easy to employ* by the application programmer were explored by both Librascope with the LGP-30 and Bendix with the G-15.

2. A form of microprogramming was used by the Bendix G-15 to provide an instruction set of over 100 entries. The LGP-30 used only 16 basic instructions. These two implementations raised the question of how sophisticated the instruction set of a small computer had to be for the computer to be useful. The LGP-30 seemed to indicate that the instruction set need not be very sophisticated at all. Table 1-3 gives the 16 basic instructions of the LGP-30.

TABLE 1-3 LGP-30 Instruction Set

Instruction*		Effect
B	m	Bring. Clear the accumulator, and add the contents of m to it.
A	m	Add contents of m to the contents of the accumulator and retain the result in the accumulator.
S	m	Subtract the contents of m from the contents of the accumulator, and retain the result in the accumulator.
M	m	Multiply the number in the accumulator by the number in memory location m, and terminate the result at 30 binary places.
N	m	Multiply the number in the accumulator by the number in m, and retain the least-significant half of the product.
D	m	Divide the number in the accumulator by the number in memory location m, and retain the rounded quotient in the accumulator.
H	m	Hold. Store contents of the accumulator in m, and retain the number in the accumulator.
C	m	Clear. Store contents of the accumulator in m and clear the accumulator.
Y	m	Store only the address part of the word in the accumulator in memory location m, leaving the rest of the word undisturbed in memory.
R	m	Return address. Add one to the address held in the counter register (C) and record in the address portion of the instruction in memory location m. The counter register normally holds the address of the next instruction to be executed.
E	m	Extract, or logical product order; i.e., clear the contents of the accumulator to zero in those bit positions occupied by zeros in m.
U	m	Transfer control to m unconditionally; i.e., get the next instruction from m.
T	m	Test, or conditional transfer. Transfer control to m only if the number in the accumulator is negative.
I	0	Input. Fill the accumulator from the Flexowriter.
P	x	Print a Flexowriter symbol. The symbol is denoted by the track number part of the address (x).
Z	t	Stop. Contingent on five switch (T1 . . . T5) settings on the control panel.

*The address part of the instruction is denoted by m when it refers to a memory location.

Source: Librascope LGP-30 Manual, Librascope, Inc., 80 Western Ave., Glendale, California. Reprinted with permission.

1.4.4 The PDP-1

In 1957, Kenneth H. Olsen, who had been associated with the Whirlwind computer development, left Lincoln Laboratories. Olsen had also worked on the MTC computer and the TX-0 and TX-1. With his brother Stanley, he founded the Digital Equipment Corporation (DEC) in a former woolen mill located in Maynard, Massachusetts. The early efforts of the company were directed toward supplying the digital logic modules used to build specialized test sets, digital controllers, or small computers by the organizations purchasing them. These modules were discrete circuit boards, incorporating such functions as AND, OR, and individual flip-flop registers. In 1959, DEC combined these logic modules to produce their first digital computer, the *Programmed Data Processor-1* (*PDP-1*). The PDP-1, which marked the emergence of DEC as a major force in the computer marketplace, was a single-address, single-instruction, stored-program computer with an 18-bit word length. It incorporated a coincident current core memory with a cycle time of 5 microseconds. The memory capacity was user-expandable in increments of 4096 18-bit words to a maximum of 65,536 words. The standard system sold for $120,000, an uncommonly low price in those days of the large, centralized digital computer. One of the most striking characteristics of the PDP-1 was the wide selection of peripherals that it supported. Figure 1-5 illustrates the I/O options of the PDP-1, and Figure 1-6 exhibits its logic organizations. The PDP-1 employed multiple-level indirect addressing, where bit 5 = 1 of the instruction word specified that the operand addressed should be treated as the address of the data instead of the data itself. At each level of memory reference, bit 5 = 1 of the addressed location's contents specified that the contents were to be treated as a new memory address. In this way, all 65,536 core locations could be accessed. Figure 1-7 gives the instruction format of the PDP-1. Ease of programming and the low cost of its rich peripheral complex made the PDP-1 an immediate success. Furthermore, DEC encouraged users of the PDP-1 to develop and annually update their software library. This stimulated additional interest in the PDP-1.

1.4.5 The CDC-160

The technology of the second generation was made part of the small computer in 1960 when the vacuum tube was replaced by the transistor and the magnetic drum memory was replaced by the coincident current core memory. Control Data Corporation's CDC-160 used this new technology, moving away from the philosophy of a fixed configuration that was embodied by the PDP-1. It should be noted that the TX-0, TX-1, and the PDP-1 were also all transistor devices. The CDC-160 permitted both the memory size and the peripheral aggregate to be expanded by the user. The CDC-160, the first commercial 12-bit computer, was an internal, parallel, binary machine with a maximum core size of 4096 words. Because of its short (12-bit) instruction word, it was the first small computer to use both relative addressing and indirect addressing. Six bits of the instruction word were used to represent a displacement relative to the location of the current instruction, where the referenced data word could be found. A

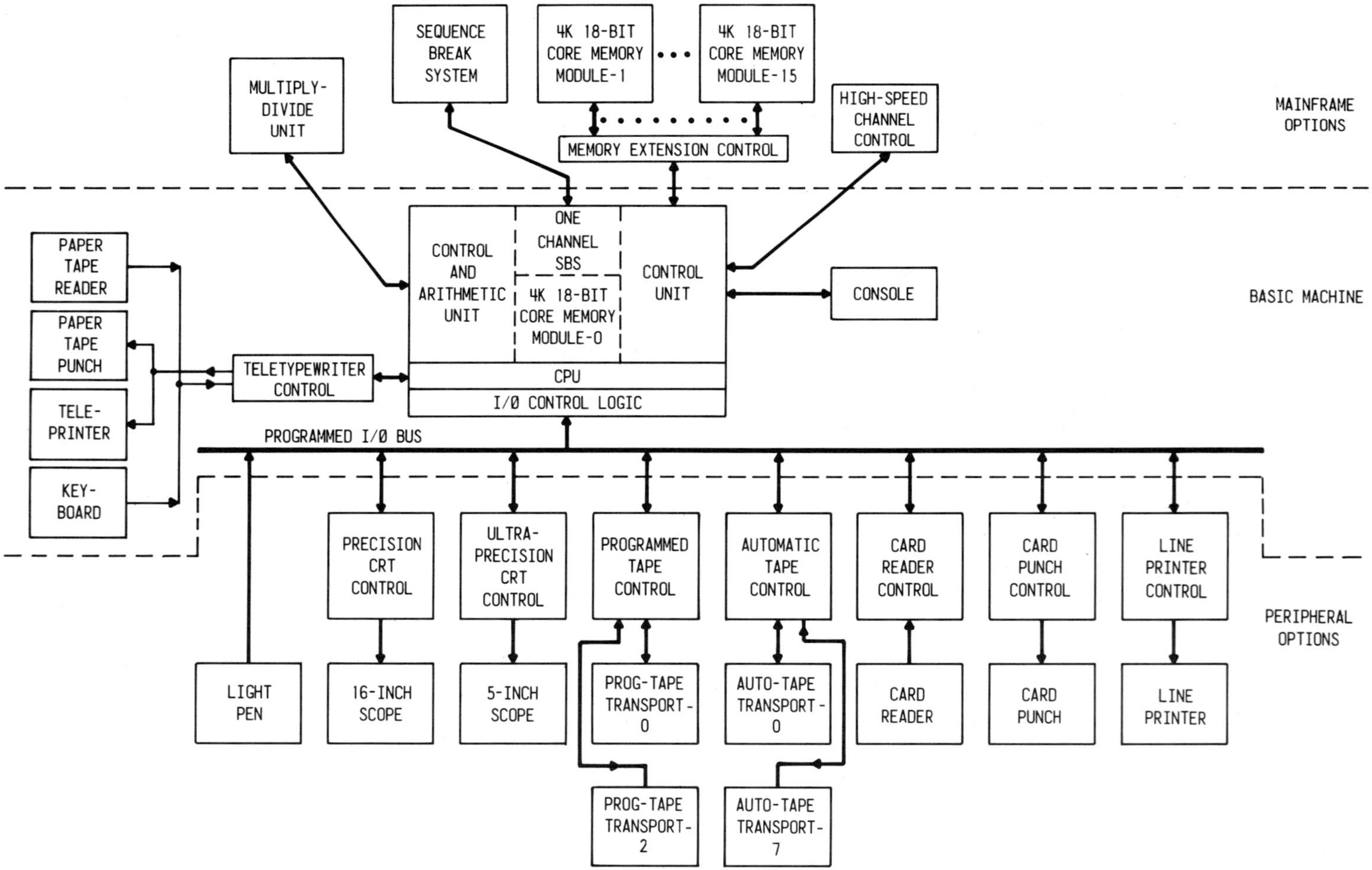

1-5 PDP-1 system block diagram exhibiting user options [Reprinted with permission of Digital Equipment Corporation]

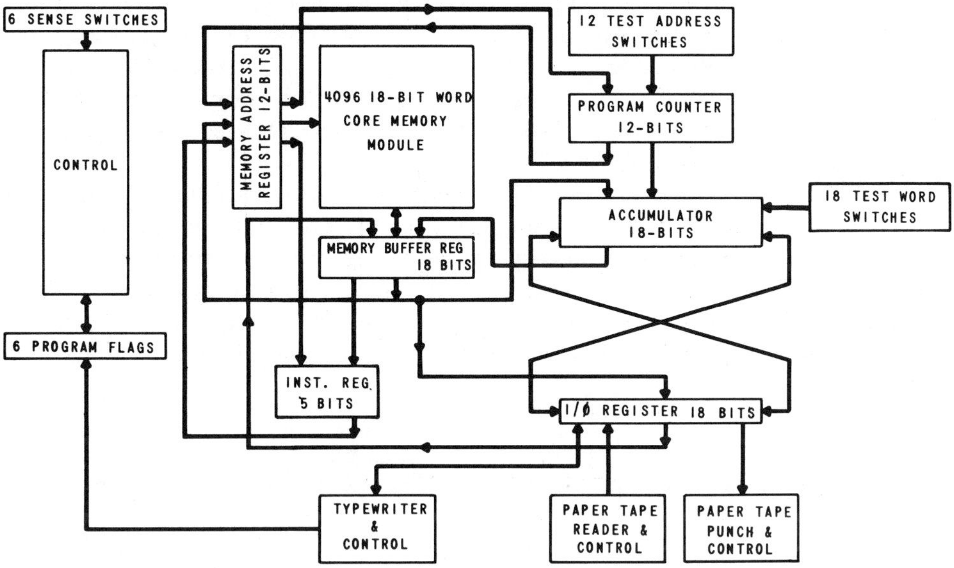

1-6 PDP-1 logical organization: the basic machine [Reprinted with permission of Digital Equipment Corporation]

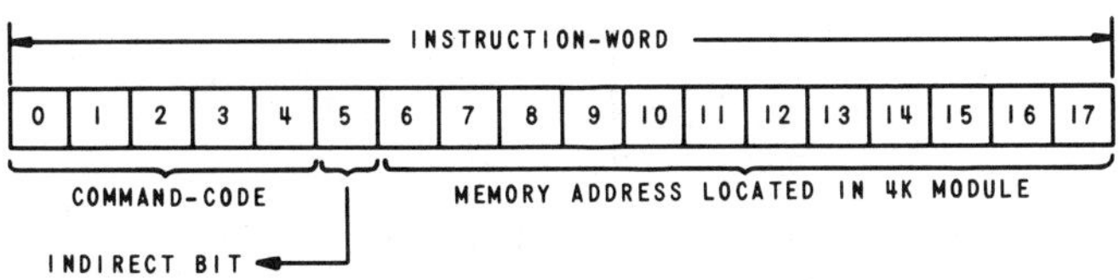

NOTE:

1. IN A MEMORY REFERENCE INSTRUCTION, BITS 6-17 SPECIFY UNIQUELY ONE OF 4096 LOCATIONS IN MAIN STORAGE.
2. AN AUGMENTED INSTRUCTION USES BITS 5-17 TO SPECIFY VARIATIONS OF THE BASIC MACHINE DIRECTIVE CALLED FOR, I.E.
   a) BIT-5 INDICATES THE DIRECTION OF A SHIFT,
   b) BIT-6 SPECIFIES WHETHER THE SHIFT IS TO BE ARITHMETIC OR LOGICAL, ETC.

1-7 Instruction format of the PDP-1 [Reprinted with permission of Digital Equipment Corporation]

seventh bit was used as a sign bit. If the sign bit was a 1, the 6 displacement bits were treated as a negative number. If the sign bit was a 0, the 6 displacement bits were treated as a positive number. By adding the 6 displacement bits with sign to the address of the current instruction, the 63 locations prior to the location of the current instruction or the 63 locations following the current instruction location could be referenced. This *relative addressing* was conditioned by a mode bit that, when set, treated the 6 displacement bits as a positive number and allowed the first 64 locations of memory to be referenced. An additional control bit allowed the referenced 12-bit data word to act as an additional address of any location in the 4096-word core memory. This technique of *indirect addressing* would be used extensively in the later minicomputers. Figure 1-8 is a block diagram of the CDC-160, and Figure 1-9 exhibits its instruction word format.

The PDP-1 represented the arrival of reasonably low-cost computation at the commercial level. The CDC-160 represented a further evolution toward inexpensive personal computing power. The industry was becoming aware that there was a market for decentralized computing. The small digital computers at the start of the 1960's had begun a trend away from the economy-of-scale philosophy for computing. It remained, however, for DEC to achieve a further technological innovation and cost breakthrough with its PDP-5 in 1963.

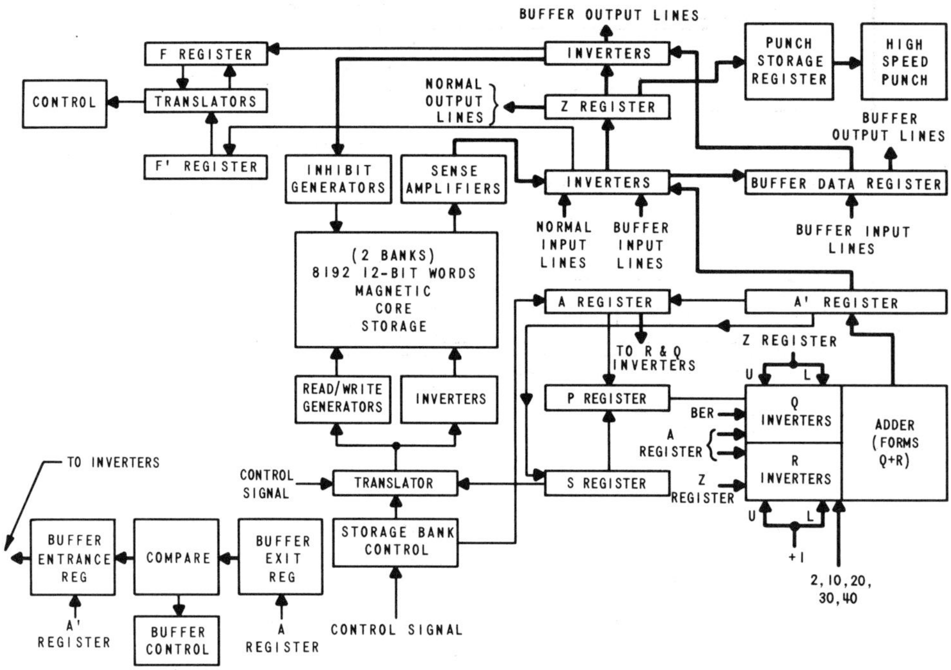

1-8 Block diagram of the CDC-160 register structure [Reprinted from the CDC-160 Reference Manual, 1960 edition, with permission of Control Data Corporation]

1.4.6 The PDP-5

The PDP-5 appears to have been a direct result of a request to DEC by the Chalk River Nuclear Laboratories, Chalk River, Ontario, Canada, for the development of a special-purpose atomic pile controller [20]. To obtain the necessary features for this

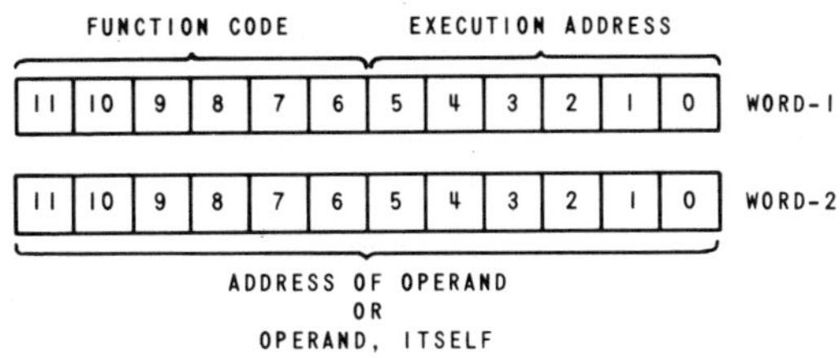

NOTE:

1. MOST INSTRUCTIONS REQUIRE ONLY ONE WORD OF STORAGE.
   a) FOR THOSE DIRECTIVES, THE FUNCTION CODE SPECIFIES THE MACHINE OPERATION & THE EXECUTION ADDRESS SPECIFIES WHERE TO FIND THE OPERAND.
2. FOR TWO-WORD INSTRUCTIONS, WORD-1 & WORD-2 MUST BE LOCATED IN SEQUENTIAL STORAGE ADDRESSES OF THE SAME BANK.
   a) HOWEVER, THE EXECUTION ADDRESS IS ALWAYS SET EQUAL TO ZERO.
   b) THE SECOND WORD WILL CONTAIN A 12-BIT ADDRESS OR OPERAND, DEPENDING ON THE INSTRUCTION.

1-9 Instruction format of the CDC-160 [Reprinted from the CDC-160 Reference Manual, 1960 edition, with permission of Control Data Corporation]

application in a reasonably inexpensive structure, DEC developed a small, simple general-purpose computer in place of the originally specified controller. The small processor proved so useful that DEC built more of them, improving the design and physical appearance. DEC called the resulting machine the PDP-5. The year was 1963, and DEC implemented the PDP-5 using the less expensive, mass-produced transistor logic and core technology that had become available. The PDP-5 sold for $30,000. It had a basic configuration consisting of a teleprinter and a paper tape reader–punch. In addition, the PDP-5 was designed to support a wide variety of peripheral devices, maintaining the philosophy established earlier by the PDP-1. Figure 1-10 gives the peripheral options available for the PDP-5. Figure 1-11 presents the basic block diagram of the PDP-5. The PDP-5 was a single-address, parallel, 12-bit, stored-program computer with a 6-microsecond memory cycle time. Core memory was available in one of two module sizes: 1024 12-bit words or 4096 12-bit words. Single-level indirect addressing was available, and location 0 in the core memory was used as the *program counter* (*PC*). A single-level interrupt was permitted, with the priority of the interrupting device established by the interrupt service routine. Furthermore, the interrupt service routine permitted one device to interrupt another (interrupt nesting) by disabling the interrupt mechanism and then reenabling the mechanism after service had begun to the interrupting device. Through the use of the single-level interrupt, *direct memory access* (*DMA*) capability, and a real-time clock, the PDP-5 provided a low-cost small computer that could administer control in *real time*. The machine

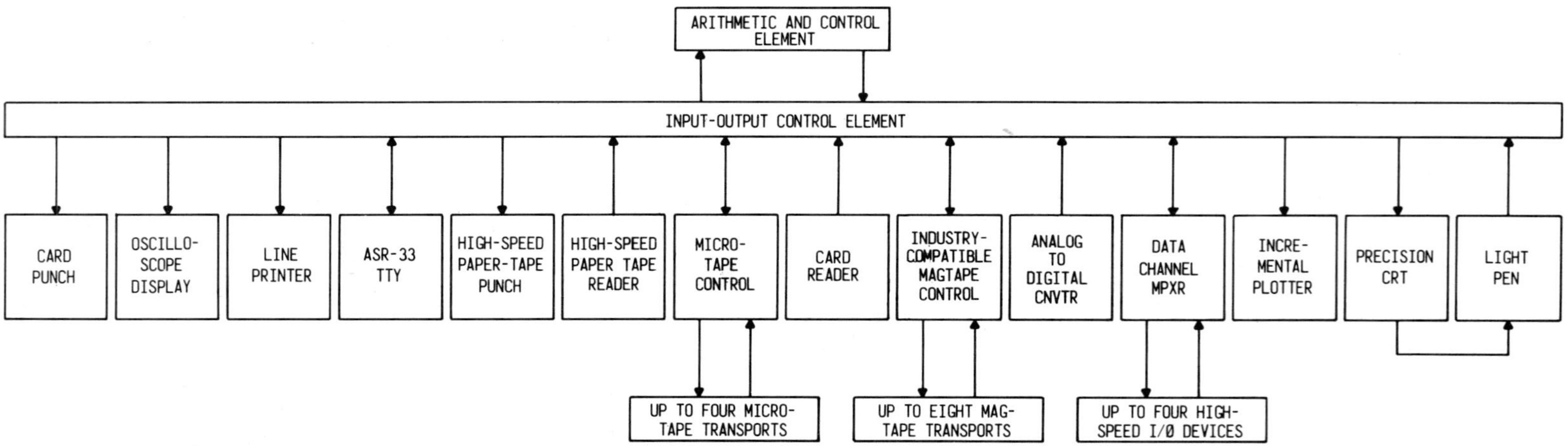

1-10 PDP-5 system components [Reprinted with permission of Digital Equipment Corporation]

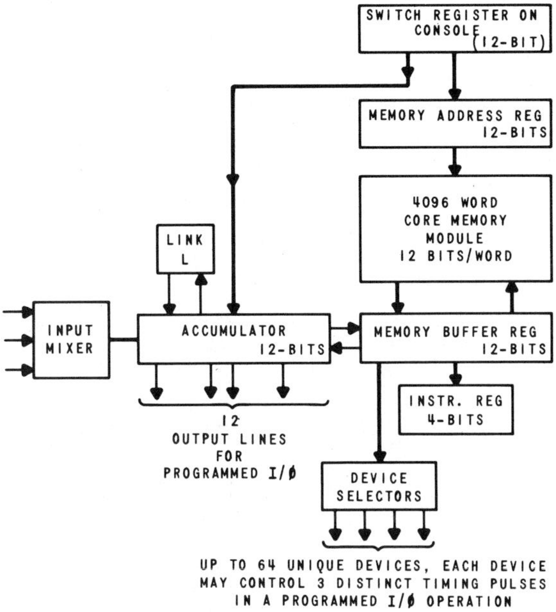

1-11 PDP-5 block diagram [Reprinted with permission of Digital Equipment Corporation]

could be event-sensitive and perform data acquisition and processing through proper use of the interrupt mechanism.

1.4.7 The PDP-8

In 1965, manufacturing techniques permitted the PDP-5 to be redesigned and produced as a new, 12-bit digital computer, the PDP-8. The PDP-8 used the basic architecture of the PDP-5 but decreased its cycle time to 3 microseconds. It sold for $18,000. Since the PDP-8 software was directly compatible with the PDP-5, an extensive program library was immediately available. Included in the PDP-8 software package was a FORTRAN II compiler, extensive I/O programs, and a limited macro assembler. Its explosive impact on the small computer market acted as a catalyst in drawing other companies into the field. In 1968, the PDP-8 was redesigned using integrated circuits (MSI) and called the PDP-8/I. It sold for $13,200. Figure 1-12 represents the functional block diagram of the original PDP-8.

1.4.8 The IBM 1800 and 1130

The 12-bit PDP-8 established a solid market for the small computer. However, the 12-bit word did not divide evenly into two 8-bit bytes. (Eight-bit bytes were the industry standard set by IBM.) To many small computer users, there was a real need

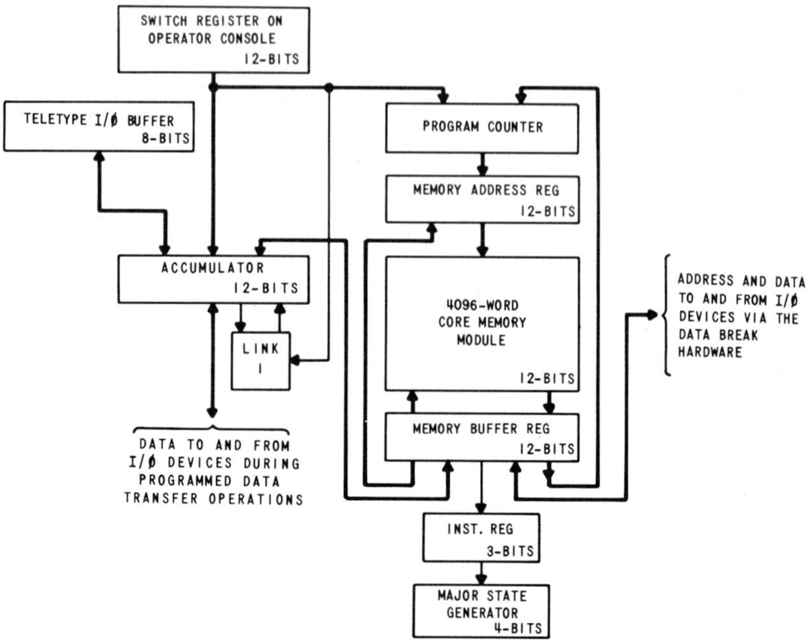

1-12 Block diagram of the PDP-8 [Reprinted with permission of Digital Equipment Corporation]

for a 16-bit machine that could function at the byte-addressable level. In early 1965, IBM introduced model 1800 for the process control industry and model 1130 for small-scale scientific applications. The 1130 quickly found wide acceptance in many business data processing applications. At the time of its introduction in February 1965, the 1130 was the lowest-priced digital computer ever marketed by IBM. The 1130, a 16-bit binary machine with a fixed word length, was limited to either 4096 or 8192 words of 3.6-microsecond core memory. Each word of memory contained 16 data bits plus 2 parity bits in the 17th and 18th bit positions. Parity checking was provided as a standard feature. I/O operations were performed in a cycle-stealing mode or a direct-program-control mode, depending on the I/O device used. In the cycle-stealing mode, the CPU initialized the I/O device, and the I/O device would then "steal" cycles from the CPU as the data transfers took place. In the direct-program-control mode, the transfer of each character between the I/O device and the CPU was individually directed by software, and the CPU was interrupted after each data transfer.

The IBM 1130 was considered to be a little brother to the IBM 1800. Both machines used a 16-bit data word with 2 additional bits associated with each word of storage in the 17th and 18th bit positions. In the 1800, the 17th bit was treated as a parity bit while the 18th bit was used as a program protect bit. The program protect bit was used to specify protected instructions and operands in main storage. The 1130 instruction set was a subset of the 1800 instruction set, differing only in the following aspects:

1. The cycle time of the 1130 was 3.6 microseconds, compared with the 4-microsecond cycle time of the 1800.
2. The 1800 used the 18th bit of its data word as a program protect bit. The 1130 used its 18th bit for a parity check.
3. The 1800 had hardware index registers and additional features that facilitated data acquisition and control applications. The 1130 did not.

Many IBM 1130 object programs could be executed directly on an IBM 1800 system with an equivalent set of I/O devices. Normally, 1800 object programs would not execute on an 1130 because of instruction set differences. Figure 1-13 gives the block diagram of the 1130.

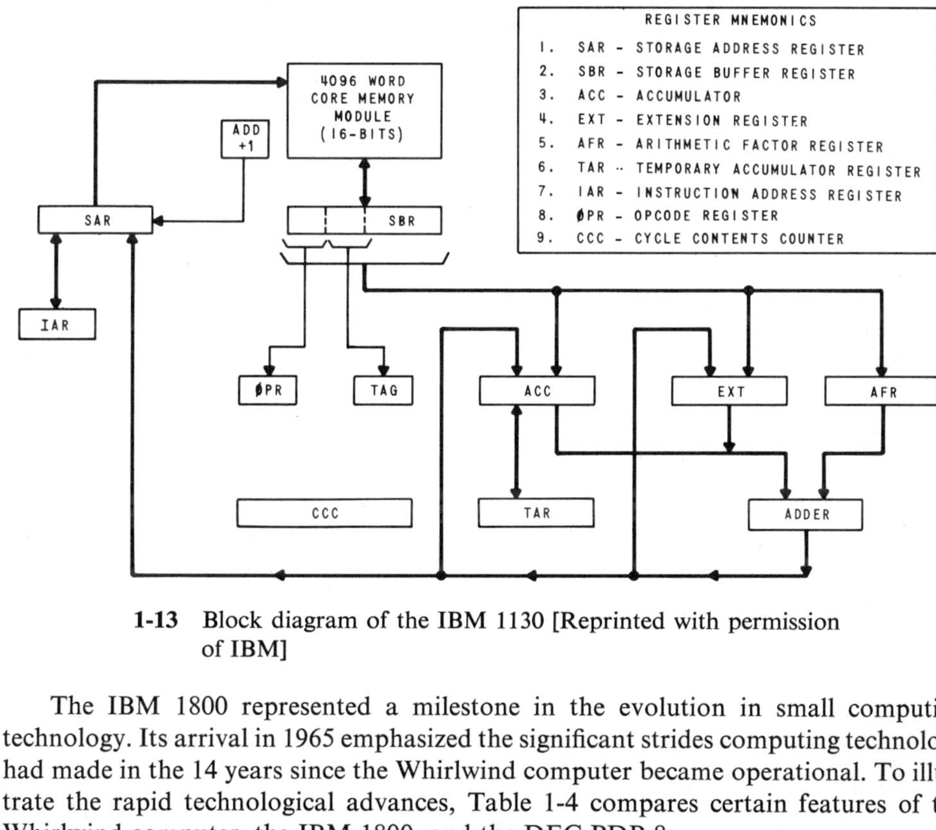

1-13 Block diagram of the IBM 1130 [Reprinted with permission of IBM]

The IBM 1800 represented a milestone in the evolution in small computing technology. Its arrival in 1965 emphasized the significant strides computing technology had made in the 14 years since the Whirlwind computer became operational. To illustrate the rapid technological advances, Table 1-4 compares certain features of the Whirlwind computer, the IBM 1800, and the DEC PDP-8.

Within this same time period (1963–1965), two additional 16-bit small computers were introduced: the DDP-16 by the Computer Control Company and the DATA 620 by Data Machines, Incorporated. (The Computer Control Company later merged with the Honeywell Computer Products Division.) The DATA 620 ultimately was marketed by Varian Data Machines as its model 620i. Each of these systems and the IBM 1800 were real-time, general-purpose computers. Each machine made use of

TABLE 1-4 Comparison of Mainframe Characteristics

	MIT Whirlwind	IBM 1800 Model 1	DEC PDP 8/e	Interdata Model 7/32
Year of Introduction	1951	1965	1970	1974
Main memory:				
Type	Electrostatic storage tube	Core	Core	Core
Word length, bits	16-bit word	16-bit word	16-bit word	32-bit word
Cycle time/word	50 μs	4 μs	1.4 μs	750 ns
Capacity, words:				
Minimum	256 words	8,192 bytes	4,096 words	8,192 bytes
Maximum	2,048 words	65,536 bytes	32,768 words	1 million bytes
Increment size	—	8K bytes/16K bytes	4,096 words	16K bytes
Parity	—	Standard	Option	—
Protect	—	Standard	—	—
Central processor: Number of internal registers	6	6	5	16-, 32-bit general registers
Number of instructions:				
Standard	27	31	56	155
Optional	—	—	71	241
Addressing:				
Direct			256 words	16 million bytes
Short	—	256 bytes		
Long	2,048 words	65,536 bytes		
Indirect	—	Long inst. only	Single level	—
Indexed	—	Yes	Autoindexing	Double
Priority interrupt system:				
Lines	—	—	1	1,024 automatic hardware vectored
Levels	—	12	1	
I/O channels:				
Programmed I/O	Yes	DPC channel	Yes	Yes
Direct memory			Yes	1 DMA bus
access (DMA)	—		1–12	16 selector
Number of channels	—	3 STD; 9 optional	Yes	channel devices
Multiplexed I/O			Application-dependent	
Number of channels				
Maximum DMA Transfer rate	—	125,000 words/s	833,333 words/s	2M bytes/s
Cost	Funded by Office of Naval Research	$113,200	$4,490	$9,990 for 32K-byte machine

multiple-level hardware priority interrupt structures. In addition, all three machines employed the concept of multiple working registers, including dual accumulators and index registers. The software for these systems was reasonably sophisticated, including macro-assemblers and FORTRAN compliers that produced relocatable code.

1.4.9 The Interdata 4

In 1966, a group of computer specialists organized Interdata, Inc., in Oceanport, New Jersey. The basic philosophy adopted by the small computer company was that the fundamental instruction set of the machine should be implemented in microcoded *read-only memories* (*ROM's*). This microprogramming implementation, now called *firmware*, allowed Interdata to pattern its basic instruction set after the IBM System/360 *basic assembly language* (*BAL*). Assembly language programming was made easy for many users who had never before dealt with a small computer. Figure 1-14 shows the block diagram of the Interdata 4, one of the first machines marketed by Interdata in the late 1960's. Hewlett Packard was also one of the early users of microprogram control in its design of the HP2100 minicomputer. Interdata appears to have been one of the first computer manufacturers of any size to exploit the *virtual machine concept*. An Interdata computer could be used to emulate an entirely different digital computer —sometimes with an actual increase in throughput—by use of the proper firmware modules. The basic word length of the Interdata 4 was 16 bits. Interdata was also one of the first small computer manufacturers to employ the technique of byte addressing. The basic architectural features included multiple-level hardware interrupts, 16 working registers, and DMA capability. Interdata processors follow the IBM System/360 method of I/O, with a selector channel DMA mode included in the hardware. Through the use of microprogramming, Interdata was able to observe strict upward compatibility in each of its later machine models, permitting software from its older machines to be used in the newer ones.

1.4.10 The PDP-11 Family

DEC, however, did not observe the philosophy of upward compatibility when it introduced its 16-bit small computer, the PDP-11, in 1969 [23]. The PDP-11 was DEC's entry into the 16-bit marketplace, but DEC had to compete with its own PDP-8 series in most application areas. The machines were not software-compatible, and it took the PDP-11 almost 2 years to firmly establish itself independent of the PDP-8. The PDP-11 series represented a family of upward-compatible, 16-bit, small digital computers. The PDP-11 family was based on the UNIBUS* concept, in which one common array of 56 wires interfaced with all devices, including the CPU and main memory. Registers in peripheral devices were addressed as though they were part of main memory. Communication took place on the UNIBUS in a master-slave mode using

*Registered in U.S. Patent Office.

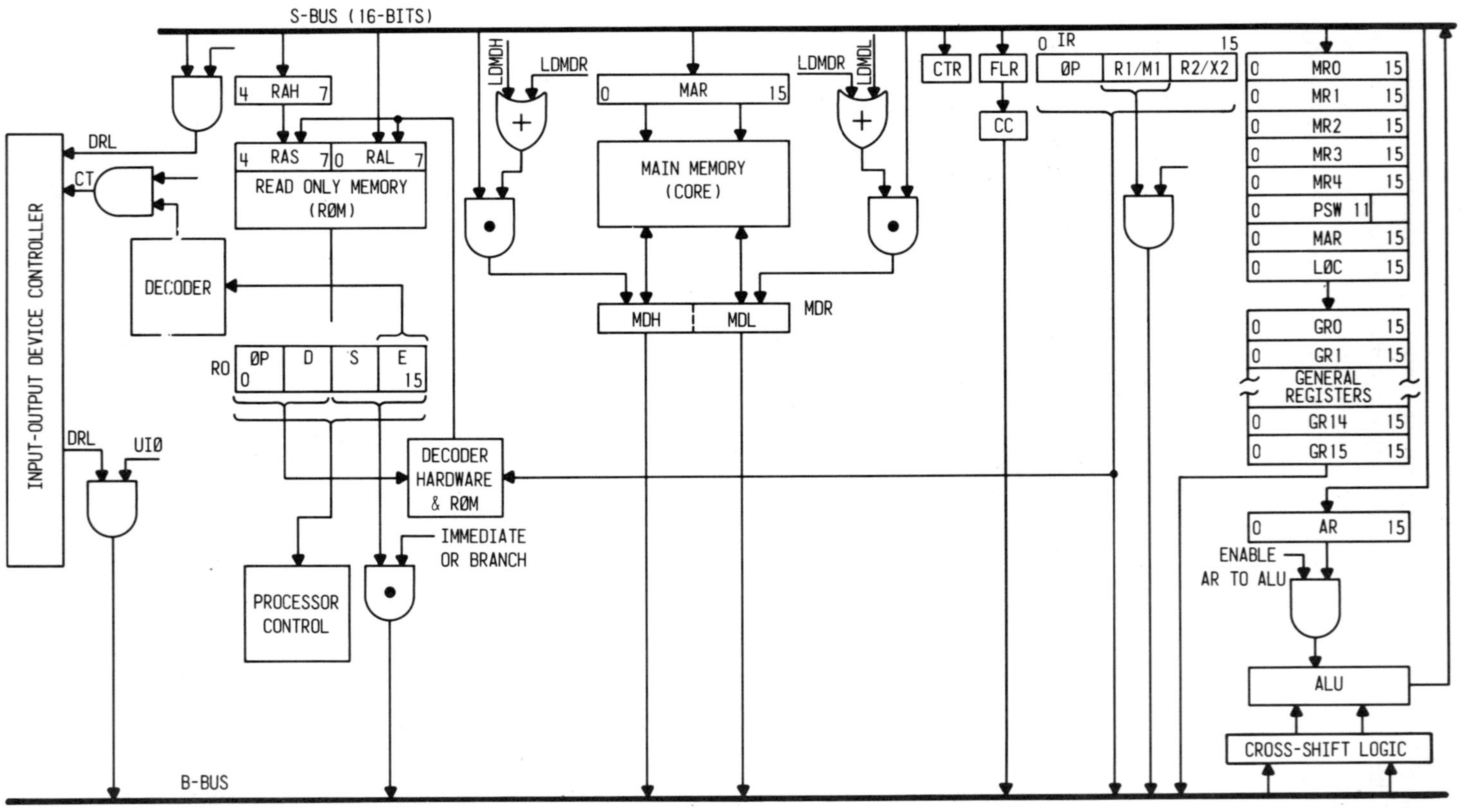

1-14 Block diagram of the Interdata Model 4 [Reprinted with permission of Interdata, a division of Perkin-Elmer]

an asynchronous handshaking protocol. In such an environment, the transaction between two devices did not proceed until the receiving device acknowledged that it received a communication from the transmitting device by returning a control signal to the sender. Each interaction between these two devices was framed in this manner until the transaction was completed. The asynchronous nature of the bus permitted devices attached to it to be technology-independent. That is, the handshaking that took place on the UNIBUS assured the proper transfer of data onto the bus, independent of the speeds of the devices attached to it. The only limiting factor was the response time of the UNIBUS itself to a bus request.

The PDP-11 family used a memory stack as part of its general architecture, permitting the possibility of indefinitely nesting interrupts. With the addition of a memory management unit, the PDP-11/40 and PDP-11/45 were capable of addressing up to 124K words of 16-bit core memory with an additional 4K words used for I/O operations and hardware register references. This provided an address space of a total of 128K words. Memory interleaving was standard on the PDP-11/45. The PDP-11/45 supported both solid-state memory and core memory with the following characteristics:

1. The cycle time for bipolar solid state memory is 300 nanoseconds.
2. The cycle time for MOS solid state memory is 495 nanoseconds.
3. The cycle time for core memory is 980 nanoseconds.

All of memory was byte-addressable; the PDP-11/50 intermixed semiconductor memory with high-speed core memory. Figure 1-15 gives a block diagram of the PDP-11/50.

1.4.11 The Data General Nova

In 1968, Edson D. de Castro, Fredrick R. Adler, Richard G. Sogge, Henry Burkhard III, and Herbert J. Richman founded Data General Corporation in Southboro, Massachusetts. Edson D. de Castro, who became president, had been closely associated with DEC during the development of the PDP-8. He was convinced of the strong need for a powerful 16-bit machine in the minicomputer marketplace. To satisfy this need, Data General introduced the Nova minicomputer. The Nova was marketed as a system component rather than a stand-alone machine. By combining this practice of component marketing with substantial discounts for large-quantity purchases, de Castro and his associates were able to build Data General into a minicomputer manufacturing company second only to DEC in terms of volume sales. Perhaps one of the strongest reasons for this achievement, aside from astute marketing, was the basic engineering decision to make all Nova family members as compatible with each other as was reasonably possible. Consequently, the primary difference between family members was memory cycle time. Data General thus attained the remarkable achievement of having all members of the Nova family *upward- and downward-compatible* in terms of software support and standard peripheral interfacing.

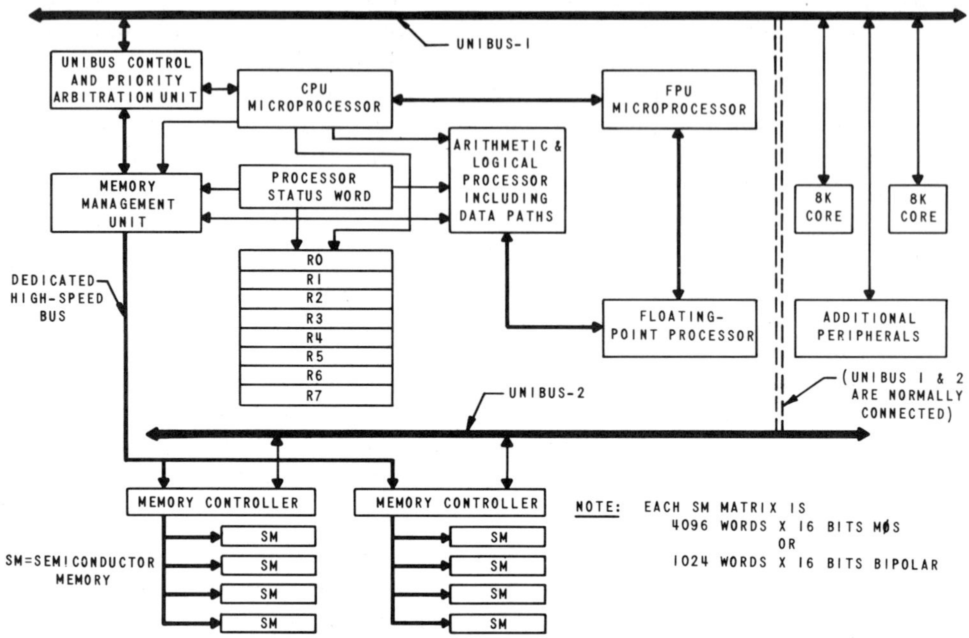

1-15 Block diagram of the DEC PDP-11/50 [Reprinted with permission of Digital Equipment Corporation]

1.4.12 The PDP-15

Following the initial success of the PDP-1, DEC evolved a series of 18-bit small computers concurrent with their development of the PDP-8 and PDP-11 lines. In rapid succession, they introduced the PDP-4, the PDP-7, the PDP-9, and finally, in 1969, the PDP-15. The PDP-15 consisted of three autonomous cooperating subsystems: the central processor, the memory, and the I/O processor. The central processor provided full arithmetic and logical operation capabilities. It permitted 18-bit, parallel, fixed-point signed and unsigned arithmetic using 1's- and 2's-complement operations. The central processor communicated with both memory and the I/O processor. The memory represented the second autonomous subsystem. Memory was organized into pages of 4096 18-bit words; two pages were paired to form a memory bank of 8192 words. The basic memory size consisted of four banks or 32,768 words. However, with the use of a memory bus multiplexer, the central processor could access a maximum of 131,768 words of core memory. The I/O processor formed the third autonomous subsystem. It permitted I/O operations to take place concurrently with the central processor. Both the I/O and central processor could reference the same memory bank, but only one of the processors at any given time was permitted to physically access the memory bank. In the event of simultaneous requests, the I/O processor was given priority over the central processor.

Figure 1-16 illustrates the system organization of the PDP-15. Figure 1-17 exhibits a simplified block diagram of the PDP-15 central processor. A basic 4K configuration of the PDP-15 cost more than $35,000 when introduced in 1969. The PDP-15 and its predecessors found substantial acceptance in the graphical applications area where *x*- and *y*-coordinates were given as 9-bit binary numbers. However, their acceptance elsewhere was limited. The reason was that the 18-bit machines were more expensive than their 16-bit counterparts. Furthermore, by 1972 the 16-bit small computer had virtually become an industry standard. While the larger word length allowed 128K words of core to be indirectly addressed, the 18-bit small computer offered few advantages, if any, over the sophisticated 16-bit machines. In terms of architectural elegance, the PDP-11/45 was just as attractive—and, in addition, it was less expensive.

1.4.13 The Interdata 7/32

In September 1973, Interdata began a new trend in the area of the small computer when it introduced the 7/32, which functioned as a 32-bit machine from the viewpoint of the user. The 7/32 uses 32 general registers (each 32 bits wide), 241 instructions, up to 1024 interrupt levels (each automatically vectored by hardware to a unique service routine), and direct addressing potential of up to 16 million bytes of main storage. This vast addressing capability substantially influenced the performance areas of DEC's PDP-11/45 and Data General's Nova. Both of these machines permitted a maximum of 64K bytes of main storage to be indirectly addressed. Expansion beyond that maximum memory size required the use of memory management and special mapping procedures. These, in turn, required the use of additional hardware and processing time to properly segment memory and map the appropriate segments. The 7/32, initially marketed with a 750-nanosecond memory, was capable of directly referencing 256K 32-bit words or 1 million bytes of main storage. Its processing capability approached that of an IBM System 370/145, but at a fraction of the cost. The basic machine, with 32K bytes of main storage, or 1K 32-bit words, sold for under $10,000. Interdata called the 7/32 a 32-bit *midicomputer*. In fact, the internal busing structure of the 7/32 was 16 bits wide instead of 32; a 32-bit word was moved between registers or memory by gating the low-order, 16-bit half-word onto the bus and then, when that transfer was complete, gating the high-order 16 bits onto the bus. By setting the appropriate bit in the *program status word* (*PSW*), all software that ran on Interdata's companion 16-bit machine, the 7/16, executed exactly the same on the 7/32. Compatibility with all of Interdata's earlier 16-bit processors (models 55, 70, 74, 80, and 85) was made possible through the use of microprogramming. Figure 1-18 gives a block diagram of the 7/32 processor.

1.4.14 The Interdata 8/32

In the spring of 1975, Interdata took another major stride forward in the minicomputer marketplace when it introduced its second 32-bit machine, the 8/32. The 8/32 used a complete 32-bit parallel architecture, including a 32-bit arithmetic unit, all

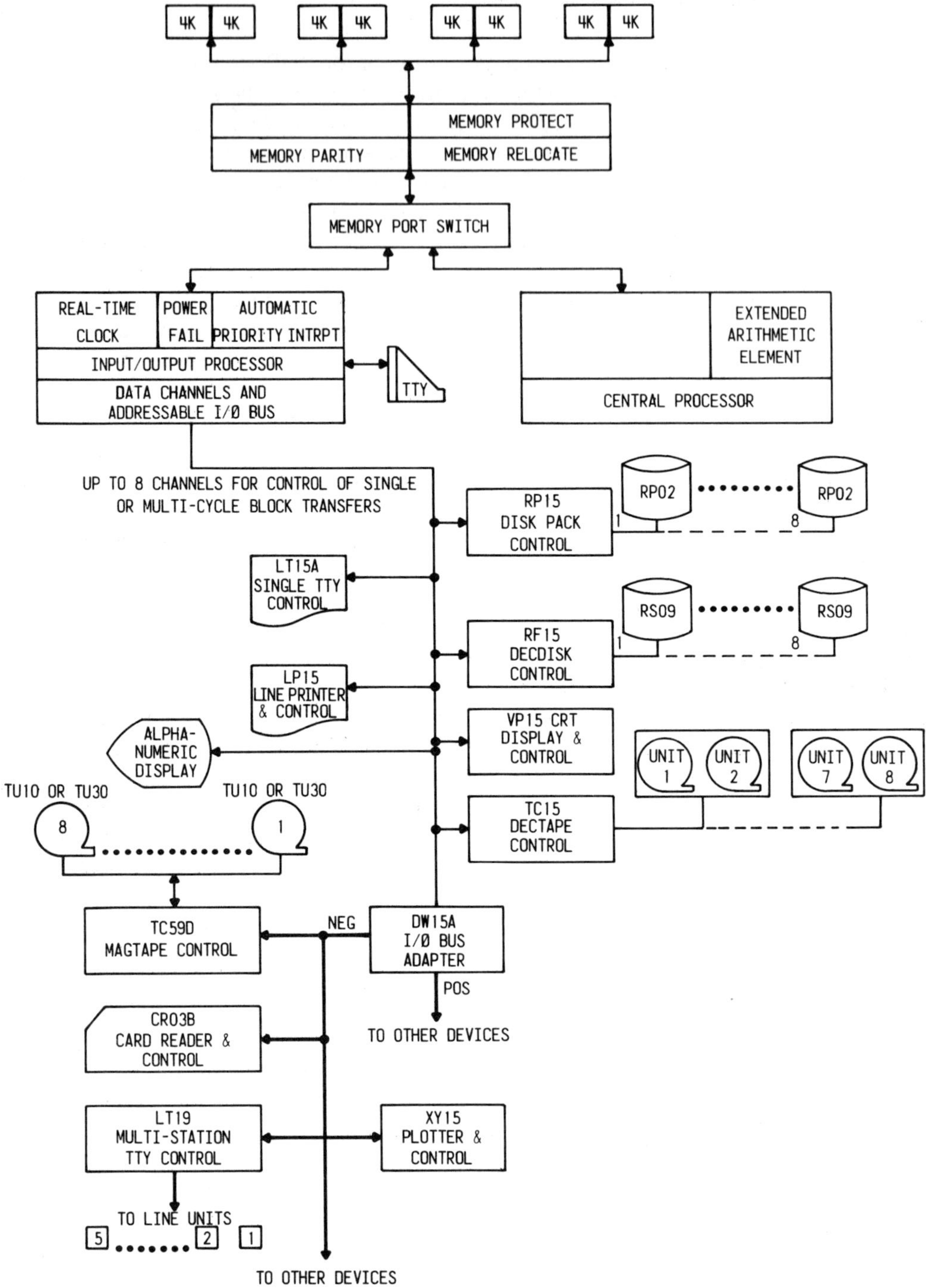

1-16 System organization of the PDP-15 [Reprinted with permission of Digital Equipment Corporation]

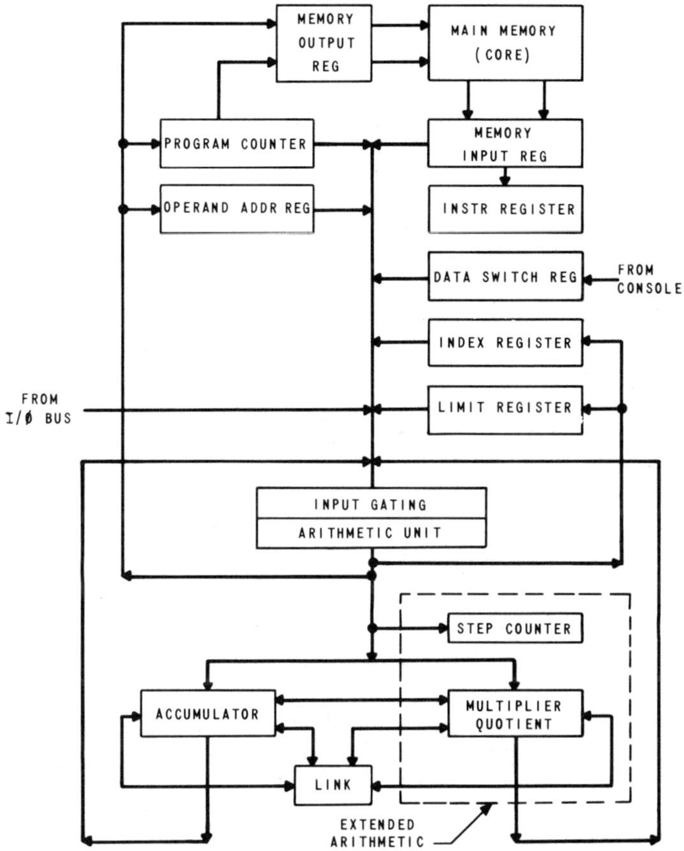

1-17 Simplified block diagram of the PDP-15 CPU [Reprinted with permission of Digital Equipment Corporation]

32-bit data paths, and the use of eight stacks of registers. Each stack contained sixteen 32-bit general registers. Rapid context switching for a heavy interrupt environment was achieved by permitting the hardware to switch automatically between appropriate register stacks. This minimized the programming overhead required by the traditional minicomputer to save all the working registers in main storage before it began to service an interrupt. Four-way interleaved memory was incorporated into the 8/32 to provide an effective 32-bit instruction time of 300 nanoseconds. In addition, a 50-nanosecond bipolar semiconductor memory was used as cache memory to enhance the overall processing time. Upward compatibility of the 8/32 with all the earlier Interdata machines was strictly observed. Interdata felt that the 8/32 and its older brother, the 7/32, were so powerful that it coined the term *megamini* to describe the category into which the two machines should be placed. An 8/32 with 128K bytes of main storage could be obtained for just over $50,000 by the summer of 1975. Figure 1-19 gives a block diagram of the Interdata 8/32.

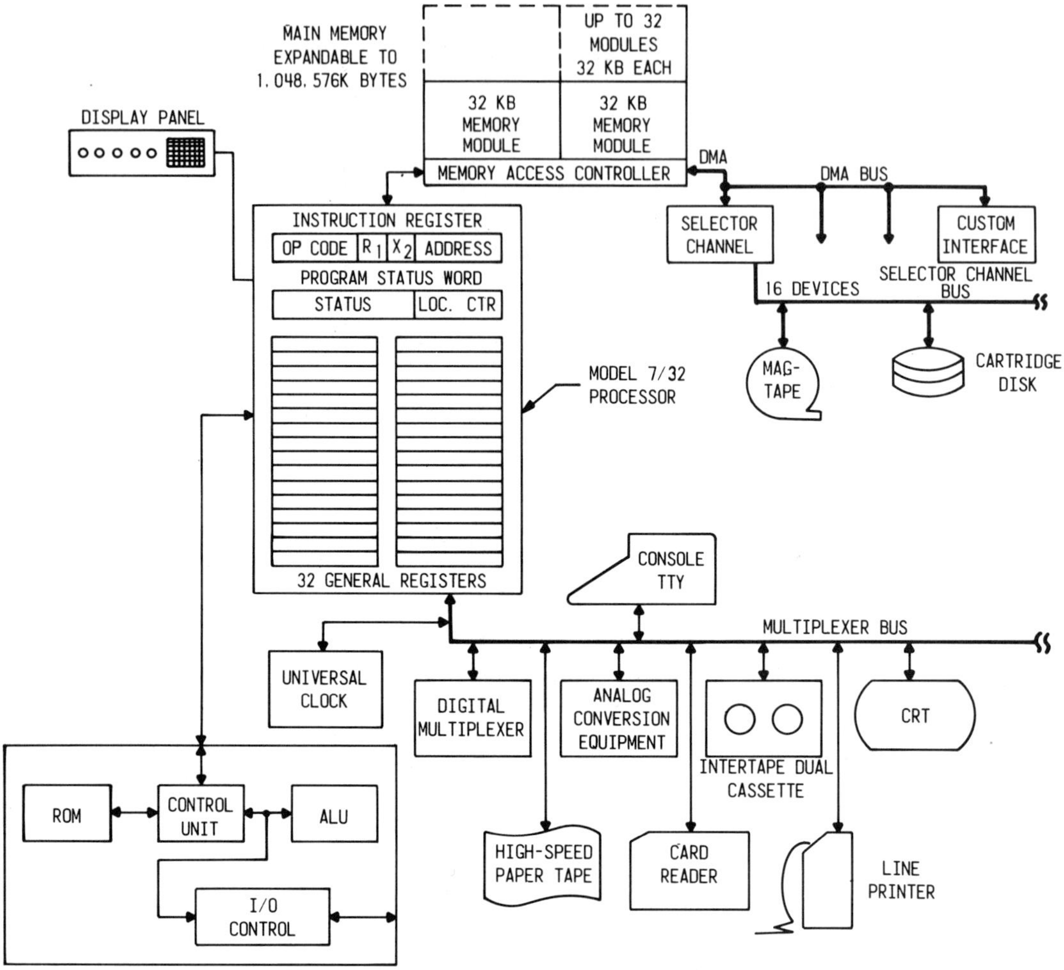

1-18 Block diagram of the Interdata 7/32 processor [Reprinted with permission of Interdata, a division of Perkin-Elmer]

Just about the time the 8/32 was introduced, DEC announced an expansion of its PDP-11 family to include a medium-scale CPU called the PDP-11/70. The PDP-11/70 was implemented to be fully upward-compatible with the earlier PDP-11 family members. The PDP-11/70, however, incorporated a high-speed, solid-state memory that functioned as a cache memory with a cycle time of 240 nanoseconds. The cache had a maximum capacity of 2048 bytes and used a 32-bit bus between the cache and main memory. A dedicated 32-bit data path was constructed between the cache and a family of high-speed peripherals that could transfer data faster than the UNIBUS. The UNIBUS architecture was retained with the 32-bit, high-speed data bus added as an

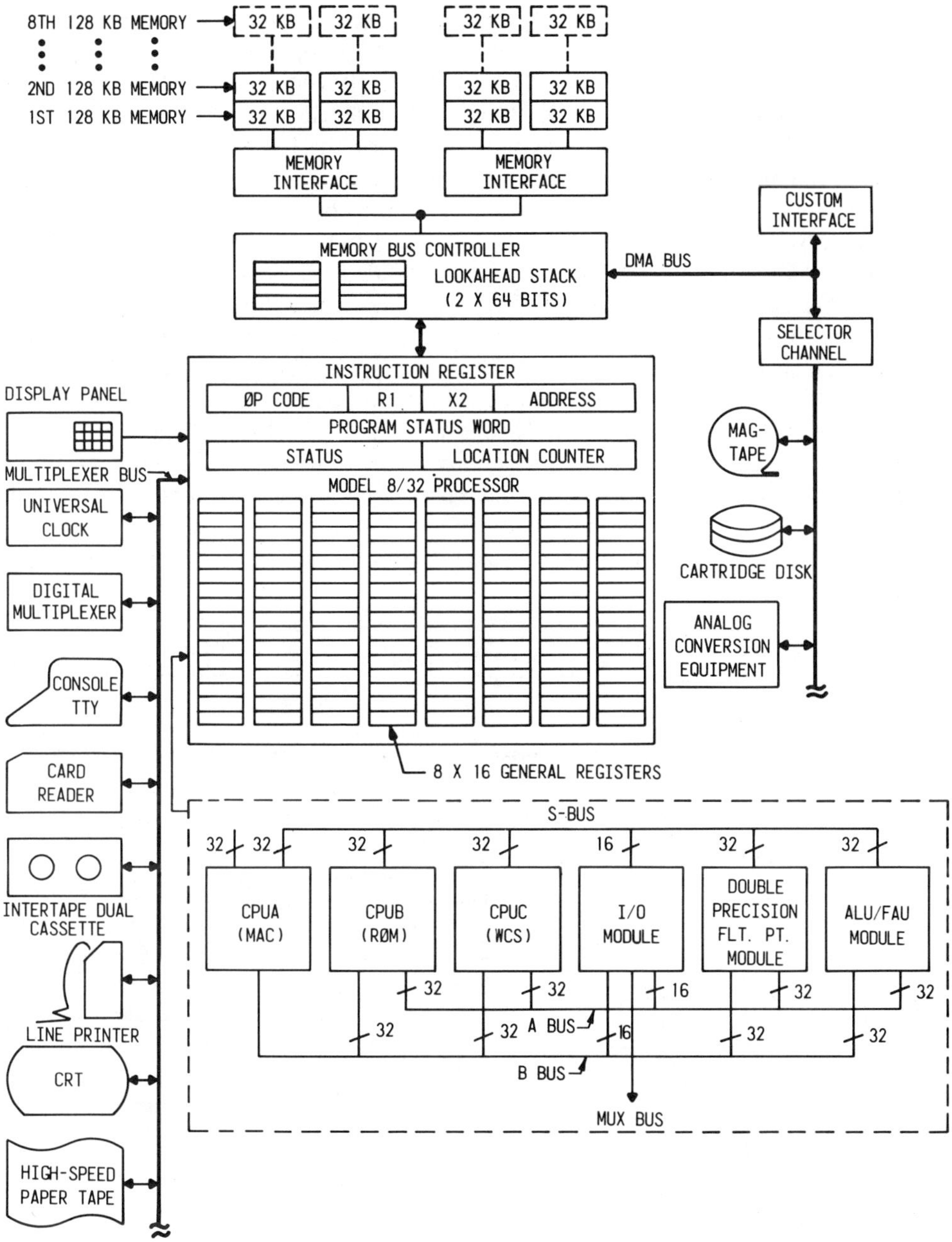

1-19 Block diagram of the Interdata 8/32 processor [Reprinted with permission of Interdata, a division of Perkin-Elmer]

overlay to the basic PDP-11 family architecture. Because of the effectiveness of the cache memory, DEC claimed that the PDP-11/70's effective memory cycle time was under 400 nanoseconds. The PDP-11/70 was designed to fill the gap that DEC felt existed between their large-scale computer, the PDP-10, which sold for just over \$800,000 in a modest configuration, and the PDP-11/50, which sold for about \$200,000 in a full-blown installation. The PDP-11/70 was not developed to be a minicomputer; it was intended to be an upward-compatible step for the PDP-11 line into the marketplace of the medium-scale computing machine or midicomputer. At the time of its announcement, a basic PDP-11/70 system consisting of the CPU, 2K-byte bipolar cache memory, 128K-byte parity core memory, and two 2K-byte disk cartridges was listed at \$72,650. An equivalent machine, Interdata's 8/32, was comparable in price. Figure 1-20 is a diagram of the general PDP-11/70 system configuration.

By the fall of 1974, the Interdata 7/16 with 8K bytes of main storage was made available at a cost of \$3200. Earlier in 1975, the MSI/T^{2}L version of the PDP-8, called the PDP-8/A (software compatible and peripheral compatible with the PDP-8/e), was marketed by DEC at a cost of \$1200 for the CPU and 4K words of main storage. In terms of sheer computational capability and cost, the philosophy of economy of scale could no longer be used to argue for centralized computing. Personal computing in terms of a dedicated small computer had become powerful enough and cheap enough to be distributed to individual users in a cost-effective manner.

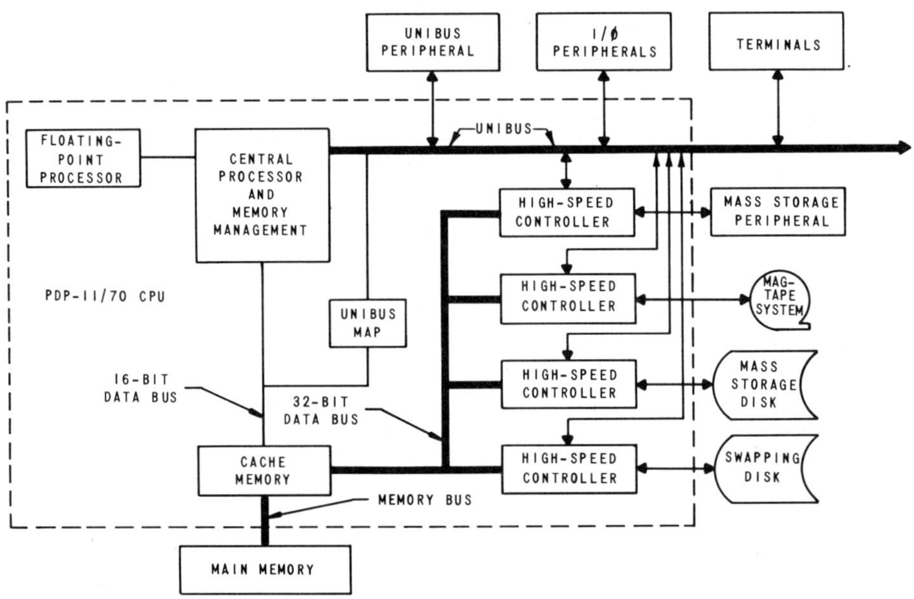

1-20 Block diagram of the PDP-11/70 [Reprinted with permission of Digital Equipment Corporation]

Because of their low cost and sophisticated computational capabilities, machines such as the Interdata 7/32, the DEC PDP-11/70, and even the PDP-8/A forced the industry to consider the definition of a minicomputer: If the PDP-8/A and 7/16 were minicomputers, could the 7/32, 8/32, and PDP-11/70 be minicomputers? Furthermore, if only the 7/32 was a minicomputer, then was the IBM 1800, the PDP-15, or the Whirlwind a minicomputer? Was it possible that even the ENIAC could be regarded as a minicomputer? In addition, how should the term "small computer" be used? At what point did a small computer cease being a small computer and become a minicomputer?

Precisely to get around this question, two national organizations that function as professional information services for the computing community have approached the definition of a minicomputer from entirely different points of view. The 1974 edition of the Auerbach Computer Technology Reports [24] defined a minicomputer as a computer that:

1. Costs less than $25,000 in a minimum stand-alone configuration.
2. Provides at least 4K or 8K bytes of memory.
3. Performs calculations under stored-program control.
4. Can be programmed in an assembly or higher-level language.
5. Can be used by a broad range of users and is not restricted to specialized applications.

The 1973 edition of the Datapro Reports on Minicomputers provided the following definition:

1. The single term "minicomputer" will be used for the entire class of stored-program, digital computers suitable for special- and general-purpose applications, whose CPU, main memory, and minimum I/O configuration are priced below $100,000. (Specifically excluded from this definition are medium- to large-scale data processing systems.)
2. In the final analysis, machine classes will be distinguishable only in terms of systems software and available peripherals.
3. Consequently, as machine classes are applications-oriented, only the way a miniaturized programmable processor is employed will ultimately provide the distinctions between machines.

By fall of 1974, the Auerbach definition was no longer entirely adequate. However, the Datapro approach, which specifically related to evolving applications features, appeared to offer a more precise clue as to exactly what a minicomputer was.

These definitions emphasized the difficulty in trying to match the features of a "minicomputer" with the accelerating rate of evolution of computing technology [25]. To a degree, it was akin to a marksman trying to hit a moving target: the next advance in technology appeared to invalidate the current concepts.

1.5 THE MINICOMPUTER: ITS APPEARANCE IN THE EVOLUTIONARY SCALE

1.5.1 Its First Identification

Auerbach [26] has pointed out that the first use of the term "mini-computer" appears in a paper written for the 1968 Fall Joint Computer Conference. The paper was called "The Mini-computer—A New Approach to Computer Design," by D. C. Hitt, G. H. Ottaway, and R. W. Shirk [27]. The hyphenated term "mini-computer" in the title was used to describe a particular small-computer application and not a class of computing machines. By 1968, however, after these small machines had emerged as a burgeoning autonomous industry propelled by the stunning success of the PDP-8, the industry seized the term "mini-computer," dropped the hyphen, and adopted it as the descriptive expression of the small-scale end of the computer industry. The minicomputer, then, has had several different meanings as the computing industry evolved. In its simplest definition, the "minicomputer" was defined as a miniature, low-cost, general-purpose digital computer. Its word size ranged from 8 bits at the lower end to 24 bits at the upper end. A 24-bit machine was not regarded as a minicomputer until 1974. The early minicomputer was characterized by small physical size (in terms of packaging), reduced processing capability (owing to its small word length), and limited software support. Beginning in 1968, substantial changes took place in the latter two areas, with the proliferation of mini's in a myriad of applications.

Perhaps the prime factor in expediting the evolution of the minicomputer was its striking annual decrease in cost. Figure 1-21 shows the cost of a basic mainframe configuration for several machines versus the cost in the year of introduction [28], starting with the CDC-160 in 1960. From this figure it can be seen that a given mainframe appeared to drop 20 to 25 percent in market price per year. With each annual decline in cost, additional features were introduced by the manufacturers in order to remain competitive. By the late 1960's, machines such as the PDP-11/20 had acquired many features traditionally associated with a medium-scale computer, but at a substantially reduced cost. A natural plateau in the cost of a basic minicomputer mainframe is inevitable since the actual purchase price will ultimately approach the hardware and assembly costs experienced by the manufacturer in making the machine. At this cost, which appears to be approximately $1000, the minicomputer will have progressed from being a computer system to being a system component or building block in a computer system.

1.5.2 A Definition Based on Main Memory Capacity

In the expansion period of the minicomputer industry from 1968 to 1974, the maximum size of main memory could have been used to determine which size category to place a computer in: small, medium, or large [29]. The tendency in the computer

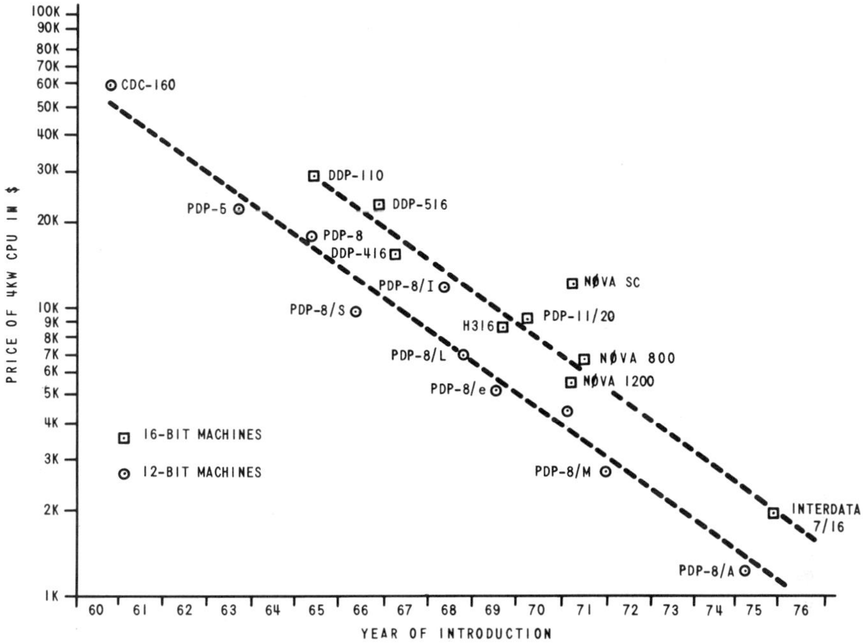

1-21 12-bit and 16-bit mainframe costs vs. year of introduction (4KW memory configuration) [From "The Effect of Low Cost Logic on Minicomputer Organization" by House and Henzel, reprinted from *Computer Design*, Vol. 10, No. 1 (Jan. 1971)]

industry has been to group machines as follows:

1. *Small Computer*. Main memory capacity: 4K words to 32K words. Examples are the DEC PDP-8, IBM 1800, and IBM System/360 model 30.
2. *Medium Computer*. Main memory capacity: 32K words to 128K words. Examples are the DEC PDP-11/45, Data General Supernova, and the IBM System/370 model 145.
3. *Large Computer*. Main memory capacity: typically in excess of 512K words. An example is the IBM System/360 model 67.

The early minicomputers, which had either 12-bit or 16-bit word lengths, permitted no more than 65K words to be used in main memory. This would place these machines in either the small computer category or the lower range of the medium computer category. The more recent minicomputers, such as the Interdata 7/32, have virtually invalidated main memory capacity as a determining attribute in identifying a minicomputer.

No precise definition of a minicomputer can really be made. Until 1974, the most obvious characteristics that distinguished a minicomputer from other digital computers were small physical size, low cost, and word length. After 1974, however, word length could no longer be used as a defining criterion. The two primary characteristics became size and cost. The major factor in creating this situation was the continuing rapid advance of computer structures brought about by technological innovation. Technology permitted the hardware features of the larger machines to be incorporated in smaller and smaller packages at continually declining costs. The advances in technology in a single year quickly outdated any definitions predicated on architectural characteristics. Only if one considers freezing technology at any given point in time can specific distinctions be made between the various classes of computing machines.

1.5.3 The Mini: A Formal Definition

Since definitions are necessary in any involved technical discussion, let a minicomputer be defined as follows: *A minicomputer is a small, general-purpose, stored-program digital computer that:*

1. *Has a word length ranging from 8 bits to 32 bits.*
2. *Provides at least 4096 words of program memory.*
3. *Sells for under $20,000 in a* minimum usable configuration, *consisting of a teletypewriter, a power supply, and a front panel to be used as a programmer's console.*

The only major differences between a minicomputer and other nonspecialized digital computers are its small size and low cost.

It would be appropriate to digress for a moment and consider the difference, if any, between the small computers discussed in Section 1.4 and the minicomputer just defined. The term *small computer* has often been used synonymously with the term *midicomputer*. Again, the two most distinguishing characteristics are size and cost. The modern minicomputer in a minimum usable configuration may be available as a desktop machine; the midicomputer may be found enclosed in a free-standing, large mainframe. In 1977, the cost differential between the two machine categories was substantial. The price of a mini varied from less than $5000 to $20,000, while the price of a midi ranged from $25,000 to $150,000. Support for machines in both categories was substantial in terms of hardware diagnostic programs and the variety of user software packages. The difference between the top-of-the-line minicomputers and various midicomputers was only in degree.

1.5.4 The Midi: A Formal Definition

Again, to establish a definition from which future discussion can proceed, a midicomputer may be defined as follows: *A midicomputer is a digital machine that:*

1. *Complies with the minimum usable configuration, as given for the minicomputer.* (Aside from physical size and cost, this statement makes the minicomputer category a subset of the midicomputer category.)
2. *Has a word length ranging from 16 bits to 32 bits.*
3. *Permits expansion of main core memory up to 250,000 words.*

4. *Permits foreground/background operations that require a sophisticated operating system.*
5. *Has a mainframe that is usually a large, free-standing enclosure* (as opposed to a simple desktop housing or rack-mounted unit).
6. *Has a minimal configuration cost between $50,000 and $150,000.*
7. *Is synonymous with the term "small computer."*

With this definition it is possible to evaluate the early digital machines that were the predecessors of the minicomputer. In terms of cost and physical size, all the early machines were midicomputers (small computers), including the LGP-30, the Burroughs E-101, and the Bendix G-15. If only processing capability is considered, both the Whirlwind and UNIVAC I would be placed in the small computer category. Since the ENIAC did not function as a stored-program machine, it would have to be excluded from this category. (Recall that programming of the ENIAC was achieved through an elaborate mechanical setup procedure; see Section 1.2.3.) However, the CDC-160 would be classified as a midicomputer because of its $65,000 purchase price. The first true minicomputer would be the PDP-5, which was the progenitor of the archetypal mini, the PDP-8. Similarly, in terms of cost and physical size, machines such as the PDP-15, the IBM 1800, 1130, System/3, and System/7, the Hewlett-Packard HP3000, and the Burroughs 1700 are true midicomputers.

1.5.5 The Maxi: A Formal Definition

To complete the spectrum of machine categories, there exists the large or maxicomputer that can differ substantially from the midicomputer. By definition, *the maxicomputer possesses the following characteristics:*

1. *Its architecture may be highly unconventional, incorporating pipelining or parallel processing structures.*
2. *It may exist in configurations well beyond the minimum usable configuration defined for the midicomputer, usually employing a rich mix of peripheral devices and the latest technologies.*
3. *Its word length may be variable, ranging from 16 bits at the low end to 64 or more bits at the high end.*
4. *It is housed in a physically imposing structure, usually consisting of several free-standing enclosures.*
5. *It offers a wide range of software for the user and multiple operating modes, including multiprogramming and multiprocessing.*
6. *The basic system configuration costs more than $150,000.*

The ILLIAC-IV and the IBM 370/195 are examples of maxicomputer systems.

In terms of marketing these various computer systems, the manufacturers have sold to three distinct customer groups:*

---

*These categories are modifications of customer groupings originally suggested by the DATA-PRO research organization [24].

1. *The original equipment manufacturer (OEM)*, who has typically purchased machines from a vendor in lots of 100 or more. The OEM incorporates the computer as a part of a larger system which the vendor sells as his own product. Often no reference is made to the inclusion of the computer in the OEM's equipment.
2. *The naive or limited-skills end user*, who normally obtains from the vendor a highly specialized computer system that is dedicated to a specific set of functions. Typically, these systems are "turn key" packages that permit the user to insert a key, turn the power on, and perform a series of prescribed operations. The naive end user, who cannot modify the system, relies on the vendor for the development of the entire system package (both software and hardware) as well as maintenance.
3. *The sophisticated or mature end user*, who buys exactly the computing system that is thought to be needed. Typically, the sophisticated end user can do all the software development, hardware interfacing, and maintenance. The user relies on the vendor for system components (CPU, memory, peripherals, etc.) which the user configures for a variety of applications.

1.5.6 The Small Mini: A Transitional Category

In 1974, General Automation (GA) introduced the LSI-12/16, a 12-bit microcomputer that used a single-chip processor employing *n*-channel *silicon-on-sapphire* (*SOS*) technology. A cross-program development system that could run on GA's SPC-16 minicomputer line was also provided. Unfortunately, the SOS technology did not prove economically feasible, and Rockwell International, the company's chief supplier, discontinued making the SOS devices the next year. This forced temporary curtailment of the development of SOS technology-based microcomputers. However, exploratory development continued at several microprocessor manufacturing companies.

By late 1973, the rapid development of LSI technology led to the appearance of several repackaged minicomputer structures [30]. These machines attempted to fill the gap that had appeared between the high-performance minicomputer and the much less expensive microcomputer. These repackaged machines represented a general structure that, for want of a better descriptive term, could be called a *small minicomputer*. The major characteristic of the small mini was a downward migration of the features of an older minicomputer structure into an LSI hardware package. The entire CPU and at least 4K words of memory were placed on a single printed circuit board. Virtually all software written for the original minicomputer could run on the small-mini version. The small mini could be interfaced with its external environment through standard interface modules, exactly as could its predecessor. Typical entries in this category were Data General's Nova-2 and DEC's PDP-8/A.

The small mini represented a *transitional category* between the maturing minicomputer and the infant microcomputer that first appeared in 1972. The rapid development of LSI was responsible not only for the appearance of the small mini, but also for the stunning development of the microprocessor from 1972 and on.

1.6 THE MICROPROCESSOR: A NATURAL CONSEQUENCE OF LSI DEVELOPMENT

1.6.1 The Emergence of MOS/LSI Technology

The emerging semiconductor technology of the 1960's refined the processes required to manufacture integrated circuits until very complicated functions could be placed on a single silicon chip. In the late 1960's, MOS/LSI technology permitted component densities of 100 or more gates to be placed on a silicon die. The cost of design, development, and tooling was substantial for each new chip. Consequently, the manufacturer required a broad range of market areas in order to spread the high initial development costs over a wide customer base. One such market area was semiconductor memory applications. At first, MOS techniques were used to manufacture semiconductor ROM's and then RAM's. Intel Corporation's 1103 semiconductor memory element with a capacity of 1K bits quickly became an industry standard. Improved fabrication techniques and increasing success in the semiconductor marketplace stimulated a steady advance in the sophistication of MOS technology. From 1969 through 1973, MOS/LSI technology progressed from a single chip with 100 transistors to a single chip containing over 14,000 transistors. This progression led to the concept of placing the central processor of a reasonably simple computer on a few chips of silicon. Using this philosophy it was possible to visualize a complete digital computer on a single printed circuit board.

The initial application of such structures was in the area of small electronic calculators. These *hand-held* calculators generally employed a serial CPU composed of one or two MOS/LSI chips. The internal structure was built around a *binary-coded decimal* (*BCD*) organization. These calculators were often capable of using word lengths that reached 100 bits, or 25 BCD digits. Perhaps their most interesting aspect was that they were designed around the *interaction time* of the human operator. Because of this, internal operations were done serially, one BCD digit at a time. Inputs to the internal processor were made through a miniature keyboard on the calculator. A keystroke operation (i.e., depressing a key) invoked a specific, internally stored function in the calculator. Consequently, the set of keystroke inputs could be regarded as a keyboard language defined by the interpretive code associated with each key and stored in the calculator's internal ROM. The calculator market was highly successful in terms of sales and future growth by mid-1971.

1.6.2 The Intel 4004 Microprocessor

In 1971, Intel Corporation developed a custom-made MOS/LSI device for calculators manufactured by Japan's Busicom [3]. However, Intel could not commit themselves to customized calculator chip development because of limited internal resources. Therefore, they opted for more general, building-block structures using four LSI circuit chips. The fundamental member of this chip set was a 4-bit CPU with a ROM chip for implementing the instruction set and a RAM chip for data storage. I/O was achieved by a shift register chip. Intel, apparently, had been initially unsure of the full dimensions of their design for Busicom. However, several companies quickly observed that the Busicom chip set not only met the needs of the calculator manufacturer, but offered the user the potential of *changing* the chip set to meet an entirely different application need simply by changing the ROM microcode. After taking a long look at the MOS/LSI central processor marketplace, Intel negotiated an agreement with Busicom whereby Intel was permitted to sell this customized CPU as long as the device was *not* used to make calculators. Consequently, the first commercial *microprocessor* was the 4-bit Intel 4004, introduced in November 1971 and patterned after the customized Busicom MOS/LSI CPU. Intel produced additional components to be used with the 4004, including a type 4001 ROM control memory, a type 4002 RAM data store, and a type 4003 10-bit shift register with enable logic. These additional circuits, implemented on *separate* chips, were used with the 4004 CPU to form a configuration that functioned as a *microcomputer*. Intel called this chip configuration, when sold as a set, its MCS-4 microcomputer. Figure 1-22 is a block diagram of the 4004 CPU. Figure 1-23 gives the timing for a basic instruction cycle.

Intel, recognizing that this new market could generate a substantial demand for semiconductor memory devices, established the philosophy that its 4004 CPU would be used to sell its standard semiconductor ROM and RAM circuits. They anticipated that for every microprocessor sold, the customer would also need an average of eight memory elements. A 1974 projection by Quantum Science Corporation [3] placed the 1977 microprocessor market in the United States at $12.6 million and the 1977 market for peripheral circuits (memories) at $92.5 million. It is easy to understand why Intel's original marketing philosophy was adopted by all of the major microprocessor manufacturers. The microprocessor opened up a broad range of applications for semiconductor memory devices with a corresponding potential for large-volume, high-profit sales.

The 4004 microprocessor was a 4-bit parallel CPU structure that performed calculations in either binary or BCD. In the BCD mode, calculation took place sequentially, one BCD digit at a time. In the binary mode, calculation took place in blocks of 4 parallel bits. The 4004 was functionally partitioned into five distinct sections. These sections consisted of a set of 16 4-bit registers used for indexing and general-purpose storage, a 4-bit ALU, an address-incrementing circuit, an 8-bit instruction register with decoder, and peripheral control circuitry. The 4004 had a basic command repertory of 45 instructions. Each instruction was made up of 8 bits that could be decoded and executed in either 10.8 or 21.6 microseconds.

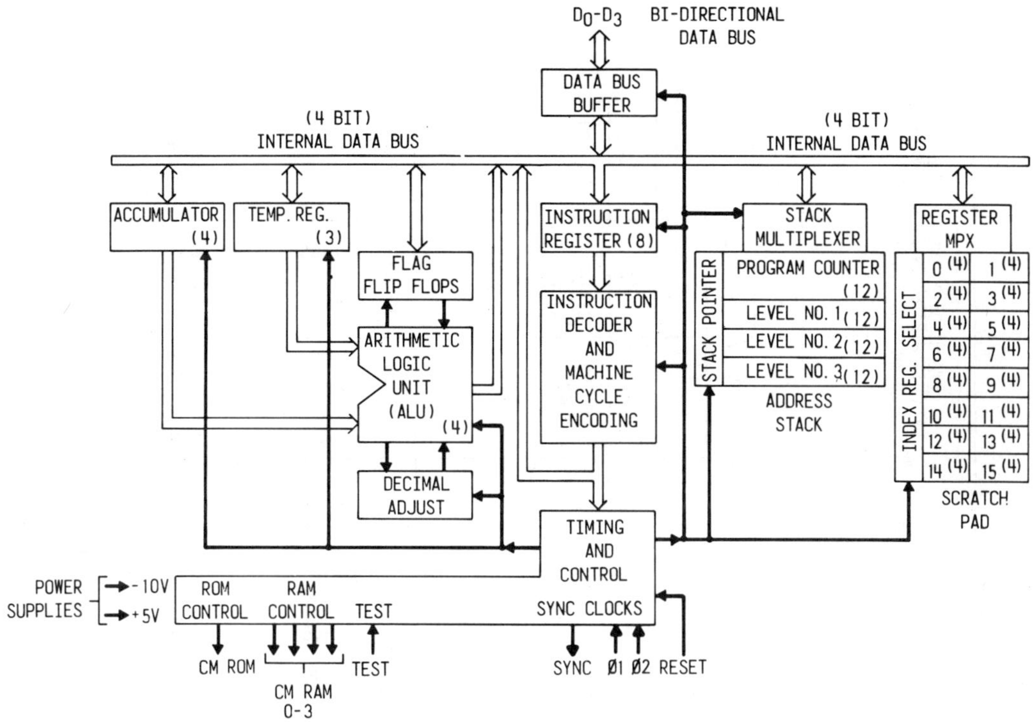

1-22 Block diagram of the 4004 CPU [Source: The Intel 4004 Microprocessor User's Manual, 1973 edition; reprinted with permission of the Intel Corporation]

Intel provided the Intellec 4 as a complete program development environment. It was built around the MCS-4 chip set and included a cabinet, power supply, programmer's panel, and *universal asynchronous receiver/transmitter* (*UART*) for teletypewriter-like I/O communications. Figure 1-23 gives a block diagram of the MCS-4 microcomputer.

1.6.3 The Intel 8008 Microprocessor

The *second* commercially available microprocessor was also developed and marketed by Intel. The Datapoint Corporation funded the development of an 8-bit microprocessor by Intel to be used in the Model 2200 Intelligent Terminal designed by Datapoint [3]. By the time the 8-bit chip set was developed, Datapoint had refined the specifications for its Intelligent Terminal and concluded that the Intel microprocessor was too slow. The project was abandoned by Datapoint after 2 years of development. Intel, however, completed the final design and marketed its 8-bit Model 8008 microprocessor in early 1972. Recognizing that the 8008 with its terminal-oriented instruc-

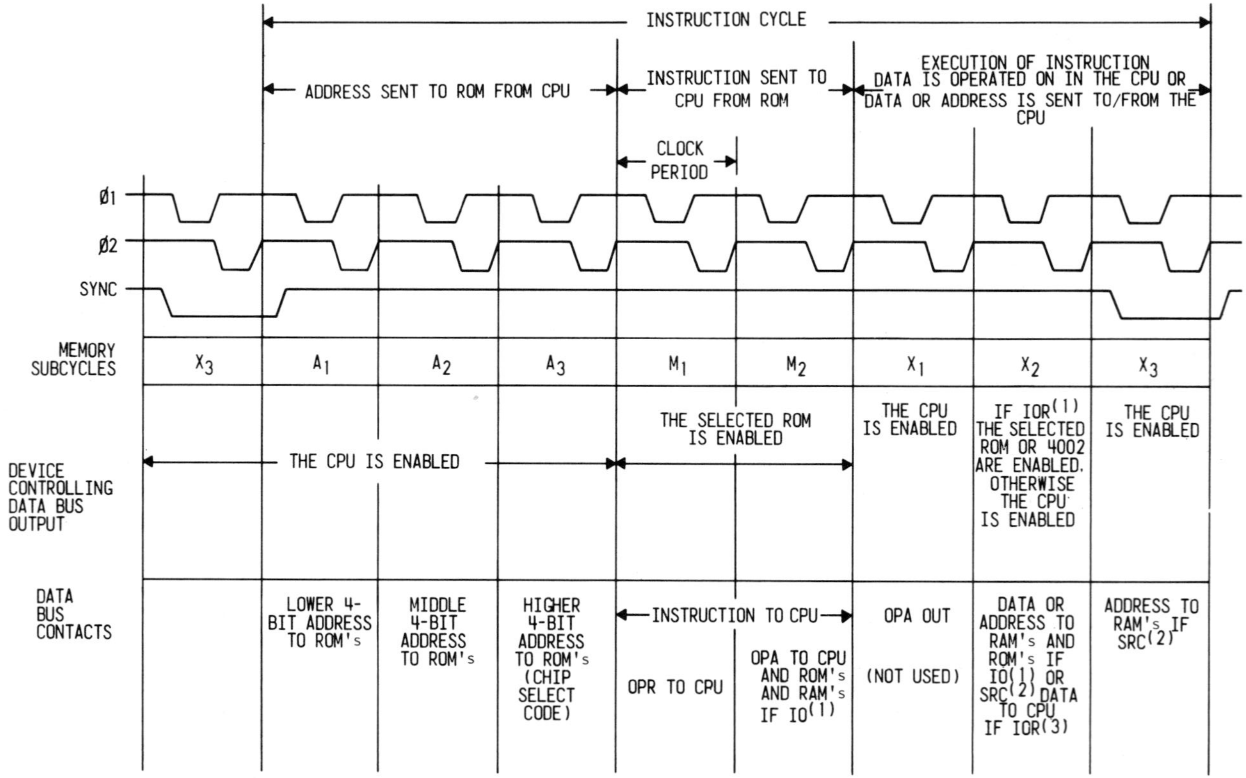

(1) IO INSTRUCTIONS CONTROL THE FLOW OF INFORMATION BETWEEN ACCUMULATOR IN CPU, I/O LINES IN ROM's AND RAM's AND RAM STORAGE. IOR STANDS FOR IO READ. IN THIS CASE THE CPU WILL RECEIVE DATA FROM RAM STORAGE LOCATIONS I/O INPUT LINES.

(2) THE SRC INSTRUCTION DESIGNATES THE CHIP NUMBER AND ADDRESS FOR A FOLLOWING IO INSTRUCTION.

1-23 Basic instruction cycle time for the Intel 4004 [Source: The Intel 4004 Microprocessor User's Manual, 1973 edition; reprinted with permission of the Intel Corporation]

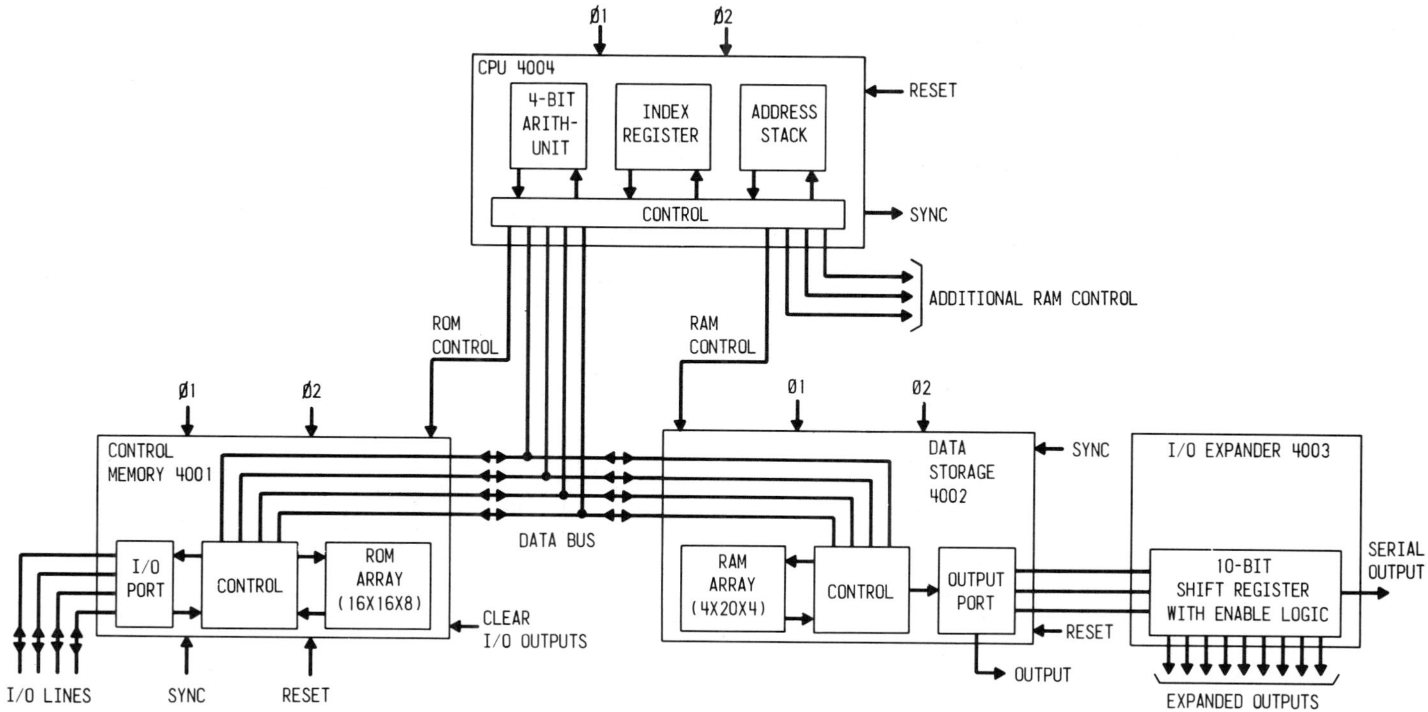

1-24 Block diagram of the MCS-4 Micro computer [Source: The Intel 4004 Microprocessor User's Manual, 1973 edition; reprinted with permission of the Intel Corporation]

tion set and 8-bit-wide busing structure had a wide marketing potential, Intel placed the 8008 in the marketplace for specialized controllers and included limited software support. The move was an immediate marketing success.

Figure 1-25 gives the internal organization of the 8008 microprocessor chip. Figure 1-26 gives a description of the 8008 basic system, including the CPU and necessary support chips. The 8008 structure was effectively an 8-bit extension of the 4004. Its CPU contained seven 8-bit registers on-chip that could be used for scratch pad memory storage; an 8-word by 14-bit address stack, and a single-level hardware interrupt lead. The 8008 was a binary-oriented internal processing machine. The 4004 could operate in either binary or BCD. The 8008 microprocessor was used in conjunction with a ROM and 20 TTL device chips to configure a minimum MCS-8 microcomputer chip set.

Both machines used 8-bit instruction words, but the 4004 had to make two ROM references to configure its 8-bit instruction. The 4004 was regarded by Intel as an equivalent replacement for 90 TTL logic packages, while the 8008 was regarded as an equivalent replacement for 125 TTL logic packages. Both the MCS-4 and MCS-8

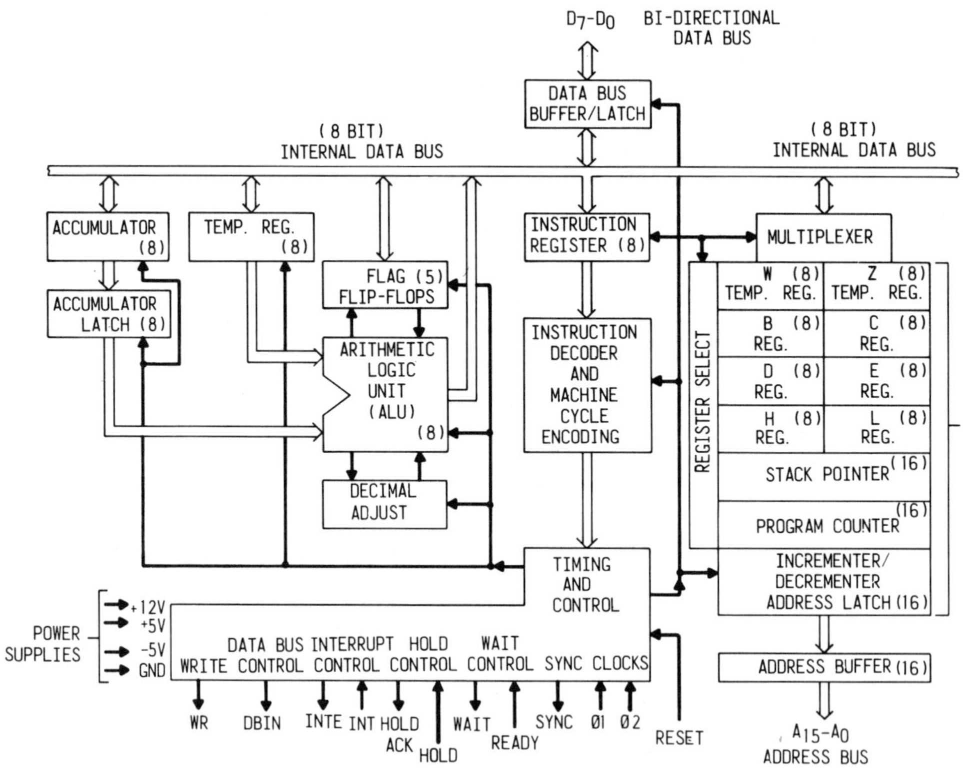

1-25 Block diagram of the 8008 CPU [Reprinted with permission of the Intel Corporation]

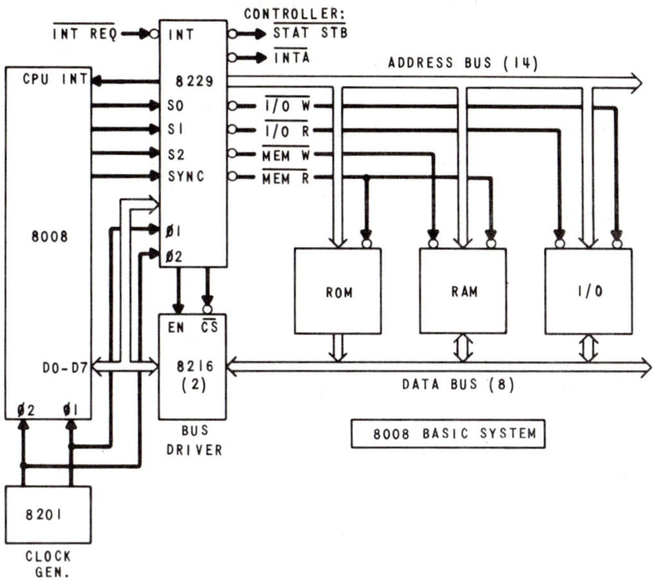

1-26 Basic 8008 system configuration [Reprinted with permission of the Intel Corporation]

microcomputers represented archetypes for their word-length categories and functioned as an initial reference point for the emerging microprocessor industry.

1.6.4 The Basic Microprocessor Structures

The success of the Intel MCS-8 microcomputer chip set prompted other semiconductor manufacturers to enter the microprocessor marketplace. A wide range of products appeared with no standardization of device features being agreed upon by the manufacturers.

The initial technology used to implement the early microprocessors had been PMOS. Later implementations took place using NMOS, CMOS, and bipolar technologies. The variety of devices available by spring 1978 could be reduced to one of three microprocessor categories [2,31]:

1. The *calculator-like structure*, which consisted of a 4-bit processor oriented toward serially processing 4 bits at a time as a BCD digit. The 4-bit processor was placed on a single silicon chip with, typically, 16 pins to interconnect the chip with the external world. The Intel 4004 was the first such IC structure.
2. The *8-bit, 12-bit, or 16-bit processor structure*, with many of the characteristics of a low-cost minicomputer's CPU, including instruction execution times of less than 5 microseconds. The 8008 was the first entry in this category. Tables 1-5 and 1-6 itemize some 8-bit and 16-bit microprocessors, respectively.

TABLE 1-5 8-Bit Microprocessors

Company	Model	Technology	Shortest Inst Time (μs)	Number of Pins on Dip
Electronic Arrays	—	NMOS	2.0	40
Fairchild	F-8	NMOS		
INSELEC	—	CMOS-SOS		
INTEL	8008	PMOS	20.0	18
INTEL	8080	NMOS	2.0	40
MOSTEK	MK5065	PMOS	4.2	40
Motorola	M6800	NMOS	2.0	40
National	IMP-8	PMOS		
RCA	COSMAC	CMOS	6.0	40
Rockwell	PPS-8	PMOS	4.0	42
SIGNETICS	2650	NMOS	5.0	40
ZILOG	Z80	NMOS	1.0	40
Western Electric	MAC-8	CMOS	0.5	40

TABLE 1-6 16-Bit Microprocessors

Company	Model	Technology	Shortest Inst Time (μs)	Number of Pins on Dip
Fairchild	9440	I^2L	1.5	40
INTEL	8086	NMOS	0.5	40
General Instrument	CP1600	NMOS		
ZILOG	Z-8000	NMOS	0.250	40–48
Texas Instruments	9900	NMOS	2.7	64
National	8900	NMOS	0.5	40

3. The *bit-sliced processor structure,* which permitted machine architectures to be configured with variable word lengths. The microprocessor used in such a configuration was partitioned into 2-bit, 4-bit, or 8-bit slices on a *single* chip. A bit-sliced chip could then be paralleled to produce a microcomputer with a word length ranging from 8 bits up to 32 bits. The overall microcomputer required the use of additional *outrigger chips* to form the complete computer structure. Typically, a bit-sliced CPU element contained a bit group of the

working register set, the ALU, status indicators, the PC, and either an on-chip hardware stack or a pointer that could be used to reference an off-chip memory stack. Multiple buses were used to interconnect the paralleled bit-sliced chips and form the overall machine. The machine instructions were implemented by the user in an external microprogrammed control memory. The user was thus able to define the machine's macroinstruction set, implement it in microcode, and generate a microcomputer with capabilities that closely approximated those of a minicomputer. Table 1-7 identifies the bipolar bit-sliced microprocessor entries as of the spring of 1978.

TABLE 1-7 Bipolar Bit-Sliced Microprocessors

Company	Model	Logic	Number of Bits	Number of Pins on Dip	Cycle Time (μs)
AMD	2901	STTL	4	40	0.10
INTEL	3001	TTL	2	28	0.1
Monolithic Memories	6701	TTL	4	24	0.2
Motorola	M10800	ECL	4	48	0.075
Raytheon	RP-16	TTL	4	48	0.6
Texas Instruments	S481	Schottky TTL (STTL)	4	48	0.10
Texas Instruments	400A/401A	I^2L	4	40	0.25

Note: Bit-sliced microprocessors offer the possibility of configuring microcomputers from the chip sets with sophisticated minicomputer capabilities.

1.6.5 The Initial Microprocessor Market Entries—After Intel

In only 4 years, microprocessors had matured through several successive development cycles (sometimes called generations). By the spring of 1975, second-generation NMOS/LSI CPU's had become available while first-generation PMOS/LSI microprocessors had just begun to be employed. Simply stated, the remarkable advance in microprocessor structures in such a short period of time was due to the rapid maturation of LSI technology [2,3,31]. This technology evolution permitted the development of economical fabrication techniques to produce standardized integrated circuits in large volumes at low cost. The characteristics of these standard IC's were changed simply by replacing one ROM with another. This provided the user with a direct replacement for hard-wired or random logic in the form of the LSI microprocessor.

The LSI microprocessor developed so rapidly that the semiconductor houses that first supplied them had difficulty in anticipating where they would be used. The primary problem with the initial microprocessors was that they had been developed by semiconductor manufacturers with virtually no experience in computer system design and no awareness as to what software support packages were required by a computer. Sophistication, however, came quickly to the microprocessor manufacturers, and by 1974 software support packages were made available by several houses. However, it was not anticipated that any LSI microprocessor manufacturer would seriously compete with the minicomputer makers in terms of overall software support. The minicomputer manufacturer had years of experience and an established software base of user programs. In addition, the semiconductor manufacturers were not strongly motivated to compete with the minicomputer makers in the general-purpose computer marketplace. The minicomputer manufacturers represented some of the biggest potential customers for the LSI microprocessor makers. This situation was particularly underscored with the appearance of the bit-sliced bipolar/LSI microprocessors and the ease with which they could be used to configure fast, architecturally sophisticated, and inexpensive minicomputers.

1.7 A COMPARATIVE CONSIDERATION OF MICRO VERSUS MINI

A fundamental difference between a microprocessor and a minicomputer is that the microprocessor is *not* a computer; it comprises only the central processing function found in a computer. In order to form a functional microcomputer, a microprocessor consisting of one or several LSI semiconductor chips requires the addition of one or more ROM's for control, one or more RAM's for program and intermediate storage, clock circuitry, I/O interface chips to operate various peripherals, and a power supply. The term "micro" has been used to denote the small physical size of the semiconductor components used to configure the microprocessor. "Micro" does *not* automatically imply that the microprocessor is a *microprogrammable* structure [2,32]. In fact, most of the original commercially available microprocessors were not microprogrammable. However, the bit-sliced bipolar/LSI chip sets that appeared in late 1974 could only be controlled by a microprogram. The microprocessor was assembled from standard LSI components and operated under stored-program control from either ROM or RAM. The standard LSI components permitted the engineer to use one hardware configuration for many different applications. Often a simple exchange of ROM's was sufficient to specialize the LSI configuration for a new application. Consequently, product modifications could be made easily even in the field, and the resulting devices were more reliable because of the fewer parts and interconnections required by the LSI configurations.

A *microprocessor*, consequently, may be regarded as the central processing portion of a computer using one or more LSI circuit chips. A *microcomputer* can be defined as a computer structure that is built around a microprocessor and uses a combination of ROM and RAM to perform instruction-oriented control. It also requires the use of I/O interface chips to communicate with devices external to the computer. In late 1974, a microprocessor could be obtained commercially for as little as $50, but the complete microcomputer configured around that microprocessor could cost several hundred dollars even for a modest system. A sophisticated system such as the Intellec 8/MDS80, which was built around the Intel 8080 microprocessor, cost more than $2000 if a teletypewriter was included for I/O operations.

The LSI microprocessor configurations that were marketed commercially by various sources [32,33,34,35] took the following forms:

1. *MOS/LSI and bipolar/LSI chip sets.* This form typically contained a microprocessor built from one or more LSI circuit chips, a RAM for program and scratch pad memory storage, a ROM for control storage, and a selection of I/O interface chips. This was the most basic form in which the microprocessor configuration was sold. The buyer was required to lay out the printed circuit boards, mount the chips on the boards, and interface the separate chips according to the manufacturer's guidelines. This form was normally used by OEM-type suppliers after a final microprocessor-based design had been debugged and was ready to be marketed. The specialized system development costs could only be absorbed if the quantity of systems to be sold by the OEM suppliers was large and the initial cash outlay could be spread over many customers.
2. *Microprocessor-based printed circuit board sets.* These boards were supplied to the buyer with the microprocessor chips and other supporting logic already mounted and interconnected by the manufacturer. In addition, the manufacturer validated all circuit boards by testing them individually and as a set before releasing them to the buyer. Such an approach proved ideal for embedded-system applications, where the board set could easily be incorporated in the housing of an existing system. In such an environment, the existing system would supply power and ground to the board set. (An intelligent instrument would represent such an application.) Designers often used the board set for initial product development. After the final product was established, a chip-set configuration would be used to optimally package the proven-in device by developing special circuit boards for the application and mounting the chip set on them. This substantially reduced the cost of mass-produced units.
3. *General-purpose microcomputer configurations.* Several semiconductor manufacturers supplied entire hardware packages, including a CPU board, ROM board, RAM board, I/O interface boards, a pluggable control panel, and power supplies in either an enclosed housing or card cage system. (A *card cage* was simply a physical frame that held the necessary circuit boards.) It was not enclosed, it had no front panel, and it was connected directly to the power supplies. Its chief function was to be embedded in a system without the user

necessarily ever knowing that it was there. Such configurations were used for prototyping or initial system development. Special breadboarding printed circuit boards were provided so that the buyer could construct logic that interfaced specifically with the application. The breadboarding boards allowed the user to construct circuits that were easily modifiable. The ability to modify circuits permitted the user to optimize the overall design before finally freezing it. In this manner, a microcomputer system could be customized by the user, intermixing the specialized interface boards with the standard logic modules in the card cage housing.

4. *Microprocessor-based minicomputers*. By late 1974, minicomputer manufacturers were incorporating microprocessors as CPU's in specialized application packages. Minicomputers had been used in such areas prior to this, but they were overpowered for the applications and were not particularly cost-effective. The bipolar/LSI microprocessor chip sets foreshadowed the possibility of constructing a microcomputer that would be equivalent to a sophisticated minicomputer, but at a fraction of the minicomputer's cost.

The minicomputer began as a modularized approach to computing that offered cost-effective computation in a wide range of application areas. They were marketed by systems-oriented manufacturers, who provided a broad range of software packages and hardware options that made the minicomputer systems easy to use. The microprocessor, in contrast, began as an offshoot of the hand-held-calculator market. They were sold as chip sets, board sets, or card cages from which a microcomputer could be built. These microprocessor hardware configurations were supplied by semiconductor houses with little software support and no standardization of interfacing procedures. The immaturity of this support was gradually reduced by the major semiconductor houses until, by the fall of 1974, they were providing a full program-development system that could run on a large host computer. Intel's software system for the 8080 was typical of such support packages. It consisted of a PL/M cross-compiler, an 8080 simulator, and an on-line editor that could be run on an IBM System/370. Most of the hardware features associated with the traditional minicomputer were being incorporated in the second-generation MOS/LSI microprocessor structures on the drawing boards or already commercially available in late fall of 1974. In addition, the bipolar/LSI, bit-sliced chip sets permitted the construction of complete, highly sophisticated computers that looked like many existing mini's.

1.8 A RATIONAL STRUCTURE OF APPLICATION CATEGORIES

1.8.1 Classification by Computer Usage

To better understand the overall implications of the emerging relationship between microprocessors and minicomputers, it is worthwhile to consider the various application areas in which these devices might be used.

The application areas of mini/microcomputers may be classified *generically*, according to the manner in which the usage of computers has evolved. Koudela [22] has identified four basic categories* into which all applications may be grouped:

1. *Process-only group.* Data are entered into a computer in a machine-readable format and processed to completion as a job by the computer. The results are displayed on a hard-copy device or a CRT terminal. This category corresponds to the batch-processing systems developed for the early computers.
2. *Data acquisition and processing group.* The computer obtains the raw data directly from the environment that it is monitoring. Standard input devices include remote data-entry terminals and on-line sensors that track the environment. In particular, this category includes on-line data acquisition systems that accept inputs directly from the area(s) where the data were created and then transmits the processed results where needed (the input devices may not be located in this area). A time-sharing system would fit into this category.
3. *Data acquisition, processing, and control group.* The computer administers the control of several external processes by acquiring data from the processes, manipulating the data according to the appropriate control algorithm, and then returning control signals back to the processes in order to direct their performance. This category specifically includes *real-time computer systems* that return the control information to the monitored process fast enough to affect the process environment at the time of data acquisition.
4. *Multiprocessor configurations.* This group treats individual processors as system resources to be allocated to a given job in either a master-slave arrangement with one specially designated processor functioning as the master, or through the use of shared memory areas common to several processors. In the strictest sense, multiprocessing is a system configuration in which more than one central processor of the same type operates in parallel. It is a field that has received remarkable impetus from the mushrooming success of the MOS/LSI microcomputer structures.

Note that categories 2 and 3 assume implicitly that multiprogramming may be involved in implementing the application system. In a multiprogramming system, several tasks may alternate execution on the central processor, interleaved between I/O operations. No two tasks are processed simultaneously. Some highly sophisticated time-sharing systems in category 3 are also complex multiprogrammed processes.

These generic classifications make no distinction between using a microcomputer and using a minicomputer. In fact, in terms of generic application features, no distinction can be made. As the microcomputers have acquired most of the sophisticated features of the traditional minicomputer, they have intruded into each generic category, displacing the underutilized minicomputers found there. They have begun to provide a spectrum of computational capability for each generic application need.

---

*The Koudela paper, while dealing exclusively with minicomputers, presents an excellent discussion of the historical evolution of the small computer and its areas of application. The authors have taken the liberty of extending Koudela's comments down to the microcomputer level.

1.8.2 Classification by Reliability Requirements

The commercial minicomputer manufacturers and microprocessor houses have given little thought to the reliability requirements of mini/microcomputer systems. The commercial vendors have not been motivated to develop highly reliable systems, since their marketing objective has always been to sell low-cost, mass produced machines that are maintained through manufacturer service contracts. When high reliability was an application requirement, total system duplication was recommended, including the mainframe and its associated peripherals. Traditionally, such high-reliability systems have found their place in the U.S. space program, military defense projects, and the telephone switching offices of the Bell System.*

Using reliability as the definitive criterion, the following application areas may be derived from the four generic application categories.

1. *Telephone network insertion.* Next to the space-borne computers and those mini/microcomputers employed in defense installations, no other application has a higher reliability requirement. In particular, the reliability requirements of a minicomputer in this situation are the same as that of the network itself. One area of potential new network applications is the use of mini/microcomputers as message switches in the emerging *value-added networks* (*VAN's*) that employ packet-switching technology. The federal government's *Advanced Research Project Agency Network* (*ARPANET*) with minicomputers used as *interface message processor's* (*IMP's*) is the prototype example of this new network technology.
2. *Switching network applique.* The minicomputer is used to monitor and/or record signals that occur within the network. Billing information has the highest reliability requirement in this case. Some billing information can be lost without seriously penalizing the common carrier. Traffic monitoring has a much lower reliability requirement than billing, but it is still important in terms of network usage, particularly in projecting peak loads and the times at which they might occur.
3. *Data communications.* The minicomputer is used to transfer information to a remotely located central data processing facility, or to function as a node in a computer network. Reliability in this case not only depends on the machine itself, but also on how the machine is interconnected to the network. Minicomputer *front-end processors* (*FEP's*) have been used to unburden large computers of all communication chores, thus freeing the large machines for number-crunching and file-management tasks. Market projections [3] have indicated that 50 to 60 percent of all minicomputers installed in the United States by 1980 will be involved in some form of data communications. In many cases, one or more microcomputers can perform the communication functions as well as a single minicomputer.

---

*In the spring of 1976, however, the TANDEM-16 was introduced by the Tandem Computing Company and was designed specifically to function in an environment requiring high reliability.

4. *Industrial automation and control.* This area is one of expanding interest because of the continuing need for cost reduction in manufacturing goods. This category includes manufacturing information systems, automated test systems, and inventory control packages. Generally, the individual minicomputers are dedicated to a given application where they are used as local loop controllers. They, in turn, may form a distributed computing network, normally using a star structure with each mini connected directly to a central supervisory computer to handle common control decision making. Manual backup can always be used in these systems, so reliability is much less than in the categories mentioned previously.
5. *Business data processing.* This category includes the use of intelligent terminals for data entry, on-line data retrieval, and specialized accounting systems. Small businesses and banks have been building up networks of terminals that access a large central computer for archival file information and automatic file updates. An airline reservation system is an example of such an application. The terminal devices may be either minicomputer-based or microprocessor-oriented. The reliability requirements on these terminals are essentially the same as in category 4, since manual backup can be employed. That is, an accounting ledger or a simple dial-up connection to a coordinator at the central computer may be used if the terminal goes down.
6. *Laboratory-based special systems.* These are installations used for research and advanced development. They would normally be found in either an engineering or a scientific environment. Local control of experiments is one application area. Reliability in such an environment is probably much lower than in the previous categories. While the system must be up for the users to complete their work, they can sustain a great deal more downtime than the switching network in a central telephone office or an automated assembly line.

1.9 TOWARD A DISTRIBUTED PROCESSING ENVIRONMENT

The early years of computer development found the basic hardware so expensive that the equipment cost had to be shared. Consequently, the resources of a single processor were allocated in an increasingly sophisticated manner using successively more complex operating systems. This was the period of the centralized, large-scale computational facilities discussed in Sections 1.1 and 1.2. The advent of the minicomputer served to decentralize computational capability in many application areas because of the decreasing processor costs. The minicomputer offered the possibility of distributing this capability among a number of smaller, less complicated machines that could interact with each other in order to implement an overall computational objective. In particular, the minicomputer stimulated consideration of distributed processing element systems—systems made up of multiple processing elements that may all operate concurrently and be physically and/or functionally distributed.

Within the category of distributed processing element systems, Joseph [36] has defined four subcategories that characterize the diffusion of computational capability provided by the maturing LSI technologies of the 1970's. These categories include:

1. *Networks of large-scale computers.* Geographically distributed, the network structure uses data communication links either over public telephone lines or by means of private high-speed cables. Minicomputers in such structures have acted as network interfaces to handle the various communication protocols.
2. *Planetary networks.* Basically, a planetary network consists of processors of different sizes, interconnected to form master-slave relationships. The classic configuration is the large, central computer that may control many satellite computers. These computers are normally separated by modest physical distances and may all be simultaneously active. By the mid-1970's the planetary-network concept was being applied at the microprocessor level. The microprocessor in many instances was responsible for data acquisition, processing, and local loop control. A minicomputer would serve as a master, coordinating the overall activity of the microprocessor-based local loops.
3. *Networks of minicomputers or microcomputers.* Normally, the machines incorporated in such structures are physically close together. The basic goal is to obtain the performance of a large-scale machine, such as a maxi, by operating the smaller-scale machines as a group, all of which may be running concurrently. Similarly, the performance of a minicomputer could be obtained by distributing its functions over an aggregate of inexpensive microcomputers.
4. *Highly parallel processors.* This subcategory was still in the exploratory stage in the mid-1970's. Perhaps the most interesting aspect of such configurations is the wide range of array-structure possibilities offered by MOS/LSI semiconductor technology.

The technology of the 1970's has been leading toward modular packages that will function as true computer components. In the future, these computer components will function as configurable modules of logic and computational capability at a virtually incidental cost. The cost of computation will be treated in the same manner as the family car. The user will pay for the luxury of all the capability that he feels he needs in a local environment, even if he seldom uses the capability. Because of this, control and computational capability will be distributed throughout a computing environment, with primary consideration being given to reliability and ease of maintenance. In most situations, repair by replacement will be performed rather than field service of any kind. Conceivably, the entire module may simply be thrown away, since it would cost too much to service.

1.10 SUMMARY

By year-end 1978, the cost of computing had dropped to a level where computational capability could be distributed locally, according to the needs of each local environment. The maturation of the minicomputer as a sophisticated computational element and the rapid evolution of the microprocessor were the primary reasons for the emergence of a philosophy of decentralized and diffused computing. This philosophy has fostered major research efforts in the areas of distributed function processing. No major distinction, aside from capability and cost, has been made between a microcomputer and a minicomputer. In fact, no major distinction can be made, including the areas in which they might be applied. This basic theme will be followed in the ensuing chapters as the detailed features of commercial and specialized mini/microcomputers are explored from various points of view.

1.11 REFERENCES

1 THE DIEBOLD GROUP, "Planning for the Fourth Generation." *Computer Decisions*, Vol. 7, No. 1 (Jan. 1975), pp. D5–D6.

2 SNYDER, F. GERALD, "The Microprocessor Shake-Out: An Engineer's Search for the Right Chip." *Digital Design*, Vol. 4, No. 9 (Sept. 1974), pp. 20–22.

3 Quantum Industry Report: "Minicomputers and Microcomputers—The Squeeze IS On." Quantum Science Corporation, 1974.

4 HEATON, JAMES E., "Computation on a Chip: What's in Store for the Control Specialist?" *Instruments and Control Systems*, Vol. 47, No. 4 (Apr. 1974), pp. 61–62.

5 LAPIDUS, GERALD, "The Computer: Now It's a Component." The Institute of Electrical and Electronics Engineers, Inc. Reprinted, by permission, from *IEEE Spectrum*, Vol. 11, No. 3 (Mar. 1974), pp. 80–82.

6 DAVIS, SIDNEY, "A Fresh View of Mini and Microcomputers." *Computer Design*, Vol. 13, No. 5 (May 1974), pp. 67–79.

7 The Annals of the Computation Laboratory of Harvard University, Vol. XVI, *Proceedings of a Symposium on Large-Scale Digital Calculating Machinery*. Cambridge, Mass.: Harvard University Press, 1948.

8 TROPP, HENRY, "The Effervescent Years: A Retrospective." The Institute of Electrical and Electronics Engineers, Inc. Reprinted, by permission, from IEEE Spectrum, Vol. 11, No. 2 (Feb. 1974), pp. 70–80.

9 ROSENBERG, JERRY M., *The Computer Prophets*, Chap. 8. New York: Macmillan Publishing Co., Inc., 1969.

10 RANDALL, BRIAN, ed., *The Origins of Digital Computers—Selected Papers*. New York: Springer-Verlag New York, Inc., 1973.

11 MOLLENHOFF, GEORGIA G., "John V. Atanasoff, DP-Pioneer." Computerworld, Inc., Newton, Mass. *Computerworld*, Part 1: Mar. 13, 1974; Part 2: Mar. 27, 1974.

12 RICHARDS, R. K., *Electronic Digital Systems*. New York: John Wiley & Sons, Inc., 1966.

13 GOLDSTINE, H. H., *The Computer from Pascal to von Neumann*. Princeton, N.J.: Princeton University Press, 1972.

14 BELL, C. GORDON, and ALLEN NEWELL, *Computer Structures: Readings and Examples*. New York: McGraw-Hill Book Company, 1971.

15 HEAD, ROBERT V., *Real-Time Business Systems.* New York: Holt, Rinehart and Winston, Inc., 1966.

16 SOLOMON, MARTIN B., JR., "Economics of Scale and the IBM System/360." *Communications of the ACM,* Vol. 9, No. 6 (June 1966), pp. 435–440. Association for Computing Machinery, Inc.

17 SHARPE, W. F., *The Economics of Computers.* The Rand Corporation. New York: Columbia University Press, 1969, by permission of the publisher.

18 ADAMS, CHARLES W., "Grosch's Law Repealed." *Datamation,* Vol. 8, No. 7 (July 1962), pp. 38–39.

19 GROSCH, H. R. J., "Grosch's Law Revisited." *Computerworld,* Vol. 9, No. 16 (Apr. 16, 1975), p. 9. Computerworld, Inc., Newton, Mass.

20 RILEY, WALLACE B., "Minicomputers Go into Action in a Myriad of Applications." *Electronics,* Vol. 46, No. 7 (Part I: Mar. 29, 1973), pp. 72–81.

21 GRABBE, EUGENE M., SIMON RAMO, AND DEAN E. WOOLDRIDGE, eds., *Handbook of Automation, Computation and Control,* Vol. 2. New York: John Wiley & Sons, Inc., 1959.

22 KOUDELA, JOHN, JR., "The Past, Present and Future of Minicomputers." *Proceedings of the IEEE,* Vol. 61, No. 11 (Nov. 1973), pp. 1526–1534.

23 BELL, C. GORDON, AND W. D. STRECKER, "Computer Structures: What Have We Learned from the PDP-11." *The 3rd Annual Symposium on Computer Architecture Conference Proceedings,* Vol. 4, No. 4 (Jan. 1976), pp. 1–14.

24 *Datapro Reports on Minicomputers—What Is a Minicomputer?* Datapro Research Corporation, Delran, N.J., Sept. 1973.

25 DAVID, JON R., "Minicomputer—Can It Be Defined?" DECUS Symposium, Proceedings, Spring 1973, Digital Equipment Corporation, Maynard, Mass.

26 *Auerbach Minicomputer Notebook.* Philadelphia: Auerbach Publishers, Inc., 1974.

27 HITT, D. C., G. H. OTTAWAY, AND R. W. SHIRK, "The Mini-computer—A New Approach to Computer Design." *Fall Joint Computer Conference,* Vol. 3, Part 1 (Fall 1968), pp. 655–662, AFIPS Conference Proceedings, Vol. 33, AFIPS Press.

28 HOUSE, D. L., AND R. A. HENZEL, "The Effect of Low Cost Logic on Minicomputer Organization." *Computer Design,* Vol. 10, No. 1 (Jan. 1971), pp. 97–101.

29 WEITZMAN, CAY, *Minicomputer Systems: Structure, Implementation, and Applications.* Englewood Cliffs, N.J.: Prentice-Hall, Inc., 1974.

30 DAVIS, SIDNEY, "A Fresh View of Mini and Microcomputers." *Computer Design,* Vol. 13, No. 5 (May 1974), pp. 67–79.

31 WOLF, HELMUT F., "Microcomputers—Revolution or Evolution." *Digital Design,* Vol. 4, No. 6 (June 1974), pp. 42–47.

32 LALIOTIS, T. A., "Microprocessors Present and Future." *IEEE Computer,* Vol. 7, No. 7 (July 1974), pp. 20–24.

33 ALTMAN, LAURENCE, "Logic's Leap Ahead Creates New Design Tools for Old and New Applications." *Electronics,* Vol. 47, No. 4 (Feb. 21, 1974), pp. 81–96.

34 WEISSBERGER, ALAN J., "Microprocessors Expand Industry Applications of Data Aquisition." *Electronics,* Vol. 47, No. 18 (Sept. 5, 1974), pp. 107–110.

35 LEWANDOSKI, ROBERT, "Preparation: The Key to Success with Microprocessors." *Electronics*, Vol. 48, No. 6 (Mar. 20, 1975), pp. 101–106.

36 JOSEPH, EARL C., "Innovations in Heterogeneous and Homogeneous Distributed-Function Architectures." *Computer*, Vol. 7, No. 3 (Mar. 1974), pp. 17–24.

37 ROBINSON, ARTHUR L., "Multiple Minicomputers: Inexpensive and Reliable Computing." *Science*, Vol. 187, No. 4174 (Jan. 31, 1975), p. 17.

1.12 PROBLEMS

1. Developments in microcomputer technology indicate that any rigorous definition of a minicomputer may be subject to serious doubts by the computing community.
   (a) Following the procedures discussed in Chapter 1, outline those features which could be uniquely associated with a minicomputer.
   (b) Can this same approach be taken with the specific areas in which a minicomputer may be used?
   (c) Do your answers to the questions above invalidate the definitions of a minicomputer and a microcomputer given in Chapter 1? If so, how should these definitions *now* be modified?

2. List the specific advantages of a multiminicomputer system over a large, centralized mainframe installation in the areas of (a) *data base management*, (b) *process control*, (c) *telephone switching*, and (d) *flight control.*

   In some cases, the centralized mainframe may be more advantageous. List examples.

3. In the late 1960's and early 1970's, the cost of the CPU and main storage was sufficiently large that a user specifically attempted to optimize the CPU and memory usage through the employment of multiprogramming techniques.

   With the advent of LSI techniques, processors and semiconductor memories have become incidentally expensive when compared with the cost of peripherals. This has led to the concept of *peripheral-sharing systems.* A peripheral-sharing system permits an expensive peripheral such as a high-speed fixed head disk to be shared by several processors.
   (a) What are the basic hardware and software features of a peripheral-sharing system?
   (b) What are the trade-offs in distributing peripherals across a mini/microcomputer system as opposed to employing a peripheral-sharing approach?
   (c) At what point, *economically*, should a peripheral be shared between processors rather than replicated, with each replica dedicated to a specific machine?
   (d) Do the requirements for privacy and restricted access change your previous answer?

4. For an established mini/microcomputer system:
   (a) What procedures should be observed to provide for equipment obsolescence?
   (b) If a replacement machine is being considered for the established system, what considerations should be given to minimizing costs?
   (c) Is it possible to obtain *true* software portability between a new machine and the established system's processor which was supplied by a different vendor? (In other words, can the existing system's software be used on the replacement machine without modifications to the source code?) If *not*, what problems and additional costs should the application engineer(s) expect?

5. Consider a mini/microcomputer system which has machines that are interconnected but located remotely from each other.
   (a) *Where* and *how* should application program development be performed?
   (b) How should application program debugging be performed?
   (c) How should the updating of application programs be performed? (This update function is called the *recent change* of the generic program.) Assume a heterogeneous mix of machines exists for this part of the problem.
   (d) How should maintenance be performed in such an environment?

   The following questions address themselves to the economic aspects of configuring and maintaining a mini/microcomputer system. In many cases, there is no *one* correct answer. Rather, there may be several acceptable answers, with the optimum solution being dictated by the application. As a rule of thumb, assume that the monthly maintenance cost of a system is 3 percent of the total hardware cost.

6. In the two cases that follow, what major capital expenditures must be considered for establishing a mini/microcomputer system aside from the cost of the CPU and peripheral equipment?
   (a) A *centralized facility* in which all machines are concentrated in one location.
   (b) A *distributed facility* in which machines may be located remotely from a central site.

   Is it possible to establish criteria to predict the economic life of mini/microcomputer hardware? If so, what is a basic set of such criteria?

7. Assume that you have been given the task of projecting the computing requirements for an organization.
   (a) Your first task will be to *define a set of criteria and establish organizational procedures* to evaluate whether or not mini/microcomputers are the *most economical* machines for a specific application when compared with (1) a large-scale central processor, (2) a time-sharing facility, or (3) a combination of the previous two arrangements.
   (b) Now readdress the entire problem with the goal of evaluating the *most reliable* system configuration.
   (c) How does the cost of ongoing maintenance (i.e., the cost of a typical maintenance contract from a commercial computer manufacturer) affect the conclusions you arrived at above?
   (d) If a *mix of equipment* from different manufacturers is used to form the associated set of peripherals for the mini/microcomputer system, do your conclusions need to be modified further?
   (e) What is the most common problem encountered in configuring and maintaining a computing system made up of equipment provided from different manufacturers?

8. While many minicomputer manufacturers supply a selection of higher-level languages and one or more general-purpose operating systems, the software associated with a microcomputer system tends to be *unique and somewhat restrictive*.
   (a) What additional costs are added to a minicomputer or microcomputer application by modifying the existing vendor-supplied software?
   (b) How are these costs modified by having the user write his own support software?
   (c) What supplementary costs are added to the project in terms of developing documentation and training procedures?
   (d) What drawbacks are encountered by an unsophisticated mini/microcomputer user attempting to develop a special-purpose application package using:

i. vendor-supplied software?
ii. application-developed software?
iii. a combination of the above?
iv. a consulting service?

9. The maintenance aspects of a mini/microcomputer project are normally the last items to be considered—if they are considered at all.
   (a) Establish a set of criteria that attempts to define the reliability of a mini/microcomputer product.
   (b) If diagnostic programs are supplied to test the CPU and its assocated peripherals, attempt to define a *measure* of the thoroughness of these diagnostics.
   (c) In general, do the reliability requirements vary as a function of the real-time nature of the application? If so, describe the way such requirements might change as the time-critical nature of the application operations changes.
   (d) What are the basic differences between the maintenance philosophies observed by a large mainframe *rental agreement* and the *field service contract* of a typical minicomputer manufacturer?
   (e) Assume that the diagnostic programs can isolate faults down to two or three circuit boards. How could simple maintenance and repair be done on LSI hardware by the end-user? How would this maintenance and repair be handled by the vendor's service force?

10. Consider for a moment an *interconnection arrangement of multiple computers.*
   (a) Which possible interconnection schemes can be utilized to lash multiple computers together?
   (b) Why would an organization want to use an interconnected multiple-computer system?
   (c) What is the difference between an interconnected multiple-computer system and a *multiprocessing system*?
   (d) Since *parallelism* or the use of concurrent processing is a significant factor in increasing system performance, which system characteristics are enhanced through the use of a multiprocessing environment? At what cost are each of these system enhancements achieved?

11. What are the major hardware interconnection techniques used to form a multiprocessor system?
   (a) Draw the interconnection scheme for each technique and describe the control philosophy.
   (b) List the advantages and disadvantages of each technique.
   (c) Which technique offers:
      i. The highest system availability?
      ii. The simplest interconnection scheme?
      iii. The most complex control requirements?

12. For a multiprocessing system to function properly, a software executive—or an operating system—should preside over the operation of the overall hardware.
   (a) Describe the major forms a multiprocessing executive might take. What are the advantages and disadvantages of each scheme?
   (b) Consider four processors connected to a common memory with four independent ports. In addition, each processor has its own private memory to be used for control or data storage.

i. Lay out the common memory so that any processor may communicate with any other processor using the common memory as a *mailbox memory*.
ii. What are the major control problems encountered when such a mailbox memory scheme is used?

13. What is a *distributed processing system*?
(a) Can an interconnection of microcomputers be a distributed processing system?
(b) Can an interconnected structure of multiple computers be a distributed processing system?
(c) Can an arrangement of computers which form a telecommunications network be a distributed processing system?
(d) What basic characteristics distinguish a distributed processing system from a multiprocessing system and a multiple-computer system? According to the characteristics you just listed, which physical parameters may be distributed in a multiple-computer environment to achieve a distributed system?
(e) What advantages may be assigned to the usage of a distributed processing system? Are there any disadvantages? If so, what are they?

14. The tremendous demand for personal computing at the consumer level has led to the conjecture that small computers will one day become commonplace household appliances, no more special than a color television.
(a) Create a list of the possible applications such a household computer might be used for. Consider both *local* applications within the home, as well as *remote* applications in which the computer would be asked to perform a control task or acquire information although many miles might separate the computer from its objective.
(b) Define the hardware and software features such a household computer might have. Sketch the physical layout of this household computer.
(c) How might software and its associated support documentation be distributed to the ordinary home user of the household computer?
(d) How might maintenance and repair be performed on this machine? Who will do the servicing and under what service schedule?
(e) What real-time response characteristics must such a machine have if *interactive intelligence* is a key feature?

15. Outline the features that you consider significant in selecting a small computer for a specific application. Consider the following applications areas:
(a) A time-sharing environment
(b) A real-time control system
(c) An instrument-based system
(d) A telephone switching system within the talking path.

16. Which of the above applications may be handled by minicomputers? Which may be handled by microcomputers? Could a single minicomputer in one of these applications be replaced by an aggregate of microcomputers? If so, indicate in block diagram form how this might be done. Discuss the possible control problems such systems might be prone to in the following cases:
(a) A homogeneous machine environment
(b) A non-homogeneous machine environment in which a mix of commercially available machines are employed.

17. What features do you feel must be met by the software supplied with a small computer to make it a useful computing component? Are these software features the same across all of the application areas mentioned above? If not, what are the significant differences when each of the application areas are considered? (That is, what software features are important for one area as opposed to another?)

18. Consider a laboratory-based environment and draw a block diagram of a data acquisition system that could be used to control an array of instruments and collect data from these instruments.
    (a) Could the controller for such an environment be a hand calculator?
    (b) Could control be distributed to each instrument and the data collected at some central analysis point? If so, how could the data be communicated to the central point?

2

Digital Logic Circuitry

2.1 DTL, TTL, AND ECL LOGIC TYPES

2.1.1 Diode-Transistor Logic (DTL)

A diode AND gate followed by a transistor inverter forms the DTL NAND gate. The basic DTL circuit is shown in Figure 2-1. Logic is performed by the input diodes. When one of the input voltages is low or near ground potential, the corresponding input diode conducts. Current flows through the bias resistor, Rl, and the diode. This action causes the potential at the anode side of the diode to have a value higher than ground. This value corresponds to the drop across a forward-biased diode, about 0.7 volt. The potential is not high enough to forward-bias the base diode and the transistor base-emitter junction. Consequently, the transistor is held in the cut-off condition, keeping the output voltage the same as the collector supply voltage. When all the input voltages are high (i.e., have a potential equal to V), the input diodes are reverse-biased. In this situation, the base diode and the transistor inverter become forward-biased. Sufficient current will then flow into the base to keep the transistor in the saturation state. The low (near ground) collector voltage gives a logical 0 at the output.

The two diodes in series with the base provide additional bias in the base circuit. This, in effect, raises the effective turn-on voltage of the transistor. Normally, a positive voltage of 0.7 volt across the base-emitter junction is required to forward-bias that junction. By inserting two additional diodes in series with the base, the potential at point X must be increased by 1.4 volts (0.7 volt for each diode) to a value of 2.1

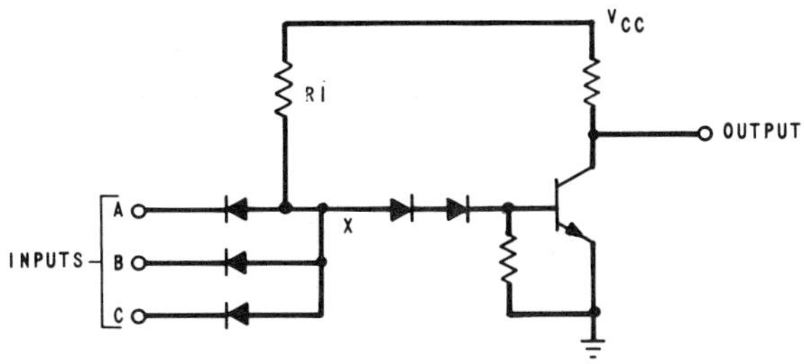

2-1 Basic DTL circuit

volts before the base-emitter junction of the transistor is forward-biased. This higher-base bias threshold provides high noise immunity for the DTL circuit.

The base diodes provide a low forward resistance for the transistor when it is turning on. This permits the switching speed of the DTL circuit to be faster than the *Resistor-Transistor Logic* (*RTL*) circuit since the time constant associated with the input capacitance will be considerably reduced. To maintain the low reverse-impedance state during the turn-off period, the recovery time of the bias diode is chosen to be longer than that associated with the transistor. This permits the storage charge at the transistor to be drawn off during the turn-off period of the transistor. A typical delay experienced by a DTL circuit with a fan-out of 8 or higher is about 25 nanoseconds. This value is obtained largely because of the high input impedance provided by each of the subsequent gates that are in the 1 state.

2.1.2 Transistor-Transistor Logic (TTL)

The TTL family is the most widely used logic series employed by logic designers. A variety of TTL circuits have evolved to meet the needs of many different applications. This broad spectrum of available TTL circuits has allowed logic designers to optimize all portions of a system in the most cost-effective manner.

The basic TTL circuit, shown in Figure 2-2, can be considered to be a direct modification of the basic DTL circuit. However, the TTL structure lends itself more readily to an integrated circuit implementation than the DTL structure. A single

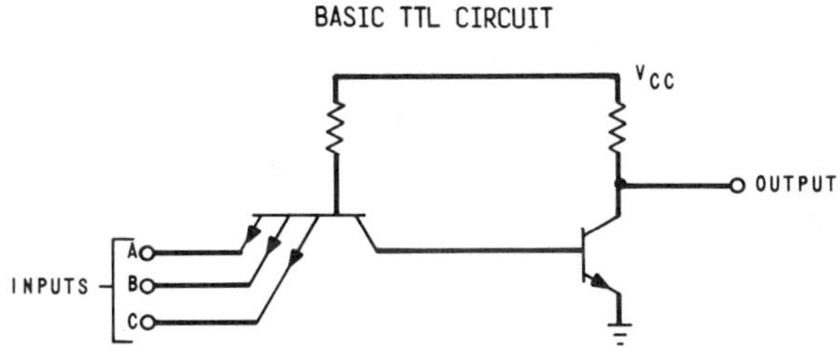

2-2 Basic TTL circuit

multiemitter transistor replaces the input diodes and series diodes of DTL. In the TTL circuit, each emitter-base junction serves as one input diode, while the base-collector junction replaces the series diode. Both the TTL and DTL circuits perform the NAND function.

Although the basic TTL circuit consists of two transistors, additional components are required to increase the circuit speed and fan-out capability. The 54/74 series started initially with three distinct, compatible families: the standard TTL series, the low-power TTL series, and the high-speed TTL series (see Figure 2-3).

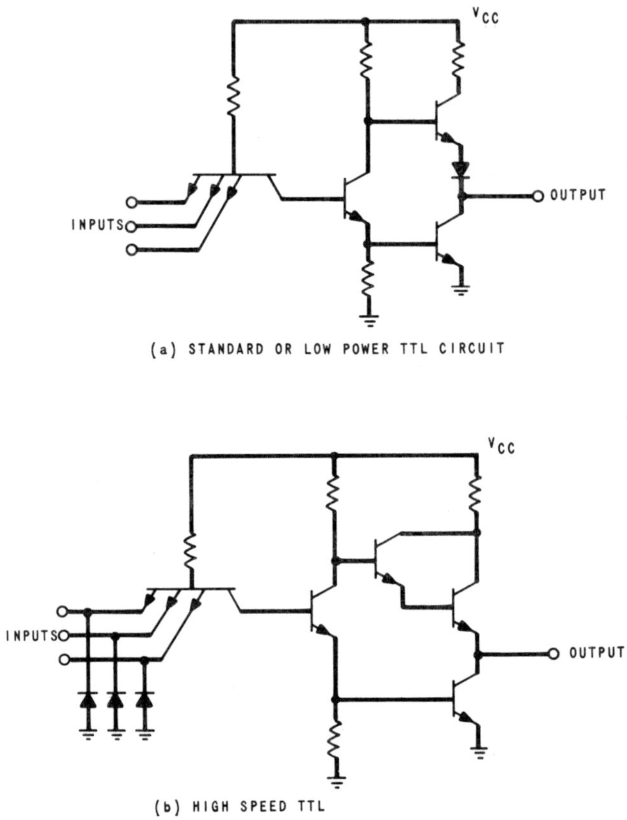

2-3 TTL standard circuits

The circuit configurations for the standard and low-power families are the same except for the resistor values, which are considerably higher for the low-power circuit. The high-speed TTL family (see Figure 2-3b) is more complex and draws more current in order to increase the switching speed of the circuit. Input clamping diodes are included to reduce transmission-line effects of ringing due to faster rise and fall times.

With the introduction of the Schottky barrier diode, two new TTL families were added to the series: one for high speed and the other for low power. The Schottky diode permits transistors to operate in the nonsaturated mode. This greatly reduces storage time and significantly improves the switching time. The two Schottky TTL circuits are shown in Figure 2-4. The high-speed Schottky TTL was developed to compete with the *Emitter-Coupled Logic* (*ECL*) series. Further evolution of Schottky technology led to the low-power Schottky TTL family in which Schottky diodes act as input elements rather than multiemitter transistor circuits. This further improved the power-delay product of the modified TTL circuit.

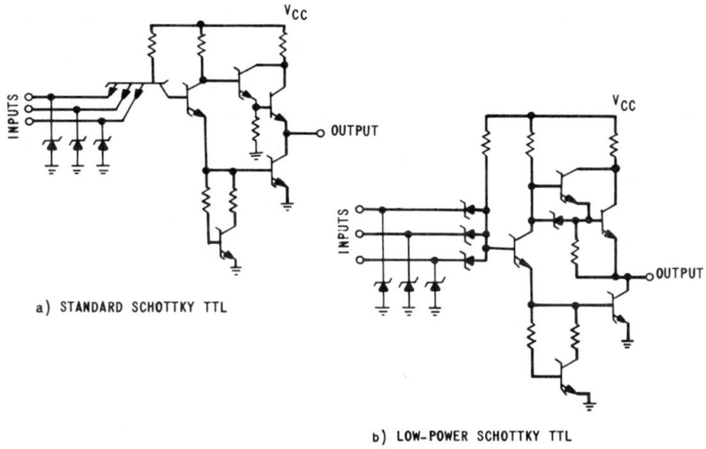

2-4 Schottky TTL Circuits

Table 2-1 shows the performance characteristics of the five TTL families. The first group, consisting of the low-power TTL series, the standard TTL series, and the high-speed TTL series, was developed using standard bipolar integrated technology. The increase in logic speed is directly related to greater power dissipation. The second group, consisting of the Schottky TTL series and the low-power Schottky TTL

TABLE 2-1 54/74 TTL Typical Performance Characteristics

	LOW POWER 54/74L	STANDARD 54/74	HIGH SPEED 54/74H	SCHOTTKY 54/74S	LOW POWER SCHOTTKY 54/74LS
POWER/GATE	1MW	10MW	22MW	19MW	2MW
DELAY/GATE	33ns	10ns	6ns	3ns	9.5ns
POWER-DELAY PRODUCT	33pJ	100pJ	132pJ	57pJ	19pJ

Source: The TTL Data Book for Design Engineers, 1977 edition. Reprinted with permission of Texas Instruments, Inc.

series, has a greatly improved power-delay product because of Schottky technology. In fact, the overall performance of the Schottky families is distinctly superior to that of the earlier TTL families.

To a large extent, the output drivers determine the speed, fan-out, and power dissipation of a logic gate. There are basically three types of output drivers: the passive pull-up (resistor), the active pull-up (transistor), and the tri-state. The passive pull-up type (see Figure 2-2) allows *open-collector outputs** to be connected in a wired-AND function, which is particularly useful in a bus structure where many outputs are multiplexed into a single output. However, the drawback of using an open-collector output is the capacitive loading which affects the speed of operation. When the gate output is switched from a low value to a high value, the capacitance load at the node must be charged through a relatively large collector resistor. A totem pole active pull-up structure is used to reduce the charging time constant for this output driver (see Figure 2-3). The totem pole arrangement provides a low-impedance path for the charging current associated with a low-to-high transition of the output voltage. A similar low-impedance path is provided for a high-to-low transition of the output voltage. The totem pole configuration also avoids power dissipation in the collector resistor when the output voltage is at ground level. It does not permit a wired logic implementation. However, the tri-state gate has a third high-impedance logic state which allows outputs to be connected in a common busing arrangement (see Figure 2-5).

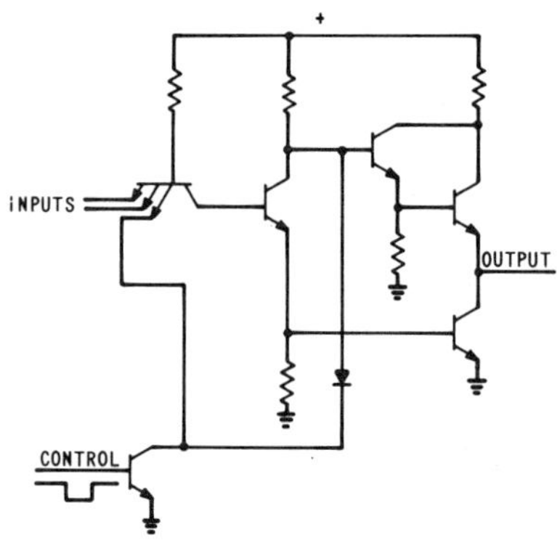

2-5 Simplified tri-state output gate

Each of the five families of commercial TTL circuits are available with any of the previously described output driver configurations. All five families are compatible and will interface directly with one another. Many of the new LSI circuits (e.g., memories, bit-sliced processor chips, etc.) are designed to interface directly with any of the TTL circuits without additional circuitry.

---

*An *open-collector output* is a logic circuit in which the collectors of individual output transistors are tied to a common load resistor.

2.1.3 Emitter-Coupled Logic (ECL)

The fastest available integrated circuit logic is emitter-coupled logic, also known as *current mode logic* (*CML*) since the circuit works on a current steering principle. The speed is obtained by operating the transistors in the nonsaturated mode. Consequently, special devices such as Schottky diodes are not required.

A basic ECL gate is shown in Figure 2-6. The input transistors (Q1, Q2, and Q3) share a common emitter resistor with the reference transistor (Q4) as in a differential amplifier. If the inputs are near ground potential, Q1, Q2, and Q3 are placed in the cutoff state. No current will flow through common collector resistor R1, and the collector potential will tend toward V_{CC}. Output transistor Q5 will follow this potential. If one of the inputs becomes positive and higher than the bias voltage, V_{BB}, the corresponding transistor will conduct. This, in turn, will cause the current flowing through R_E to switch from reference transistor Q4 to the input transistor—hence the name "current-mode switching logic." The collector voltage, in turn, will drop, giving a logical 0 output. The logical output of the ECL gate is the same as the NOR function. If another output transistor is connected to the collector of the reference transistor, a complementary output is obtained, which gives a dual-rail output. That is, both the logic signal and its complement are available.

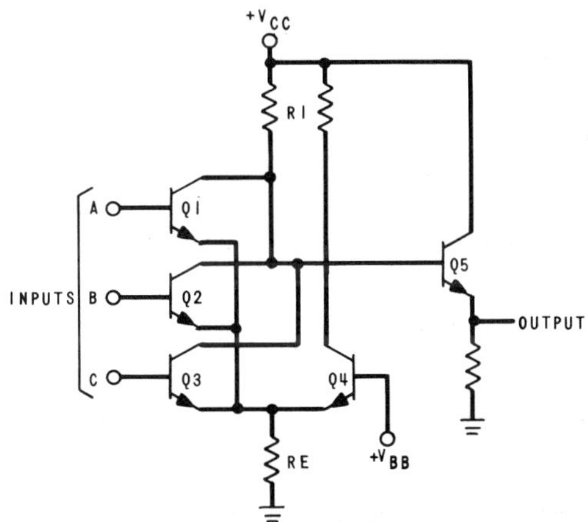

2-6 Basic ECL circuit

As mentioned previously, an ECL circuit is structured to operate in the nonsaturated mode. The result is a very fast switching speed, typically only a few nanoseconds. However, this speed is realized at the expense of relatively high power dissipation. So far, ECL has been used in only the largest computers. There are many disadvantages in working with such high-speed, high-power circuits because of the increased noise sensitivity and temperature problems associated with the higher power dissipation.

2.1.4 Speed-Power Comparison

For small computers, the TTL family has been used almost exclusively and is generally accepted as the industry standard. Figure 2-7 summarizes the relationship between the propagation delay and power dissipation for the various TTL logic families. The high performance of Schottky TTL circuits is clearly shown in the figure.

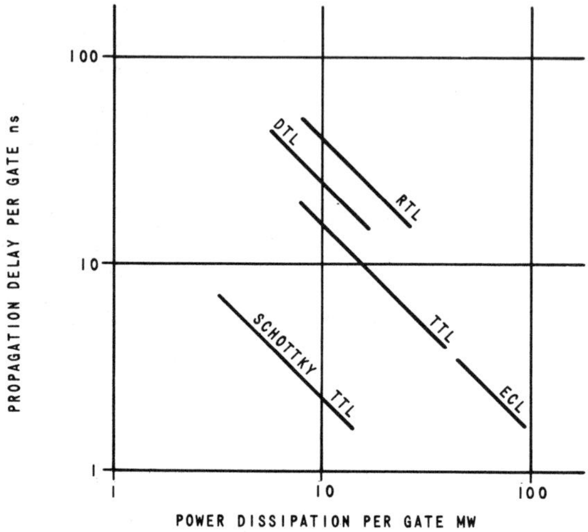

2-7 Speed versus power dissipation of logic families [Source: The TTL Data Book for Design Engineers, 1977 edition. Reprinted with permission of Texas Instruments, Inc.]

2.2 LOGIC FUNCTIONS

2.2.1 Basic Logic Gates

The implementation of digital control logic requires certain logical operators. The three basic logic operators commonly used are the OR function, the AND function, and the NOT function. The NOT function, in conjunction with either the OR function or the AND function, is sufficient to implement any logical operation. The combined OR and NOT (invert) functions form the NOR gate. Similarly, the combined AND and NOT functions form the NAND gate.

OR gate

Each input and output of a digital circuit can be in one of two distinct states, 0 or 1. Some logic gates are also designed to have a third output state, the high-impedance state. The following discussion, however, will deal only with 2-state logic gates.

Two conventions are normally used to represent these logic values. The first convention, which uses the more positive voltage level to represent the 1 state, is called *positive logic*. The second convention, which uses the less positive potential to represent the 1 state, is called *negative logic*. The positive logic convention is more common and will be used throughout this text. In the case of the TTL series logic gates, the 0 state corresponds to near ground potential, and the 1 state corresponds to about 3 volts.

The OR circuit is arranged so that the output is in the 1 state when any one of its inputs is in the 1 state. The truth table and the logic symbol for the OR gate are shown in Figure 2-8a.

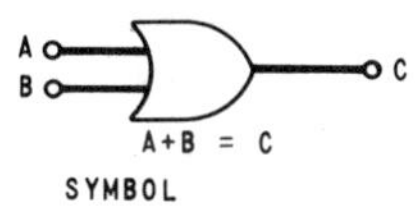

INPUT		OUTPUT
A	B	C
0	0	0
0	1	1
1	0	1
1	1	1

TRUTH TABLE

(a) OR GATE

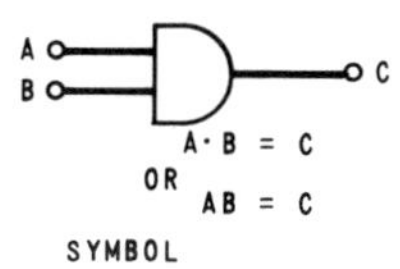

INPUT		OUTPUT
A	B	C
0	0	0
0	1	0
1	0	0
1	1	1

TRUTH TABLE

(b) AND GATE

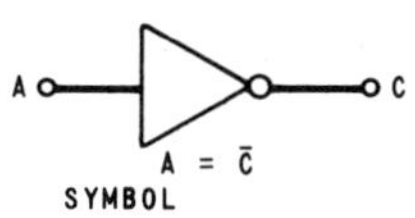

INPUT	OUTPUT
A	C
0	1
1	0

TRUTH TABLE

(c) NOT GATE

2-8 Basic logic gates

AND gate

The AND circuit requires all its inputs to be in the 1 state to produce a 1 output. The truth table and logic symbol for the AND gate, shown in Figure 2-8b, indicate whether or not all the AND gate's inputs are in the 1 state at the same time.

NOT gate

This circuit is an inverter. Its one input and one output are complementary. The truth table and logic symbol for the NOT circuit are shown in Figure 2-8c. The NOT function is one of the necessary operations required to implement more complex logical functions.

NOR and NAND gates

In most logic circuits, the logical operation is performed by the input elements such as diodes. The input stage is then followed by an output stage. This is necessary to provide proper signal levels and adequate drive capability (fan-out). The output stage is usually of the type that provides inversion of the signal. As a result, the combined OR and NOT function is called the *NOR gate*. In some circuit configurations, both inverted and noninverted outputs can be obtained from a single gate (this is called two-rail logic), implying that OR and NOR are implemented by the same gate. The truth table and logic symbol are shown in Figure 2-9a. Since the two-rail outputs facilitate logic implementation, there is no need to go through another NOT stage to generate the proper output, which would be necessary if a single output were provided.

Similarly, the AND circuit followed by the NOT circuit configuration is called the *NAND gate*. Figure 2-9b shows the truth table and logic symbol for the NAND gate. The gate symbols for the NOR and the NAND are the same as for the OR and the AND except for a small bubble at the output, which denotes signal inversion.

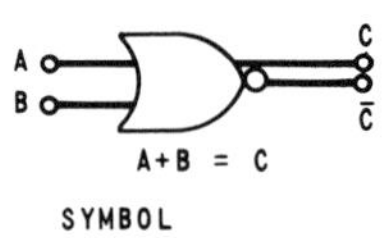

INPUT		OUTPUT	
A	B	$\bar{C}$	C
0	0	1	0
0	1	0	1
1	0	0	1
1	1	0	1

TRUTH TABLE

(a) NOR GATE WITH TWO-RAIL OUTPUTS

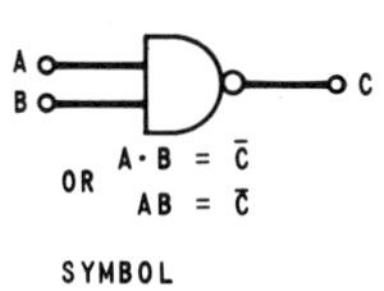

INPUT		OUTPUT
A	B	C
0	0	1
0	1	1
1	0	1
1	1	0

TRUTH TABLE

(b) Nand gate

2-9 Other basic gates

Gate representations

The basic gate symbols for OR, AND, and NOT circuits are shown in Figure 2-10. The OR and AND functions are denoted by the shape of the symbols. Although the NOT is defined by the triangular symbol, the inversion of the input signal is indicated by a small bubble at the output. The single-input NOT function can be expressed by any of the three symbols shown in Figure 2-10a.

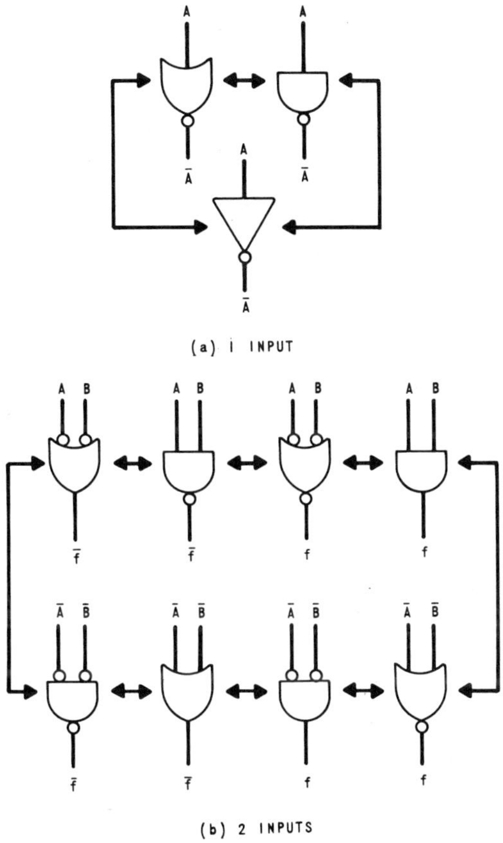

2-10 Gate representations

OR and AND gates, combined with possible signal inversions either at the input or the output, are shown in Figure 2-10b. The gates with the same inputs and outputs are equivalent. The duality of DeMorgan's theorem,

$$\overline{A + B + C} = \bar{A} \cdot \bar{B} \cdot \bar{C} \tag{1}$$

or

$$\overline{A \cdot B \cdot C} = \bar{A} + \bar{B} + \bar{C} \tag{2}$$

is a valuable aid in logic design, especially for complementing logic functions and expressions. It can be shown that the AND functions are easily converted to OR functions with the appropriate conversions. For example,

$$f = \bar{A} \cdot B + A \cdot \bar{B} \tag{3}$$

$$\bar{A} \cdot B = \overline{(A + \bar{B})} \tag{4}$$

$$A \cdot \bar{B} = \overline{(\bar{A} + B)} \tag{5}$$

$$f = \overline{(A + \bar{B})} + \overline{(\bar{A} + B)} \tag{6}$$

By the use of DeMorgan's theorem, equation (6) can be expressed as

$$\bar{f} = \overline{\overline{(A + \bar{B})} + \overline{(\bar{A} + B)}} \tag{7}$$

which is a NOR-gate realization. By rewriting the original expression [equation (3)], it may be expressed as

$$\bar{f} = \overline{[\bar{A} \cdot B + A \cdot \bar{B}]}$$

$$\bar{f} = \overline{(\bar{A} \cdot B)} \cdot \overline{(A \cdot \bar{B})} \tag{8}$$

and, forming the complement of $\bar{f}$,

$$f = (\bar{\bar{f}}) = \overline{(A \cdot \bar{B})} \cdot \overline{(\bar{A} \cdot B)} \tag{9}$$

which is a NAND-gate realization.

2.2.2 XOR Gate

The *exclusive-OR* (*XOR*) function of two variables is given by the following logic expression:

$$f = \bar{A} \cdot B + A \cdot \bar{B} \tag{10}$$

Its implementation can be realized by various circuit arrangements formed from the standard logic gates previously described. One such circuit is shown in Figure 2-11a. According to the truth table (see Figure 2-11c), the XOR circuit gives a 1 output whenever its input signals are different ($A = 1$, $B = 0$; or $A = 0$, $B = 1$). The sum of two binary digits gives the same corresponding outputs as the XOR circuit when the carry is neglected. For this reason, it is sometimes called a *modulo-2 adder* or a *half-adder circuit*. The symbol for the XOR gate is shown in Figure 2-11b. A full adder may be built using a second XOR gate. The output of the first circuit and the carry-in from the preceding stage are used as the inputs to the second XOR gate. An XOR of 3-input variables is obtained by cascading two XOR circuits. The parity check function utilizes XOR circuits in a tree-type structure since XORing n input variables gives a final output of 1 if an odd number of the input variables are 1's (see Figure 2-12). Although the XOR gate is realized with a composite of several logic gates, a func-

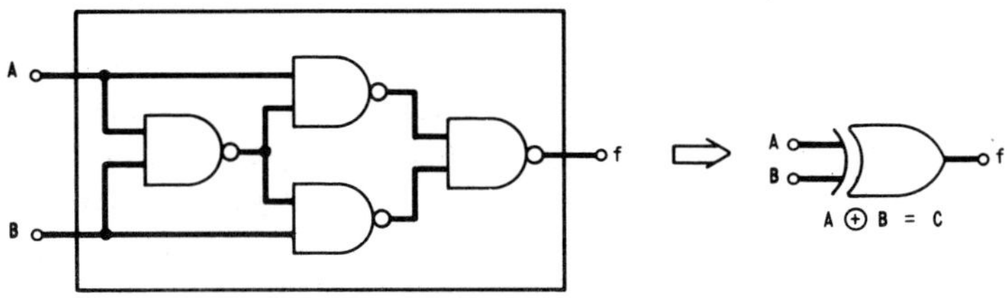

(a) A LOGIC CONFIGURATION (b) SYMBOL

INPUT		OUTPUT
A	B	f
0	0	0
0	1	1
1	0	1
1	1	0

(c) TRUTH TABLE

2-11 XOR function of two-input variables

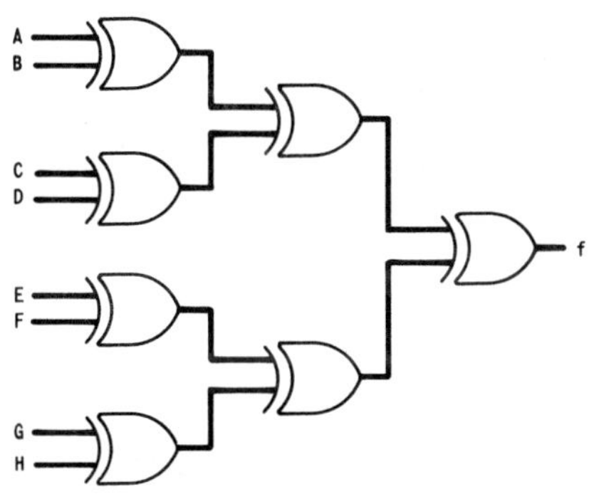

$$f = A \oplus B \oplus C \oplus D \oplus E \oplus F \oplus G \oplus H$$

2-12 XOR *n*-input variables

tional symbol has been adopted to denote the logical operation because of its wide usage in logic design.

Another commonly used logic function of 2-input variables is the exclusive-NOR circuit, which is the inverse or complement of the XOR function. The logic symbol is the same as the XOR symbol except that a small bubble is inserted at the output, indicating an inversion of the output signal. This circuit is also referred to as a *comparator*, since both inputs must be in the same state for the output to be a 1.

2.2.3 Wired Logic

Some logic families have gates with wired logic capability. When such gates have their outputs connected together, an extra stage of logic is introduced without an additional gate being needed. This type of logic depends on the operating characteristic of the circuit used. For the negative-OR function (negative logic), connecting outputs together results in an output of 0 if any one of the connected outputs is a 0. If this effect is examined from the viewpoint of positive logic, the resultant output will be a 1 only when all the connected outputs are in the 1 state. The positive logic arrangement forms the AND function. Another possible effect of connecting outputs together is that the resulting output will be a 1 when one of the connected outputs is a 1. In this situation, the output tie gives an OR function. Not all outputs can be connected because of the operating characteristic of the circuit. This will be elaborated on in the following section.

The wired-AND function is more commonly used in logic design since the wired-AND capability is an inherent part of the TTL family. The symbol for the wired-AND is given in Figure 2-13. If NAND gates are used in a logic implementation, the wired-AND capability eliminates a gate delay in the logic chain. If the same logic function is to be obtained with NAND gates but without using the wired-AND capability, two additional stages of logic are required. If NOR gates are used instead, the wired-AND capability has the effect of increasing the number of inputs to the NOR gate.

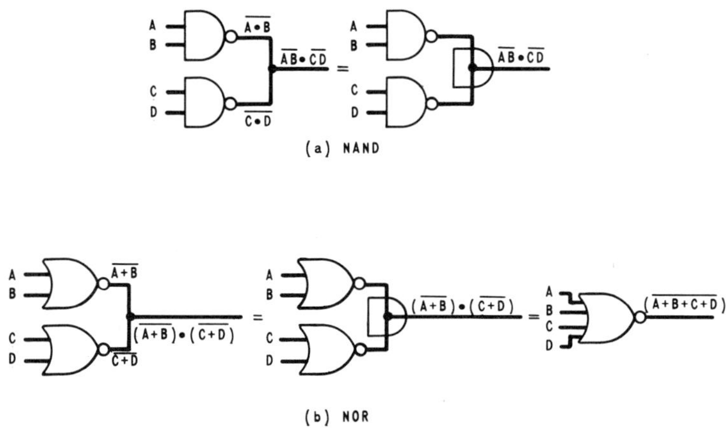

2-13 Wired-AND connection

2.2.4 Application of Wired Logic

One of the more important applications of wired logic is in implementing bus structures for data transfers that occur within the processor. The use of a common data bus is an excellent means of transmitting data signals from one register to another. In most instances, the data transfer involves selecting a source of data from a group of possible data registers and then transferring that data to a selected destination register. The destination register may be part of the same group as the data source register, or it may be part of an entirely different group of registers. The circuit that selects the source information and places it on the bus is called a *multiplexer*. A *demultiplexer* is a circuit that takes the bus data and transfers it to the selected destination register.

Figure 2-14 shows 1 bit of a data bus structure using a multiplexer and a demultiplexer. The wired connection in the multiplexer is a very efficient way to form a data bus by merging many outputs into one physical signal line. This operation is feasible because only the selected source data will appear on the bus, while all the nonselected sources will be disabled or inhibited. A particular advantage of the NAND gate is that the outputs of multiple NAND devices may be tied together to form a bus for multiplexing and demultiplexing logic signals.

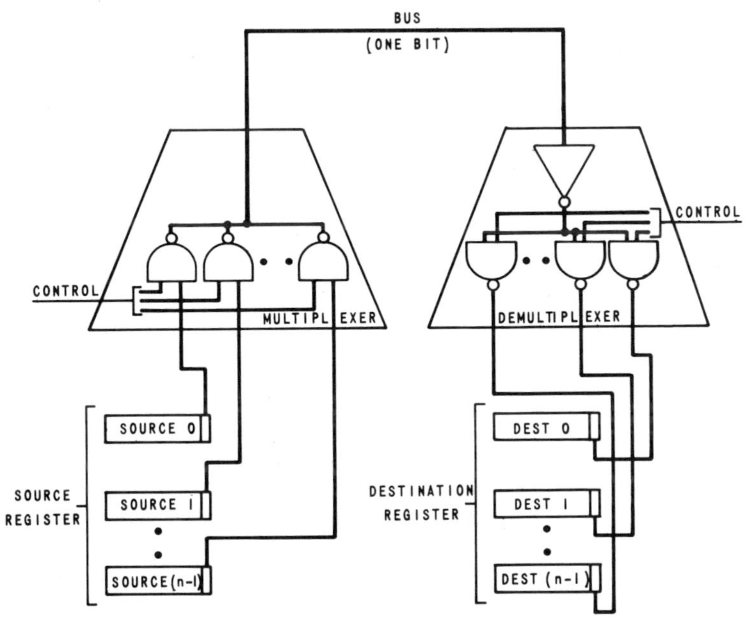

2-14 Bus application of wired logic

2.3 STORAGE ELEMENTS

2.3.1 The Characteristics of a Flip-Flop

A storage element characterized by having two different stable states is known as a *flip-flop*. It is capable of storing binary states 1 and 0 for an indefinite period. An ordered set of these circuits, called a *flip-flop register*, is used to store a word instead of single bits. In its most basic form, a flip-flop consists of two NAND (or NOR) gates cross-connected with the output of one connected to the input of the other and vice versa (see Figure 2-15). Its two inputs, R and S, are normally in the inactive 1 state. When S becomes 0, the flip-flop is set to the 1 state, with the Q output high and the Q′ output low. The information will remain in this state even after S returns to the 1 state. This circuit falls into the category of flip-flops known as *RS latches*, which form the nucleus of the more complicated flip-flops.

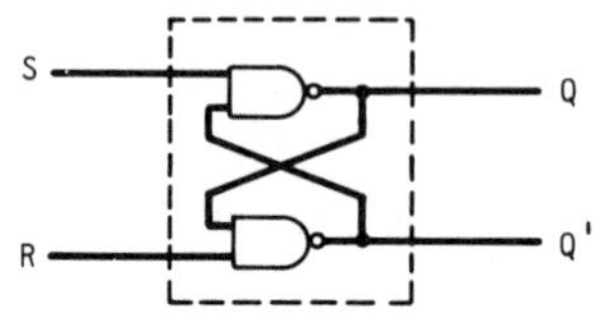

2-15 Basic RS flip-flop (latch)

Flip-flops are designated in the same manner as inputs. For example, designations JK, D, and T represent inputs to flip-flops with the same designations, respectively. The inputs imply the operating characteristics of the flip-flops.

2.3.2 Latch Operation

When data are transferred into an RS latch, the operation is usually synchronized with a clock pulse (see Figure 2-16). During the clock period, the R and S input signals are transferred directly to the outputs of the latch. Both signals may be a 1 during this interval, but the signal that has been 1 the longest prior to the termination of the clock pulse will be retained and latched to that state until the next clock period. When both R and S input signals are held in the 1 state for the entire clock period, the RS latch may be placed in an indeterminate state at the end of the clock pulse. Figure 2-16 illustrates this condition during the first clock pulse in which both the R and S inputs are in the 1 state. When the clock goes low, the RS latch will settle in one of two possible states, depending on the relative speed of the input gates and the corresponding side of the latch. The latch may oscillate a little and finally settle to the steady state (indicated by the solid line) or the opposite state (indicated by the dashed lines). Consequently, the control logic should not allow both R and S inputs to be in the 1 state near the end of the clock pulse. It is permissible, however, for both inputs to be 1 near the beginning of the clock period.

2.3.3 Generalized Flip-Flop

The latch type of flip-flop forms the basic storage element from which more sophisticated flip-flops are constructed. In general, the different arrangements of the input circuits determine the operating characteristics of a flip-flop. Figure 2-17 shows the generalized form of flip-flop circuit with a latch providing the outputs. Some of the

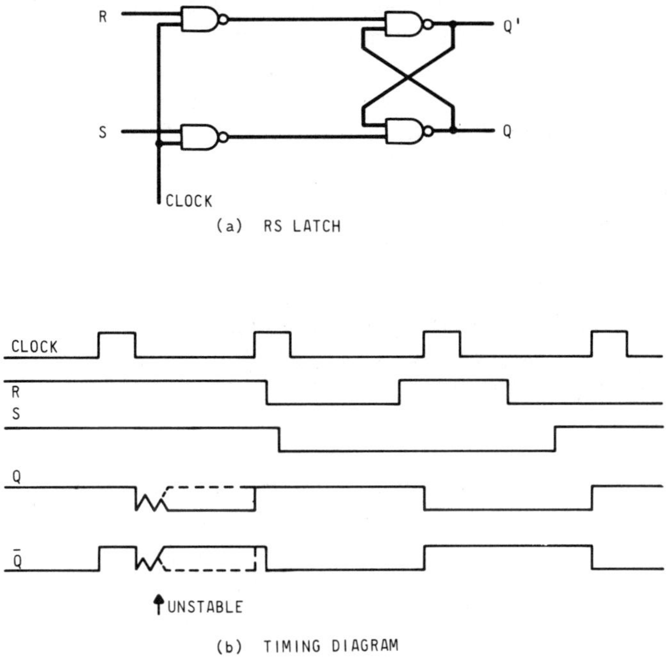

2-16 RS-latch circuit and operation

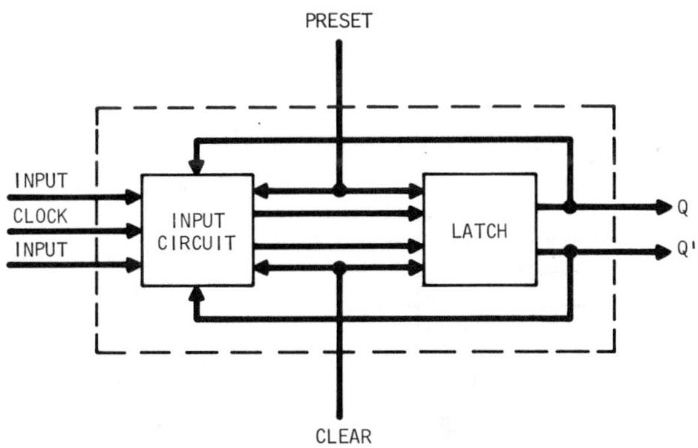

2-17 Generalized flip-flop

input connections indicated may or may not be present. For example, feedback paths are used by the JK flip-flop but are not used by the RS and D types. The feedback paths are essential for the complementing or toggling function that the JK type of flip-flop can perform when its inputs are in a predefined state. There are two other modes of input operation in addition to the straightforward PRESET and CLEAR functions that force the latch to a specified state. One mode of operation is the master–slave type, in which the data entering the input circuit are withheld from propagating to the output for the duration of the clock pulse. This action is particularly useful in the operation of sequential circuits in which an output is combined with other system conditions to generate control signals that direct specific functions *and* also cause the state of the flip-flop to be changed. The logic delay is necessary to keep the output stable during the clock period. In addition, the logic delay eliminates the race condition of having the flip-flop output fed back directly to the input. The other mode of operation is the edge-trigger type, in which data are transferred on either the positive- or negative-going edge of a clock pulse. The input is required to be stable only during the transition interval. Flip-flops that operate as edge-trigger devices are often used in counters and shift registers. In these two modes of input operation, the input circuit is actually more complex than the output latch.

RS flip-flop

The RS flip-flop is designed to operate under clock control. Its functional representation and truth table are shown in Figure 2-18. It may have either a CLEAR or PRESET asynchronous input, or both. Normally, these inputs are in either the inactive state or at a logic 1 level. If the CLEAR becomes a 0 or grounded, the flip-flop is forced to the 0 state. If the PRESET input is grounded, the flip-flop is set to the 1 state. The operation of the flip-flop is shown by the truth table, which includes the state of the R and S inputs prior to the clock pulse and the state of the Q output immediately after the clock pulse. Because the output is not predictable if both the inputs are in the 1 state, it is necessary to avoid this condition when data are transferred into the flip-flop. When both inputs are in the 0 state, the flip-flop will remain in the same state regardless of the clock.

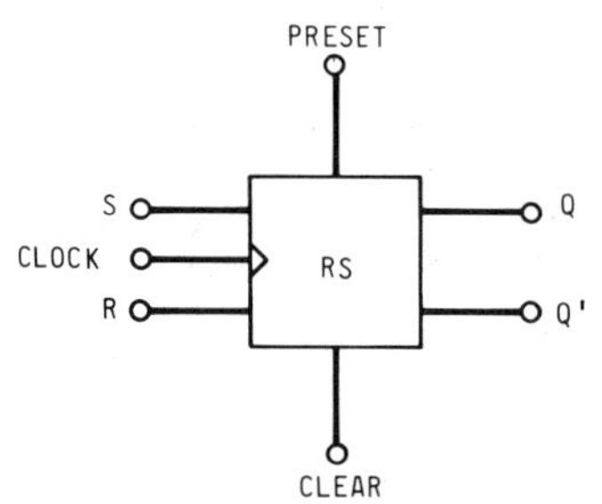

R	S	Q
0	0	Q
0	1	1
1	0	0
1	1	*

= TRIGGER ON POSITIVE EDGE * INDETERMINATE

= TRIGGER ON NEGATIVE EDGE

(a) FLIP-FLOP (b) TRUTH TABLE

2-18 RS flip-flop and truth table

JK flip-flop

The operational characteristics of the JK flip-flop are the same as those of the RS type except for the fourth input condition: J = K = 1. When this input condition exists and the flip-flop is clocked, the output changes to the opposite state and the flip-flop toggles. The functional representation and the I/0 truth table for the JK flip-flop are shown in Figure 2-19. Many of the commercial JK flip-flops available on a circuit chip have incorporated additional J and K inputs to eliminate the need for external gates. The JK flip-flop is considered the most versatile logic circuit available in terms of its ability to implement different memory elements.

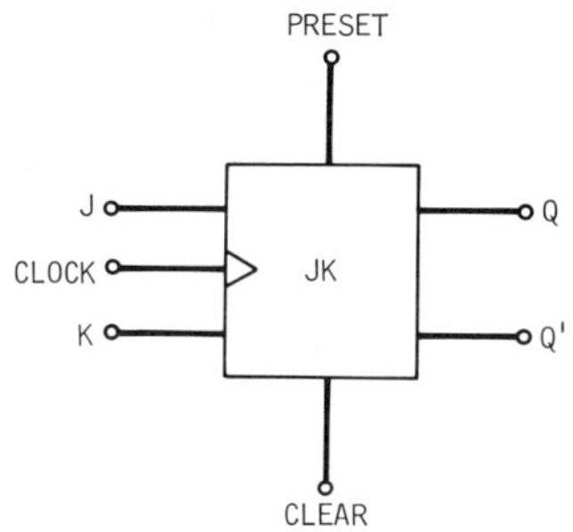

(a) FLIP-FLOP

J	K	Q
0	0	Q
0	1	0
1	0	1
1	1	Q'

(b) TRUTH TABLE

2-19 JK flip-flop and truth table

T flip-flop

The operation of a T flip-flop, which has a single data input and a clock input, is quite simple (see Figure 2-20). When the T input is at a 1 level, the occurrence of the clock will cause the flip-flop to toggle to its opposite state: hence the name T flip-flop. When the T input is at the 0 level, the flip-flop will remain in the same state regardless of the clock signal. It may also have a CLEAR or PRESET input to jam-set the flip-flop to a fixed state. The JK flip-flop, which possesses the toggle function, is often connected to operate as a T flip-flop. As indicated in Figure 2-20a, the flip-flop toggles on the positive transition of the clock pulse. Two clock transitions are needed to cause one transition in the output. This inherent divide-by-2 feature is required in many binary counter circuits.

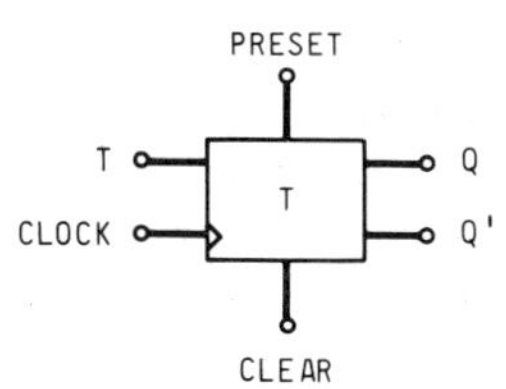

(a) FLIP-FLOP

T	Q
0	Q
1	Q'

(b) TRUTH TABLE

2-20 T flip-flop and truth table

D flip-flop

The D flip-flop is basically an RS flip-flop with only one data input (D) and a clock input. Figure 2-21 shows its functional representation and associated truth table. The positive edge of the clock strobes in the data input and switches the flip-flop to the same state as the D input. The two other possible input conditions found in the RS flip-flop, the 00 state and the 11 state, do not exist in the D flip-flop.

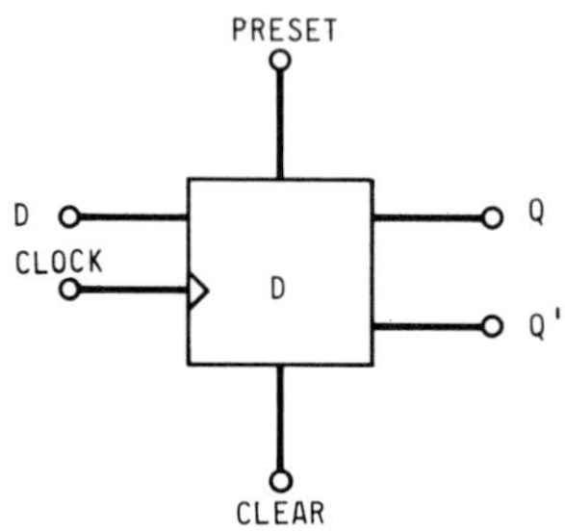

(a) FLIP FLOP

D	Q
0	0
1	1

(b) TRUTH TABLE

2-21 D flip-flop and truth table

2.3.4 Master–Slave Operation

A master–slave flip-flop consists of two latches, called the *master* and the *slave*, connected in series (see Figure 2-22). The transfer of data is accomplished in two steps. During the clock period, the input data are gated into the master latch and the gates between the two latches are simultaneously disabled. This action, effectively, isolates the output latch from the inputs. At the termination of the clock pulse, the state of the master is transferred to the slave. Figure 2-22 shows the RS master–slave flip-flop and the timing diagram of its operation. The two inputs, R and S, are normally complementary. When the input gates are enabled by the clock pulse, the inputs are transferred directly to the master latch. The master will remember and hold the last state prior to the termination of the clock pulse. When the clock goes low, the input gates to the master flip-flop are disabled and the input gates to the slave flip-flop are enabled to transfer the data from the master to the slave. For the RS type of flip-flop or latch, the R and S inputs cannot both be in the 1 state when the clock pulse goes low.

An indeterminate condition results when both the R and S inputs are in the 1 state and both are gated concurrently into the master latch. If another set of inputs is provided which prevents the R and S gates from simultaneously becoming active, the indeterminancy does not exist. This condition can be satisfied by feeding back outputs Q and Q′ from the slave latch in the cross-connected arrangement shown in Figure 2-23. The inputs are now changed from R and S to K and J, respectively, to indicate that both inputs may legitimately be in the 1 state. This flip-flop is referred to as the *JK master–slave*.

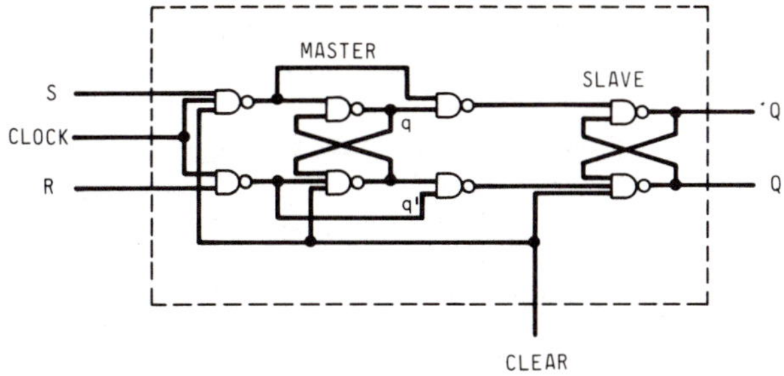

(a) RS MASTER-SLAVE FLIP-FLOP

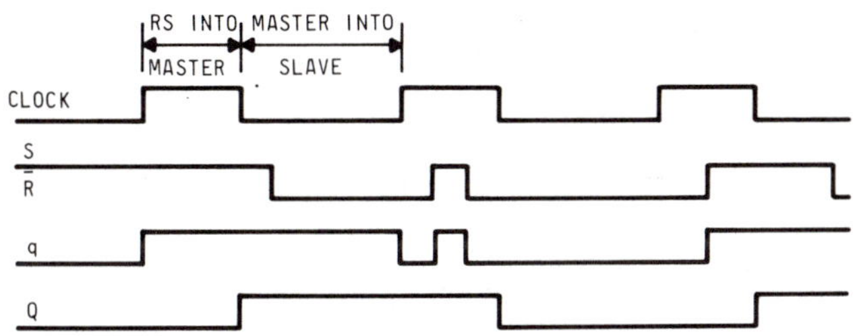

(b) TIMING DIAGRAM

2-22 RS master–slave flip-flop and timing diagram

When both J and K are in the 1 state, the feedback cross-connections allow the complement of the output data to be gated into the master latch during the clock pulse. At the end of the clock, the master data are transferred to the slave. This is the same, in effect, as toggling the slave to the opposite state. The J and K inputs must be stable during the entire clock interval. Otherwise, if both inputs momentarily become 1's during the clock pulse, the complementary state of the output will be stored in the master latch and remain in that state. Consequently, the wrong data will be transferred to the output at the termination of the clock. As indicated in Figure 2-23a, a CLEAR signal can reset both the master and the slave latches to the 0 state. This is often necessary to ensure that a flip-flop is in the cleared state. Similarly, a PRESET (not shown in the figure) can also be incorporated into the circuit to set the flip-flop to the 1 state. A timing diagram illustrating the JK master–slave operation is shown in Figure 2-23b.

2.3.5 Edge-Trigger Operation

The edge-triggered clock operation depends on the voltage level at which a positive or negative transition occurs. Either a positive or a negative transition is used in a single flip-flop circuit bit, but not both. This type of clocking enables the input data to be transferred directly to the outputs. Edge-triggered operation requires that an input be stable only during the transition period. This, in turn, results in a higher

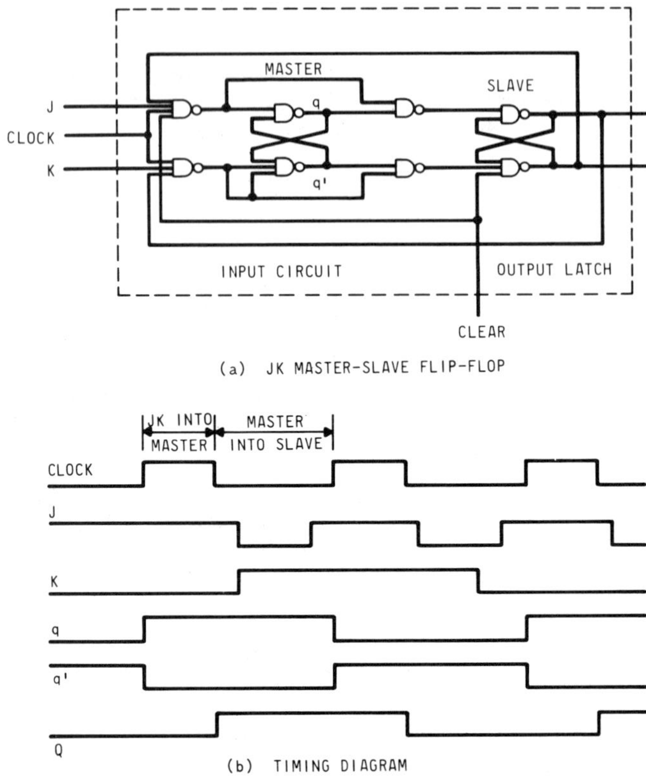

2-23 JK master–slave flip-flop and timing diagram

speed of logic operation. The inputs may also change during other periods without altering the information. The data are strobed into the output latch during a level change of the clock. The level change may be either positive or negative, depending on the logic circuit. The input circuitry is arranged to remember the input data during this transition. Any further input changes will not affect the inputs to the output latch.

The positive edge-trigger RS flip-flop implemented using standard NAND gates is shown in Figure 2-24. The input circuitry consists of interlocking latches with the outputs connected directly to the output latch. When the clock is in the low state, these outputs are held in the inactive or high-output condition. Any changes in the R or S input signals have no direct effect on the gates connected to the output latch. Prior to the positive transition of the clock, the two inputs must be stable and complementary or both must be in the 0 state for the circuit to work properly.

The RS edge-trigger flip-flop reacts the same way as the RS master–slave flip-flop when both the R and S inputs are in the 1 state at the time of the clock transition which transfers data into the output latch. This unstable condition can be corrected by feeding the output back in combination with the inputs. This ensures that the resul-

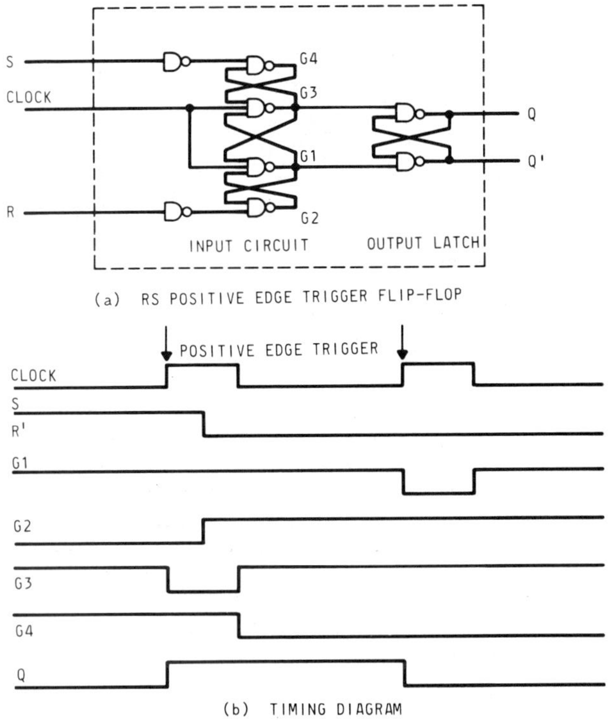

2-24 RS positive edge-triggered flip-flop and timing diagram

tant inputs to the set and reset latches are not both active. This is shown in Figure 2-25a, where the outputs are fed back to the input circuit in a cross-connected arrangement. This configuration is referred to as a *JK positive edge-triggered flip-flop*. When inputs J and K are both in the 1 state on the positive clock transition, the output latch will toggle to its complementary state. The timing diagram of this action is shown in Figure 2-25b.

The possibility of having both inputs in the 1 state can also be eliminated by having a single data input. If this input is a 1 or a 0, there can be no conflict from multiple inputs. The circuit for this *D positive edge-triggered flip-flop* is shown in Figure 2-26.

2.3.6 Flexibility of the JK Flip-Flop

The basic storage element of any of the flip-flops is still the simple latch circuit. The various input circuit configurations determine the operating characteristics of the flip-flop in response to its input signals. The input circuit may be arranged to transfer data into the storage element upon a transition of a clock pulse. This feature allows all types of counter applications and shift registers to be implemented using the more

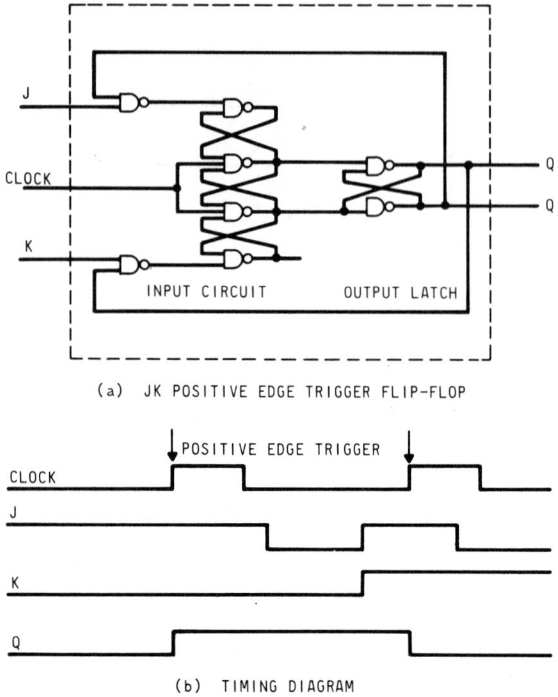

2-25 JK positive edge-triggered flip-flop and timing diagram

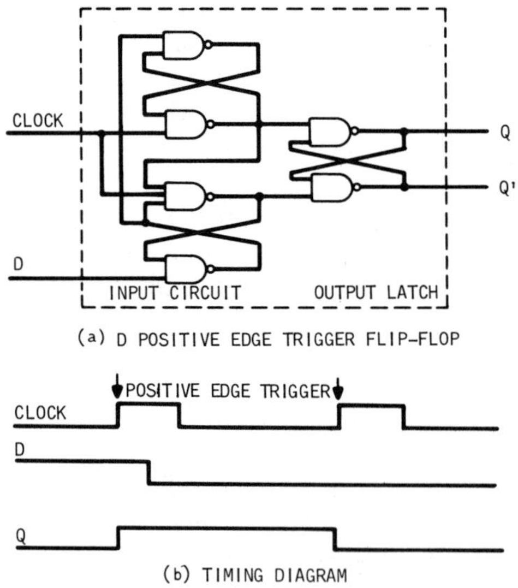

2-26 D positive edge-triggered flip-flop and timing diagram

complex flip-flop configurations. Because of the wide flexibility of the JK flip-flop, it is used to implement many of the special registers. It can also be used to implement both the D and T flip-flops very easily. As illustrated in Figure 2-27a, the D flip-flop is produced by using an inverter between the J the K inputs, while the T flip-flop is formed by tying the J and K inputs together (see Figure 2-27b). Also, the JK flip-flop can replace the RS type directly since it behaves in the same manner and has the additional capability of complementing the output when both of the inputs are in the 1 state.

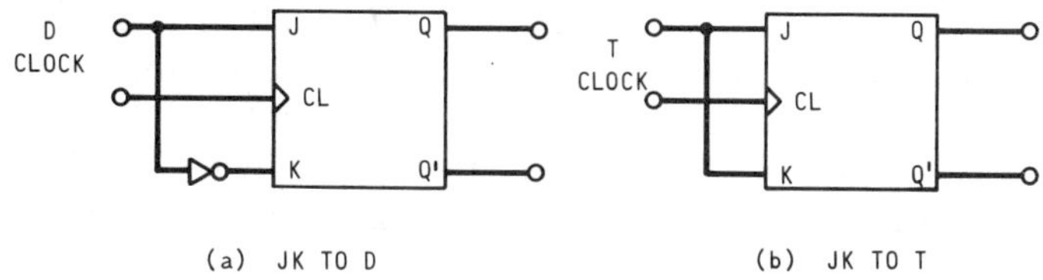

2-27 Versatility of the JK flip-flop

2.4 INTEGRATED CIRCUITS

2.4.1 The Level of Integration on a Chip

In addition to the fabrication of a logic gate on a silicon chip, the chip itself had to be encapsulated in a suitable package. It soon became apparent to semiconductor manufacturers that several gates fabricated on a single chip required very little additional cost. Therefore, the next step was to increase the number of gates on a single chip. However, as a chip grows larger, its circuitry increases, affecting the device yield. This is due to imperfections, generally scattered randomly throughout the chip, which are in the silicon slice during the manufacturing process. The larger the chip, the greater the probability that a defect exists. The yield therefore varies inversely with the size of the chip. The defect density has been reduced as technology and manufacturing processes have improved.

The area of a chip depends not only on the number of gates and their interconnection, but also on the number of leads going off the chip (also called the *pin-out count*). Considerable ingenuity has been applied to circuit design to minimize the number of off-chip leads. In some instances, a reduction of leads is possible by incorporating additional gates on the chip or by performing more functions serially. The primary objective, of course, is to pack as much circuitry as possible on a given size chip while at the same time allowing it to be manufactured economically.

The level of integration has been increased steadily by achieving a larger packing density of gates per unit area through improvements in processing techniques. The primary motivation for higher levels of integration is cost. Although individual chips may cost more, the cost per gate goes down dramatically with each higher scale of integration. In addition, the size and weight of the equipment incorporating the chips are reduced considerably. More significantly, equipment reliability is increased since fewer parts and interconnections are required.

2.4.2 Small-scale Integration (SSI) Circuits

The early manufacturers of integrated circuits were concerned with the placement of several gates on a single chip. Most of these circuits were partitioned on a unit-logic basis; that is, all inputs and outputs for each gate were brought off the chip. They were then interconnected on the circuit board level to form the desired logic function. Such SSI circuits have been used as standard building blocks in various logic designs. Typical of these circuits are the quad 2-input NAND gates, quad 2-input NOR gates, dual 4-input NAND gates, and single 8-input NAND gates. A quad circuit refers to four identical logic gates on the same chip with their respective inputs and outputs brought out to the external world. Similarly, a dual SSI circuit refers to two identical logic gates on the same chip. The great attraction of such SSI devices is that every gate can be fully utilized, since there are no interconnections among gates on the same chip.

2.4.3 Medium-Scale Integration (MSI) Circuits

MSI is the next level of integration encountered by the logic designer; 12 to 100 gates are partitioned and placed on a single chip. These circuits are general purpose and have wide use throughout a computer's design. With the proper interconnections, they can be used as building blocks to expand a small, logical structure into a larger functional unit. For example, a 4-bit full adder can be expanded to any length by connecting individual 4-bit full adders together. A 16-bit full adder, for example, can be made with four 4-bit full adders.

The common MSI parts used as standard building blocks are the 4-bit ALU (arithmetic/logic unit) chip, look-ahead carry circuit, multiplexers, decoders, counters, shift registers, and latches. They form the functional blocks that are used to implement more complex computer systems. The MSI chips permit more interconnections to be made internally rather than on the circuit board level. The number of circuit parts is reduced accordingly. Except for semiconductor memories, minicomputers in the late 1960's and early 1970's were implemented exclusively with MSI and SSI parts.

2.4.4 Large-Scale Integration (LSI) Circuits

Memory devices had the greatest impact on the market for LSI circuits because of their great sales potential. They were also reasonably easy to manufacture because of their regular structure. Consequently, the early work on LSI devices was directed toward this area.

As mentioned earlier, the chip area required increases as more and more circuits are placed on a single chip. However, there are basically three constraints which may cause difficulties in chip implementation. They are the number of external leads required, the number of circuits to be placed on the chip, and the power that must be dissipated. These constraints are all interrelated, since both the number of external leads and the number of circuits occupy silicon area. Furthermore, power dissipation increases with the number of circuits.

The choice of MOS technology for LSI implementation was based on its high packing density and low power dissipation. A logic function implemented using MOS technology requires a much smaller area of silicon on the chips than the same logic function implemented using bipolar technology. For example, a 3-input gate made from NMOS technology requires a chip area of about 3.5 mil^2. This may be compared with the same gate made from low-power Schottky TTL technology, which requires a chip area of 20 mil^2. Similarly, power dissipation for an NMOS device is less by a factor of 5 to 10 than the same devices using TTL. However, this reduced power dissipation is at the expense of reduced switching speed for the NMOS device. The two factors of chip area and power dissipation have strongly favored MOS technology for use in LSI implementations.

The number of external leads going off of a chip has remained a limitation. As more and more functions are incorporated on a single chip, there is a further need to increase the number of pin-outs. The number of pins, like the gates per chip, has increased (but at a much slower rate). The original Intel 4004, a 4-bit microprocessor, was a 16-pin device. In 1975, Texas Instruments introduced its TMS9900, a 16-bit microprocessor with 64 pins.

In the bipolar area, various manufacturers concentrated on obtaining a processor chip set for use in higher-performance minicomputer systems. This was done to stay within the limitations imposed by a practical chip size, the number of pins that could be usefully provided for external connections, and allowable power dissipation. At the same time, it provided an alternative to the slower MOS microprocessor structures.

2.5 LSI CONTROL STORAGE: ROM (READ-ONLY MEMORY)

2.5.1 Characteristics of ROM Devices

Control functions in the past were largely implemented with random logic. SSI circuit parts were used, with the design of the control section tailored to meet each individual timing and control requirement. In contrast, the LSI solution to random logic has been to employ a host of ROM's. Because a ROM offers the logic designer a combination of low cost, high speed, and system flexibility, it has become an important part of many digital systems.

ROM's are intended to store nonchanging information and, because of their regular logical organization, are well suited to LSI manufacturing processes. The circuitry associated with a ROM device is much less complex than the circuitry required by a RAM. This simplicity in physical organization permits a ROM to be implemented using either the bipolar or MOS manufacturing processes. The availability of high-speed ROM structures makes possible the implementation of microprogram techniques for the control section of a computer.

In a microcomputer, ROM's are used to store fixed user programs. The rapid growth in the microprocessor field has been directly related to the development of inexpensive ROM's. They are also widely used in many other applications (e.g., code converters, character generators, and look-up tables). Because of their cell simplicity, ROM's are capable of achieving very high bit packing densities.

2.5.2 ROM (Read-Only Memory)

A semiconductor ROM is an array of diodes or transistors. In the discrete component era, the elements could be resistors, capacitors, or transformers. The information contained in the ROM is specified by the interconnection pattern of the array. Figure 2-28 shows a simplified 16-word by 1-bit array of diodes. The 16 diodes are organized in a 4 × 4 array, with four rows and four columns. Half of the address

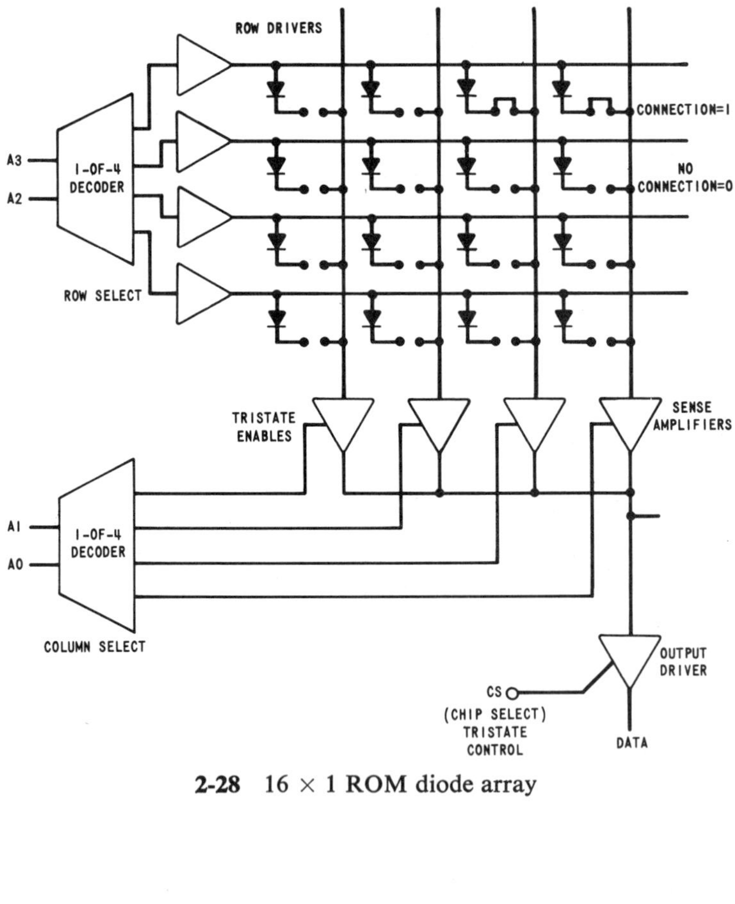

2-28 16 × 1 ROM diode array

lines are decoded and used to energize one of the four rows. The signal on the selected row is passed through those diodes connected to the corresponding columns. As indicated in the figure, a closed connection represents a 1 for that bit position, and an open connection represents a 0. The remaining address lines are decoded and used to enable one of the four sense amplifiers associated with the columns. The symbol used for the sense amplifiers represents a tri-state control device in which the signal appearing at the input of the selected sense amplifier is transmitted to the output driver. The nonselected amplifiers are kept in the high-impedance state. This permits all four outputs from the sense amplifiers to be connected together. The signal from the column selected by the address lines is passed on to the output driver; the output signals from the other three columns are not enabled. In this arrangement, the 4 × 4 array is organized into a 16-word by 1-bit array. The output driver is itself another tri-state gate, with the enable lead designated as a chip select signal. The tri-state output allows outputs from other ROM chips to be connected together to extend the word size. If the chip select is a 1, the data are gated to the output by the output driver. In a mask-programmable ROM, the encoding of information is accomplished by selectively including or omitting the small conducting jumper shown between the diode and the bit line in Figure 2-28. This is done during the final phase of fabrication. Because of the simplicity of these memory elements, a large number of bits can be packed into a single ROM chip.

The small diode array can be expanded into a larger ROM chip as indicated in Figure 2-29. The 32 × 32 array gives a 1024-bit ROM, which is organized into an arrangement of 256 words by 4 bits. The 5 high-order address bits are used to select one row out of 32 in the top array. The 32 columns are divided into four 8-bit groups. The three low-order address lines are used to select one output from each of these four groups, giving a total of four outputs. The tri-state output gates allow other ROM chips to be connected at their outputs to form larger memory arrays.

The ROM chips can be fabricated using either bipolar or MOS technology. The primary differences between a bipolar ROM and an MOS ROM are in the access time required by the chip decoding logic and the number of bits that may be placed on a chip. The access times for bipolar ROM's range between 50 and 90 nanoseconds, while the access times for MOS ROM's are an order of magnitude higher. Bipolar ROM's are available in 1K-bit to 16K-bit packages; MOS ROM's may be obtained in modules that range in size from 1K bit to 64K bits. The two primary reasons for increasing the density of devices on a ROM chip are (1) to reduce the number of ROM packages on a board, and (2) to increase the number of functions in a ROM package. This is normally accomplished by using the lower-cost MOS process, which also yields a higher device density.

2.5.3 PROM (Programmable Read-Only Memory)

PROM's are generally constructed using bipolar technology. They are organized in the same array structure as ROM's, with either diodes or transistors as memory elements. Included with each memory element is a fusible link. A simple 2 × 2 PROM

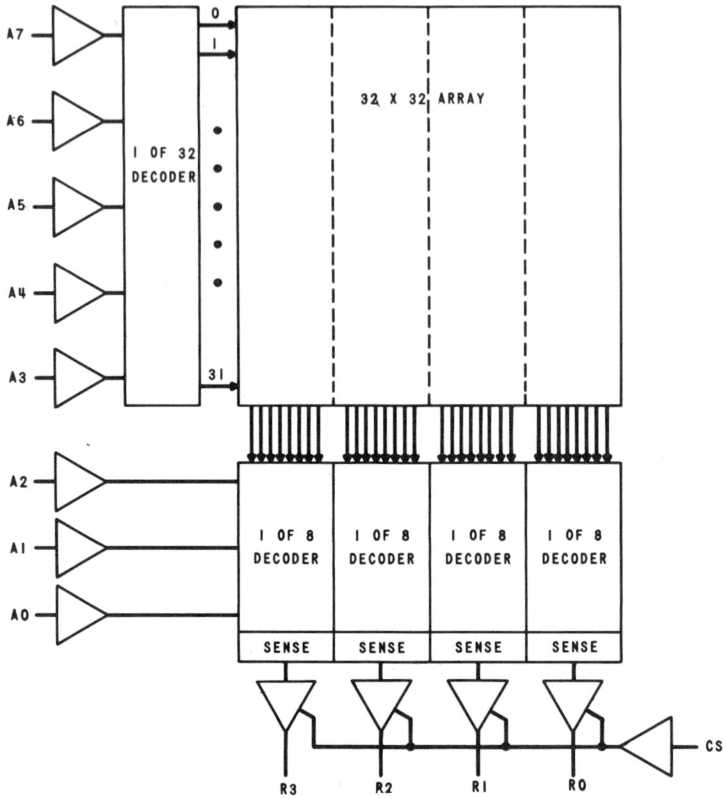

2-29 256-word by 4-bit ROM block diagram

transistor array is shown in Figure 2-30, with a fuse link connecting the emitter of each transistor to the bit line (column). Programming is accomplished by directing a sequence of current pulses, which typically range between 20 and 30 milliamps, to the selected fusible link until it is blown. This action changes a logical 1 to a 0. Consequently, programming of PROM's may be done directly by the user.

Because the current levels required for the fusing operation are incompatible with MOS impedance levels, encoding by fusing does not work readily with MOS devices. Thus, an MOS device is not a good candidate for incorporation in a fusible PROM structure. The two most commonly used fuse technologies for PROM's are nichrome and polysilicon fusing. Nichrome is an alloy of nickel and chrome. Nichrome fuses are deposited as very thin film links to the column lines (see Figure 2-30). When a heavy current is forced to flow through this thin nichrome film, the film blows and opens the connection between the row and column lines. The most difficult problem associated with nichrome fuse technology was the phenomenon of *growback*, which occurred during the programming of the first production units. Growback, the

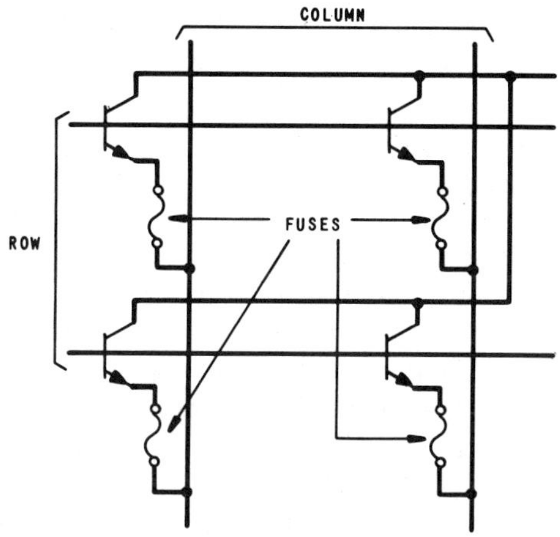

2-30 2 × 2 transistor array

reversal of the programming process, occurs when a fuse "grows back" and begins to conduct again. A programmed 0, for example, would return to the 1 state. The reliability problems associated with nichrome fuses have all been related to fuse processing. It should be noted, however, that not all nichrome-fuse PROM's have had the growback problem. In general, this problem has been solved by better processing techniques.

The second common type of fuse technology uses polysilicon fuses. These work in the same manner as the nichrome fuses except that the fusing material is polycrystalline silicon. The silicon is deposited in a thick layer as a link between each row and column line. The fuse is blown with a train of current pulses which range between 20 and 30 milliamps. During this fusing operation, temperatures of 1400°C are reached. At these temperatures, the silicon oxidizes and forms silicon dioxide, an insulating material. The early production polysilicon fuses did not have the same growback problem that the first nichrome fuses had.

The largest bipolar PROM's provide 16K bits of storage, organized in a 2K × 8 configuration. These chips are commercially available from several manufacturers with the same pinouts and electrical characteristics. The existence of multiple sources of an LSI device is a very important consideration in guaranteeing the device's continued supply at the most competitive cost. The 4K PROM typically features an access time of 70 nanoseconds and is TTL-compatible on both its inputs and outputs.

The inclusion of fusible links makes PROM chips more complex and, therefore, more expensive than ROM's. However, they do not require a special mask. The PROM is particularly convenient for small-to-moderate quantity applications, and it is also preferred during preliminary design of early models in which considerable changes are expected. In these cases, PROM's are used until the system design has been proven, at which time the capital investment needed to produce an initial mask for a ROM is justified. Consequently, some semiconductor manufacturers make equivalent-density PROM/ROM compatible pairs using the same pinout and packaging configuration. This allows direct replacement of PROM's with ROM's.

2.5.4 EPROM (Erasable Programmable Read-Only Memory)

The greatest flexibility in changing a ROM program at the design stage is provided by EPROM's that allow more than a one-time program change. There are several techniques for EPROM implementation. One of the better known is the *floating-gate avalanche MOS (FAMOS) charge storage device*. It is essentially a silicon gate field-effect transistor in which no connection is made to the silicon gate. The write operation involves applying a high-voltage pulse between source and drain, which removes positive carriers from the floating gate. The isolated negative carriers on the gate create a conducting channel. This operation depends on charge transport to the floating gate by avalanche injection of electrons from either the source or drain. After the applied junction voltage is removed, no discharge path is available for the accumulated electrons. The presence or absence of charge (logical 1 or logical 0) can be sensed by measuring the conductance between the source and the drain. This electronic charge is cleared (discharged) by exposing the floating gate to ultraviolet radiation.

Another technique is based on metal nitride oxide silicon technology. A layer of silicon nitride placed between the metal gate and oxide insulator retains a charge introduced by a high-voltage pulse. This charge will remain for years in the absence of any externally supplied power. The advantage of this technique is that the data stored in the form of a charge may be cleared and then reprogrammed in a manner similar to writing data into a RAM, without removing the device from the circuit board.

The trapped-charge EPROM's are made exclusively from MOS technology. They rely on the high-impedance state of the memory cell to retain their stored charges for long periods of time. EPROM's are available in modules of various sizes ranging up to 64K bits with an access time of 500 nanoseconds.

2.6 PLA (PROGRAMMABLE LOGIC ARRAY)

There are many standard MSI and LSI building blocks for simplifying a design. Nonetheless, a good deal of decoding and control logic must be implemented with SSI parts. The PLA is intended specifically for replacement of random logic.

Figure 2-31 shows a simple PLA circuit consisting of two arrays of diodes. The first array forms a set of AND gates that realize product terms in a logical expression. Each column functions as an AND gate, with an input diode at each intersection of a row and a column. Both primed and unprimed inputs are generated by inverters on the PLA chip to reduce the number of input terminals. A diode connection provides either the primed or unprimed inputs to the AND gate formed by each column. The outputs from the first array are connected as inputs to the second array. This connec-

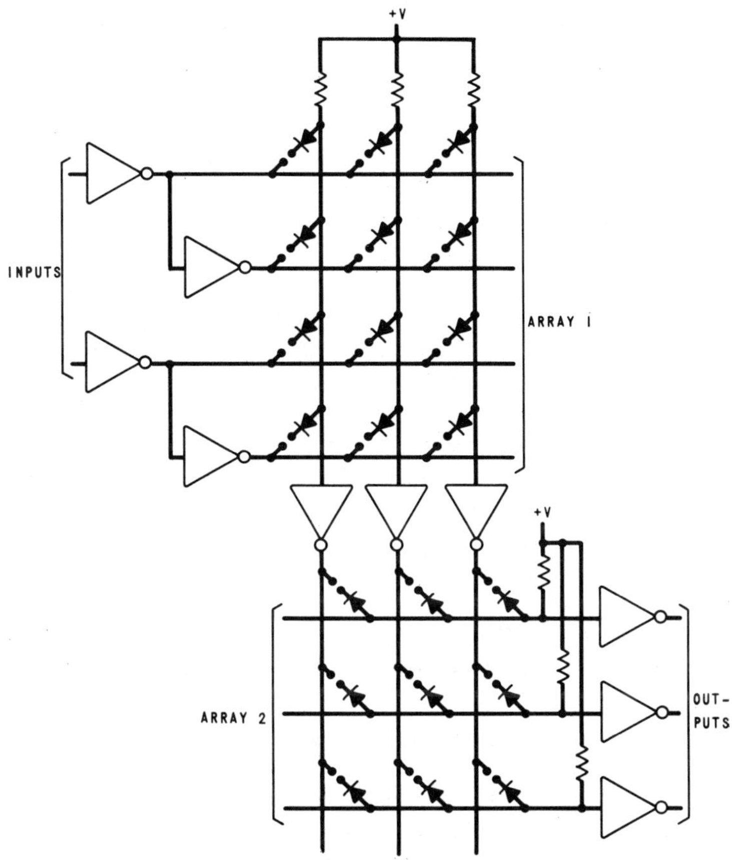

2-31 Simple PLA circuit

tion performs the logical ORing (or summing function) of the product terms. The connection of a diode in the second array to a particular column allows the output of that product term to be transmitted to the final output. Any logical function can be realized by the PLA structure. Its use in implementing the control section of a computer is described in Chapter 7.

A standard PLA has 14 inputs, 96 product terms, and 8 outputs. The circuit is functionally equivalent to a collection of 96 14-input AND gates which may be ORed at any of the circuit's 8 outputs. The PLA's are fabricated using bipolar technology, with a switching speed between 50 and 100 nanoseconds. The masked-programmed PLA's are more costly when compared with ROM's and PROM's, and the slow turnaround time required to program a PLA makes it inflexible for design changes. However, nonprogrammable PLA's with built-in functions are much more flexible than ROM's, and they can be substituted for nonstandard logic circuits at a relatively low cost. Typical functions that are well suited to preprogrammed PLA's include code conversions (i.e., gray code to BCD code), a modulo-10 counter, and trigonometric function generation.

Another important development is the *field-programmable logic array* (*FPLA*). It is structurally the same as the PLA except that each diode contains a fusible link. The fusible link for the FPLA functions in the same manner as the fusible link for the PROM. Programming is done by blowing fuses with high current pulses. To gain access to each fuse, additional access circuitry must be provided so that the high current can be directed only to the selected fuses. Because the extra circuitry required by the FPLA and the fuse links take up a large amount of chip area, the number of product terms is reduced from 96 to 48 to accommodate the added components. The FPLA allows an engineer to breadboard a system in little time. These devices bridge the circuit gap between standard MSI and LSI parts.

There are some difficulties in the use of FPLA's. Often the devices are difficult to program and test. More software and hardware design aids are needed to facilitate the programming of the chips. Although the FPLA and the PLA have the same package size and pin configuration, they are not always directly interchangeable because of the reduced number of product terms available from the FPLA's.

2.7 LSI DATA STORAGE: RAM (RANDOM-ACCESS MEMORY)

2.7.1 The Development of RAM Devices

Semiconductor memory costs have declined rapidly since 1967, primarily because of the increasing density of LSI RAM chips. The limits of LSI have not yet been reached and further improvements are leading to larger, higher-density memory devices. The cost per bit has continued to fall while bit density has continued to increase. Semiconductor memories also offer the advantage of high speed. Continuing developments are increasing the speed of memory operation even further.

An important feature of a semiconductor memory is the ease with which it may be interfaced with other parts of a digital system. Most of these memory devices are compatible with standard computer logic. Individual packages may be easily combined in a modular size and then grown into very large capacity configurations as the need arises.

The development of RAM devices has been directed toward both MOS and bipolar technologies: MOS for high density and bipolar for speed. There is a wide choice of RAM's available for a variety of applications, each of which may have different requirements in speed, size, and power dissipation. In mid-1978, bipolar RAM's were of the static type; they were used most frequently as scratch pad or buffer memories. Larger memories made use of MOS technology.

A RAM memory cell can be either static or dynamic. A static memory cell is similar to a bipolar memory cell in that it functions as a latch with two stable states. These states are used to store logical 0's or 1's. A dynamic memory cell is essentially a capacitor with a stored charge used to represent a 1 and no charge used to indicate a 0. Since the charges eventually tend to leak off, they must be periodically refreshed: hence the term *dynamic RAM*. The refreshing function requires special timing signals and extra power supplies. This need for extra equipment is a distinct disadvantage. However, if the additional circuitry required for the refresh function is spread over a large memory configuration, the lower cost of the denser, dynamic type of RAM justifies its use. On the other hand, for the small memories usually encountered in microcomputer applications, the static MOS memories may prove to be more economical, since no additional logic is required to realize the refresh circuitry (the static RAM requires no refresh operation). The use of a static or dynamic RAM, therefore, is dictated by the requirements of the application system.

2.7.2 Static MOS RAM Cell

Figure 2-32 shows a static MOS memory cell. It is a typical latch flip-flop in which the cross-coupled transistors, Q1 and Q2, form the basic storage elements. Transistors Q3 and Q4 replace the collector resistors, while Q5 and Q6 serve as gates that connect the collectors of Q1 and Q2 to the digit lines. The memory cell is read by turning on gates Q5 and Q6 by means of the word line. The stored data are transferred to the digit lines. The outputs that appear on the digit lines are complementary, and the read operation is nondestructive. The write operation is carried out in a similar manner by turning on gates Q5 and Q6. This action sets the logic state of the RAM cell to correspond to the voltages that appear on the digit lines. The storage cells, Q1 and Q2,

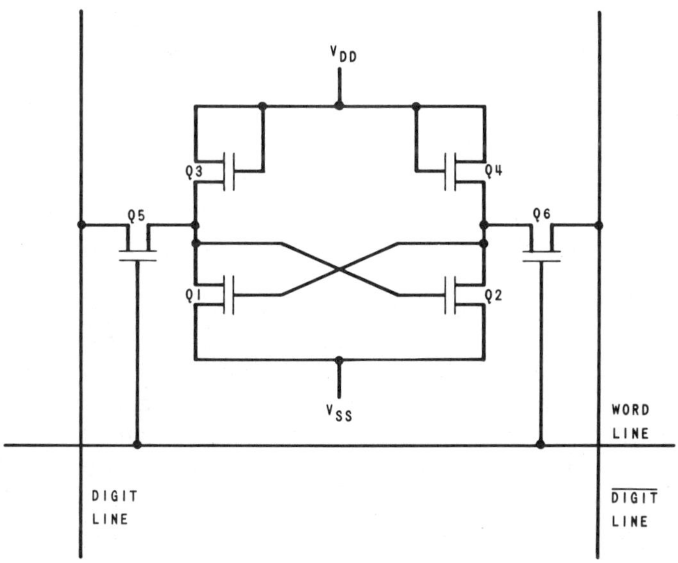

2-32 Static MOS memory cell

will assume the same logical state as those that appear on the digit lines. Power dissipation could be reduced by clocking the power supply from low voltage to high voltage only during the memory-access interval. If the memory chips are not selected during a memory operation, they will remain in the low-power quiescent state. The major disadvantage of the six-transistor static cell is the large cell size required by the six transistors. However, cell size has been reduced by using NMOS technology. One of the more popular 1024-bit static RAM's has been widely used in peripheral, terminal, and microprocessor applications. Most static RAM's are organized on a 4-bit slice (i.e., 256 $\times$ 4), which fits modularly with the 4-bit, 8-bit, and 16-bit microprocessors. This also allows memory units to grow in smaller modules, thereby keeping the number of parts as few as possible. Higher-density static RAM's are organized on a single-bit slice (i.e., 4K $\times$ 1) to keep down the number of external pins required by the memory chip, and a 4-bit slice (i.e., 1K $\times$ 4) to allow microprocessors to grow in smaller modules.

2.7.3 Dynamic MOS RAM Cell

The extremely high input resistance of an MOS device provides a temporary storage node which can be used to reduce the number of components in a memory cell. Because the junction leakage currents are so small, charges can be stored on both the gate capacitance and gate parasitic capacitances for hundreds of milliseconds. Since the charges do leak out slowly, they must be refreshed periodically before data are lost.

The transition from a static RAM cell to a dynamic cell is accomplished by simply removing the load transistors (Q3 and Q4 in Figure 2-32), which reduces the memory cell from six to four transistors. This is shown in Figure 2-33a with the two-gate transistors, Q5 and Q6, operated as load transistors when the cell is accessed. Writing is accomplished by forcing the appropriate bit line to ground with an external applied signal. When transistors Q5 and Q6 are activated, the data appearing on the digit lines are transferred into the cell. The cell will hold the information that has been set into it by this operation. When transistors Q5 and Q6 are turned off, the charge on the appropriate capacitance will gradually leak off. The cell will eventually lose its information content and must be refreshed. This is done simply by turning both Q5 and Q6 on.

As shown in Figure 2-33a, there are two storage capacitances. The data are represented by the capacitance, which contains the charge. A further simplification can be realized by utilizing only one capacitance. In this case, data will be represented by the presence or the absence of charge on this single capacitance. This configuration, shown in Figure 2-33b, utilizes three transistor cells. The state of transistor Q2, the information storage element, depends on the charge stored on capacitor C. Transistor Q3, when activated by the read select control, transfers the data onto the read data line. In writing, the data are applied to the write data line. Transistor Q1 is activated to either charge or discharge the capacitor C. Transistor Q1 is also used for refreshing

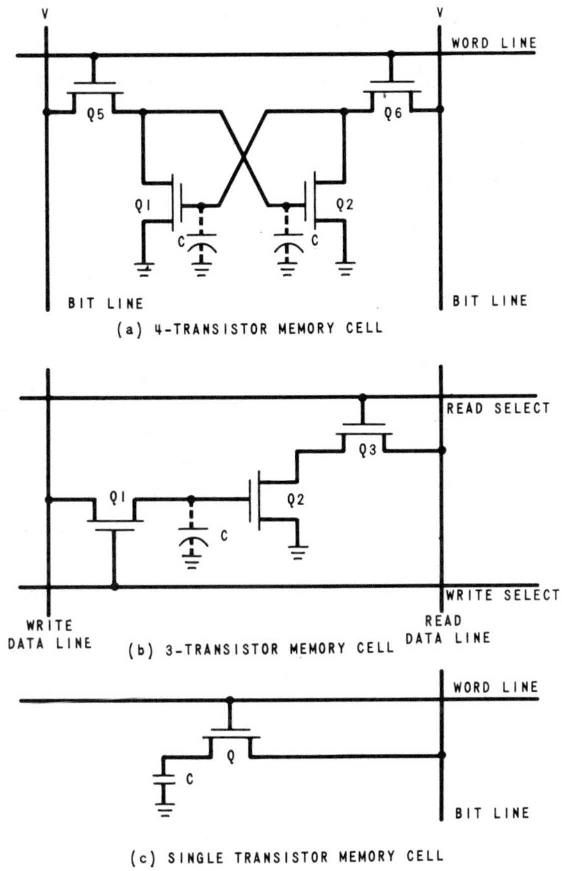

2-33 Dynamic MOS memory cells

information storage element Q2. This is done by a clocked refresh amplifier that is connected between the read and write lines (not shown in the figure). This permits read information to be fed back onto storage element Q2. The information to be refreshed must be read first and then written. This results in a longer refresh cycle. A single refresh amplifier is normally incorporated on another chip to serve an entire column in the array of storage elements.

The early 1024-bit dynamic RAM's were constructed using either the 4-transistor or the 3-transistor cell structure. Because the 1103 dynamic RAM introduced by Intel in 1970 was, perhaps, the most popular semiconductor memory device in that period, it was quickly accepted as an industry standard. The 1103 used P-channel MOS technology and employed the three-transistor-cell structure shown in Figure 2-33b.

The simplest storage cell, shown in Figure 2-33c, consists of single transistor and a capacitor. The data are written by establishing the signal level on the bit line and then activating the gate transistor. The information is transferred from the bit line onto the capacitor by means of the gate transistor. The read operation is performed by connecting the capacitor, by means of the gate, to the bit line and sensing the charge on the bit line. A special design is required to increase the sensitivity of the sense amplifiers. The readout of this particular cell is destructive since the stored charge redistributes itself between the cell and the bit line capacitance. It is necessary to internally rewrite the data into the cell after they are read. The same circuitry is also used to refresh the cell at periodic intervals. The major problem associated with a single transistor cell is to obtain a large enough voltage swing to easily read the information out of the cell. This is due to the large value of the bit line capacitance which exists relative to the cell storage capacitance. However, the real advantages of such a cell structure are its simplicity and the small area it occupies. Considerable development effort has gone into solving many of the problems associated with a single transistor cell. All 4096-bit dynamic RAM's use this simple structure to realize the large number of bits required in going from a 1024-bit device to a 4096-bit device. The first 4096-bit dynamic device was introduced commercially in 1974 using N-channel polysilicon technology.

The 16,384-bit RAM became commercially available at the beginning of 1976. This bit density was achieved by using an enhanced N-channel silicon gate technique. A double level of polysilicon conductors was used to shrink the memory cell to less than half the cell size encountered in the densest 4K-bit RAM. The 16K chip is an

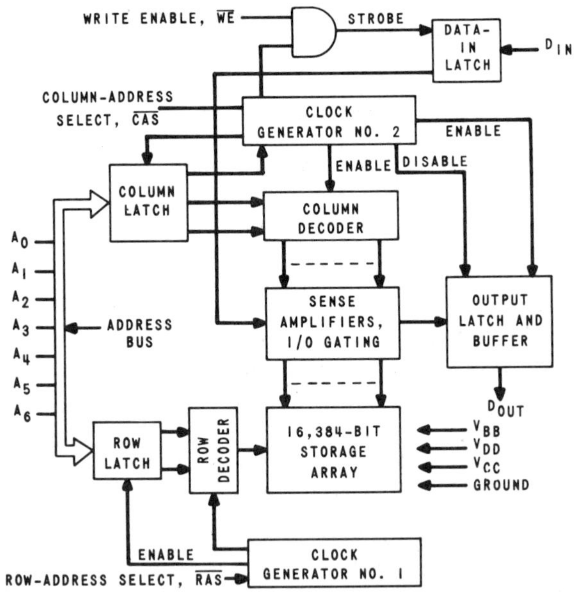

2-34 Intel 16K dynamic RAM chip (2116)

extension of, rather than a radical departure from, the N-channel process used in the standard 4K devices. The organization of the Intel 2116 16K dynamic RAM chip is shown in Figure 2-34. It is laid out as two 8192-bit RAM's sharing a column decoder. The address lines are multiplexed to limit the number of pinouts on the chip to 16. This approach was chosen so that the 16K RAM would be compatible with Intel's existing 16-pin model 2104 4K RAM's. Because of this pin arrangement, a memory designed with the 2104 can be updated easily with 16K RAM's to quadruple the memory size on a circuit board.

The 64K dynamic RAM's were introduced commercially in late 1978. It is expected that 256K dynamic RAM's will be available in the mid-1980's.

2.7.4 Bipolar Static RAM Cell

For high-speed applications such as scratch pad memories, RAM's must operate at logic-compatible speeds. For this purpose, RAM's are generally of the faster, more costly bipolar type rather than the slower, less expensive MOS variation. The size of bipolar RAM's ranges from 64 bits to 4096 bits. A typical bipolar RAM cell is shown in Figure 2-35. It is a basic flip-flop structure in which the cross-coupled transistors

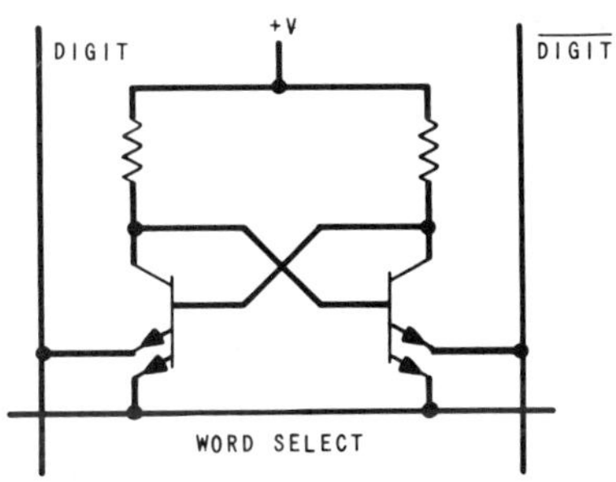

2-35 Static bipolar memory cell

have multiple emitters to facilitate reading and writing. In the memory array, all cells in a column share the same digit line while all cells in a row are selected by a common word line. Digit lines are normally held at a higher potential than the word line, which reverse-biases the emitter junctions. In the read operation, the potential of the word line is raised, causing one of the digit line emitters to conduct current to the digit line. The information stored in the cell is sensed by detecting the current flow. In the write operation, data are written by raising the word line potential and lowering one of the two digit lines, which causes the flip-flop to assume the appropriate state. Bipolar memories are manufactured by processes similar to those used in logic circuit production (TTL and ECL). The static devices do not need to be refreshed nor do they need the long cycle times required by the dynamic MOS RAM's.

2.8 SUMMARY

Semiconductor technology has progressed at an explosive rate. Innovations in processing techniques have led to higher performance circuits and denser chip structures. This evolution has occurred in both MOS and bipolar technology. These technology advances have occurred to meet the needs of a variety of applications. For example, 64K dynamic RAM's, more powerful microprocessors, and improved processor chip sets emerged from this semiconductor development to become commercially available products.

Figure 2-36 summarizes the various semiconductor technologies and their circuit applications at the chip level. As indicated, the technologies are divided into two areas: MOS and bipolar. Although MOS technology had been around for many years, its potential was not realized until the early 1970's, when Intel introduced its model 1103 1K RAM chip and its model 4004 microprocessor chip. The early LSI chips were developed with PMOS technology. Since then, great strides have been made with NMOS and CMOS. NMOS is just an extension or second generation of PMOS technology. It is well suited for LSI RAM's and microprocessors (see Appendix A).

In the bipolar area, the early design efforts were pointed toward providing SSI and MSI high-performance logic families, RAM's, and LSI ROM's. Bit-sliced LSI processors became a reality. Most of the minicomputer CPU's were produced with MSI-level, low-power Schottky TTL. The machines became more and more sophisticated, moving up to compete with the low end of the large mainframe machines.

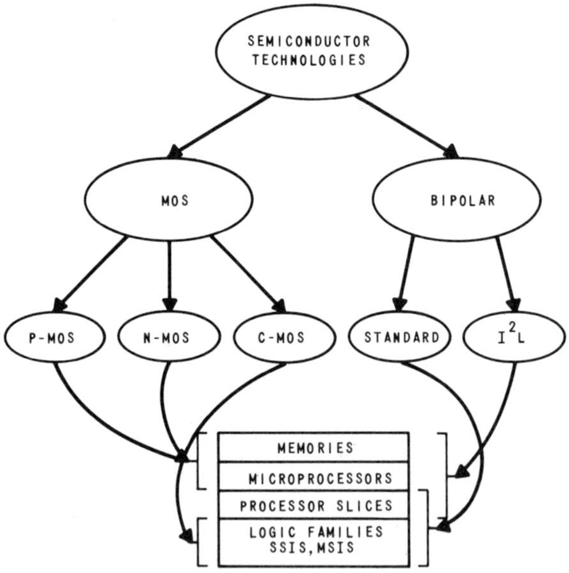

2-36 Semiconductor technologies

2.9 REFERENCES

1 MORRIS, R. L., AND J. R. MILLER, *Designing with TTL Integrated Circuits*, Texas Instrument Electronics Series. New York: McGraw-Hill Book Company, 1971.

2 GSCHWIND, H. W., AND E. J. MCCLUSKEY, *Design of Digital Computers*. New York: Springer-Verlag New York, Inc., 1975.

3 CRAWFORD, R. H., *MOSFET in Circuit Design*, Texas Instrument Electronics Series. New York: McGraw-Hill Book Company, 1967.

4 PENNEY, W., AND L. LAU, *MOS Integrated Circuits*, America Microsystems Engineering Staff. New York: Van Nostrand Reinhold Company, 1972.

5 DAVIS, S., "Selection and Application of Semiconductor Memories." *Computer Design*, Vol. 13, No. 1 (Jan. 1974), pp. 65–77.

6 GREENE, B., AND D. HOUSE, "Designing with Intel PROMs and ROMs," *Intel Application Note, AP6*. Intel Corp., Santa Clara, Calif., 1975.

7 HODGES, D. A., "Trends in Computer Hardware Technology." *Computer Design*, Vol. 15, No. 2 (Feb. 1976), pp. 77–85.

8 BERGER, H. H., AND S. K. WIEDMANN, "The Bipolar ISI Breakthrough, Part 1: Rethinking the Problem." *Electronics*, Vol. 48, No. 18 (Sept. 4, 1975), pp. 89–95.

9 EATON, S. S., "Sapphire Brings Out the Best in C-MOS." *Electronics*, Vol. 48, No. 12 (June 12, 1975), pp. 115–120.

10 ALTMAN, L., "Special Report: C-MOS Enlarges Its Territory." *Electronics*, Vol. 48, No. 10 (May 15, 1975), pp. 77–88.

11 HUU, A. N., "Advances in C-MOS Device Technology." *Computer Design*, Vol. 14, No. 1 (Jan. 1975), pp. 87–92.

12 HART, C. M., A. SLOB, AND H. E. J. WALMS, "Bipolar LSI Takes a New Direction with Integrated Injection Logic." *Electronics*, Vol. 47, No. 20 (Oct. 3, 1974), pp. 111–118.

13 PEDERSEN, R. A., "Integrated Injection Logic: A Bipolar LSI Technique." *Computer*, Vol. 9, No. 2 (Feb. 1976), pp. 24–29.

14 BERGER, H. H., AND S. K. WIEDMAN, "The Bipolar LSI Breakthrough, Part 2: Extending the Limits." *Electronics*, Vol. 48, No. 20 (Oct. 2, 1975), pp. 99–103.

15 ALLAN, R., "Components: Microprocessors Galore." *IEEE Spectrum*, Vol. 13, No. 1 (Jan. 1976), pp. 50–56.

16 TORRERO, E. A., "Focus on Semiconductor Memories." *Electronic Design*, Vol. 23, No. 7 (April 1, 1975), pp. 98–107.

17 ALLAN, R., "Semiconductor Memories." *IEEE Spectrum*, Vol. 12, No. 8 (Aug. 1975), pp. 40–45.

18 ALTMAN, L., "Specifications of 16K RAM Memories Beginning to Emerge." *Electronics*, Vol. 48, No. 26 (Dec. 25, 1975), pp. 29–30.

19 COE, J. E., AND W. G. OLDHAM, "Enter the 16,384-bit RAM." *Electronics*, Vol. 49, No. 4 (Feb. 19, 1976), pp. 116–121.

20 HEMEL, A., "The PLA: A Different Kind of ROM." *Electronic Design*, Vol. 24, No. 1 (Jan. 5, 1976), pp. 78–84.

21 ALTMAN, L., "The New LSI Bipolar Chips Are Best Buy for Designers of Fast Systems." *Electronics*, Vol. 48, No. 14 (July 10, 1975), pp. 81–85.

22 HORTON, R. L., J. ENGLADE, AND G. MCGEE, "I²L Takes Bipolar Integration a Significant Step Forward." *Electronics*, Vol. 48, No. 3 (Feb. 6, 1975), pp. 83–90.

23 DAVIS, S., "Selection and Application of Semiconductor Memories." *Computer Design*, Vol. 13, No. 1 (Jan. 1974), pp. 65–77.

24 HODGES, D. A., ed., *Semiconductor Memories*. New York: IEEE Press, 1972.

25 LUECKE, G., J. P. MIZE, AND W. N. CARR, *Semiconductor Memory Design*, Texas Instruments Electronics Series. New York: McGraw-Hill Book Company, 1973.

2.10 PROBLEMS

1. A 32-bit arithmetic unit is made up of eight cascading 4-bit ALU slices. An all-0 output detector circuit is required for setting the Z-flag.
   (a) Design an all-0 output detector circuit using NOR gates. Assume that each NOR gate has four inputs.
   (b) Design an all-0 output detector circuit using NAND gates. Assume each NAND gate has four inputs.
   (c) Design an all-0 output detector circuit using XOR gates. Assume each XOR gate has two inputs and that open-collector outputs are used.
   (d) Design a circuit that will detect both the all-0's condition and the all-1's condition. (The all-0's condition and all-1's condition represent the 0-number in the 1's-complement arithmetic.)
2. Figure 2-11a shows the logic implementation of the XOR circuit. For this exercise, assume that open-collector outputs are used.
   (a) Redesign the circuit so that it gives the exclusive-NOR function.
   (b) Connect eight exclusive-NOR circuits to form an 8-bit comparator with an output of 1 for the matched condition and an output of 0 for the nonmatched condition.
3. In Figure 2-14, the control signals of the multiplexer select one-out-of-*n* data sources to be gated onto the bus.
   (a) Where are the control signals decoded? Support your answer by sketching the implementation and listing the reasons for your decision.
   (b) The bus output is inverted so that it gives the correct signal to the demultiplexer. The inverter should be placed at the output of the multiplex. Why?
4. Assume that the RS latch shown in Figure 2-16a is made up of NOR gates instead of NAND gates. Draw the corresponding timing diagram, using Figure 2-16b as an example.
5. The basic flip-flop consists of two cross-connected NAND (or NOR) gates. The circuit shown in the figure below consists of three interconnected NAND gates. The delay between input and output is ΔD.
   (a) Sketch the waveforms of the Q_0, Q_1, and Q_2 outputs.
   (b) What is the usefulness of this circuit?

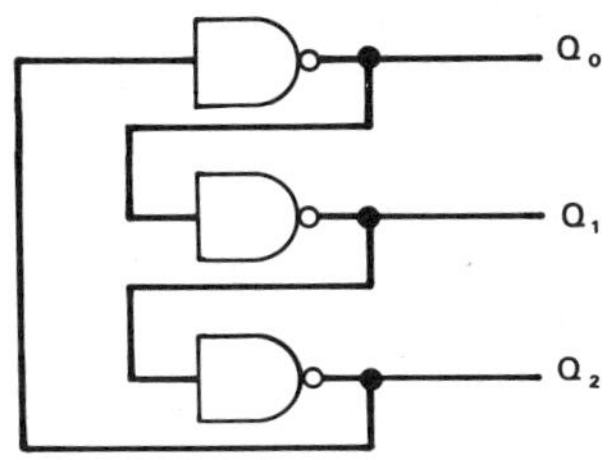

Fig. 2-5

6. In the RS latch circuit shown in Figure 2-16a, an unstable state may exist when both inputs (R and S) are in the 1 state and the clock signal returns to the 0 state. Without increasing the number of logic gates, arrange the RS latch circuit so that it may store a 1 in the latch ($Q = 1$ and $Q = 0$) when both inputs (R and S) are in the 1 state at the *termination* of the clock signal. (The number of input gates may be increased to solve this problem.)

7. Using the JK flip-flops shown in Figure 2-25 as building blocks, interconnect four cells to function as
   (a) a serial ripple binary counter, and
   (b) a shift register.
   Draw timing diagrams for both implementations.

8. RS latches are often grouped together as a data register. An example of this implementation would be a PSW (program status word). The outputs normally fan out to various circuits to control the internal operation of the CPU (central processor unit). The signal leads usually go off from one circuit board and onto other circuit boards via the backplane interconnections. It is good design practice to provide buffers (drivers) for the latch outputs as shown in the figure below. *Why* is this a good practice?

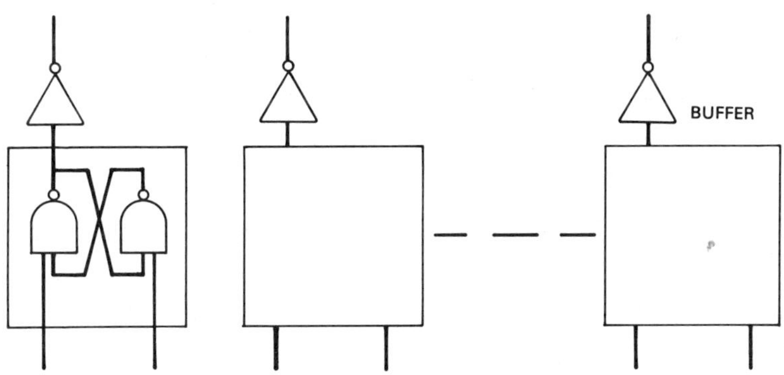

P 2-8

9. Design a decimal digit counter which counts from 0 to 9, in sequence, using JK-positive edge-triggered flip-flops (see Figure 2-25). Sketch timing diagrams for the clock input and the counter outputs.

10. A byte of data (eight bits) plus a parity check bit give odd parity, meaning there are an odd number of 1's in the nine bits. Using a 1K × 4 ROM circuit, design a parity checker that would generate an error indication if the nine bits give even parity.

11. Using two 1K × 4 ROM circuits, design a 4 × 4 multiply circuit which allows multiplication of two 4-bit binary numbers with an 8-bit result.

12. Using a standard PLA (14 inputs, 96 product terms, and 8 outputs), design a 4 × 4 multiply circuit that allows multiplication of two 4-bit binary numbers with an 8-bit result.

13. In the figure below, the data gated onto the bus by the tri-state gate is determined by the 2-bit binary number (A and B). One and only one of the four tri-state gates should be enabled at any one time. However, under trouble conditions, two or more decoder outputs may become active (low potential), enabling two or more tristate gates simultaneously. It is possible to damage the selected tristate gates under this trouble condition. Devise a scheme that would ensure that no more than one tristate gate would be enabled when a fault occurs in the decoder.

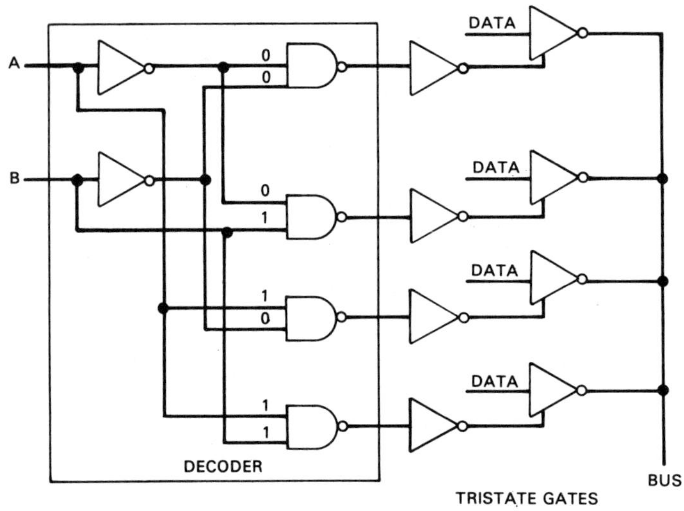

P 2-13

14. Using the 16 × 1 ROM diode array shown in Figure 2-28 as a model, lay out the following multidimensional ROM arrays:
    (a) A 16 × 4 ROM
    (b) A 32 × 4 ROM
    (c) A 256 × 4 ROM
    (d) A 1024 × 8 ROM

15. Any combinational network can be realized using a ROM. Consider a 16 × 4 ROM and implement the following logic functions, where the symbol $\oplus$ implies $x \oplus y = x\bar{y} + \bar{x}y$.
    (a) $f = \overline{(A \oplus B) + (\bar{C} \oplus D)} + C$
    (b) $g = A + (C \oplus \bar{B}) + D$
    (c) $h = A \oplus (B \oplus C)$

16. Design a 4-bit decimal counter that counts in the pattern shown below, (a) using conventional D-type flip-flops and NAND gates and (b) using a 16 × 4 ROM array and any additional circuitry that you may think is required.

Decimal Number	5	3	1	1
0	0	0	0	0
1	0	0	1	0
2	0	0	1	1
3	0	1	0	0
4	0	1	1	0
5	1	0	0	0
6	1	0	0	1
7	1	0	1	1
8	1	1	0	0
9	1	1	0	1

3

Architectural Features

3.1 THE BASIC COMPUTER STRUCTURE

3.1.1 The Components of a Machine

The internal organization of the digital computer has been in a state of continuous evolution since the appearance of the first calculating machines in the 1940's. Howard Aiken's electromechanical calculator, the Mark I, embodied certain basic concepts that were found also in the operation of the ENIAC, the first electronic digital computer. These basic concepts were:

1. Both machines required inputs to operate on. The Mark I, for example, received input data from either punched cards or an array of 60 registers, each of which could be manually set to a different constant. The ENIAC received input data from punched cards and used three function tables for the storage of tabular data. Each function table made use of a portable function matrix with switches that could specify 104 values for an independent variable.
2. A set of instructions or procedures was required to control the overall operation of the machines during the computational process. The ENIAC used some 6000 multiposition switches as well as a host of plug wires to establish the control environment for a specific problem. The Mark I, on the other hand, was controlled by a paper tape facility. The instructions were arranged in sequential order on 24-column paper tape and read one at a time into the machine. The Mark I required operator intervention in order to skip over certain instructions

on the control tape. This was achieved by having the operator move the control tape forward or backward in the tape reader.

3. The ENIAC and the Mark I characterize the structure of the earliest machines: they were externally programmed machines. The Mark I possessed the unique characteristic of separating control from input data. In a sense, the paper tape served as a procedure memory while the punched cards functioned as an operand memory. The logic associated with the tape reader mechanism acted as a control unit for the system. This physical separation of program from data in separate storage units has come to be associated with the Mark series of machines developed at Harvard. The ENIAC also effectively achieved a complete separation of program and data.
4. A processing section was essential in order to perform arithmetic and logic operations upon the input data. Both machines used internal decimal counters to perform the necessary calculations. Both the ENIAC and the Mark I employed the accumulator concept, and each functioned as a high-speed calculator. In terms of actual internal processing speed, the ENIAC could out-perform the electromechanical Mark I by a factor of approximately 500.

   The implementation of a new program on the ENIAC required an elaborate rewiring of the machine's control section. This difficulty caused von Neumann and his associates to conjecture that instructions and data could be operated on interchangeably in the main memory of the machine. He visualized that they were essentially equivalent when regarded as simply the contents of different main storage locations. To minimize the need for rewiring when reprogramming became necessary, he recommended that the separate facilities for procedure and operands be combined into a single, common memory. Effectively, the program and its data could be entered at the same time through the punched card facility supplying input to the system. This philosophy, which permitted instructions and data to share the same memory, also allowed a program to modify itself. This idea was incorporated into virtually all major computer structures developed from that point on, until the MOS/LSI calculators made their appearance in the early 1970's.
5. Some form of local storage was required in these early machines to act as a temporary record, or scratch pad memory, of intermediate data. Such a memory could retain frequently used operands and the partial results of calculations.
6. Finally, some form of output medium was required to communicate the finished results. Both the ENIAC and the Mark I employed punched cards and teletypewriters as primary output facilities.

The basic structure embodied by these early machines is shown in Figure 3-1. Note that three distinct forms of storage are indicated: operand, procedure, and temporary (or intermediate). Note also that the communication paths between each unit are clearly displayed. These paths, which form the internal busing structure of the system, define how the units interconnect and characterize individual computing systems. A *bus* may be defined as a parallel array of wires linking a number of source

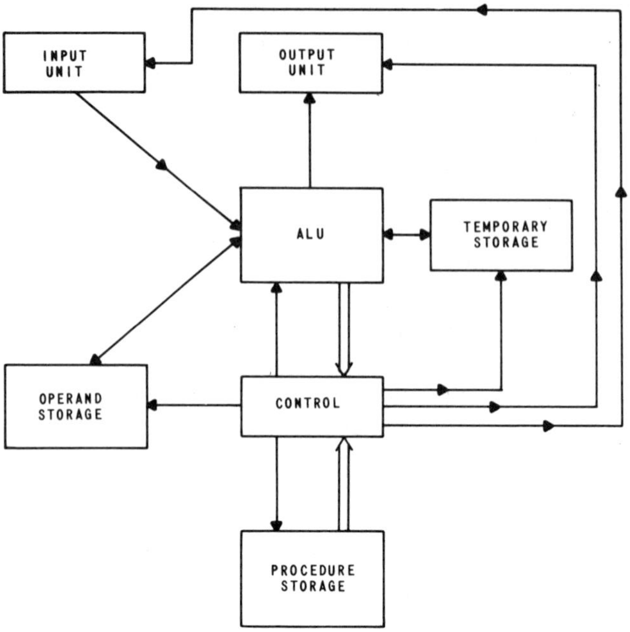

3-1 Basic computer structure

units and destination units. Any single source may transmit data onto the bus at a given time; any one, or several, destination units may remove the data from the bus. Consequently, a computer structure may consist of one or more address buses, one or more data buses, at least one control bus, and an I/O communication bus. An address bus could be used to access procedure memory as well as operand memory and intermediate storage.

Figure 3-2 represents an intermediate step between the calculator structure of the Mark I (shown in Figure 3-1) and the machine structure proposed by von Neumann. Note that the intermediate (temporary) storage unit has been combined with the *arithmetic and logic unit* (ALU), while the operand store and program store have been grouped together into a single unit. A further modification is achieved (see Figure 3-3) when the control unit is grouped with the ALU. This combination is commonly called the *central processing unit* (*CPU*) and forms the core of the computer. The machine shown in Figure 3-3 consists of a CPU communicating with a memory block which may include both procedure and operand storage as well as an I/O facility. This figure represents the traditional computer block diagram. Each of the units in this basic computer configuration represents a refinement of the three basic units originally implemented in the early computing machines. These basic units are:

1. The *memory unit*—which is used to store procedures or operands and may also function as a form of intermediate storage. All items placed in memory are entered in binary form.

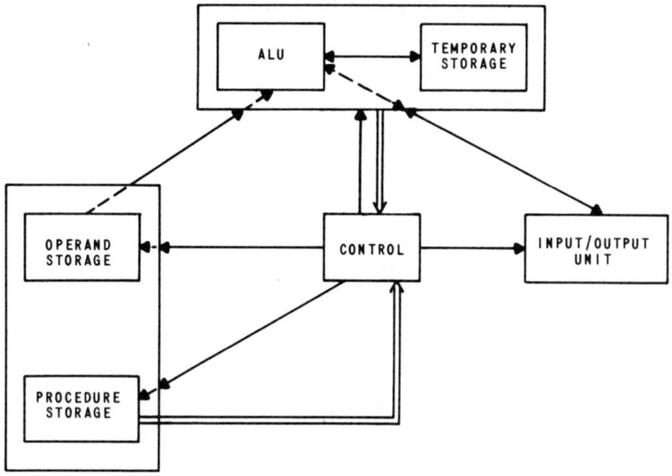

3-2 Fundamental computer arrangement

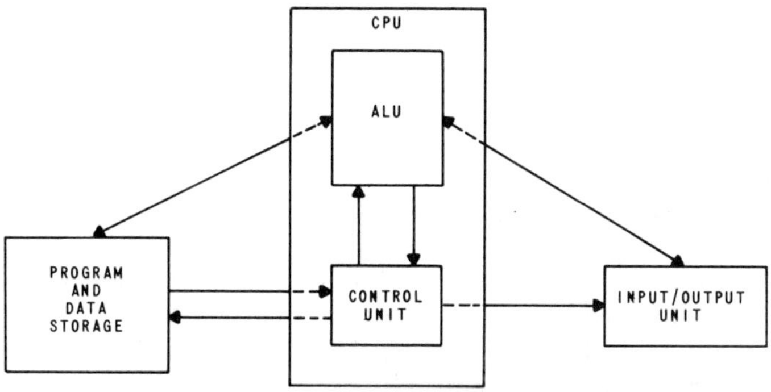

3-3 Modern computer block diagram or von Neumann architecture

2. The *central processing unit (CPU)*—consisting of one or more high-speed registers, the ALU, the control unit, and the circuitry necessary to perform bus control.
   (a) The *arithmetic and logic unit (ALU)*—which is used to perform all processing functions involving arithmetic and logic operations as well as the generation of partial results for a calculation.
   (b) The *control unit*—which coordinates the operation of all units. The overall operation is controlled by a system clock, which is closely synchronized to the memory cycle speed. The control unit receives directives in a logical sequence from the memory unit. This logical sequence of instructions defines a program that will execute on the machine. The control unit, in

conjunction with the ALU, provides for branching as decision points are encountered in the program sequence.

(c) The *bus control circuitry*—which provides communication paths for address, data, and control within the machine. In a time-multiplexed bus structure, this circuitry determines when information on a single bus will be treated as an address rather than data or control signals.

3. The *input/output unit*—which provides a means for the machine to communicate with its external environment. This unit links the machine with its operator and allows an orderly exchange of information to take place.

The term *architecture* has been used to describe the interconnection of these three major units that form a digital computer. The associated set of machine directives is generally included in the definition of architecture. The distinction between architecture and implementation in the following sections follows closely that given by Hellerman [1]. *Architecture* denotes the logical properties of a computer organization. Included in this definition are addressing modes for obtaining operands, the instruction repertoire, and I/O procedures. *Implementation* describes how a given architecture is physically realized. This definition includes all circuitry, firmware, and programs necessary to realize the characterized machine. Architecture is user-oriented; implementation is technology-oriented. Unless otherwise specified in the following discussions, the configurations under consideration will represent architectures.

3.1.2 The Harvard Machine and Princeton Machine Categories

The architecture shown in Figure 3-1 not only describes the early computing machines, but also the calculator and microprocessor structures which emerged in the early 1970's. In the Mark I, machine directives were read in sequentially from paper tape while data were concurrently being input from punched cards. In effect, the procedure (program) memory was kept isolated from the operand (data) memory since separate storage media were used for each. The procedure memory communicated with the CPU over a private pathway (the paper tape input mechanism) that did not physically connect with the operand memory. Similarly, the operand memory communicated with the CPU over a second private pathway (the punched card input mechanism) that did not interconnect with the procedure memory. This configuration, known as a *Harvard machine structure*, is illustrated in Figure 3-4. In this machine type, not only are separate memories employed for program and data, but each memory is accessed by the CPU from a separate, independent store bus. Although separate buses for instructions and data are expensive in terms of additional hardware, a potential speed advantage may be achieved by the concurrent use of both memories by the CPU. If the program memory and the data memory both communicate with the CPU over the same bus, execution can take place only by the sequential access of the procedure memory (for commands) and the operand memory (for data). While this is the most common form of program execution in a computer, various applications have throughput

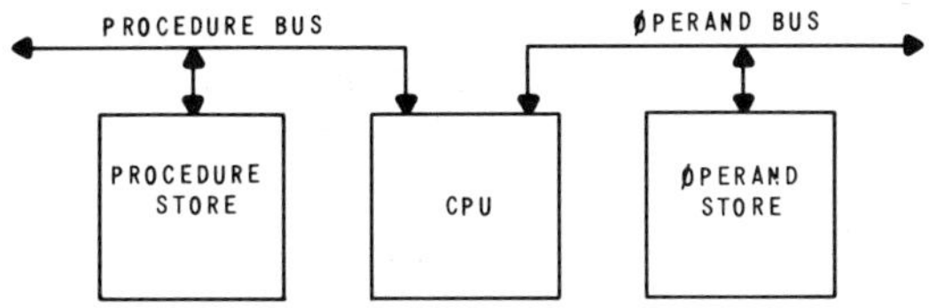

NOTES:
1. SEPARATE MEMORY MODULES ARE USED FOR INSTRUCTION STORAGE AND DATA STORAGE.
2. SEPARATE AND INDEPENDENT BUSES ARE USED TO FORM DISTINCT COMMUNICATION PATHS BETWEEN THE CPU AND EACH STORE.

3-4 Strict Harvard machine structure or the Harvard machine type—class I

requirements that require an enhancement in the execution speed. The Harvard machine structure provides the potential to achieve this goal.

For the purpose of future discussion, the architecture shown in Figure 3-4 will be referred to as a *strict* or *class I Harvard machine*. It will be defined as possessing the following two characteristics:

1. Separate memory modules are used to store instructions and data; instructions and data are not permitted to intermix in either store module.
2. Separate and independent buses are provided which permit the CPU to communicate privately with each store; the CPU-procedure store bus is physically and logically independent of the CPU-operand store bus.

A variation of the Harvard architecture, shown in Figure 3-5, consists of a separate address bus and information bus. Both the procedure store and operand store are accessed from the same address bus, and both receive or transmit data from the same information bus. Consequently, both buses are time-shared by the program store and

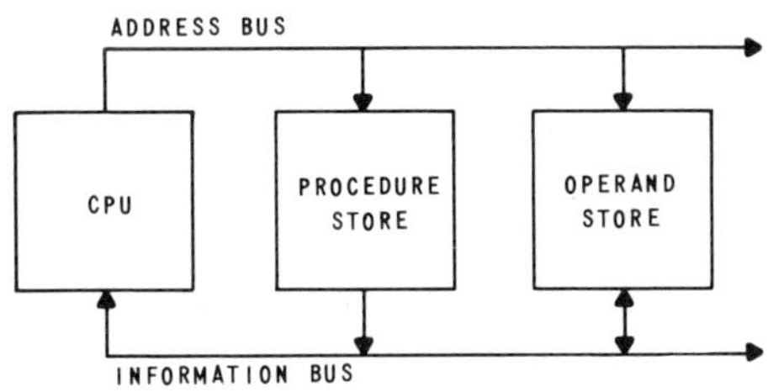

NOTES:
1. THE USE OF SEPARATE MEMORY MODULES FOR INSTRUCTION STORAGE AND DATA STORAGE.
2. THE USE OF A DUAL-BUS ARRANGEMENT TO PROVIDE CONCURRENCY OF OPERATIONS.

3-5 Variation of the Harvard machine structure or the Harvard machine type—class II

data store. A form of concurrent operation may be obtained from this configuration by overlapping the operation of the two store modules (see Section 3.4). Both stores may be buffered in hardware registers so that while one store is being accessed, the data from the other store buffer can be gated onto the information bus. Note that the concept of a hardware buffer precludes having to specify the technology employed in implementing the stores (e.g., the overlapped operation is not dependent on the READ followed by RESTORE cycle of a core memory). This holds equally true for a semiconductor memory implementation. However, if the hardware buffers are removed, the basic operation of this configuration is no different from a single-bus arrangement that is time-shared by both memories.

For future reference, the variation of the Harvard architecture shown in Figure 3-5 will be referred to as a *class II Harvard machine*. It will be defined as possessing the following characteristics:

1. Separate memory modules are used to store instructions and data; instructions and data are not permitted to intermix in either store module.
2. A common address bus is used to access both memory modules. A second, common bus transfers data between either store and the CPU.
3. Both buses are time-shared by the procedure store and operand store. A form of concurrent operation may be obtained through the use of a hardware buffer attached to each memory module, which permits an overlapped memory operation to be performed on each store. This enhances the apparent processing speed of the machine.

In general, the Harvard architecture exhibited by both the class I and class II machines provides a higher throughput capability than a single-memory bus machine. If the feature of overlapped store operations is removed from the class II machine, the access of one store module must be completed before the other module may be referenced. This mode of operation causes the configuration shown in Figure 3-5 to appear

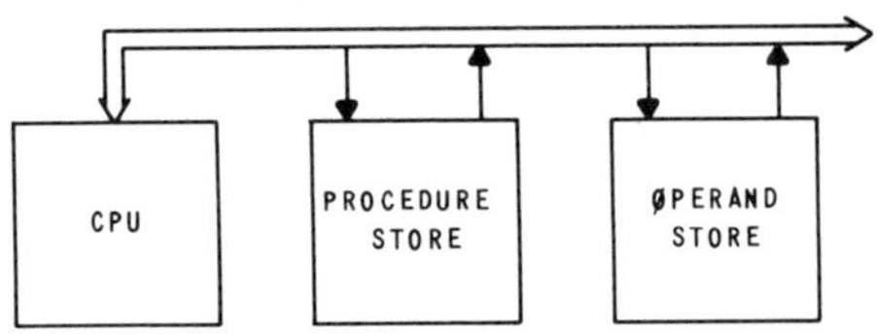

NOTES:

1. SEPARATE MEMORY MODULES ARE USED FOR INSTRUCTION AND DATA STORAGE.

2. A SINGLE-BUS STRUCTURE IS USED TO COMMUNICATE BETWEEN BOTH MEMORY MODULES AND THE CPU. THIS PRECLUDES CONCURRENCY OF OPERATION. CONSEQUENTLY, THIS IS NOT A STRICT HARVARD MACHINE.

3-6 Harvard machine type—class III

as the single-store bus machine illustrated in Figure 3-6. The address bus and information bus have been combined into one general busing structure that is time-shared by the procedure store and the operand store. The partition of program and data into separate memory modules has been maintained in this single-store bus machine.

Within the computing community, the term *Harvard architecture* has often been used to characterize a machine of the type shown in Figure 3-6, which does not permit programs and data to share the same physical memory. This structure precludes concurrent operation of the store modules and does not represent a strict Harvard architecture. However, such a structure has gained wide acceptance as a representative of the Harvard class of computing machines. Because of this, the machine configuration shown in Figure 3-6 will be referred to as a *class III Harvard machine*. It will be defined as possessing the following characteristics:

1. Separate memory modules are used to store instructions and data; instructions and data are not permitted to intermix in either store module.
2. A common store bus is time-shared by the program memory and the data memory; both memories cannot use the store bus concurrently.
3. If separate groups of signal leads are used to transmit address information and data, this configuration becomes interchangeable with the class II Harvard machine, provided that hardware buffering of each store and memory overlapping are also implemented.

The common characteristic appearing in all three of these definitions is the complete separation of memory modules; the instruction store is kept physically removed from the data store. There are, however, some specific considerations that need to be reviewed when a machine's architecture physically attempts to isolate the program area of main memory from the data area. First, the strict definition of a Harvard machine does not require that the procedure store be a *read-only memory* (*ROM*). Nor does the definition state that data will exist only in a dynamically alterable memory or *random-access memory* (*RAM*). The procedure store may be implemented entirely in ROM, entirely in RAM, or in some combination of the two. The operand store, however, will normally be implemented entirely in RAM. In special cases, a combination of RAM and ROM might be used. However, operand storage will not be exclusively ROM since some form of scratch pad storage is usually required by most machines. Consequently, if both stores may be some mixture of ROM and RAM, it is only in the way that a memory reference is performed that determines if a machine is of the strict Harvard class (e.g., instructions cannot be treated as data, and vice versa). It is possible to reference the procedure store during the EXECUTE portion of an instruction and treat the information obtained as data. Similarly, it is possible to reference the operand store during the FETCH portion of an instruction and treat the information obtained as a machine directive. In fact, the distinction between the contents of a main storage location being interpreted as an instruction rather than data is determined solely by when the memory reference is made in the instruction cycle. This simple fact establishes the equivalence or interchangeability of instructions and data.

The intermixing of instructions and data in the procedure store of a strict Harvard machine leads to a hybrid architecture, which will be discussed shortly.

As a result, the single-bus structure exhibited in Figure 3-6 could treat the procedure store as being contiguous to the operand store in the address space of the machine. In effect, program and data would share the same memory. Such a configuration, shown in Figure 3-7, is referred to as a *Princeton machine structure*. The name is derived from the IAS computer built at Princeton in the late 1940's.

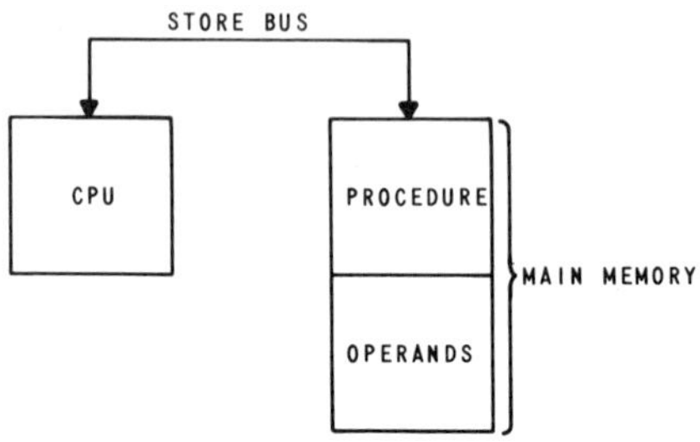

NOTES:

1. PROCEDURE AND OPERANDS SHARE THE AVAILABLE MEMORY SPACE OFF THE SINGLE STORE BUS.
2. INSTRUCTIONS AND DATA MAY BE INTERMIXED THROUGHOUT MAIN STORAGE

3-7 Princeton machine structure

For the purpose of future discussion, the architecture shown in Figure 3-7 will be referred to as a *strict Princeton machine*. It will be defined as possessing the following characteristics:

1. All physical memory can be used to store both instructions and data; these quantities can be intermixed throughout any store and are distinguished only when they are referenced in the instruction cycle.
2. A single store bus communicates between the CPU and main memory. An instruction memory can no longer be considered a separate physical item that is distinct from the physical memory used to store data. Instead, the procedure store and operand store share a common physical memory space.

Because of its lower cost and programming versatility, the Princeton architecture has been used in a wide range of commercial computers at the maxi, midi, and mini levels.

Interestingly enough, the first commercial microprocessor, the Intel 4004, fell into the category of a class III Harvard machine. Both it and the Mark I were originally developed as calculator structures; the 4004 was intended for the calculator marketplace while the Mark I was developed to perform automatic computations. This is not to say that the Harvard architecture was entirely neglected during the years between the development of the Mark I and the appearance of the 4004. In fact, the Bell System adopted a variation of it when they began the design of the No. 1 Electronic Switching System (ESS).

The ENIAC, the Mark I, and the Intel MCS-4 microcomputer structures represent the first appearance of a computing structure in a particular technology. Figure 3-8 compares the basic features of these first calculators. Note that each machine appears to be a variation of the Harvard architecture.

The Harvard machine and Princeton machine categories have come to be regarded as generic types by which a computer structure may be classified. This is obviously a simplistic attitude toward basic machine structures, since many computer architectures employ the features of both categories. However, these generic types have continued to prove useful as descriptors at the mini/microcomputer level. Although the exact distinctions between these two basic machine types have already been given, it is worthwhile to consider their variations. For instance, using the Princeton machine structure, program and data may be separated by a wide gap in the available memory space of the machine. However, if instructions and data reside in the same physical store, the machine still remains a Princeton type (see Figure 3-9). In a variation of this situation, shown in Figure 3-6, instructions have been placed in a procedure store and data in an operand store. If data and instructions are permitted to intermix in each store, that configuration is also considered to be a Princeton type. If data and program are *not* permitted to be intermixed, the configuration becomes a class III Harvard machine. This configuration could be regarded as a Princeton structure with the control program placed in a write-protected area of main memory. The use of a ROM for program storage, however, removes the structure in Figure 3-6 from the strict Princeton machine category. It also underscores the difficulty in attempting to categorize a simple machine configuration.

There are machines such as the Bell System No. 2 ESS (see Figure 3-10) that combine the features of both the Harvard and Princeton architectures. The No. 2 ESS has two separate memory buses; one bus communicates with the read-only program store and the other bus communicates with the RAM data store. Translation tables, which are kept in the program store, act as data for the call processing programs. This arrangement makes the machine a Princeton type. However, only data are kept in the data store. No instructions are executed from the data memory since the word length of the program store and data store are not the same. This makes the machine a Harvard type.

In the most widely used minicomputer architecture, the CPU communicates with main memory over a high-speed store bus; all program-controlled operations involving external devices are required to take place over a separate I/O bus (see Figure 3-11). With its PDP-11 series, the Digital Equipment Corporation (DEC) pioneered the use of the single-bus concept (shown in Figure 3-12). Using a single-bus architecture, all registers in peripheral devices were treated as though they were locations in main memory. A separate class of I/O instructions was not required, since all I/O operations appeared to the programmer as regular memory reference instructions.

THE ENIAC

(ELECTRONIC NUMERICAL INTEGRATOR AND CALCULATOR)

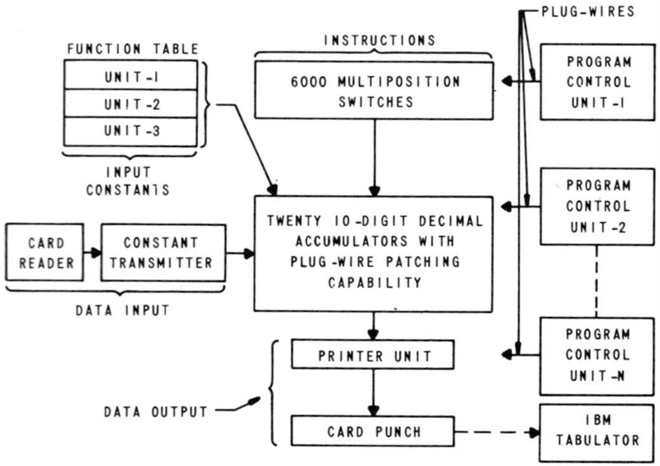

1. FIRST OPERATIONAL ELECTRONIC DIGITAL COMPUTER.
2. CONTAINED APPROXIMATELY 18,000 VACUUM TUBES.
3. CONSIDERED FULLY OPERATIONAL IN 1945.
4. PLUG-WIRES WERE USED TO CONNECT THE ACCUMULATORS AND PROGRAM CONTROL UNITS TOGETHER TO SEQUENCE CONTROL.
5. THE FUNCTION TABLES PROVIDED MEMORY FOR TABULAR DATA.
6. RESULTS OF INTERMEDIATE CALCULATIONS COULD BE PUNCHED OUT ON CARDS AND RELOADED LATER VIA THE CARD READER.
7. THE MACHINE PERMITTED THE SIMULTANEOUS PERFORMANCE OF SEVERAL OPERATIONS (PARALLELISM IN COMPUTATION).
8. PROGRAMMING WAS HIGHLY COMPLEX.
9. DEVELOPED BY THE MOORE SCHOOL OF THE UNIVERSITY OF PENNSYLVANIA UNDER CONTRACT WITH THE ORDINANCE DEPARTMENT OF THE U.S. ARMY.

THE MARK-I

(THE AUTOMATIC SEQUENCE CONTROLLED CALCULATOR)

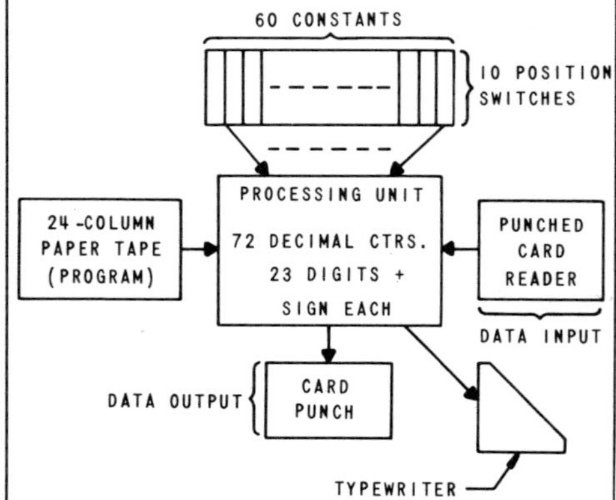

1. FIRST OPERATIONAL ELECTROMECHANICAL DIGITAL COMPUTER.
2. CONSIDERED FULLY OPERATIONAL IN AUGUST 1944.
3. MACHINE WAS CONTROLLED BY MEANS OF INSTRUCTIONS PUNCHED ON 24-COLUMN PAPER TAPE.
4. THE FIRST TRUE PROGRAMMING TECHNIQUES WERE DEVELOPED ON THIS MACHINE.
5. DEVELOPED AT HARVARD UNIVERSITY WITH FUNDS SUPPLIED BY IBM.

THE MCS-4

THE MICROCOMPUTER SYSTEM BASED ON THE 4004 μP

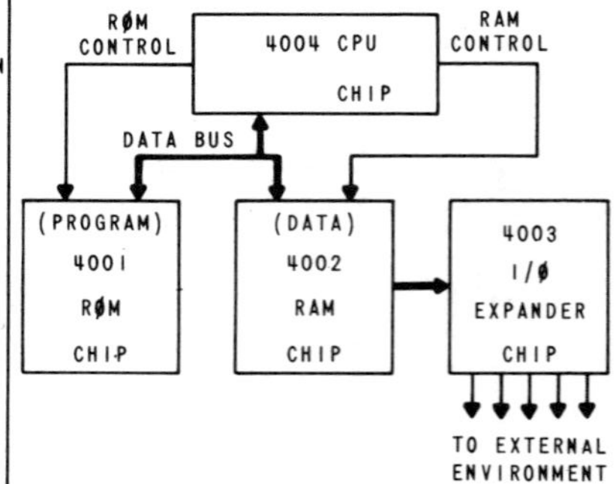

1. FIRST COMMERCIALLY AVAILABLE MICROPROCESSOR.
2. INTRODUCED BY INTEL IN FALL 1972.
3. INSTRUCTIONS PLACED IN RØM.
4. INPUT OR OUTPUT COULD BE A TELETYPEWRITER OR ANY SERIALLY-ORIENTED DEVICE.
5. 4-BIT PARALLEL CPU.
6. STANDARDIZED INSTRUCTION SET WITH 45 COMMANDS.
7. DESIGNED TO SPECIFICALLY HANDLE BCD NUMBERS WITHOUT CONVERTING FROM BINARY.
8. MINIMUM CONFIGURATION OF 1 CPU AND 1 RØM COST $50 IN QUANTITIES OF 100 IN NOV. 1972.

3-8 Comparison of three original computing machines

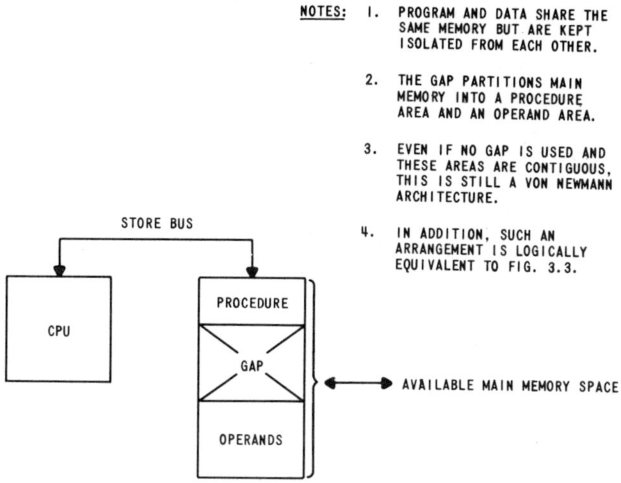

3-9 Variation of the Princeton machine structure

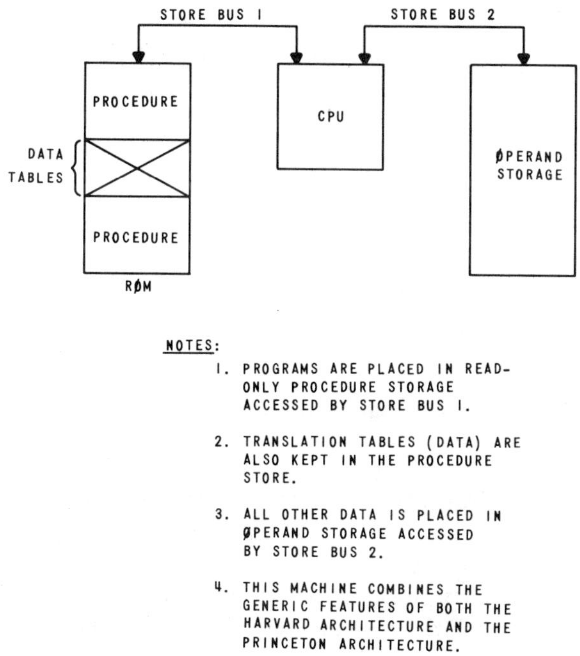

3-10 Machine structure of the Bell System No. 2 ESS

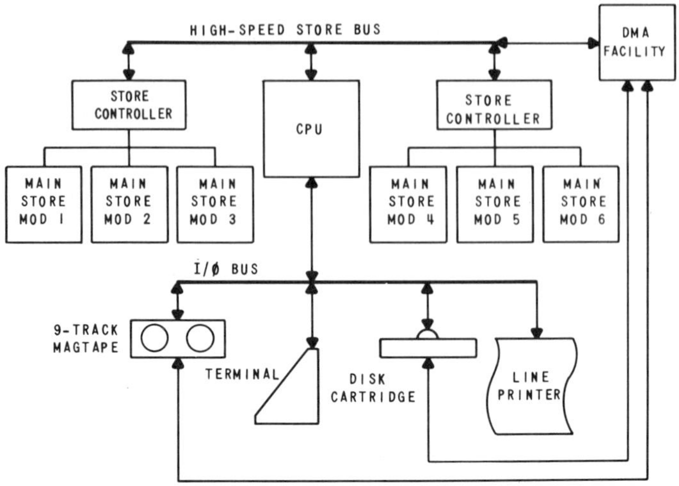

3-11 Typical dual-bus minicomputer architecture

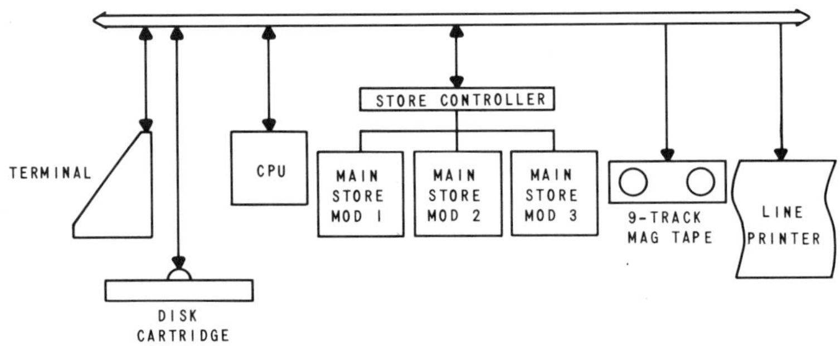

NOTE: THE DMA FACILITY IS NORMALLY OBTAINED AS AN INHERENT FEATURE OF THIS STRUCTURE.

3-12 Typical system configuration using a single-bus architecture

3.1.3 The Principle of Locality of Reference

A careful study of programs being executed on machines of various sizes has established the property of *locality of reference*. This is a characteristic of a program segment, spanning several instruction cycles, in which all references to memory for operands or directives tend to cluster in localized areas of storage. Hellerman [1] has pointed out that "this property suggests that the highest speed of reference and access may only be necessary to a relatively small area of storage." The physical realization of this concept was the utilization of a cache memory (see Figure 3-13). The cache-oriented machine uses hardware to examine the operand address and the address for the

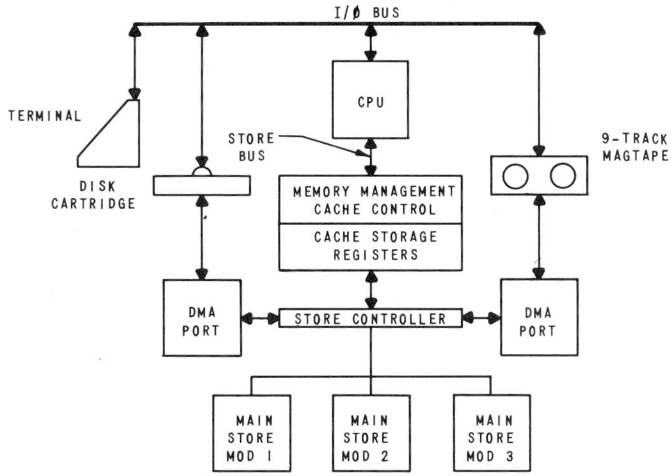

3-13 Use of a cache memory in a dual-bus I/O structure

next instruction. If the segment of memory containing the desired quantity is in the cache, execution proceeds at a very high rate, since a typical cache cycle time is less than 250 nanoseconds. If the referenced item is not in the segment of memory currently occupying the cache, the cache hardware control logic automatically locates the required segment on system bulk storage and loads it into the cache. The newly loaded cache segment will contain the referenced item as well as the block of contiguous code surrounding the item. Because of the automatic administration of memory, a typical system will often exhibit a cycle time approximately equal to that of the cache. The Data General Eclipse series and the DEC PDP-11/70 both incorporated cache memories when they were introduced in late 1974 and early 1975, respectively.

3.2 INTERNAL ORGANIZATION

3.2.1 The Execution Cycle

The previous section exhibited the characteristic configuration of a generalized computer, as shown in Figure 3-3. The basic elements of any computing machine were identified as the CPU, the program and/or data memory, and the facilities provided for input and output. Using the stored program concept, the procedure memory is used as a store for machine instructions. These directives are binary-encoded data words that are fetched by the CPU and then decoded to determine the precise activity that the CPU will perform. This decoding operation is commonly called the *execute phase* of the machine cycle and is used by the CPU to perform such operations as operand referencing in main memory and arithmetic/logic processing.

A sequence of logically associated instructions stored in procedure memory is called a *program*. The operand memory is used to store the data to be processed by the CPU. As mentioned earlier, the partitioning of memory into a procedure store and an operand store was observed by several of the early microprocessor structures. Typically, a ROM was used as the program memory, and a semiconductor RAM was used as the data memory. The evolving minicomputer structures have followed the classical Princeton machine format (i.e., program and data sharing the same memory). In whatever machine configuration memory is employed, the basic organization of the RAM or ROM is an array of sequential storage slots. Each slot is identified by a unique address and may contain either binary data or a machine instruction. Two registers are always used in conjunction with a memory to perform the function of intermediate storage between the CPU and the memory itself. The first register is the *memory address register* (*MAR*), which contains the binary address of the slot in memory and where information will be either read from or written into by the CPU. The second register is the *memory data register* (*MDR*), which holds the data word to be exchanged with memory.

Both data and instructions may be modified by the CPU when either a Harvard or Princeton architecture is observed. However, the strict Harvard architecture does not permit direct modification of the procedure store's contents by an executing program. Recall that the procedure store will be referenced only during the FETCH portion of an instruction cycle. In such a case, the procedure store functions as an effective ROM for the executing program. Modification of the program store's contents requires either manual intervention (e.g., the processor is halted and the operator physically loads the desired data in the appropriate memory locations) or a replacement of the store contents. In the latter case, the control memory is removed from the CPU and a new ROM inserted in its place. In particular, interchanging an old ROM for a reprogrammed ROM can convert a microprocessor configuration to a new application. In some cases, this may be done without ever modifying any of the I/O connections. Consequently, a Harvard machine would be used primarily as an algorithmic controller or dedicated processor. This is typical of the hand-held calculators and numerical machine controllers sold commercially. If the procedure store is a read/write memory, its contents may be modified by an instruction that directs an area of the program memory to be overwritten from a system device. This permits a variety of programs to be brought in from a bulk storage device. Also, by not allowing the procedure store to be written into when data are being manipulated, the executing program is protected from mutilation. It is the program protection provided by the Harvard machine that has made a variation of that architecture attractive in telephone switching systems.

The Princeton machine has been used in applications that require program modifications. In these cases, the CPU must have the capability of accessing all of main memory, including ROM and RAM. If sufficient storage is not available to contain all the program and data required for a given application, the CPU must administer its main memory in conjunction with the larger, slower bulk storage. Typically, the CPU will move the required data and/or instructions it needs from a peripheral storage device (such as a disk or magnetic tape unit) into RAM. This information will have previously been saved as a file on the peripheral unit. Consequently, a computer system requires one or more I/O channels to permit the CPU to communicate with the external world.

3.2.2 The Central Processing Unit (CPU)

The CPU is the administrator of the entire computer system; it unifies the system. The CPU in most microprocessor structures functions as a special-register processor. Usually one of the operands specified in an instruction word is found in memory, the other operand is located in a special register. The special registers are as follows:

1. One or more accumulator registers, any one of which may accept the output of the ALU.
2. An accumulator-extension register, which is linked to the accumulator in such operations as multiplication, division, and multiple precision arithmetic.
3. One or more index registers, any one of which may be used in the effective address generation of an operand.
4. An address-extension register, which permits more than one bank of ROM or RAM to be referenced by the CPU.

The early minicomputers, such as the PDP-8, also functioned as special-register processors. The sophisticated minicomputers and the bipolar/LSI microprocessors have a CPU structure that functions as a general-register processor. Instead of dedicating each user-addressable register to a given function, the general-register processor structure allows any one of the *general-purpose registers* (*GPR's*) to be an index register, generalized accumulator, or base register. The GPR concept has been extremely useful in improving the throughput of large-scale computing machines and the evolving mini/microcomputers. Each member of IBM's System/360 family provided a set of 16 GPR's as part of the CPU. DEC adopted this feature in its PDP-11 family of minicomputers. Each general register could be used as an index register, relocation register, accumulator for fixed-point arithmetic, or for specific logical operations. The GPR's provided increased flexibility in register usage; no register was dedicated to performing a specific function. More significantly, a large number of fetch and store operations were removed when arithmetic functions were performed. In this mode, the storage accesses to main memory for the arithmetic operands were replaced by register-to-register operations in which the required operands were placed in different GPR's. This enhanced the processing time of the computer since the time involved for register-to-register operations is much less than that required for operations that involve references to main storage.

For machines that function as general-register processors, a register function designator is needed as part of each directive that specifies a register operation. For instance, if one of the GPR's is to be used as an accumulator, the instruction employing that GPR must designate the register and specify its function as that of an accumulator. Typically, a bit pattern in the instruction word would be used to name the GPR, and another bit pattern of the same directive would be used to specify the function of the named GPR (i.e., base register, index register, accumulator, etc.). Such designators reduce the number of available bit patterns in the operand portion of a machine directive. For example, if 16 GPR's were available as either accumulators or index registers, a 4-bit register designator would be needed to name the register (GPR-0, GPR-1, etc.) in each instruction. In addition, a single-bit designator would be required to distinguish the register function (i.e., an accumulator or an index register). Consequently, 5 bits of the operand portion of an instruction would be dedicated and unavailable as additional code space. Such situations reflect themselves in the coding efficiency of the instruction repertoire.

The ALU is the processing section of the CPU. It is here that all arithmetic and logic operations are performed. The features found in an ALU can vary considerably, depending on the sophistication of the microprocessor or minicomputer architecture. Typically, the ALU is a parallel, binary 2's-complement arithmetic processor that forms the sum of two inputs and produces an output. The most fundamental operation performed by the ALU is binary addition. An accumulator normally holds one of the operands to be manipulated by the ALU; the other operand is taken from a general register or main memory. The accumulator may be regarded as a register in which the total of a series of numbers may be accumulated. The result of the ALU operation is placed back in the accumulator, overwriting the previous operand stored there.

Typically, the ALU provides additional functions: shift-rotate capabilities, Boolean logic operations, and subtraction. Subtraction is performed by expressing the number to be subtracted (the negative number) in 2's-complement form and adding the result to the minuend in the ALU. This operation, aside from encoding the subtrahend as a 2's-complement number, is identical to addition. The 2's-complement form* has been used almost exclusively in mini/microcomputer ALU's because it provides a unique binary representation for 0. Zero is treated as the binary number containing 0's in all its bit positions. The 1's-complement form,† which may be used instead of 2's-complement, provides two representations for 0: the binary number may either contain all 0's, or it may contain all 1's. Additional logic is required to check for a 0 in the ALU.

---

*The *2's-complement form* is achieved by complementing every bit position in a binary word and then adding 1 to the result. The most-significant bit is treated as a sign bit to designate either a positive number (sign bit = 0) or a negative number (sign bit = 1).

†The *1's-complement form* is achieved by complementing every bit position in a binary word. A 1 is not added to the result. The sign bit convention is identical to the 2's-complement form. Consequently, if $T(N)$ represents the 2's complement of the binary number N, and $i(N)$ represents the 1's complement, the following relation always holds:

$$T(N) = i(N) + 1$$

where $i(N)$ is formed by complementing each bit position in N. The unique representation for 0 in the 2's-complement form permits one more negative number to be represented than there are positive numbers. The most negative number that can be represented has 0's in all bit positions except for the sign bit position; the sign bit is a 1. The positive value of this negative quantity cannot be represented in the same number of bits used to represent the negative number. Consequently, a 12-bit data word can represent any signed number between −2048 and +2047. A similar analogy may be drawn for 16-bit and 18-bit data words with the following results:

1. A 16-bit data word may represent any signed number between −32,768 and +32,767.
2. An 18-bit data word may represent any signed number between −131,072 and +131,071.

The accumulator may be implemented as a dedicated location in main memory, with the result of the ALU operation automatically directed to this slot as a memory reference. Some of the older single-address machines used this type of accumulator. Modern accumulators are always found implemented as hardware registers in any of the MSI/T^2L, MOS/LSI, or bipolar/LSI CPU structures.

3.2.3 The Control Unit

The ALU may also contain certain status bits which indicate (1) whether or not the accumulator has reached 0, (2) if an arithmetic overflow has occurred, (3) if a carry has been generated, or (4) if any other specialized test conditions have occurred. The user program may test any of these status bits and perform a conditional branch in the execution of control, depending on the state of the bits. The administration of these status bits is done in conjunction with the control section of the CPU. It is the control circuitry which directs the proper sequencing of machine states for any processing application.

The control section is normally made up of the following elements, which direct the execution of a program:

1. *The CPU.* The CPU possesses a dedicated register which functions as a counter and contains the address of the next machine instruction in program memory. The CPU increments this program counter (PC) by 1 after fetching a new instruction. This technique is the simplest method for achieving sequential program flow. An entirely different technique would be for each current instruction word to explicitly contain the address of the next instruction. This technique has not been applied at the macroinstruction level because of the cost of expanding main memory. However, this concept has been widely exploited at the microinstruction level.
2. *The fetch of a machine directive.* The fetch of an instruction is achieved in two separate control phases. In the first phase, the contents of the PC are sent to the program memory. In the second phase, the memory controller returns the accessed instruction word to the CPU, which, in turn, places the machine directive in the instruction register. The instruction register retains the directive and uses it to define the machine operation(s) that will take place during the execution portion of the current instruction cycle.
3. *A translation mechanism.* This mechanism is used to decode the contents of the instruction register and issue the appropriate timing pulses to implement the current machine directive. The instruction decoder and its control sequencer are used to translate the machine command residing in the instruction register into the necessary internal timing signals required by the CPU.

The control section of the early minicomputers was implemented using hard-wired or random logic. Typically, a random-logic implementation consisted of many individual logic circuit packages with a large number of interconnections between the packages. Random-logic design made use of both small-scale integration (SSI) and medium-scale integration (MSI), employing either TTL or ECL technology to obtain high-speed logic functions. The large number of *dual in-line packages* (*DIP's*) required for random-logic implementations was made necessary by the limited number of logic functions available on a standard discrete integrated circuit (IC). This led to a design that was both costly and unreliable, the unreliability being directly related to the number of interconnections. In addition, the hard-wired interconnections between components made the design relatively inflexible and difficult to service.

The control sections of many minicomputers and microprocessors have been constructed using the latest concepts in microprogramming. Microprogramming has offered the user flexibility in specifying the instruction set, ease of maintenance, and high reliability. These advances have been made possible by using MSI/LSI technology to produce the control ROM's that contain the processor microcode. Figure 3-14 illustrates the general structure of a microprogrammed machine. Note that the control section of a conventional computer has been replaced by a control store (or microprogrammed ROM) and sequencing logic to access the ROM. Typically, a macroinstruction residing in program memory is fetched into the instruction register, and its operation code is used to derive a pointer to the starting address of a microcode segment located in the control ROM. The microcode segment interprets the macroinstruction residing in the instruction register at the basic gate level of the machine. When the microcode segment is complete, control is returned to fetch the next macroinstruction in program memory. Figure 3-15 illustrates the interpretation operation that the microcode segment performs. A macroinstruction is fetched from the program memory and placed in the instruction register. The operations code field is modified by the

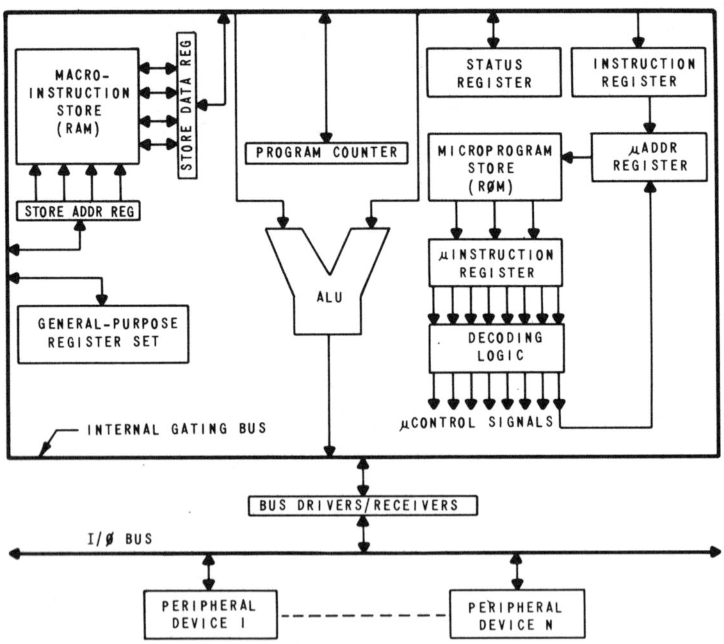

3-14 General structure of a microprogrammed machine

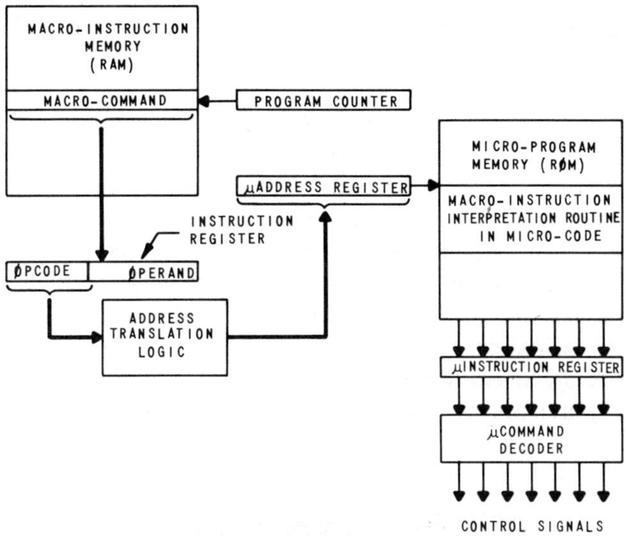

3-15 Microcode interpretation sequence of a macroinstruction

address translation logic to generate an address for the microprogram store. This number represents the starting address of a microcode routine that realizes the macroinstruction in the specific hardware of the machine. When the microcode routine has completed, it returns control to the fetch routine so that the next macroinstruction may be obtained and the interpretation process can be repeated.

3.2.4 Typical Microprocessor Chip Structures

The basic CPU configuration, consisting of the general register set, the ALU, and the ALU's associated control section, can be placed on either a single MOS/LSI chip or a configuration of five or fewer silicon chips. The major difficulty in placing a CPU on a single chip has been in providing enough pins for the CPU to communicate off-chip with the other elements of its chip set. As the number of pins on an integrated circuit package are increased, the circuit yields of the manufacturing process substantially decrease, resulting in an increase in manufacturing costs. Understandably, semiconductor manufacturers have tried to minimize the number of signal leads leaving the CPU chip. The result, called *pin multiplexing*, permits the CPU to use a single pin for more than one type of communication signal. Pin multiplexing is observed in most of the MOS/LSI microprocessors. For example, the early microprocessors were initially found in 16-pin DIP's with the address and data bits multiplexed on a bidirectional data bus. The Intel 4004 was configured in this manner using a 16-pin DIP and a 4-bit data bus. Semiconductor manufacturers have resolved the pin limitation problem for single-chip microprocessors by (1) producing larger silicon chips containing additional functional units, and (2) placing more pins on each DIP. Again, Intel is a particularly good example of a manufacturer's approach.

The bipolar-LSI bit-sliced microprocessor chip sets were developed by the semiconductor manufacturers to permit the design of 4-bit, 8-bit, 16-bit, 32-bit, and even larger CPU's. These structures function under control of a microprogrammed memory. The bit-slice approach requires each *central processing element* (*CPE*) *chip* to contain a 2-bit or 4-bit slice of every register in the CPU. Multiple gating paths are used to minimize bus contention and decrease the cycle time of the processor. An N-bit instruction word machine would be formed by paralleling either $N/2$ 2-bit or $N/4$ 4-bit CPE's. Figure 3-16 exhibits a 16-bit CPU formed by four paralleled 4-bit CPE's. It forms a natural building block for a minicomputer CPU. For a CPU constructed of a bipolar-LSI chip set, the difference between a CPE and a CPU is simply that the CPE is the bit-sliced element that is used to form the complete CPU by paralleling two or more CPE's to obtain the desired processor word length. Bipolar/LSI CPU's of this type are faster than their MOS/LSI equivalents. In addition, they may be used to construct a variety of minicomputer central processors that are fast, powerful, and inexpensive.

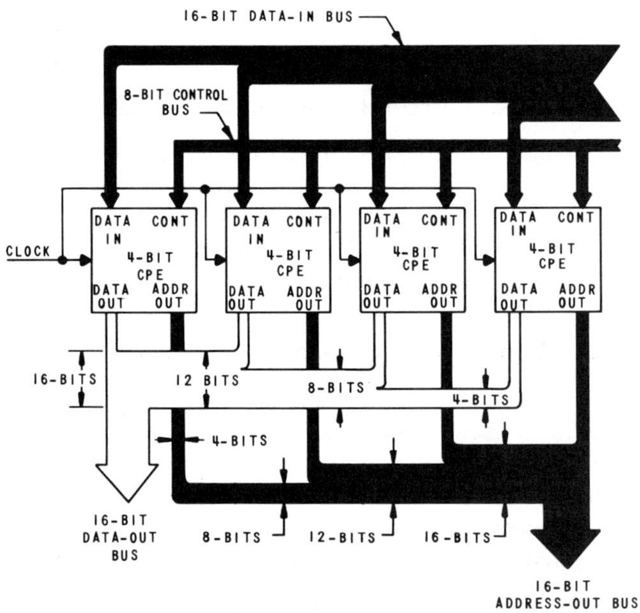

3-16 16-bit CPU made from four 4-bit CPE's

3.3 DATA TRANSFER GATING LOGIC

3.3.1 Register Interconnection Logic

The processor is composed of a large collection of registers in addition to the control circuitry and the arithmetic unit. The data stored in one register may either be modified by the ALU, transferred to another register, or used directly to perform specific functions. A systematic communication structure is essential to facilitate the data flow and simplify the control of these registers.

As the scale of integration of logic circuitry increases, the number of interconnected leads becomes increasingly important in the design of the system. The use of a common data bus is an excellent method of transmitting data signals within the processor. It is very flexible, while keeping the number of internal leads to a minimum.

The transfer of data from one register to another is usually accomplished by means of standard gates. Consider the example in Figure 3-17. In transferring the data from register A to register B, destination register B is first cleared to the all-0's state by a common reset signal, and the gates are immediately enabled, allowing the 1's in register A to be transmitted from register A to register B. This method of transferring data is referred to as *single-rail gating*. Similarly, the destination register can first be set to all 1's so that 0's can be gated into it. Since the gating path is unidirectional, from register A to register B, another set of gates is necessary for transmission in the reverse direction. Because a large number of flip-flop registers and associated gates are required for data transfers, a significant savings in the number of gates and leads can be realized if

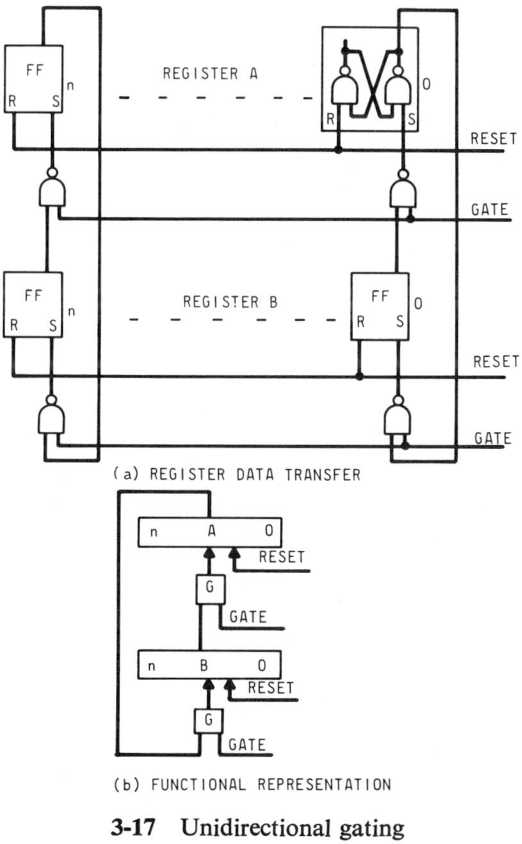

3-17 Unidirectional gating

only one set of gates is used for transmission in both directions. The concept of bidirectional gates or switches has been widely used in core store-access circuitry, where the read current is sent through the core winding in one direction and the write current is sent in the reverse direction. However, the application of bidirectional gates in digital logic has not been fully exploited.

In a bidirectional gate, the input and output circuits must have electrical symmetry. This allows the two circuits to be interchanged functionally without degradation in transmission of the data signal. The IGFET (insulated gate field effect transistor) unipolar transistor shown in Figure 3-18a exhibits electrical symmetry in its source (input) and sink (output) circuits. However, the bipolar transistor does not, since the current gain alpha for normal current flow is usually much larger than the alpha for current flow in the inverse direction. Electrical symmetry in bipolar devices can be obtained with two transistors connected as shown in Figure 3-18b. The collector of one transistor and the emitter of the other are connected together to form either the input or the output circuit. A resistor is inserted in each base to reduce current hogging* when the transistor is operated in the inverted mode.

The method of data transfer between two flip-flops using the proposed bidirectional gate is illustrated in Figure 3-19. To effect bidirectional transfer of data, the source impedance at the output of a flip-flop must be substantially different for the flip-flop being in the binary-1 state as opposed to the flip-flop being in the binary-0 state. The 0 outputs of the flip-flops are connected to the I/O leads of the bidirectional gate. In a data transfer, the receiving flip-flop is cleared prior to enabling the bidirectional gate. The resulting function is a single-rail operation in which a 1 is transferred from the transmitting flip-flop to the receiving flip-flop. For example, in transferring the information from flip-flop A to flip-flop B, the B flip-flop is cleared first, causing the 0-side output (b′) to be at a positive potential. If flip-flop A contains a 0, the enable gate signal will not turn the bidirectional gate on, and the state of the B flip-flop will remain unchanged since outputs a′ and b′ are at the same positive potential. If flip-flop A contains a 1 (a′ being near ground potential), the bidirectional gate will turn on, causing output b′ to assume nearly the same potential as a′. In this case, output a′ is in the low-impedance state. When output b′ falls below the threshold of the gates comprising the flip-flop, B will switch to the 1 state, accomplishing the data transfer from flip-flop A to flip-flop B. To gate information from flip-flop B to flip-flop A, flip-flop A is cleared instead of flip-flop B. The direction of signal flow is determined by which flip-flop is cleared so that the cleared flip-flop may act as the receiving flip-flop.

**Definition: Current hogging*—this physical behavior occurs in direct-coupled transistor logic (DCTL) gates. Unless the input characteristics of each of the load transistors are carefully matched, one load transistor will tend to draw most of the current supplied by the driving transistor. This is because several base-emitter junctions are being driven from the same point. Variations in the current–voltage (IV) characteristics of the individual transistors will cause one base-emitter junction to turn on, or conduct, first. The first junction to conduct may then "hog" the current supplied by the driving transistor. This "current hogging" may be sufficient to prevent the other load transistors from turning on. This problem is generally resolved by placing a resistor in series with the input base circuit of each load transistor. This makes the base current of each load transistor less dependent in the variations of the base-emitter voltage (V_{be}) characteristic of that transistor.

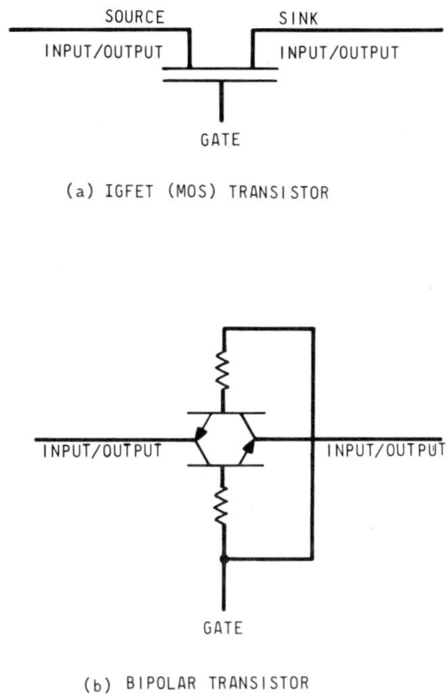

3-18 Bidirectional switch

The receiving flip-flop is reset prior to the enabling of the bidirectional gate. This, in turn, determines the data transfer path.

The use of bidirectional gates reduces the number of gates required by 50 percent when compared with the single-rail gating technique discussed previously. This reduces the number of interconnections in the system by the same factor. In addition, the bidirectional gate is normally held in the off state. As a result, no power is dissipated in the nonactive state. System application of bidirectional gates is discussed further in the following sections.

3.3.2 Dedicated Data Paths and Time-Shared Common Data Bus

There are several arrangements for transferring the content of any one register to any other register in a digital machine. The most efficient way to perform such data transfer operations requires that parallel data paths exist between all registers; every register must have direct access to all other registers. All bits in the transmitting register are then transferred in parallel to the receiving register. As shown in Figure 3-20a, $n(n - 1)$ sets of gates are required for n registers. If n is relatively large, the number of gates becomes excessively high. For example, when $n = 16$, 240 sets of gates are needed. This tends to create a complex interconnection problem. This problem is further complicated by the fact that each flip-flop may fan out to 15 logic gates and handle a fan-in

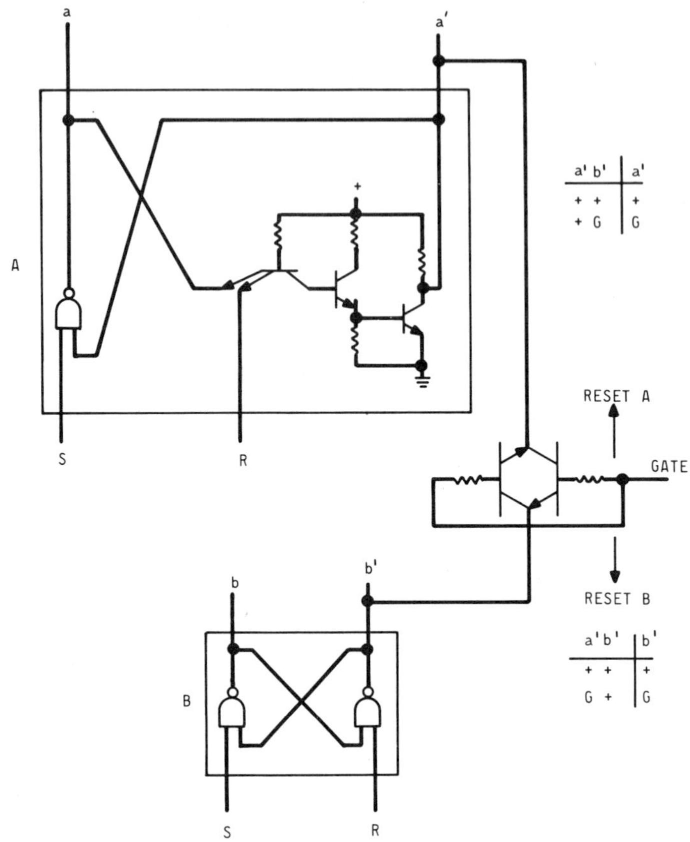

3-19 Data transfer using bidirectional gate

of 15 gate outputs.* The use of bidirectional gates reduces the number of gates associated with the fan-in and fan-out characteristics of a flip-flop. As shown in Figure 3-20b, the flip-flop may accommodate a large fan-out if the receiving logic circuitry is made up of bidirectional gates. Typically, as the fan-out increases, the cumulative ac loading associated with each logic gate also increases. This ac loading tends to degrade the speed of flip-flop's operation. The use of bidirectional gates reduces the ac loading problem by reducing the fan-out of the flip-flop.

This simultaneous transfer of many sets of data words using parallel busing paths is not characteristic of small systems. Instead, data transfer operations normally occur in serial fashion, with one data word at a time being transferred between the source and destination registers. All bits in the data word are transferred in parallel in a single gating operation. This permits time sharing of a common data bus. Figure 3-21a

***Definitions: Fan-out* refers to the number of output connections driven by a single gate. *Fan-in* refers to the number of input connections received by a single gate.

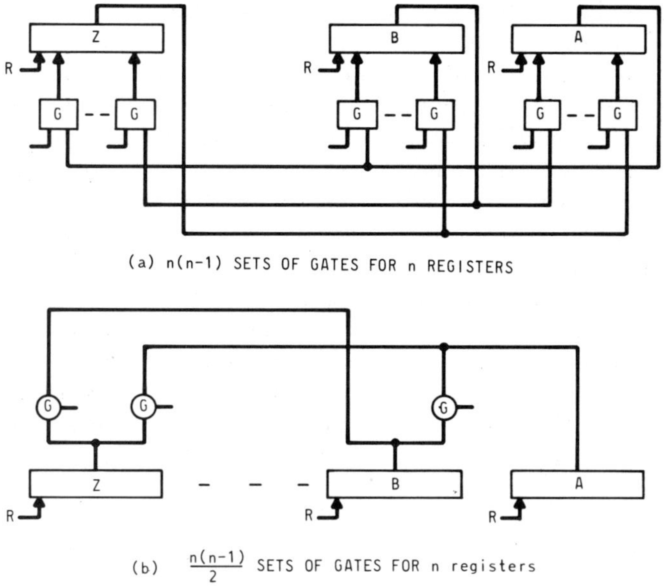

(a) n(n-1) SETS OF GATES FOR n REGISTERS

(b) $\frac{n(n-1)}{2}$ SETS OF GATES FOR n registers

3-20 Dedicated parallel data paths

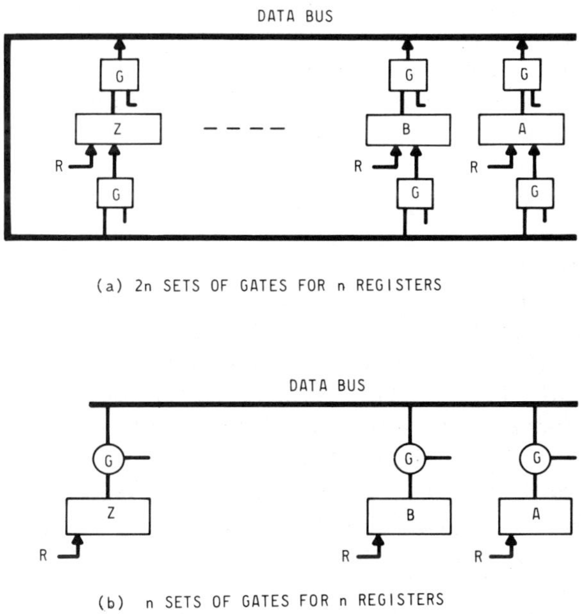

(a) 2n SETS OF GATES FOR n REGISTERS

(b) n SETS OF GATES FOR n REGISTERS

3-21 Time-shared common data bus

shows a single data bus arrangement in which the content of any register can be transferred to any other register in the system. Two sets of gates are needed: an input set and an output set. In transferring information from register A to register B, for example, the output gates associated with register A are enabled, allowing the data to flow onto the bus. Register B must then be set to 0 or cleared by a common reset signal. The data from the bus are gated into register B by enabling the input gates of register B as the last step in the data transfer operation. For n registers, $2n$ sets of gates are required to implement the data bus if conventional, commercially available gates are used by the logic designer.

The busing arrangement shown in Figure 3-21b, which uses bidirectional gates, is very attractive for several reasons: (1) it is a simple interconnection of logic gates; (2) it requires only one set of gates per register; (3) it consumes no dc power; (4) it simplifies the fan-in and fan-out problems; and (5) it minimizes the interconnections between logic gates. The choice between using bidirectional gates as opposed to unidirectional gates in a busing structure depends upon the ease of implementing such a logic arrangement using commercially available SSI, MSI, and LSI logic building blocks (such as AND gates, OR gates, and flip-flops). These basic building blocks allow the construction of control patterns that are highly regular in their physical arrangement. If a bidirectional gate is used in such a control logic configuration, the physical gating arrangement can become more irregular in its interconnection pattern and more difficult to implement. The use of bidirectional gates appears to be quite attractive when implementing a busing structure using MOS technology. Since the bidirectional gate offers a symmetric input characteristic, it more closely matches the logical parameters of MOS structures than those gating arrangements implemented using bipolar technology. Figure 3-22 shows a busing arrangement used to gate data from one flip-flop register to another. The entire circuit arrangement has been made from MOS logic circuitry. This structure lends itself easily to the modern microprocessor in which the entire processor is placed on a single silicon chip.

3.3.3 Single-Rail Versus Double-Rail Gating

The method of transferring data mentioned in the previous section is referred to as *single-rail gating*. Its most common implementation requires that the destination register be cleared before the contents of the source register are gated into it. In this case, bits that are in the 1's state in the source data word are gated into the destination register. An alternative implementation requires that the destination register be set to the all-1's state before the data word is transferred. In this case, only those bits in the 0's state in the source data word are gated into the destination register. The final decision as to which of the two previous implementations is used in a register transfer operation depends upon the logic of the bus—that is, whether the bus is designed to physically gate a logical 1 or a logical 0 into the target register. Generally, the 1's-rail gating scheme shown in Figure 3-23a is the one most commonly used.

Double-rail gating, shown in Figure 3-23b, is performed as a single-step operation in contrast to the two control steps required to gate a data bit into a register using the

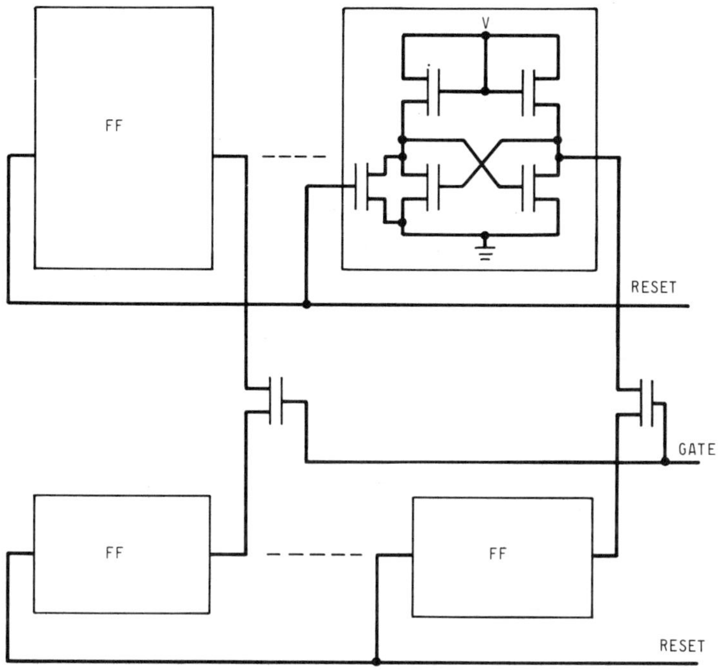

3-22 Data transfer with MOS circuits

single-rail gating technique. As shown in Figure 3-23b, two sets of gates are necessary to implement double-rail gating: one set gates the 1's of the source data word into the target register; the other set gates the 0's. The transfer of the 0's and 1's of the source data word into the target register occurs as a parallel gating operation. While the double-rail gating operation is faster than the single-rail approach, the increased speed of logic operation is gained at the expense of an extra set of gates and an extra set of input leads. If a particular silicon chip is limited by the number of I/O pins going off the chip rather than by the number of gates on the chip, it may be advantageous for the logic designer to trade gates for I/O pins. In this situation, the second rail may be derived from the first rail using inverters as shown in Figure 3-23c. The second rail acts as the logical complement of the signal provided by the first rail. A more efficient method of implementation is shown in Figure 3-23d.

An important consideration in data transfer is the settling time of the flip-flop outputs associated with the destination register. This settling time can also be equated with the speed with which the data are transferred to the receiving flip-flop. This determines how soon the received information can be used for data processing. The speed of single-rail operation is inherently slower than the speed of double-rail gating. Therefore, double-rail gating appears to be ideally suited for high-speed operation. The reason for the delay in single-rail gating is the sequential action of first clearing (setting) all flip-flops in the destination register and then setting (resetting) the appropriate bits in the target register. This situation is illustrated in Figure 3-24. When the

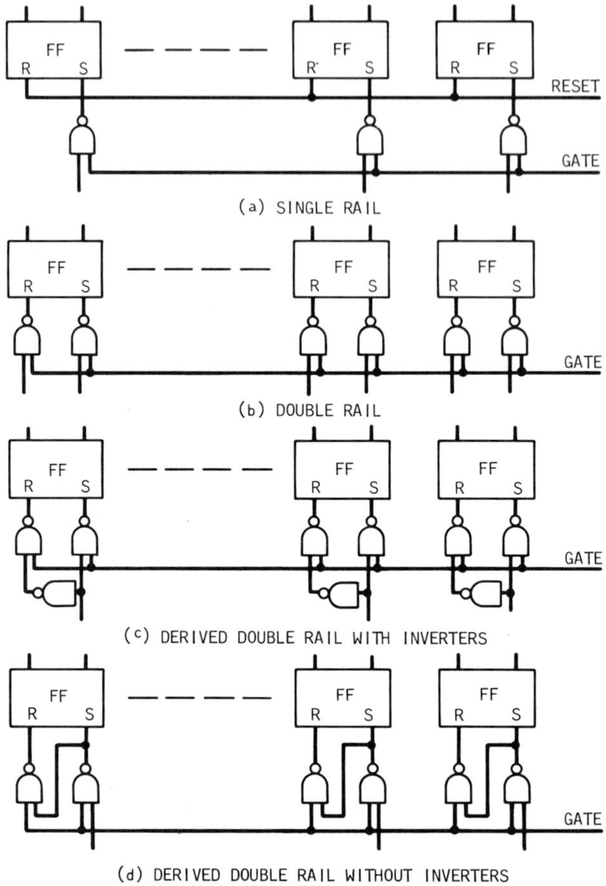

3-23 Circuit variations in data transfer

input is a 1, both set and reset signals are applied to the flip-flop simultaneously during the first part of the gating interval. The outputs of the flip-flop (Q and Q′) are both held at a plus potential. In order to use the Q′ output, the system must wait until the reset signal is no longer present and the Q′ output has reached the correct state of ground potential. The time required for the Q output signal to stabilize is affected only by the propagation delay of the input gate and the turn-on time associated with the set side of the flip-flop. If the Q side of the flip-flop is fed through an inverter stage to generate the Q′ output, an enhanced speed of logical operation can be obtained. In terms of minimizing off-chip interconnections, this approach is completely compatible with the general philosophy of MSI circuit design. Furthermore, the speed of logical operation obtained from this implementation is equal to the speed achieved through the use of the dual-rail gating scheme.

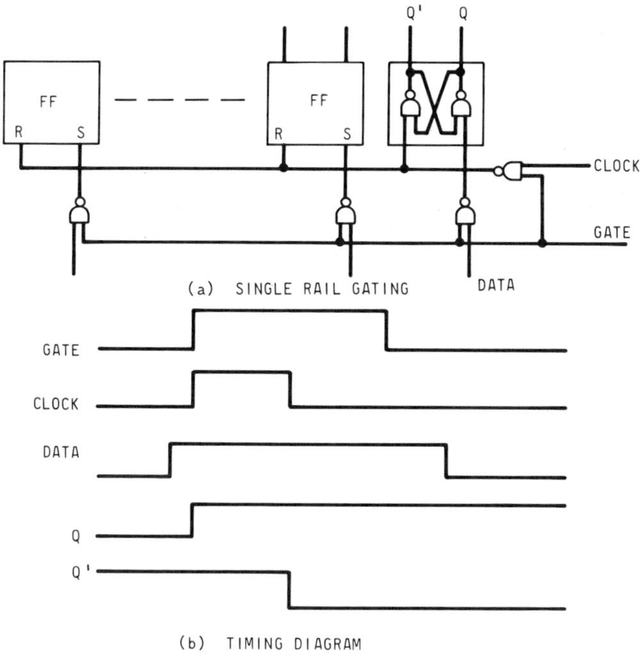

3-24 Single-rail gating and timing diagram

If flip-flops that employ open collectors are used, the input gates can be connected directly to the outputs. This arrangement is equivalent to the wired-AND function since the resultant output is high (or in the 1's state) only when both inputs are high. The output connection is commonly referred to as a *collector tie*, in which a common load resistor is shared by the output gates. The ability to form a collector tie, with the flip-flops comprising a processor register, offers the designer additional variations in implementing the data transfer logic, using either single-rail or double-rail gating techniques. Figure 3-25 shows the circuit variations used to perform data transfer when the wired-AND or collector-tie capability is provided. These gating structures are similar to those shown in Figure 3-23. However, they do *not* permit the individual flip-flops to use the collector-tie feature. If the individual gating structures are compared with each figure, it can be seen that the collector-tie capability eliminates a state in the logic chain required to transfer data into the target register. The elimination of this logic stage results in a faster register-to-register data transfer operation. The arrangement shown in Figure 3-25a may be compared with the single-rail implementation in Figure 3-23a, which does not use the collector-tie capability. The physical procedure for transferring data using the circuit of Figure 3-25a is as follows:

1. Both a SET and a RESET signal are applied simultaneously to the same side (Q′) of the flip-flop.
2. The RESET signal holds output G1 in the high state at the same time that the SET signal holds output G2 in the low state.

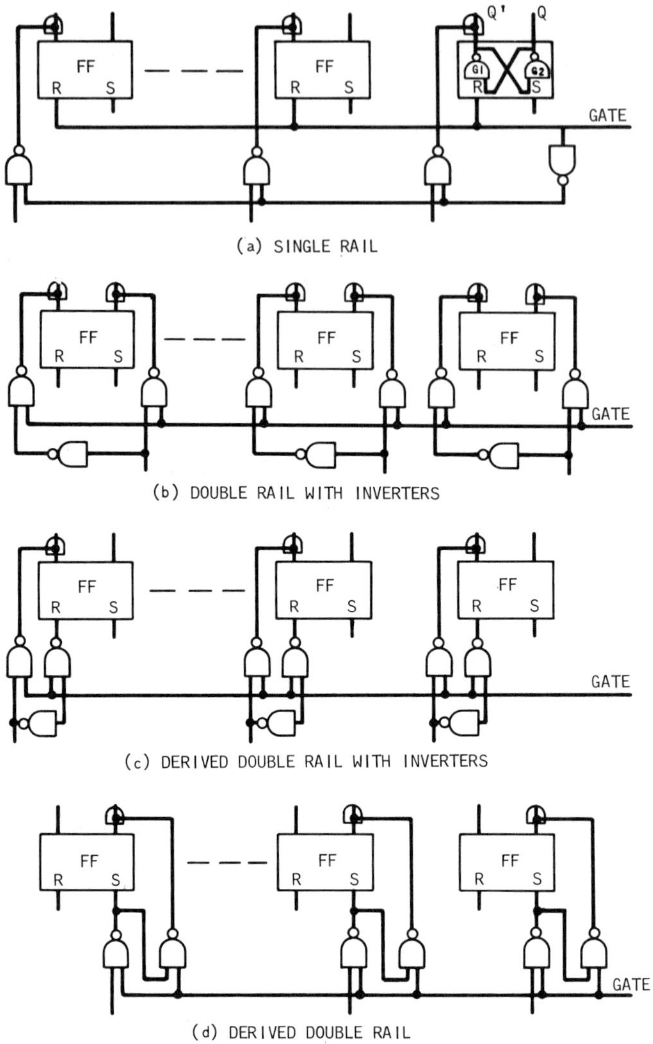

3-25 Circuit variations in data transfer with wired-AND capability

3. The resultant output, Q, is low, which indicates that a logical 1 has been transferred into the flip-flop.
4. As the control signal returns to the inactive or high state, the two outputs also change states. G1 switches to the low state first, followed by G2 switching to the high state.
5. There is a momentary overlap when both outputs are in the low state because of the longer delay associated with the logic path of G2. This overlap is necessary to keep the flip-flop in the set state upon termination of the control signal.

Each of the other data transfer arrangements shown in Figure 3-25 can be compared with the single-rail circuits shown in Figure 3-23 to obtain a more detailed picture of how the collector-tie capability may be used to move data between registers.

3.3.4 Data Bus Arrangements

The time-shared data bus described earlier is shown again in Figure 3-26. The outputs of the corresponding bits are connected to form a 16-bit data bus. Because of the inversion of going through a stage of NAND logic, the Q′ output is used as the data to be transferred, to preserve the correct polarity signal on the bus. Some circuit difficulties accompany this arrangement if either the number of collector ties or the fan-out of the bus becomes excessive. The output impedance of the pull-up resistor must be within a certain range in order to maintain the proper voltage values for logic 1 and logic 0. This value is significantly greater than that of the active pull-up totem pole output. The operating characteristics of open-collector gates affect their performance in terms of switching speed and noise margin. Typically, it is possible to wire-AND five collectors and still maintain a fan-out of eight. As the number of collector ties increases, the fan-out capability is proportionately reduced. The switching speed will be degraded appreciably by the capacitive load at the common output node.

To alleviate the capacitive loading effects of the collector tie and, at the same time, to improve the fan-out capability, the data bus can be structured as shown in Figure 3-27. Instead of connecting many collectors together and providing a correspondingly large number of fan-outs, the two output requirements can be separated by adding another logic stage capable of driving the high fan-out. At the same time, the collector ties can be subdivided into small groups and logically combined, as indicated in the figure. The data signal must be taken off the Q side of the flip-flop because of the additional stage of logic. In this manner, the electrical requirements of the bus can be met without any difficulties.

The shortcoming of the open-collector gate is that the value of the pull-up resistor must be kept relatively high to maintain the proper logic level at the output. This limits the number of collector ties that can be used, as well as the fan-out capability of the

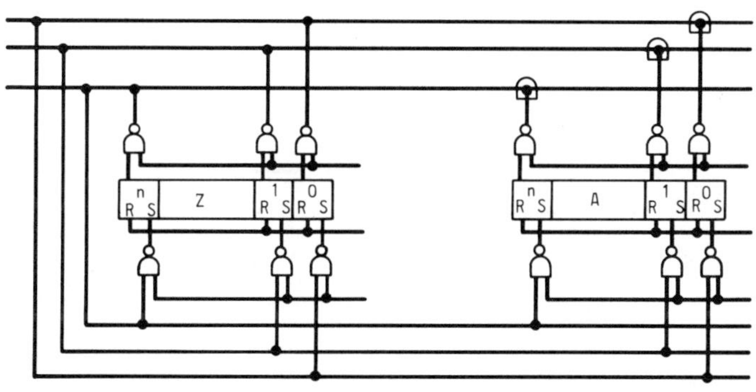

3-26 Data bus arrangement with wired-AND capability

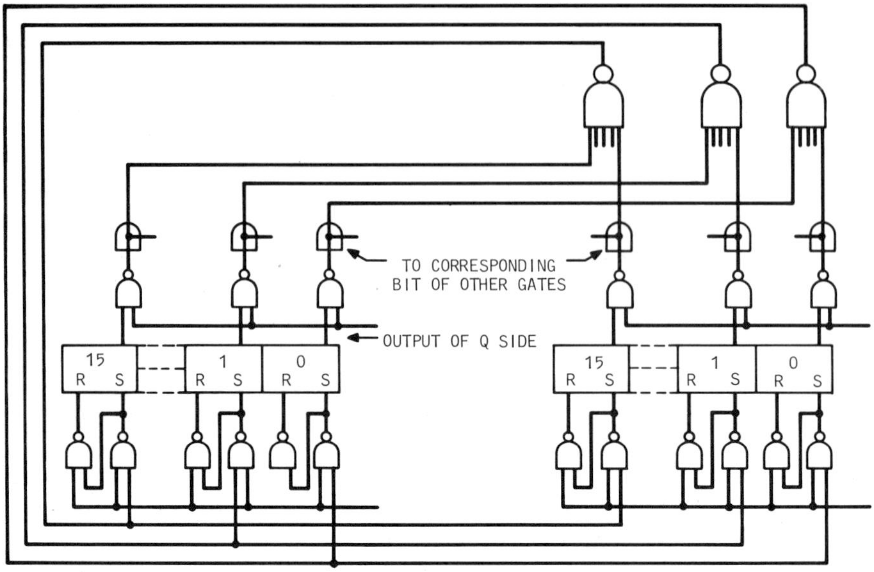

3-27 Data bus arrangement with limited collector ties

gate. The gates with an active totem pole output stage (see Figure 3-28) offer a low-impedance drive for both logic 1 and logic 0. Since one of the two output transistors will be in the low-impedance state, it is highly effective in driving capacitive loads (unlike gates with a passive output stage). The active pull-up circuit configuration, however, is not well suited for use in a wired-AND logic connection.

If the wired-AND connection was implemented using gates with totem pole drive, as shown in Figure 3-29, a single output in the 0 state would have to sink current from all the other active pull-up transistors. Because of the low resistance offered by the collector circuit of the output transistor, an extremely high output current is generated.

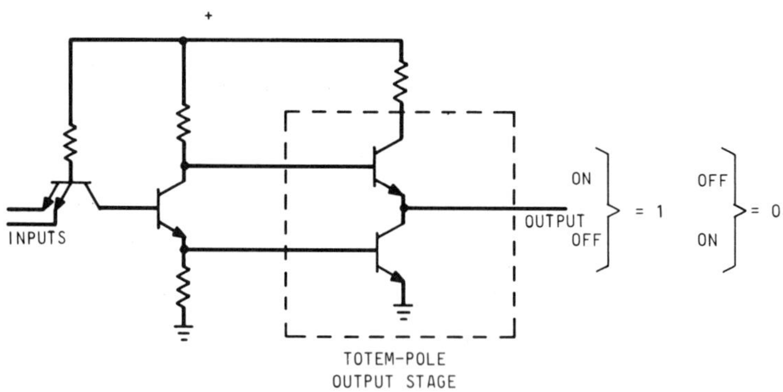

3-28 NAND gate with totem pole output stage

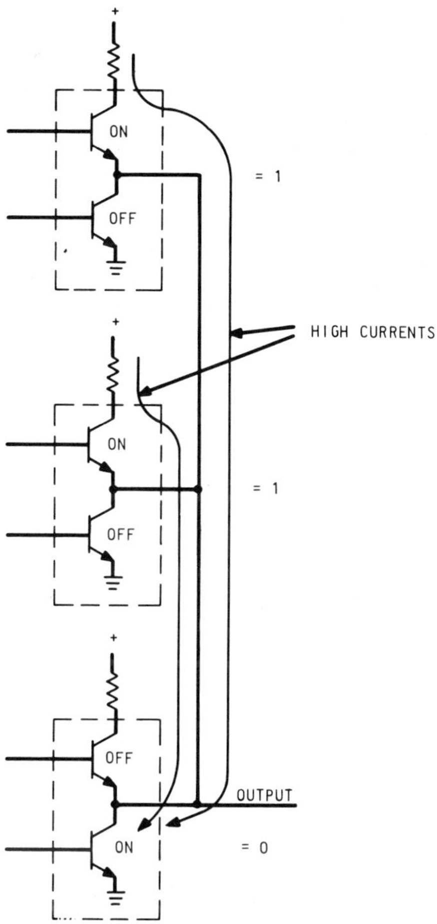

3-29 Wired-AND connection of gates with totem pole outputs

This high current must be absorbed by the output transistor. Under these conditions, it is very probable that the transistor will be damaged, since it is not designed to handle high current. If it is not damaged, the high current may degrade the logical-0 output voltage to a point where the associated logic circuitry will not recognize the output voltage as a logical 0. For these reasons, totem pole outputs are not used to implement the wired-AND function.

Consider the totem pole circuit arrangement shown in Figure 3-29. The two output transistors that form the totem pole structure can be in one of two possible pairs of states. If a logical 1 output is being produced, the top or pull-high transistor is ON and the bottom transistor is OFF. Similarly, if the output is a logical 0, the top transistor will be OFF and the bottom transistor will be ON. There will be a high current flow occurring from the ON state of the pull-high transistor to the output transistor. In a bus structure formed from totem pole gates, the normal or idle state for each output transistor is a logical 1. If the idle state for each totem pole gate can take the form in which both the top and the bottom transistors are in the OFF state, a three-level output or tri-state gate is obtained. In this state the three-level gate will appear to be an open circuit of very high impedance to the output node. Since each three-level gate appears to be an open circuit when the gate is in its idle state, an almost unlimited number of outputs from separate tri-state gates can be connected in a wired-AND connection. When a particular tri-state gate is selected or rendered active by the bus control logic, the gate will transfer a logical 0 or logical 1 to the output node; no current is drawn from all other tri-state gates connected to the output node. This situation is illustrated

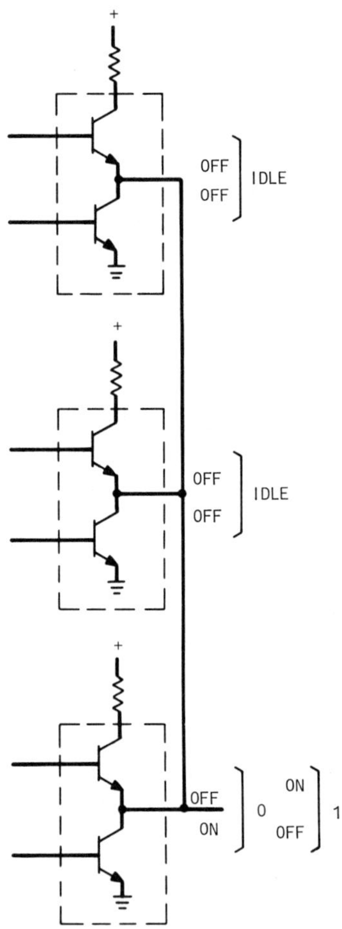

3-30 Wired-AND connection of gates with three-state output

in Figure 3-30. The totem pole output circuit configuration also provides a high current capability for driving low-impedance loads in both the logical 0 and logical 1 states. This, in turn, meets the high fan-out requirement for a gate structure that is used in a busing arrangement.

The realization of the tri-state or three-level output gate is shown in Figure 3-31. In the normal two-level totem pole output configuration, the disabled or idle state is a logical 1, with the pull-up transistor in the ON state and the output transistor in the OFF state. If the output is in the logical 0 state, the application of the control signal will set the output to the logical 1 state. If additional control circuitry is added as indicated in Figure 3-31, the control signal will also switch the pull-up transistor to the OFF state. This action produces the OFF–OFF state configuration of the pull-up transistor and the output transistor that represents the idle or disabled state of the three-level output gate.

The high-impedance state of the tri-state gate isolates the gate from the output node. Proper logical operation requires that only *one* of the tri-state gates used in the wired-AND configuration be enabled at any time. Otherwise, the possibility of a high current flow between the outputs of the two active tri-state gates exists. This high current flow may damage the transistors through which it flows, or it may give an indeterminate output voltage. The requirement that only one tri-state gate in a wired-AND connection be active at any time does not affect the usage of these gates in a busing structure. Since only one tri-state gate is ever active at a time, the output node or wired-AND connection point is time-shared by all the three-level gates tied to that point,

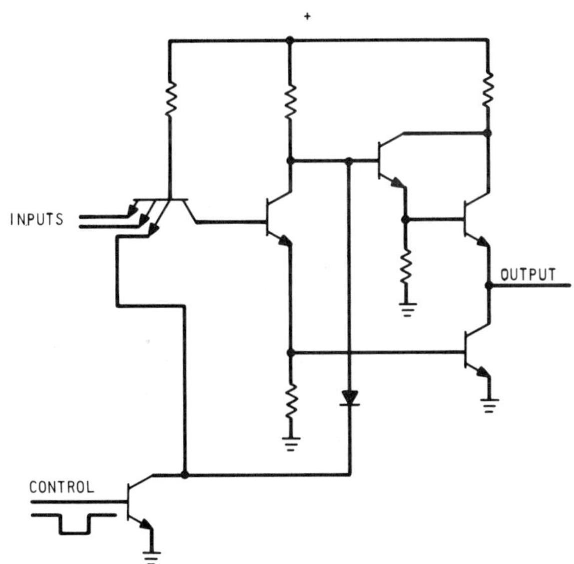

3-31 Simplified three-level output gate

with only one data transfer occurring over the bus at a time. The tri-state gate offers a high fan-out capability and permits an almost unlimited number of outputs to be tied together in a wired-AND configuration.

3.4 BUSING SYSTEMS

3.4.1 Initial Considerations

The internal data bus organization depends on how fast the designer wishes to have the data transfer operation take place and how much the designer wishes to pay for the higher-speed logic circuitry to obtain an enhanced performance. These considerations involve design trade-offs in which the cost of logic circuitry is balanced against the speed of logic operation desired by the designer. The speed of data transmission along the internal data bus is directly related to the number of bits that are transferred in parallel. If this number is less than the number of bits in a full word, multiple bus transfers must occur before the data word can be moved from the source register to the destination register. For high-speed transfer operations, either more bits must be moved in parallel or higher-speed logic circuitry must be used to reduce the time required to move blocks of data. Obviously, if full words are involved exclusively in data transfer operations and very high speed logic circuitry is used in implementing the busing structure, the maximum transfer rate is obtained. However, the cost of such an arrangement can be prohibitive when compared with a busing structure made from less expensive and slower logic circuitry.

One of the primary functions of a computer is to process and convert binary data into more useful results for the user, such as performing arithmetic or logic operations on sets of data. For example, the most frequent arithmetic operation, addition, involves forming the sum of two operands. These numbers may be available in hardware registers or fetched sequentially from main memory. Either a single-bus or multiple-bus structure could handle the data transfers involved in the arithmetic operation. The choice of the busing structure, again, depends on the values assigned by the designer to the desired speed of data transfers and the cost of the circuitry.

3.4.2 Single-Bus Structure

In a single data bus arrangement (see Figure 3-32), all hardware registers are connected to the same bus so that data may be transferred between any two registers or between any register and the ALU. If more than three registers are to communicate with each other, a common bus to which all registers are connected is more economical than dedicated gating paths that interconnect privately between two registers. This economy is measured in terms of fewer gates and interconnections. If the common bus arrangement is used, only one operand at a time can be presented to the ALU. Furthermore, the bus must be time-shared by the individual operands required by the ALU. Consequently, hardware buffer registers must be provided to temporarily store any

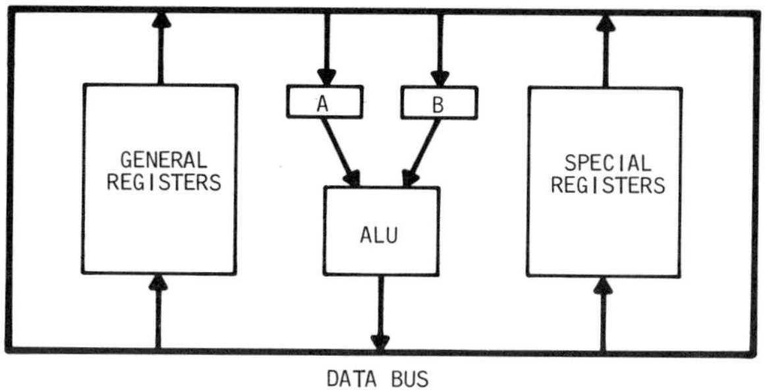

3-32 One-bus oriented toward ALU

operands directed to the ALU. In the case of addition, the two operands must be transferred to these two buffers on separate operations. The first operand must have successfully reached the first ALU buffer register before the second operand can be gated onto the bus and into its ALU buffer register. The outputs of these buffer registers are processed by the ALU; the result is available since the buffer registers are not disturbed. A third data transfer operation is necessary to gate the sum from the output of the ALU into the destination register.

The serial nature of a common bus may or may not increase the time required to perform an arithmetic operation on two binary numbers. For example, if the instruction specifies that the two operands are to be obtained from memory and the result is to be stored in memory, then the memory access time is, in all likelihood, the limiting factor in moving the data to the ALU. However, since each operand must be fetched separately from main storage because of the serial nature of the common bus, the ALU operation is not delayed. If data *were* available in the hardware registers, the sequential steps required to calculate the address of an operand would add directly to the execution time of the operation. This represents a loss of real time, which degrades the instruction execution rate and, consequently, the throughput of the system.

Since the operand transfer for an arithmetic operation is divided into several steps, additional sequencing logic is required to control the flow of data. Although more sequencing logic is needed, the overall control is simplified and reduced since there is only one bus to manipulate and control.

3.4.3 Two-Bus Structure

Two operands that are presented simultaneously to the ALU offer the most natural way to perform arithmetic operations. The ALU operates on both operands in a single control step and provides the resultant at the ALU output in that same control step. This process allows the ALU to immediately perform the required arithmetic operation rather than wait for the second operand to be loaded in an ALU buffer register. Figure 3-33 shows a two-bus arrangement in which an output from each bus is provided as a separate input to the ALU. The information on each bus is supplied

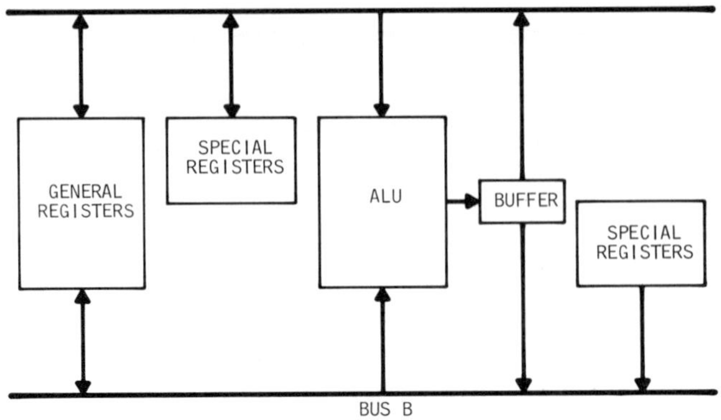

3-33 Two-bus oriented toward ALU

by separate internal registers. Each bus may receive an output from either a general register or a special register. In particular, the special registers are divided into two groups; one group is connected to bus A, and the other is connected to bus B. No two registers within the same group are used as operands simultaneously. For example, the memory output register and the PC are in separate groups, so that one register may be gated onto bus A and the other onto bus B for the purpose of being operated on by the ALU circuitry. The general registers, however, must be connected to *both* buses. This is done to permit any general register to be combined with any register of *either* special register set in an arithmetic operation. If it is necessary to obtain both operands from the same group of special registers, one of the operands must first be moved into a general register so that each operand can be put on a different bus. This initial operation requires an additional machine instruction, which must be included in the program prior to the command to execute an ALU operation.

The output of the ALU must be directed somewhere. Since the possibility exists that both of its buses may be occupied, a natural arrangement would be for the machine to store the ALU output in a buffer register as shown in Figure 3-33. The ALU output may also be directed to both buses, allowing the arithmetic result to be gated back to either a special register or a general register. This procedure means that an arithmetic operation would require two steps. The first step would gate both operands onto separate buses, add the operands in the ALU, and store the result in the ALU output buffer register. The second step would gate the buffered sum into the designated destination register. The latter step could be removed if a third bus were used on which the ALU output could be gated directly to the destination register. The additional bus saves the time required for the second control step, but at the expense of additional hardware.

The data from the bus are fed directly to the ALU as inputs (see Figure 3-33). No input buffer registers are necessary if both sets of input data are held long enough for the correct result to be strobed into the ALU output register. However, if input buffer registers are provided, any gating into the ALU becomes simply a register-to-register transfer operation. In this case the ALU output buffer register would be stable as long as the data in the input registers remained unchanged. The ALU can then be gated directly onto either bus A or bus B.

Although it is not shown in Figure 3-33, there are other dedicated, private gating paths within the processor to provide quick data transfer to one or more of the special registers. For example, a direct path from the PC to the memory address register (MAR) is usually provided, since the data transfer between these registers is done with nearly every instruction fetch.

Another two-bus variation is shown in Figure 3-34. It is arranged to facilitate single operand operations. The single operand arithmetic and logic portion of the ALU has been removed and is incorporated as a separate bus-modifier unit. The bus modifier can be programmed to operate on all data that flow through the unit. It can be directed to perform the operations of increment, decrement, shift, rotate, or complement upon the data words gated to it. In addition, the bus modifier may appear transparent to the data entering it. In this case, the data will simply pass straight through without modification to the second bus. The bus modifier connects the two buses together, allowing data from the SOURCE bus to be modified on the "fly" to the DESTINATION bus in a single control step. For this bus arrangement, a two-operand arithmetic operation requires three control steps. The first two steps load the operands into the ALU input buffer registers. The third step performs the arithmetic or logic operation and then transfers the result to the destination register. The two-operand operation is, therefore, identical to the one-bus arrangement. The main advantage of this bus organization which uses a bus-modifier unit is that a single operand can be transferred and modified as it is gated from one register to another in a single control step.

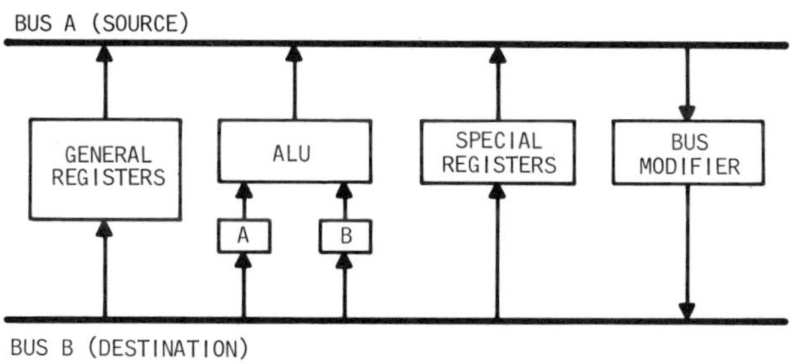

3-34 Two-bus oriented toward single operand operation

3.4.4 Three-Bus Structure

A third data bus can be added to reduce to one the number of control steps in an ALU operation. This three-bus structure is shown in Figure 3-35. It is similar to the two-bus arrangement, except that the output of the ALU is directed to the third bus instead of a buffer register. The third bus may be used to direct the result of the ALU operation to any general register or special register.

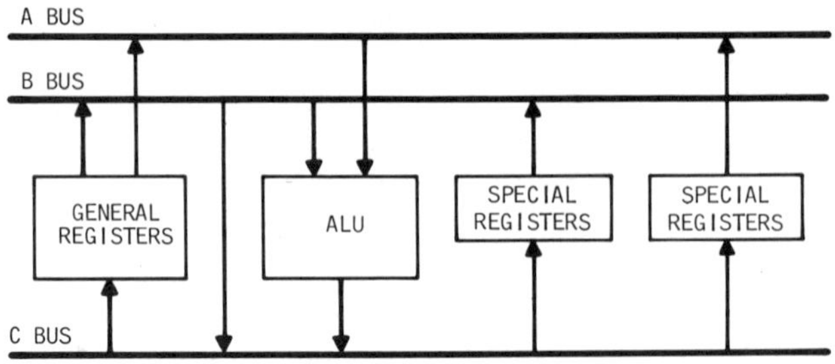

3-35 Three-bus oriented toward ALU

Before the correct result is available on the third bus, a delay will be incurred while the operands are gated to the ALU and operated on by it. The gating of data from the third bus must be timed to account for this delay. Only data to be modified by the ALU will be directed through the unit; otherwise, a direct path from bus B to bus C bypasses the ALU. In this case, the delay of the operand is reduced, and the timing of the data transfer is different in that the control logic does not have to anticipate either the settling time of the operand or the logic delay introduced by the ALU before the resultant data word is available.

By means of the third bus, the result can be gated to any general register or special register.

3.4.5 The Unified I/O and Memory Bus Concept

The Digital Equipment Corporation (DEC), in 1969, introduced the concept of using an external *single-bus structure* at the small computer level with its announcement of the PDP-11 family of minicomputers. The single bus employed by the PDP-11, commonly referred to as the UNIBUS,* used a parallel run of 56 physical-signal leads to which the CPU, main storage, and all peripheral devices were interfaced. In general, the signal leads of a single-bus structure may be partitioned into two physical groups of leads: the first group forms the set of address leads; the second group forms the set of data leads. The number of signal leads in the address set defines the width or number of bits in the address word. Similarly, the number of signal leads in the data set defines the size of the data word. The widths of the address word and the data word do not have to be equal. In one form of the single-bus structure, the same set of signal leads is used to transmit the address information first and the data next. Consequently, address and data are time-multiplexed on the same set of signal leads for such a physical arrangement.

The address space of a single-bus structure may be defined as *the maximum number of main memory locations that may be referenced using all the bits in an address word.* Thus, a 16-bit address word provides an address space of $2^{16} = 65{,}536$ memory locations. In general, no one device may have continuous control of the single-bus structure except in a seizure of the busing arrangement for a maximum-speed *direct memory*

*Registered in U.S. Patent Office.

access (DMA) operation. Typically, control will be delegated to any device that requests the bus to establish a communication path between itself and another device interfaced to the single bus. The delegation of control is handled by a *bus arbitration unit*. In the basic single-bus structure, the bus arbitration unit is always part of the CPU, with the CPU remaining in control of the single bus, except during DMA transfers. In addition, the basic single-bus structure treats memory reference instructions and I/O operations as separate classes of machine directives. Consequently, I/O address space is kept distinct from program and data storage space.

The single-bus structure may be refined by reserving a portion of the total bus-address space for all I/O transactions. This reduces the total amount of main memory that may be referenced by the locations dedicated to the usage of I/O operations. However, this permits one address space to accommodate instruction, data, and peripheral device I/O operations. In effect, the separate categories of memory reference instructions and I/O commands are eliminated using this form of the single-bus arrangement. Both of these categories are replaced by a single directive classification that can best be described as *I/O reference instructions*. These instructions control all communication that takes place between the central processor, main memory, and various peripherals. I/O transactions using this structure make use of the entire memory-reference class of instructions. This variation of the single-bus structure has been called a *unified-bus structure*. Figure 3-36 illustrates the basic single-bus concept and the unified-bus concept. In this figure, the CPU is in control of the bus.

The unified-bus concept may be expanded to permit devices other than the CPU to gain control of the bus. The device in control of the bus is referred to as the *bus*

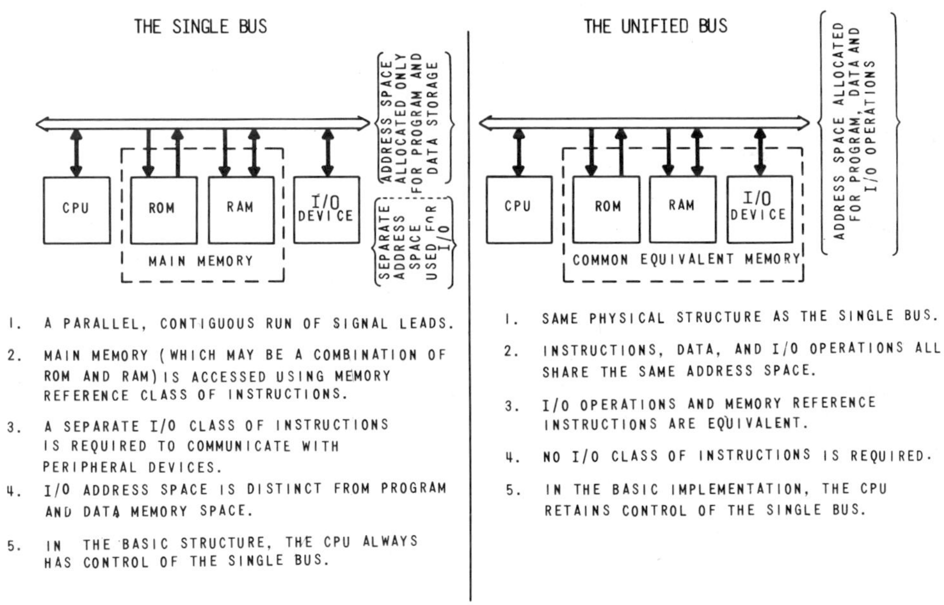

3-36 Basic single-bus concept and unified-bus structure

master. Those devices with which *the bus master* communicates are referred to as *slaves*. Thus, all devices that can function as a bus master, including the CPU, issue bus requests at preestablished priority levels. A bus arbitration unit resolves the bus request contention and assigns the bus to a specific device, permitting *that* device to become bus master. A bus master communicates with any peripheral device register just as though it were a register in main storage. This procedure removes the need for I/O instructions, since addressing any peripheral device register appears to the system as though a reference to a location in main memory is being made.

An *asynchronous, handshaking communication mode* is associated with the single-bus structure which permits a bus transaction to take place between the bus master and a slave device in a step-by-step handshaking manner. The master (slave) is not permitted to continue its dialogue until a reply has been received from the slave (master). This reply is determined by the response characteristics of the device involved and not by a system clock (hence, the term, *asynchronous, handshaking mode*). This asynchronous communication mode permits the user to mix memories and peripherals of various speeds in the same system. Such a system is said to be *technology independent*.

3.4.6 Microprocessor Busing Structures

Two levels of busing systems have evolved for configuring a computer structure from an MOS/LSI microprocessor chip set. In terms of a single-chip CPU, an internal busing system has been developed which allows various on-chip elements of the CPU to communicate with each other. An external busing arrangement has been used off-chip to permit the CPU to interact with the various members of the chip set and form a microcomputer structure. Normally, the external busing configuration does not differ substantially from the on-chip internal busing arrangement.

Because of the limited amount of chip real estate available for an internal busing structure, the most common on-chip busing configuration has been the single bidirectional bus on which addresses and data are multiplexed. Data located in any internal register may be gated onto the bus and moved into any other internal register. Control, however, takes place over a series of private signal leads from the timing and control section to each functional unit on the chip. Figure 3-37 illustrates a typical microprocessor configuration implemented in a DIP that uses a single internal gating bus. This configuration is fairly general, and virtually all single internal-bus microprocessor devices may be represented by it, with the appropriate insertion or removal of special registers. As an example, Figure 3-38 shows the architecture of the Intel 4040 microprocessor, which uses a single internal gating bus. Address and data are multiplexed to the internal bus as needed in 4-bit segments. The ALU functions as an accumulator which communicates with the internal data bus on the CPU chip. Notice, however, that for the 4040, only one 4-bit busing path leaves the chip; this path must supply both address and data to the external world. Figure 3-39 illustrates the architecture of the Motorola M6800 microprocessor. It also uses a single bidirectional internal gating bus, but the bus is 8 bits wide instead of 4 bits wide as in the 4040. The M6800 provides

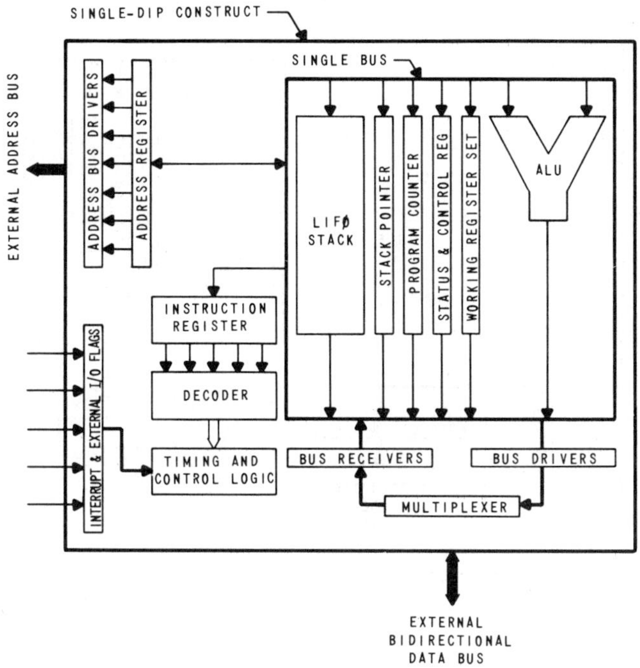

3-37 Typical single-DIP microprocessor configuration

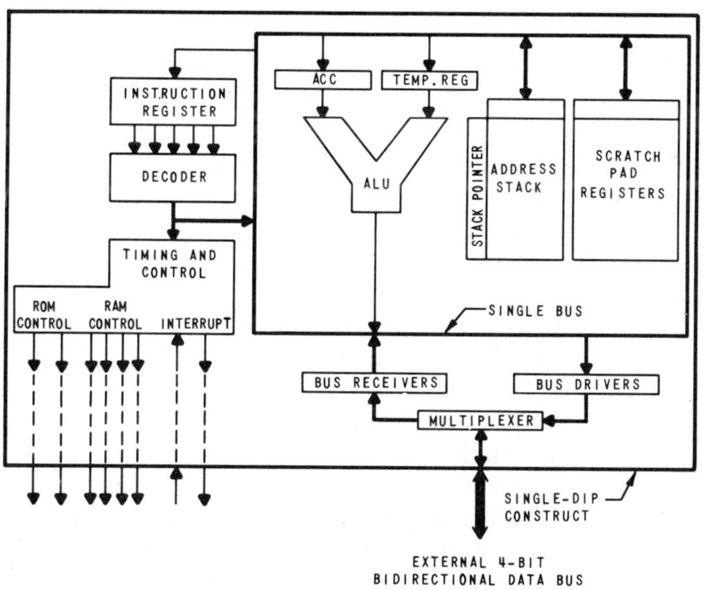

3-38 Intel 4040 μP exhibiting internal and external busing arrangements [Reprinted with permission of Intel Corporation]

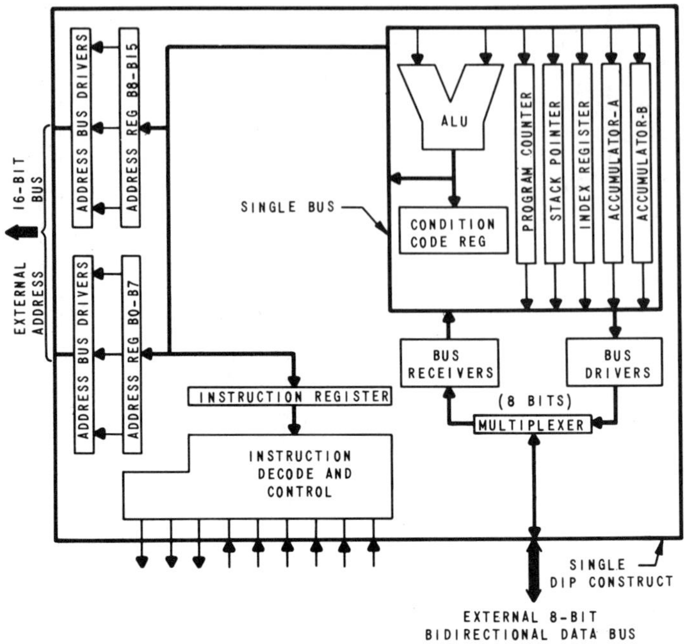

3-39 Motorola M6800 μP exhibiting internal and external busing arrangements [Adapted, with permission of Motorola Semiconductor Products, Inc.]

a 16-bit address bus for off-chip references and an independent 8-bit data bus for bidirectional data communication between the microprocessor and the attached members of its chip set.

The National Semiconductor PACE microprocessor provides a good example of a dual internal-bus structure that has been successfully implemented on a single CPU chip. Figure 3-40 illustrates the PACE architecture, which employs the concept of a source (operand) bus and destination (result) bus. Note that the PACE has a 16-bit bidirectional gating bus to communicate with the external world. The single and dual internal-bus structures exhibited by the 4040, M6800, and PACE represent the two categories into which on-chip microprocessor busing structures may be placed.

Two distinct, external, off-chip bus arrangements have been used in a similar fashion. The first type is characterized by the Intel 4040 implementation in which a single, external bidirectional bus is used. The width of the external bus is the same as the width of the on-chip single bus; the external bus appears as an extension of the internal bus. To achieve off-chip communications, address and data are multiplexed from the internal data bus to the bidirectional output bus. This communication takes place in 4-bit segments which are transferred from the internal bus to the external I/O bus of the microprocessor. Effectively, this is the basic single-bus structure discussed earlier, with the CPU remaining in control of the bus.

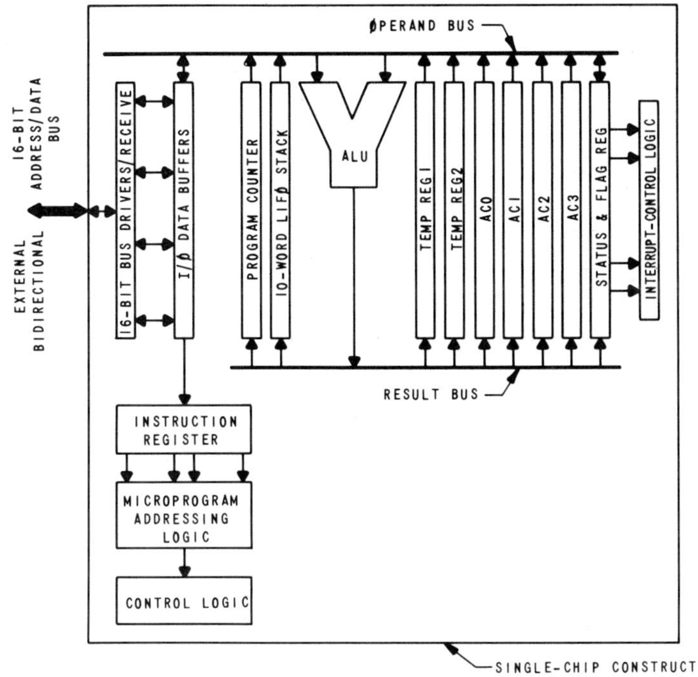

3-40 National Semiconductor PACE μP exhibiting internal and external busing arrangements [Adapted from *PACE User's Manual* with permission of National Semiconductor Corp.]

The use of two distinct address and data buses for off-chip communications in a microprocessor structure has become common. Figure 3-41 shows a typical external busing arrangement. Note that the address word is a different width (16 bits) than the data word (8 bits). Using the single-bus concept developed earlier, Figure 3-40 may be redrawn to resemble an equivalent single-bus configuration, shown in Figure 3-42. The basic single-bus concept simply requires that all devices interface with a common run of signal leads. That requirement is fulfilled by changing the layout of the external address and data buses of a microprocessor-based system. A generalized, single external bus configuration may be drawn for an arbitrary microprocessor-based system (see Figure 3-43). This structure is not a unified-bus structure per se, but if I/O transactions are treated as memory reference instructions, this figure can relate to a unified bus as well.

The disadvantage of the single-bus structure at the minicomputer level has been that memory operations and I/O transactions must be alternated; they cannot run concurrently. DEC solved this problem by incorporating a high-speed private memory bus in their PDP-11/45 so that the overall throughput could be increased. A microprocessor normally does not have high throughput requirements because of the more circumscribed areas that it is used in. Consequently, it appears that the single-bus structure offers the speed required by microprocessor applications. It also appears

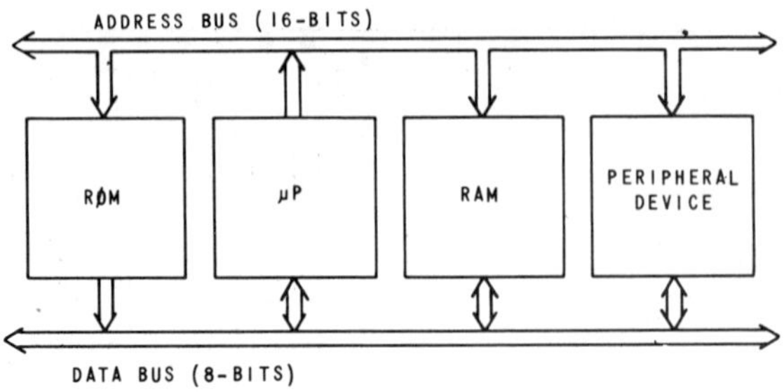

3-41 Typical separate address bus and data bus configuration for a μP system

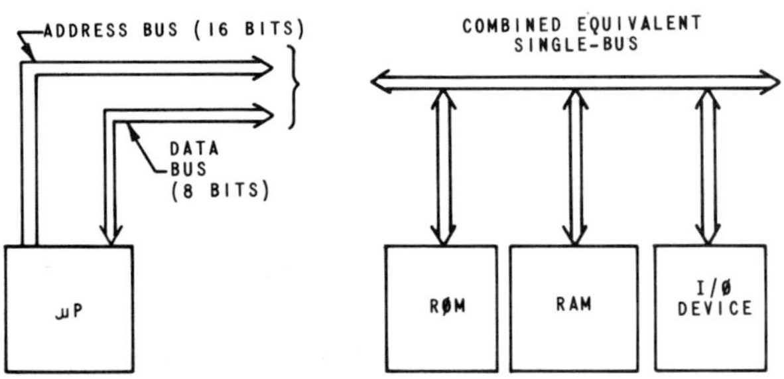

3-42 Equivalent single-bus configuration of a μP bus system

that the consolidation of instructions, data, and I/O operations into one contiguous memory address space through the use of the unified bus has become a fairly standard concept.

As a final comment on busing structures, microprocessors may be classified according to their external busing scheme and use of memory. For instance:

1. The early microprocessor-based calculators used a single external bus arrangement and partitioned instructions and data into separate stores (ROM and RAM, respectively). A separate class of I/O instructions was used. The PPS-4 and 4004 are representative of this class.
2. The second-generation microprocessors used a single external bus but permitted program and data to share the same memory. They continued to employ a separate class of I/O instructions. This class was characterized by the 8080 and the PPS-8 MOS/LSI CPU's.
3. The mature microprocessor structures adopted the unified-bus approach, in which program, data, and I/O operations shared the same address space. This approach has been typified by the PACE and M6800 devices.

The evolution of these classes occurred as the actual physical implementation of various microprocessor features developed at the chip level. The single-bus approach

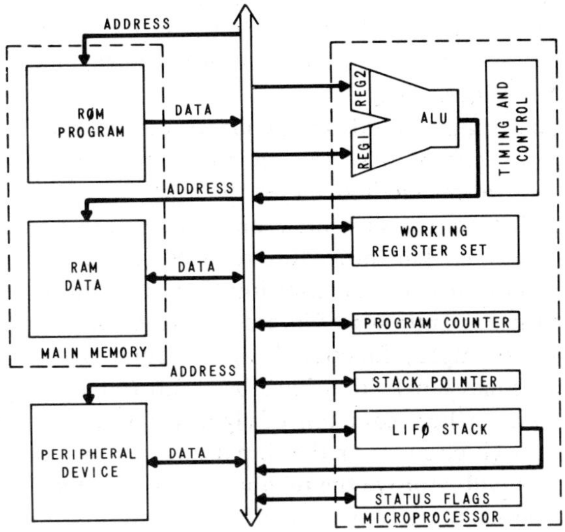

NOTE: IF I/Ø OPERATIONS ARE TREATED AS MEMORY REFERENCE OPERATIONS THIS SINGLE BUS STRUCTURE IS REFERRED TO AS A UNIFIED BUS.

3-43 Generalized single external bus configuration for μP systems

was a natural outgrowth of trying to interconnect piece parts (members of the chip set) in a reasonably simple manner to an MOS/LSI CPU. The unified-bus technique was a natural outgrowth of the single-bus structure, which greatly simplified the programming of the microprocessor.

3.5 PARTITIONING OF DATA TRANSFER CIRCUITS

Three different scales of integrated circuits have been used to implement the logic circuitry of a processor. They are:

1. *Small-scale integration* (*SSI*). The equivalent of 10 or fewer logic gates are placed on a single chip.
2. *Medium-scale integration* (*MSI*). More than 10 but fewer than 100 logic gates are placed on a single chip.
3. *Large-scale integration* (*LSI*). More than 100 logic gates are placed on a single chip.

Some SSI circuits are packaged so that *all* the inputs and outputs of each logic gate are brought off the chip. A logic configuration is formed by individually interconnecting all appropriate inputs and outputs associated with the separate gates used in the logic design. In this method, called the *unit logic approach*, each gate is individually identifiable in the hardware realization. Unit logic circuits usually contain one to six gates on a chip and provide the logic designer with the flexibility of realizing infrequent or unusual logic configurations.

In many logic designs, it is advantageous for the designer to minimize the number of off-chip interconnections, since this enhances the reliability of the logic structure being implemented. In this method, called the *lead-reduction approach*, the inputs and outputs of several logic circuits are interconnected before a signal lead is sent off-chip to the next package level. This procedure reduces the number of pins required by the integrated circuit and provides a denser logic structure on the IC chip.

To further reduce the number of interconnections between IC's, it is necessary for the logic designer to employ functional logic circuits. The *functional-logic approach* makes use of functional blocks that have been fabricated on separate IC chips. This method results in a further reduction of signals that are sent off-chip and a higher packing density of logic circuitry on the chip itself. Removing many of the interconnections between chips will improve the reliability of the system, since these interconnections are the primary sources of malfunctions. In addition, the higher density of logic circuitry will reduce the signal delays associated with long interconnections, which were required when two gates communicated in an off-chip environment. When both gates are placed on the same chip, the reduction of delays improves both circuit and system performance. All MSI and LSI chips are implemented using the functional-logic partitioning method.

One of the problems in MSI and LSI design is to define functional blocks of sufficient size and generality so that they may be used repetitively throughout the system. The general registers and their associated input and output gates meet these requirements for a logic structure that forms an acceptable functional block. Figure 3-44 shows the three ways in which the general registers and their associated circuitry may be grouped to form functional logic configurations. These arrangements, which are essentially register building blocks, take the following forms:

1. A word-organized structure.
2. A bit-organized structure.
3. A structure that is a combination of the previous two structures.

Figure 3-45a illustrates the word-organized building block. A 16-bit word, including all the associated input and output gates for each bit position, is shown as the functional logic element. The functional unit possesses 34 external signal leads, consisting of 16 leads for input data to the register, 16 leads for output data from the register, and two control leads that enable either the input gates or the output gates. A set of 16 general registers, each with a 16-bit word length, can be implemented by stacking 16 such word-organized building blocks together. The inputs and outputs of each register element must be connected together to form a bus structure for data transfers between registers.

Figure 3-45b illustrates the bit-organized configuration in which one bit from each of 16 different registers is included in the functional grouping. In addition, the input

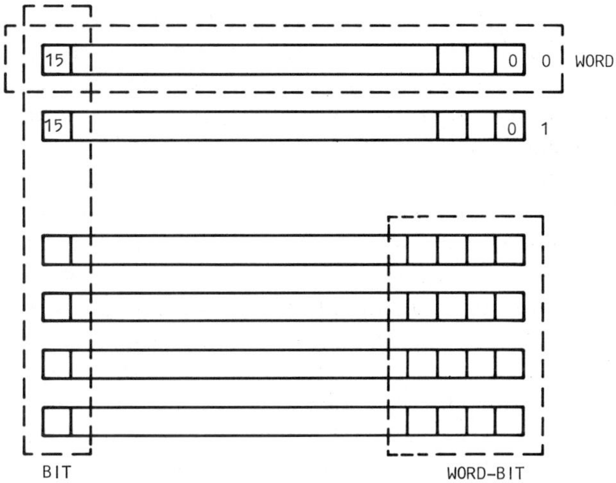

3-44 Data register partitioning

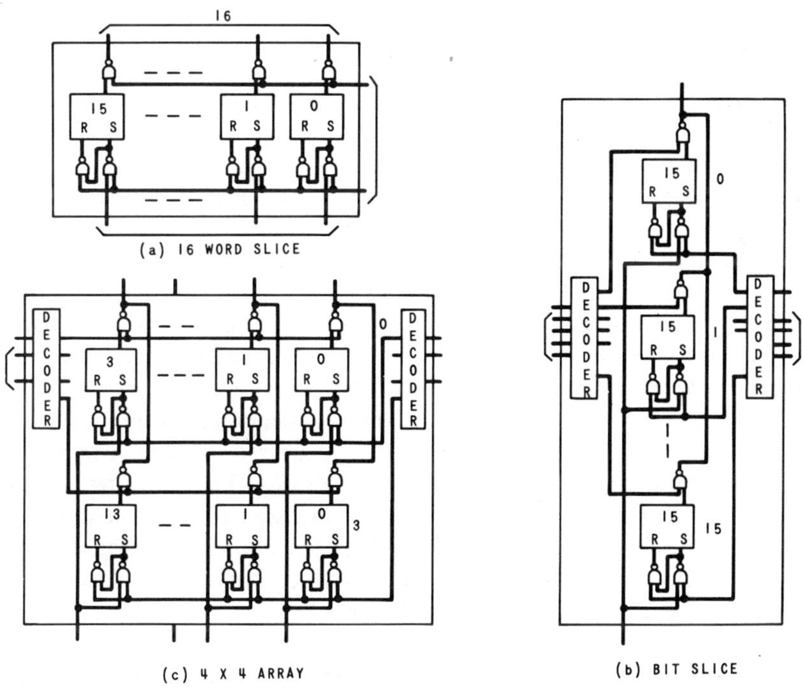

3-45 16-bit partition

and output interconnections from each bit and the additional logic circuitry required to decode the control signals for each register are included. If this decoding logic were not included, 32 individual control signals would be required, one for each input gate and one for each output gate. In this case, the number of external signal leads extending off the bit-organized arrangement would be the same as for the word-organized arrangement. A more compact binary decoding scheme can be used to take advantage of the fact that only one of the 16 input gates and one of the 16 output gates are enabled at any one time. The local decoding (within the functional block) reduces the number of leads considerably, at the expense of replicating the decoding function for each bit. The designer, in this case, must make a trade-off between the number of gates available on a functional chip and the number of external signals that must communicate with the chip through its arrangement of input and output pins, or *pinouts*. These considerations are particularly important when functional logic circuits are partitioned and implemented as an array of interconnected gates on a single IC chip. It is possible to replace the 16 individual control signals by five signals, four of which represent a decoded 4-bit binary number. The fifth signal is required to synchronize the decoding and gating operations. This situation is shown in Figure 3-45b, in which the total number of signal leads has been reduced to 12 (as compared with the word-organized configuration).

A functional logic structure can be more easily fabricated as an integrated circuit if the structure can be organized in a physical-array configuration. The symmetry of an array allows the metalization processes to be done in a reasonably straightforward fashion. Consequently, a more attractive arrangement for a register building block is the 4×4 array structure shown in Figure 3-45c. This array consists of 4 bits from four different registers, a total of 16 bits associated with the register building block. The number of data signals that enter or leave the building block increases directly with the size of the array. That is, the number of external data leads is a function of the word size used in the register building block. For instance, a 2×2 array requires four external connections; a 3×3 array requires six external connections; a 4×4 array requires eight external connections. In the case of the 4×4 array illustrated in Figure 3-45c, four input data leads and four output data leads are required since the data in and the data out are bused to all registers on the building block. Local decoding of the gating signal to strobe data into one of the four registers is performed as part of the building block. Similarly, local decoding of the gating signal to strobe data onto the output bus is also done. Consequently, the number of selection leads required to control the building block is six, with three leads required for input control and three leads required for output control. The total number of I/O pins required by the 4×4 array structure is 14. This arrangement may be contrasted with the bit-sliced organization shown in Figure 3-45b, which requires 10 I/O signal leads made up of one input lead, one output lead, four input control leads (which are decoded locally), and four output control leads (which are also decoded locally).

The number of terminals or pins available on most MSI dual in-line packages has been 14, 16, up to 24. Two pins in each of these packaging arrangements have already been assigned for power and ground. Consequently, there are actually two fewer terminals available than the numbers shown on each package. The choice of how a functional building block is partitioned so that it may be implemented in a dual in-line package will be strongly influenced by the number of terminals available on the package. Figure 3-46 shows the number of pins required on a package as a function of the word size for a 16-bit array structure used as a register building block. The signal leads are divided into two categories: data leads and control leads. The control leads are decoded locally within the register building block to minimize the number of control signals passed between the register elements. The total number of terminals or pins is simply the sum of the data pins and control pins required. In the case of an array structure that uses either a 1-bit or a 2-bit word length, the total number of pins required is the same (i.e., 12), as indicated in Figure 3-46. In this instance, the increase in data signals is compensated for by the reduction in required control signals. Beyond the array structure that uses a 2-bit word length, the increase in required data leads far exceeds the decrease in required control signals.

If the number of I/O terminals on a package is constrained to 16, the choice of partitioning a register building block will be determined by the number of bits to be included in the building block. For a 16-bit building block, either the bit slice or the array structure may be used. A word slice will not be applicable since the total number of pins required by a 16-bit structure will exceed the 16 available on the package. The bit-sliced organization allows a word of any size to be constructed by adding 1 or more bits to the existing register(s). The additions must be in blocks of 16 words. An array of four register elements (4 bits each) allows the number of bits in a register to grow in increments of 4 bits. The number of registers can similarly be expanded by the same number. A set of sixteen 16-bit hardware registers would require the same number of circuits for both the bit and the array organization. However, if the processor required

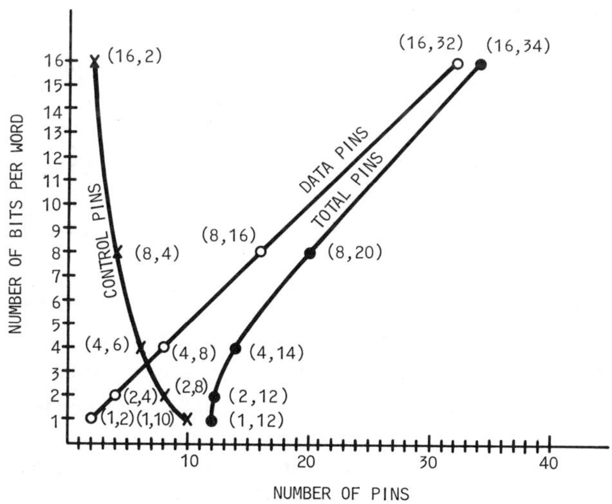

3-46 Number of pins as function of bits per word with a total of 16 bits

only eight 16-bit words, one-half as many circuits would be needed for the array organization.

For special registers such as the PC or status registers, in which the input and output logic varies with the function each register is to perform, only one register normally performs these functions. Consequently, the bit-sliced organization or the array structure is not appropriate for building the special registers since the array structure is oriented toward multiple-register implementations. In spite of the large number of external leads required, the word-organized configuration is more suitable for the implementation of the special registers. In contrast, the bit-sliced organization is particularly applicable in the area of large-size memories, where the size of the functional logic block is *not* tens of words but thousands of words. Such a structure lends itself to LSI organization, and the bit-sliced organization is ideally suited to minimize the number of leads or terminals that are required.

In general, there is a requirement for all three levels of integration in a machine that uses more than a few integrated circuit chips. For specialized functions where the need is limited, SSI building blocks partitioned on a partial-word configuration provide the best implementation. In the case of a general register stack involving 8 or 16 register elements, MSI building blocks organized in an array configuration will keep the number of terminals within reasonable limits. Finally, LSI building blocks are used to greatly increase the number of bits on a chip. In this case, the bit-sliced organization is necessary to minimize the number of signal leads that go off the chip.

3.6 THE FAMILY CONCEPT AND FUNCTIONAL MODULARITY

3.6.1 The Philosophy of Compatibility

One of the prime concepts that has emerged from the evolution of computing structures during the late 1960's and early 1970's has been the realization that a computer system should continue to have a useful life even in the presence of accelerated technological change. A newer model should at least support the software developed for an older model originally marketed by the same manufacturer. This is the concept of software compatibility, which may be observed by a line of machines in either of two ways.:

1. Each successive, more sophisticated model of a given machine will run all the software supported by the earlier models. However, portions of software written for the more sophisticated model will not run on the less sophisticated members of the line. Generally, this situation arises because a richer instruction set is used on the more sophisticated machine, and an expanded form of I/O operation is employed. This situation is called *upward compatibility in terms of software*. Strict upward software compatibility would permit all software and peripherals used on an earlier model to be used on a later model, but not vice versa. However, a line of computing machines may be upward compatible in

terms of software and *upward/downward-compatible in terms of peripherals*; that is, any machine in the line may be interfaced with the full set of associated peripheral devices. This requires that the administration of control to the peripherals be both program-compatible and I/O-signal-compatible across all machines in the line. DEC's PDP-11 line of minicomputers was an excellent example of this last case, prior to the introduction of the PDP-11/70. Certain high-speed peripherals were designed to interface directly with the cache memory used by the PDP-11/70 and did not employ the UNIBUS* for burst-type data transfers. Consequently, the earlier machines, which did not employ a cache memory, could not use the high-speed peripherals designed for the PDP-11/70.

2. All models of a given machine type will run all software. It does not matter if the software was developed for the top-of-the-line model or the most elementary model. Any machine in the line may also be interfaced with the full set of associated peripherals. Such machines are said to be *upward/downward-compatible in terms of software and peripherals*. The Data General Nova line was developed and marketed with this philosophy in mind.

3.6.2 The Idea of a Computer Family

The advantages of preserving an established software base and using mature, familiar peripheral devices that are well understood by maintenance personnel are obvious. The large mainframe manufacturers such as IBM recognized this in the early 1960's when they introduced the concept of a *computer family*, or line of successively more sophisticated machines. A computer family is characterized by each family member using the same basic instruction repertoire, fundamental I/O operations, and data formats (such as the 8-bit byte). Also, each member supports the same basic system software package. For an upward-compatible computer family, each more sophisticated machine contains the instruction sets of the less sophisticated members as a subset of its instruction set. The main differences between family members are (1) the size of main memory supported by each member, (2) the cycle time of the associated main memory, (3) the selection of peripheral devices that may be directly interfaced with the machine, (4) the way each member is physically packaged, and (5) the maximum capacity of the power supply associated with the mainframe. For an upward/downward-compatible computer family, these differences are just the basic considerations of memory cycle time, packaging, and available electrical power in the mainframe.

The family concept is an easily accepted idea since the user of a computer structure does not have to pay a severe penalty for moving up to a more sophisticated model as application requirements become more mature. Consequently, many of the commercial minicomputer manufacturers such as DEC, INTERDATA, MODCOMP, and Hewlitt-Packard have adopted the computer family concept. In addition, the family concept has been observed at the microprocessor level by Intel in the architecture of

---

*Registered U.S. Patent Office.

both the 4040 CPU and the 8080 CPU. The features of the Intel 4004 are included as a subset of the 4040, and the 8080 contains the 8008's features as a subset of its characteristics.

In the late 1960's, the minicomputer manufacturers produced separate machines for each computational level in their computer family line. It was to their financial advantage to sell a minimal system that could be configured into a more sophisticated model by simply adding features to the mainframe. These additional features were implemented on separate circuit boards that could be plugged into the mainframe connector slots. Each feature was individually priced and could be bought separately once the user had obtained the mainframe associated with the desired family member. Consequently, one of the early characteristics of the commercial minicomputers was the ease with which additional memory and peripheral devices could be added to the system configuration. This approach offered a graceful expansion into a more powerful system. Figure 3-47 shows a minicomputer mainframe that exhibits how such options were plugged into the I/O bus. In addition, the I/O bus itself is shown as being expandable through use of a bus extender module that is cabled to the power and I/O bus located in the mainframe.

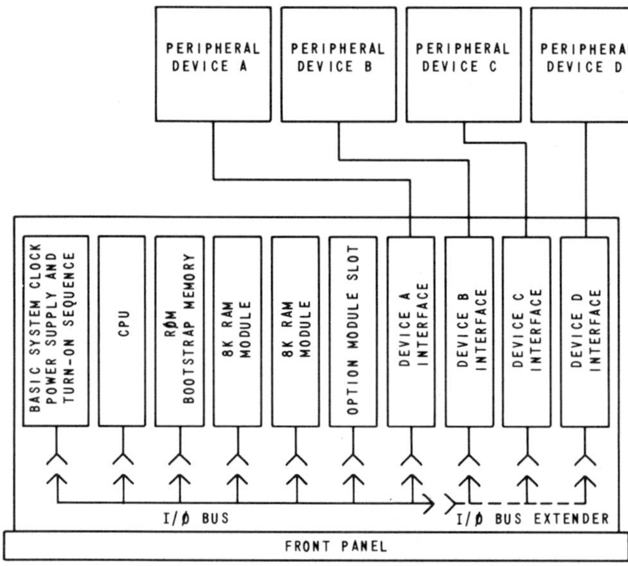

3-47 Physical packaging for adding mainframe features

3.6.3 Mainframe Options

The need for ease of expansion led to the philosophy of *functional modularity* [19]. Typically, the circuit cards were functionally independent; their insertion or removal in the mainframe did not disturb the overall operation of the system. Since these functional modules represented an array of hardware options that could be appended to the mainframe, they allowed the user to start with a basic system arrangement and to tailor the configuration to meet application requirements. These functional modules were called *mainframe options* by the manufacturers who attempted to offer a broad range of such units.

By the 1970's, a minicomputer user could start with a basic CPU and add functional modules to obtain a reasonably sophisticated system. To obtain the next higher family member, however, usually required replacement of the basic CPU.

With the accelerating development of LSI technology in the early 1970's, functional modularity offered the computer designer a new flexibility. It became possible to functionally partition separate features on individual circuit boards such as the working register set, the entire ALU, the hardware interrupt logic, memory, and the overall control logic. Thus, a computing structure could be built by interfacing a selection of these same units; a more sophisticated structure could be built by using a broader selection. These functionally oriented units represent circuit boards that may be directly interfaced to the system; they have been partitioned for optimum usefulness and not simply for ease of manufacturing. This permits the upgrading of an existing system by simply removing one set of circuit boards and adding another.

A second design concept is that of *technology independence* [19]. Compliance with this concept requires that a given functional module can be replaced by a higher-performance module made from a new technology without the system being aware of the difference. An example of this is the trend toward replacing magnetic core memory with LSI semiconductor memory as the main store in various families of computing machines. To accommodate such functional replacements, the timing of the system must be adaptable to the new module. This is achieved by requiring that the timing associated with each of the functional modules be asynchronous with respect to the system clock. Consequently, each functional module must dialogue with the CPU in an asynchronous handshaking manner; each communication from the CPU requires a corresponding acknowledgment from the addressed functional module.

The concept of functional modularity provides the facility for generating a computer family with the following characteristics:

1. Each family member is hardware-compatible with all other members. A basic set of functional modules defines the fundamental member; higher-level members are generated by adding to the basic set from a selection of other functional modules. Each family member shares the same basic technology and interconnection techniques. However, the more sophisticated machines may use faster memories and more advanced technology to implement certain of their functional options.
2. Upward/downward software compatibility may be realized in such a family arrangement. In particular, instructions executed on the higher-level machines, which are not implemented in microcode on the lower-level machines, may be trapped as they are executed on the more limited machines. The trap directs execution to take place in a subroutine which interprets the instruction. This

software facility permits program integrity to be preserved on the smaller machines.

In essence, functional modularity protects the user's financial commitment to a machine type at both the hardware and software levels. It is both design-effective and cost-effective.

3.7 SUMMARY

The two classical machine categories have been discussed from the perspective of how each machine type uses main storage. The strict Harvard machine was defined as one that did not intermix instructions and data; a distinct memory module, which was separate from another module used to hold operand information, was used to contain machine directives. In contrast, the Princeton machine was defined as one that permitted instructions and data to be intermixed anywhere within main storage.

The internal organization of a computer was found to be composed of the CPU, including the arithmetic-logic unit (ALU), and the control unit. The most common structure encountered within the CPU is the data transfer gating logic or the register-interconnection logic.

The use of bidirectional gates was shown to simplify the data transfer logic. In addition, the advantages and disadvantages of using single-rail gating versus double-rail gating were discussed. In general, the data transfer logic was found to lead to considerations in the area of busing structures. The busing systems used by microprocessors were shown to consist of an internal gating bus that communicated with an external structure that could be reasonably different from the on-chip busing arrangement.

The partitioning of data transfer logic into one or more functional building blocks was also discussed. The actual partitioning was shown to be very dependent on the number of terminals or pins that are available on the building block. Too few pins can require a highly complex logical building block to configure the proper data transfer paths.

Finally, the advantages of the family concept were reviewed from the point of view of both the user and the machine designer. The family concept allowed software to be preserved and moved over to the more powerful machine once it was developed on a less powerful family member. The family concept was shown to have been observed at the microprocessor level as well as the minicomputer level of control.

3.8 REFERENCES

1 Hellerman, H., *Digital Computer System Principles.* New York: McGraw-Hill Book Company, 1973.

2 Gschwind, H. W., *Design of Digital Computers.* New York: Springer-Verlag New York, Inc., 1967.

3 Foster, C. C., *Computer Architecture.* New York: Van Nostrand Reinhold Company, 1970.

4 FREEDMAN, M. D., *Principles of Digital Computer Operation.* New York: John Wiley & Sons, Inc., 1972.

5 HILL, F. J., AND G. R. PETERSON, *Digital Systems: Hardware Organization and Design.* New York: John Wiley & Sons, Inc., 1973.

6 RICHARDS, R. K., *Electronic Digital Systems.* New York: John Wiley & Sons, Inc., 1966.

7 HOLLINGSWORTH, D., *Minicomputers—A Review of Current Technology, Systems, and Applications,* Document No. AD-783-316. National Technical Information Service (NTIS), The Rand Corporation, Santa Monica, Calif., 1974.

8 CUSHMAN, R. H., "EDN's First Annual Microprocessor Directory, 1974." *Electronic Design News,* Vol. 19, No. 22 (Nov. 20, 1974), pp. 31–41.

9 MARTIN, DONALD P., *Microcomputer Design.* Martin Research Ltd., Chicago, 1975.

10 *A Manual of Operation for the Automatic Sequence Controlled Calculator,* Annals of the Computation Laboratory of Harvard University. Cambridge, Mass.: Harvard University Press, 1946.

11 NICK, J. R., "Using Schottky 3-State Outputs in Bus-Organized Systems." *Electronic Design News,* Vol. 19, No. 23 (Dec. 5, 1974), pp. 35–39.

12 MRAZEK, DALE, "Bus-Connectable TTL Adds a New State to Binary Logic." *Electronic Design News/Electronic Equipment Engineering,* July 15, 1971.

13 *The TTL Data Book for Design Engineers.* Texas Instruments, Inc., Houston, Tex., 1973.

14 MORRIS, R. L., AND J. R. MILLER, *Designing with TTL Integrated Circuits.* New York: McGraw-Hill Book Company, 1971.

15 BEUSCHER, H. J., AND W. N. TOY, "Check Schemes for Integrated Microprogrammed Control and Data Transfer Circuitry." *IEEE Transactions on Computers,* Vol. C-19, No. 12 (Dec. 1970), pp. 1153–1159.

16 NORDQUIST, W. R., AND W. N. TOY, "A Novel Rotate and Shift Circuit Using Bidirectional Gates." *IEEE Transactions on Computers,* Vol. C-19, No. 9 (Sept. 1970), pp. 802–808.

17 *Intel 4040 Microprocessor User's Manual,* Intel Corporation, Santa Clara, Calif., 1975.

18 *M6800 Microprocessor Applications Manual,* Motorola, Inc., Phoenix, Ariz., 1975.

19 *MODCOMP IV Reference Manual,* Modular Computer Systems, Fort Lauderdale, Fla., 1974.

20 Stone, H. S., *Introduction to Computer Architecture.* New York: McGraw-Hill Book Company, 1975.

21 THURBER, K. J., E. D. JENSEN, L. A. JACK, L. L. KINNEY, P. C. PATTON, and L. C. ANDERSON, "A Systematic Approach to the Design of Digital Bussing Structures," *Proc. AFIPS 1972 Fall Jt. Computer Conf.,* AFIPS Press, Montvale, N. J., 1972.

3.9 PROBLEMS

1. A small computer has 16 general-purpose registers, with each register containing 24 bits. Each register communicates with every other register.
   (a) Assume bidirectional data lines are used between each register and all data transfers are done in parallel. What is the total number of data lines that are required so that

each register may communicate privately with every other register? Note: Include the gate-out and gate-in control signals for each register.

(b) Assume, instead, that 32 general-purpose registers are used, with each register containing 16 bits. *Now* what is the total number of data lines that are required so that each register may communicate privately with every other register?

(c) Now assume that the 32 general-purpose registers communicate via a bidirectional common bus. How many leads are in the common bus and how are the source register and destination register selected in the gating operation?

2. Consider three central processing units (CPU's) that are to be interconnected in a triple-redundancy configuration for error detection and correction.
   (a) Draw a block diagram of the interconnection arrangement.
   (b) In any such structure, the synchronization of operations must be carefully controlled. Describe the type of synchronization signals that should be used.
   (c) Draw a logic diagram of the error detection logic and the switching logic.
   (d) What steps can be taken to prevent the error detection logic and the switching logic from introducing faults into the system?
   (e) When one of the three CPU's has been rendered inoperative through some system fault of its own, is this triple-redundancy scheme still useful? How can the faulty machine be distinguished from the two remaining operational CPU's? Is a simplex arangement (i.e., one processor running with the other two processors removed from service) more advantageous than a degenerate triple-redundancy scheme? Give reasons for your answer.

3. Consider a typical 4-bit bipolar microprocessor slice. Design the error checking logic so that two such devices could be run in a *step-by-step match mode* with one bit-sliced CPU *shadowing* the operations of the other (i.e., the on-line CPU performs all calculations and supplies data to the external world while the shadow CPU performs the same calculations *but* provides data *only* to be used by the error checking logic).
   (a) If an error is detected, to which processor can the error be attributed? Describe the logical scheme necessary to identify the failing processor.
   (b) If the failing machine is the *shadow processor*, what should the response of the error checking and switching logic be?
   (c) If the failing machine is the *on-line processor*, what should the response of the error checking and switching logic be?
   (d) Assume that a repair has been implemented. What procedure should be used to bring the processors "up in step" in the corresponding correct initial state?

4. Consider a typical 4-bit bipolar microprocessor slice. Is it possible to run two such devices in the *hot, standby mode* (i.e., one CPU functions as the on-line processor, performing all calculations and I/O, while the other CPU is held in the powered-up state waiting to be switched in as the new on-line processor if the present on-line machine experiences one or more hard faults)?
   (a) What kinds of errors, if any, can be detected from this bit slice?
   (b) Are these errors sufficiently significant to justify using a hot, standby approach, or would a better approach be to use a step-by-step matching arrangement?

5. For each of the machine configurations shown below, indicate whether Harvard architecture or Princeton architecture is being observed or whether the structure is a variant of both. In each case, carefully state the reasoning behind your conclusions.

(a)

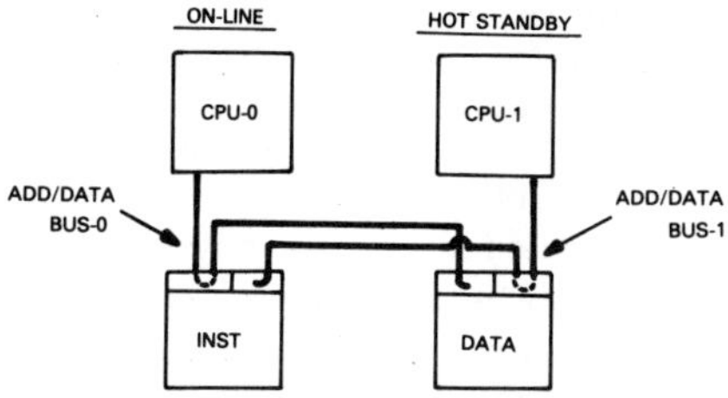
ON-LINE
HOT STANDBY
CPU-0
CPU-1
ADD/DATA BUS-0
ADD/DATA BUS-1
INST
DATA

(b)

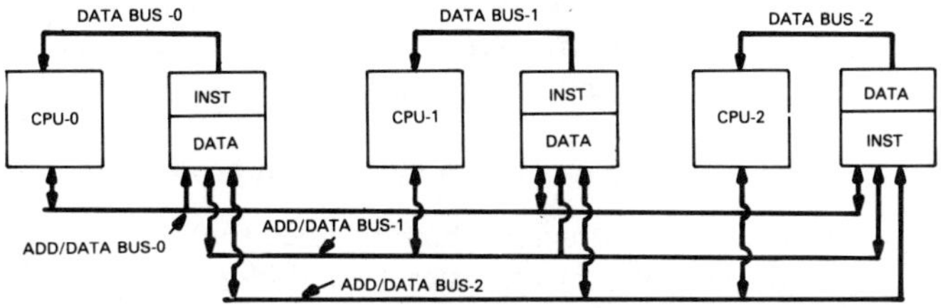
DATA BUS -0
DATA BUS-1
DATA BUS -2
CPU-0
INST
DATA
CPU-1
INST
DATA
CPU-2
DATA
INST
ADD/DATA BUS-0
ADD/DATA BUS-1
ADD/DATA BUS-2

(c)

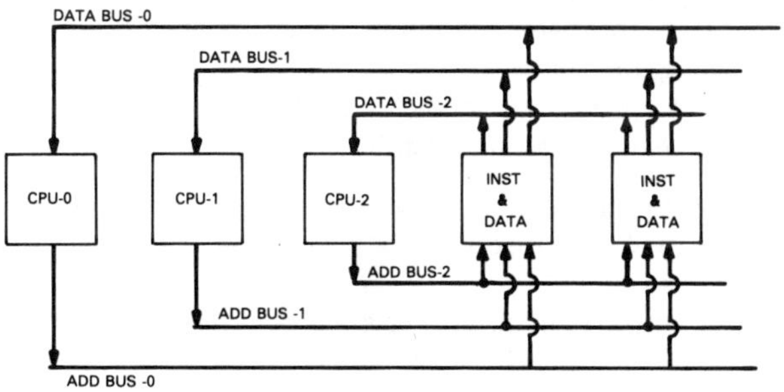
DATA BUS -0
DATA BUS-1
DATA BUS -2
CPU-0
CPU-1
CPU-2
INST & DATA
INST & DATA
ADD BUS-2
ADD BUS -1
ADD BUS -0

(d)

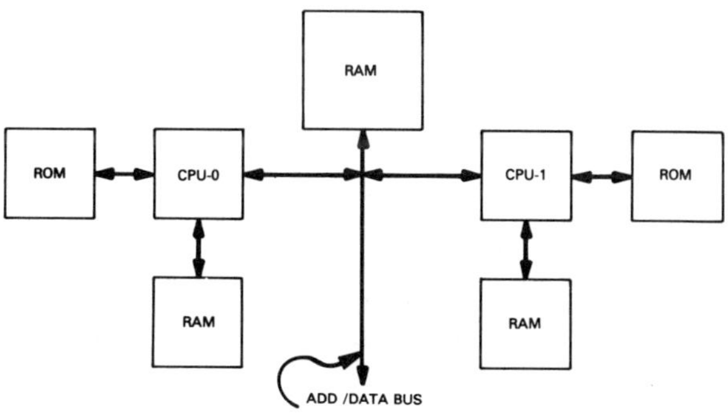
RAM
ROM
CPU-0
CPU-1
ROM
RAM
RAM
ADD /DATA BUS

(e)

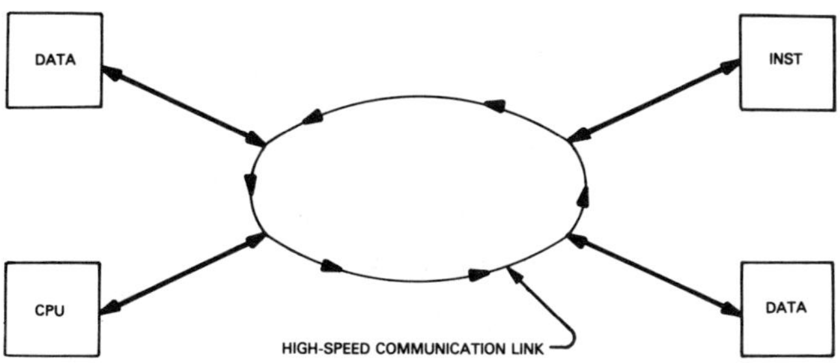
DATA
INST
CPU
DATA
HIGH-SPEED COMMUNICATION LINK

Convert the above structure into a strict Harvard machine structure using the serial communication link concept.

6. Busing structures may be separated into two main categories: the *dedicated* bus structure and the *nondedicated* bus structure. A dedicated bus may be *physically dedicated*, *functionally dedicated*, or both. Similarly, a nondedicated bus may be physically nondedicated but functionally dedicated *or* both physically and functionally nondedicated.
   (a) List the advantages and disadvantages of a physically dedicated bus structure. Give an example of how this has been used at the microprocessor level.
   (b) Contrast the functionally dedicated bus with the physically dedicated bus.
   (c) Describe the features of a busing structure that is both physically and functionally dedicated. Is such a structure typically encountered at the mini/microcomputer level of machine design?
   (d) List the advantages and disadvantages of a nondedicated bus structure.

7. (a) How has the *reliability* of busing structures been handled traditionally?
   (b) Is parity checking at the end of a bus transfer a good idea? Should this be used in conjunction with bus replication?
   (c) Is *replication* a reasonable approach to obtain reliability in a machine that uses physically dedicated busing structures?
   (d) Describe a cost-effective, replicated, nondedicated busing arrangement that could be used to speed up concurrent I/O transactions.

8. (a) What are the advantages and disadvantages of the following bus control schemes?
      i. A *centralized* bus control structure using a *fixed-hardware priority* bus request scheme.
      ii. A *decentralized* bus control structure using a *fixed-hardware priority* bus request scheme.
      iii. A *decentralized* bus control structure using a *dynamic priority* bus request scheme.
   (b) How is the priority of bus requests administered in each of the preceding cases?
   (c) Which of these bus control techniques is:
      i. The simplest in terms of hardware implementation?
      ii. The fastest?
      iii. The least expensive?
      iv. The most reliable?

9. Bus *timing* conventions are physical procedures that are used between a source device acting as a *transmitter* and a destination device acting as a *receiver*. These timing conventions represent physical conditions that must occur to transfer information on the bus between the transmitter and the receiver.
   (a) Describe the *synchronous bus* communication technique.
   (b) Contrast the previous technique with the *asynchronous bus* communication method.
   (c) What factor(s) determine the choice of a bus communication method?

10. For each of the following *bus control schemes* [21] describe (a) how the control mechanism functions, (b) the major advantages of the control scheme, and (c) its most significant weakness. In addition, you are to address the question of how the *reliability* of each bus control scheme may be improved. Suggest a simple, low-cost modification to the bus control scheme for each case—if at all possible—that improves reliability.

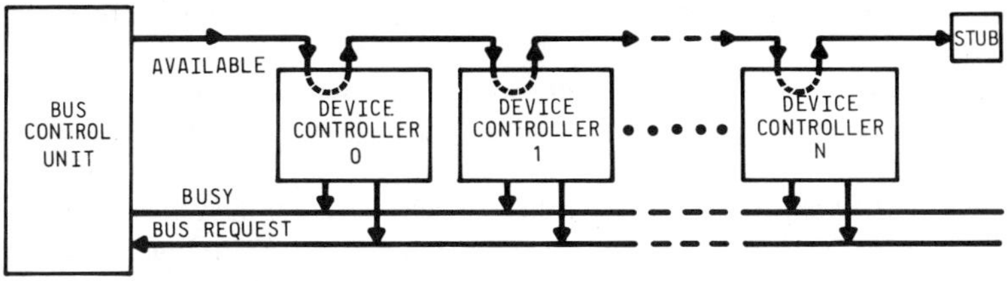

P3-10(a) Daisy-chained centralized bus control

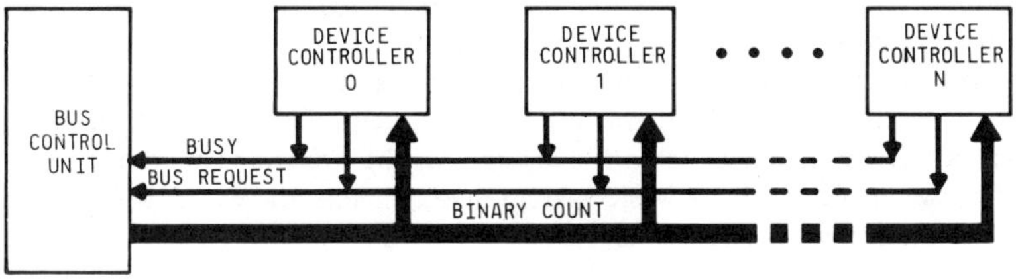

P3-10(b) Polled centralized bus control

Is it possible to do away with the BUS REQUEST line using the approach shown in the above figure. If so, how is priority established?

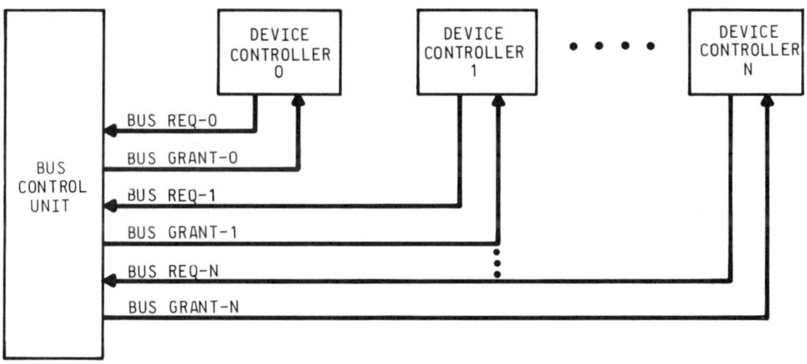

P3-10(c) Independent centralized bus control

11. The most significant advantage of the *unified bus* is the ease with which modules may be added to the system. The modules are simply plugged directly into the bus (where they pick up all the necessary communication signals to dialogue with the processor). As was mentioned in this chapter, it is characteristic of the unified bus that the internal registers associated with each I/O device are treated as though they were *addressable locations in main storage*.
    (a) Consider a machine built around a unified bus with a maximum addressing range of 65,536 bytes. Assume that 2048 main storage addresses have been reserved for I/O device registers.

i. How many bytes of physical main storage may actually be referenced by the processor?

ii. If memory modules are normally sold in 8K byte increments, what is done with the area of main storage that would be accessed by the 2048 dedicated unified-bus addresses?

(b) What *practical* approach may be taken to relieve the unified bus of the condition in which the request/response loop has opened and caused the bus to "hang" because an acknowledge signal is not returned during a bus dialogue?

(c) List the major features of the unified bus.

12. The development of microprocessor peripheral chips has closely followed the philosophy of *mainframe options* developed by the minicomputer manufacturers. Mainframe options are functional modules that are implemented on individual circuit cards. Each of the circuit cards are functionally independent; their insertion or removal in the mainframe does *not* disturb the overall operation of the system. Since these functional modules represent an array of hardware options that can be appended to the mainframe, they allow the user to start with a basic system arrangement and tailor the configuration to meet the application requirements.

In many minicomputers the front panel is treated as a user option. Describe how a digital system would be used for each of the following front panel options:

(a) *No* front panel exists. A key-operated on/off switch is provided to apply primary power to the mainframe.

(b) A *limited* front panel exists. A display register(s) is provided along with the key-operated on/off switch.

(c) A *complete* front panel exists. A key-operated on/off switch is provided as well as all necessary display registers and the facility to (i) halt the processor, (ii) manually examine all of main storage or the working register set, (iii) manually change the content of any location in main storage or the working register set, and (iv) manually force program execution to begin at any location in main storage.

(d) How would program debugging be done in each of the previous front panel option cases?

(e) Is there any advantage to having a front panel located remotely (several miles away) from the processor? How would such front panel operations be controlled?

4

The Organization of Memory

4.1 THE ADMINISTRATION OF INTERNAL STORAGE

4.1.1 A Hierarchy of Storage Facilities

The CPU is composed of semiconductor logic gates with response times measured in nanoseconds. Main storage is made up of either semiconductor memory modules with typical response times in excess of 100 nanoseconds or magnetic core modules with typical response times of one to several microseconds. The great difference between the real-time response characteristics of the CPU and its associated main memory represents a degradation in the potential processing capability of the CPU. In effect, the CPU must constantly wait for the response from main storage when any main memory access takes place before it can proceed to the next processing step. To more closely match the processing capability of the CPU with the response time of the available memory technology, a structured organization of storage facilities has evolved. This organization can be broken down into four categories. Each category may be distinguished by its speed of response, the technology employed to implement the devices found within the category, and the complexity of the control environment required by the associated devices. In essence, these categories form a hierarchy of storage facilities that may *all* exist on a particular computing system. Each category is distinguished by the response time of the memory device found within it.

In general, memory facilities associated with a computing environment may be classified into the following four categories:

1. The first category, represented by very high speed internal storage devices, might contain the working register set and a cache-type memory structure. Specific functions performed by members of this memory group include temporary storage of data and instructions and the intermediate results of calculations. To optimize their speed of response, these memories are usually made from semiconductor devices.
2. The second category is represented by the main internal memory of the processor. These memories may be made from either semiconductor devices or magnetic core modules. Typically, such memories will have cycle times ranging from 650 nanoseconds to 2 microseconds. The main internal memory is used to store the data and instructions of the currently executing program.
3. The third category, represented by on-line mass storage devices, usually includes electromechanical devices (e.g., a magnetic tape unit or magnetic disk storage). These mass storage devices are used for storing large files of programs and data that normally do not have to be resident in main storage. Speed of access is of less importance than the capability to store large amounts of data.
4. The fourth category is represented by off-line bulk storage devices. Typically, such devices are used to store extremely large data files that are accessed very infrequently. The frequency of use is so low that manual intervention is required to load the storage media on the appropriate system device before the required data may be referenced by a program. Magnetic tape, cartridge disk packs, punched cards, and paper tape fall into this category.

It is a characteristic of a device in this memory hierarchy that *its speed of response is inversely related to the complexity of its implementation*. In addition, *the capacity of the device varies inversely with the speed of its response*. For example, the working register set has the fastest response time of any memory element and is implemented using straightforward logical gating circuits and electronic gating paths. In contrast, a magnetic tape unit can store millions of bits of data on a single reel of tape. However, the tape must be retrieved from off-line storage and mounted on the tape drive, and the system must then be alerted that the appropriate reel has been loaded. Also, the magnetic tape system consists of a controller and one or more tape drives; each is usually housed in a separate enclosure, making the overall system highly complex.

In general, a memory device may be represented by the timing diagram shown in Figure 4-1. A read or write operation involving the memory device begins with an initiation signal from the processor. The time interval between the original appearance of the initiation signal and when the desired datum's address has been located is called the *latency* of the device. The time required to perform the indicated read or write operation after the latency period is called the *data transfer time*. The combination of the latency interval plus the data transfer time is referred to as the *access time* of the device. The access time may also be thought of as the time interval between the appearance of the memory-initiate signal and the completion of the desired memory operation. The *recovery time* is the period required by the memory device to restore

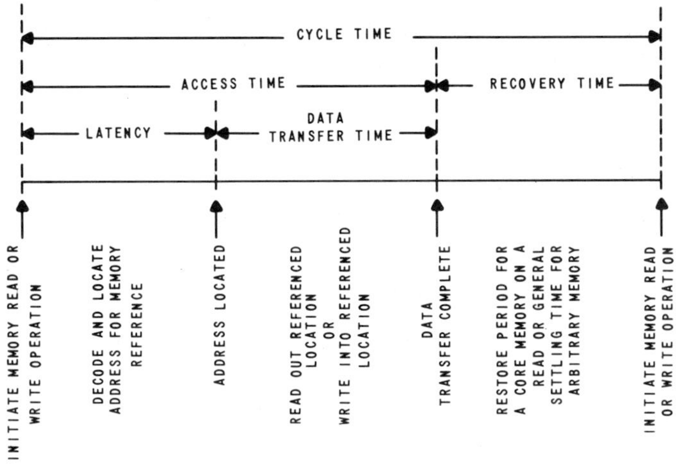

4-1 Terminology used in a general memory reference

itself to a stable internal state such that the next memory reference may be performed in a reliable manner. For a core memory device this is equivalent to the write-back or data-regeneration period required after a memory word is read. Finally, the *cycle time* of the memory device is the time required to perform two consecutive memory references. *Cycle time*, by this definition, is a composite of the memory device's access time and recovery time. It has become customary to partition storage into successively smaller quantities, each of which may be referenced individually by a sophisticated CPU. These quantities, which have become closely associated with the terminology of the IBM System/360 and System/370 machines, are illustrated for a 32-bit full word in Figure 4-2. The classifications of these successively smaller items of information are given by:

1. A full word (32 bits).
2. A half-word (16 bits).
3. A byte (8 bits).
4. A nibble (4 bits).
5. A bit.

A *random-access memory* (*RAM*) is a device in which data may be written into storage or obtained from storage at any location. The time required to access an address is the same for all addresses in the storage device. For instance, a ROM that would normally be placed in category 2 of the processor memory structure is also a RAM. At the microprocessor level, it became convenient to abbreviate the name for dynamic internal storage from a random-access read/write memory to simply a RAM. If there is some question as to the type of internal storage actually being used, the term *R/W memory* will be used to distinguish a dynamically alterable random-access memory from a read-only RAM.

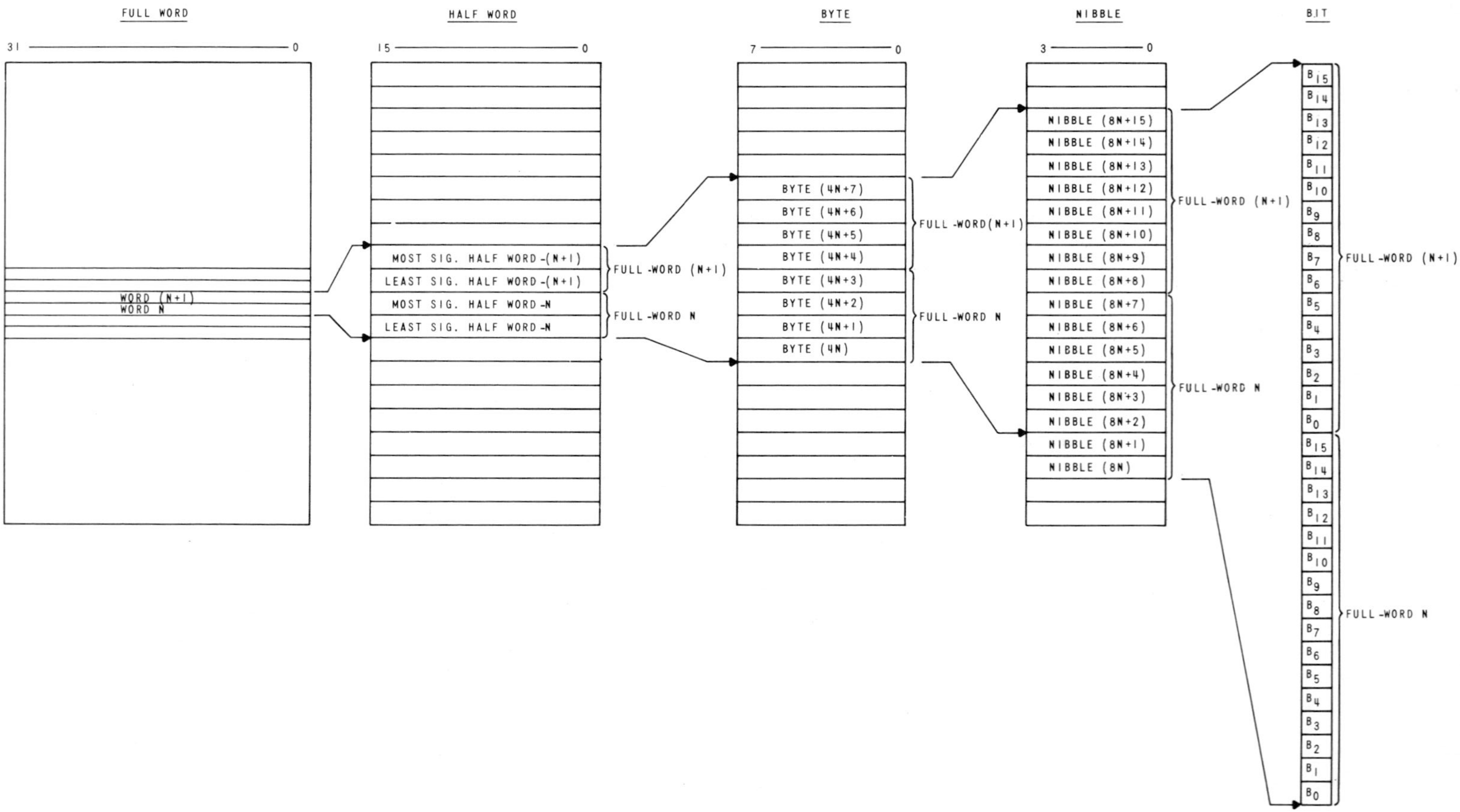

4-2 Levels of memory reference in main storage

4.1.2 Overlapped Memory Operations

One of the prime reasons for processor idle time has been the RESTORE phase required after each read of a location in core memory. During this phase, the early core-based machines entered a WAIT state until the next sequence in the instruction cycle could be entered. During this state, the data word read from a particular core location was written back into that location. Figure 4-3 illustrates the individual operations that are required in a full machine instruction cycle. In the FETCH phase, the instruction word that was read out is restored in the core location just addressed by the processor. Similarly, in the EXECUTE phase, the operand obtained from the data memory is restored to the location from which it was just read. Both of these restoration phases cost execution time if the processor is unable to perform useful work.

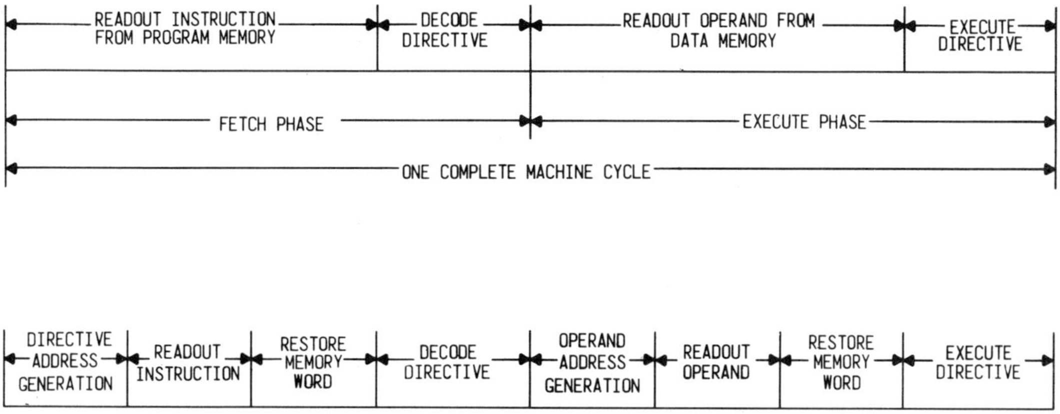

4-3 Memory operations associated with a full machine cycle

As an example, assume that main memory has been implemented using two separate storage modules, as shown in Figure 4-4. These modules are also called *memory banks* or *memory fields*. Imagine that each module has been assigned its own *memory data register* (*MDR*). The even addresses for this structure have been placed in module 0, and odd addresses have been placed in module 1. It is now possible to let module 1 begin a memory operation during the RESTORE phase of module 0. This form of memory operation is referred to as *overlapping* and the storage configuration is called *two-way memory interleaving*. By employing two interleaved memory modules, the effective readout time of successive memory references can be significantly improved. For consecutive reads, this technique doubles the memory-transfer rate. The basic advantage of interleaving is the apparent speed enhancement obtained for a RAM.

It is possible to extend the interleaving concept to 8-way, 16-way, and larger configurations. Figure 4-5 illustrates an 8-way interleaving structure. In this configuration, the CPU can obtain information from eight consecutive data words concurrently.

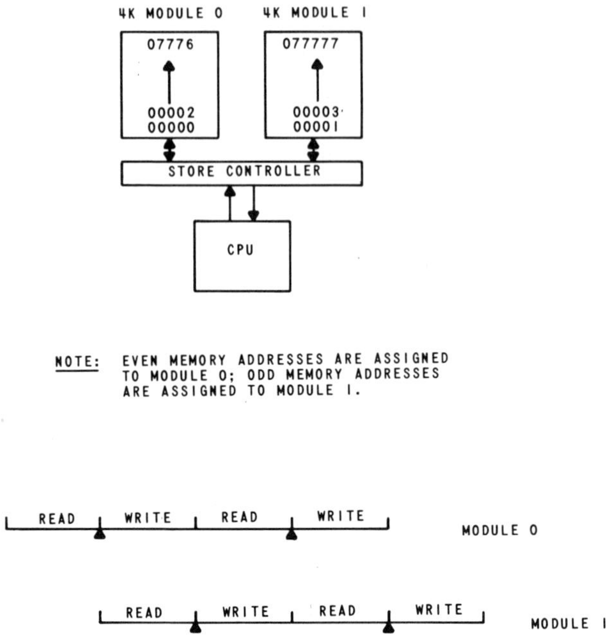

4-4 Two-way interleaved memory operation exhibiting overlapping

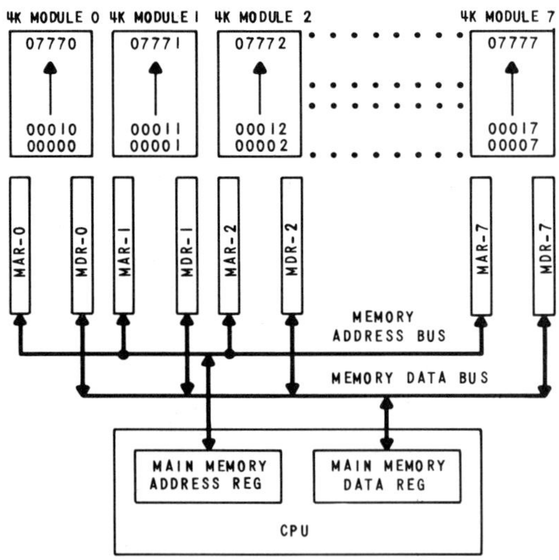

4-5 Eight-way interleaved memory configuration

Each unique MDR acts as a private buffer for its associated memory module. The contents of each buffer will be transferred back to the main data register of the main store controller (MSC) at a time determined by the sequencing logic of the CPU. The determining factor of this arrangement's effectiveness is the difference between the basic CPU clock period and the time at which information becomes available in each memory module after the module has been accessed by the central processor. The larger this difference is, the greater the number of CPU operations that can be performed per individual memory reference.

Interleaving, in its most general sense, does not have to be done exclusively with core memories, where advantage is taken of the RESTORE phase in each memory reference. Interleaving may also be accomplished using semiconductor memories. However, the advantage gained from such a structure will depend on the occupancy of the single store bus between the MSC and the individual storage units. The MSC will initiate memory operations in those units that contain addresses needed by the CPU for reference in the currently executing program. If those units are busy, the MSC will be forced to wait in its *consecutive address generation process* until it can initiate a new transaction with the presently occupied unit.

The primary requirements for effective overlapped memory operations are:

1. A reasonable difference between the basic clock interval of the CPU and the access time of an individual memory module.
2. The ability of the central processor to request a block of information stored in consecutive memory locations.
3. The ability of the CPU to initiate the operations to obtain this block of information concurrently from each of the separate memory modules.

The basic drawback of interleaving is the availability of the system under a fault condition that invalidates a memory module. If a module experiences a fault that causes it to fail totally, those storage locations associated with that module are lost. Unfortunately, a reconfiguration of the system's main memory arrangement is not normally possible because of the distribution of memory addresses over multiple storage modules. For the small computer, this means that all of main storage can be lost until the faulty module is identified and replaced.

4.1.3 The Working Register Set

The early minicomputers were organized around a small number of *special-purpose registers*. These included the *instruction register* (*IR*), the *memory address register* (*MAR*), and the *program counter* (*PC*). In addition, one or more other registers were provided that could be associated with a specific register operation other than those just mentioned. These registers could normally be placed in one of three types: an *accumulator*, an *index register*, or a *base register*. A typical early minicomputer might have used one or two accumulators, with index registers placed at dedicated locations in main memory. An indirect memory reference through one of these locations was required to implement the indexing function. In several instances, the accumulator was also incorporated as a part of main storage. The reason for limiting the number of hardware registers or incorporating their features into main memory was based on simple economics. Because hardware was expensive, serious cost trade-offs had to be considered in terms of the machine's complexity in order to produce a viable market item. Core registers, on the other hand, were immediately available as a part of main storage.

The remarkable development of integrated circuit (IC) technology in the late 1960's completely altered these cost considerations. Hardware became an inexpensive item relative to the overall implementation. The hardware register set became a low-cost feature that could be included in a minicomputer design. Similarly, the evolution of microprocessors permitted this feature to be added at the MOS/LSI chip level by the mid-1970's. These hardware registers provided a faster, more efficient addressing environment since they functioned as accumulators, index registers, and base registers. With a slight increase in control logic and some additional cost, a hardware register could be used to perform all three of the previous register operations. As a result, a portion of the hardware register set evolved from being a collection of special-purpose registers into a group of independent, general-purpose registers directly addressable by a programmer. Such a register set is called a *general-purpose register* (*GPR*) set. A set of 8 to 16 general registers, also referred to as *file registers* (see Section 4.2), may be provided as part of the processor. For these machines, which include a register file, the selection of one register from the file must be explicitly indicated by the instruction.

The major significance of a hardware register set lies in the faster access time that the processor can achieve for operands when they are placed in the GPR set. This leads to a faster execution time for a program since the GPR's are not part of main storage and do not incur the cycle-time delay associated with a core memory. The use of GPR's to facilitate operand fetching provides a mode of memory referencing called *general register addressing*. The GPR set acts as a high-speed buffer memory between the CPU and main storage. Memory references are designed with such a structure so that the majority of operands will be found in the GPR set rather than in main storage. By skillful programming, it is possible for the average access time of an operand to closely approximate the access time of the GPR set. When used in this fashion, the GPR set is also referred to as a *scratch pad memory*. Consequently, a scratch pad memory is a high-speed storage array that is much smaller than the main storage facility and serves as a temporary work space for the programmer. Using the general-register addressing concept, a scratch pad may also be regarded as a front end to main storage in which all memory references are administered. Figure 4-6 illustrates this view of the scratch pad memory concept. The GPR set also permits register-to-register operations among its own elements as well as certain special-purpose registers located within the processor. Normally, these register-to-register operations yield a smaller program with a faster execution time than a program written to function exclusively in a core memory environment.

One or more special hardware registers may also be incorporated in a general computer structure to assist the CPU in processing. While special registers such as the

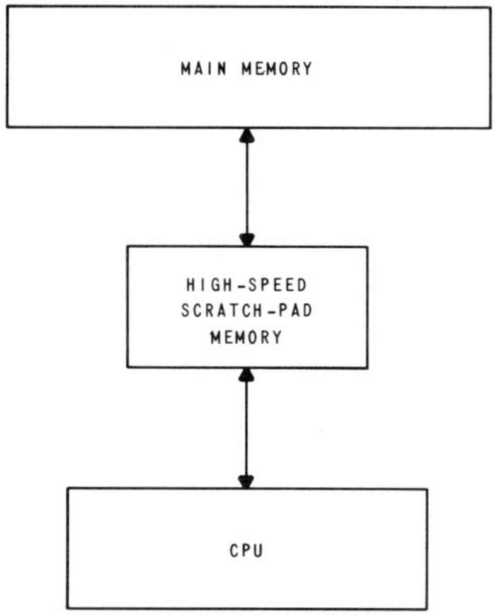

4-6 Scratch pad concept

IR and PC can be manually loaded by the programmer, they are unavailable to the programmer during the execution of a program. Other special registers are manipulated by the control logic during the execution of a machine instruction but appear transparent to the programmer. These registers act as buffers during information transfers within the machine to meet internal timing requirements. The programmer is not aware of the presence of such registers in either a manually initiated instruction or a normal program environment. Such registers will be called *internal buffer registers* to distinguish them from the class of special registers that may be controlled by the programmer. The *working register set* will be defined as the group of registers directly accessible by the programmer. By this definition, the working register set consists of both the GPR set and those special registers that may be controlled by the programmer. The terms *working register set* and *general-purpose register set* are often used interchangeably in the literature of the small computer field. Strictly speaking, they are not equivalent, and the use of these terms in future discussions will strictly observe the previous definition.

In addition to ease of programming, registers are also provided to facilitate sequencing and control of the instruction. In the case of microprogrammed control, these registers are for the convenience of microprogramming. By providing several of these registers, the more complicated microprogram sequence may be shortened, reducing the number of microprogram memory words and at the same time speeding up the execution time. The main instruction has no linkage with these hardware registers, which are used mainly by the microprogram sequence. This means that the microinstruction format must include the appropriate fields to control the data flow of these registers in addition to the general registers. Rather than having a separate field in the microinstruction for each register, a more efficient arrangement is to com-

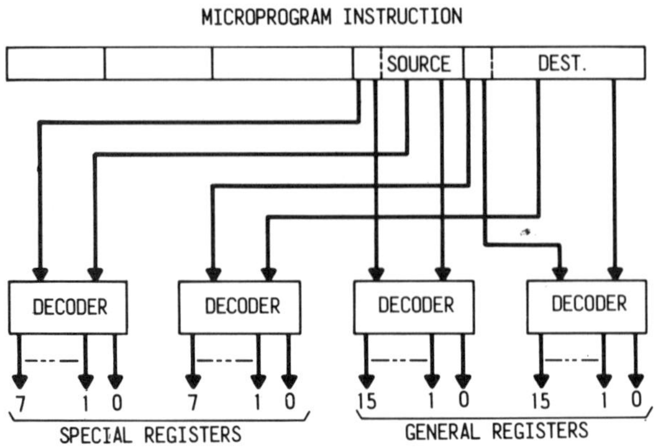

4-7 Data transfer control

bine them, as shown in Figure 4-7. Assume that there are 16 general registers for the main program and eight for the microprogram. The operand field that specifies the general register requires only 4 bits in the instruction format. On the other hand, the microinstruction must be capable of selecting 1 bit out of a possible 24. In this situation, 5 bits are required by the microinstruction rather than the 4 bits used by the main instruction. As indicated in the figure, the fifth bit in the microinstruction field can be used to identify the group of registers (general or microprogram); the other 4 bits select a specific register in the group.

4.1.4 Special Registers

Special registers found within the CPU are dedicated to specific functions. These functions are normally associated more frequently with hardware operations than software control sequences. Consequently, the storage elements that make up these special registers may be more complex than the simple latch-type flip-flop used to realize the general registers. The special registers, in general, do not lend themselves to being implemented as large-scale integration (LSI) chip structures. This is due to the irregular pattern of control logic signals that govern the behavior of the special registers. Typically, unique inputs are associated with the special registers. In addition, the outputs from these registers are used directly to generate individual logic signals. The outputs may also be tied into the normal busing path, which allows data to flow between the general registers and the special registers. Each of the unique inputs may undergo logic operations such as shifting or binary counting prior to being gated into the destination register(s). The memory output register, memory address register, PC, system status register, and I/O data register are members of the special register set.

The memory data and address registers are functionally dedicated to the main memory, as shown in Figure 4-8. As a result, the output control signals from each register go directly to the memory. Since the output register is usually used for writing

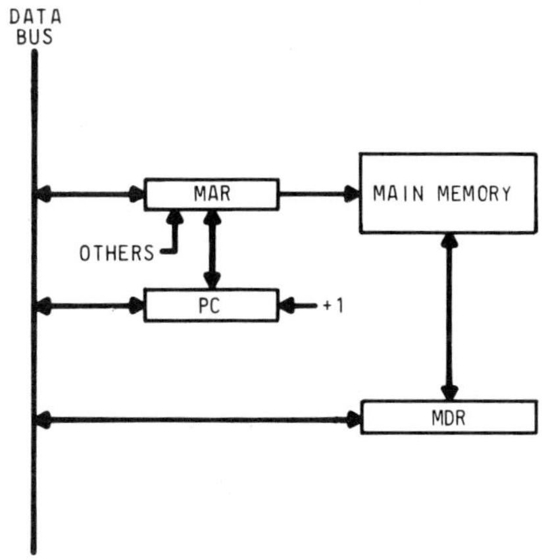

4-8 Registers associated with main memory

into the memory, the data for the memory data output register (MDR) is obtained by means of the processor's internal bus. Similarly, the *memory address register* (MAR) may obtain its data directly from either the PC for sequential addressing or via the processor's internal bus for branch or data addressing. Other direct inputs may be connected to the MAR, such as the switch inputs from the control panel. Consequently, other inputs may be directed to these functional registers in addition to signals from the processor's internal bus.

The PC is characterized by the requirement of additional logic to perform binary counting. The counting logic may be incorporated as a part of the storage element. Again, the PC is connected to the bus to allow *information flow* to and from other registers. In the case of an interrupt, the PC is gated by means of the processor's internal bus to the memory data register to be stored in memory. Upon completion of the interrupt, the contents of the PC are restored from memory by means of the previous busing path.

4.2 REGISTER FILE ORGANIZATION

4.2.1 Read/Write Register Array

The 4 × 4 register array shown in Figure 4-9 provides the basic building block from which a set of general registers can be constructed in multiple blocks of four words. This functional array possesses independent access capability that permits a word to be read from any one of the four registers in the array and to be written simultaneously into any one of the array registers. It is possible to read and write different data into the same register word if the storage elements are the RS master–slave type.

This arrangement allows data to be read out, modified, and written back into the same memory location. However, for increased LSI packing density, the storage element normally used to build a register array is the simple RS-latch type. Using this implementation, it is not possible to simultaneously read and write different data into the same register. This operation, using RS-latch type flip-flops, requires two steps. The data word must be read from the desired location and then modified during the first step. The modified data word is then written back into the original location during the second step.

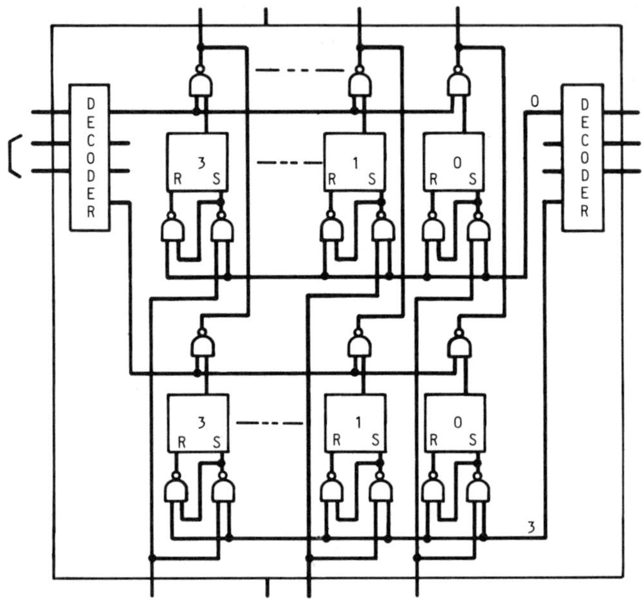

4-9 4 × 4 array

The building block is the 4-bit by 4-bit circuit shown schematically in Figures 4-9 and 4-10a. A general register set of 16 words, each 16 bits wide, can be configured as shown in Figure 4-10b. Two address fields of 4 bits each are required to select two of the 16 registers: one for writing and one for reading. These two fields represent the source and the destination of the data if the transfer takes place within the set of general registers. The two signals that control the input and output enable the operations of reading and writing to be performed independently so that either one or both can be active simultaneously. Also, if neither operation is enabled, no action will be performed. The 4-bit address field, as indicated in Figure 4-10b, is divided into two groups of 2 bits each. The low-order 2 bits go directly to the circuit chip to select one of the four words. The high-order 2 bits are decoded into a control signal in which only one out of the four outputs is active and enabled by the respective input or

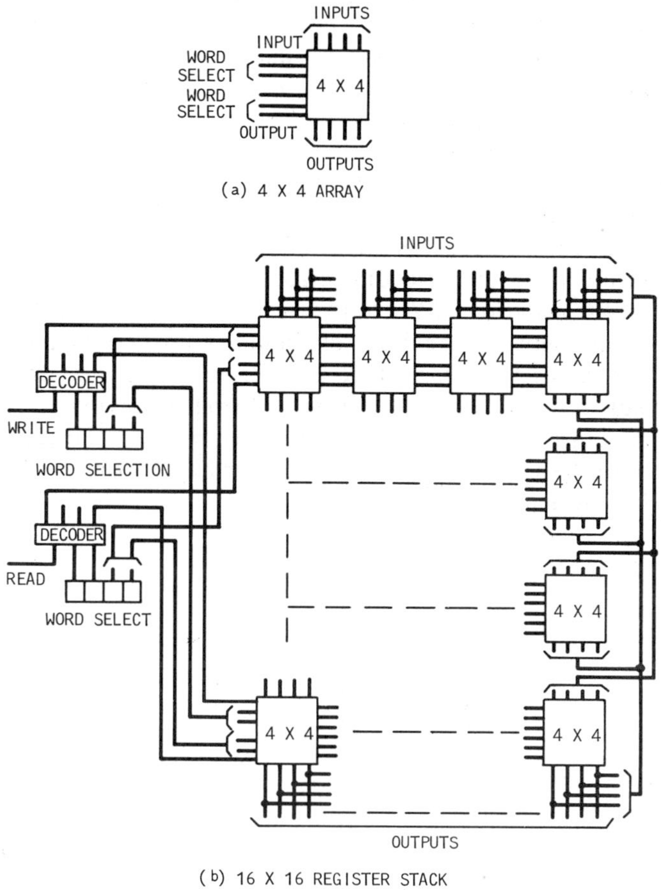

4-10 16 × 16 register stack using 4 × 4 bit circuit

output control signal. These outputs are used to select the circuit chip and initiate the read or write function. Other register array sizes can be configured by providing the proper addressing and decoding fields.

4.2.2 Single-Access Register Array

The 4 × 4 register array has been designed to facilitate logic implementation of the data transfer circuitry. A set of input gates and output gates is provided for each word. Simultaneous access is permitted to both sets of gates. If the input and output access capability is eliminated and only reading or writing at any given time is allowed, the two 2-bit address fields can be combined into a single 4-bit field. This 4-bit field can be used to address all 16 words of the register array. The number of terminals required by this configuration remains the same as that used by the 4 × 4 register array. The scale of integration, however, increases from a 16-bit data register to a 64-bit memory module. The commercially available 16 × 4 register file produced by Texas Instruments (as device *SN7489 TI*) is shown functionally in Figure 4-11 and in more detail in Figure 4-12. The ENABLE lead provides the control signal to initiate either the read or write operation specified by the R/W function lead. The 4-bit address specifies one of the 16 words in the register file. With this as the basic building block, a set of 16 × 16 general register files may be realized by simply interconnecting four 16 × 4 register arrays to a common set of address and control leads (see Figure 4-13). This avoids any additional decoding associated with the previous arrangement, which uses a 4 × 4 register array. While it is a simple matter to build large register files using this arrangement, the capability of simultaneously reading and writing data into the file is sacrificed. Data cannot be transferred within the set of words in a single step. Instead, any data transfer must be accomplished in two steps: (1) the outputs must be temporarily stored in an output buffer register, and (2) the data must then be written into the selected word in the register file. This method is the same as that used to write into main storage.

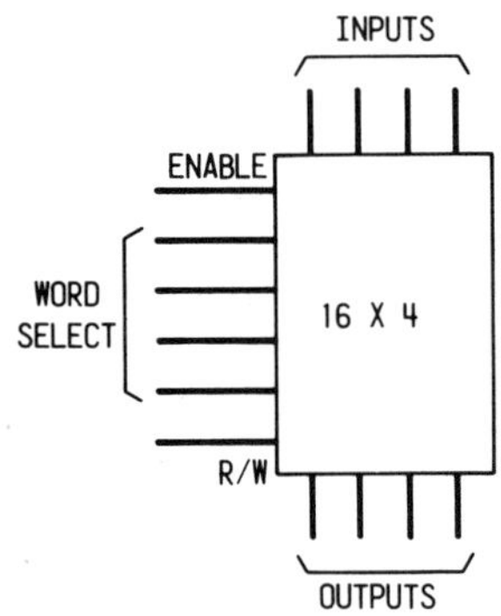

4-11 16 × 4 register file: functional diagram

4.2.3 Dual-Port Access RAM

As described in Section 3.4.4, a three-bus structure permits two operands to be added together and the resulting sum to be directed to a specified destination register as a single, concurrent machine operation. This type of bus arrangement facilitates single-step arithmetic operations which result in a higher instruction-execution rate, on the average, than a single-bus structure. A dual-port access RAM (AMD29705) available in 1977 could be used to implement the general registers arranged in a three-bus structure.

Figure 4-14 shows the functional logic diagram of the AMD29705, a 16-word by 4-bit two-port RAM. The circuit provides two independent output ports. The 4-bit *A* address field selects any one of the 16 words to be read out on one port. Similarly, the

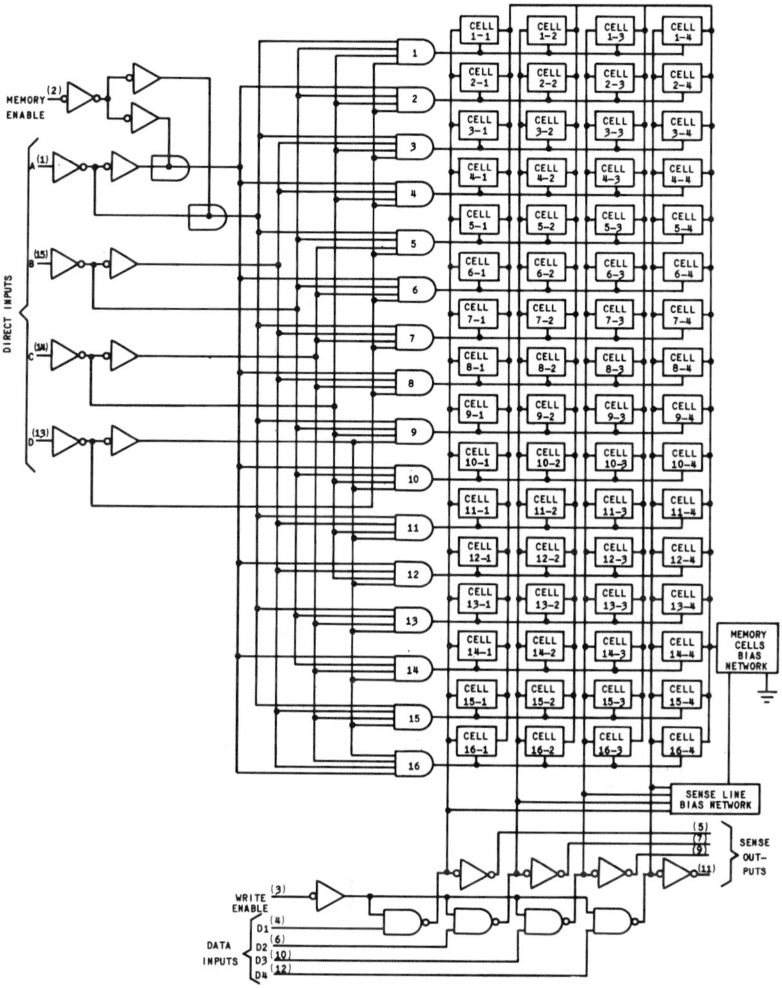

4-12 16 × 4 register file: detailed diagram

B address field selects any one of the 16 words to be read out on the second port. The two address fields permit any two 4-bit words to be read from the RAM simultaneously. The RAM outputs are latched in flip-flops under control of a common latch-enable (LE) signal lead. The device has two write-enable $\overline{(WE)}$ inputs. Wiring together the write-enable 1 $\overline{(WE1)}$ and the latch-enable (LE) leads gives the apparent effect of edge-triggered flip-flop operation. The bar on top of $\overline{WE1}$ and $\overline{WE2}$, as indicated in Figure 4-14, implies that ground potential is the active signal on these leads. When both $\overline{WE1}$ and $\overline{WE2}$ are at ground, the data appearing on the D0 to D3 leads will be written into the word addressed by the *B* field. The LE signal, on the other hand, is active in latching the RAM outputs when the LE signal is held at high potential. Using the same signal to control the latch and the write operation ensures that both

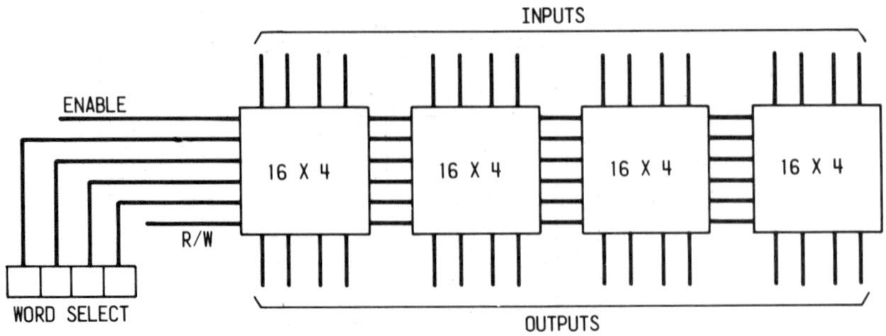

4-13 16 × 16 register stack using a 16- × 4-bit circuit

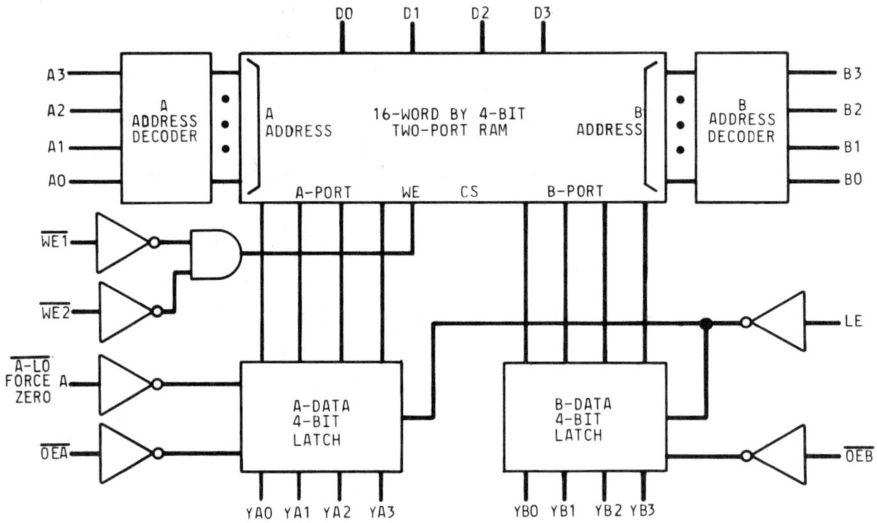

4-14 16-word by 4-bit two-port RAM (AMD29705) [Reprinted (adapted) with permission of Advanced Micro Devices Inc.]

operations will not occur at the same time. This allows two operands specified by *A* and *B* to be made available simultaneously to the ALU. The results of the ALU operation can then be written into the word specified by *B* without the possibility of any race condition occurring. The RAM outputs are sensed by tri-state output latches with a separate control for each port $(\overline{OEA}, \overline{OEB})$. The word size of the RAM can be expanded by connecting the corresponding outputs together. Because of the second port, the device requires 28 pins instead of 16 for the standard 16-word by 4-bit RAM.

The two-port RAM used as a set of general registers in a 3-bus type of structure is shown in Figure 4-15. The *A* and *B* signal groups are the source buses which provide the two simultaneous operands to the ALU. The two operands can both come from the general registers or one from the general registers and one from the special registers. The ALU outputs can be directed to any one of the general registers or one of the special registers. As indicated in Figure 4-15, it is also possible to transfer data from the special registers into the general registers by means of the direct gating path shown rather than by using the ALU as the communicating link between the two register groups.

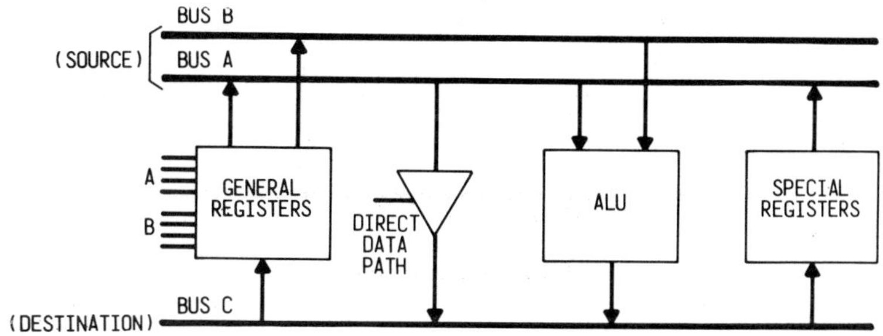

4-15 Three-bus arrangement

4.2.4 Register Banks

As more general registers are used to facilitate the programming capability of the system, the housekeeping chore of storing the register file into memory when an interrupt is serviced and restoring the file after the interrupt has been serviced increases with the number of registers in the file. If the interrupts occur frequently enough, it may be desirable to minimize this overhead by providing multiple register files. Each file would be dedicated to a program-execution level. This is shown in Figure 4-16 with a 64-word RAM divided into four banks of register files. A 2-bit up–down file counter automatically points to the proper bank of file registers as the program goes from one execution level to another. The file counter is incremented upon entry into an interrupt service routine. This directs the program to use the next sequential bank of file registers and leaves the interrupted program intact with its data in the previous bank of file registers. When the interrupt is completed, the interrupt service routine decrements the file counter so that it points to the previous set of file registers. By having multiple banks of file registers, up to four programs can reside within the system without the CPU being required to move the data in the file registers into main storage upon an interrupt. For this example, the system will support four independent sets of file registers: one set for the main program and one set for each of three separate interrupt levels. The lower 4 bits of the RAM address are used to select a specific word in the register file pointed to by the file counter. These bits are under program control.

If the system is restricted to three levels of interrupts and subroutines are prohibited from sharing the register bank or stack facilities, four banks of file registers are adequate to handle all possible program conditions. A better arrangement, however, is to provide adequate hardware stacks to process interrupts and subroutines for

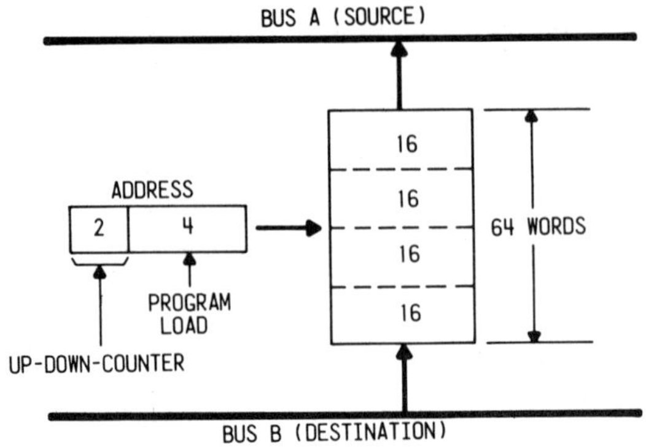

4-16 Register banks

the majority of the situations that may occur, and to have the hardware extend the register files into main memory to take care of infrequent situations. When subroutines are allowed to use the register stack facility, it is often difficult to predict the maximum number of nested subroutines that may be encountered by the system. To accommodate this situation, the address capability of the up–down file counter must be extended to include the register banks in memory. As shown in Figure 4-17, adding 1 more bit to the file counter, to make 3 bits, doubles the addressable number of banks. This extended addressing range permits four register banks to be placed in hardware and four in main storage. As long as there are available hardware registers for the interrupt program, the pointer generated by the file counter automatically points to the right file.

In Figure 4-17a, the main program is interrupted by a level-5 interrupt. When the interrupt service routine is entered, the file counter, which is incremented by 1, points to the second register file. The INT 5 service routine has complete freedom in its usage of this register set, while execution of the MAIN program is halted with all associated data preserved in the first register file. The INT 5 service routine is interrupted by a higher-level interrupt occurring at level four. The file counter is again incremented by 1. It, in turn, points to the next available register file for use by the INT 4 service routine. The INT 5 service routine is suspended, with its associated data saved in the second register file. Now let this same process occur again, with a level-3 interrupt request becoming active. The INT 3 service routine will use the last bank of hardware registers. The file counter will have been incremented to a count of 011. When a level-2 interrupt is recognized by the system, the counter will advance to a count of 100. The interrupt service program will check the third bit of the counter. If it is a 0, as in the case of the first three interrupts, the service program will proceed with processing since the counter points to an idle register file. However, the third bit of the counter will no longer be a 0 but a 1, since the four available hardware register files have all been assigned to lower-priority programs. When the file counter goes to 100, the first 2 bits of the count will wrap around and point again to the first register file. The service program will check to see if the high bit of the file counter is a 1. If it is,

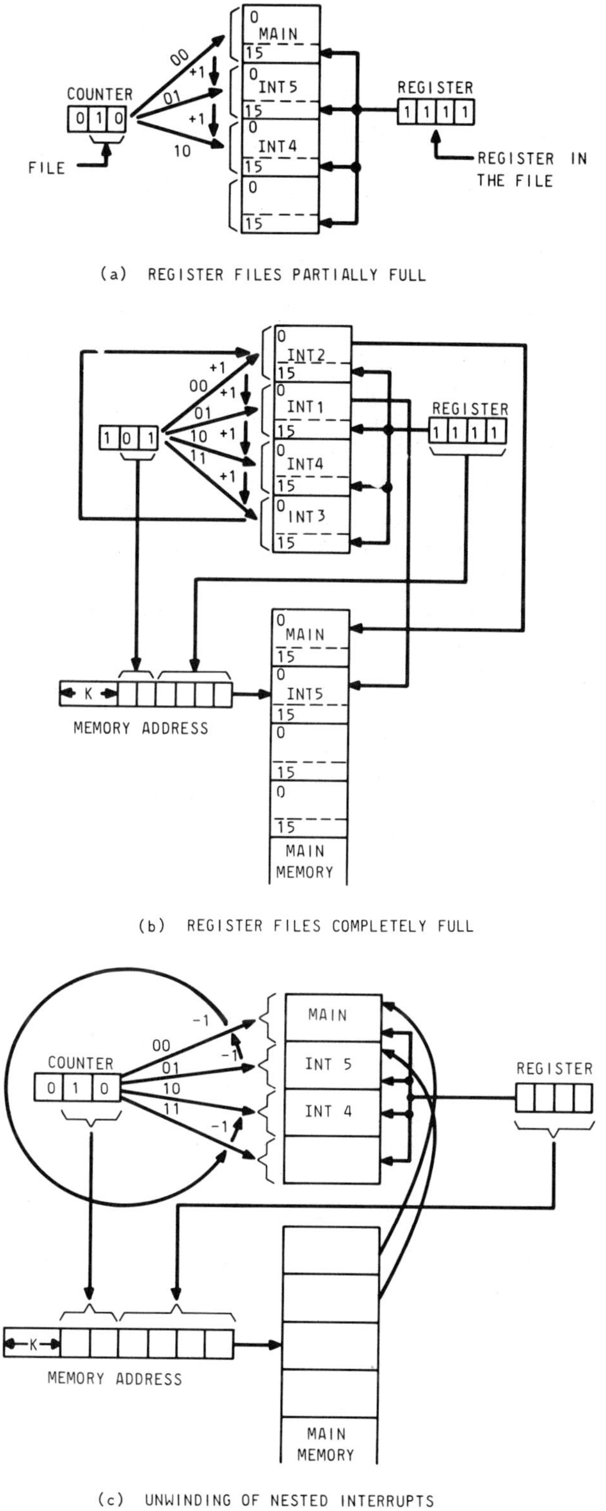

4-17 Multiple register and memory files for nested interrupts

the service program must save the contents of the first file hardware register in main storage. In this example, the first register file is associated with the MAIN program. As shown in Figure 4-17b, a dedicated area in main storage has been assigned specifically to extend the set of register files. Space has been allocated in memory to contain four 16-word register files.

The mapping of the memory address is indicated in Figure 4-17b. The low-order 6 bits of the address are identical to the address for a word in any one of the four files. The first 4 bits of the address select the word in the file. The 2 high-order bits select the specific register file to be used. The remaining high bits of the memory address are assigned a fixed value, depending on the location of the register files in main storage. The high bit of the up–down counter is used by the interrupt service program to determine if the current register file should be saved in main storage. After the content of the first file has been saved in the corresponding file in memory, the INT 2 service program can use the hardware registers for its processing. For example, assume that in executing the INT 2 service program, the highest interrupt, INT 1, occurs. The counter is incremented to a count of 101, pointing the interrupt service program to the second file. Since the high-order bit of the counter is a 1, the program must save the file in its corresponding area in main memory. After that is done, the INT 1 service program can use the second file to process its program. Since the highest-priority interrupt is that associated with the level 1 interrupt, the processor will complete the program without any further interruption. When INT 1 processing is done and the high-order bit of the file counter is a 1, the service program will restore the register file from the corresponding file save area in main storage. Control will then exit the interrupt service program and decrement the file counter to a count of 100. Processing will continue from this point in the interrupted INT 2 service program. Similarly, when processing is completed in the INT 2 program, the same procedure of unwinding the nested interrupt service routines will be observed, as indicated in Figure 4-17c.

It is possible that the combination of nested interrupts and subroutines both using the register stack facilities might exceed the memory space allocated for the register files. If it does, the contents of the file counter wraps around completely on itself and resets the file counter. As a result, the data belonging to the previously interrupted programs are lost. To detect this possibility, 1 more bit can be added to the counter, to inform the system that a file counter overflow has occurred.

4.3 THE PUSHDOWN STACK

4.3.1 Characteristics of a Stack

One of the most powerful features of internal memory referencing at both the micro and the mini level has been the use of a *last-in-first-out* (*LIFO*) *buffer* or *pushdown stack*. The device derives its name from the fact that items may be added to the stack in sequential order and then retrieved from the stack in reverse order. A stack operation implicitly references the operand at the *top of the stack* (*TOS*). If the operation involves the saving of an operand, the item to be saved pushes down each of the other items in the stack one position from their former locations. Consequently, a stack-write operation is called a *push*. In a similar manner, if an item is removed from the stack, it appears as though each item in the entire stack has been moved up one position from its former location. A stack-read operation is referred to as a *pop*. Once an item has been "popped" from the stack, its stack location becomes available for future use. Items are always entered on or withdrawn from the TOS. Because of this characteristic, a stack reference does not require a specific memory address to obtain an operand. By careful programming, the stack can be used as a temporary storage facility with the next item to be referenced always placed at the TOS. Figure 4-18 illustrates the basic administration of a logical stack using push and pop operations. Conceptually, all data enter the logical stack and leave it from the same end. Information appears to successively move down one position on each push operation and up one position on each pop operation. The TOS appears to remain fixed while the entire stack moves down or up as data are loaded onto the stack or removed. Physically, however, it is not practical to implement a stack by moving the entire contents of the stack up or down each time a push or pop operation is performed. Instead, the actual hardware stacks use an up–down counter as a pointer to the TOS. Using this method, the entire stack is never physically moved in memory. Rather, the TOS is moved up or down in memory as the stack pointer is incremented or decremented. Since the stack pointer always points to the TOS, the results of the last stack operation are immediately available to the program without an explicit memory reference.

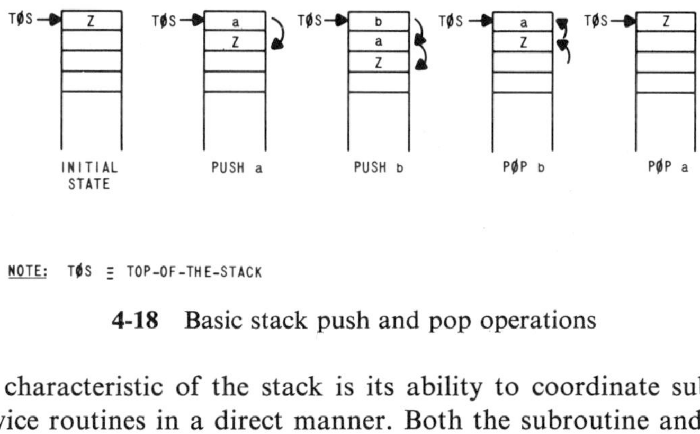

NOTE: TØS ≡ TOP-OF-THE-STACK

4-18 Basic stack push and pop operations

Another characteristic of the stack is its ability to coordinate subroutines and interrupt service routines in a direct manner. Both the subroutine and the interrupt require linkage information to be saved by the machine so that control may be returned to the point from which it was diverted after the interrupt processing is complete. Typically, all the necessary linkage information will be loaded onto the stack automatically when either a subroutine call is executed or an interrupt request is recognized by the processor. In the case of a subroutine, linkage information will be contained in either the PC or in one of the registers in the working register set prior to the execution of the subroutine call. The contents of the linkage register will be pushed onto the

TOS and the PC will be loaded with the starting address of the subroutine. Execution will then proceed from that point. Each successive subroutine call will push the contents of its linkage register onto the TOS until a subroutine return instruction is executed. The subroutine return command will specify which member of the working register set is to be used as the recipient of the linkage information located at the TOS. This command will take the current contents of the designated linkage register and place it in the PC. The contents of the TOS will then be popped and placed in the linkage register. Execution will commence from that point. Using this technique, one subroutine may call another subroutine several levels deep within the executing program, and each return will be made automatically to the proper calling subroutine. The return sequence for the stacked subroutines will be the inverse of the order in which they were called. The process of automatically stacking the return linkage information is referred to as the *nesting of subroutine calls.*

Interrupts are quite similar to subroutine calls in that they both represent transfers of control during program execution. A subroutine call will be encountered as part of the normal program flow generated by the program designer. An interrupt, on the other hand, is a forced break in the execution of a program. The interrupt may be generated by an event occurring internal to the processor, such as memory parity check failure, or by an event produced by the external environment, such as a terminal requesting service by the processor. The interrupt requires that the entire state of the machine prior to the occurrence of the interrupt be preserved so that the interrupted program may be restored without mutilation. The contextual information on the machine state may be kept in a single processor status word (PSW), or it may be retained in the entire working register set of the processor. Figure 4-19 illustrates the nested usage of a stack by combining subroutine calls and processor interrupts. Steps 5, 6, and 7 show the sequence of events that occur during the execution of a subroutine when the call specifies the PC as the linkage register. In this case, the PC's content is pushed onto the TOS, and none of the general registers are disturbed. The associated return instruction for the subroutine must specify the PC as the linkage register also. In this case, the contents of the TOS are moved directly into the PC on the return, and execution is forced to continue from that point. This particular technique is typical of the PDP-11's subroutine servicing operation.

4.3.2 TOS Administration

The administration of a stack in terms of pushing and popping is handled by means of a register called the *stack pointer*, which always points to the TOS. The control of the stack is determined by how the hardware is to interpret the contents of the TOS.* This, in turn, determines when the stack pointer is to be incremented or decremented. The hardware designer must consider these three specific cases:

1. *The contents of the TOS occupy the first free or unoccupied location in the stack.* In this case it is the location into which the next item of data will be pushed.

---

*Private communication from J. E. Sylvester of Bell Laboratories.

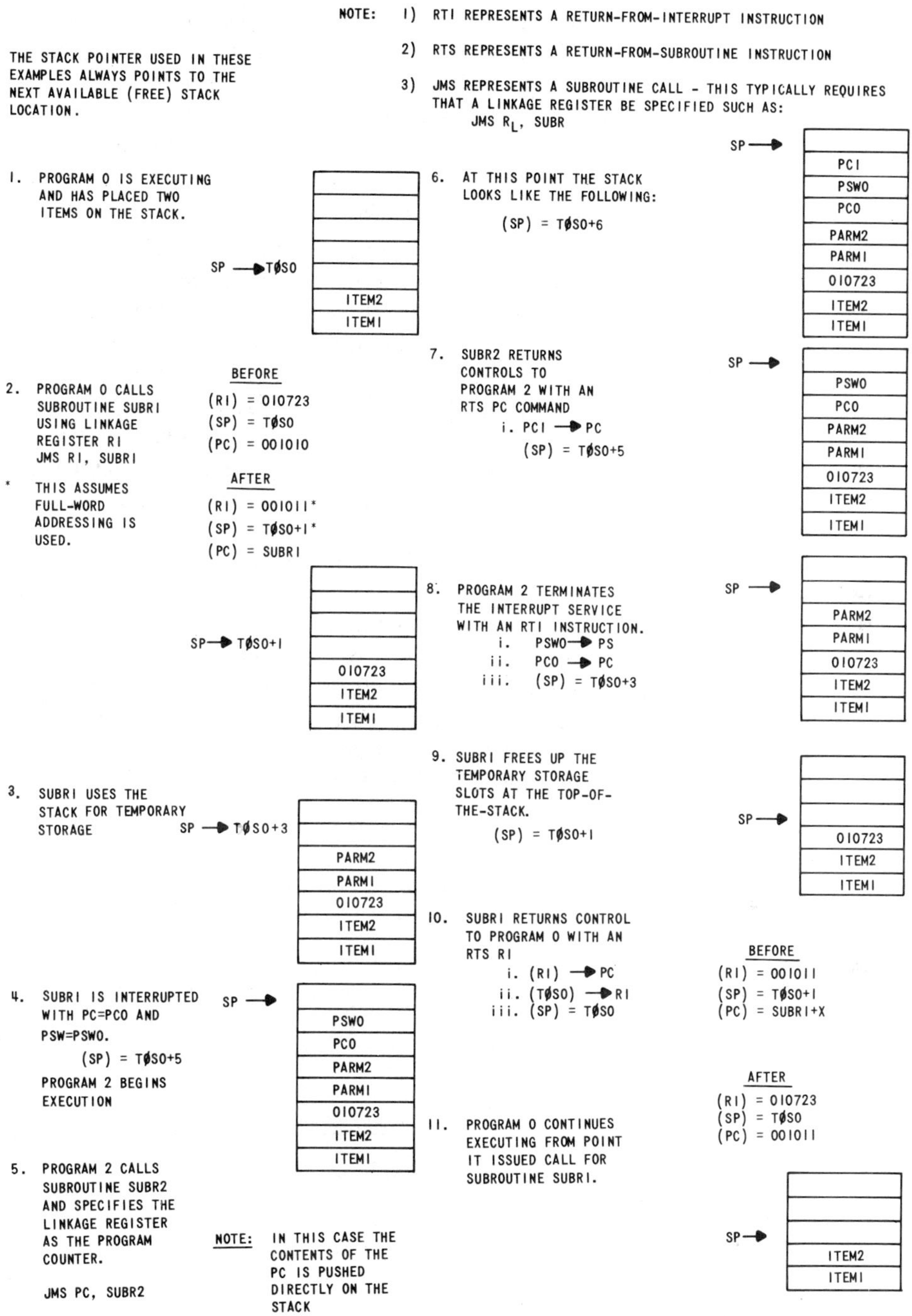

4-19 Nested usage of a stack by a combination of subroutine calls and processor interrupts

2. *The contents of the TOS represent the last item of data placed on the stack.* This data item could represent (a) a constant, (b) the contents of the linkage register for a subroutine call, or (c) the PSW for an interrupted process.
3. *The contents of the TOS are determined by the last operation performed by the stack hardware.* This technique is sometimes called the *time-saver method*, since the stack pointer is administered only when two consecutive operations of the same type are performed on the stack.

In each of the preceding cases, the point of concern is the instant of time when the stack pointer will be incremented or decremented during the control of a stack memory reference. In case 1, data may be pushed immediately onto the stack. The stack pointer will be incremented after the push operation. In contrast, a pop operation requires that the stack pointer first be decremented and the contents of the TOS moved from the stack. Figure 4-20 illustrates the control procedure for case 1. In case 2, data may be popped immediately from the stack. The stack pointer will be decremented after the pop operation. However, a push operation requires that the stack pointer first be incremented and the item of data placed on the stack. Note that case 2 is simply the complement of case 1 in terms of the sequence of operations. Figure 4-21 illustrates the control procedure for case 2. In case 3, the stack control logic is required to remember whether its last operation was a push or a pop. If the last operation was a push, the TOS contains the most recent item of data available on the stack. Consequently, if the next operation is a pop, data may be obtained immediately from the TOS and the content of the stack pointer will be left unchanged. However, if the next operation is a push, the stack pointer must first be incremented by 1 before the data item may be placed on the stack. The inverse situation holds if the last operation was a pop. In this case, if the next operation is a push, data may be added immediately to

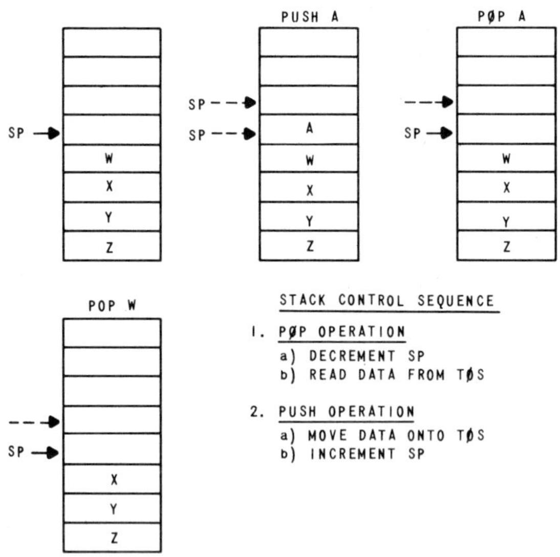

4-20 TOS is the first unoccupied location in the stack

the TOS and the content of the stack pointer will be left unchanged. However, if the next operation is a pop, the stack pointer must first be decremented before the data item may be removed from the stack. Case 3 takes the best features of both case 1 and case 2. However, control implementation is more complicated than in the previous two cases because of the need for the stack hardware to remember whether the last operation was a push or a pop. Figure 4-22 illustrates the control procedure for case 3.

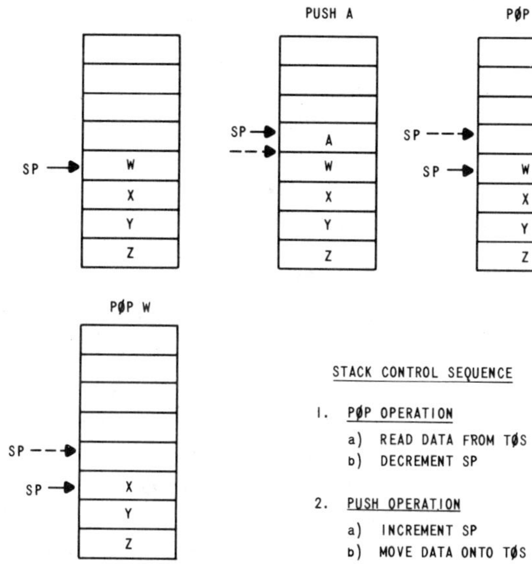

4-21 TOS is the last item of data placed on the stack

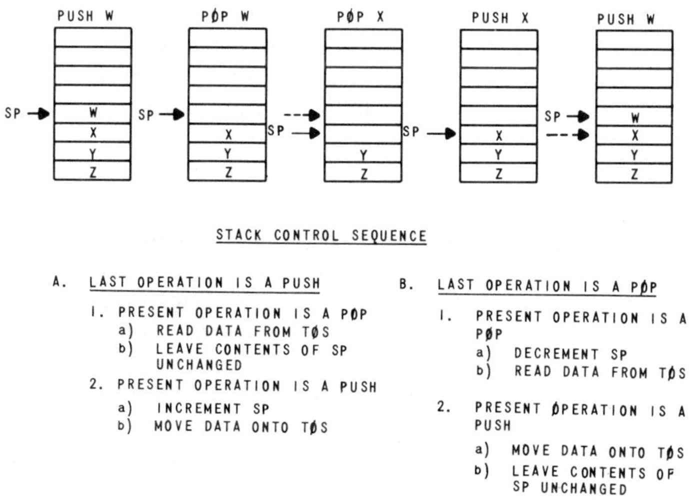

4-22 Contents of the TOS are determined by the last stack operation

In administering the stack, some machines permit any general register to function as a stack pointer. More than one general register may be used simultaneously in this manner. A machine directive must be used to produce each push or pop of the stack. The directive must designate the register to be used as an additional stack pointer and whether a push or pop is to be performed. One advantage of this implementation is that any register used as a stack pointer may peer into the stack without automatically being used by the stack hardware in push and pop operations. In a multiple pointer environment such as this, one register is specifically reserved as a *hardware stack pointer.* This is a hardware register that automatically establishes the necessary linkage information at the TOS when a subroutine call is executed or an interrupt request is recognized by the processor. It is the specific register administered by the stack control logic.

4.3.3 Stack Hardware Implementation

The physical implementation of a stack takes one of several forms:

1. *The stack may be located entirely in main memory.* In this case, a portion of main memory is set aside to be used as the *stack build area.* The stack may "build" (i.e., push items onto the TOS) starting with the lowest physical address (which defines the bottom of the stack). It will expand linearly upward to the highest physical address (which defines the TOS). The PDP-11 family is implemented so that it builds its stack in exactly the inverse manner—it starts at the highest address reserved for the stack and expands linearly downward to the lowest reserved stack address. Figure 4-23 illustrates these two variations in the stack-build procedure. Typically, the stack pointer will be the only hardware register supplied by the manufacturer. The user programs must be provided with sufficient intelligence to check when a push operation causes the stack to overflow its build area. The software overhead to perform this checking can become quite expensive in terms of real-time usage. Most MOS/LSI microprocessor structures function with only a hardware stack pointer. This is characteristic of both the Intel 8080 CPU and the Motorola M6800 CPU.
2. *The stack may be configured entirely from a set of dedicated hardware registers.* The hardware stack does not spill over into main storage when it is filled to capacity in this case. A separate hardware register or stack pointer is used to keep track of which register is functioning as the TOS. Depending on the implementation of the stack, when the last register in the stack is loaded so that the stack is full, the stack control logic may do either of the following:
   (a) *No notice may be taken of the stack having reached the full condition.* In this case it is the responsibility of the program to test the stack pointer prior to each push to see if the stack limit has been reached. If the stack limit is reached, the program must set a software flag so that no further push may be made under program control. If a further stack push is permitted, the stack pointer overflows or resets to point to the first register in the stack.

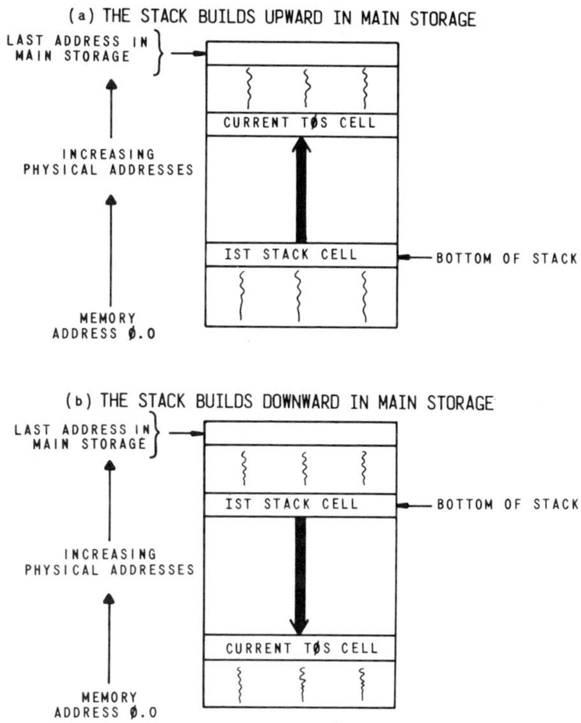

4-23 Stack build procedure in main memory

The contents of that location are overwritten with the item just placed on the stack. This causes an information loss and possible destruction of processor control, since the linkage information for a subroutine or an interrupt will be destroyed on the reset of the stack pointer. The Intel 4040 uses an on-chip address stack that is 12 bits wide and eight locations deep. Upon a subroutine call or an interrupt request, the PC is automatically pushed onto the stack. Since the PC occupies one location in the stack, seven levels of nested subroutines and/or interrupts may be accommodated. However, it is the application program's responsibility to maintain an awareness of the nesting depth and provide sufficient stack locations to meet the system's heaviest interrupt load. If an eighth push of the address stack is experienced, the first address stored on the stack is lost since the stack pointer resets.

(b) *A stack-full flag is set and further stack access of any kind is prohibited.* If another stack push is attempted for any reason, a stack overflow flag is set and further processing is prohibited. This terminates further control until the program and/or interrupt environment is modified.

3. *The problem of exceeding the number of hardware registers allocated to form the stack may be removed if the hardware stack is allowed to expand into main*

memory. In this case the hardware registers act as a buffer for the top locations of the stack and provide increased speed of access to items located in the stack itself. The stack facility of the Microdata 3200 minicomputer has been implemented in this manner. In this realization, an up–down counter is used as the stack pointer for the hardware register portion of the stack. A separate stack pointer is used for the memory portion of the stack to provide a more flexible accessing arrangement. The memory locations allocated to the stack are directly under the control of the application program since the main memory stack pointer is a full-width address word. The structure of the pushdown stack for this implementation is organized in such a manner that the movement of data between the hardware register portion of the stack and its extension in main memory is transparent to the programmer. The instructions that concern the stack automatically transfer data as needed without regard to where the data are kept in the stack. This is accounted for in the control sequences of the instructions that manipulate the stack. The advantage of this stack organization is its capability of restructuring the stack to any size to meet the needs of the application. It permits use of a fixed hardware register stack that automatically extends into main memory as the depth of the stack expands.

The Intel 8080 MOS/LSI microprocessor uses a 16-bit stack pointer which is resident on the CPU chip to reference an external stack located off-chip and entirely within main memory. The use of an on-chip stack pointer to reference main memory for stack operations has sometimes been called a microprocessor's *pointer mode of operation*. The most sophisticated stack implementation at the MOS/LSI microprocessor level is the incorporation of a dedicated set of hardware registers as an on-chip CPU stack. When the hardware register stack is full, this stack automatically spills over to an off-chip stack located in the set of main memory chips. The control for such a structure is the same in concept as that discussed for the Microdata minicomputer.

4.3.4 Stack Control Logic

The implementation of a pushdown hardware stack is rather straightforward. The register file in which a single read or write operation is used (discussed in Section 4.2) may be employed to form this stack. An up–down counter is required to point to the TOS as push and pop operations are performed. Figure 4-24 gives the functional block diagram for a hardware stack which has been incorporated into a three-bus structure. The output of the stack is shown directed toward one of the ALU's two input buses. Any arithmetic or logic operation applied to data would normally be restricted to operands stored in the push-pop stack. Arithmetic and logic operations would not be permitted in combination with data in any of the special registers. The stack output will normally be directed to only one of the two buses. However, the processor may need to place the operand from the stack in either the bus A buffer register or the bus B buffer register. Another gating path from the bus A buffer register

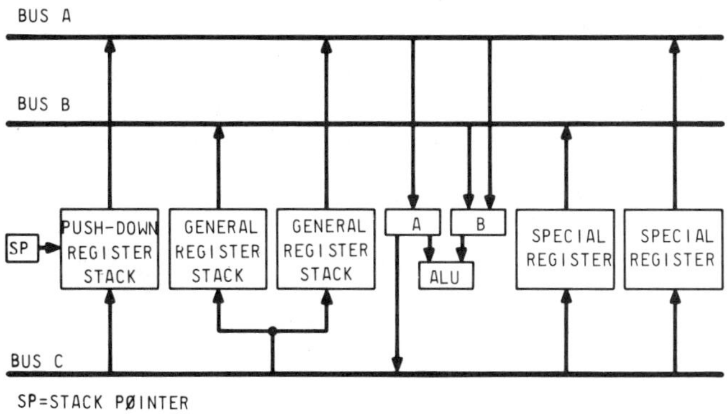

4-24 Three-bus arrangement incorporating a hardware stack

to the bus B buffer register may be added to provide this feature, as indicated in Figure 4-24. With this arrangement, the TOS can be popped into either the A register or the B register. The content of either of these registers may be used as the operand(s) for the ALU.

Figure 4-25 shows another possible implementation scheme for the hardware stack. The major difference between this scheme and the earlier one is the mechanism used to transfer data between the register file and main storage. In this scheme, when the hardware portion of the stack is full, a push into a file register is automatically preceded by a transfer of the data in the bottom register of the file into a dedicated portion of main storage. The major purpose of this scheme is to limit the stack activity to the hardware register. This arrangement maximizes the real-time performance of the stack.

Separate pointers are used to keep track of the TOS in the hardware register file and in main storage. Figure 4-25 shows four hardware registers that form a stack and the stack's memory extension into main storage. The area in main storage allocated for the stack is limited by the address capability of the memory pointer. The two pointers always point to the top word in the respective part of the stack. As data are pushed into the stack, the associated pointer is incremented by 1 with each push operation. In addition to the two pointers, a 4-bit status word (1 bit in the status word is associated with each word in the hardware register file) is provided to indicate whether or not the respective word is filled. When A and B are pushed into the stack as indicated in Figure 4-25a, the corresponding bits of the status word are set to 1. Two more successive pushes fill the hardware stack completely. The up–down counter then makes a complete revolution and again points to the beginning of the stack as the top word (see Figure 4-25b). With each push the hardware sequence (or microprogram sequence) is directed by the corresponding status bit for the hardware register to be loaded. If the status bit is a 0, a push onto the TOS will take place. If the status bit is a 1 (see Figure 4-25c), the bottom word of the register file becomes the top of the hardware register stack. The original data in the bottom word must be transferred into the

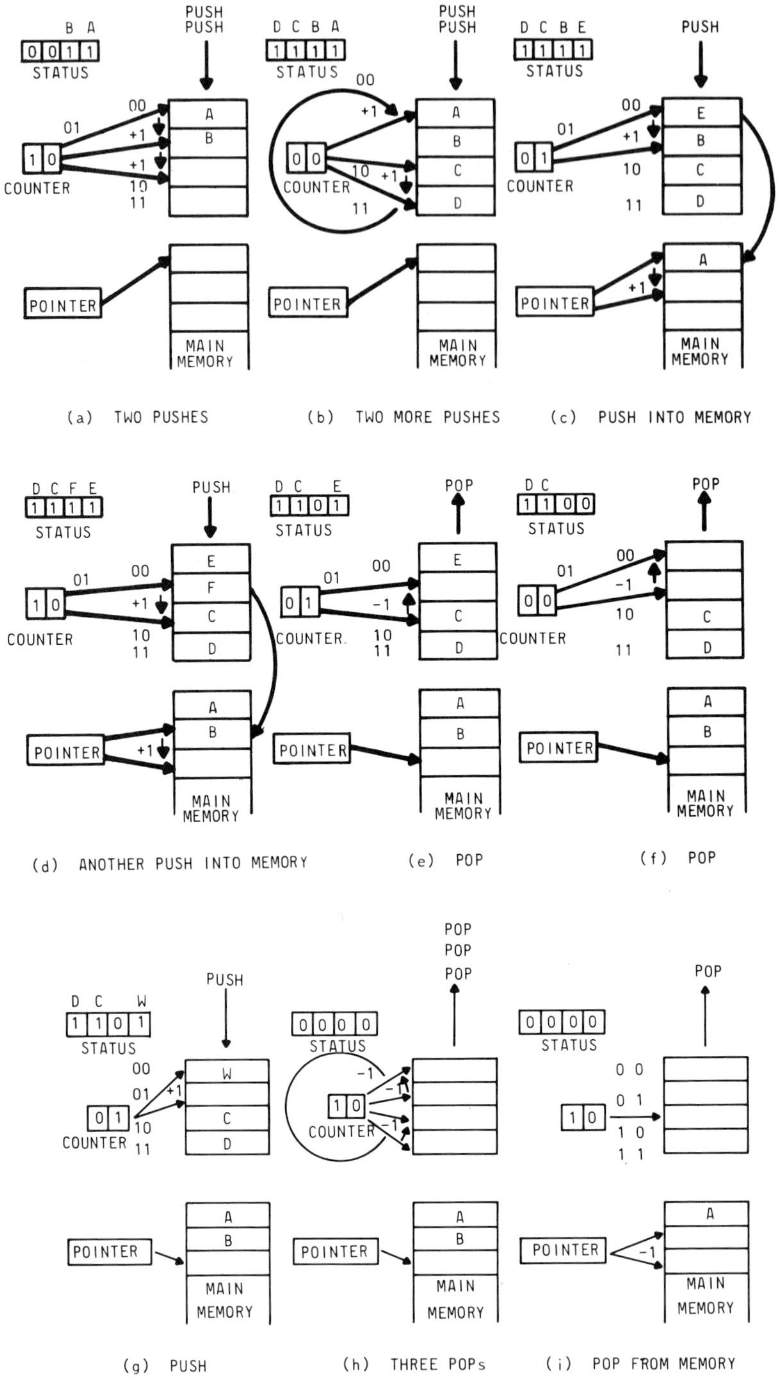

4-25 Push-pop operation

memory extension at the location specified by the memory stack pointer. After the transfer of the contents of the bottom word into main storage, the push of data E onto the TOS is carried out. If another push is to be performed and the status bit indicates that the hardware register stack is filled, the procedure above is repeated (see Figure 4-25d). In the case of a pop operation (see Figure 4-25e), after the data are taken off the stack, the corresponding status bit is changed to a 0, to indicate that a location in the register stack is available. The stack data in main storage are left intact. In the earlier scheme, the contents of the TOS in main storage would be restored to the emptied word of the hardware file. If another operation occurred, this same procedure would be repeated (see Figure 4-25f). Since the status bit corresponding to the top word of the stack is idle, a normal push would be performed (see Figure 4-25g) if a push occurred at this time. Although there are data words already in the memory stack, push and pop operations will be carried out within the hardware stack as long as there are available words in the stack. This limits the program activity to the local registers without requiring accesses to main storage for data. After all the data words have been pushed onto the stack in main memory, the status word is set to all 0's, indicating that the hardware register stack is empty (see Figure 4-25h). If a pop operation is requested when the status bits are all 0, the control sequence directs the FETCH operation to take place from the stack in main storage (see Figure 4-25i). Consequently, the pop operation does not have to transfer data from main storage unless the hardware stack is completely empty.

The data transfers to and from the hardware register stack are largely dependent on the contents of the status bits. These bits are continually updated with each push and pop operation. The update of the status bits occurs at the same time that the up–down counter is updated. The associated logic circuitry is shown in Figure 4-26. As indicated in Figure 4-25, the pointer always points to the next available slot in the stack and the corresponding bit in the status register. When a push occurs, the data are loaded into the pushdown stack and the binary decoder is enabled. The appropriate status bit is set during the first part of the normal push operation as indicated in the timing diagram of Figure 4-26b. After the data have been loaded onto the hardware stack and the status bit has been set, the up–down counter is incremented by 1 to advance to the next word in the stack. When a pop operation occurs, the reverse functions are carried out. The counter, consequently, points to the first occupied location at the TOS rather than the next available location in which data may be stored on the stack. The data are then transferred from the TOS to the appropriate CPU register. Following this action, the second set of binary decoder gates is enabled. The output of the decoder clears the corresponding bit of the status register during the second part of the pop operation.

Two different schemes for keeping track of the stack's state have been described: the first is a rather rigid control scheme which requires minimal additional logic, while the second is a more flexible hardware design with additional logic to facilitate stack operation. The use of the first scheme for nesting interrupts and/or subroutines is probably quite satisfactory if not too many levels of nesting are permitted. The second

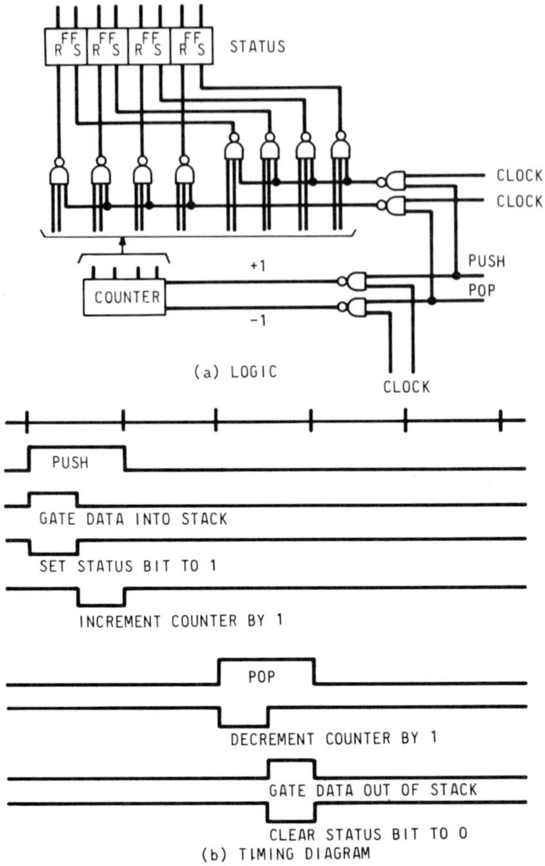

4-26 Counter and status update logic

approach is more advantageous for a CPU environment in which stack operations occur at fairly frequent intervals. Any increase in the efficiency of administering the stack will be directly reflected in the overall performance of the system. Consequently, it is important for the designer to use a more flexible and faster scheme for stack administration—even at the expense of additional control logic.

Most of the traffic into and out of a stack involves only the top few stack locations. Typically, several hardware registers are adequate to keep the stack's push operations from spilling over into the stack extension located in main storage. For a few applications, there may be a need for a bigger hardware stack, in which case the stack extension may be entirely satisfactory. However, the overhead of storing and retrieving the data in the stack whenever an interrupt occurs increases as the number of hardware registers found in the CPU is increased unless a separate bank of stacks is provided for each interrupt level.

4.4 SUMMARY

The hierarchy of storage facilities associated with a computing system has been identified, including the concept of overlapped memory operations to enhance the processing speed of a CPU. The storage hierarchy involves the use of special- and general-purpose registers to provide the CPU with additional processing capabilities. The hardware register set may be further refined to take the form of a register file organization. A register file arrangement may be built from standard LSI building blocks because of the regular pattern of the file organization. An extension of the register file structure is a hardware register stack. The hardware stack permits operand saves (pushes) and operand retrieves (pops) to be done without reference to main storage. This feature allows a higher processing speed until the stack overflows. Two ways to deal with stack overflow were discussed. The first way simply permits the stack to recycle and overwrite information in the earlier stack locations. In this case, the application software is expected to detect this situation and provide an error routine to deal with the problem. The second approach was shown to be the more attractive. It prevents the hardware stack from recycling. In this case, the hardware stack is permitted to extend into main storage. Further push operations just move data from the bottom hardware register onto the TOS located in main storage. Additional hardware control logic is required, but the possibility of a disastrous loss of information associated with the stack is removed.

4.5 REFERENCES

1 STONE, HAROLD S., *Introduction to Computer Architecture*. Chicago: Science Research Associates, Inc. (a subsidiary of IBM), 1975.

2 GEAR, C. W., *Computer Organization and Programming*. New York: McGraw-Hill Book Company, 1969.

3 HILL, F. J., AND G. R. PETERSON, *Digital Systems: Hardware Organization and Design*. New York: John Wiley & Sons, Inc., 1973.

4 BLAKESLEE, T., *Digital Design with Standard MSI and LSI*. New York: John Wiley & Sons, Inc., 1975.

5 BURNS, R. and DON SAVITT, "Microprogramming, Stack Architecture Ease Minicomputer Programer's Burden," *Electronics*, February 15, 1973.

6 KORN, G. A., *Microprocessors & Small Digital Computer Systems for Engineers & Scientists*. New York: McGraw-Hill Book Company, 1977.

7 PEATMAN, J. B., *Microcomputer-Based Design*. New York: McGraw-Hill Book Company, 1977.

8 KLINGMAN, E. E., *Microprocessor Systems Design*. Englewood Cliffs, N.J.: Prentice-Hall, Inc., 1977.

9 HILBURN, J. L., and P. M. JULICH, *Microcomputers/Microprocessors: Hardware, Software, and Applications*. Englewood Cliffs, N.J.: Prentice-Hall, Inc., 1976.

10 WEST, J. T., "Lasting Computer Designs Exploit Standard Parts," *Electronics*, November 13, 1975, pp. 130–136.

4.6 PROBLEMS

1. The core memory cycle time is divided into approximately two equal intervals (read/write) as was shown in Figure 4-4. For a semiconductor memory, the recovery time or the write interval is close to zero. A memory cycle for the read operation is nearly equal to the read interval. Design a 2-way overlapped memory structure for a semiconductor memory. Draw a detailed block diagram and a timing diagram.
2. A cache system is a memory hierarchy used to improve the effective main memory speed. It accomplishes this by inserting a small high-speed buffer between a slower main memory system and the CPU. A cache may be classified as one of three types: *fully associative*, *direct mapping*, and *set associative*.
   (a) A *fully associative cache* is organized so that any word in the main memory can be in any word in the high-speed buffer. Sketch a detailed block diagram for this structure.
   (b) A *direct mapping cache* is organized so that if a given word in the main memory is in the high-speed buffer, it should be in a fixed word of the buffer. This location is determined by some low-order address bits of the memory word. Sketch a detailed block diagram for this implementation.
   (c) A *set associative cache* is organized so that if any memory word is in the buffer, it will be confined to a fixed subset of buffer words. A fully associative cache and a direct mapping cache represent two extremes of a set associative cache. Sketch a detailed block diagram of a set associative cache implementation.
   (d) When the referenced word is in the high-speed buffer, the condition is said to be a *hit*. If the referenced word *is not* in the high-speed buffer, the condition is said to be a *miss*. One major problem in a fully or set associative cache is the replacement algorithm, which determines which member of the set (set associative) or which word in the buffer (fully associative) is to be replaced with the new word. Design three schemes implementing the replacement algorithm, and state the advantages and disadvantages of each scheme.
3. Using the dual-port access RAM (see Figure 4-14), implement a 16-bit general-purpose register structure as shown on the left side of Figure 4-15. Do not include the ALU or the special registers. Specify a microinstruction format that contains the necessary controls to effect a data move from one of 16 GPR's, specified by A, to another GPR, specified by B.
4. Using the 16×4 RAM (see Figures 4-11 and 4-12), implement the stack structure (64 words $\times$ 16 bits) as shown in Figure 4-16. Specify a microinstruction format which controls the *PUSH* and *POP* operations. Show timing diagrams for each function.
5. The administration of a stack in terms of pushing and popping is handled via the stack pointer. The control of the stack is determined when the stack pointer is to be incremented or decremented. Consider case 3 described in Section 4.3.2 (TOS Administration).

The contents of the TOS are determined by the last operation performed by the stack hardware. Design the control logic to administer the stack pointer in terms of pushing and popping. Specify the clock signals required for the implementation.

6. The stack structure as shown in Figure 4-25 consists of four hardware register files and extends into the main memory. The push and pop operations, illustrated in the figure, show when the last item, A, is popped from the stack (see Figure 4-25i.) The stack pointer for the main memory port points to the top of the stack. However, the stack pointer for the hardware register file points to the middle address (10) rather the beginning address (00). Explain why this is so.

7. In the usage of a stack, two conditions are significant for the proper administration of the stack. They are a *stack overflow error* and a *stack underflow error*. In a stack overflow error, the contents of the stack pointer exceed the numerical value of the stack limit register (the contents of which assign the maximum address in main storage allocated to the stack). In a stack underflow error, the contents of the stack pointer are less than the numerical value contained by the stack lower boundary register (the contents of which define the lowest address in main storage allocated to the stack).
   (a) Describe the possible responses of the processor to the occurrence of both a stack overflow error and a stack underflow error.
   (b) Is there any advantage to permitting the stack overflow logic and stack underflow logic to be enabled or disabled under program control?
   (c) Suppose the stack overflow logic is disabled and the stack exceeds its upper limit. Is there any way for the system to recover gracefully—will the system even know if it is still sane? What is the most practical way to handle this situation, as a system designer?

8. A hardware stack is to be used in an 18-bit small computer. The hardware stack is to be implemented using an LSI building block which functions as a 6-position shift register (see Figure P4-8).
   (a) How are *stack overflow* and *stack underflow* error conditions sensed by the stack control logic?
   (b) What modifications need to be made to the shift register building block so that an executing program could "peer into the stack" without disturbing the top of the stack (TOS)?
   (c) Design the control logic to implement the ability to "peer into the stack."

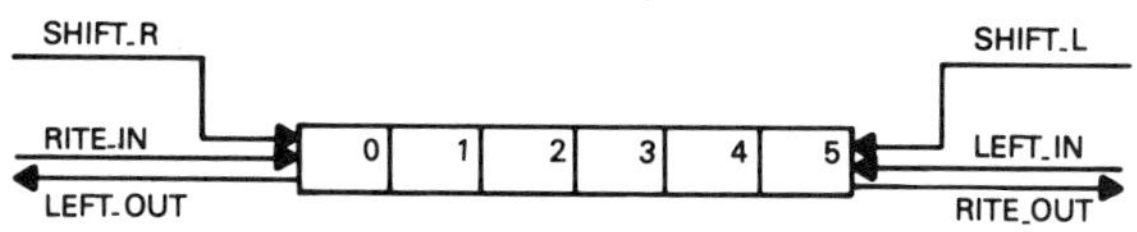

P4-8

In Figure P4-8, note that: (1) shift_L is a pulsed control line that shifts a data bit one position left for each shift_L pulse; (2) shift_R is a pulsed control line that shifts a data bit one position right for each shift_R pulse; (3) rite_in represents an input bit lead for right shift; (4) rite_out represents an output bit lead for right shift.

9. Using the hardware stack designed in the previous problem, design a stack arithmetic logic unit (ALU) to perform the following operations:

(a) Data words stored in the top two locations of the stack (i.e., TOS and TOS-1) will be manipulated arithmetically and the result will be placed back in the TOS.
   i. On an ADD instruction, the addend will be found at the TOS; the augend will be found at TOS-1.
   ii. On a SUB instruction, the subtrahend will be found at TOS-1; the minuend will be found at the TOS.

   Consider the possibility of arithmetic overflow.

(b) The logic operations of AND, OR, XOR and NOT are to be handled by this ALU. For each logical function, the top two locations of the stack will be manipulated; the result will be placed in the TOS.

10. Consider the problem of stack overflow when a stack limit register is *not* employed.
    (a) Is there an advantage to dedicating the stack to either subroutine usage exclusively or interrupt usage exclusively?
    (b) Assume that nesting of *either* interrupts *or* subroutines is permitted. How can the condition of stack overflow be handled?
    (c) If the nesting of *both* interrupts and subroutines is permitted, how are the conclusions for Problem 10b modified?
    (d) Let enough intelligence be placed in the memory referencing logic so that an out-of-range memory address can be recognized. Describe the procedure to be used to detect a stack overflow in the case of the CPU attempting to reference *nonexistent memory*. What should be the response of the system to a stack overflow in this case?

11. Consider a processor that dedicates a separate stack in main storage to service subroutines exclusively; another stack in main storage is dedicated exclusively to servicing interrupts.
    (a) Describe the control logic that would allow the interrupt stack to build on the subroutine stack if the interrupt stack overflowed. How would the processor know it was administering an interrupt in the subroutine stack? How would it know when to leave the subroutine stack because it had exhausted the interrupts that had been nested there and return to the interrupt stack to unwind interrupts nested there?
    (b) Is Problem 11a a realistic approach to handling a heavy interrupt load? With the cost of commercial RAM sufficiently low, wouldn't it be simpler to merely extend the area of main storage allocated to the interrupt stack? Is there a reasonable maximum size to a hardware stack allocated exclusively to interrupts (i.e., how many words of main storage should be dedicated to the interrupt stack so that the probability of a stack overflow error occurring is small)?

12. Consider a processor in which one hardware register is used as the stack pointer for a stack used by both interrupts and subroutines. It is possible to let the processor build the stack in noncontiguous areas of main storage by setting the contents of the stack pointer to a new value under program control. Once the stack pointer has been changed, all interrupt and subroutine linkages will build in the new stack area in main storage—until the stack pointer is restored to its old value.

    Assume that four distinct stack-build areas are permitted for a particular processor structure. Describe the control philosophy used to allow *switching between different stacks* in main storage. Provide a detailed layout of main storage for any data structures associated with implementing this control philosophy.

Prelude to Problem 13. Arithmetic procedures are customarily expressed using a notational convention called *infix notation.* This simply means that any operation to be performed between any two variables is indicated by placing an operator *between* these variables. An example, is the expression

(A+B)*(C+D)

If an arithmetic expression is written in infix notation, it is necessary to scan back and forth over the expression to determine which operation is to be performed next.

The Polish mathematician Jan Lukasiewicz demonstrated that the restriction requiring that variables *must* be separated by operators in an arithmetic expression may be removed. The notational convention adopted by Lukasiewicz places the operator *before* the variables that it operates on. This convention, called *prefix notation*, is often referred to as *Polish notation*. As an example of this notational convention, the previous arithmetic expression may be rewritten in the following manner:

*(+AB)(+CD)

An alternative notational expression places the operator *after* the variables on which it operates. This convention, called *postfix notation*, is often referred to as *reverse Polish notation*. The previous arithmetic expression may be rewritten in postfix notation as:

(AB+)(CD+)*

In particular, the postfix notation is in a form that allows an arithmetic expression to be easily manipulated by a stack. No parentheses need to be used in an arithmetic expression employing postfix notation since an operator is always associated with the two immediately preceding variables or operational results.

A convenient way of representing an arithmetic expression is by a graphical construct called a *tree*. Such an *evaluation tree* consists of nodes and branches. A *node* represents a specific arithmetic operation, while a *branch* represents a variable name. An evaluation tree is read from left to right and from bottom to top. A tree allows an arithmetic expression to be decomposed into its appropriate postfix representation.

Consider the expression (A*(B/C+D*E)/F. Its evaluation tree takes the form shown in Figure P4-13.

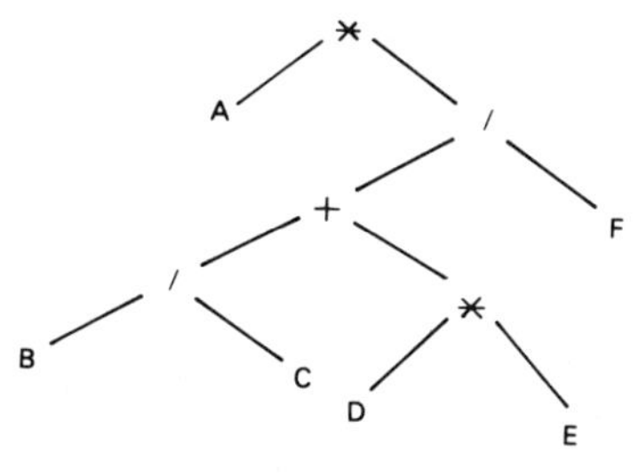

P4-13

13. Consider a hand-held calculator. What are the advantages of permitting the keyboard entry of arithmetic expressions using:
    (a) infix notation as opposed to prefix notation?
    (b) infix notation as opposed to postfix notation?

(c) prefix notation as opposed to postfix notation?

Do these conclusions need to be moderated if we assume that the user will be a highly naive, unskilled person rather than a mathematically sophisticated scientist or engineer?

14. Convert the following numerical expressions into reverse-Polish notation, and show the stack operations for evaluating the results:
    (a) A*B/C+D
    (b) A+[C*(D*E−F)/G−H]
    (c) (A+C)*(D+E/F*(B−G))

15. Express the following infix expressions in *both* their correct prefix (Polish) and postfix (reverse-Polish) notations:
    (a) A−(B+C)/(D−E*F/G*H)
    (b) A+(B−C)+(D/(E−F)*(G−H))
    (c) A/(B*C−(D*(E+F)/(G+H)))

    Consider expression c and indicate how it would be evaluated by a machine using a stack. Show the intermediate states of the stack as the evaluation proceeds.

16. Neither the cycle time of main storage nor the CPU cycle time can be regarded as good measures of a digital system's performance. They represent specialized measures that do not account for a variety of additional factors that affect the processing speed of the system. A more realistic measurement of system performance is the *bandwidth of the digital system. The system bandwidth* is defined as the word length of the memory multiplied by the number of words that can be referenced by the system in one second. In general, the result of this computation is expressed in terms of bytes per second.
    (a) For a 32-bit word length memory and a 600-ns memory cycle-time, calculate the bandwidth of the memory.
    (b) If the internal busing structure of the machine permits only a 16-signal lead bus instead of a 32-signal lead bus to interconnect the CPU with main storage, will the calculation of the system bandwidth be affected? If so, how? Is the *memory bandwidth* the same as the *system bandwidth*?
    (c) If a 200-ns cache memory was used as a "front end" to the 600-ns main memory, would the memory bandwidth change? If so, how?

17. For Figure P4-17 assume a main store cycle time of 1.2 μs and a CPU cycle time of 200 ns.

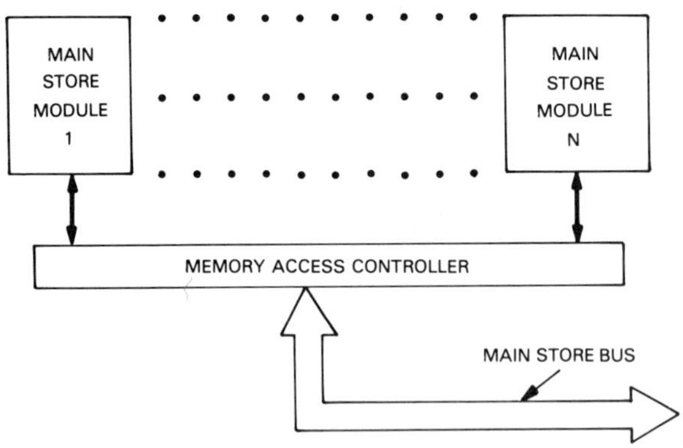

P4-17

(a) What is the practical level of memory interleaving that may be used with this system?
(b) Draw an execution diagram showing the FETCH and EXECUTE phases occurring under one main store cycle.
(c) Show the address assignments for each main store module.
(d) Assuming that successive memory references do not access the same main store module, what factors associated with the software degrade the performance of the system (ie., CPU instruction interference)? What factors associated with hardware degrade the system's performance (i.e., what must be the minimum bandwidth of the main store bus)?

5

Memory Referencing Techniques

5.1 WORD-LENGTH CONSIDERATIONS

5.1.1 Initial Concerns

The clever and imaginative design of instruction sets that could be efficiently used by machines with a short word length has remained a fundamental problem area for the development of each new mini/microcomputer.

Before the word length of a given machine is determined, the designer must consider the format of the instructions that make up the programs and the data formats used by the machine for internal operations and I/O transactions. Instructions and data must be stored and manipulated internally by the computer. This, in turn, affects the amount of storage that is required for a program and how rapidly that program may be executed. For a given amount of main memory, as the word length used for an instruction increases, the number of words that need to be stored decreases, since more machine operations may be incorporated in a single command. This reduces the number of memory locations required in a storage unit at the expense of a large, complicated instruction format. In terms of data word length, as the length of the data word increases, the precision of the numbers used in a numerical calculation also increases. The trade-off is that large data words require a large amount of memory to save single items of data. This means that as the size of the data unit increases, the number of data units that can be handled at one time decreases.

The evolution of the most useful data unit has been strongly influenced by IBM's 8-bit character or byte structure. Within this category of the 8-bit byte, two distinct *character codes* have received wide acceptance. The first is the *Extended Binary Coded Decimal Interchange Code* (*EBCDIC*) used extensively by IBM in its various machine types (shown in Table 5-1). The other character code is the *United States of America Standard Code for Information Interchange* (*USASCII*) used by virtually all the mini/microcomputer manufacturers (see Tables 5-2a and 5-2b).

TABLE 5-1 Extended Binary-Coded Decimal Interchange Code (EBCDIC—8 Bits)

MS-HEX DIGIT \ LS-HEX DIGIT	0	1	2	3	4	5	6	7	8	9	A	B	C	D	E	F
0	NUL	SOH	STX	ETX	PF	HT	LC	DEL			SMM	VT	FF	CR	SO	S1
1	DLE	DC1	DC2	TM	RES	NL	BS	IL	CAN	EM	CC	CU1	IFS	IGS	IRS	IUS
2	DS	SOS	FS		BYP	LF	ETB	ESC			SM	CU2		ENQ	ACK	BEL
3			SYN		PN	RS	UC	EOT				CU3	DC4	NAK		SVB
4	SP										¢	.	<	(	+	|
5	&										!	$	*	)	;	¬
6	-	/										'	%	–	>	?
7										`	:	:	@	'	=	"
8		a	b	c	d	e	f	g	h	i		{	≤	(	+	+
9		j	k	l	m	n	o	p	q	r		}	⌑	)	±	■
A	~	s	t	u	v	w	x	y	z			└	┌	[	≥	.
B	0	1	2	3	4	5	6	7	8	9		┘	┐	]	≠	-
C		A	B	C	D	E	F	G	H	I						
D		J	K	L	M	N	O	P	Q	R						
E			S	T	U	V	W	X	Y	Z						
F	0	1	2	3	4	5	6	7	8	9						

The first microprocessor structures were heavily influenced by the success of the hand-held calculators that operated on binary-coded decimal digits (each digit required four bits to represent the numbers 0 through 9). Consequently, the early microprocessors were parallel, 4-bit machines. The 4-bit data unit is often referred to as a *nibble* rather than an 8-bit byte. As a result, various small machines permit individual elements of information to be addressed at the byte level, the nibble level, or the single-bit level.

5.1.2 Single-Word Versus Multiple-Word Instructions

The word length reflects itself not only in the size and cost of the main memory modules but also in the width of the internal busing structure of the machine and the control logic required to handle the larger word size. The wider buses and additional control logic require more hardware in their implementations. Up to the early 1970's,

TABLE 5-2a United States of America Standard Code for Information Interchange (USASCII—8 Bits)

MS-HEX DIGIT \ LS-HEX DIGIT	0	1	2	3	4	5	6	7	8	9	A	B	C	D	E	F
0	NUL	SOH	STX	ETX	EOT	ENQ	ACK	BEL	BS	HT	LF	VT	FF	CR	SO	S1
1	DLE	DC1	DC2	DC3	DC4	NAK	SYN	ETB	CAN	EM	SUB	ESC	FS	GS	RS	US
2	SP	!	"	#	$	%	&	'	(	)	*	+	,	–	.	/
3	0	1	2	3	4	5	6	7	8	9	:	;	<	=	>	?
4	@	A	B	C	D	E	F	G	H	I	J	K	L	M	N	O
5	P	Q	R	S	T	U	V	W	X	Y	Z	[	\	]	¬	–
6	'	a	b	c	d	e	f	g	h	i	j	k	l	m	n	o
7	p	q	r	s	t	u	v	w	x	y	z	{	:	}	~	DEL

NOTE: HEXADECIMAL POSITIONS 80 THROUGH FF ARE UNUSED.

TABLE 5-2b United States of America Standard Code for Information Interchange (Terminal-Oriented; No Communication Codes Used)

MS-HEX DIGIT \ LS-HEX DIGIT	0	1	2	3	4	5	6	7	8	9	A	B	C	D	E	F
0	NUL	↑A	↑B	↑C	↑D	↑E	↑F	↑G	↑H	TAB	LF	VT	FF	CR	↑N	↑O
1	↑P	↑Q	↑R	↑S	↑T	↑U	↑V	↑W	↑X	↑Y	↑Z	ALT MODE	CTRL SHIFT L	CTRL SHIFT M	CTRL SHIFT N	CTRL SHIFT O
2	SP	!	"	#	$	%	&	'	(	)	*	+	,	–	.	/
3	0	1	2	3	4	5	6	7	8	9	:	;	<	=	>	?
4	@	A	B	C	D	E	F	G	H	I	J	K	L	M	N	O
5	P	Q	R	S	T	U	V	W	X	Y	Z	[	\	]	↑	←
6		a	b	c	d	e	f	g	h	i	j	k	l	m	n	o
7	p	q	r	s	t	u	v	w	x	y	z	{	|	}	ESC	DEL

NOTE: HEXADECIMAL POSITIONS 80 THROUGH FF ARE UNUSED.

hardware was expensive and memory very costly. Consequently, the word length of a small computer was kept within the bounds of 8 to 18 bits. These word lengths provided a reasonably limited class of instruction sets that still offered the programmer a rich-enough mix of machine directives for useful application software and an efficient means of addressing memory to obtain the necessary operands.

The simplest single-word instruction consists of a field called the *operation code* (*opcode*) and another field called the *operand address* (see Figure 5-1). The opcode is used to specify what operation the machine is to perform. The operand address portion points to the location in main memory where the operand is stored. In several instances,

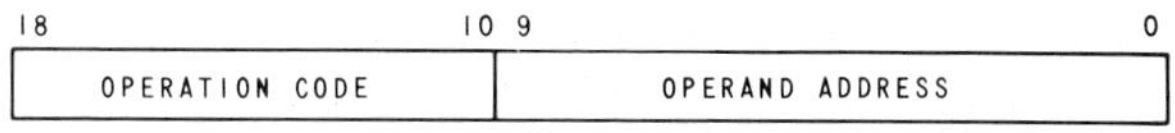

5-1 Basic single-word instruction format

the instruction may not reference an operand at all and the address portion is used for immediate data.

The phenomenon known as *locality of reference* permits most machines with a short word length to use only a portion of the bits available in the instruction word for direct addressing. Because of this, two distinct memory reference modes have evolved at the small machine level:

1. The first mode permits direct addressing of a subset of the total number of locations available if the full instruction word is used as an address, since instructions tend to cluster; this allows use of single-word, short-word-length (8- to 18-bit) instructions.
2. The second mode permits addressing of all available memory locations by using the full instruction word as an address. This can be done only if a second data word is available in a main storage location or in a working register, since part of the instruction word must be dedicated to the opcode field. In this case the portion of the instruction word containing the opcode specifies that the contents of another memory location is to be used as the address of the operand.

The implication of this observation is that at least one additional field is required in the instruction word to specify how a memory reference will be performed; this is the *address mode field.* The modified instruction word is shown in Figure 5-2. The full details of these conclusions are examined in Section 5.3 when the entire problem of referencing memory using a short-word-length instruction is considered.

There has been a strong motivation toward keeping the data word length equal to the length of the instruction word. This has particularly been the case with the Princeton class of machines, where data and instructions share the same memory. However, development of the Harvard class of microprocessor structures appears to indicate a movement away from data and instruction word compatibility. In several cases, the data store is a different width than the instruction store, indicating that consideration is being given to more fully meeting the separate requirements of the data and the machine directives.

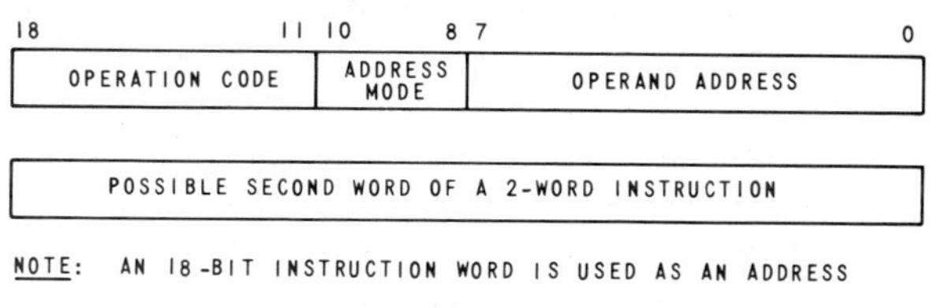

5-2 Inclusion of an address mode field

If multiple-word instructions are used, a sequence of memory references must be made before the instruction may be completely executed. These additional memory references increase the idle time of the CPU and reduce the *throughput* (the number of instructions that may be executed in unit time) of the machine. For high throughput, therefore, it is advantageous to use an instruction format consisting of a single word. Furthermore, the efficiency of memory utilization is increased when single-word instructions are employed, since less memory is normally required to store a program sequence. For small-word-length machines, two instruction formats have been employed to optimize throughput and storage utilization. These are a *short command format* and a *long command format*, which provide the two memory reference modes described earlier. The long format corresponds to a two-word instruction, where the second word is the operand address. This second word may be located any place in available main storage. The short format is the one most commonly executed to obtain high throughput. The long format is normally used only when it is necessary to reference an operand in main storage.

5.1.3 Trade-Offs in Assigning Word Length

In determining the word length of a given machine, the manufacturer has traditionally been influenced by the marketplace. Typically, the manufacturer has tried to sell a general-purpose machine that will perform efficiently in a wide range of applications at the most marketable selling price. The minicomputer has had to remain competitive both in terms of the pricing structure of the marketplace and the number of hardware features incorporated in the mainframe. These cost considerations have dictated the selection of a short word length. The shorter word length, in turn, has meant a smaller core module size, resulting in a cheaper memory cost per word as measured in fractional cents per bit. However, the shorter the word length, the more the speed of processing may be reduced, since double- and even triple-word instructions may have to be used. To enhance the speed at which a machine may execute instructions, it is desirable to have most instructions contained in a single word. The more bits that are assigned to these instruction words, the more sophisticated each instruction can be. Additional bits in the instruction word permit the procedure of referencing data in memory to become more straightforward and less difficult. Consequently, as the word length increases, the number of bits available for opcodes and operand addresses increases in a proportional manner. If limited computational ability is required and the data is byte-oriented, a shorter word length will often prove quite satisfactory. If, as was discussed earlier, arithmetic operations are to be performed, a longer word length may be required to enhance the precision of the calculations.

The microprocessor instruction word sizes have been influenced by both the available markets and the current state of the technology. The 8-bit microprocessors appear to be a compromise between the 4-bit microprocessor structures used as calculators and the minicomputer CPU configurations that could be reasonably implemented using MOS/LSI technology. The bipolar LSI microprocessor chip sets offer the capability of constructing a personal microcomputer and employing a macroinstruction word length of the user's own choosing. In particular, such bipolar LSI chip sets allow the user to concatenate bit-sliced CPE's to construct a CPU with an arbitrary word length at the macroinstruction level. In effect, word length becomes a secondary consideration in such designs. The primary concern is the utility of the macroinstruction set in relation to the application the machine will be used in (i.e., how easy it is to use, and how easy it is to modify).

5.2 INSTRUCTION FORMATS

5.2.1 Operation Code Considerations

The great difficulty encountered when considering a machine with a short word length, particularly one with a processor word length of 4 or 8 bits, is that most instructions must span more than one memory word. Instruction formats are used to accommodate this need for varying word-length commands. The instruction formats specify the way each machine directive is represented and define the instruction repertoire of a given machine.

In general, there are many different classes of instructions. Each instruction requires its own unique combination of bits in the opcode portion of the command word. In order for an instruction to reference an operand, another portion of the command word must be reserved for address information. Consequently, the number of unique bit patterns available to specify the machine directive and the operand is limited if a single-word instruction is used. If eight unique opcodes are required, 3 bits of the instruction word must be dedicated to this function. For an 8-bit instruction word, this leaves 5 bits available for operand referencing. However, only $2^5 = 32$ memory locations may be uniquely addressed using these 5 bits, an extremely limited addressing range. For practical applications, this requires that the 8-bit machine either use an augmented addressing scheme or employ multiple-word instructions. The various addressing schemes employed by the general class of small-scale computers is discussed in Section 5.3. However, Figure 5-3 illustrates three possible classes of instructions for an 8-bit machine; each class is characterized by a different instruction word length. For instance, a *class II instruction* is a double-word command requiring two consecutive memory references to configure the complete machine directive. Additional memory references are characteristic of multiple-word instructions. For applications where real time and processor throughput are not major concerns, multiple-word instructions and a short-word-length machine can be quite effective. However, it is the instruction formats that determine the effectiveness of an instruction set for a given machine, whether that machine is a microprocessor or a large-scale computer.

5.2.2 The Four-Address Command Format

The instruction format must contain either explicitly or implicitly all the information necessary for a machine to execute a given command. Typically, this information will consist of:

1. The opcode representing the current machine directive that is to be executed.
2. The address of the first operand involved in the machine operation.

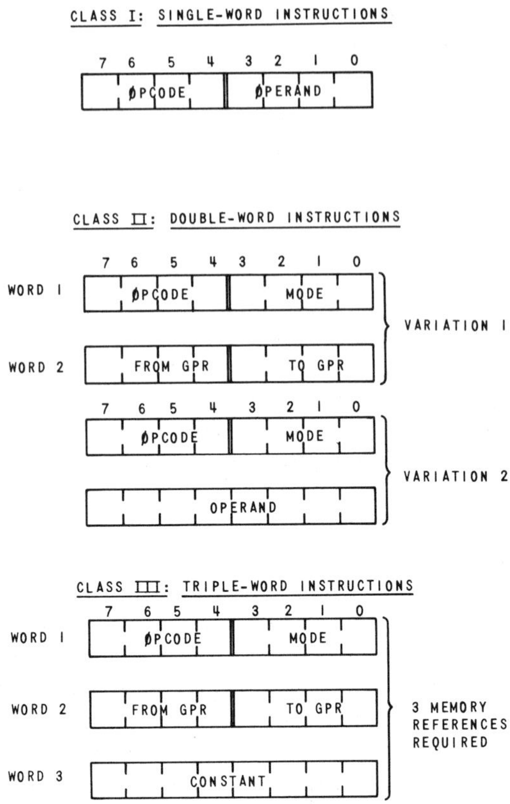

5-3 Three possible instruction classes for an 8-bit machine

3. The address of the second operand involved in the machine operation.
4. The address of the result (where the result is to be stored within the machine).
5. The location of the next instruction to be fetched at the conclusion of the current execution cycle.

If all these parameters are explicitly identified in the machine directive, the arrangement is called a *four-address instruction format* (see Figure 5-4). Perhaps the most significant advantage of such a format is that there is no need to employ a BRANCH instruction in the machine's command repertoire. Every instruction carries with it the explicit location of the next instruction to be executed.

In addition, since the address of the participating operands and the resultant are explicitly identified, they may be individually located throughout main storage. The four-address instruction will handle all these variables in a single instruction cycle

OPERATION CODE	ADDRESS OF ØPERAND 1	ADDRESS OF ØPERAND 2	ADDRESS OF RESULT	ADDRESS OF THE NEXT INSTRUCTION

5-4 Four-address instruction format

without the need to use intermediate storage. However, this single instruction cycle may involve several memory references if the individual operands are located in main storage and the resultant operand is to be placed there also.

Table 5-3a exhibits a generalized program that uses four-address instructions to implement solution of the equation

$$A = \frac{B + C + (D \cdot E)/F}{G \cdot H} \tag{1}$$

TABLE 5-3a Four-Address Command Format

OPCODE	OPERAND-1	OPERAND-2	RESULT	NEXT INST.

```
4-ADDRESS PROGRAM              INTERNAL MACHINE OPERATIONS

I1.  MUL  G,H,T1,I2            1.  T1 <-- G*H;  NXT-INST-REG <-- I2-ADDR
I2.  MUL  D,E,T2,I3            2.  T2 <-- D*E;  NXT-INST-REG <-- I3-ADDR
I3.  DIV  T2,F,T3,I4           3.  T3 <-- (D*E)/F;  NXT-INST-REG <-- I4-ADDR
I4.  ADD  C,T3,T4,I5           4.  T4 <-- [C+(D*E)/F];  NXT-INST-REG <-- I5-ADDR
I5.  ADD  B,T4,T5,I6           5.  T5 <-- [B+C+(D*E)/F];  NXT-INST-REG <-- I6-ADDR
I6.  DIV  T5,T1,A,I7           6.  A <-- [B+C+(D*E)/F]/(G*H);  NXT-INST-REG <-- I7-ADDR
I7.  HLT                       7.  HALT ALL MACHINE OPERATIONS
```

COMMENTS

1. LOCATIONS T1,T2,T3,T4 & T5 ARE TEMPORARY STORAGE LOCATIONS. THEY PERMIT ALL VARIABLES USED IN THE PROGRAM TO REMAIN UNCHANGED.
2. EACH INSTRUCTION ACTS AS AN INNATE BRANCH COMMAND SINCE THE ADDRESS OF THE NEXT INSTRUCTION ALWAYS ACCOMPANIES THE COMMAND.
3. CONSEQUENTLY, INSTRUCTIONS DO NOT HAVE TO BE EXECUTED CONSECUTIVELY.

Note that each instruction is an innate branching command and that instruction execution does not have to take place using consecutive memory locations.

The major disadvantage of the four-address format is the required width of the memory word. As an example, if each address required 12 bits for a unique specification, 48 bits would be required just to characterize the four required addresses. When the opcode bits are included, the four-address format produces a large word size, one that particularly has not been considered for mini- or microcomputers because of the cost of memory and associated hardware. However, the four-address format has been used in microprogram control to achieve higher processor performance at the expense of using a wider microprogram store word.

5.2.3 The Three-Address Command Format

Normal program flow occurs largely as the sequential execution of a series of consecutive commands. The only break in the program sequence is encountered when a branching command or JUMP instruction is executed. Because a program may be regarded as an ordered sequence of instructions, a counter may be used to keep track of which instruction is to be executed next. In normal program execution, 1 will be added to this counter at the completion of the current instruction. If a conditional or unconditional BRANCH instruction is encountered, the contents of the instruction counter will be changed to point to the location in program memory to which control is to branch. By using this type of instruction referencing, the next address is automatically accounted for by the machine control logic. Effectively, the next address location is implied or understood by the programmer. Figure 5-5 illustrates this arrangement, which is usually referred to as a *three-address instruction format*. If a program branch command is encountered, the operand-1 and operand-2 fields will be ignored and the contents of the result address field will be used as the address in memory to which control is to branch. The removal of the next instruction field reduces both the size of the machine command word and the total number of bits required by a main storage module.

OPERATION CODE	ADDRESS OF OPERAND 1	ADDRESS OF OPERAND 2	ADDRESS OF RESULT

5-5 Three-address instruction format

Table 5-3b exhibits a program that uses three-address instructions to implement a solution to equation (1). Note that while the same number of instructions are required for this solution as for the four-address instruction program, a separate BRANCH command must be employed to change the direction of program flow. Consequently, an additional instruction and memory location will be required for *each* point in the program that involves a control decision.

TABLE 5-3b Three-Address Command Format

OPCODE	OPERAND-1	OPERAND-2	RESULT

3-ADDRESS PROGRAM			INTERNAL MACHINE OPERATIONS
I1.	MUL	G,H,T1	1. T1 ← G*H; PC ← PC+1
I2.	MUL	D,E,T2	2. T2 ← D*E; PC ← PC+1
I3.	DIV	T2,F,T3	3. T3 ← (D*E)/F; PC ← PC+1
I4.	ADD	C,T3,T4	4. T4 ← [C+(D*E)/F]; PC ← PC+1
I5.	ADD	B,T4,T5	5. T5 ← [B+C+(D*E)/F]; PC ← PC+1
I6.	DIV	T5,T1,A	6. A ← [B+C+(D*E)/F]/(G*H); PC ← PC+1
I7.	HLT		7. HALT ALL MACHINE OPERATIONS

COMMENTS

1. INSTRUCTIONS MUST BE EXECUTED SEQUENTIALLY.
2. THE PROGRAM COUNTER (PC) IS INCREMENTED BY 1 AT THE COMPLETION OF EACH NONBRANCHING INSTRUCTION.
3. A SEPARATE BRANCH COMMAND MUST BE EMPLOYED TO CHANGE THE DIRECTION OF PROGRAM FLOW.

NOTE: I1,I2,..., ETC. ARE INSTRUCTION ADDRESSES.

5.2.4 The Two-Address Command Format

A further savings may be achieved if the concept of the program counter (PC) is retained but one of the three fields in the three-address instruction format is left to be implied by the instruction. This convention leads to the *two-address instruction format* shown in Figure 5-6. Two variations of the two-address command format have been implemented. Version I uses the third instruction field for the address of the result.

(VERSION I)

OPERATION CODE	ADDRESS OF ØPERAND 1	ADDRESS OF RESULT

(VERSION II)

OPERATION CODE	ADDRESS OF ØPERAND 1	ADDRESS OF ØPERAND 2

5-6 Two-address instruction format

Version II uses the third instruction field for the address of the second operand. Version I has been constructed by dedicating a processor register to hold the second operand implicitly. This procedure requires that the second operand be placed in the *implied processor register* (*IPR*) before a two-address command is executed. Typically, the IPR will be the main accumulator of the machine. The instruction will explicitly identify the first operand and the location at which the results of the machine operation will be stored. Table 5-3c, which illustrates a program using two-address instructions, observes the version I convention and implements a solution to equation (1). Note that neither operand is destroyed when one of these instructions is executed, since the address of the result is directly specified in the instruction word.

Version II uses the third instruction field to specify the location of the next instruction. Operand 2 is still required to be placed in the IPR before a two-address command is executed. However, the IPR in this case functions as both an implied source and destination register. The result of the machine operation is automatically placed in the IPR, overwriting the original operand that had been stored there. Table 5-3d gives a program using two-address instructions that observes the version II convention and implements a solution to equation (1). Note that both versions of the two-address instruction class require the introduction of two special instructions to manipulate the contents of the IPR. The MOV instruction clears the IPR and then transfers the contents of a specified location into the IPR. The STORE instruction clears a specified location and then transfers the contents of the IPR into that location. The initial contents of the IPR will normally be destroyed during execution of a version II, two-address command. The primary function of the IPR in such instructions is to perform the replacement operation; that is, it retains the implied source operand only until the result has been generated and then acts as an implied storage location for the result by replacing the implied source operand with the result.

As a means of comparison, four additional commands are required by the version II solution over the version I solution. More interesting, however, is the fact that neither the second operand nor the location of the result needs to be explicitly identified for a useful program to be written. Furthermore, it has been established that use of a PC removes the need for the next instruction field in the instruction word. This

TABLE 5-3c Two-Address Command Format (Version I)

OPCODE	OPERAND-I	RESULT

2-ADDRESS PROGRAM			INTERNAL MACHINE OPERATIONS
I1.	MOV	H,IPR	1. IPR ← H; PC ← PC+1
I2.	MUL	G,T1	2. T1 ← G*H; PC ← PC+1
I3.	MOV	E,IPR	3. IPR ← E; PC ← PC+1
I4.	MUL	D,T2	4. T2 ← D*E; PC ← PC+1
I5.	MOV	F,IPR	5. IPR ← F; PC ← PC+1
I6.	DIV	T2,T3	6. T3 ← (D*E)/F; PC ← PC+1
I7.	MOV	C,IPR	7. IPR ← C; PC ← PC+1
I8.	ADD	T3,T4	8. T4 ← [C+(D*E)/F]; PC ← PC+1
I9.	MOV	B,IPR	9. IPR ← B; PC ← PC+1
I10.	ADD	T4,T5	10. T5 ← [B+C(D*E)/F]; PC ← PC+1
I11.	MOV	T1,IPR	11. IPR ← G*H; PC ← PC+1
I12.	DIV	T5,A	12. A ← [B+C+(D*E)/F]/(G*H); PC ← PC+1
I13.	HLT		13. HALT ALL MACHINE OPERATIONS

NOTE: a) MOV X,Y FIRST CLEARS LOCATION-Y AND THEN PLACES THE CONTENTS OF LOCATION-X IN LOCATION-Y

b) IPR ≜ IMPLIED PROCESSOR REGISTER

COMMENTS

1. THE 2ND OPERAND MUST BE PLACED IN THE IMPLIED PROCESSOR REGISTER (IPR) BEFORE A 2-ADDRESS COMMAND IS ISSUED.
2. SINCE THE ADDRESS OF THE RESULT IS EXPLICITLY CONTAINED IN THE INSTRUCTION WORD, NEITHER OPERAND IS DESTROYED WHEN THE INSTRUCTION IS EXECUTED.
3. THE PC IS AUTOMATICALLY INCREMENTED BY 1 AT THE COMPLETION OF EACH NONBRANCHING INSTRUCTION.
4. A SEPARATE BRANCH COMMAND MUST BE EMPLOYED TO CHANGE THE DIRECTION OF PROGRAM FLOW.

means that a further reduction in the size of the command word and an associated reduction in the cost of main storage modules may be obtained.

5.2.5 The Single-Address Command Format

The PC may be used to implicitly point to the location of the next instruction while the second operand and the location of the result can then be implied by the current instruction. Such an arrangement, called a *single-address instruction format*, is shown in Figure 5-7. Typically, the single address instruction explicitly references one of the operands that will be found either in main memory or in one of the working registers. If a second operand is called for by the current machine directive, it must have been

OPERATION CODE	ADDRESS OF OPERAND 1

5-7 Single-address instruction format

placed by a previous instruction in an implied register location such as an accumulator. As in the two-address command, the result of the operation will be used to overwrite the second operand in the accumulator. A very close analogy exists between the operation of a single-address instruction and the operation of a version II, two-address command. Table 5-3e presents a program solution to equation (1) which uses single-address commands. With the exception of the next instruction address field employed

TABLE 5-3d Two-Address Command Format (Version II)

ØPCØDE	ØPERAND-1	NEXT INST.

2-ADDRESS PROGRAM			INTERNAL MACHINE OPERATIONS
I1.	MØV	H,I2	1. IPR ← H; NXT-INST-REG ← I2-ADDR
I2.	MUL	G,I3	2. IPR ← G*H; NXT-INST-REG ← I3-ADDR
I3.	STORE	T1,I4	3. T1 ← IPR; NXT-INST-REG ← I4-ADDR
I4.	MØV	D,I5	4. IPR ← D; NXT-INST-REG ← I5-ADDR
I5.	MUL	E,I6	5. IPR ← D*E; NXT-INST-REG ← I6-ADDR
I6.	STORE	T2,I7	6. T2 ← IPR; NXT-INST-REG ← I7-ADDR
I7.	MØV	F,I8	7. IPR ← F; NXT-INST-REG ← I8-ADDR
I8.	DIV	T2,I9	8. IPR ← (D*E)/F; NXT-INST-REG ← I9-ADDR
I9.	STORE	T3,I10	9. T3 ← IPR; NXT-INST-REG ← I10-ADDR
I10.	MØV	C,I11	10. IPR ← C; NXT-INST-REG ← I11-ADDR
I11.	ADD	T3,I12	11. IPR ← [C+(D*E)/F]; NXT-INST-REG ← I12-ADDR
I12.	ADD	B,I13	12. IPR ← [B+C+(D*E)/F]; NXT-INST-REG ← I13-ADDR
I13.	STORE	T4,I14	13. T4 ← IPR; NXT-INST-REG ← I14-ADDR
I14.	MØV	T1,I15	14. IPR ← G*H; NXT-INST-REG ← I15-ADDR
I15.	DIV	T4,I16	15. IPR ← [B+C+(D*E)/F]/(G*H); NXT-INST-REG ← I16-ADDR
I16.	STORE	A,I17	16. A ← IPR; NXT-INST-REG ← I17-ADDR
I17.	HLT		17. HALT ALL MACHINE OPERATIONS

NOTE: a) MØV X,I0 CLEARS THE IPR AND THEN MOVES THE CONTENTS OF LOCATION X INTO THE IPR; PROGRAM EXECUTION CONTINUES AT LOCATION I0.

b) STORE Y,I1 CLEARS LOCATION Y AND THEN MOVES THE CONTENTS OF THE IPR INTO LOCATION Y; PROGRAM EXECUTION CONTINUES AT LOCATION I1.

COMMENTS

1. THE 2ND ØPERAND IS USED AS BOTH AN IMPLIED SOURCE AND DESTINATION.
2. THE 2ND ØPERAND MUST BE PLACED IN THE IMPLIED PROCESSOR REGISTER (IPR) BEFORE A 2-ADDRESS COMMAND IS ISSUED.
3. THE INITIAL CONTENTS OF THE IPR WILL NORMALLY BE DESTROYED DURING EXECUTION OF THE COMMAND.
4. EVERY INSTRUCTION IS INNATELY A BRANCH COMMAND.

by the solution using two-address commands, Tables 5-3d and 5-3e appear identical. However, had control decision points been encountered in the program, the single-address command implementation would have required a separate BRANCH instruction for each decision. A single-address BRANCH command automatically overwrites the contents of the PC, with the address explicitly called for in the instruction. Execution then begins at that address at the completion of the instruction.

TABLE 5-3e Single-Address Command Format

OPCODE	OPERAND-1

1 - ADDRESS PROGRAM	INTERNAL MACHINE OPERATIONS
I1. MØV H	1. IPR ← H; PC ← PC+1
I2. MUL G	2. IPR ← G*H; PC ← PC+1
I3. STORE T1	3. T1 ← IPR; PC ← PC+1
I4. MØV D	4. IPR ← D; PC ← PC+1
I5. MUL E	5. IPR ← D*E; PC ← PC+1
I6. STORE T2	6. T2 ← IPR; PC ← PC+1
I7. MØV F	7. IPR ← F; PC ← PC+1
I8. DIV T2	8. IPR ← (D*E)/F; PC ← PC+1
I9. STORE T3	9. T3 ← IPR; PC ← PC+1
I10. MØV C	10. IPR ← C; PC ← PC+1
I11. ADD T3	11. IPR ← [C+(D*E)/F]; PC ← PC+1
I12. ADD B	12. IPR ← [B+C+(D*E)/F; PC ← PC+1
I13. STORE T4	13. T4 ← IPR; PC ← PC+1
I14. MØV T1	14. IPR ← G*H; PC ← PC+1
I15. DIV T4	15. IPR ← [B+C+(D*E)/F]/(G*H); PC ← PC+1
I16. STORE A	16. A ← IPR; PC ← PC+1
I17. HLT	17. HALT ALL MACHINE OPERATIONS

NOTE: a) MØV X CLEARS THE IPR AND THEN MOVES THE CONTENTS OF LOCATION X INTO THE IPR.

b) STORE Y CLEARS LOCATION Y AND THEN MOVES THE CONTENTS OF THE IPR INTO LOCATION Y.

COMMENTS

1. THE 2ND OPERAND IS USED AS BOTH AN IMPLIED SOURCE AND DESTINATION.
2. THE 2ND OPERAND MUST BE PLACED IN THE IMPLIED PROCESSOR REGISTER (IPR) BEFORE A SINGLE-ADDRESS COMMAND IS ISSUED.
3. THE INITIAL CONTENTS OF THE IPR WILL NORMALLY BE DESTROYED DURING EXECUTION OF THE COMMAND.
4. THE PC IS AUTOMATICALLY INCREMENTED BY 1 AT THE COMPLETION OF EACH NON-BRANCHING INSTRUCTION.
5. A SEPARATE BRANCH COMMAND MUST BE EMPLOYED TO CHANGE THE DIRECTION OF PROGRAM FLOW.
6. WITH THE EXCEPTION OF THE NEXT-INST-ADDR FIELD, THE SINGLE-ADDRESS COMMAND AND THE 2 ADDRESS COMMAND FORMAT (VERSION II) ARE EQUIVALENT.

5.2.6 The Zero-Address Command Format

A still-further reduction in the required size of memory modules used for program storage may be achieved if the instruction word is used to deal entirely with implied operands. The physical structure to implement this concept is the LIFO stack that was discussed in Section 4.3. Any mathematical or logical operation will manipulate the top two stack locations. The result of the machine operation will be put in the location directly below the TOS. The stack will then be popped, leaving the result of the machine operation as the top element in the stack. A PC is used to implicitly point to the next instruction; it is incremented by 1 at the completion of each nonbranching instruction. The push and pop operations are actually single-address instructions that require the specification of an operand in main storage. Table 5-3f exhibits a program that uses a stack to implement a solution to equation (1). Note that the loading of the stack (a push operation) requires the specification of the address in main storage of the operand that is to be placed on the stack. Similarly, the unloading of the stack (a pop operation) requires the specification of the address in main storage where the contents of the TOS are to be placed. Consequently, the pure stack architecture actually requires a mixture of zero-address and single-address instructions to implement a program. The Burroughs B5500, a midicomputer, represents a commercial machine that has been implemented using a zero-address instruction format.

5.2.7 The Single-Address Machine

Most computers execute a mixture of instruction types. However, in terms of programming efficiency, one type may be executed predominantly. This instruction type is then used to characterize the machine. For example, the stack machine required the use of zero-address and single-address instructions. Data movement operations (pushes and pops) required single-address commands. Data manipulation operations (arithmetic and logical functions) used zero-address commands. Such commands represented the important operations the machine had to perform. Consequently, the stack machine is often referred to as a *zero-address machine.*

The most common format, however, that has been encountered at the mini/microcomputer level has been the single-address command. There is a fundamental reason for this. The single-address format will normally produce a reasonably simple machine structure that is efficient in terms of the memory area required to store each individual instruction. Also, it will economize on hardware since complicated instructions will not be employed. However, the single-address format will require more memory references to execute a given program because of the more limited capability of the single-address instructions.

The limited word size of the early small computers' processor encouraged the use of the single-address scheme, which was the only viable format in terms of cost effectiveness. The traditional minicomputer has been developed as a low-cost, general-purpose computing machine. It has achieved a substantial cost reduction by incorporating simplified architectural features, such as a single accumulator and modular

TABLE 5-3f Zero-Address Command Format

	0-ADDRESS PROGRAM (OPCODE)	STACK-STATE BEFORE	STACK-STATE AFTER
I1	PUSH D		D
I2	PUSH E	D	E D
I3	MUL	E D	D*E
I4	PUSH F	D*E	F D*E
I5	DIV	F D*E	(D*E)/F
I6	PUSH C	(D*E)/F	C (D*E)/F
I7	ADD	C (D*E)/F	C+(D*E)/F
I8	PUSH B	C+(D*E)/F	B C+(D*E)/F
I9	ADD	B C+(D*E)/F	B+C+(D*E)/F
I10	PUSH G	B+C+(D*E)/F	G B+C+(D*E)/F
I11	PUSH H	G B+C+(D*E)/F	H G B+C+(D*E)/F
I12	MUL	H G B+C+(D*E)/F	G*H B+C+(D*E)/F
I13	DIV	G*H B+C+(D*E)/F	[B+C+(D*E)/F]/(G*H)
I14	PØP A	[B+C+(D*E)/F]/(G*H)	
I15	HLT		

COMMENTS

1. A MATHEMATICAL OR LOGICAL OPERATION MANIPULATES THE TOP TWO STACK LOCATIONS, PUTS THE RESULT IN THE LOCATION DIRECTLY BELOW THE TØS AND POPS THE STACK, LEAVING THE NEW RESULT IN THE TØS.
2. BOTH THE PUSH AND POP OPERATIONS ARE ACTUALLY SINGLE-ADDRESS INSTRUCTIONS.
   i. PUSH X OBTAINS THE CONTENTS OF MEMORY LOCATION X AND PUSHES IT ONTO THE TØS.
   ii. POP Y POPS THE CONTENTS OF THE TØS AND PUTS IT IN LOCATION Y.
3. THE PC IS AUTOMATICALLY INCREMENTED BY I AT THE COMPLETION OF EACH NONBRANCHING INSTRUCTION.
4. A SEPARATE BRANCH COMMAND MUST BE EMPLOYED TO CHANGE THE DIRECTION OF PROGRAM FLOW.

packaging concepts. The microprocessor structures have maintained this philosophy of elegance in performance through simplicity in design.

5.3 ADDRESSING SYSTEMS

5.3.1 The Concept of Address System Design

The execution of a machine directive involves specification of the location of the operand referenced by the instruction. Typically, such operand information is contained within the operand field of the instruction itself. However, the operand or the address of its location in main storage may also be placed in a processor register that is referenced by the instruction. The actual technique employed to locate the operand is a function of the instruction word size of the machine and the sophistication of the addressing logic which operates on the instruction word.

The simplest addressing technique is for the bits in the operand field to be used to explicitly specify a unique address in main storage. Figure 5-8 illustrates this situation. Note that the width of the memory address register (MAR) is equal to the width of the operand field in the instruction word. Consequently, the length of the address word and the length of the instruction word are not equal. Furthermore, the maximum size of main storage that may be referenced by a single instruction is dictated by the number of bits in the operand field. For this example, the operand field contains 12 bits and the maximum size of main storage available for this instruction type is $2^{12} = 4096$ locations. To reference an operand stored in a location other than one of the first 4096 main storage slots (addresses 0_8 through 7777_8) would require the use of another instruction. This instruction would switch the address logic to the appropriate 4096-word memory bank before the following instruction referenced the desired operand. Consequently, the number of operands that may be referenced by a single instruction is limited by the size of the address field in the instruction word. This restriction can be

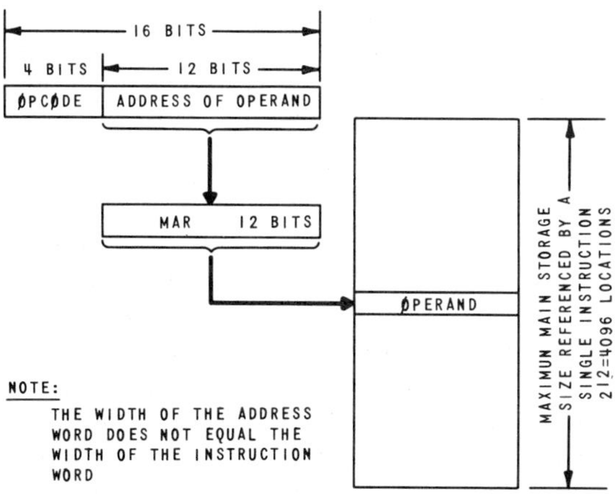

5-8 Instruction explicitly specifies the location of the operand

severe if no double- or triple-word instructions are permitted since the operand field cannot expand. For short-word-length instructions (8 to 16 bits), it is common to find 256 to 1024 locations accessible to the machine using this addressing convention. Since the early large-scale computing machines employed instruction words of sufficient length, this addressing technique was not inconvenient. For instance, the 32-bit instruction word found in the IBM System/360 series permitted 20 or more bits to be used to define the location of the operand. In this case, a single instruction could directly reference in excess of 1,048,576 storage locations. Thus, even though the address word was shorter than the instruction word, a wide span of memory could be accessed directly by the machine.

The capability of directly addressing an extensive amount of main storage did not necessarily make such large machines easier to program. Variations in addressing memory were incorporated for use on the large computing machines to provide flexibility of programming for the user. These variations in addressing took the form of operations performed on the address field of the instruction word before the operand was referenced in main storage. Typically, an algorithm was applied to the address field using hardware to produce a physical memory address. The primary purpose of such techniques was twofold:

1. To provide programming versatility for the user.
2. To economize on the area required in main memory to store the program by keeping the number of address bits in an instruction to a reasonable size.

Address system design, consequently, incorporates various algorithms to modify or interpret the operand address field in the instruction before the operand is actually referenced. In employing a particular addressing convention, the address that a machine actually uses for finally referencing main storage is called the *effective address*. In the addressing technique shown in Figure 5-8, the operand address found in the instruction word is also the effective address. In general, the techniques used to generate an effective address are dictated by the performance requirements placed on a given machine and the cost of implementing these techniques in a given architecture. Occasionally, a particular addressing technique will either complicate the programming of a given machine or require a sufficiently complex logical implementation to not justify its inclusion in the set of machine features.

The basic concepts of address system design are common across the spectrum of computing machines from the large maxicomputer to the microcomputer made from a single-chip microprocessor. However, addressing techniques may be incorporated in a small computer design that may not be used in a large computer implementation. The reasons for this have to do with the special problems encountered when working with the limited-size instruction word of a small computer.

One of the most striking characteristics of many of the microprocessor structures is that the length of the address word and the length of the data word are not the same. For example, the address bus of the Rockwell PPS-8 microprocessor has a width of 15 bits while the data bus has a width of only 8 bits. Although typical of modern microprocessor structures, this is contrary to the concept observed by most minicomputers, in which the address word and the instruction word are both the same length. The address word length of a microprocessor is normally greater than the length of the data word. The extended address word permits a wide range of main storage to be referenced by an effective address generated by a single instruction. At the same time, the microprocessor handles data as 8-bit bytes of information. This dichotomy is also observed at the microprocessor level in terms of dedicating certain processor registers to handling only data words and separating these from one or more other processor registers that administer only address words. Typically, selected on-chip registers will be reserved for data handling with their word length set equal to the data word length. In addition, another set of on-chip registers will be used for address calculations, with the word length of these registers set equal to the length of the address word.

In an attempt to circumvent the limited addressing capability of a small computer, various addressing strategies originally developed for use on large-scale computers have been adopted by the designers of small machines. These strategies are also called *addressing modes* and are typically selected by a bit group specified in the instruction word. The mode bits are normally partitioned off from the bit group used to form the operand address field, as shown in Figure 5-9. A common occurrence is for a specific instruction to implicitly employ an addressing mode as opposed to explicitly identifying the mode in the instruction word, as shown in Figure 5-10. This approach provides additional bit combinations that may be used to expand the opcode or operand fields.

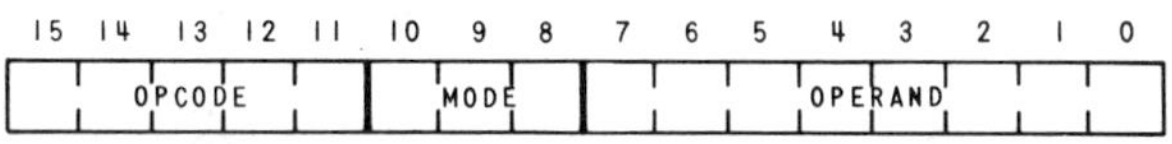

5-9 Use of an address-mode field

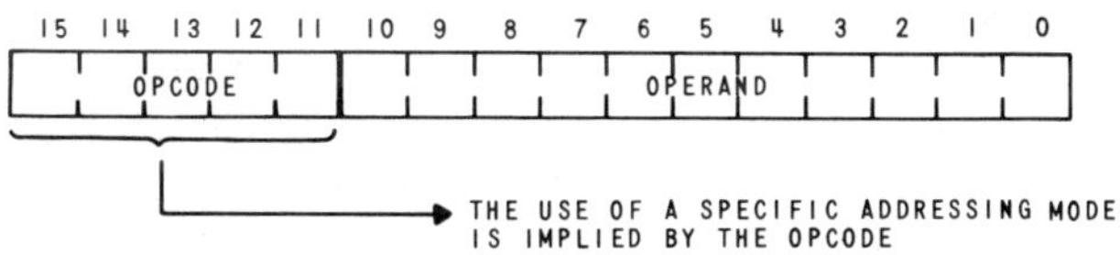

5-10 Use of an implied address mode

In many machine operations, the contents of the operand field are often added to the contents of a memory location or a processor register to generate the effective address. Essentially, the operand field acts as a signed number that specifies how many memory locations from a fixed storage address the operand is actually located. The operand field functions as a signed displacement, as shown in Figure 5-11. As a consequence, the operand bit group is often referred to as the *displacement field of the instruction word.* This expression has been widely accepted by users of the IBM System/360 and System/370 machines, where the operand section of an instruction is usually much shorter than the actual effective address used to reference memory. The terms *displacement* and *operand address field* will be used interchangeably in future discussions.

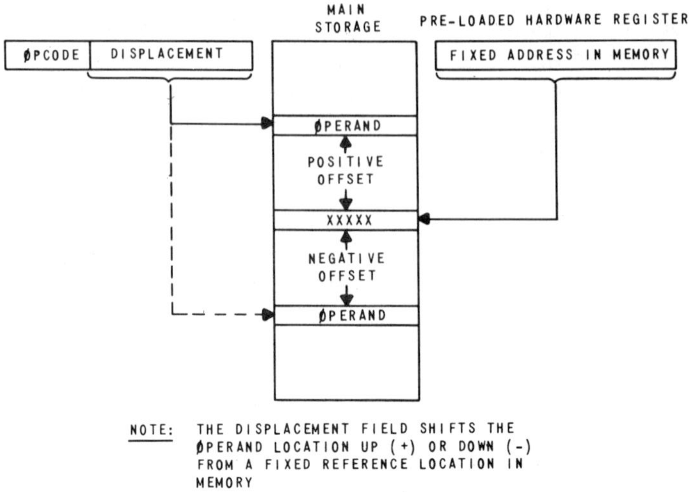

5-11 Concept of the displacement field

5.3.2 Direct Addressing

The most common form of memory addressing encountered at any level of machine design is *direct* or *absolute addressing*. This technique uses the displacement bits of the instruction word as the effective address of the desired operand. Typically, the displacement is moved directly into the memory address register and the associated operand is then fetched into the memory data register. The address word in many machines is normally longer than the displacement. Consequently, the displacement is inserted in the MAR in the low-order bit positions of that register, with the remaining positions filled with 0's. Figure 5-12 illustrates this addressing technique.

Direct addressing, as employed at the microprocessor level, often refers to the use of an instruction word that is wide enough to include a displacement that may reference any location in main memory. If the displacement is not of sufficient width to access all of memory, a variation of direct addressing, called *abbreviated addressing*, may be employed. In this case, the displacement contains only the least significant bits of the operand address. The most significant portion of the address is contained in an independent register that may be part of the CPU. This register must be loaded by a separate instruction. The effective address is formed by the concatenation of this offset register and the displacement in the MAR. Figure 5-13 shows the implementation of abbreviated addressing. Abbreviated addressing is a form of *base register addressing*, which is discussed more fully in Section 5.3.7.

A further variation of direct addressing is *immediate* or *literal addressing*. In this technique, the displacement portion of the instruction word is not treated as an address. Instead, the address displacement bits are assigned the actual value of the desired operand. Typically, these immediate data will be used in an intermediate calculation or routed to one of the processor data registers. Immediate addressing can enhance

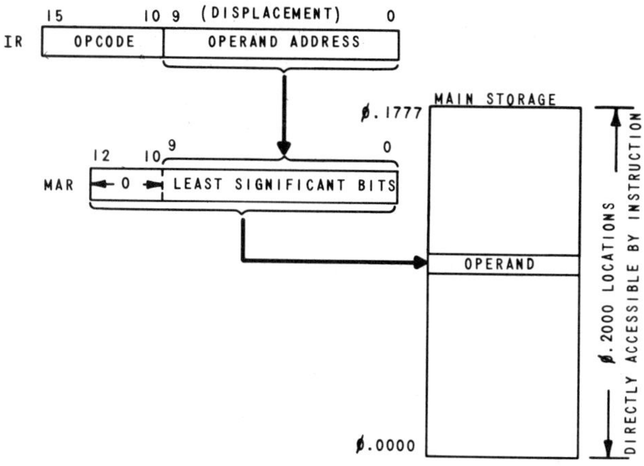

NOTES:

1. MOST SIGNIFICANT BITS OF MAR (B10-B12) MUST BE PRELOADED BY A SEPARATE INSTRUCTION.
2. DISPLACEMENT SIZE PERMITS 1024 STORAGE LOCATIONS TO BE REFERENCED BY THE INSTRUCTION.

5-12 Implementation of direct addressing

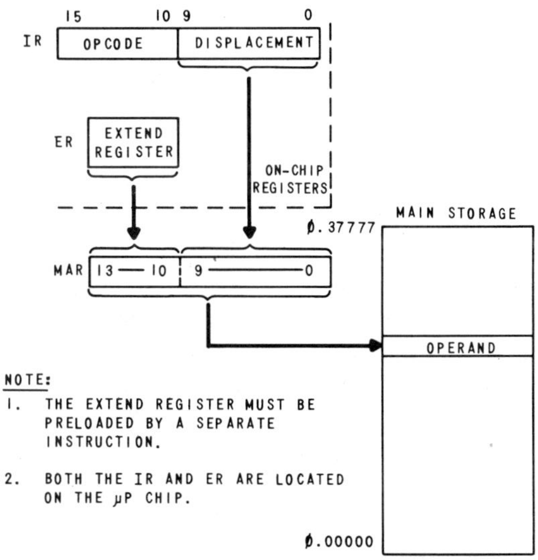

5-13 Abbreviated addressing

the execution time of a program by reducing the number of memory accesses required to fetch the associated operands, since these operands are stored as part of the instructions that use them. The PDP-11 family uses an immediate addressing mode in its instruction set to provide a time enhancement for accessing constant operands by including the constant in the memory location immediately following the instruction word. In this case, the PDP-11 instruction functions as a double-word, two-cycle immediate address command. Figure 5-14 exhibits the technique of immediate addressing.

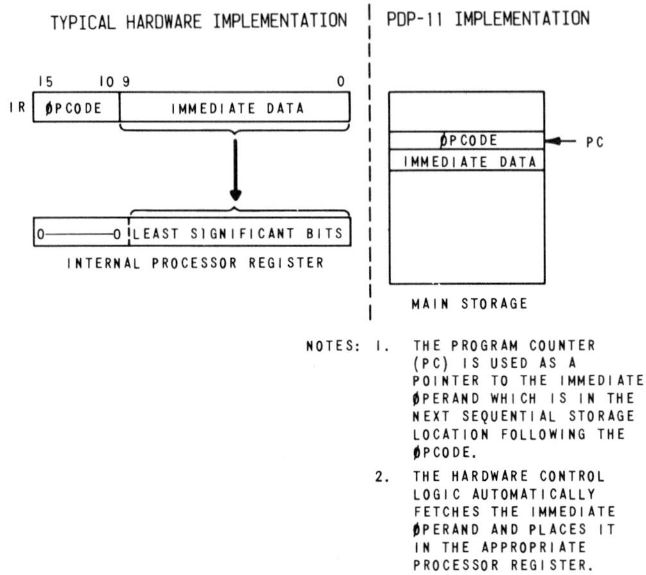

5-14 Immediate or literal addressing

The major disadvantage of direct and immediate addressing is the limitation placed by the size of the instruction word on the maximum range of main storage that may be referenced by a single-word directive. Since the opcode field requires a portion of each instruction word, all available memory often cannot be accessed unless either abbreviated addressing is used or the instruction is configured from two or more words in memory. Virtually all 4-bit and 8-bit microprocessors employ some form of double-word and even triple-word instructions. The primary disadvantage of multiple-word instructions is that additional memory accesses are required to configure the instruction. Each n-word instruction must increment the PC n times to obtain the entire instruction word. Consequently, multiple-word instructions require a more sophisticated control section than single-word commands, and multiple-word instructions require additional memory. However, they can expand and enrich a machine's command repertoire. For many years, the cost of main memory discouraged the use of multiple-word instructions in commercial minicomputers. However, the appearance of low-cost semiconductor memories and the successful implementations of 4-bit and 8-bit microprocessors led to the routine use of multiple-word instructions in the instruction repertoire of mini/microcomputers.

In general, addressing modes may be classified into one of two categories, based on the number of words required to be used with an instruction to reference an operand:

1. *Short-form addressing*. This group uses only the displacement bits in the instruction word to either represent the operand itself or to define an address relative to either location 0 in main memory, the PC, or a dedicated register that may be directly accessed by the processor. Direct addressing, abbreviated addressing, and immediate addressing, when a double-word instruction is not employed, all fall within this category.
2. *Long-form addressing*. This group makes use of extended addressing techniques through multiple-word instructions to reference main memory. The long-form group will be elaborated on in the following sections.

5.3.3 Indirect Addressing

Indirect addressing makes use of two (not necessarily contiguous) storage locations to access any word in a memory field. The operand portion of a short-form instruction is used to point to a memory location that does not contain the desired data but, rather, the effective address of the storage location containing the data. A second memory reference must then be performed by the processor to obtain the operand. During this second memory reference, the execution of the instruction is deferred until the operand has been fetched. Because of this, the PDP-11 family refers to its implementation of indirect addressing as *deferred addressing*. The terms may be used interchangeably. Its chief disadvantage is that it costs execution time in the form of an additional access of main storage to obtain the operand. However, it may be implemented very economically and is found as a standard mode on virtually all microprocessors and minicomputers. Indirection may also be performed using the contents of a general register as the effective address of the operand. In this case, the instruction specifies the general register and the fact that address indirection is to be performed using the register contents. This variation is more fully discussed in Section 5.3.11.

Single-level indirect addressing is specified by a dedicated bit in the instruction word. If the indirect bit is set, the contents of the location pointed to by the displacement is treated as an address. The processor enters an instruction-deferred state, delays execution of the current instruction, and uses the obtained address to perform a second memory reference or first-level indirection operation to fetch the operand. If the indirect bit is cleared, the contents of the location pointed to by the displacement are treated as the desired operand. Indirect addressing permits a program to be written that will reference a table of effective addresses for data. The actual table entry is made by means of an indirect address pointer. This implies that the operand obtained by the table access should be treated as the effective address of the required data instead of the data themselves. The table entries may be changed prior to program execution to point to new data or to relocate the original data. In either case, the program itself does not have to be modified. Figure 5-15 illustrates single-level indirect addressing, and this situation in particular.

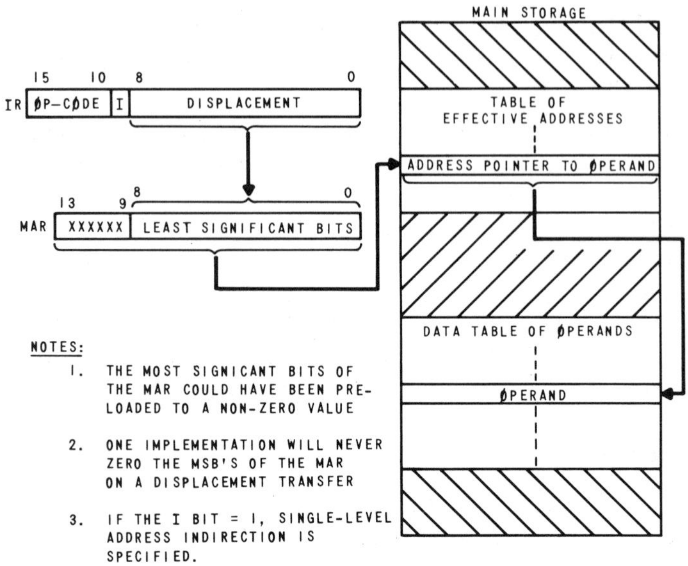

5-15 Single-level indirect addressing

Hellerman [1] has pointed out that indirect addressing may be employed for an entirely different reason—to improve the instruction fetch rate from a memory with a given bandwidth. *Bandwidth*, in this case, refers to the number of storage accesses per unit of time (bits per second) that a memory is capable of supplying. For a given program, most instruction types will only be permitted to be of the short-form addressing group. Since this requires that most operands be referenced by the displacement portion of the instruction word, the program is confined to execute in a highly restricted address range of memory. Indirect addressing may be used to fetch those occasional operands that cannot be fitted within the limited area of memory permitted to the program. Consequently, if the vast majority of the instructions are kept within the short-form address group, only one memory reference will be required per instruction, and a high instruction fetch rate may be obtained. For those few operands that lie out of the direct addressing range of the program, the occasional extra memory cycle required to perform indirection should have little effect on the overall execution time of the program.

For most mini/microcomputers, the instruction fetch rate is not the determining factor in a system application. The most significant factor, aside from the cost, is the required system response. This, in turn, is related to the ability of the processor to perform the required internal computations and I/O operations effectively. Instruction fetch rate is actually secondary to instruction execution time unless a great many indirect memory references are made. Because of this, indirection as applied at the mini/microcomputer level has been used to extend the addressing capability of the machine rather than to optimize the instruction fetch rate.

5.3.4 Multilevel Indirect Addressing

An extension of indirect addressing that allows more than one indirect address reference by a single instruction is known as *multilevel indirect addressing*. In this case, a bit in each word of memory is treated as an address indirection indicator or INDIRECT bit. By convention, this bit is normally taken as the same bit employed by the instruction word to specify an indirect memory reference. Typically, the most significant bit of each memory word during the operand FETCH portion of an instruction is treated as the INDIRECT bit. If the INDIRECT bit is set at the referenced location, the contents are treated as a memory address in an indirection chain. The final location in the indirection chain will have its INDIRECT bit cleared, indicating that the content of that location is the effective address of the desired operand. Figure 5-16 depicts the general details of multilevel indirect addressing. For each level of indirect addressing, at least one additional memory cycle is required to fetch the contents of the next location to be referenced. Multilevel indirection may be specified by the programmer at assembly time through the use of a macro or pseudo-op (see Appendix C) to indicate indirect references beyond single-level indirect addressing.

There are three major programming areas where multilevel indirection can be meaningfully used. The first area is the linking of table entries to point to an operand stored in a specially organized logical structure. The second area is the passing of parameters between a string of subroutine calls. A subroutine nested several levels deep may need a parameter that was passed from subroutine A to subroutine B. The nested subroutine may just link backward through a series of memory indirections to the original parameter pointer passed at the first level of subroutine calls. The entire

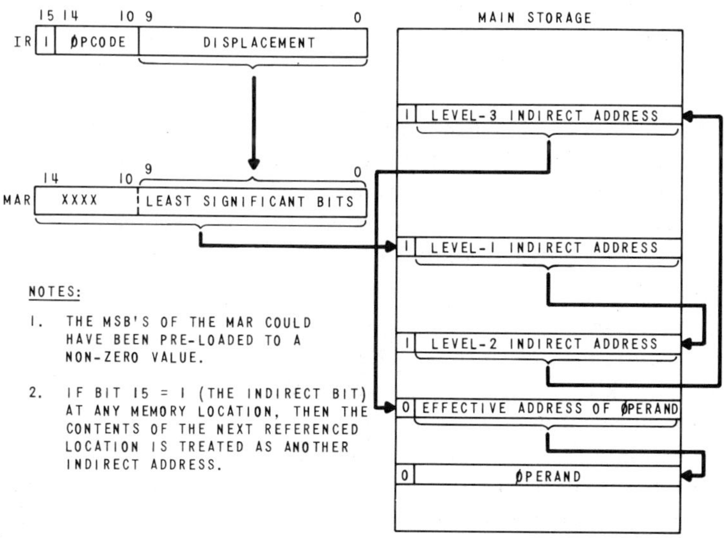

5-16 Multilevel indirect addressing

indirection chain may be set up by a macro issued in conjunction with the nested subroutine call. The third area is in the design of a relocatable assembly language program. Using multilevel indirection in a fixed sector addressing structure (refer to Section 5.3.9), the program may be written without concern for the sectors in which it will be stored. When the program is being loaded, the loader provides indirect addressing whenever it detects an operand that does not fall in either the current sector or sector 0. The loader substitutes a reference to sector 0 and then stores an indirect address in this referenced location. References to the same operand from other pages will be linked through the same location in sector 0. The Honeywell 516, the System Engineering Laboratories SEL-810B, and Hewlett-Packard HP2100 series all used multilevel indirection by assigning bit 15 of the memory word as an indirect bit. This halves the maximum allowable locations in main memory that may be accessed by a user program without resorting to bank switching of memory modules.

Multilevel indirect addressing has not been used widely in most mini/microcomputers for several reasons. First, the dedication of a bit in each storage word to specify indirection reduces the maximum size of memory that may be referenced by a single instruction. Second, an additional memory reference is required for each new level of indirection. These additional memory cycles can represent a serious real-time consideration if the machine is being used in an event-sensitive environment. Event sensitivity is normally obtained by using the hardware interrupt mechanism of the machine to respond to critical events that have occurred in the external world. It is a characteristic of most machines that employ multilevel indirection that the hardware interrupt mechanism is disabled until all levels of multilevel address indirection have been completed. It is possible to encounter an indirection chain of sufficient length that it compromises the interrupt response time required by the application. It is the responsibility of the application system designer to anticipate such cases and prevent their occurrence through programming techniques that do not use excessively long indirection chains.

Perhaps the most serious concern confronted by a programmer when multilevel indirection is used is the possibility that the executing program may chain into a nest of indirect addresses with the last address in the chain referencing the first address in the chain. In effect, the program forms a closed indirection loop and indirects around the chain forever. Two possible solutions to this situation are usually considered by the machine designer:

1. The programmer is alerted that the possibility of endless indirection exists by the instruction manual of the machine. It is left as the programmer's responsibility to check the program and ensure that this condition will never arise.
2. Since for most programmers simple program analysis will still not guarantee that the situation of endless indirection has been caught, a *trap circuit* is also provided in the control hardware to sense this condition. When the first level of indirection is entered, signified by the machine entering the instruction DEFER state, a hardware timer is initialized to run for sufficient time so that every location in the current memory field can be accessed by a chain of indirect addresses. When the timer reaches the preset count, signifying that one entire field of

memory has been completely indirected through, a trap or internal interrupt to an indirection fault service routine is generated. The service routine sets the appropriate error flag and aborts the program.

5.3.5 Autoindex Addressing

An interesting variation of single-level indirect addressing is called *autoindexing*. In this structure, several main storage locations are reserved as autoindex registers. The control hardware permits this operation to take place only when an instruction makes an indirect reference to one of these locations. If an indirect reference is made, the effective address is generated by the machine, which automatically increments or decrements the contents of the referenced autoindex register. In autoincrement addressing, the contents of the memory location are incremented by 1 immediately *before* the instruction is executed. In autodecrement addressing, the contents of the memory location are decremented by 1 immediately *following* execution of the instruction.

Typically, special locations in memory consisting of 8 to 16 core registers are reserved for autoindexing. In the PDP-8, for example, locations 10_8 through 17_8 of sector 0 in each memory field function as autoincrement registers. Autoindexing is an inexpensive technique that may be used to access successive locations in an array. No index registers (see the following discussion) need to be employed. For the early minicomputers, this saved hardware and reduced costs. In addition, no instruction word bit is used to produce autoindexing. This provides a larger set of possible opcodes by doubling the number of available bit combinations. Only one extra memory cycle is required to implement autoindexing. However, the autoindex main storage registers are not used for normal address indirection.

5.3.6 Indexed Addressing

The concept of autoindexing is actually part of a larger scheme known as *indexed addressing*. Indexing is an addressing strategy that permits rapid, repetitive calculations on large arrays of data. The early digital computer designers found that address modification for referencing large array structures occurred very frequently in many programs. To improve the speed of program execution, they removed this function from program control and had it performed automatically by hardware. To avoid using a memory reference, the address words were placed in one or more dedicated registers and the indexing operation was invoked implicitly when one of these registers was referenced by an instruction. The indexing function uses the displacement portion of the instruction word and the contents of the referenced register. It automatically adds or subtracts (depending on how the indexing function is implemented) the displacement to the register contents to form the effective address of the operand. The number added to the displacement is called the *index quantity* and the register containing the index quantity is referred to as an *index register*. Just as with indirect addressing, a bit in the instruction word may be dedicated to signify whether the referenced address should be indexed before the operand is fetched.

The actual index registers may be either located in dedicated memory locations, as discussed in the previous section, or implemented as hardware registers independent of main memory. If dedicated memory locations are used, an extra memory cycle is required for each indexing operation. In this case, actual execution time is considered secondary to the advantage of having multiple, low-cost index registers. Hardware register indexing requires only a small portion of the memory cycle and minimizes the time required to calculate the effective address of the operand. The SEL-810B assigns a dedicated bit in every memory location to indicate that the contents of that location should be indexed by unity. The SEL-810B also dedicates a bit of every memory word to signify memory indirection. Consequently, every memory reference instruction may involve both multilevel indirection and multilevel indexing. This technique costs 2 bits of every memory location, since they perform dedicated machine functions. In addition, multilevel indirection can become excessive in its use of memory cycles. For these two reasons, this addressing convention has not been observed by most other commercial machines. Figure 5-17 illustrates the general indexed addressing concept.

Indexing can provide the same features as single-level indirection. However, because less hardware is required, indirect addressing can be implemented in a less costly manner than indexed addressing. This appears to be the major reason why indirect addressing was used on most of the early minicomputers. Virtually all microprocessors and most minicomputers use the adder found in the ALU for indexing operations, thus economizing on hardware and cost. In addition, an index register can function as an accumulator and also serve as an intermediate storage register. The width of the index register is normally the width of the machine instruction word. Consequently, indexed addressing can specify any location in main storage provided that the size of available storage is not greater than the memory field size dictated by the number of bits in an instruction word. If more than one field of memory is

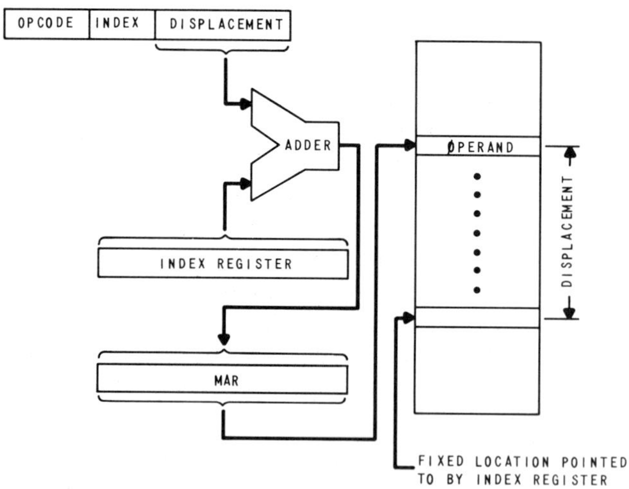

5-17 Indexed addressing

employed, indexing must be used in conjunction with a field switching instruction to access all of main memory.

Indexed addressing is now performed in most mini/microcomputers using either preindexing or postindexing. Both methods function identically when the direct address of an operand is generated; the displacement points to the actual operand on a direct memory reference. However, when an indirect memory reference is made, preindexing generates the indirect address in a manner different from postindexing. Preindexing immediately adds the address bits of the instruction word to the contents of the specified index register to generate a pointer to the location in main storage that contains the effective address. Preindexing performs the indexing operation first. The results of this operation are then used to obtain the indirect address of the operand. Figure 5-18 illustrates this situation. Postindexing, on the other hand, performs the indirection operation first. This is accomplished by using the address bits generated by the instruction word as an indirect pointer to a location in main memory. The contents of this location are treated as a displacement quantity for the effective address of the operand. This displacement is added to the contents of the specified index register to generate the effective address. Figure 5-19 shows the postindexing operation. Postindexing is the technique more commonly encountered in various mini/microcomputer designs. The use of multiple index registers offers several advantages. In general, they permit

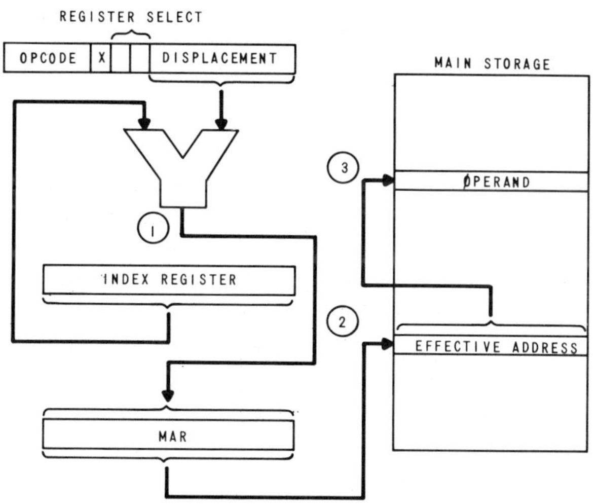

NOTE: MORE THAN ONE INDEX REGISTER MAY BE AVAILABLE, IN WHICH CASE THE INSTRUCTION WORD WILL OFTEN USE A REGISTER SELECT FIELD.

1. DISPLACEMENT ADDED TO PRESENT CONTENTS OF INDEX REGISTER.
2. RESULT PLACED IN MAR AND POINTS TO THE EFFECTIVE ADDRESS.
3. THE EFFECTIVE ADDRESS USED TO FETCH THE OPERAND.

5-18 Preindexed addressing

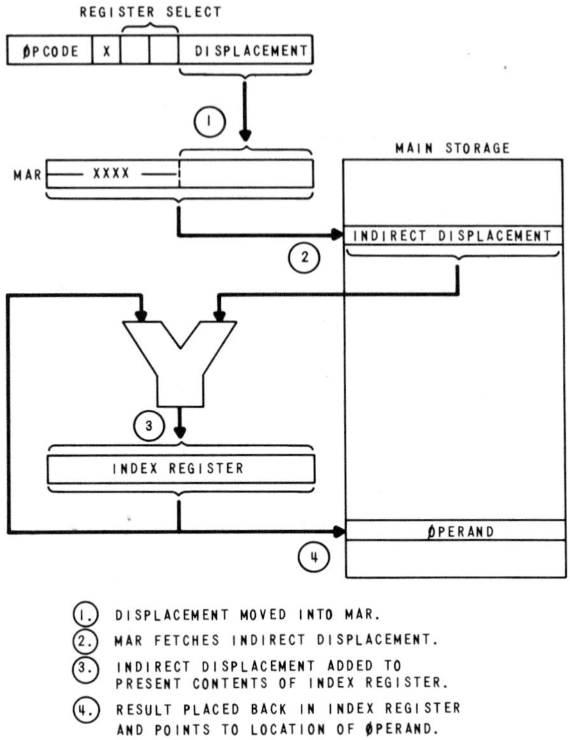

5-19 Postindexed addressing

involved address calculations to be performed by the control hardware. This reduces the number of address calculations that must be made by a program and, consequently, reduces the number of instructions required by a specific program. This reduction in machine instructions reflects itself in less main storage area being required for the program and a faster execution time. At both the mini- and microcomputer levels, multiple index registers are routinely incorporated in the machine design. For instance, the Intel 4040 microprocessor uses a total of 24 4-bit index registers organized into three eight-register banks for easy access by the programmer.

5.3.7 Base Register Addressing

Base register addressing, conceptually, is almost identical to indexing and, in several large computing machines, the same hardware has been used to implement both. In this mode, a base register separate from the instruction counter is normally employed. The address displacement in the instruction word is added to the contents of the base register to obtain the effective address of the operand. The displacement may be a signed binary number so that the operand may be found at an address above or below that contained in the base register. In concept, this operation appears the same as preindexing. In fact, several minicomputers have employed base register addressing as an alternative to preindexing. The primary differences that exist between the two are philosophical. Base registers are used to solve the problems of program relocation and the limited addressing range permitted by a small computer word. Index registers are used to reference data words contained within an executing program. In the larger computing machines, base registers are administered by the supervisory control program using privileged instructions. The user programs are not permitted to modify the base registers. At the microprocessor level, however, base registers are now being used to contain the effective address of the operand. Typically, the address word found in the base register will be longer than the word size used for data. The index registers are used to manipulate data words and, consequently, have the same length as the data. The base register supplies an extended addressing capability. Figure 5-20 illustrates base register addressing.

Program relocation is achieved with base addressing by first writing the program so that its starting location in memory is either 0 or a preestablished constant. During program execution, the base address, placed in a specific base register, is added to each program location. This feature permits the supervisory control program to arbitrarily relocate the application program in memory prior to its execution. It does this by loading the base register, with the address representing the offset in memory to which each program location should be referred.

The situation encountered in many of the microprocessor structures is that the instruction word length is insufficient to address all of the available main storage. Consequently, a larger address word is formed by using a base register and adding the displacement portion to the contents of the base register. This register may not be on the same chip as the CPU, but it has sufficient width to generate an effective address that can span all of available main storage. If the cost of additional execution time and

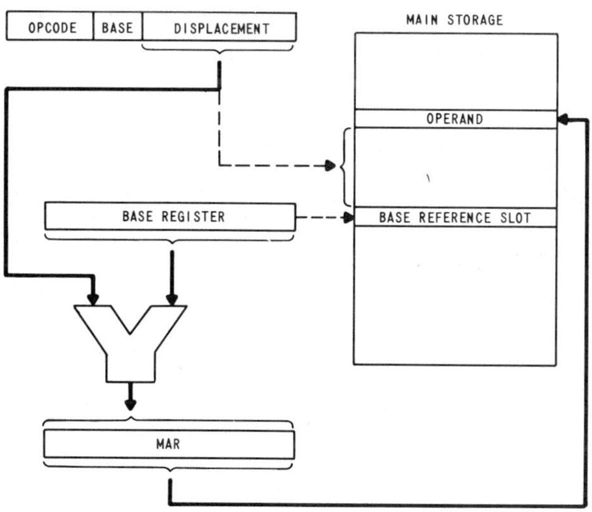

5-20 Base register addressing

hardware is too expensive to justify adding the displacement to the contents of the base register, a variation of base register addressing is used, called *page* or *sector addressing*. Main storage is divided into sectors or pages. Each sector has a maximum size equal to the addressing range of the displacement. A sector address register is preloaded with the high-order bits of the effective address. The full effective address is formed by concatenating the high-order bits in the sector address register with the displacement bits; the displacement forms the least significant bits of the effective address. This technique is often called *pagination* or *sectorization* and is discussed in detail in Sections 5.3.9 and 5.3.10. Figure 5-21 illustrates the principle of sector addressing. The addressing technique called *abbreviated addressing* is simply sector addressing using a base register. More than one page register may be used in a given machine implementation. In such a case, the instruction word specifies the page register to be used as well as the value of the displacement. The primary functional difference between a page register and a base register is that the contents of the displacement field are concatenated with the contents of a page register, whereas the contents of the displacement field are added to the contents of a base register. Figure 5-22 exhibits the use of multiple page registers. The primary advantage of both procedures is the larger address word that may be obtained.

A further variation of base register addressing uses the instruction counter as the base register. The displacement is normally treated as a signed binary number so that the effective address may be situated above or below the address contained in the instruction counter. The actual range of memory that a program may directly reference is defined by the addressing range of the displacement. Figure 5-23 illustrates this case. The range of directly addressable memory defines a sector that appears to follow the instruction counter. For this reason, this technique is often referred to as *program relative addressing* or as a *floating sector*.

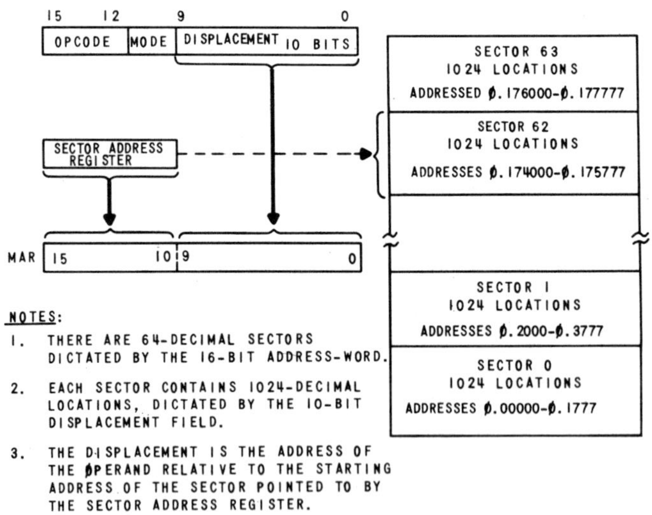

5-21 Fixed page or sector addressing

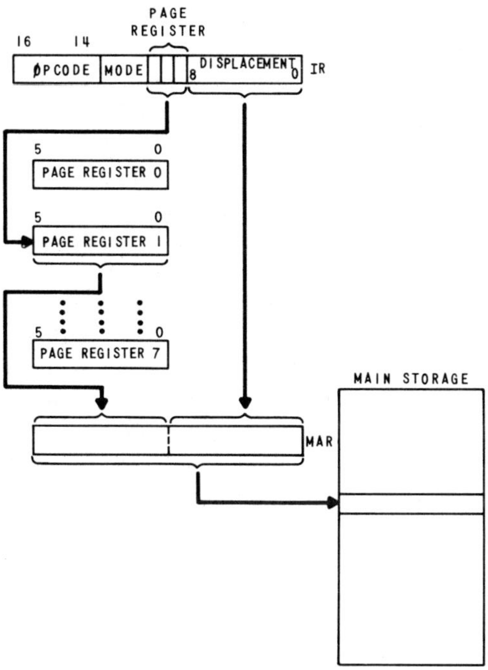

5-22 The use of multiple page registers

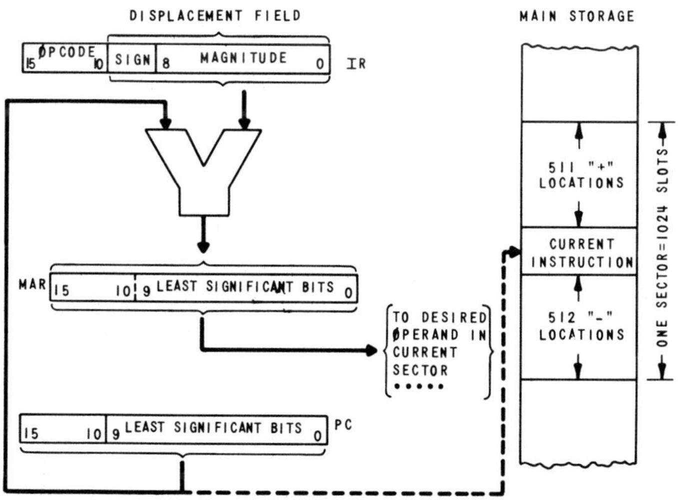

NOTE: THE MOST SIGNIFICANT BITS OF THE PC ARE USED TO DEFINE THE CURRENTLY AVAILABLE SECTOR

5-23 Program relative sectorization

Another variation of base register addressing, called the *pointer address mode*, is used at the microprocessor level, permitting a machine with a small instruction word to address a wide range of memory. The address word is obtained by placing the high-order bits of the address in a special register by means of a separate instruction. The contents of the special register are then concatenated with the displacement field of the instruction word to form the effective address. The pointer address register may be implemented on-chip or it may be an off-chip hardware device referenced by the microprocessor. As an example, consider Figure 5-24, which diagrams a microprocessor with its working registers located in main storage as opposed to being incorporated on the microprocessor chip. The number of working registers is taken to be 16, and they may be located anywhere in main memory. The application program references them by preloading the *working register group pointer* (*WRGP*) with the most significant bits of the address, where the working registers can be found in memory. Note that the size of the WRGP is 12 bits and that the register field in the instruction word must be 4 bits to specify 16 registers. Consequently, the WRGP points to a specific area of main storage that is 16 words wide. The register field selects the specific location in this 16-word area that is referenced by the instruction. Furthermore, this 16-word group may be relocated in main storage simply by changing the contents of the WRGP. In this example, main storage is laid out so that an area in low memory contains the starting address (base address) of each group of 16 consecutive addresses that are to be treated as a separate working register set. The WRGP is initially loaded with the starting address of the basic working register set. Thereafter, the application program overwrites the contents of the WRGP with a new base address only when a new group of working registers is to be used. The program itself must check for out-of-range addresses; no protection is provided in hardware for a new working register set being written in a critical data area of main storage. The 4-bit register field of the instruction word is moved into a 4-bit counter which is then concatenated with the contents of the WRGP. From this example, it should be apparent that the pointer address mode is another form of abbreviated addressing.

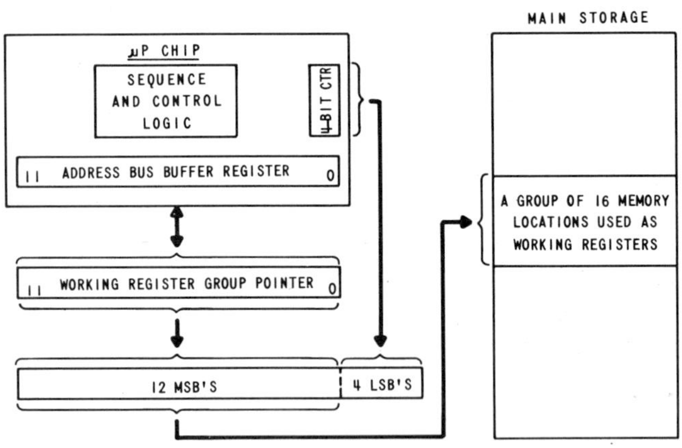

5-24 Pointer address mode

Extended addressing is a form of base register addressing in which an extension register is used to form the effective address. The contents of the extension register are concatenated with the instruction word displacement field to indicate the selected word in main storage. Typically, this extension register will be smaller than the displacement width, although the extension register could just as easily be larger. Its primary function is to provide an address word of sufficient width to access all available memory. Consequently, abbreviated addressing, pointer mode addressing, and sector addressing are all equivalent to extended addressing.

5.3.8 Generalized Bank Switching

Generalized bank switching has been observed at both the mini- and microcomputer level to permit the CPU to reference an extended address range of main storage. In particular, bank switching is an application of extended addressing where the maximum size of main storage is larger than the range of unique addresses possible when a full machine address word is employed. Using the PDP-8 as an example, its 12-bit word length permits a maximum of 4096 words to be referenced. However, its main core memory may be built up to a maximum size of 32,768 words using eight 4096-word memory modules. Each module represents a memory bank or field with the memory fields being numbered from 0 to 7. Field 0 is used to designate the first 4096 words of main storage.

Typically, a *memory field register* (*MFR*) is used to indicate the bank from which an operand is to be referenced or an instruction fetched. The memory address register then distinguishes which location in that bank contains the desired element of information. One instruction is used to change the contents of the MFR. A second instruction then directs program flow to branch to the new memory bank or reference an operand in the new field.

The PDP-8 uses two special 3-bit registers to achieve its bank switching capability. These two registers are called the *instruction field register* (*IF*) and *data field register* (*DF*). Depending on the portion of the instruction cycle being executed, the IF or the DF will be concatenated with the contents of the PC to permit a total of 2^{15}, or 32,768, memory locations to be addressed. The IF determines the field from which all instructions will be fetched. In addition, for all memory reference instructions that employ direct addressing, the IF specifies the field from which the associated operands will be obtained. The DF dictates the memory field from which operands are taken for all memory reference instructions that use indirect addressing. The PDP-8 employs two instructions to administer the contents of the IF and the DF:

1. The *change instruction field* (*CIF*) *command* tells the machine to change the contents of the IF to the specified field number. The new field number is kept in a 3-bit buffer register that is transparent to the programmer until a JUMP INDIRECT instruction is encountered. The buffer register contents are moved into the IF at the completion of this command to avoid an execution race condition. Figure 5-25 illustrates an example of how control is transferred to a

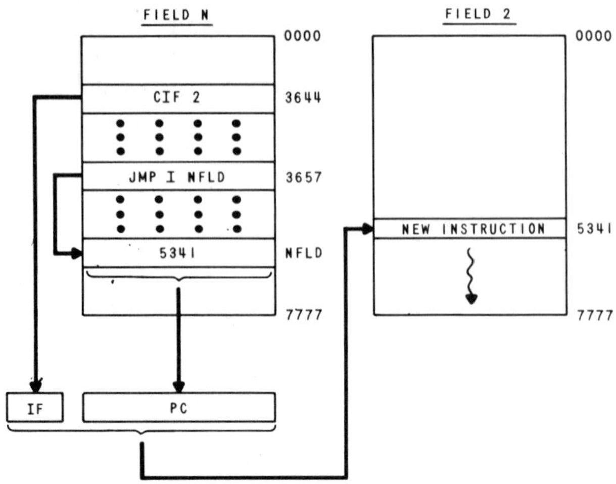

5-25 Transfer of control in the PDP-8 to a different memory bank [Reprinted (adapted) with permission of Digital Equipment Corporation]

different field. At location 3644, the program issues a CIF 2 command, which alerts the hardware to change the contents of the IF to 2 when a JUMP INDIRECT instruction is executed. At location 3657, such an instruction is encountered. The hardware uses the contents of location NFLD as an indirect pointer to location 5341, with the IF set to 2. The PC is loaded with the address 5341, and execution begins at the point in field 2.

2. The *change data field* (*CDF*) *instruction* loads the DF immediately with the new field to be used for data fetches. An operand, however, will be obtained from the new field only when an indirect memory reference is made. Figure 5-26 demonstrates how an operand is obtained from a field different from the field the program is executed in. At location 2415, the program indicates that future indirect operands are to be taken from field 3. However, it is not until location 2421 that the program issues a command that makes an indirect memory reference. In this case, the program obtains the contents of location SAM by making an indirect memory access through location PJOE in field 1. Since the DF already points to field 3, the hardware obtains the contents of location SAM in field 3. Note, however, that program execution continues in field 1. A CIF instruction must be used to redirect control to a new memory field.

Different field sizes have been used by various minicomputers other than the PDP-8. For instance, the SEL-810B uses a field size of 16,384 16-bit words. Only 14

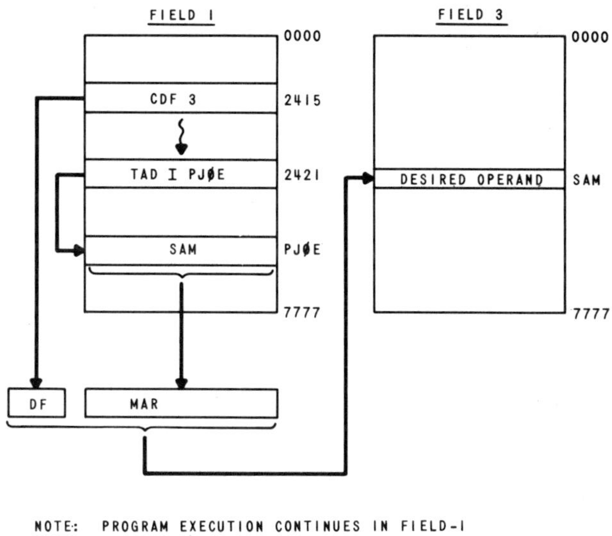

5-26 PDP-8 operand referencing in a field different from the field of the program [Reprinted (adapted) with permission of Digital Equipment Corporation]

bits of the SEL-810B address word are used for the specification of a location in main storage. Consequently, the physical memory bank size was set at $2^{14} = 16{,}384$ words. In each case, bank switching was employed as a means of expanding the maximum range of main storage that could be referenced by the minicomputer. Bank switching has been employed at the microprocessor level for both ROM and RAM accessing. A typical ROM bank encountered in a microprocessor chip set is a 28-pin DIP that contains 1024 8-bit words. Normally, a 12-bit address word is used by the CPU to reference a location in ROM. This provides for a maximum of 4096 8-bit ROM locations. Depending on whether the microprocessor is a 4-bit or 8-bit CPU, one of two addressing techniques is used to reference ROM:

1. *A separate address bus is used to transmit the full ROM address to the ROM chip group.* The address is decoded at the chip level with the chip number selectable by a wiring option provided by the manufacturer. All address bits are transmitted at the same time by the CPU when a ROM reference is performed. Such microprocessors as the Intel 8080 and the Motorola M6800 have employed a full 16-bit address word to reference either ROM or RAM.
2. *A common bus is used to transmit both address and data information.* The Intel 4040 is a good example of such an arrangement at the 4-bit microprocessor level. The 12-bit ROM address is configured by multiplexing nibbles of the address word, one at a time, to the bus. Each ROM chip configures an 8-bit address during the first two nibbles. The last nibble is used to transmit the two most significant bits of the ROM address and a 2-bit chip-select code. This chip-

select code will match the preprogrammed metal-option code of only one of the chips in the ROM bank if the ROM bank is made up of several chips. Only the selected chip will be permitted to send data back to the CPU.

In each memory reference technique, the CPU has functioned as a memory controller. It administers data in the ROM and RAM modules it controls. If the unified-bus concept is employed, in which all peripheral device registers are assigned main memory addresses, the CPU can further be regarded as a generalized digital interface in which the devices controlled by the CPU look exactly like an extension of main memory.

5.3.9 Fixed-Page Addressing

Short-form addressing has been implemented in several different minicomputers such as the 12-bit PDP-8 using a technique called *fixed-page addressing* or *sectorization*. As discussed in Section 5.3.7, main storage is divided up into equal areas, which are called pages. Each page contains the same number of memory locations. That fixed number represents the physical page size and is given by the addressing range of the displacement. A special register that functions as the page register is used to locate the operand in memory. The effective address is formed by concatenating the contents of the page register and the displacement. This technique is identical to the procedure described under extended addressing, including the requirement that the page register must be preloaded by a separate instruction before the effective address is generated.

An integer relation must exist between the size of a memory field and the minimum size of the page register. Refer to Figure 5-27 during the following discussion. Let

$F =$ number of storage locations in the memory field

$P =$ number of bits in the page register

$N =$ number of bits contained in the displacement

Then, the minimum size of the page register in bits is given by

$$(2)^P \geq F \div (2)^N \tag{2}$$

$$P \geq \log (F) - N \tag{3}$$

For the memory field to be exactly divisible by the page size, P must satisfy the equation above as an integer, with F expressed as an integer power of 2.

For the PDP-8, $F = 4096 = 2^{12}$ and $N = 8$,

$$P = \log (2^{12}) - 8 = 12 - 8 = 4 \text{ bits} \tag{4}$$

As an alternative to using a separate page register, the high-order bits of the PC may be decoded to determine the page number. Such an arrangement saves on hardware and is the addressing scheme used by the PDP-8 family. In the fixed-sector scheme,

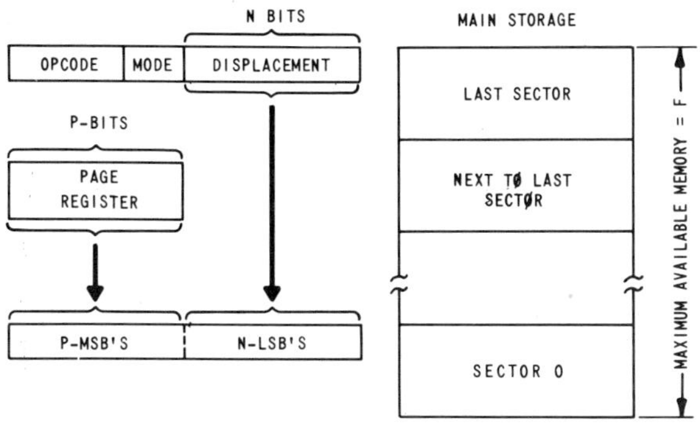

NOTES:

1. $2^{(P+N)} \geq F$
2. $2^{P} . 2^{N} \geq F$
3. $2^{P} \geq (\frac{F}{2^{N}})$
4. $P \geq \log_2 (F) - N$
5. SECTOR SIZE = 2^{N} LOCATIONS

5-27 Concept of paging or using a page register

an additional bit in the instruction word is used to specify page 0 or the current page. If N represents the number of memory locations on a fixed page, page 0 is defined by addresses 0_8 through $(2^N - 1)_8$. The current page is defined by the contents of the page register. If the high-order bits of the instruction counter function as the page register, the current page is defined by the contents of the instruction counter. If a separate page register is employed, the contents of the instruction counter can be quite different from the page register. In such a case, the user's software is required to administer the base register before an operand FETCH is performed.

The PDP-8 uses a hierarchy of fixed memory structures to permit its 12-bit instruction word to access all 32K words of available main storage. Main memory is organized into eight fields of 4096 words each. Each field contains 32 decimal pages of 128 words each. Figure 5-28 shows the memory organization of the PDP-8. All fixed-sector machines approach memory organization in a similar manner. However, the number of words per page, the number of pages per field, and the maximum number of fields supported by a given machine may be quite different from the PDP-8.

To reference an operand not contained in page 0 or the current page, indirect addressing is employed. The reason for this is quite simple. If short-form addressing is used and the operand does not lie in page 0 or the current page, it cannot be directly referenced by an instruction. What is required is a long-form addressing technique that will permit the operand to be referenced. Indexing could be used, but that requires additional hardware. For the PDP-8 and several similar computing machines, the least costly approach was to use address indirection. Using this convention, an indirect pointer is placed on either the current page or page 0; the pointer contains the address

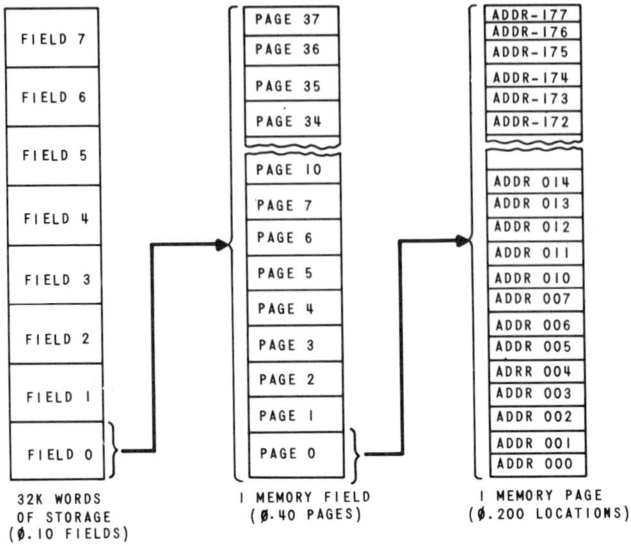

5-28 Memory organization of the PDP-8 [Reprinted with permission of Digital Equipment Corporation]

of the desired operand. This convention has one weakness and that occurs when page 0 is completely filled. An indirect pointer to an off-page operand can only be placed on the current page. This requires the programmer to direct execution to branch over the pointer so that the pointer will not be executed as an instruction. Normally, this situation is handled by the machine language assembler, which automatically generates the necessary single-level indirect pointers and flags them for the programmer. However, if one operand is referenced off-page by several different instructions (with each instruction located in a different page and page 0 filled), a separate indirect pointer must be created on each page to point to the same operand. In this case, if the machine does not support multilevel indirection, the most the assembler can do for the programmer is to flag such operand references as illegal double-level indirections. The burden of creating the necessary assembly language pointer is placed in the hands of the programmer. The programmer must use additional symbols to define the same location. Each symbol explicitly exists on its current page and functions as a pointer to the desired operand. When many such operand references exist, this technique can quickly use up valuable symbol table space in the assembler if program development is done on the target minicomputer system.

5.3.10 Program-Relative Paging

In several machines (the Data General Nova series is an example), the displacement is treated as a signed binary number, and a memory reference is made relative to the contents of the PC. This technique is often referred to as *program-relative paging* or *floating sectorization.* If N is the number of bits in the displacement, the full page size is given by 2^N, as in the case of fixed sectorization. However, the normal convention of using a signed displacement permits $[2^N - 1]$ memory locations to be directly addressed in the forward direction and 2^N locations in the backward direction. The sign bit permits one additional address to be accessed in the backward direction. In this configuration, the current page appears to move with the instruction counter. Consequently, this technique is sometimes described as *making use of a floating page.* A condition bit is employed in the instruction word just as in the fixed-page scheme to specify whether sector 0 or the current sector is to be referenced. An address in sector 0 will always be treated as a positive number. A variation of program-relative paging in which the displacement is treated as a positive binary number can also be implemented. In this case, there is no backward direct referencing capability on the current page. But this really presents no serious drawback since, with either convention, the programmer is responsible for placing an operand or its pointer near the instruction word. Both the signed and unsigned floating-page conventions require the insertion of instructions between operands that include BRANCH commands to connect the separated program segments together. In a further variation, the concept of page 0 may be abandoned. Instead, the directly addressable range of a command is simply the area surrounding the instruction word itself. In each of these variations, indirect addressing is used just as in the case of the fixed-sector scheme to reference an operand not located in either sector 0 or the current sector. The most common form of program-relative paging used at the mini/microcomputer level appears to be the signed displacement convention using both the current sector and sector 0.

5.3.11 General Register Addressing

As was pointed out earlier, the reason for the evolution of a general-purpose register set at both the mini- and microcomputer level was the speed enhancement achieved on executing instructions that referenced operands stored in individual registers in the GPR set. This improvement in execution time was significant when contrasted with executing instructions that referenced those same items placed in main storage. In addition, the use of GPR's offered the application programmer added flexibility in writing useful and efficient software. Because of these two facts, consideration has been given to exactly how many GPR's should be incorporated in a specific machine design. The optimum number of GPR's to be employed in a given machine is not a well-defined number. Generally, if a single-word instruction (16 bits) is used and a displacement field must be designated in the instruction, a maximum of eight GPR's has been employed. This allows 3 bits in the instruction word to be dedicated to specify the GPR, with the remaining bits divided between the opcode group, the addressing mode group, and the displacement. Figure 5-29 illustrates the case where 16 GPR's have been used and the instruction is a single 16-bit word. Note that the displacement is confined to 16 possible memory positions, which is a highly limited direct addressing range. Obviously, the 16-bit displacement field can be used in conjunction with the contents of a GPR to perform useful memory references. However, if an additional bit in the instruction word is assigned to the displacement field, the range of available operand references is doubled. This situation is shown in Figure 5-30. In terms of the cost of hardware and efficiency of programming, several machines including the PDP-11 family and the General Automation SPC-16 series have been implemented with eight registers as the size of their GPR file. The cost of hardware became so inexpensive by mid-1975 that multiple GPR files could be incorporated in a given machine structure very simply. However, the restrictions of a small instruction word still limited the effectiveness of such hardware features when single-word instructions were performed.

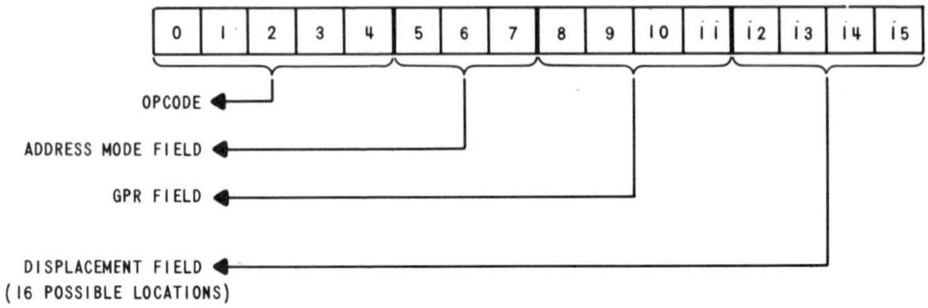

5-29 Specification of 16 GPR's in a 16-bit instruction word

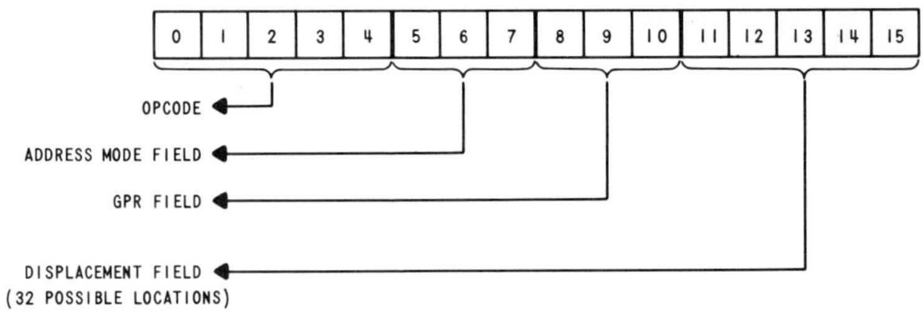

5-30 Specification of 8 GPR's in a 16-bit instruction word

There are two ways to extend the instruction-word capability when the word length is fixed:

1. The first is to use multiple-word instructions where necessary to provide additional code space for both the opcode and the displacement.
2. The second is to eliminate entirely the specification of a displacement value in a single-word instruction. If a displacement value is appropriate, a two-word instruction is used instead.

The PDP-11/20, introduced in 1970, was an unusual machine in that it implemented these two concepts at the minicomputer level for the first time. Prior to the appearance of the PDP-11/20, the minicomputers of that period had used the conventional memory addressing techniques outlined earlier (e.g., indirection, indexing, and base relative addressing). The PDP-11/20 used eight registers to form its GPR set; each of the registers could be employed by an instruction as either an accumulator or an index register. In particular, if an operand was placed in an accumulator, it did not require a reference to be made to main memory by the instruction; the specific accumulator could be referenced directly by the processor, saving a memory cycle in terms of instruction execution. In addition, the PDP-11/20 operation was built around the use of a processor status word that contained the most recent information on the state of the machine. The processor status word was implemented in a separate hardware register that contained the processor condition codes in bits 0 through 3 and the priority level of the currently executing program in bits 5 through 7. The condition codes were 4 flag bits that specified the result of arithmetic and logic operations. If an interrupt was received from a higher-priority process, the hardware pushed the current processor status word and PC onto the processor stack; a new processor status word and PC were then swapped in from a dedicated area of main storage to service the interrupt. At the conclusion of the interrupt service routine, the earlier state of the processor was reestablished by popping the previously stored processor status word and PC off the stack and forcing execution to continue at the location to which the PC pointed. The use of the processor status word permitted the PDP-11/20 to be shared by several concurrently executing programs in a multiprogramming environment. The actual contents of the processor status word could only be changed by executing a privileged instruction; the privileged instruction, in turn, could only be executed by a special executive program. Each new member of the PDP-11 family incorporated the addressing facilities found in the original PDP-11/20 so that an upward-compatible line of machines was obtained.

The PDP-11 is a 16-bit instruction word computer that has no direct addressing capabilities. Instructions may be one, two, or three words long. All memory referencing is done by using the eight GPR's found in the basic PDP-11 configuration (shown in Figure 5-31). A single-word instruction has no displacement field. Instead, it consists of a 9-bit opcode and a 6-bit destination address field (see Figure 5-32). The destination address field is broken up into a single bit to specify indirection, a 2-bit address mode field, and a 3-bit register address field. If two operands are required by an instruction, a single instruction can specify two distinct addresses through use of the GPR set. A two-operand instruction is shown in Figure 5-33. It uses 4 bits for the operation code, a 6-bit source operand field, and a 6-bit destination address field. Each address field is composed of a 3-bit address mode group and a 3-bit register address group. The destination field acts as the implied source of the second operand and specifies the location at which the result of the operation will be placed. Both operands may be located in separate GPR's; they may both be placed in main storage, or one operand can be placed in main storage with the other positioned in a GPR. The procedure observed in calculating each address is as follows:

1. The source address is generated first using the register field of the source operand in conjunction with the 2 most significant bits of the address mode to produce a basic address.
2. The least significant bit of the address mode group is then used to determine if the basic address is to be used as a direct address or treated as an address indirection.

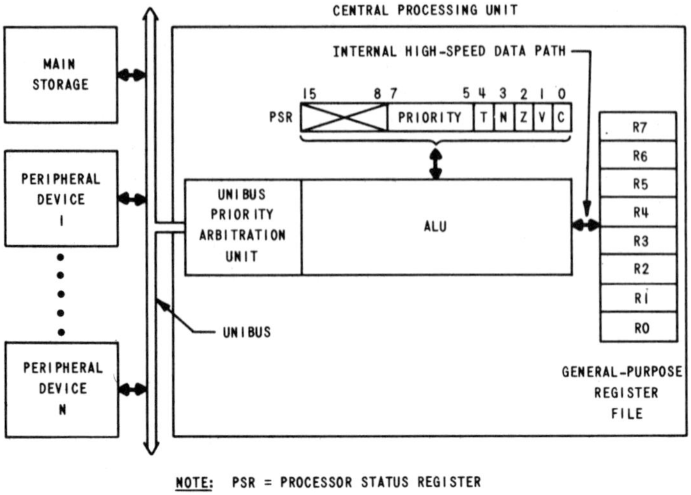

5-31 Basic PDP-11 configuration

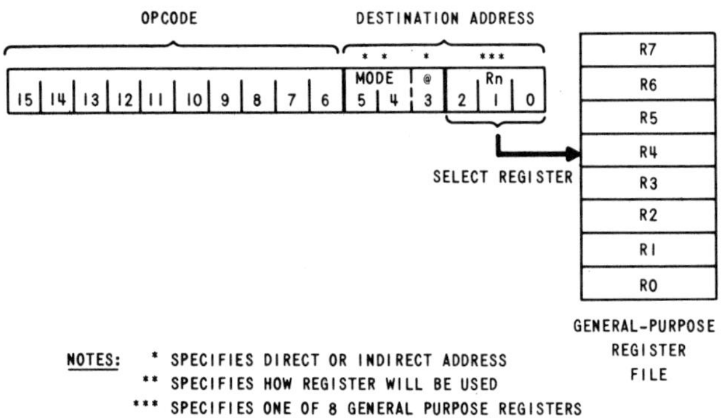

5-32 Single-operand instruction for the PDP-11 family [Reprinted with permission of Digital Equipment Corporation]

3. The destination address is then generated, proceeding through the same two calculation steps used for the source address. Recall, however, that this address acts as both the source of the second operand and the final destination of the result.

Figure 5-34 illustrates the four basic direct addressing modes performed by the PDP-11, while Figure 5-35 depicts the associated indirect addressing modes. An interesting additional feature in the PDP-11 addressing structure is that the PC may be manipulated in the same manner as a GPR. Figure 5-36 shows the additional addressing modes obtained when the PC is administered in this fashion.

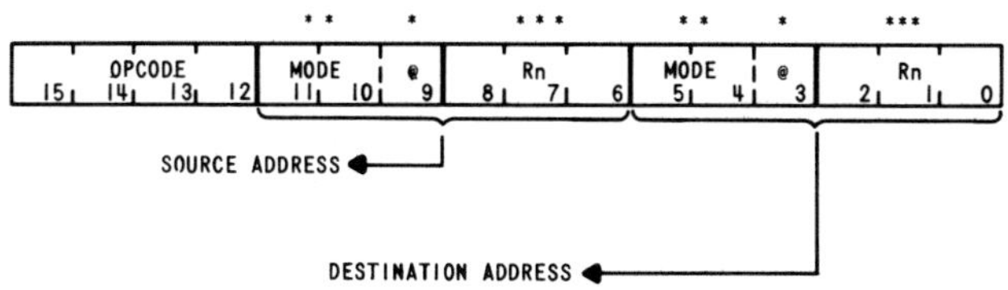

NOTES:

* DIRECT OR INDIRECT BIT FOR SOURCE AND DESTINATION ADDRESSES

** SPECIFIES HOW SELECTED REGISTERS ARE TO BE USED

*** SPECIFIES A GENERAL REGISTER

5-33 Double-operand instruction for the PDP-11 family [Reprinted with permission of Digital Equipment Corporation]

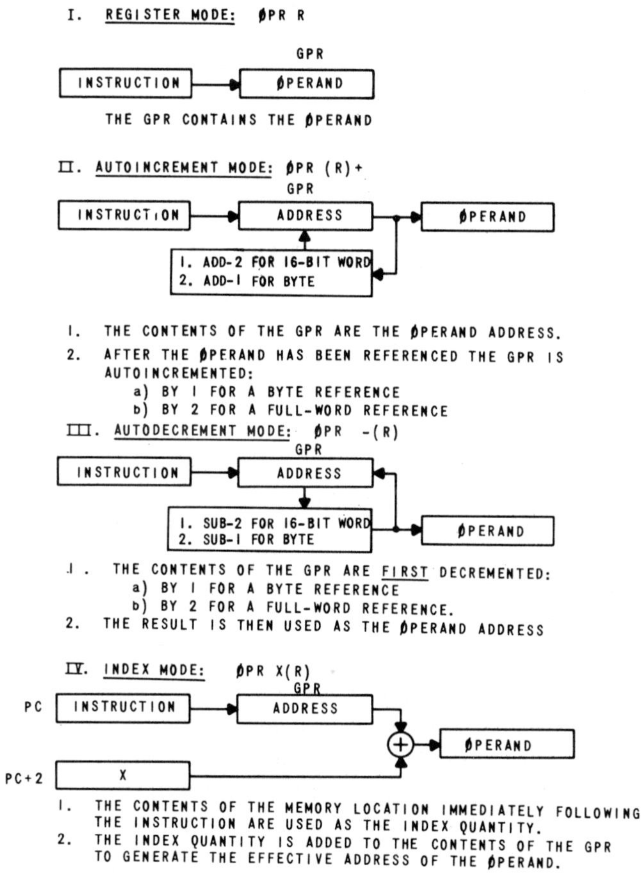

5-34 Four GPR direct addressing modes of the PDP-11 [Reprinted with permission of Digital Equipment Corporation]

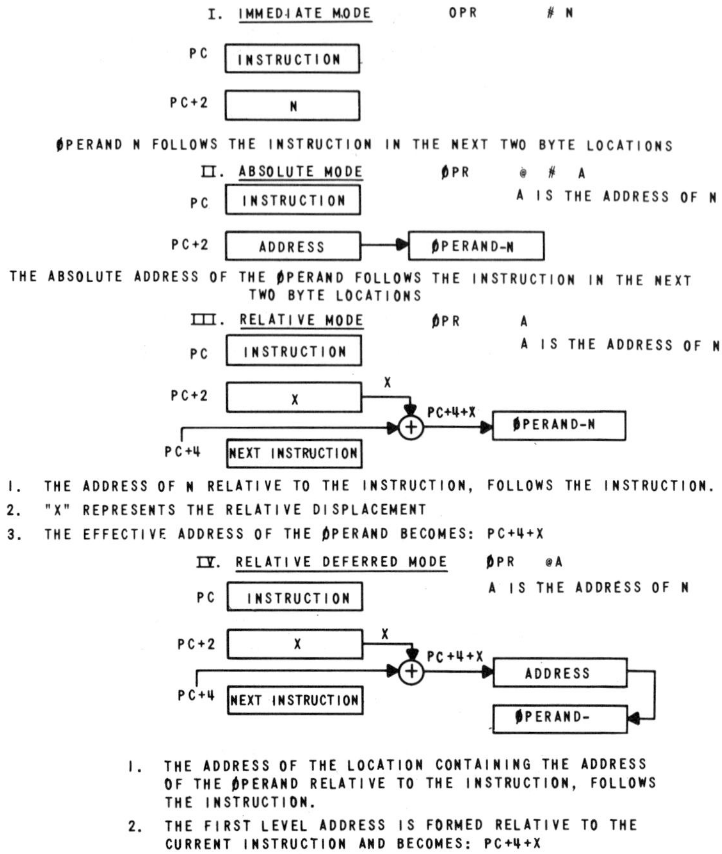

5-35 Four GPR indirect or deferred addressing modes of the PDP-11 [Reprinted with permission of Digital Equipment Corporation]

5.4 SUMMARY

A close relationship has been shown to exist between the word length of an instruction, the formats used to characterize the instruction, and the addressing modes that can be used with the instruction. The longer the word length, the more sophisticated the instruction repertoire may become. In addition, the longer word length will also support a wider variety of addressing modes, which, in turn, offer a more versatile programming environment.

In general, the modern small-scale computer makes use of either short-form instructions (only a single memory word is used) or long-form instructions (multiple memory words are used) to configure the instruction word. Long-form instructions

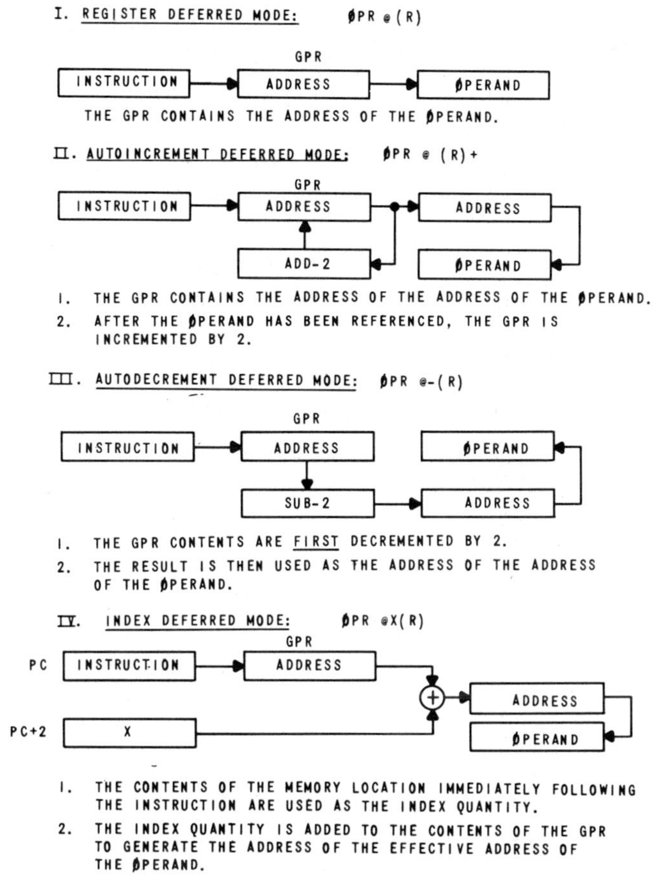

5-36 Program counter addressing modes of the PDP-11 [Reprinted with permission of Digital Equipment Corporation]

are characteristic of microprocessor structure, where real time is not considered a major area of concern. Single-address or short-form instructions are the dominant command elements in a minicomputer system, where the real-time response of the system is critical.

5.5 REFERENCES

1 HELLERMAN, H., *Digital Computer System Principles.* New York: McGraw-Hill Book Company, 1967.

2 FOSTER, C. C., *Computer Architecture.* New York: Van Nostrand Reinhold Company, 1970.

3 RICHARDS, R. K., *Electronic Digital Systems.* New York: John Wiley & Sons, Inc., 1966.

4 *Computer Systems Architecture*. Auerbach Computer Technology Reports, Special Report 100.0000.700. Philadelphia: Auerbach Publishers, Inc., 1974.

5 SWEET, W. B., "Addressing Technique Unlocks Minicomputer's Extended Memory." *Electronics*, Vol. 46, No. 23 (Nov. 8, 1973), pp. 107–112.

6 HOLLINGSWORTH, D., *Minicomputers—A Review of Current Technology, Systems, and Applications*, National Technical Information Service (NTIS) Document No. AD-783-316. The Rand Corporation, Santa Monica, Calif., 1973.

7 *PDP8/E, PDP8/M and PDP8/F Small Computer Handbook*. Digital Equipment Corporation, Maynard, Mass., 1973.

8 *PDP11/45 Processor Handbook*. Digital Equipment Corporation, Maynard, Mass., 1973.

9 *Auerbach on Minicomputers*. New York: Petrocelli Books, 1974.

10 MARTIN, DONALD P., *Microcomputer Design*. Martin Research Ltd., Chicago, 1975.

11 *The Microprocessor Handbook*. The Texas Instruments Learning Center, Texas Instruments, Inc., Houston, Tex., 1975.

12 HILL, F. J., and G. R. PETERSON, *Digital Systems: Hardware Organization and Design*. New York: John Wiley & Sons, Inc., 1973.

13 KORN, G. A., *Microprocessors and Small Computer Systems for Engineers and Scientists*. New York: McGraw-Hill Book Company, 1977.

14 GEAR, C. W., *Computer Organization and Programming*. New York: McGraw-Hill Book Company, 1969.

15 STONE, H. S., *Introduction to Computer Architecture*. New York: McGraw-Hill Book Company, 1975.

16 WEITZMAN, C., *Minicomputer Systems: Structure, Implementation and Applications*. Englewood Cliffs, N.J.: Prentice-Hall, Inc., 1974.

5.6 PROBLEMS

1. When a particular computer is called an *N-bit machine*, it has traditionally been assumed that the main internal bus widths of the machine are parallel, *N*-bit wide data paths.
   (a) What requirements, if any, does this viewpoint place on the number of bits that must be in:
      i. The memory address register (MAR)?
      ii. The memory data register (MDR)?
   (b) What implication does a *difference* between the number of bits contained in the MDR and the number of bits contained in the main internal bus of the machine have on any definition of *word length*? Specifically, how does the processor handle the case in which the internal busing structure contains *fewer* bits than the number found in the MDR?
   (c) Is it possible to define the word length of a machine in terms of the *width* (or number of bits) of the registers that form the GPR set of the machine? Explain your answer.
   (d) Define an *N*-bit machine.

2. Various trade-offs are adopted in determining the specific memory addressing modes of a digital machine. In particular, what are the considerations in each of the following situations?
   (a) It was indicated in the text that single-level indirect addressing was an approach taken when a hardware index register was considered quite expensive. Given the incidental cost of hardware with the advent of LSI technology, is it more advantageous now to use an index register(s) or is it better to continue employing single-level indirection? (This assumes one technique or the other may be used, but *not* both.)
   (b) An even more perplexing situation arises in an instruction format that permits *both* indirect addressing and immediate addressing to be specified in the same instruction. How should this situation be handled by the effective address generation logic?
   (c) Given a 16-bit small computer with 16 general-purpose registers, is there a simple hardware design convention that would permit 20-bit memory addressing using specific members of the GPR set? How would the participating registers be identified? Can this procedure be generalized to include any two registers in the GPR set?

3. The design of a new processor is under consideration. It is undecided what the exact word length of the machine should be. Two separate candidate word-lengths are to be reviewed: 16 bits versus 24 bits in the instruction word.

   The hardware features of the processor include: (1) Two base registers (20 bits are contained in each register). (2) Two sets of general-purpose registers. Each set contains 16 individual registers. (3) Multilevel indirect addressing is permitted.
   (a) What are the advantages and disadvantages of using a 16-bit word-length instruction over a 24-bit word-length instruction?
   (b) Is the choice influenced by the different applications the processor will be used in?
   (c) If a 24-bit instruction word length is chosen, is there any reason to retain the base registers?
   (d) What should the optimum length of the base registers be, in terms of number of bits? Is there really an optimum length?

4. A small computer has the following processor structure: (1) Locations 20_{16} thru 27_{16} are autoindex registers. (2) There are two 18-bit base registers. (3) There are two 18-bit accumulators. (4) Multilevel indirect addressing is permitted.

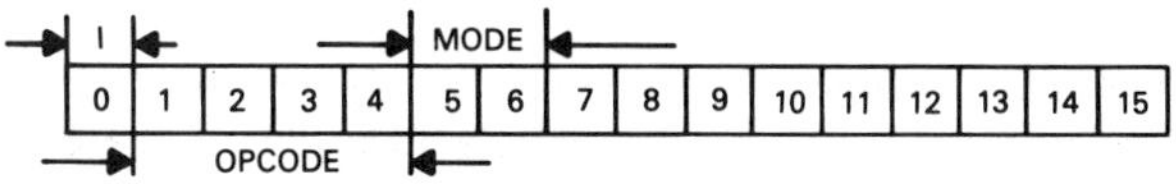

I	
0	DIRECT
1	INDIRECT

MODE	
0	ABSOLUTE
1	IMMEDIATE
2	RELATIVE TO BASE REGISTER 1 (BR1)
3	RELATIVE TO BASE REGISTER 2 (BR2)

P5-4

(a) See Figure P5-4, and derive the equation for the effective address in each of the following situations and indicate the maximum size of memory that may be referenced.
   i. Direct, absolute
   ii. Direct, immediate
   iii. Direct, relative to a base register
   iv. Indirect, absolute
   v. Indirect, immediate
   vi. Indirect, relative to a base register
   vii. Indirect, absolute, autoindex
   viii. Indirect, immediate, autoindex
   ix. Indirect, relative to a base register, autoindex

(b) Is this a particularly useful addressing technique? What are its drawbacks, if any?

5. Consider the processor architecture shown in Figure P5-5.

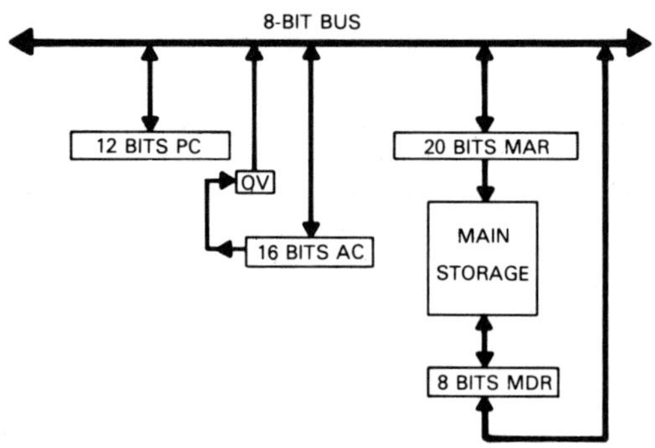

P5-5 *Allocated to memory:* (1) two 12-bit index registers that do *not* have to be referenced indirectly to cause indexing; (2) two 20-bit base registers. *Note:* Bit 07 of each location in main storage is used to indicate that the contents function is an indirect address pointer (bit 07 = 1).

(a) What hardware changes would be required to permit these registers to be relocated anywhere in main storage—the precise location of the current register set being determined by an executive control program?

(b) Using a control scheme of your choice, flowchart the execution sequence for a base-relative, 3-level, indirect, indexed addressing procedure.

(c) If each gating operation involving the bus (a transfer of data from one register to another) takes 100 ns, calculate how much time would be required to execute the previous control scheme. (Assume a memory with a cycle time of 1 μs is used to store *both* instructions and data.)

6. A small-scale processor, depicted in Figure P5-6, has the following instruction word format: (1) The *maximum size* of a memory module used for main storage is 16,384 words.

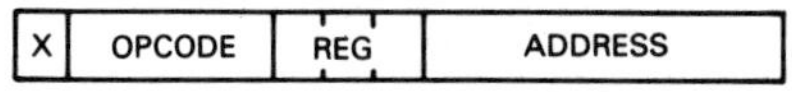

P5-6

(2) Three bits of each instruction word are *dedicated* to specifying a general-purpose register (GPR). Each GPR contains 12 bits. (3) The *most significant bit* of each instruction is used to indicate that the specified GPR should function as an index register ($X = 1$).

(a) Suppose we want to be able to directly reference every operand in main storage *without* the use of a GPR. Assume also that the *minimum* acceptable number of useful opcodes is seven. How many bits should be assigned to the ADDRESS field? How many bits should be assigned to the OPCODE field? How many bits are in the instruction word?

(b) Suppose the condition $X = 0$ *and* the usage of a GPR were specified. Let this situation indicate that the specified GPR should function as a base register. *Adopt a hardware convention* that will allow the named GPR to reference every location in a main storage module.

(c) Suppose main storage must be expanded beyond 16,384 words. What hardware convention could be used to accommodate this situation? Is indirect addressing a practical solution to this problem, assuming that the hardware is already laid out?

7. A computer has the instruction word format shown in Figure P5-7. For each of the following addressing modes, derive the expression for the effective address and indicate the maximum number of words that can be addressed.

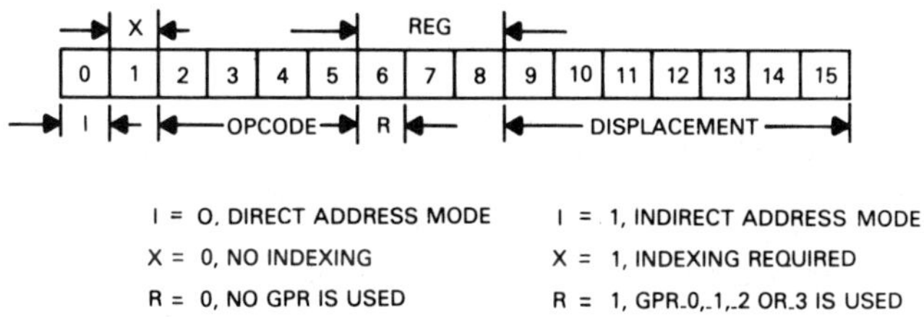

P5-7 Note: Four general-purpose registers (GPR's), each 16 bits long, are available. One index register (IXR), 8 bits long, is provided. The program counter is 16 bits long.

(a) Direct, absolute, no indexing, no GPR
(b) Direct, absolute, indexed, no GPR
(c) Direct, absolute, indexed, GPR
(d) Direct, no indexing, no GPR
(e) Direct, indexed, no GPR
(f) Direct, no indexing, GPR
(g) Direct, indexed, GPR
(h) Indirect, absolute, no indexing, no GPR
(i) Indirect, absolute, indexed, no GPR

(j) Indirect, absolute, no indexing, GPR
(k) Indirect, absolute, indexed, GPR
(l) Indirect, no indexing, no GPR
(m) Indirect, indexed, no GPR
(n) Indirect, no indexing, GPR
(o) Indirect, indexed, GPR

Note: For any mode combinations which appear to be imcompatible, identify the reasons for the imcompatibility and tell what steps should be taken to resolve the situation. Multilevel indirect addressing is permitted.

8. Consider the 8-bit processor of Figure P5-8 in which both data and instructions are placed within the same RAM unit. The processor uses multiple-word instructions and multilevel indirect addressing. For an indirect memory reference, the most significant bit of the current memory word is used to specify indirection. A double-word instruction is executed, specifying that the desired operand will be found after a base-relative, three-level, indirect, indexed addressing calculation is performed.

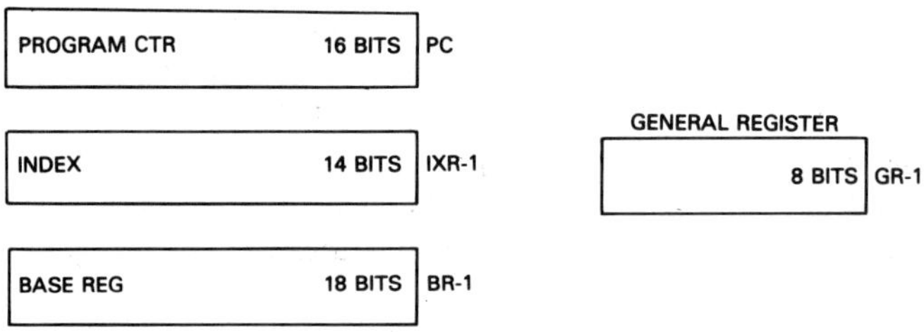

P5-8

If the time required to execute the *entire* control sequence from the initial fetch of the first byte of the instruction until the operand has been located *and* placed in a general register is 15 μs, what is the cycle time of the random access memory? Assume all logic operations between registers (i.e., gating, add, Boolean, etc.) each take 100 ns.

9. Consider the following 12-bit processor construct which functions as a single-address machine:

Allocated to Hardware	Allocated to Memory
The program counter (PC) : 12 Bits	A single accumulator: 12 Bits
The memory address register (MAR) : 12 Bits	Two index registers: 12 Bits each
The memory data register (MDR) : 12 Bits	An overflow bit

Note: Multilevel indirect addressing is permitted, with bit 11 of each location functioning as the indirect bit.

(a) If three bits of the instruction word are allocated to the opcode, what is the maximum range of memory that may be directly addressed using a single-word instruction?
(b) What is the maximum range of memory that may be directly addressed using a double-word instruction?

(c) Draw the control flow chart for a two-level, indirect, indexed addressing sequence.

(d) Assume that there is a 1-μs memory cycle time and that RAM is used for *both* instruction and data storage. Calculate the time required to execute a two-level, indirect, indexed addressing sequence.

(e) What hardware addition(s) would be required to allow this processor to address a maximum range of 64K bytes of memory?

10. Because of the low cost of integrated circuitry, general registers are provided as an integral part of the processor *rather* than assigning these registers locations in main storage. However, in certain microprocessors, such as the TMS9900 supplied by Texas Instruments, the general register set has again been placed in main storage.
    (a) Explain the rationale behind this design decision.
    (b) What are the advantages and disadvantages of having only a single accumulator in the processor?

6

The Elements of an Instruction Set

6.1 THE INSTRUCTION REPERTOIRE

6.1.1 The Definition of a Macroinstruction

The basic operations that a machine may perform are specified by its set of machine directives or instructions. These instructions form the order-code repertoire of the machine. To distinguish these instructions, which form the *executable object program module* (*OPM*), from the microinstruction set associated with a microprogrammed machine, the term *macroinstruction* will be used (see Appendix C). The reason for this is that programs in a microprogrammed machine execute at two distinct levels. The macroinstructions are analogous to assembly-language commands. A single macroinstruction may be broken down by a microprogrammed computer into a sequence of microinstructions. Each macroinstruction has an established microinstruction sequence that interprets the detailed steps of the macroinstruction execution. It is the macroinstruction set, however, that the assembly language programmer sees. He is not aware of how each macroinstruction is implemented at the microcode level.

For a given application, certain machine operations may facilitate software development and make one macroinstruction set more attractive than another. Since both minicomputers and microprocessors have been designed for use in a wide range of applications, instruction sets provided by the various manufacturers have been general purpose, often lacking the specific operations needed for a given application. To contend with this situation, the instruction set special features have traditionally been placed as subroutines in main memory. This approach has been acceptable provided that the operations within the subroutines are not highly repetitive and do not consume a great deal of execution time. Otherwise, consideration has to be given to augmenting the instruction set by expanding the command repertoire or selecting a different machine. Augmentation can take the form of an additional hardware package that is invoked by a designated opcode. One such package is the hardware floating-point multiply–divide module provided as an option on most minicomputers. An alternative augmenting technique has been used on various microprogrammed machines. In this technique, an area in the available microcode address space is reserved for special functions identified by the user. These functions are placed in ROM and are invoked by specific opcodes. This ROM is added to the basic ROM set, thus extending the instruction set of the original machine.

6.1.2 Length-Group Categories

For machines that are not microprogrammable, the extension of the existing instruction set can be a very difficult, if not impossible, job. This raises the question of whether or not an optimum instruction set can be defined for a given machine. Unfortunately, an order-code structure cannot be divorced from the application areas in which the machine was designed to function. Thus, a general-purpose computer will not be able to include all features that would be attractive to users in, for example, both the data communications field and the process control industry. The primary reason for this is the limited number of instructions that may be obtained from a machine with a short word length. For instance, a single-word instruction must provide code space for both the operations code and the location of the operand. In Section 5.3, it was shown that if a single-word instruction does not provide an adequate addressing range for all memory, then some addressing strategy must be employed to calculate the effective address. This permits the operand to be referenced at an arbitrary location in main storage. Effectively, the single-word instruction is required to use a second word to find the operand; the second word is stored in an index or base register and is implied by the instruction. This underscores one of the basic characteristics of both minicomputers and microprocessors: multiple-word instructions are employed to expand the instruction repertoire and facilitate the referencing of operands. These multiple-word directives form length groups into which various instructions may be placed. These length groups are (1) single-word instructions, (2) double-word instructions, (3) triple-word instructions, and so on.

For example, the Intel 8080 uses 1-byte, 2-byte, and 3-byte instructions, where the 8-bit byte is the width of the data bus from the program ROM. The Interdata 7/32 uses one-word, two-word, and three-word instructions, where 16 bits is the width of an interleaved memory module. A four-word instruction is entirely possible but has not been commonly implemented at the commercial minicomputer level because of the fourth memory reference required to configure the instruction. Obviously, if a machine designer is willing to trade execution time for word length, a long instruction word may be built up from many memory references.

The philosophy of machine design that has evolved from the real-time systems of the 1960's is to optimize in favor of execution time and employ short-form or single-word instructions, since virtually all computer programs can be implemented with very simple order-code structures. The classic example is the instruction set for the PDP-8 family which has eight fundamental commands or opcode states (see Table 6-1).

6.1.3 The Classification of Operation Codes

While it is not obvious what constitutes the "best" instruction set, it *is* possible to identify classes of operations that must be handled by a machine. How these operations are implemented, or if they are even included in the instruction repertoire, is a decision that must be made by the machine's designers. A reasonable design philosophy, however, is for the hardware or firmware to be designed so that it provides a versatile and easy-to-use assembly language. The operation code may be broken up into the following classifications, with the extended function category being implemented as either an add-on hardware module or a series of microroutines in ROM.

1. *Data movement.* The storage and retrieval of data within the computer.
2. *Computation.* Data are operated on numerically or logically to obtain a final result. The SHIFT and ROTATE functions are included in this category.
3. *Input/Output.* Communication of information between the environment external to the processor and the processor itself.
4. *Control.* The actual direction of the processor operations, including program-controlled branching.
5. *Special operations.* These are specialized functions that may not form part of the standard instruction set. One example is the testing of individual bits found in a specific processor register to determine whether each individual bit has been set or cleared.
6. *Extended functions.* These are actual instructions added to the basic instruction set to extend the command repertoire for a specific application. The calculation of the *cyclic redundancy-check character* (*CRCC*) for data communications is often implemented as a command that is an extension of the standard instruction set.

Table 6-2 illustrates the breakdown of the operation code into these six categories. Note that several of these categories may be common for a given machine. For example, the PDP-11 treats I/O operations as though they are memory reference instructions. In the Motorola M6800 microprocessor, any instruction that uses a memory address assigned to the I/O port of a *programmed interface adapter* (*PIA*) may be regarded as an I/O instruction.

In evaluating the effectiveness of a specific instruction set for a given application, the total number of available instructions cannot normally be used as a good measure of the command repertoire. The most effective approach is the employment of *weighting factors.* A weighting factor may be regarded as an index of merit that would

TABLE 6-1 PDP-8/I Instruction List*

Group†	Mnemonic	Operations Code	Operation Peformed	Time (μs)
Basic instructions	AND	0000	Logical AND	3
	TAD	1000	Two's-Complement Add	3
	ISZ	2000	Increment and Skip If Zero	3
	DCA	3000	Deposit and Clear AC	3
	JMS	4000	Jump to Subroutine	3
	JMP	5000	Jump	1.5
	IOT	6000	Input/Output Transfer	4.25
	OPR	7000	Operate Group	1.5
Group 1, micro-operations	NOP	7000	No-Operation	
	CLA	7200	Clear AC	
	CLL	7100	Clear Link	
	CMA	7040	Complement AC	
	CML	7020	Complement Link	
	RAR	7010	Rotate AC and Link Right One	
	RAL	7004	Rotate AC and Link Left One	
	RTR	7012	Rotate AC and Link Right Two	
	RTL	7006	Rotate AC and Link Left Two	
	IAC	7001	Increment AC	
Group 2 micro-operations	SMA	7500	Skip on Minus AC	
	SZA	7440	Skip on Zero AC	
	SPA	7510	Skip on Plus AC	
	SNA	7450	Skip on Non-Zero AC	
	SNL	7420	Skip on Non-Zero Link	
	SZL	7430	Skip on Zero Link	
	SKP	7410	Skip Unconditionally	
	OSR	7404	Inclusive-OR Switch Register with AC	
	HLT	7402	Halt the Program	
	CLA	7600	Clear AC	

*Reprinted with permission of Digital Equipment Corporation.

†The microoperation groups are used to define logical sequences that can occur during one cycle: group 1 is used primarily for clear, complement, rotate, and increment operations; group 2 is used primarily to check the contents of the AC and link.

be assigned by the applications engineer charged with evaluating a given instruction set. For example, a set of values between 0 and 5 could be used. The number 5 would represent the highest merit value (i.e., an absolutely essential command), while 0 would denote an instruction that would normally not be used by the application. Let I_{mk} represent the kth instruction of the command repertoire for machine m. Let W_{mk} represent the index of merit assigned to that instruction by the applications engineer. Let S_m represent the weighted sum or figure of merit of the instruction set for machine m. Then,

$$S_m = W_{mi} + W_{m2} + \cdots + W_{ml} \tag{1}$$

TABLE 6-2 Six Basic Categories of Instructions

Data Movement	Control	Computation	I/O	Special Functions	Extended Functions
		Arithmetic:			
Memory to register	Branch	Add	Set flag	Set bit *N*	Communications instructions
Register to memory	Branch on condition	Subtract	Clear flag	Clear bit *N*	Process control instructions
Memory to memory	Branch to subroutine	Multiply	Test flag	Test bit *N*	Automatic testing instructions
Register to register	Return from subroutine	Divide	CPU $\longrightarrow$ device	Find least zero	
Push stack	Return from interrupt	Increment by 1	CPU $\longleftarrow$ machine	Compare byte strings	
Pop stack	Return from trap	Decrement by 1		Count number of ones in a word	
	Micro-operations	Compare			
		Logic:			
	Halt	AND			
	No-op	OR			
	Execute	Exclusive-OR			
	Mark	Complement			
	Trap	*Manipulational:*			
	Wait	Shift			
	Reset	Rotate			

where l is the number of instructions in the instruction repertoire for machine m.

Equation (1) may be rewritten to obtain equation (2):

$$S_m = \sum_{i=1}^{l} W_{mi} \qquad (W_{mi} = 0, 1, 2, 3, 4, 5) \tag{2}$$

By a similar line of reasoning, the figure of merit for the instruction set for machine n would be given by

$$S_n = \sum_{i=1}^{k} W_{ni} \qquad (W_{ni} = 0, 1, 2, 3, 4, 5) \tag{3}$$

where k is the number of instructions in the instruction repertoire for machine n.

The cumulative weighted sum for one machine can then be compared to the weighted sum of another machine. A comparison of these weighted sums made over a selection of machines will establish an ordering of these machines for a given application in terms of instruction set features. That is, the figures of merit may be arranged in an order that commences with the largest number and ends with the smallest number.

The largest figure of merit would represent the machine most applicable for the user—in terms of instruction set features. Although this procedure is highly subjective, it does force the applications engineer to clearly identify the instructions that are most critical for his particular use.

For the purpose of instruction-set evaluation, it is worthwhile to consider the possible instruction types in each of the six basic instruction categories. No real distinction will be made between microprocessor instruction sets and the command repertoires associated with a minicomputer. Since a small-scale machine may be implemented at the byte-addressable level, the basic command features will stay the same when considering either an 8-bit microprocessor or a 16-bit minicomputer. In short, both machines may employ single-operand instructions and multioperand instructions. It will, however, take an 8-bit microprocessor longer, in terms of one or more additional memory references, to configure a multioperand instruction that is equivalent to a minicomputer multioperand command.

6.2 MACHINE COMMAND GROUPINGS

6.2.1 The Data Movement Class

The data movement class is characterized by four basic data transfer operations that are listed below. The first three operations are classified as *memory reference instructions*.

1. Memory to memory (the slowest category).
2. Memory to register.
3. Register to memory.
4. Register to register.

Each of these data transfer operations may be either byte-oriented or word-oriented. As a matter of convention, the letter B is often appended to the command word if a byte operation is required. For instance, byte operations in the PDP-11 always access the low-order byte of the specified register. Typical memory reference operations take the form shown in Table 6-3, block (A).

The register-to-register category forms the class of operations known as *non-memory reference instructions*. Typically, such instructions take the form of a MOVE command, shown in Table 6-3, block (B). Generally, such operations transfer a full word rather than a single byte. The transfer of immediate data from the displacement field of the instruction word to a specified register also falls into the class of non-memory reference instructions. Typically, such an instruction takes the form of a LOAD IMMEDIATE (LOADI) command, shown in Table 6-3, block (B).

If a hardware stack is used with the processor, the two instructions used to administer the stack should be included in the data movement category. The stack manipulation directives may be considered memory-reference instructions. The stack administration commands take the form shown in Table 6-3, block (C).

TABLE 6-3 Data Movement Instruction Class

	Type of Instructions	Command String	Operation Performed
(A)	Typical memory reference	LOAD GPR, MEMLOC	Transfer the contents of main storage location, MEMLOC, into the hardware register specified by the GPR field.
		STORE GPR, MEMLOC	Save the contents of the hardware register specified by the GPF field in main storage location, MEMLOC.
		MOVE MLOC2, MLOC1	Transfer the contents of main storage location, MLOC1, into main storage location, MLOC2, and leave the contents of MLOC1 unchanged.
(B)	Typical nonmemory reference	MOVE GPR1, GPR2	Move the contents of the hardware register specified by the GPR2 field into the hardware register specified by the GPR1 field.
		LOADI GPR, CONST	Load the value specified by the CONST field into the lower-order bits of the hardware register specified by the GPR field.
(C)	Stack administration	PUSH ITEMA	Place the contents of location ITEMA (a memory location or a GPR) onto the top of the stack and add one to the stack pointer.
		POP ITEMB	Subtract one from the stack pointer and remove the contents of the top of the stack. Place the contents in location ITEMB (a main storage location or a GPR).

6.2.2 The Computation Class

The computation class may be further divided into the arithmetic instruction class and the logical function class. The arithmetic instruction class consists of the following operations:

1. Addition.
2. Subtraction.
3. Increment by 1.
4. Decrement by 1.
5. Comparison.
6. Multiplication.
7. Division.

Since subtraction may be achieved on a binary machine by representing the subtrahend as a 2's-complement number and adding the representation to the minuend, the subtract command is often omitted from the mini/microcomputer instruction set. However, if the subtract command is available, the programmer is not held responsible for providing the correct complement representation of the subtrahend. This feature can make the machine easier to program.

If addition is performed on individual bytes, it is necessary to indicate that the carry produced by the previous addition be used in the current byte addition. Many microprocessors employ an *add-with-carry* command to accommodate this situation. The addition command may take either of the two forms shown in Table 6-4, block (A).

TABLE 6-4 Computation Instruction Class

	Type of Instructions	Command String	Operation Performed
(A)	Typical add instructions	ADD X,Y	Add the contents of location X to the contents of location Y. If a carry overflow is generated, set the appropriate status bit or flag in the machine. (a) A carry overflow implies that the sum is greater than the capacity of the machine. (b) X and Y may be two locations in main storage, two hardware registers, or a hardware register and a main storage location.
		ADDC X,Y	Add-with-carry the contents of byte location X to the contents of byte location Y. X and Y will normally be locations in main storage.
(B)	Typical subtract instructions	SUB X,Y	Subtract the contents of location Y from the contents of location X. If an outgoing borrow is generated, set the appropriate flag in the machine. (a) An outgoing borrow indicates that the difference is negative. (b) X and Y may be two locations in main storage or two hardware registers.
		SUBB X,Y	Subtract-with-borrow the contents of byte location Y from byte location X. X and Y will normally be locations in main storage.
(C)	Unity operation instructions	INC1 NUM1	Increment the contents of location NUM1 by unity. If a carry overflow is generated, set the appropriate flag bit in the machine.
		DEC1 NUM1	Decrement the contents of location NUM1 by unity. If an outgoing borrow is produced, set the appropriate flag bit in the machine. *Note:* For both case 1 and case 2, NUM1 may be either a GPR or a full word in main storage.
(D)	Typical add-immediate and subtract-immediate instructions	ADDI X,CONST	Add the value of the constant field to the least-significant bits of location X.
		ADDCI X,CONST	Add-with-carry the value of the constant field to the contents of byte location X.
		SUBI Y,CONST	Subtract the value of the constant field from the least-significant bits of location Y.
		SUBBI Y,CONST	Subtract-with-borrow the value of the constant field from the contents of byte location Y.

TABLE 6-4 ***(cont.)***

	Type of Instructions	Command String	Operation Performed
(E)	Typical compare instructions	CMP X,Y	Compare the contents of location X with the contents of location Y on a bit-by-bit basis. (a) Set the appropriate status indicators $(X = Y, X \neq Y, X < Y, X > Y)$ but do not change the contents of either location. (b) X and Y may be main storage locations or GPRs.
		CMPB X,Y	Compare the contents of byte location X with the contents of byte location Y on a bit-by-bit basis. Set the appropriate status indicators $(X = Y, X \neq Y, X < Y, X > Y)$ but do not change the contents of either location.
(F)	Typical compare-with-mask instructions	CMPM X,Y	This instruction is identical to that given above except that the use of a mask register is included in the execution of the command.
		CMPMI, X,Y,MASK	Compare-under-immediate-mask functions the same as the previous instruction except that the mask is included explicitly in the instruction.
(G)	Typical logical function instructions	AND X,Y	Logically AND the contents of location X with the contents of location Y; set the proper condition-code bits if the result is all zeros.
		OR X,Y	Inclusive OR the contents of location X with the contents of location Y; set the proper condition-code bits if the result is all zeros.
		XOR X,Y	Exclusive OR the contents of location X with the contents of location Y; set the proper condition-code bits if the result is all zeros.
		COMP X	Complement the contents of location X. This instruction changes the state of each bit found in the associated data word.
(H)	Typical data manipulational instructions	SHIFTR X,N	Shift the contents of location X right *N* places and insert the result back in location X.
		SHIFTL X,N	Shift the contents of location X left *N* places and insert the result back in location X.
		ROTR X,N	Rotate the contents of location X right in a clockwise fashion *N* places and insert the result back in location X.
		ROTL X,N	Rotate the contents of location X left in a counterclockwise fashion *N* places and insert the result back in location X.

The subtraction command is normally implemented in a manner similar to the addition instruction. Subtraction may take place on two full-length data words or between two bytes of data. If the latter case is encountered, the *subtract-with-borrow* command must be included to accommodate the case where the previous subtraction generated a borrow as shown in Table 6-4, block (B).

The increment-by-1 and decrement-by-1 instructions are provided to operate explicitly by 1 on the contents of a memory location or a GPR. These are shown in Table 6-4, block (C).

A variation of the add or subtract instruction is the *add-immediate* or *subtract-immediate commands*. In this case, a constant specified in the displacement portion of the instruction word is added to or subtracted from the indicated GPR or main memory location. These instructions take the form shown in Table 6-4, block (D).

If the value of the immediate operand field is a full word in width, the value is normally placed in the address immediately after the instruction. A carry overflow or an outgoing borrow will set the appropriate status indicators on an add-immediate or subtract-immediate operation.

The instructions for multiplication and division have normally not been found as standard commands in the repertoires of most commercial minicomputers and microprocessors. If either command has been desired, it has been implemented as a subroutine call rather than an operation code specification. The minicomputer vendors have included multiplication and division as part of a floating-point hardware package that is added to augment the instruction set. The PDP-11/45, however, includes 16-bit multiply commands and 32-bit divide commands as elements of its basic instruction repertoire. For higher accuracy and faster processing, the user is encouraged to move up to the hardware floating-point processor developed for the PDP-11/40 and PDP-11/45 family members.

Comparison may be achieved through the use of the subtract instruction. However, the most common implementation of this instruction is a direct bit-by-bit comparison of the two specified operands. Typically, the compare instruction will simply set the appropriate status flags but not change either of the operands involved. A conditional branch instruction customarily will follow the compare command. Table 6-4, block (E), illustrates the compare instruction forms.

Masking may be performed in conjunction with the comparison operation. Masking permits only those bits of specific interest to be compared in two data words. The comparison with masking operation may be implemented in either of two ways:

1. A separate instruction is required to load the internal processor register that functions as the mask register. When the comparison instruction is executed at either the full data word level or byte level, the mask register is automatically included as part of the compare operation. Typically, if a 1 is placed in bit position N of the mask register, no comparison is made between the Nth bits of the two data words being compared. A 1 is then forced in the Nth bit of the result, thus masking the effect of the compare operation on the Nth bits of the two data words. If a 0 is placed in bit position N of the mask register, the comparison between the Nth bits of the two data words is allowed to take place. The following two rules are observed for each individual bit position:
   (a) If the 2 bits compare, a 1 is placed in the Nth bit of the result.
   (b) If the 2 bits do not agree, a 0 is inserted in the Nth bit of the result.

Each individual bit position is handled in this fashion simultaneously when the compare-under-mask instruction is executed.

2. A single instruction is used to specify the comparison operation, the two operands, and the mask. Such an instruction, which may be referred to as a *compare-under-immediate-mask instruction*, will normally require two words in memory to implement the command. The first memory location will contain the operation code and the addresses of the two operands; the second location will contain the actual mask to be used. This mask will automatically be included in the comparison operation. All other execution features are the same as (a). Table 6-4, block (F), lists the various compare instructions.

The comparison operation emphasizes the need for various *status indicators* or *condition flip-flops* that the machine can set as critical situations arise during the course of program execution. Several such conditions have already been mentioned and are included in the following list:

1. Carry overflow.
2. Outgoing borrow.
3. Result equals 0.
4. Result is positive.
5. Result is negative.
6. $(X) = (Y)$.
7. $(X) \neq (Y)$.
8. $(X) > (Y)$.
9. $(X) < (Y)$.

Note: The notation (M) is read "the contents of M," where M may be a memory location or a GPR.

Variations of these conditions have been included in the instruction sets of virtually all minicomputers and microprocessors as well as conditions not identified in the previous discussion. Because of the variety of possible conditions that can be considered, a group of flip-flops is normally dedicated to specifying which condition has occurred for each instruction. These flip-flops, usually called *condition-code bits*, are often incorporated in the program status word. The condition-code flip-flops range from the single LINK bit encountered in the PDP-8 family to the 4 condition bits found in the DEC PDP-11 family and the Intel 8080 microprocessor. Figure 6-1 defines the PDP-11 flag bits and Figure 6-2 describes the status indicators used by the 8080.

The logical function class of instruction is made up of the following operations:

1. AND.
2. Inclusive-OR.
3. Exclusive-OR.
4. Complement.

The AND instruction may be used to mask the bits of a data word that will not be involved in a specific calculation. A 1 must exist in the Nth bit position of each

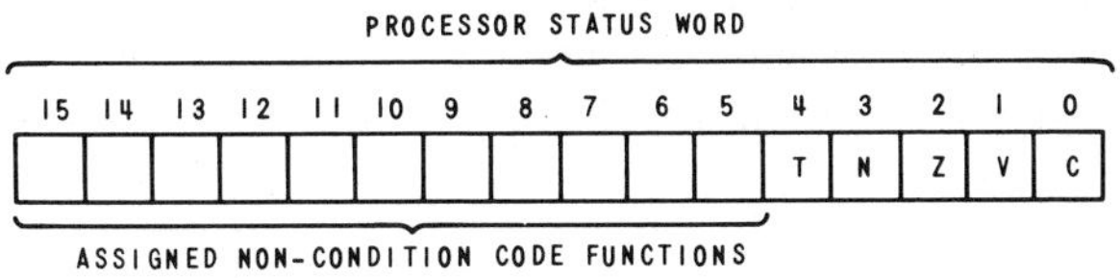

CONDITION CODE BIT	ASSOCIATED FUNCTION
1. C = CARRY BIT	1. SET BY THE PREVIOUS OPERATION IF A CARRY WAS CAUSED OUT OF THE MOST SIGNIFICANT BIT POSITION.
2. N = NEGATIVE BIT	2. SET IF THE RESULT OF THE PREVIOUS OPERATION WAS NEGATIVE.
3. Z = ZERO BIT	3. SET IF THE RESULT OF THE PREVIOUS OPERATION WAS ZERO.
4. V = OVERFLOW BIT	4. SET IF THE RESULT OF THE PREVIOUS OPERATION RESULTED IN AN ARITHMETIC OVERFLOW.
5. T = TRAP BIT	5. MAY BE SET OR CLEARED UNDER PROGRAM CONTROL; SERVES AS A DIRECT METHOD OF INSTALLING BREAKPOINTS WHICH ARE USEFUL IN PROGRAM DEBUGGING.

6-1 PDP-11 condition code bits [Reprinted with permission of Digital Equipment Corporation]

FLAG FLIP-FLOP	ASSOCIATED FUNCTION
1. CARRY	1. THE PREVIOUS OPERATION PRODUCED EITHER A CARRY-OVERFLOW OR A CARRY UNDERFLOW IN THE RESULT.
2. ZERO	2. THE RESULT OF THE PREVIOUS OPERATION IS ZERO.
3. SIGN	3. THE MSB OF THE RESULT IS A ONE.
4. PARITY	4. THE PARITY OF THE RESULT IS EVEN.

6-2 Intel 8080 flag flip-flops [Reprinted with permission of Intel Corporation]

operand to produce a 1 in the *N*th bit of the result. The inclusive-OR operation will produce a 1 in the *N*th bit position of the result if a 1 exists in the *N*th bit of either operand. The exclusive-OR operation is also known as the *logical mismatch function.* It evaluates the following logical expression formed for each bit position of the two operands:

$$R \text{ (result)} = \bar{X} \cdot Y + X \cdot \bar{Y}$$

A 1 is produced in the *N*th bit position of the result if the *N*th bits of the two operands do not agree.

The complement operation changes the state of each bit found in the designated operand; that is, 0's are changed to 1's and 1's are changed to 0's. Using the complement operation, the OR function may be obtained from the AND function, and vice versa.

$$X + Y = (\overline{\bar{X} \cdot \bar{Y}}) \qquad X \cdot Y = (\overline{\bar{X} + \bar{Y}})$$

This is a simple application of DeMorgan's theorem and allows either the AND operation or the OR operation to be excluded from the instruction set without paying a severe penalty. However, additional instructions are required to form the necessary complements. For each of the instructions in the logical function class, X and Y may be both main memory locations, one a main memory location and the other a GPR or both GPR's. Table 6-4, block (G), lists the various logical function instructions.

The data manipulation subclass consists of the shift and rotate directives. The shift instruction may be implemented as either an arithmetic shift or a logical shift. Furthermore, the shift operation may move the bits of the register involved to the right or to the left. Two versions of the arithmetic shift are encountered. In the first version, an arithmetic right shift preserves the state of the sign bit in the most significant bit (MSB) position but shifts 0's into low-order bit positions on successive operations, starting with the next-most-significant position. Figure 6-3 illustrates this case, which is the implementation used by the PDP-11 family. This permits the sign information to be retained on right shifts if the number to be used is negative. In the second version, an arithmetic right shift propagates the sign bit successively into succeeding low-order bit positions; 0's are not inserted in the vacated MSB positions. Figure 6-4 illustrates this technique, used by the General Automation SPC-16/40.

In both cases, an arithmetic left shift propagates the MSB into the LINK bit and shifts all other bits one position to the left; a 0 is placed in the least-significant-bit position. On successive arithmetic left shifts, this operation repeats itself so that the sign bit is lost. Figure 6-5 gives an example of an arithmetic left shift. Note that a right shift is equivalent to dividing the number found in the shift register by 2, while a left shift is equivalent to multiplying the number in the shift register by 2. The left shift may also be achieved by adding the number in the shift register to itself.

If the shift register is considered to form a carousel as shown in Figure 6-6, with a LINK bit used to loop the least significant bit (LSB) of the register into the MSB, the shift operation becomes a *rotate operation*. The rotate instruction preserves the state of the overall data word but rotates the bits in the data word either right or left

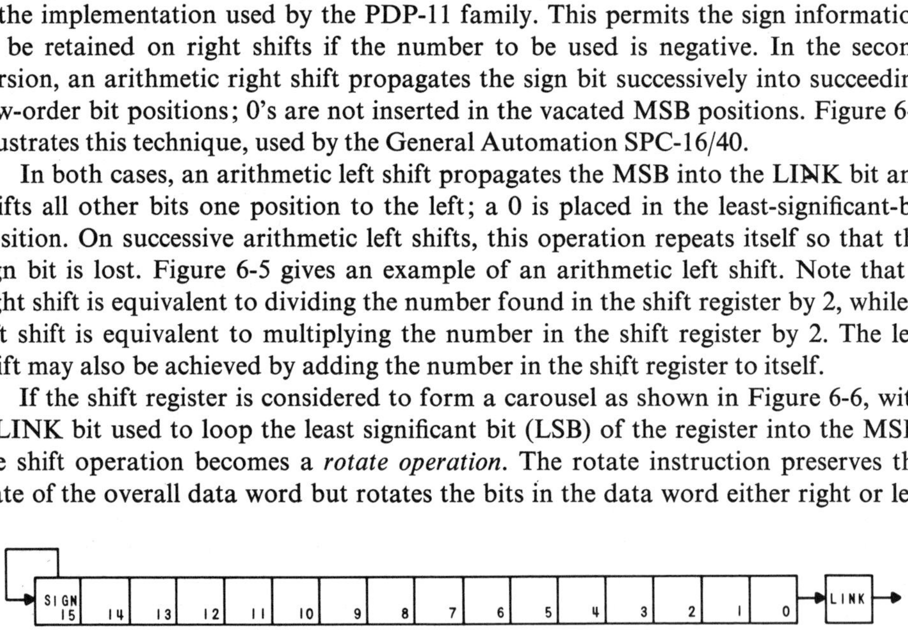

NOTES:
1) THE STATE OF THE SIGN BIT IS PRESERVED.
2) ZEROS ARE INSERTED ON SUCCESSIVE SHIFTS IN THE VACATED HIGH-ORDER BIT POSITIONS AFTER THE SIGN OR MSB POSITION

6-3 Arithmetic shift right, version 1

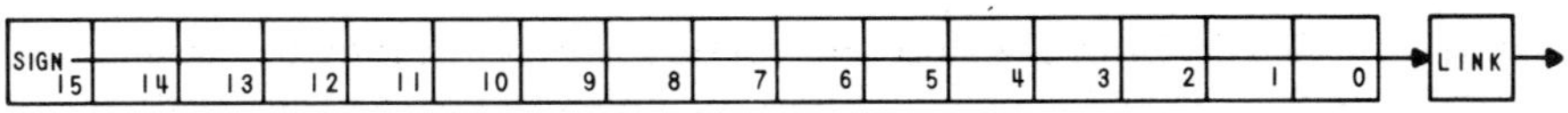

NOTES:

1) THE STATE OF THE SIGN BIT IS PRESERVED.
2) THE SIGN BIT IS PROPAGATED ONE POSITION RIGHT ON SUCCESSIVE SHIFTS.
3) THE CONTENTS OF THE VACATED HIGH-ORDER BIT POSITIONS DO NOT HAVE ZEROS SHIFTED INTO THEM.

6-4 Arithmetic shift right, version 2

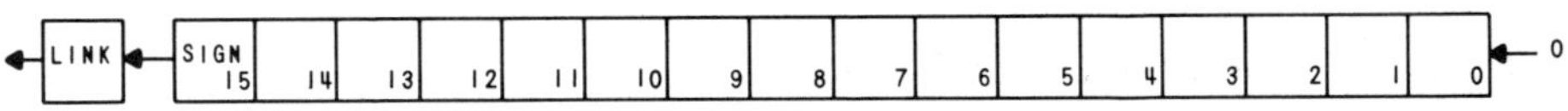

NOTE:

1) ON THE FIRST SHIFT THE SIGN BIT IS MOVED INTO THE LINK AND A ZERO IS SHIFTED INTO BIT 0.
2) ON SUCCESSIVE LEFT SHIFTS, THE ZERO IS PROPAGATED TO THE LEFT INTO THE VACATED HIGHER-ORDER BIT POSITIONS.

6-5 Arithmetic shift left

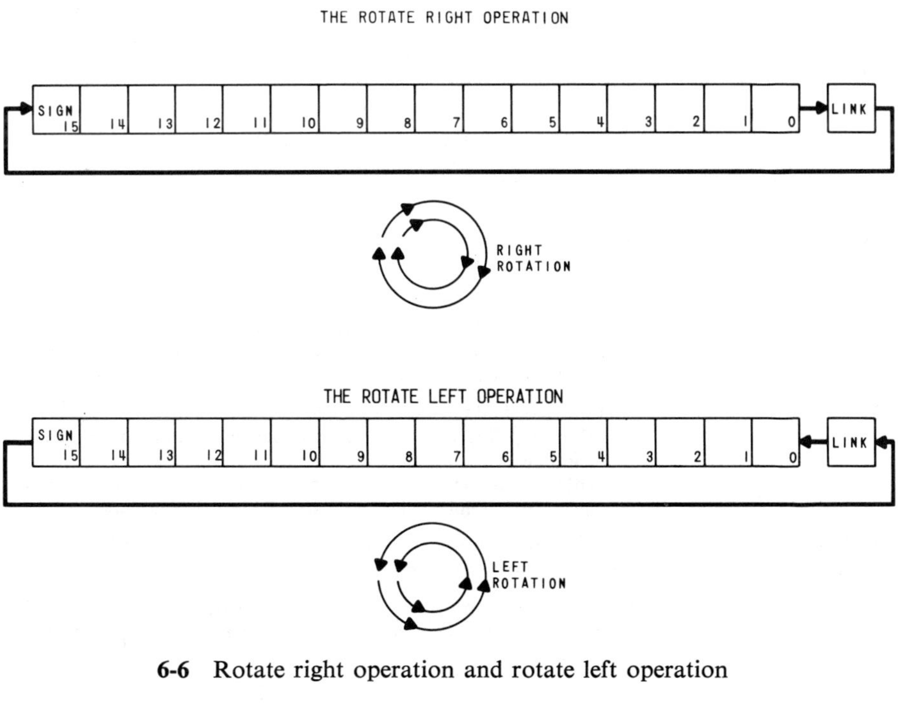

6-6 Rotate right operation and rotate left operation

through the LINK bit. Both the shift and rotate instructions may be used to identify a bit for testing if the machine does not possess individual bit test instructions.

It is particularly desirable for both the shift and rotate instructions to possess a multiposition shift/rotate feature. This feature allows multiposition shift or rotate operations to be specified by a single instruction. Consequently, a 10-position shift/rotate operation *does not* require the execution of 10 individual single-shift or rotate operations. Instead, it requires one instruction that explicitly specifies a 10-position operation. This reduces the required number of main memory locations (only one instruction is used instead of 10) and also improves the execution time of the program (only one memory reference is required instead of 10). Table 6-4, block (H), lists the forms that typical data manipulation instructions may take.

6.2.3 The Input/Output Class

The input/output class of instructions typically consists of the following set of commands:

1. Set the device flag.
2. Clear the device flag.
3. Test the device flag.
4. Transfer data into a device register from the computer.
5. Transfer data into the computer from a device register.

These instructions also form the category of operations known as *programmed I/O*. Each instruction, which must be executed by the computer, allows the computer to communicate with its external environment under program control. Typical I/O command elements are given in Table 6-5.

TABLE 6-5 Input/Output Instruction Class

Command String	Operation Performed
SETF DEVFF	Set a control flip-flop in the peripheral device to establish a communication path from the computer to the device.
CLRF DEVFF	Clear the specified control flip-flop in the peripheral device. This procedure may be performed to initialize the device or restart an information transaction between the computer and the device.
TST DEVFF	Test the specified flip-flop in the peripheral device. (a) If the flip-flop is in the 1's state, set the appropriate condition code bit(s). (b) Often the test instruction incorporates an implied skip of the next instruction if the flip-flop indicates that the device is not busy.
XMT DEVRG,GPR	Transmit the contents of the register specified by the GPR field into the peripheral device register specified by the DEVRG field.
RCV GPR,DEVRG	Receive the contents of the peripheral device register specified by the DEVRG field in the internal register of the computer specified by the GPR field.

On machines that treat all I/O operations as memory reference instructions, arithmetic and logical operations may be performed implicitly on data being moved between the peripheral device register and the current contents of the addressed internal register of the computer. Technically speaking, instructions that individually enable or disable the interrupt logic in each peripheral device should be placed in the category of I/O operations since they control the interrupt enable flags found in each device. Machines that employ unique I/O instructions generally observe the command format shown in Figure 6-7. Note that the instruction consists of five distinct fields:

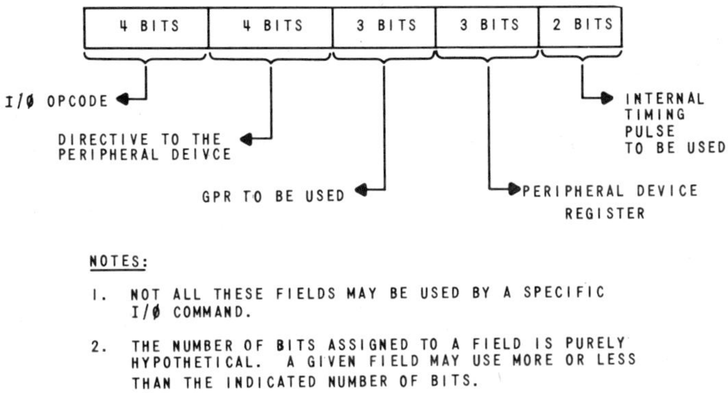

6-7 Generalized I/O instruction format

1. The I/O operations code.
2. The GPR involved in the transaction.
3. The directive to the device which specifies the operation to be performed, such as transmit data to the peripheral device register or receive data from it.
4. The actual peripheral device register involved in the transaction.
5. The internal timing pulse of the computer specifying when the operation is actually performed.

There are many variations of this instruction format. For example, the PDP-8 family uses 6 bits to specify the device selector that interacts with the external device register. The device register itself is not named. Three bits are used to identify the I/O operations code. The remaining 3 bits specify which of eight unique timing operations will be used by the device selector. These last 3 bits, in conjunction with the device selector specified, actually dictate the I/O operation that will be performed.

6.2.4 The Control Class

Perhaps the most interesting instruction class encountered is in the category of control. The control class consists of the following command elements:

1. Branch unconditionally.

2. Branch and save the return address.
3. Return from subroutine.
4. Execute the instruction found at the specified location.
5. MARK (special PDP-11 command).
6. Return from interrupt.
7. TRAP.
8. Return from TRAP.
9. Perform no operation at all.
10. Reset the system.
11. Halt all program-controlled operations.
12. WAIT (special PDP-11 command).
13. Micro-operations.
14. Branch on condition.

The unconditional branch operation takes two basic forms. The first form is a direct branch to the specified address. The direct branch loads the program counter (PC) with the effective address calculated by the command. The second form is the SKIP command, which permits the machine to simply jump over the next consecutive instruction. The SKIP instruction increments the PC by 2 to jump over the next sequential instruction. Condition bits are normally used with the SKIP command to perform conditional transfers of control. Table 6-6, block (A), illustrates these two basic types of unconditional branch instructions.

A powerful variation of the unconditional branch instruction is the *branch-and-save-return-address command.* This instruction causes the following action to take place:

1. The current contents of the PC are incremented by 1 for a word-addressable machine and by 2 for a byte-addressable machine. This creates a pointer to the next sequential instruction following the branch-and-save command; this pointer is sometimes called a *return pointer.*

TABLE 6-6 Control Instruction Class

	Type of Instructions	Command String	Operation Performed
(A)	Typical unconditional branch	BR NEWLOC	Unconditionally branch control to the location in main storage specified by the NEWLOC field. (a) An explicit or implied addressing mode will normally be used to generate the target address. (b) This instruction jams the address of NEW-LOC into the program counter and causes execution to continue from that point. The former contents of the PC are lost.
		SKP	Branch over the next consecutive instruction and continue program execution from that point.

TABLE 6-6 *(cont.)*

	Type of Instructions	Command String	Operation Performed
(B)	Typical subroutine related	JSR SUBR	Unconditionally branch control to the effective address of SUBR. (a) For a non-stack-oriented machine, the return pointer will be saved as the contents of the first location in the subroutine. (b) For a stack-oriented machine, the contents of the linkage register and the return address pointer will be saved as consecutive items on the processor stack.
		RTS GPRN	This is a return-from-subroutine command executed on a stack-oriented machine. This instruction loads the return pointer from the stack into the program counter and restores the linkage register specified by the GPRN field using the information stored on the stack.
		EXECUTE NXTINS	Execute the instruction found at the effective address of NXTINS.
		MARK N	Perform a subroutine exit from the processor stack; *N* parameters precede the mark *N* instruction on the stack.
(C)	Typical interrupt and trap related	RTNI	Automatically pop the old PSW and old PC from the processor stack to exit from an interrupt service routine.
		TRAP	Push the current contents of the PSW and PC onto the processor stack. The fixed address of the trap service routine is loaded into the PC and the associated PSW is placed in the processor status register.
		RTNT	Disengage any trace trap mechanism, then automatically pop the old PSW and old PC to exit from a trap service routine.
(D)	Typical special control	NO-OP	Cause the processor to do nothing for one full instruction cycle.
		RESET	Reinitialize the system to its post power-up state; this includes both the mainframe and peripherals.
		HALT	Terminate all further processing at this point and relinquish control to the front console. The console could be located remotely from the mainframe and peripherals. In this case, communications between the processor and front console may have to take place over a data link facility if the separation is wide enough.
		WAIT	Disengage the PDP-11 processor from competing for usage of the UNIBUS. Control is returned to the processor after exiting from an interrupt service routine.

2. The return pointer is saved as the contents of the effective address to which control is to branch.
3. 1 is added to the effective address and the result is jam-set into the PC.
4. Program execution then continues at the main memory location given by the effective address plus 1. Note that the return address has been saved at the entry location of this block of code.

This entire sequence of events forms the jump-to-subroutine operation and permits execution to return to the original program after the subroutine has completed its task. To return from the subroutine, either of two techniques is normally employed:

1. A branch-indirect instruction is executed. This command jam-sets the return pointer into the PC and causes control to return to the original program.
2. A return-from-subroutine instruction is executed. The details of this command execution are discussed later in this section.

A much more sophisticated version of the branch-and-save instruction is encountered on a stack-oriented machine. In such a machine, the subroutine call does not change the contents of any location in main memory. Consequently, more than one interrupt handler may share the same subroutine since no handler modifies the instructions or data that compose the subroutine. Such code is called *pure-procedure* or *reentrant coding*. In addition, a stack-oriented machine can permit an indefinite nesting of subroutines. No unusual procedures must be observed to save or restore the subroutine linkages at any level of nesting. This is done automatically by the hardware.

A subroutine call in a stack-oriented machine requires the specification of the working register that will be used as a linkage pointer. The subroutine command explicitly designates this register. The execution of the subroutine call automatically performs the following functions:

1. It pushes the contents of the linkage register onto the top of the processor stack.
2. It adds 1 to the current contents of the PC but does not place the result in the PC; this is the return address to be used when the subrouting has completed.
3. The return address is pushed onto the top of the processor stack. It becomes the top item in the stack and pushes the linkage register contents one level down.
4. The effective address of the target branch location is jam-set into the PC.
5. Execution is then forced to continue from this point in main memory.

The *return from subroutine* (*RTS*) *instruction* is used to direct execution back to the original program. In particular, this command loads the PC with the return pointer found at the top of the stack (TOS), and then restores the contents of the linkage register to its original status.

A special EXECUTE command has been included in several instruction sets permitting an instruction to be executed out of sequence, with control returned to the next consecutive instruction following the EXECUTE command. This feature allows insertion of an instruction not initially included in the execution sequence. Effectively, the EXECUTE command behaves the same way as a single-instruction subroutine, but without the overhead of explicitly designating when the return-from-subroutine instruction is executed.

The PDP-11 family uses a special instruction to facilitate the details of unloading the stack when a subroutine exit is performed. The MARK command requires one variable to be specified in its command format. This variable is the number of parameters that are to be placed on the stack to be used by the subroutine. The MARK instruction is actually loaded on the stack as the first item after the current contents of the PC (see Figure 6-8). The procedure for employing the MARK instruction is as follows:

1. The linkage register is pushed onto the stack as the first item of the subroutine call.
2. Each individual parameter is separately pushed onto the stack. If there are *N* distinct parameters, *N* stack locations will be occupied by data words after the linkage register contents.
3. The actual binary representation of the MARK instruction, including the number of parameters passed, is pushed onto the stack. The format is MARK *N*, where the MARK *N* command is expressed in binary.

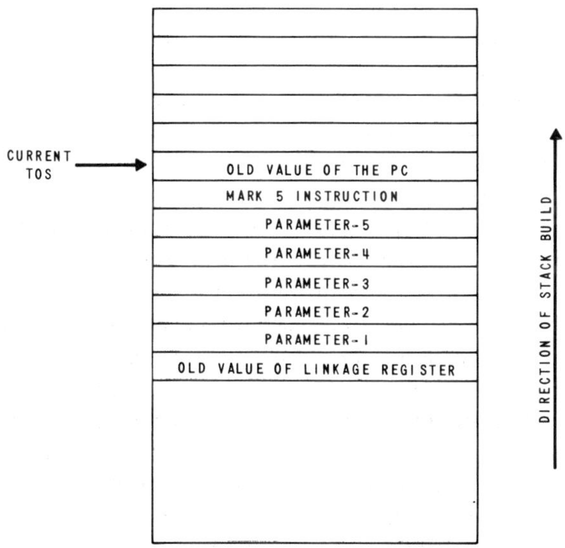

NOTE: AT THE COMPLETION OF THE PUSH OF ALL THE ELEMENTS ASSOCIATED WITH THE MARK 5 LOAD, THE LINKAGE REGISTER WILL POINT TO THE LOCATION OF THE MARK 5 INSTRUCTION IN THE STACK.

THE QUANTITY "5" REPRESENTS THE NUMBER OF PARAMETERS PUSHED ON THE STACK BEFORE THE MARK INSTRUCTION WAS LOADED.

6-8 MARK command in the PDP-11 stack

4. The linkage register contents are then overwritten with the actual stack address of the MARK *N* instruction. This completes the stack-build preamble of the main program.
5. The main program now issues a subroutine call that saves the contents of the current PC at the TOS, and execution is redirected to the subroutine.

The subroutine completes its processing by executing an RTS instruction that specifies the linkage register used in the preamble. The RTS instruction automatically loads the PC with the contents of the linkage register and then places the return address or the old contents of the PC in the linkage register. This points the PC to the stack location containing the MARK *N* instruction and forces execution to continue at that location.

When the MARK *N* instruction is executed, the following sequence of events automatically takes place:

1. The stack pointer is decremented *N* times to point to the original linkage register information saved on the stack.
2. The present contents of the linkage register, which correspond to the return address in the main program, are loaded into the PC.
3. The original linkage register information is popped from the stack and loaded into the linkage register, completing the subroutine exit.
4. Execution continues at the return address loaded into the PC. Table 6-6, block (B), describes the functions of these subroutine-related instructions.

An interrupt is similar to a subroutine call, except that it represents an externally forced branch in program control. It typically forces control to branch to a software service routine that handles the interrupt. In a non-stack-oriented machine, the return address to the interrupted program is saved in the first location of this service routine. If the processor employs a processor status word (PSW), the old value of the PSW is saved in the next location of the service routine. If a stack-oriented processor is employed, the PC and the PSW are pushed successively onto the stack. The interrupt service routine, except for the manner in which it is invoked, is identical to a subroutine. Exit from the interrupt service routine is normally accomplished by executing either a branch-indirect instruction using the contents of the first location in the service routine as the return pointer, or a *return from interrupt* (*RTI*) *instruction*. In the former case, the restoration of the PSW is left as the service routine's responsibility before a return to the interrupted program is performed. In the latter case, the contents of the old PC and the old PSW are automatically restored to the current PC and PSW.

A *trap* is essentially a software-generated interrupt. Consequently, a similar service routine may be used to handle the trap. A trap service routine may be exited by executing either a return from interrupt command or a *return from trap* (*RTT*) *instruction*. Table 6-6, block (C), gives typical interrupt- or trap-related instructions.

The ability to cause a machine to do essentially nothing for an entire instruction cycle is particularly useful in program debugging. Virtually all machines have a NO-OP instruction, which causes the processor to consume a full instruction cycle and not perform any other control activities. In program debugging, an unwanted or undesirable instruction can simply be overwritten with the NO-OP command without forcing the rest of the program module to be rewritten. At the microprocessor level, a sequence of NO-OP's or a NO-OP loop can function as a preestablished delay in a precise timing loop. This technique is not the best since the timing loop is critically tied into the actual device employed. If the microprocessor were replaced by a device with different operating characteristics, the timing loop would normally have to be rewritten.

Several machines permit the processor and system to be reinitialized by a single software command in addition to the normal hardware initialization that usually takes place when power is brought up. This command resets the system to the state in which each system device is placed after power-up. Its mnemonic representation normally takes the form RESET.

Virtually every machine at the micro or mini level possesses a HALT instruction which stops all execution at that point in the program flow. Typically, for those systems that possess consoles, the console panel is given control of the machine. The PC contains the address of the next instruction to be executed. Processor execution is resumed by the operator manually pressing the EXECUTE or CONTINUE key located on the console. In this situation, no system initialization is generated when processing is continued since it is assumed the operator wants the state of the machine left unchanged from the point at which processing was halted.

The PDP-11 family contains an unusual instruction called WAIT, which suspends the processor from the UNIBUS* until an external interrupt is experienced. The processor does not contend with other UNIBUS devices for bus usage when placed in this state. Consequently, much higher data transfer rates may be achieved between a peripheral device and main memory. The PC is set to point to the next instruction to be executed following the WAIT command. An interrupt will automatically place this value of the current PC and PSW on the processor stack. When the exit is made from the interrupt service routine, the old PC is automatically placed in the current PC. Execution then proceeds from the instruction following the WAIT command and the processor is reactivated.

A special instruction group is implemented by several manufacturers and referred to simply as *microoperations*. The PDP-8 family uses this instruction group to specify a series of operations that may all be done within the space of one memory cycle. These operations are specified by individual bits in the microoperation instruction and include such functions as clearing the accumulator, clearing the link bit, complementing the accumulator, and skipping the next instruction on the occurrence of a specified condition.

An internal hard-wired sequencer interprets the operations to be performed and the sequence in which they are to be executed. The hard-wired sequencer then executes these microoperations within one instruction cycle. The microoperation instruction permits several elementary operations to be combined into one instruction. This is not microprogramming in the classical sense defined by Maurice Wilkes. Table 6-6, block (D), illustrates this group of special control commands.

---

*Registered U.S. Patent Office.

No transfer-of-control command set would be complete without the inclusion of a class of *branch-on-condition instructions*. These instructions take two basic forms:

1. *Skip-on-condition*. In this case, the PC is incremented the correct number of times to skip over the next sequential instruction, providing that the stated condition has occurred. Otherwise, the next sequential instruction is executed.
2. *Branch-on condition*. This command permits branching to any permissible location in main memory, providing that the stated condition has occurred.

Both these commands test internal processor flags which have normally been set by the execution of the immediately preceding instruction. In each case, the status bits of the machine are automatically set during the execution of the preceding instruction. An additional instruction(s) is then required to examine the status bits and determine if a specific condition has occurred.

To clarify or determine the state of the processor, one of several *test-and-compare instructions* may be used. In each case, the appropriate status flags are set and may be tested by a branch-on-condition instruction. The test-and-compare instructions may be broken down into three types. They may be identified as:

1. A *straight comparison* of two words in memory. The contents of two separate hardware registers, or the contents of a hardware register and the contents of a word in memory, are compared.
2. An *arithmetic operation* between the contents of two words in memory, the contents of two separate hardware registers, or the contents of a hardware register and the contents of a word in memory. The result of the arithmetic operation sets the appropriate status flags.
3. A *logical operation* between the contents of two words in memory, the contents of two separate hardware registers, or the contents of a hardware register and the contents of a word in memory. The result of the logical operation sets the appropriate status flags.

Several microprocessors and minicomputers make a distinction between the operation of a branch instruction and the operation of a jump instruction regardless of whether they are unconditional or conditional commands. The branch instruction without indirection is simply a *program relative jump*, which is confined to an area surrounding the immediate instruction. For instance, the PDP-11 family permits branching of up to 255 locations ahead of the current instruction and 256 locations behind it. This case is often called a *short-branch operation*. The jump instruction is treated as a *double-word command*, with the second word specifying the effective address to which control is to branch. This case is often called a *long-branch operation*.

Virtually all machines minimize the effect of these instruction types by permitting address indirection. A short branch, however, does not require an additional word in storage, nor does it require an additional memory reference. It is particularly useful at the microprocessor level, where RAM is being conserved and cycle time optimized. Table 6-7 illustrates some of the possible conditions under which branching may take

TABLE 6-7 Possible Conditions Under Which Branching Might Occur

Machine overflow (result greater than machine's capacity)/no machine overflow
Normal carry generated/no carry generated
Outgoing-borrow/no borrow
Parity odd/parity even
Equal/not equal
Positive/not positive
Minus/not minus
Zero/not zero
Greater than/not greater than
Less than/not less than
1's/not 1's—this is often used after a test-bit-under-mask instruction.

place. In the 8080 microprocessor, a jump to a subroutine may be made conditional on the occurrence of an explicit processor flag. Most minicomputers and microprocessors have implemented some form of the *numeric signed conditionals* shown in Table 6-8. In particular, the branching instructions usually test the results of a previous

TABLE 6-8 Numeric Signed Conditionals

Sign	Meaning
$>$	Greater than
$\geq$	Greater than or equal to
$<$	Less than
$\leq$	Less than or equal to
$=$	Equal to

operation in which the operands involved are treated as signed 2's-complement quantities.

Signed conditional transfers of control are achieved in two steps:

1. An arithmetic operation that specifically involves signed 2's-complement arithmetic is performed. Depending on the results of this operation, certain internal flags are set.
2. A test-and-branch instruction is then executed, which causes the processor to sample the set of internal flags to determine if one or more of the explicitly designated conditions has occurred. If the condition(s) has occurred, control branches to the effective address produced using the contents of the operand field in conjunction with the specified addressing mode. Otherwise, the next

sequential instruction is executed by the machine. Table 6-9 lists typical branching constructs that may be generated using signed conditionals.

TABLE 6-9 Typical Signed-Conditional Branch Instructions

Instruction	Condition	Operand	Description
BR	G / GE / EQ / LE / E	NEWLOC	If the designated condition has occurred, branch to the effective address of NEWLOC.
BRN	G / GE / EQ / LE / E	NEWLOC	If the designated condition has not occurred, branch to the effective address of NEWLOC.

Often the major internal condition flags are kept as a single group and incorporated as part of the PSW, as in the PDP-11. These flags, called the *condition-code bits*, describe the results of the last CPU operation. Successive instructions may then interrogate these bits to determine if a condition has occurred that requires a branching operation. Each of these individual condition bits may be set or cleared separately or as members of a group, using the condition-code instruction that is part of the bit-oriented special instruction class.

6.2.5 The Special Function Class

Many minicomputers permit an additional ROM package to be inserted, which expands the basic instruction set supplied with the machine. This additional instruction package is a vendor-supplied option, and the actual implementation of the instructions at the microlevel is not specified by the end-user. These commands form the special instruction category and may consist of the following functions:

1. *The operation by the CPU on an individual bit or bits in a particular processor register.* Both the bit(s) and register can be specified by the instruction. However, the register may be implied by the specific operation to be performed.
2. *The location of first or least significant 0 in a processor register.*
3. *The determination of the total number of 1's in a processor memory location or internal register.*
4. *A comparison of two separate strings of bytes in memory.*

Any one or several of these special commands may be implemented as standard items in a given machine instruction repertoire. However, these directives normally represent special functions supplied by the vendor that must be requested by the end-user. This characteristic distinguishes this category from the extended instruction set category in which the user specifies the additional directives required by the application and *how* these directives should be implemented. In some cases, the user actually develops the microcode sequences to interpret the macroinstructions and supplies them to the manufacturer to have the microsequences programmed into ROM.

Instructions that test individual bits in a given register have proven quite useful in the process control industry and in an automated manufacturing environment. In both areas, individual bits indicate the state of ongoing processes such as the bounds on the temperature of a melt and whether or not a wire-wrapping tool has completed its current operation. In each case, a single small-scale computer controls many of these processes simultaneously and monitors the progress of each variable by sampling the individual status bits. The most common bit-oriented instructions take the following forms:

1. Set bit N in memory location MMEM1.
2. Clear bit N in memory location MMEM1.
3. Test bit N in memory location MMEM1.
4. Complement bit N in memory location MMEM1.

Several variations of these instructions employ a mask. The mask word bits have a one-to-one correspondence with the data word to be operated on. If bit N is in the 0's state in the mask word, then bit N of the data word will be manipulated. Otherwise, bit N of the data word will be left unchanged by the instruction. Consequently, all those bits in the mask word that are in the 0's state permit the corresponding bits of the data word to be administered by the machine command (see Section 6.2.2. for further details). The mask permits a specific operation to be performed on a group of bits simultaneously instead of a single bit at a time. These bit command variations take the forms:

1. Set bits under mask in memory location MMEM1.
2. Clear bits under mask in memory location MMEM1.
3. Test bits under mask in memory location MMEM1.
4. Complement bits under mask in memory location MMEM1.

In each of these instruction types, memory location MMEM1 could equally well be one of the registers in the working register set. Table 6-10, block (A), lists typical bit-oriented instructions that do not involve memory references; Table 6-10, block (B), lists typical bit-oriented instructions that involve memory references.

These instruction types form the category of *bit operations under a mask* and function the same as the single-bit manipulation commands just described for setting and clearing. The only difference is that all bits that fall under the mask will be set for the set-under-mask command and zeroed for the clear-under-mask command. All other bits in the specified word will remain unchanged. Similarly, all bits that fall under the mask will be complemented for the complement-under-mask command. The test-bits-under-mask command, however, presents a much more involved situation. Typical command types are given in Table 6-10, block (C).

The ability to search a register by starting from the least significant end and looking for the first occurrence of a 0 has been a very powerful instruction in the area of electronic switching. This instruction is called the find-least-zero (FLZ) instruction. Such a feature permits a processor to locate the first available line in a telephone

TABLE 6-10 Special Function Instruction Class

	Type of Instructions	Command String	Operation Performed
(A)	Typical bit-oriented instructions (nonmemory reference group)	SETBR REG1,BITK	Set BITK in register 1; all other bits of register 1 are left unchanged.
		SETR REG1,REG2	Set the bit in register 1 determined by 4 least-significant bits of register 2; all other bits of register 1 are left unchanged.
		CLRBR REG1,BITK	Zero BITK of register 1, but leave all other bits unchanged.
		CLRR REG1,REG2	Zero the bit in register 1 determined by the 4 least-significant bits of register 2; all other bits of register 1 are left unchanged.
		TSTBR REG1,BITK	Set the appropriate status flag to the condition of BITK in register 1.
		TSTR REG1,REG2	Set the appropriate status flag to the condition of the bit in register 1 specified the 4 least-significant bits of register 2.
(B)	Typical bit-oriented instructions (memory reference group)	SETB MMEM1,BITK	Set BITK of the memory word found at the effective address of MMEM1; all other bits at that memory location are left unchanged.
		CLRB MMEM1,BITK	Zero BITK of the memory word found at the effective address of MMEM1; all other bits are left unchanged.
		TSTB MMEM1,BITK	Set the appropriate status flag to the condition of BITK of the memory word found at the effective address of MMEM1; all other bits of MMEM1 are left unchanged.
(C)	Typical test-bits-under-mask instructions	TSTMM MMEM1,MASK	Test all bits in the memory word found at the effective address of MMEM1 that are enabled by the contents of the associated mask register. (a) If one or more of these bits is in the 1's state, set the appropriate status flag. (b) This is a memory reference instruction in which the contents of the memory word are left unchanged by the operation.
		TSTBM REG1,MASK	Test all bits in register 1 which are enabled by the contents of the associated mask register. (a) If one or more of these bits is in the 1's state, set the appropriate status flag. (b) All bits in register 1 are left unchanged.
(D)	Find-least-significant-zero instruction	FLZ REG1,REG2	Find the first occurrence of a zero in register 1, starting from the least significant end, and record the position of the zero in register 2. If a zero is found: (a) Its location is translated into a 4-bit binary number that is placed in bits 0 through 3 of register 2.

TABLE 6-10 (*cont.*)

	Type of Instructions	Command String	Operation Performed
(D)			(b) Bits 4 through 15 of register 2 are set to zero. (c) The appropriate status flag(s) is set to 1. (d) The zero in register 1 is set to 1. (e) If a zero is not found, the status flag(s) is cleared to 0 and register R2 is left unchanged.
(E)	Find-the-total-number-of-bits-in-the 1's-state instruction	FNO REG1,REG2	Find the total number of bits in the 1's state occurring in register 1. (a) This count is placed in register 2. (b) If no 1's are found, the appropriate status flag is set and a zero count is placed in register 2.
		FMNO MMEM1,REG2	Find the total number of bits in the 1's state occurring at the effective address of MMEM1. (a) This count is placed in register 2. (b) If no 1's are found, the appropriate status flag(s) is set and a zero count is placed in register 2.
(F)	Compare-2 byte-strings instruction	CLC STR1,STR2	1. Compare the 2-byte strings located in main storage. (a) The starting address of the first byte string is given by the contents of location STR1. (b) The starting address of the second byte string is given by the contents of location STR2. 2. A prior instruction will have loaded an internal counter with the number of bytes that are to be compared on a byte-by-byte basis. 3. If a byte comparison fails at any point prior to the end of the strings (i.e., the internal counter has not reached zero): (a) An internal status flag is set. (b) The number of bytes left to be compared are stored in an implied internal register. (c) The instruction execution is terminated at that point. (d) Control is returned to the regular instruction sequence. 4. If the byte-by-byte comparison is successful (i.e., the internal counter reaches zero): (a) A different internal status flag is set. (b) Zero is stored in the implied internal register. (c) Control is returned to the regular instruction sequence.

switching environment. This represents a standard command in a small-scale switching processor that would be a special instruction or an extended instruction on a commercially supplied machine. Table 6-10, block (D), illustrates this command.

The PDP-11/40 and PDP-11/45 machines possess a special opcode sequence for individually setting or clearing the condition-code bits. In addition, the user may select combinations of these bits to be set or cleared as a group. These instructions are part of the standard command group for these minicomputers and do not fall in the special instruction category defined here. However, they are bit-oriented operations and are placed in this section solely for that reason.

The ability to automatically determine the total number of bits in the 1's state in a specified register may also be useful in the process control industry. This command is, effectively, a variation of the FLZ instruction discussed above [see Table 6-10, block (E)].

The facility to compare two separate strings of bytes, both located in main storage, has been found quite useful in the area of data communications, where a transmitted character may be represented by an 8-bit byte. A message stream being received by a communications processor or terminal may automatically be checked against an expected message that has been preloaded. This feature can substantially expedite the processing capability of the terminal or small computer. The Texas Instrument Model 980A minicomputer employs such a command as an element in its instruction repertoire. This instruction is described in Table 6-10, block (F).

6.2.6 The Extended Functions Class

The major distinction between the special instruction category as used in this discussion and the extended instruction category is that in the latter case the user specifies precisely what applications-oriented commands are needed. These instructions are not usually standard options supplied by the manufacturer. If they are, these directives should actually be placed in the special instruction category. It is not uncommon for users to also specify the micro-level implementation of the commands they request for this category.

The most convenient method of examining instructions in this class is through examples. For several machines such as the Microdata 3200 and the HP-21MPX, data communications instructions are standard options. However for most other machines, such instructions must still be specified by the user. This requirement would place such instructions in the extended command set. Consider two of the possible types of instructions that might be requested to perform data communications more efficiently:

1. Translate the character residing in a specified register. This translation might be from BAUDOT to USASCII, from EBCDIC to USASCII, or BAUDOT to EBCDIC. The inverse translations are also possibilities.
2. Generate the *cyclic redundancy check character* (*CRC*) associated with a block of data characters. The CRC characters are produced using modulo-2 arithmetic and a generating polynomial. Typically, different CRC characters will be

generated for *binary synchronous control* (*BSC*) *protocol* as opposed to *synchronous data link control* (*SDLC*) *protoccl.*
These commands are implemented in firmware (microcode), according to the specifications of the user's requirements.

6.3 THE DESIGN OF AN EFFICIENT INSTRUCTION SET

No theoretical limit exists to the number of instructions that may be included in the command repertoire of a given machine. For instance, by using multiple-word instructions, a wider opcode field may be provided. For each additional bit assigned to the opcode, the total number of possible commands in the instruction repertoire is doubled. Thus, a substantially more versatile instruction set is obtained by allowing the opcode field to increase slightly. This may be achieved by employing a slightly wider instruction word or going to multiple-word instructions. However, if a large and comprehensive instruction set is implemented on a given machine, the programmers associated with the machine will have a tendency to use a subset of the overall instruction set. This is one of the observed characteristics of human nature. In addition, the more sophisticated the individual instructions are, the more likely it is that several instructions may perform portions of the same operation. This reduces the actual efficiency of the instruction set itself. However, the more sophisticated an instruction set is, the faster the programs should execute on the machine since the number of memory references for individual instructions should be appreciably reduced.

The design of an efficient instruction set can have a pronounced effect on a mini- or microcomputer structure. In particular, a considerable savings in the actual amount of memory required to store a user program may be achieved. In addition, the execution time required for the program may be reduced, provided that the number of main memory references is kept to a minimum. A general-purpose instruction set often will be too powerful and may actually represent an overkill or lack sufficient features for the intended application. For this situation, the instruction set is inconvenient to use and an awkward tool for implementing useful programs. Agraval [8] has defined an efficient instruction set as "one which meets the requirements of different applications in such a way that the average user pays a minimum penalty for the features which are unwanted or are rarely used by him."

It is a characteristic of virtually all computing machines that the individual instructions that make up the command repertoire are not found in various programs with the same frequency of occurrence. Information theory indicates that any instruction set should have a maximum utilization when instructions are used with the same frequency, a situation that is not encountered in the real world of computing. However, an instruction set may be designed in such a manner that the penalty paid by a programmer for seldom-used instructions is minimized. In particular, Agraval determined that a sampling of programs for the PDP-10 indicated that about 10 percent of the elements in the instruction set accounted for 80 percent of the total written code. This observation indicates that if statistical information can be incorporated in the frequency of utilization of the individual directives, a more efficient implementation of the instruction set could be achieved. One means of achieving this is by requiring that high-utilized instructions should be kept to a single memory word in length and coded in a manner that optimizes the use of bits in the short-form directive. Consequently, the area in main storage required by a user program may be reduced and the execution time of the program can then be improved.

6.4 ALTERNATIVE APPROACHES TO INSTRUCTION SET OPTIMIZATION

Several other approaches may be considered for achieving some optimization in instruction set design. The first and perhaps the simplest is the use of microoperations. This technique uses individual bits or groups of bits to combine a number of elementary operations that may all be performed in one instruction cycle. These elementary operations do not involve memory references, and the sequence in which they are executed is defined by the hard-wired control logic that implements them. A single instruction word is used to specify the microoperations, and the operand field is interpreted as an extension of the operation field. Execution time and main storage are conserved at the expense of the additional complexity required by the control logic to produce these functions.

A second approach is to divide the instruction set up into opcode groups. Each group of opcodes is essentially mutually exclusive. The opcode groups are formed by identifying instruction classes which are normally never mixed. Each group is given a unique prefix number which sets it apart from the other groups. After a particular group has been selected by the machine as the source of the instruction stream, the prefix number is used as a designator of the individual commands in that group. Consequently, fewer bits are required by each instruction since the prefix numbers are stored separately in some internally designated flip-flops that act as an extension of the operation field in the instruction register. To permit the program to execute from an instruction group other than the one currently directing program flow, an escape command must be employed. The execution of the escape command automatically switches control to the new instruction group. For good program performance, this technique requires that excursions between instruction groups be kept to a minimum. This, in turn, minimizes the number of escape instructions that must be executed and reduces the execution time of the program. The size of the operation-code field is reduced using this opcode grouping procedure. However, additional main storage is required to accommodate the escape commands and an additional level of complexity is required in the decoding logic.

Foster and Gonter [9] have proposed using an instruction set that is predicated on the conditional interpretation of the associated opcodes. Using this procedure, the present opcode being executed dictates the opcodes that may be permitted to follow it. They have shown that *not* all opcodes are equally likely to be encountered after a particular opcode has been executed. In effect, the instruction set may be designed such that only selected opcodes will be permitted to follow other opcodes. Such a machine would have to use the present state of the machine to interpret how the next instruction is to be executed. Foster and Gonter have shown that if only a small number of instructions are permitted to follow any arbitrary instruction, the required length of the opcode field may be substantially reduced. This approach would permit a traditional minicomputer with a limited word size to have an extensive instruction repertoire. However, no economy of main storage is achieved and an extreme level of complexity is introduced at the machine-language level. This complexity, in turn, complicates the assembler and its use by the application programmer.

Each of these techniques, with the exception of the use of microoperations, has not been adopted by the minicomputer or microprocessor designers for a very specific reason: the techniques have increased the complexity of the operations required by the user. The trend in modern small-scale computing is to remove complexity and provide the user with a straightforward, easily administered system. The ultimate direction pointed to by many manufacturers and systems houses is a totally "turnkey" package that is supplied to the user. In scientific and engineering computing, such systems would be dedicated controllers or special-function calculators. But in even the more sophisticated processing systems, the trend is to relieve the user from involved manual operations through applications-oriented firmware and a software base, including an instruction set, that is easy to understand. The instruction set, in turn, incorporates features that allow programs to be gracefully written by a reasonably unsophisticated user.

6.5 SUMMARY

The instruction sets found at the small computer level have been heavily influenced by the short word length used by these machines. However, if multiple-word instructions are employed, the sophisticated command elements of a much larger machine can be used. This chapter surveyed the wide range of command elements that could be used at the small computer level. The survey classified instruction types into six categories and characterized the members of each of these groups. Perhaps the strongest single feature that can be associated with instruction set development at the minicomputer or microcomputer level is the concept of ease of usage. That is, a set of command elements which are relatively easy to use by an application programmer should be identified for a given machine. Such directives permit software modules to be gracefully written, which also make efficient usage of main storage.

6.6 REFERENCES

1 RICHARDS, R. K., *Electronic Digital Systems*. New York: John Wiley & Sons, Inc., 1966.

2 *Intel MCS-40 User's Manual for Logic Designers*. Intel Corp., Santa Clara, Calif., 1975.

3 *Intel 8080 Microcomputer System Manual*. Intel Corp., Santa Clara, Calif., 1975.

4 *Motorola XC6800 Product Review* (Document NP-24). Motorola, Inc., Phoenix, Ariz., 1974.

5 *PDP8/E, PDP8/M and PDP8/f Small Computer Handbook.* Digital Equipment Corporation, Maynard, Mass., 1973.

6 *PDP11/45 Processor Handbook.* Digital Equipment Corporation, Maynard, Mass., 1975.

7 *The Value of Power . . . and How It Saves You Money on Your Minicomputer Systems.* General Automation Corporation, Anaheim, Calif., 1973.

8 AGRAVAL, DURGA P., *Design of an Efficient Instruction Set.* Master's degree thesis, Department of Computer Science, Carnegie-Mellon University, 1972.

9 FOSTER, CAXTON C., AND ROBERT GONTER, "Conditional Interpretation of Operation Codes." *IEEE Transactions on Computers,* Vol. C-20, No. 1 (Jan. 1971), pp. 108–111.

10 WEISS, C. D.: private internal BTL communication, Fall 1974.

11 WILSON, T. C., private internal BTL communication, 1967.

12 KORN, GRANINO A., *Microprocessors and Small Digital Computer Systems for Engineers & Scientists.* New York: McGraw-Hill Book Co., 1978.

13 HILBURN, JOHN L., and PAUL M. JULICH, *Microcomputers/Microprocessors: Hardware, Software, and Applications.* Englewood Cliffs, N.J.: Prentice-Hall, Inc., 1976.

14 KLINGMAN, EDWIN E., *Microprocessor Systems Design.* Englewood Cliffs, N.J.: Prentice-Hall, Inc., 1977.

6.7 PROBLEMS

1. As a processor's structure becomes more sophisticated, various instruction elements are proposed as additional commands for the instruction repertoire.
   (a) How *significant* are the following hardware instructions for a small machine that has been earmarked for the commercial, general-purpose, small computer market?
      i. Byte addressing
      ii. 32-bit *multiply* and *divide*
      iii. Variable length *rotate*
      iv. *Block search* through a list of items
      v. *Block move* of a list of items
      vi. Double-length GPR operations
   (b) What *simple* redundancy schemes may be used to increase the reliability of the instructions executed and the data referenced by the processor (e.g., parity checks, etc.)?

2. Shown in Figure P6-2 are the instruction formats and addressing modes that are available on a 16-bit machine that contains two 20-bit base registers, four 16-bit index registers, and sixteen 16-bit general-purpose registers.
   (a) Which operation is performed in the shortest time by the processor?
   (b) Which operation is performed in the longest time by the processor?
   (c) Can there ever be a situation when the execution time of case 2 will be equal to the execution time of case 3?
   (d) Suppose the opcodes for case 1, case 2, and case 3 are as follows:

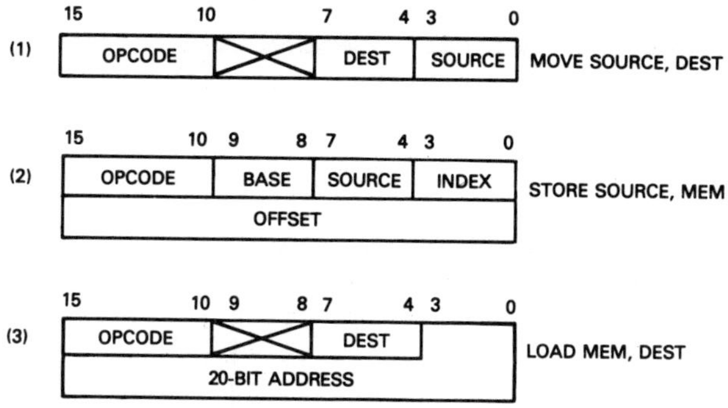

P6-2 *Note:* (1) SOURCE and DEST are GPR's. (2) MEM is a location in main storage.

$$\text{MOVE} = (\text{A})_{16} \qquad \text{STORE} = (1\text{B})_{16} \qquad \text{LOAD} = (3\text{C})_{16}$$

What operations are implied by each of the hexadecimal instruction words given below?

i. $(\text{F0F1})_{16}(\text{3CD2})_{16}$
ii. $(\text{28CC})_{16}$
iii. $(\text{6FD6})_{16}$
iv. $(\text{1C2})_{16}$

Are any of the above instructions improperly coded? If so, how should they be corrected so that they represent legitimate instructions that may be executed on the processor under consideration?

3. The processor shown in Figure P6-3 observes the following design conventions: (1) *All* instruction words are 18-bits long. (2) The width of the opcode field is fixed at 2 bits. (3) All arithmetic operations take place with the contents of accumulator, AC0, participating as one of the operands; the result is placed in AC1. Neither AC0 nor AC1 needs to be specified. (4) The data store is 16 bits wide. (5) The maximum size of the data store is 65,536 words. (6) Any operand specified by one of the four *legitimate* opcodes may be directly addressed in the data store. (7) The width of each GPR is 16 bits. (8) The four legitimate opcodes are: *LOAD* AC0 from memory location AAA $= (00)_8$; *STORE* AC0 into memory location AAA $= (01)_8$; *ADD* AC0 to contents of memory location AAA $= (10)_8$; *UNASSIGNED* $= (11)_8$. (9) The maximum size of the instruction store is 16,384 words.

(a) How many bits are in each of the following registers?

i. The program counter (PC).
ii. The ROM address register (RAR).
iii. The ROM data register (RDR).
iv. The instruction register (IR).
v. The memory address register (MAR).
vi. The memory data register (MDR).
vii. Accumulator AC0 or AC1.
viii. Index register IX0 or IX1.

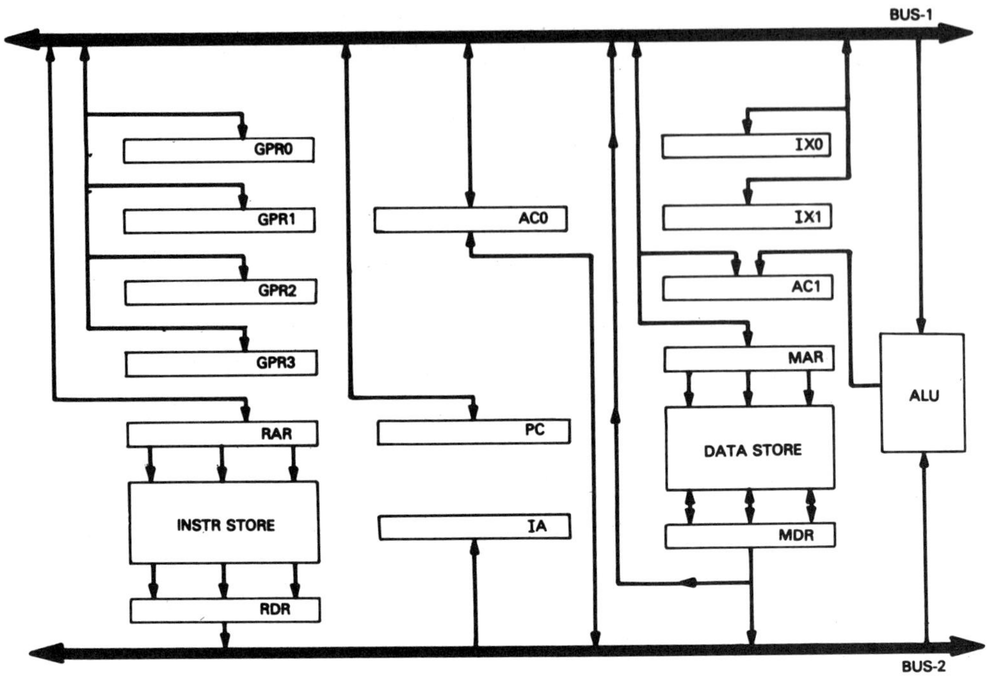

P6-3

(b) Assume we want to *expand* the data store beyond 65,536 words. The instruction word remains fixed in length, and memory indirection will *not* be allowed. What simple modification to the existing set of memory registers may be made to permit extended memory to be addressed?

(c) How may additional command elements be added without disturbing the fixed length of the opcode field? Is the use of microoperations appropriate here? Could an "extended" opcode field be implemented?

(d) Assume an extended opcode field is employed. Lay out the instruction formats for the following operations:

 i. The contents of a GPR is *added* to the contents of AC0.

 ii. The contents of AC0 is placed in the data store at the location specified by the sum of the contents of an index register and an OFFSET.

(e) Now let all arithmetic operations take place between the contents of any location in the data store *and* any register accessible from BUS-1. Lay out the instruction formats for the following operations:

 i. The contents of a GPR is *added* to the contents of another GPR.

 ii. The contents of a GPR is *added* to the contents of a location in the data store that is specified by the sum of the contents of an index register and an OFFSET.

 iii. The contents of a location in the data store is added to the contents of a location in the instruction store.

(f) Draw the timing diagram for the instruction described above in subpart ii of part e.
(g) Is there any need for a base register addressing mode?

4. Consider a 24-bit processor structure that has the following hardware features: (1) The internal bus is 24 bits wide and may be used for either address or data. (2) The GPR set consists of sixteen 24-bit registers. (3) Memory addressing is done using two 20-bit base registers. (4) The opcode field is made up of six bits. (5) The instruction word may be either 16, 24, or 32 bits long. (6) A 16-bit index register may be used in the effective address calculation.

   For each of the following situations, lay out the addressing mode or instruction format as it would *appear* in main storage:
   (a) A 16-bit *load-immediate instruction* that moves a nibble into a specified general register.
   (b) A load-immediate instruction that moves a 24-bit data word from a specified general register *into* main storage. An *offset* quantity may be used with the appropriate base register to form the effective address.
   (c) A register transfer command that loads the destination register from the specified source register. A 24-bit *immediate mask* is supplied for operating on the transferred data.
   (d) A load register command that transfers data *from* a location in main storage into the destination register. Both indexing and an offset quantity may be used with the appropriate base register to form the effective address.
   (e) A *group move command* that transfers a group of bytes starting at the location specified by base register RB1 to a group starting at the location specified by base register RB2. The number of bytes to be moved is placed in a specified general register.
   (f) *Store the right-most 8 bits* of data in a specified general register into the indicated effective byte address in main storage. Both indexing and an offset quantity may be used with the appropriate base register to form the effective byte address.

5. Consider the machine architecture shown in the Figure P6-5a. Assume the instructions shown in Table P5 are available:

TABLE P5

ADD I,X,AAA	Where the contents of the AC are added to the contents of Location AAA and the results are placed back in the AC.
JMP I,X,BBB	Branch unconditionally to location BBB.
JMS I,X,CCC	Subroutine branch to location CCC. The return address is placed on the top of the hardware stack.
RTS	Return from a subroutine. The contents of the top of the hardware stack is placed in the program counter and control-directed to continue execution from that point.
RTI	Return from an interrupt. The contents of the five top locations of the hardware stack are placed in the following registers, successively: AC, IXR1, BR1, IM, and PC. The IM is the interrupt mask register.

Instruction:	LOAD	STORE	ADD	JMP	JMS	RST	RTI
Opcode:	$(3)_8$	$(4)_8$	$(5)_8$	$(6)_8$	$(7)_8$	$(10)_8$	$(11)_8$

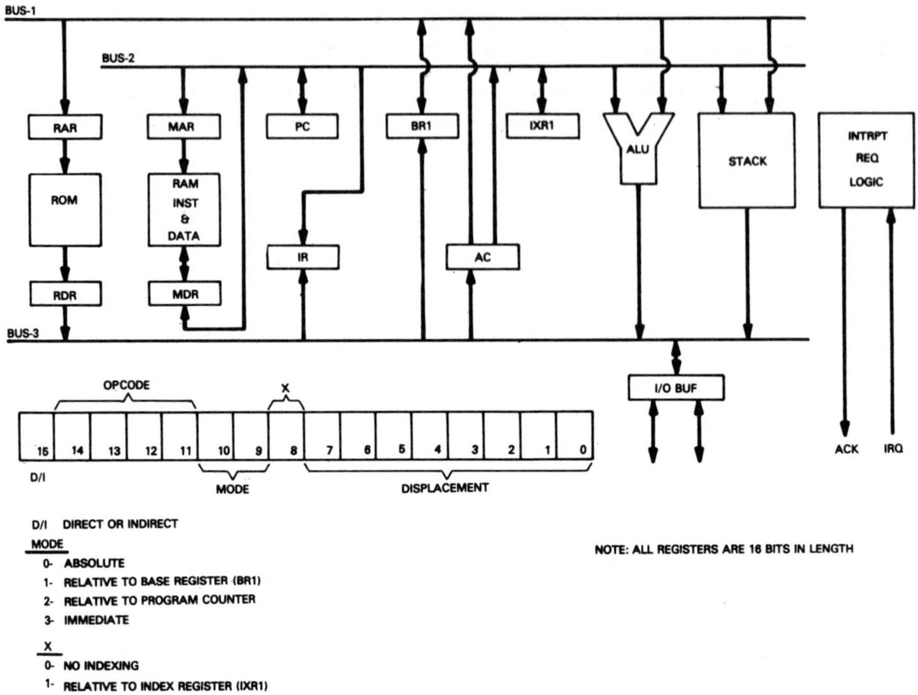

P6-5a

(a) Consider the machine state shown in Figure P6-5b. Describe the resultant behavior of the processor as execution continues from the point indicated by the program counter (PC).

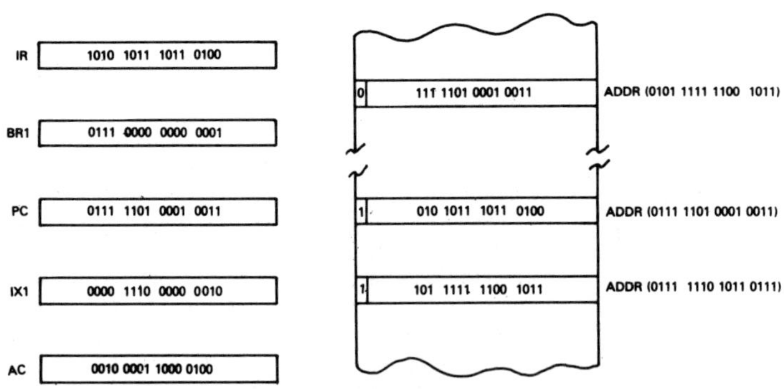

P6-5b

(b) Study the machine state shown in Figure P6-5c. Assume that address indirection is the final address modification performed in the calculation of an effective address for the operand. Describe the resultant behavior of the processor as execution continues from the location indicated by the program counter (PC).

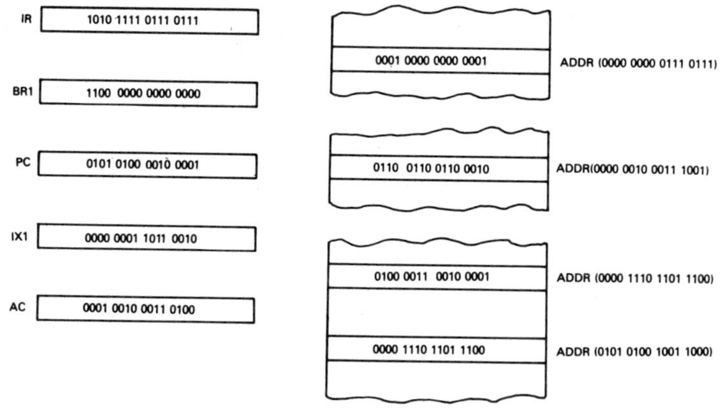

P6-5c

If address indirection is the first operation performed in the effective address calculation, how does this change your answer.

(c) Study the machine state shown in Figure P6-5d and describe the behavior of the processor as execution continues from the location indicated by the program counter (PC).

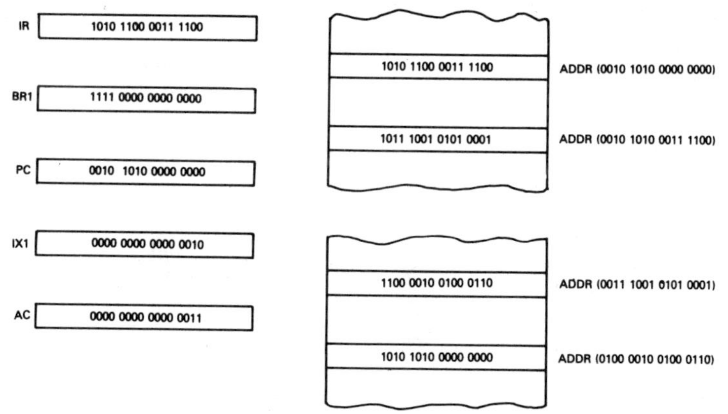

P6-5d

Is the behavior of the system under these conditions unusual? If so, what possible mechanism (hardware or software) could be used to alleviate this problem?

(d) Consider the machine state shown in Figure P6-5e. Notice that the top five locations of the hardware stack are explicitly given. Starting at Location $(8756)_{16}$, where does execution continue after the instruction at Location $(8758)_{16}$ is executed?

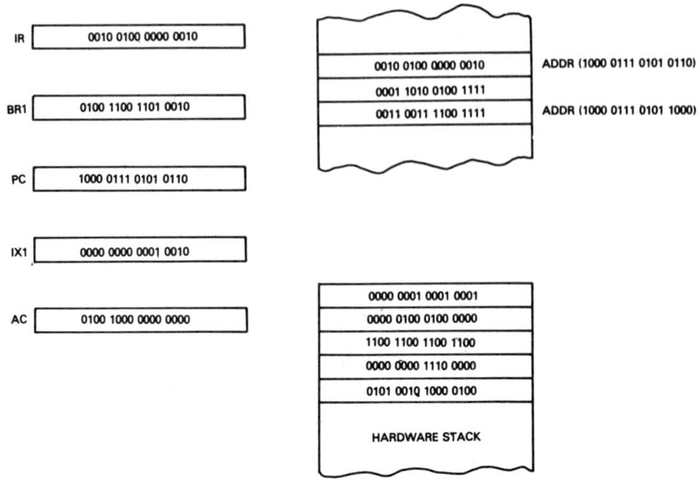

P6-5e

6. While studying the machine architecture shown in Figure P6-6, consider the following:

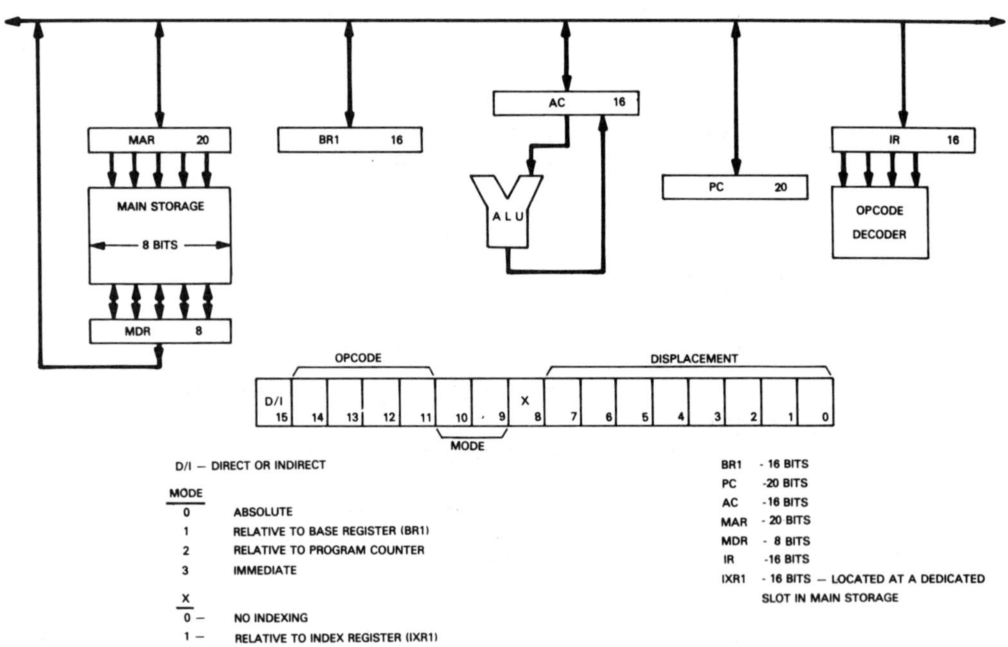

P6-6

(1) Indexing is always done before indirection. (2) Multilevel indirection is permitted. If an 8-bit word has its D/I bit set, the next consecutive memory location is used to derive a

16-bit address; otherwise, this procedure is observed repeatedly until the effective address is found.

(a) The ADD instruction for this machine takes the form of

ADD I,X,DISP

where DISP is the operand that is to be used. By implication, the contents of the AC are added to the operand specified by the instruction; the result is placed in the AC. Consider the following instruction [where the ADD opcode is (0101) = (5)8]:

1	0	1	0	1	0	1	1	0	1	1	1	0	1	1	0

Assuming 200 ns for each operation involving the ALU and 100 ns for each gating operation involving the bus (i.e., gating onto the bus and gating off of the bus), what is the total amount of time required to execute this instruction if a main memory with a cycle time of 2 ms is employed?

(b) Consider an identically structured machine, except that the width of all registers and the gating bus is 16 bits. Let IXR1 be a separate hardware register as opposed to being located in main storage. Call this machine *machine B* and the previous machine *machine A*.

If a 16-bit memory with a cycle time of 2 ms is used with machine B, what must the cycle time of the 8-bit memory used with machine A be to achieve the identical execution time for the ADD instruction executed by machine B? *Note:* Only a single-level indirection is required by the ADD instruction.

7

Conventional and PLA Control

7.1 INTRODUCTION

A general-purpose CPU may be considered as being divided into four functional units: a *control section*, a *memory facility*, an *arithmetic logic unit* (*ALU*), and an *I/O section*. The control section is the heart of the system; it interprets and executes stored instructions from main memory. The implementation of the instruction set, which is unique to each design, defines the control section of the machine.

Three techniques are used to implement the control section in hardware: *conventional* or *random logic*, *programmable logic array* (*PLA*), and *microprogram control*. Random logic is an outgrowth of the discrete component era; logic gates are minimized to reduce the hardware cost. This gives rise to an irregular structure; control signals are scattered throughout the entire machine in an apparently random manner. An LSI approach to random logic is the PLA. The logic structures generated by random logic and the PLA's are equivalent.

The design aspects of control functions implemented using random logic and PLA's are covered in this chapter. The third technique, microprogram control, differs considerably from the other two and will not be discussed in detail in this volume.

7.2 CONTROL FUNCTIONS

Control operations may be classified into four basic categories: *instruction fetch*, *instruction decode*, *operand fetch*, and *instruction execute*. These operations dictate the necessary control signals required to implement the control functions defined by the instruction set of a computing machine.

The instruction fetch operation, which provides the control linkage from instruction to instruction, allows a continuous flow of instructions to be executed. Instructions are normally grouped into several types: for example, *register-to-register* (*RR*), *register-to-storage* (*RS*), *storage-to-register* (*SR*). The decode function identifies the various classes of instructions that have common control sequences. This permits different instructions with identical operations to share the same hardware.

For instructions requiring a memory reference (i.e., RS or SR types), a data fetch (commonly referred to as an *operand fetch*) is required to obtain the prescribed data from memory. The number of operand fetches depends on the instruction set (see Section 5.1).

To implement an instruction, various control signals are required to coordinate the activities occurring at different times. Each action is an elementary operation and, by itself, may not accomplish the desired result. However, the "orchestration" of the various actions into a well-organized sequence results in the operation specified by the instruction. The number of control signals for a given instruction depends on its complexity and the internal structure of the machine. Since each instruction performs a unique function, the control sequences differ from instruction to instruction.

Figure 7-1 shows the relationship of basic control functions. They implement not only the execution of instructions but also perform the addressing operation of sequencing from instruction to instruction to form a *program sequence*. The address modification applies to both operand and instruction fetches. The many ways of altering an instruction sequence or performing a data fetch illustrate the strength and flexibility provided by a stored program. Figure 7-2 illustrates the flow of data or instruction from the main memory. The address modification logic for program or data normally shares the ALU hardware when indexing operations are to be performed under the control of the execution logic.

7.3 INSTRUCTION SEQUENCING

Instruction sequencing provides a continuous flow of instructions to the execution circuitry. The basic timing associated with each instruction and the general machine structure interconnecting the various functional units must be considered prior to and during the design of the control logic. In early systems, the memory cycle was generally used as the basic machine cycle time. The primary reason for this choice will become obvious as the access and cycle time of core memory systems are discussed further.

Typically, a core memory cycle is divided into two approximately equal intervals: a *read operation* and a *write operation* (see Figure 7-3). The read interval represents the operation time required by the memory to decode the address, switch the cores, and sense the outputs before the data are presented to the CPU. This interval is defined as the *access time*. As the information stored in memory at that address is read from the cores, it is either destroyed or cleared. To restore the data, the information must then be written back into the cores immediately following the read interval. With a cycle time in the range of 1 to several microseconds, nearly all control operations required

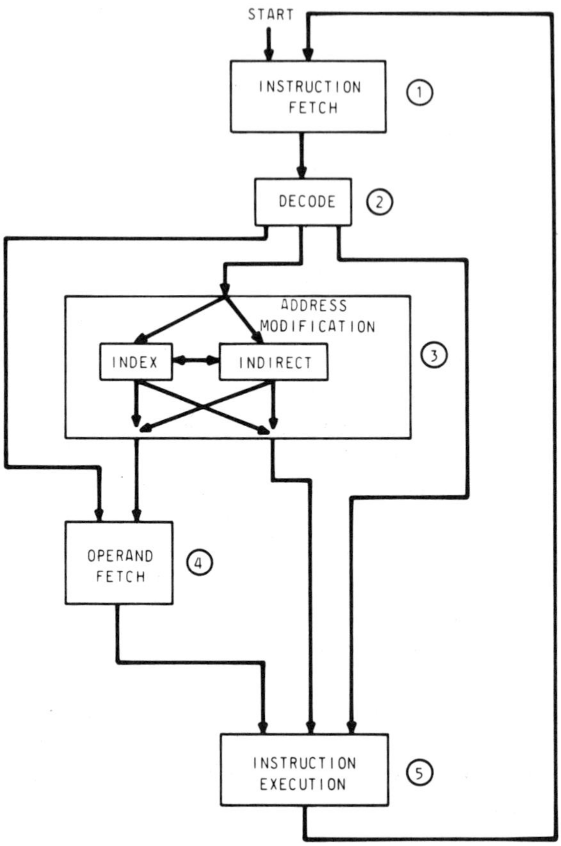

7-1 Basic control functions

by the instruction can be completed during the write interval and subsequent read interval. This implies that the memory access rather than the control operations is the limiting factor in the instruction-execution rate of a processor. However, this is not true for more complicated instructions, such as multiplication or division. These instructions require many cycles of repeated operations without any memory access.

By organizing the basic machine cycle to coincide with the memory cycle, the maximum data transfer rate between main storage and the processor may be realized. Figure 7-4 shows a timing sequence of simple instructions that can be fully implemented during the write and read intervals. The overlap operations of instruction fetch and execution keep the memory access rate at the 100 percent level. Figure 7-5 shows an instruction requiring an operand fetch. In both cases, the memory access and the instruction execution are completely synchronized to use the memory at its fastest possible rate.

An adequate number of clock pulses must be provided to synchronize the different control operations that occur at various times during a machine cycle. Since most of

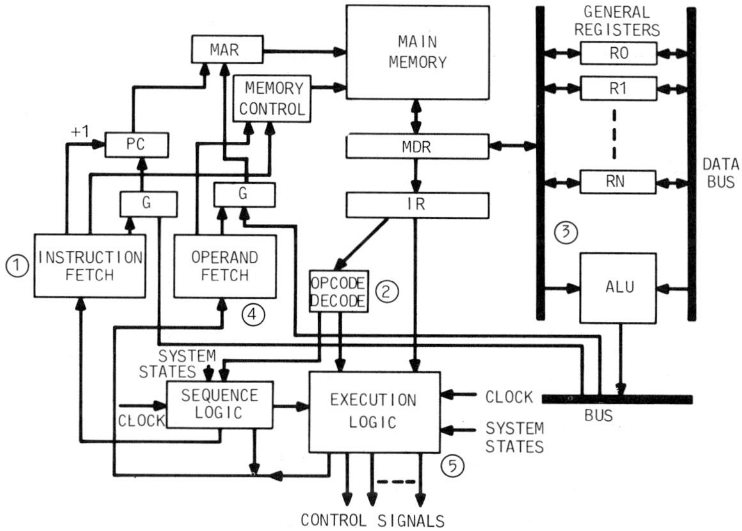

7-2 Simplified block diagram of instruction and data flow from main memory

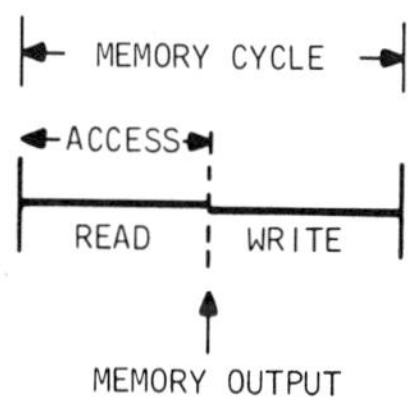

7-3 Memory fetch operation: memory cycle

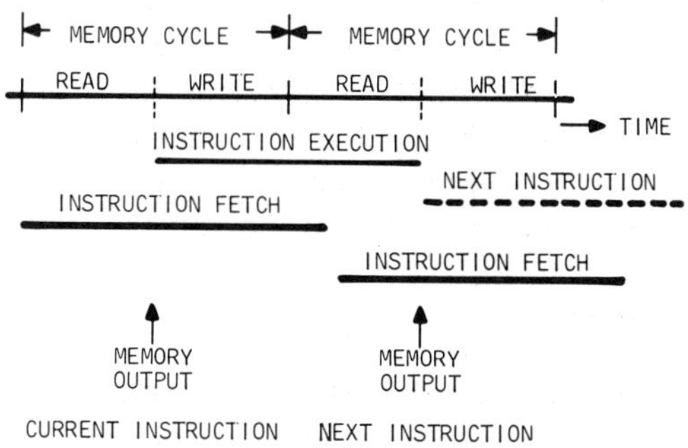

7-4 Memory fetch operation: instruction cycle

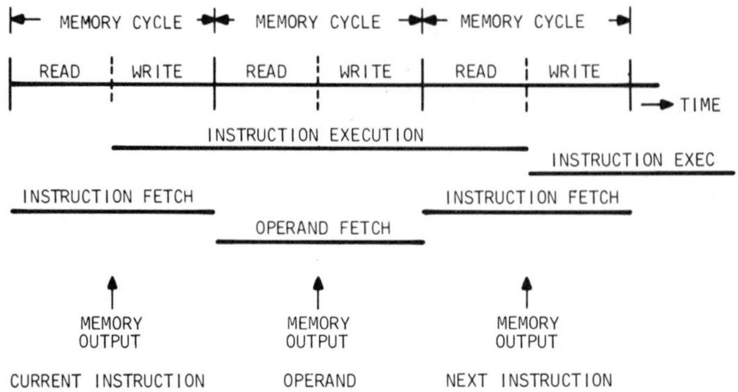

7-5 Memory fetch operation: instruction cycle with operand fetch

the instructions can be executed in one machine cycle, the period must be divided into sufficient intervals to allow processing of the most complex sequence of operations within the cycle. The number of clock pulses needed, therefore, is directly related to the number of sequential steps found in the machine cycle.

In the case of semiconductor memory, the read is a nondestructive operation. This results in an access time that is nearly equal to the cycle time. For the following control logic discussion, it is assumed that core memory is used and the memory cycle is divided into read and write intervals. This should not affect the basic technique of control logic design. When the semiconductor memory is used, one of the two intervals becomes zero. Section 7.10 covers the possible uses of both semiconductor and core memory in a CPU.

7.3.1 Sequential Addressing

A program sequence is normally executed in consecutive order with the program address incremented by one count each time an instruction is fetched from memory. At times, it is necessary to branch from the regular program sequence and jump to a new one. The address of the next instruction found in the program counter (PC) will be changed to correspond to the entry point of the new program sequence. Figure 7-6 and 7-7, respectively, show the hardware and the timing chart of a sequential instruction fetch. The PC is automatically incremented by one count after its content is transferred to the memory address register (MAR). A serial counter rather than a high-speed parallel binary counter can be used in the implementation of the PC, since the count does not have to be settled until the next PC-to-MAR transfer.

7.3.2 Operand Fetch

Not all memory fetches are for instructions. In many instances, fetches for data words are interleaved with instruction fetches. In such cases, there must be a pause of one memory cycle in the sequential access to allow the operand fetch to "steal" a cycle.

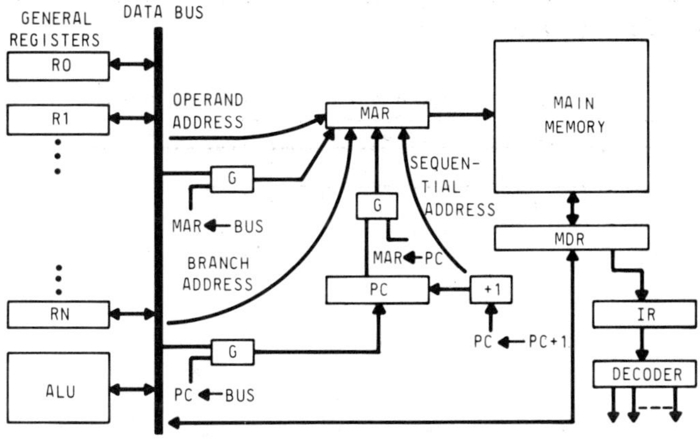

7-6 Memory addressing: functional diagram of memory addressing

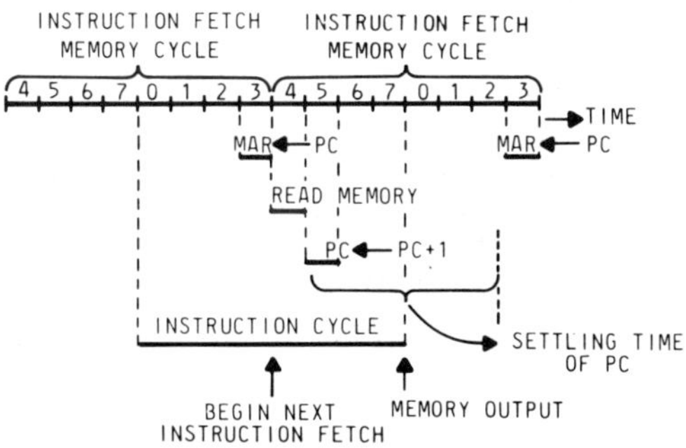

7-7 Memory addressing: timing sequence of simple sequential addressing

The normal PC-to-MAR data transfer and add-one-to-PC operation are not done during the scheduled clock phase. The information concerning the operand fetch operation can be derived directly from the instructions by means of the decode logic. Figure 7-8 shows a diagram of the interleave relationship between the instruction and operand fetches. The operand address is assumed to be one of the internal registers gated onto the bus, although this relationship is not shown in the diagram. When the operand address is ready at the regular clock phase, the information is gated directly to the MAR by means of the data bus, as indicated in the figure. In some cases, the addressing may undergo several gating steps plus an arithmetic operation (i.e., indexing by means of the ALU). Under this condition, the operand address will not be ready at the prescribed interval, and the memory operation will be delayed until the address modification has been completed. The operand address is gated into the MAR one cycle later by means of the data bus, as shown in Figure 7-9. The control logic signals, which add one count to the PC and transfer the operand address to the MAR, are synchronized with the instruction decode and execution logic to achieve the maximum memory-to-CPU data transfer rate.

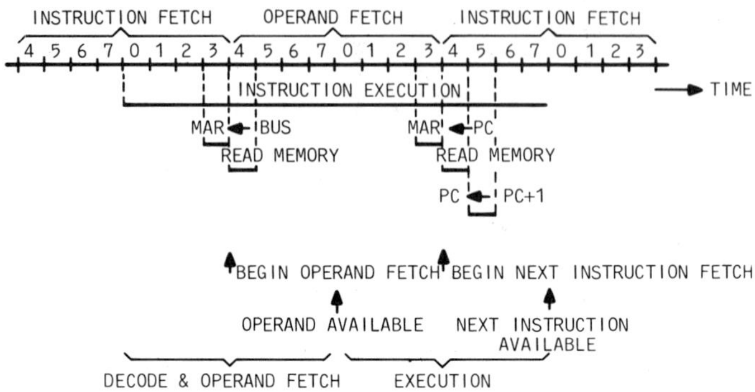

7-8 Memory addressing: timing sequence with operand

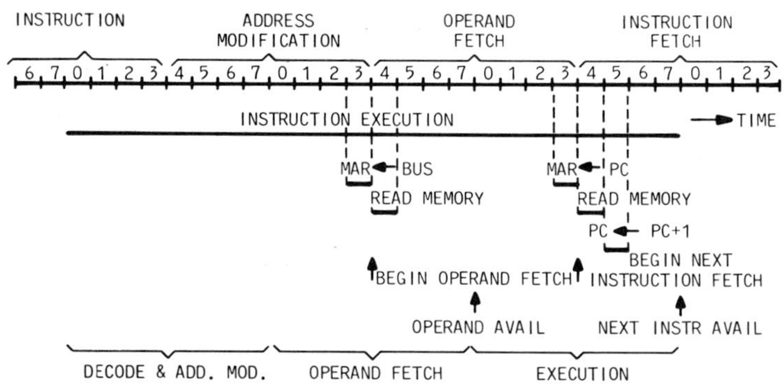

7-9 Memory addressing: timing sequence with operand address modification

7.3.3 Unconditional Branch

When a program breaks from a normal execution sequence and jumps to a new memory location, the hardware must provide an alternative data path in order to gate the new address into the PC. This is usually accomplished by means of the common data bus in the same manner as the addresses used for data, except that the information gates directly into the PC instead of the MAR. Figure 7-6 shows the hardware used when the branch address is gated into the PC by means of the bus and, hence, into the MAR. The operation assumes that the new address from any of the internal registers is ready immediately upon instruction decoding. If this is not the case, the memory fetch logic must pause for a cycle until the address *is* ready.

Many addressing modes are used for branching as well as for data. *Indirect branching* is an example in which the branch address is stored in memory. To retrieve the address, it must be fetched as an operand. Figure 7-10 shows the timing chart for the memory operation of an indirect branch instruction. The branch address is fetched as an operand and used as the next program address; therefore, an extra memory cycle is necessary.

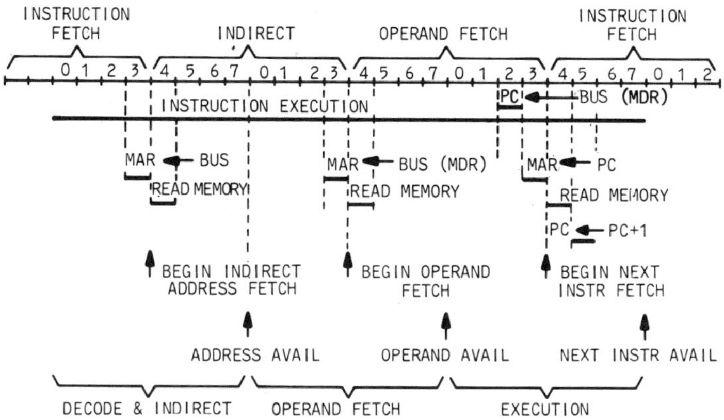

7-10 Memory addressing: timing sequence with indirect operand

7.3.4 Conditional Branch

Another class of branching instructions is the *conditional type*, which depends on the state of the machine at the time the branch instruction is executed. If the specified conditions arc satisfied, the program executes a branch in control. Otherwise, the program continues with the next sequential instruction. Figure 7-11 shows the two program addressing paths, sequential and branch. For a conditional branch instruction, the decision to redirect the flow of execution depends on the specified system condition(s). Usually, it is assumed that the conditions(s) have been stabilized prior to execution of the instruction.

In some cases, certain logic or arithmetic operations are performed, with the conditional branch based on the result. Because of the additional manipulations required, the results of the specified operation are not immediately available. Consequently, the branch decision cannot be determined until the result has been obtained. This means that a possible wait of one or more memory cycles must occur before the branch can take place. If the branch is not taken, this wait represents a loss in execution time. Alternatively, the system can be designed such that the fetch of the next sequential instruction is processed immediately. If the branch is not taken, no time is lost. If the branch *is* taken, the prefetch of the next sequential instruction can be discarded without any loss of execution time. This action assumes that the operation and the decision logic require almost the entire cycle to complete execution. If this is

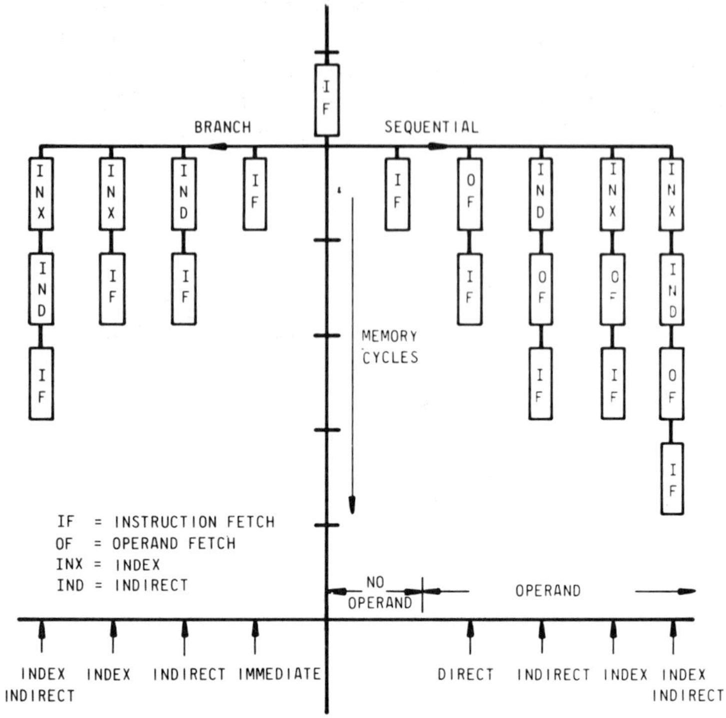

7-11 Instruction and operand fetch sequences

not the case, the prefetch may delay the branch operation. The design choice depends on whichever method results in a faster execution rate and is easier to implement.

The instruction and operand fetches, as described, are completely synchronized with the instruction execution. Although the operation of each sequence is relatively straightforward, the different possible combinations of operand and instruction fetches make the circuitry somewhat irregular and perhaps not the easiest to maintain. Figure 7-11 shows a flow diagram of various combinations of instruction and operand fetch sequences. It is assumed that a single operand instruction requires a single memory cycle to perform address modification (indexing). For simplicity, postindexing using a specified index register and multilevel indirect addressing is not included in the example. Otherwise, many other combinations are possible.

7.3.5 Interrupt Addressing

Interrupt facilities are provided in most minicomputers and microcomputers to handle I/O and external interrupts. Breaking into a normal program sequence must be done at the appropriate time to preserve the continuity of the interrupted program sequence. The operation is almost identical to the branch instruction, except that the next instruction address must be saved either in a hardware register or in main memory. This is necessary to allow the return of the interrupted program at the completion of the interrupt. The operation is analogous to a subroutine call.

Before an interrupt can direct execution to transfer to a new program sequence, the contents of the current PC must be saved immediately. This allows the PC to be set to the address corresponding to the interrupt sequence. Figures 7-12 and 7-13, respectively, show the functional diagram and timing sequence for this arrangement. The fetching of the next instruction is a common routine for all instructions. A specially derived timing signal, called an *end-of-instruction* (*EOI*) *signal*, occurs during the last cycle of each instruction. It is used to initiate the next instruction fetch and advance the PC to the next address. The interrupt logic, in combination with the clock and EOI signals, generates the controls that save the contents of the PC in a special hardware register called the *return program counter* (*RPC*). The interrupt logic then jam-sets the PC to the interrupt address. It is this address that will be gated into the MAR in order to fetch the next instruction. Following this action, the normal instruction fetch sequence is performed. The PC and the MAR are now set to the new interrupt address with the current program address saved in the RPC. The next instruction read from memory is the one at the entry address of the interrupt service routine. This corresponds to the beginning of a new program sequence.

If the system has only a single-level interrupt facility, there is no need to transfer the contents of the RPC into memory. However, in a multilevel interrupt arrangement in which a higher-priority interrupt may suspend the execution of a lower-priority service routine, the hardware RPC register serves only as a temporary buffer until the program has a chance to store the return address in memory. Consequently, it would be advantageous to eliminate this buffer entirely and store the return address directly in memory or into an *LIFO* (*last-in-first-out*) *hardware stack*.

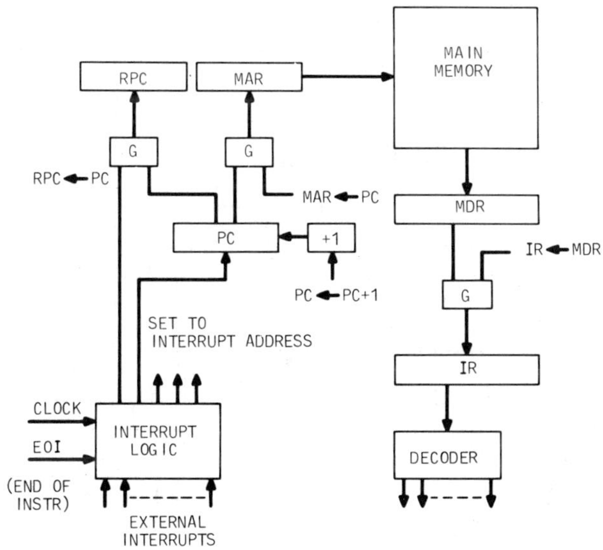

7-12 Interrupt by address replacement: functional diagram

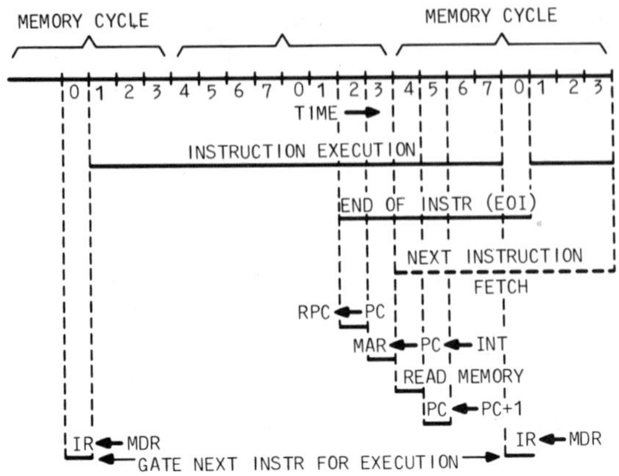

7-13 Interrupt by address replacement: timing sequence

Figure 7-14 shows an arrangement in which the normal procedure of fetching the next instruction is inhibited, preserving the current PC. The interrupt logic in combination with the clock and the EOI signals generates a control which jam-sets a special interrupt instruction directly into the IR. This is done when the next instruction from the MDR is gated into the IR. During this time, the normal data transfer is inhibited by the jam-set control signal. The replacement of the next instruction by a special one is synchronized with the instruction sequencing. This allows a smooth interrupt entry into the system. The INT signal is a special branch-and-save instruction. Its execution

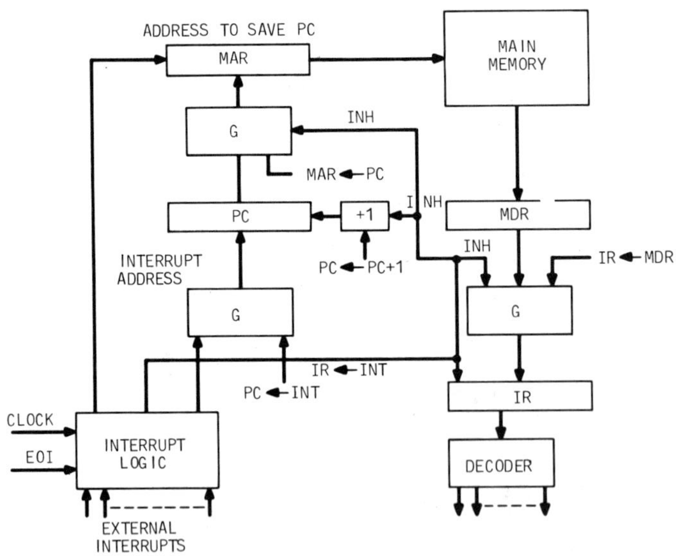

7-14 Interrupt by instruction replacement: functional diagram

results in saving the current PC in memory and performing a branch to the location specified by the interrupt logic. The sequence of operation is shown in Figure 7-15. The INT signal could be the same as the BRANCH-to-subroutine instruction.

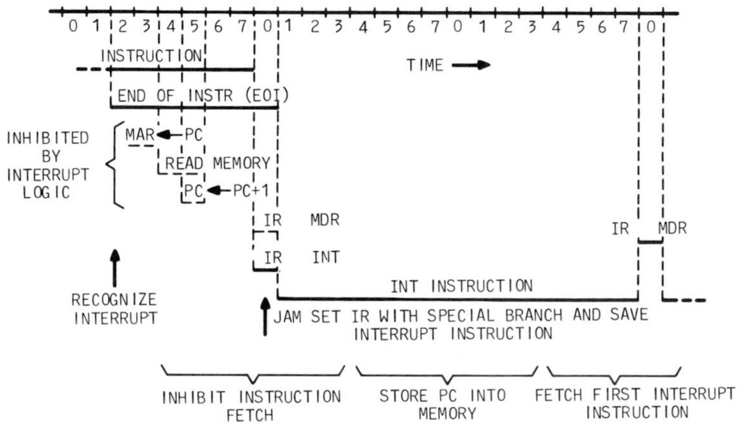

7-15 Interrupt by instruction replacement: timing diagram

7.3.6 Instruction Prefetch

The operations of memory read and write are essential parts of the instruction execution sequence. Different addressing modes improve programming efficiency and provide the flexibility of storing and retrieving data from memory. Address information may be used either directly or in modified form, according to specifications given by the instruction. If it is used directly, the operand fetch can be processed immediately without delay (see Figure 7-8). The memory is then operated at 100 percent of its duty cycle. When indexing is performed, several gating steps plus the associated arithmetic operation may require an additional cycle (see Figure 7-9). Under these conditions, the memory is idle during the additional cycle. The fetching of the next instruction could be accomplished while the operand address is being modified, maximizing the utilization of the memory and execution rate. This prefetching strategy requires an additional hardware register to hold the next instruction while the current one is being executed (see Figure 7-16). The data and the instruction are separated and directed into independent registers as they are fetched from memory. The extra buffer provides the flexibility of prefetching the next instruction at any convenient time. In the previous arrangement, which does not use prefetching, the next instruction is always fetched at the end of the current instruction. The memory data register (MDR) serves as a buffer to hold the information until it is gated into the IR. Figure 7-17 shows that the instruction execution is decreased from three to two cycles by prefetching the next instruction during the time the memory address is being modified. However, it is not always possible to save an extra cycle by prefetching. For example, if the instruction is a memory read rather than a memory write, additional time may be required to process the data.

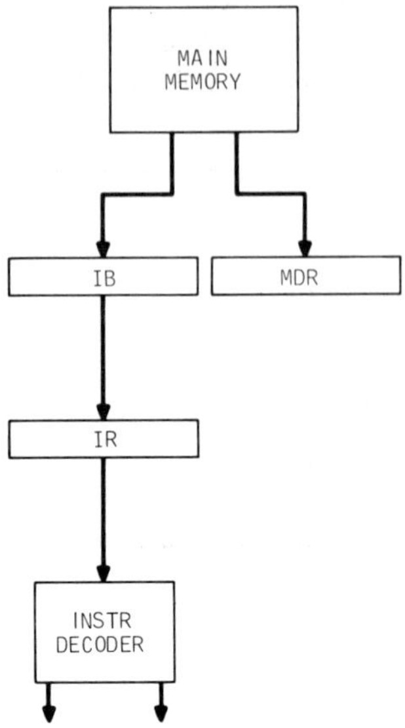

7-16 Instruction prefetch: separate buffer for data and instruction

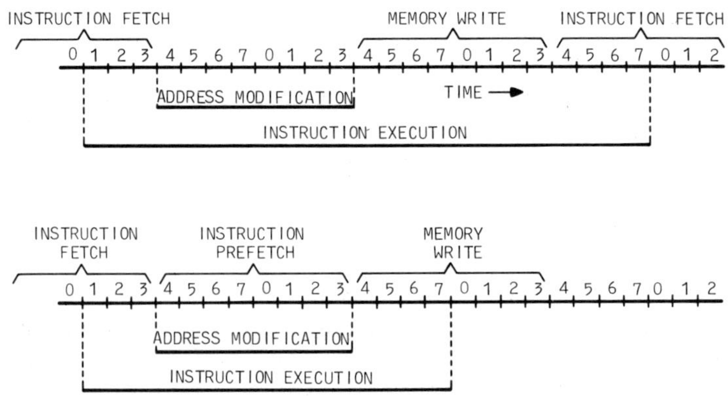

7-17 Instruction prefetch: timing diagram for an instruction prefetch

7.3.7 Instruction Decode and Execute

For small machines, the processor decodes and executes only one instruction at a time. The decoding of simple instructions leads directly to the desired control actions without any additional logic circuitry. In more complex instructions, the decoder outputs are logically combined with appropriate system conditions and clock signals to generate a composite set of sequential control signals. These, in turn, implement a given instruction. Figure 7-18 shows a general diagram of control signals. The outputs may be divided into two types: those associated with instruction sequencing and those associated with individual instructions.

The ultimate source of the timing signals is the clock. The clock's output frequency is very accurately controlled by a highly stable crystal oscillator. The number of clock phases or pulses within a machine cycle is dictated by the maximum number of steps required to process the data from memory or perform certain logic or arithmetic operations. A *single phase clock* (one clock pulse) arrangement is widely used in microprocessor design because of its simplicity of logic circuitry. The arithmetic or logic operation is normally enabled during the clock interval and the result is strobed into a destination register at the trailing edge of the clock pulse. When more than one clock pulse is provided, the clock is normally referred to as a *multiphase clock*. The oscillator output drives a chain of counter circuits or shift registers with outputs logically combined to form a set of repetitive signals. Figures 7-19, 7-20, and 7-21, respectively, show the general block diagram of a clock circuit and two sets of clock pulses that could be used as timing signals. The spacing and the width of the pulses

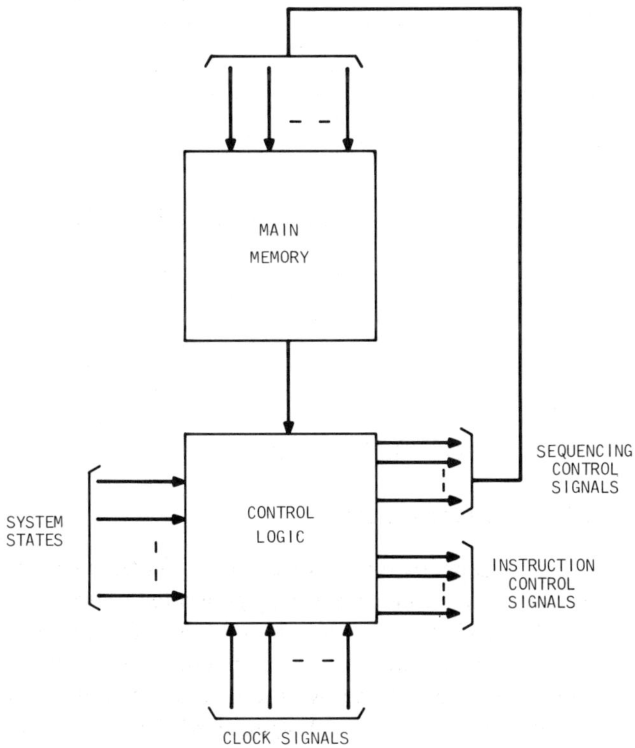

7-18 General diagram of control logic

are determined by the logic structure of the machine. For one-cycle instructions, the number and arrangement of the clock pulses should be adequate to process the operations required within a single cycle. However, multicycle instructions require additional clock pulses that are unique. The normal procedure is to generate a set of cycle-timing pulses as shown in Figure 7-22. These pulses in combination with the clock signals provide the timing pulses necessary to implement the instruction.

7-19 Clock timing: clock block diagram

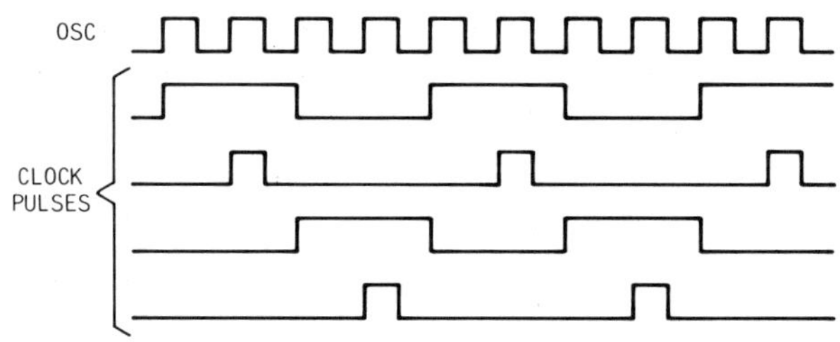

7-20 Clock timing: clock pulses

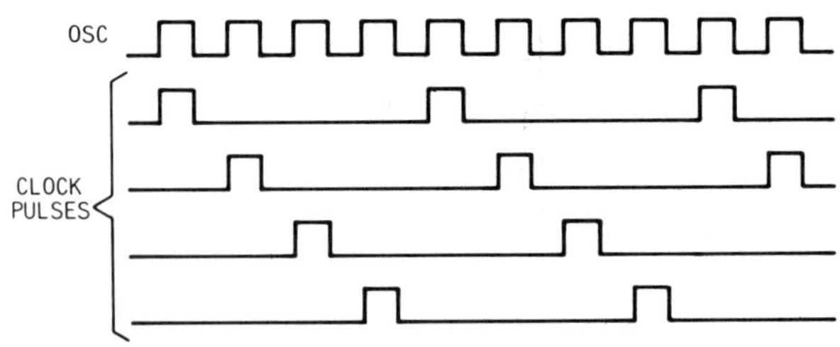

7-21 Clock timing: clock pulses

7.3.8 Cycle Timing Generation

The number of cycles depends on the instruction. As the instruction is being executed, cycle-timing pulses must be automatically generated to provide the required timing signals. The opcode implicitly contains the number of cycles allocated to a given instruction. This means that the outputs of the opcode decoder may be used to derive the cycle-timing signals. Figure 7-23 shows the decoder outputs sorted and grouped according to the number of machine cycles required for instruction execution. The outputs from the groups are encoded into a binary number representing the cycles. The clock provides eight consecutive pulses, C0 through C7 (see Figure 7-24). At the

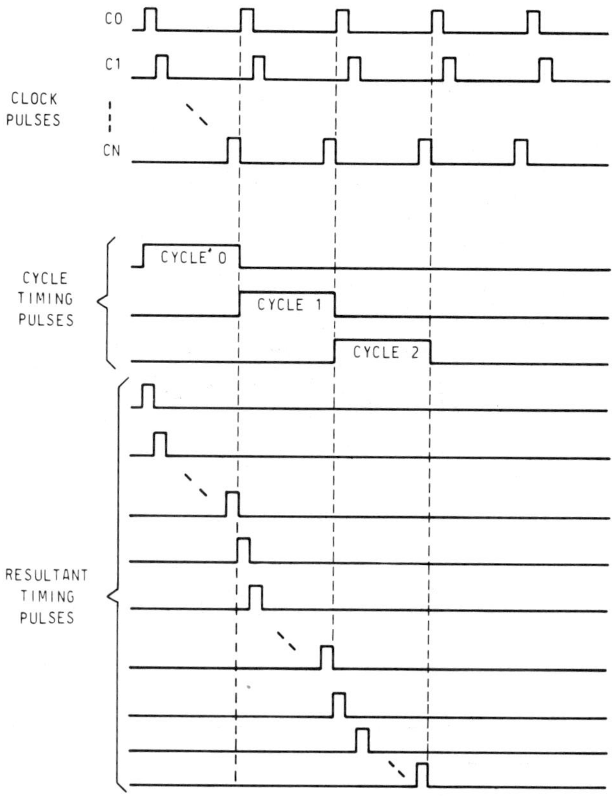

7-22 Multicycle timing pulses

beginning of each cycle, the binary counter is advanced by one clock phase (C0). After the counter has been stabilized, the count is compared to the encoder outputs during clock phase C2. When the two numbers agree, a signal is generated to set the EOI flip-flop. This condition will be used to clear the counter to the initial zero state instead of advancing it to the next count. The EOI output is also used to initiate the fetch of the next instruction and gate the memory output from the MDR into the IR. This sequence of operation is always accomplished during the last cycle of each instruction, assuming that no hardware is provided for prefetching. A new instruction is decoded, and the process is repeated for the next instruction. The number of cycles per instruction is predetermined by the encoder output.

When the counter changes state, it is possible for the outputs to assume many different values during the transition because of variations in the delays of various counter stages. As a result, extraneous spikes could be generated in the decoder outputs. If this is detrimental to the system's operation, the counter can be configured to count in a special gray code in which only one bit will be changed for each new count.

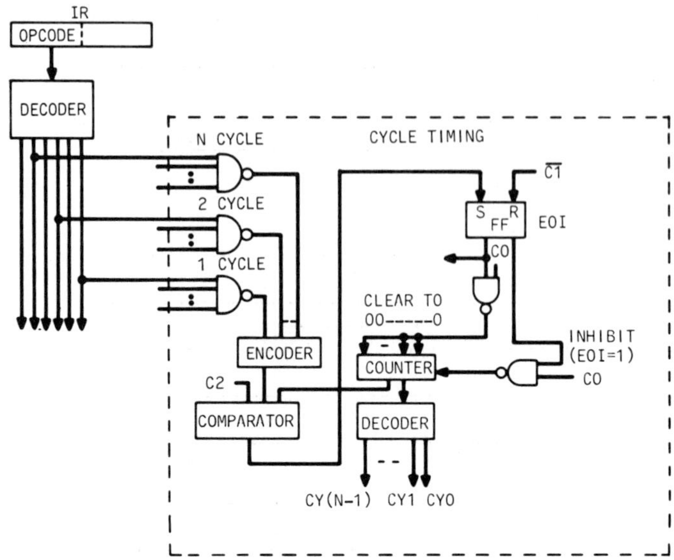

7-23 Cycle timing with counter circuit: cycle-timing circuit

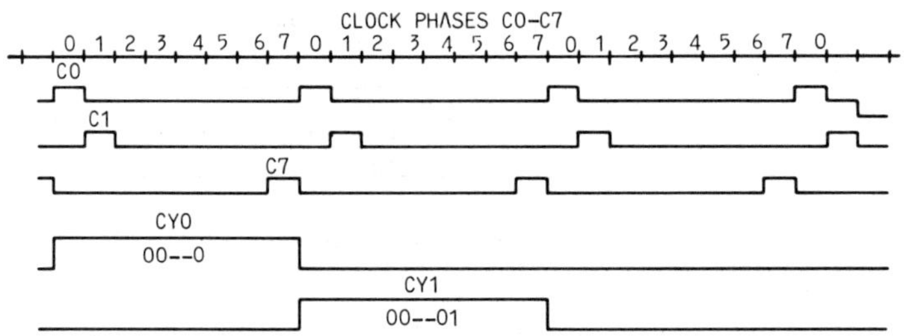

7-24 Cycle timing with counter circuit: cycle-timing sequence

7.3.9 Use of Shift Register

Another implementation is shown in Figure 7-25. A shift register or ring counter is used instead of the binary counter and decoder. A considerable simplification in the cycle-timing logic is obtained by assigning 1 bit of the shift register to each cycle timing pulse. This procedure also eliminates the need for the encoder. The cycle output is taken directly off the shift register. The number of bits in the shift register represents the maximum number of cycles possible for the instruction set. At the end of each instruction, the shift register is initialized with the first bit set to 1 and the remaining bits set to 0 (0 . . . 001). The clock pulse C0, occurring once per cycle, successively shifts the 1 in the register to the left by one bit position. This action generates a set of sequential pulses. The last pulse for each instruction is determined by comparing the shift register outputs with the sorted decoder outputs (see Figure 7-25). When a 1 is shifted into the last cycle bit position, the EOI flip-flop is set. This action terminates the sequence and reinitializes the cycle-timing logic for the next instruction.

The use of a shift register eliminates the appearance of spurious spikes that occur in the output. A shift register also eliminates the need for encoding and decoding circuitry. The penalty paid for this realization is an increase in the number of bits required in the shift register. The ready commercial availability of many bits of a shift register on a single silicon chip makes this implementation quite attractive.

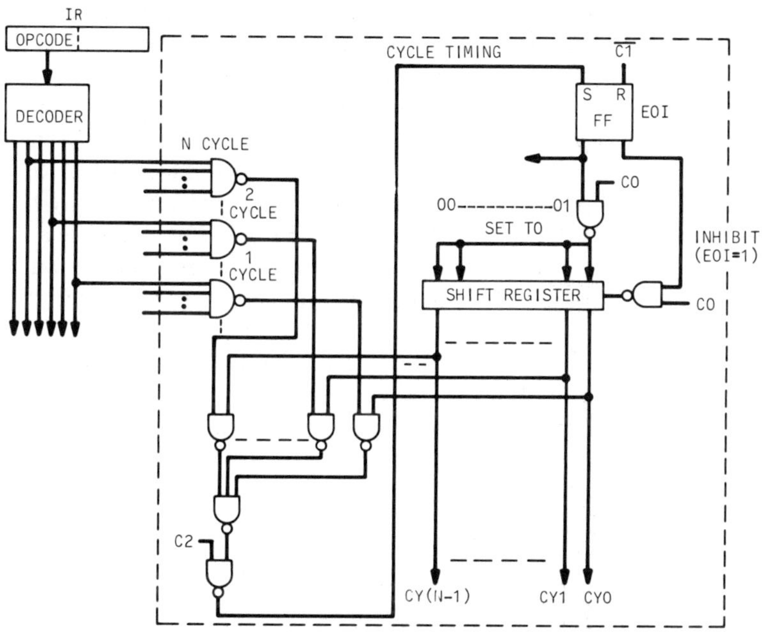

7-25 Cycle timing with shift register

7.3.10 Instruction Cycle Allocation

As indicated in Figures 7-23, 7-24, and 7-25, the decoder outputs are also used in the cycle-timing circuit. They control the number of cycles allocated for each instruction. The outputs are combined into functional groups according to the number of cycles. If the opcode is 6 bits wide, there are 64 decoder outputs to combine and sort. This involves a complex interconnection of high fan-in gates. To minimize a circuit's *fan-in* (*number of inputs*) and *fan-out* (*number of outputs*) leads, it is desirable to assign the opcodes in a manner that would facilitate the cycle grouping procedure. For example, if more than half of the opcodes belong to the same group, 32 of them could be assigned codes with the most significant bit of the opcode having a value of 1. Instead of collecting 32 outputs directly from the decoder outputs, it is necessary only to examine the most significant bit. This technique is basically the classical minimization of combinational circuitry. The disadvantage of this simplification is that it produces a more irregular logic structure and places a constraint on the opcode assignments.

7.3.11 Common Instruction Fetch Cycle

The instruction fetch cycle provides the proper timing and control signals to step the program along one instruction at a time. Each instruction fetch must be accomplished during the last cycle of the current instruction if no additional register buffer is provided to store the prefetched instruction. The whole sequence of addressing, reading the memory, and gating the output from the MDR to the IR can be carried out whenever the EOI flip-flop is set (see Figures 7-26 and 7-27). As an example, assume that the new address of a branch-type instruction is the result of an arithmetic calculation. This value appears as the output of the ALU. When the branch is taken, the content of the ALU is gated by way of the data bus into the PC. It, in turn, is gated into the MAR. The PC, normally, is automatically incremented by 1 in preparation for the next sequential address. However, if the next instruction is a branch, the target address may be stored in any one of several hardware registers found in the CPU rather than the ALU. The decoded instruction will select the register that acts as the source for the data to be directed onto the data bus. The destination register is pre-established by the instruction and follows the path through the PC and into the MAR. The control signal for gating the data from the bus into the PC would be provided by the ORing of all decoded branch operations timed to occur before the PC is gated into the MAR.

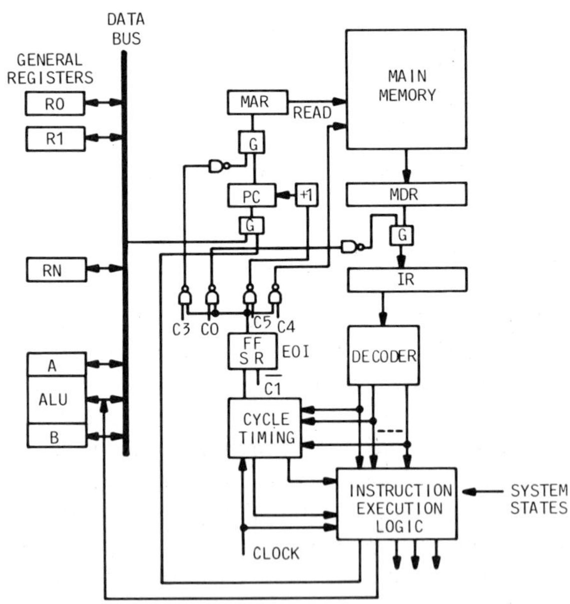

7-26 Instruction sequencer: instruction fetch sequence functional diagram

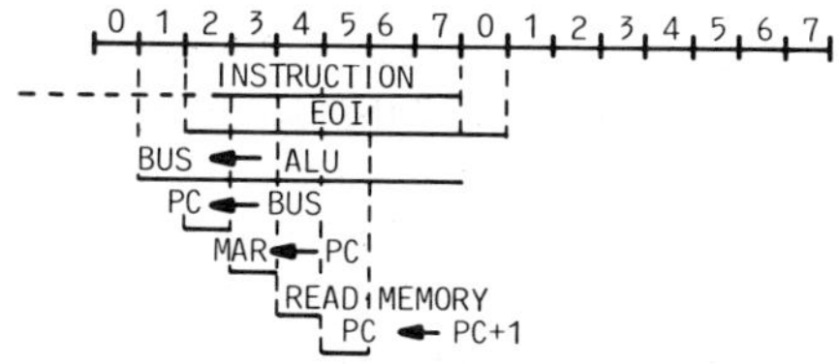

7-27 Instruction sequencer: instruction fetch timing sequence

7.3.12 Decoder Design Using Logic Gates as Building Blocks

Decoders are logic circuits commonly used within a computer. Their input and output specifications are well defined. These features provide decoders with the capability of functioning as one of the basic building blocks for address selection and control logic design. Consequently, MSI decoders in several sizes (2 to 4, 3 to 8, or 4 to 16 outputs) have been available commercially, but they are usually restricted to smaller configurations than the 4- to-16-line decoder because of the excessive number of output pins required by the latter. The smaller decoders can be used, however, as building blocks to implement larger and more complex decoders.

In implementing a microprocessor, the design objective of using logic gates as basic building blocks provides a greater degree of flexibility in optimizing such parameters as speed, number of gates, complexity in interconnection, and power dissipation. There are several logical arrangements that may be used in designing decoders. Figure 7-28 shows one method of decoding a 4-bit binary number (ABCD) using two predecoders. It requires 24 2-bit gates and eight inverters to provide three stages of logic delay. Another method (see Figure 7-29) uses one predecoder with sixteen 3-bit gates. In still another method, the decoder is implemented directly with sixteen 4-input

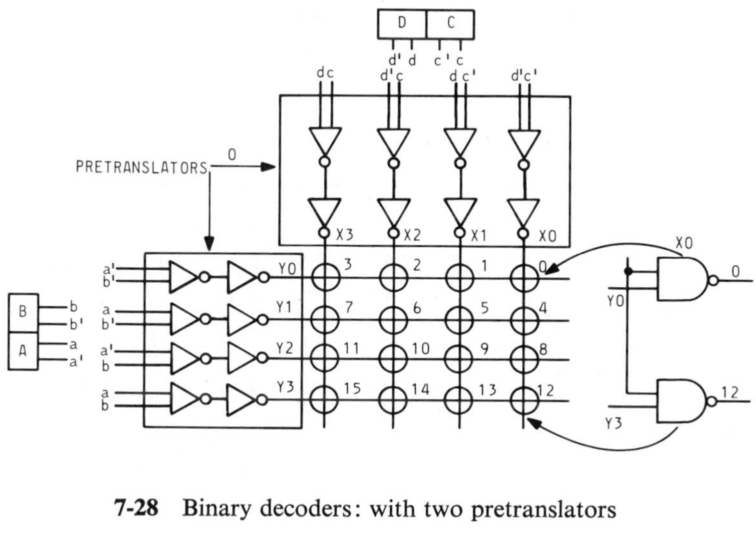

7-28 Binary decoders: with two pretranslators

gates (see Figure 7-30). The choice of implementation depends on many factors (e.g., fan-in, fan-out, speed, and maintenance). The MSI decoders that have been available commercially are of the form shown in Figure 7-30.

The decoder outputs may be used to enable other decoders. As an example, assume that the instruction in Figure 7-31 is a MOVE instruction. It transfers data from one register to another within the set of general registers. The 6-bit opcode specifies the MOVE operation, and the two 4-bit fields specify the source and destination of the data transfer. The opcode decoder output representing the MOVE instruction is used to enable two 4-bit decoders. One 4-bit decoder provides the set of signals used to select one of 16 general registers to be gated onto a common data bus. The other 4-bit decoder provides the set of signals used to gate the contents of the data bus into one of the same 16 general registers, as shown in Figure 7-32. The two 4-bit decoders, the registers, the input gates, and the output gates are available commercially on a single DIP package as a two-port, 16-word by 4-bit RAM. A set of 16 registers, each 16 bits wide, including associated access circuitry, can be implemented using four of these DIP's.

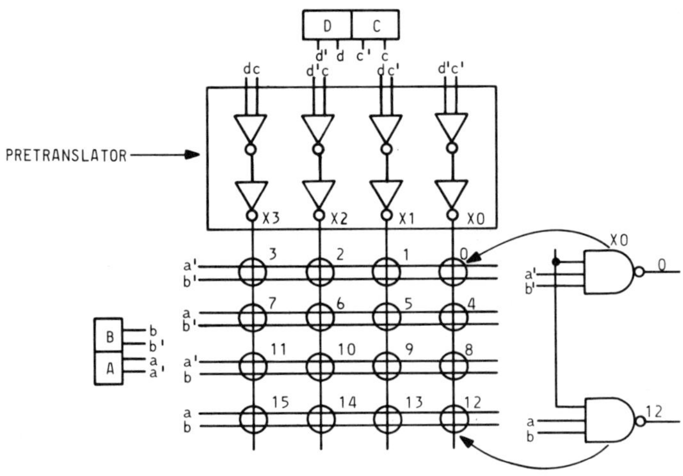

7-29 Binary decoders: with one pretranslator

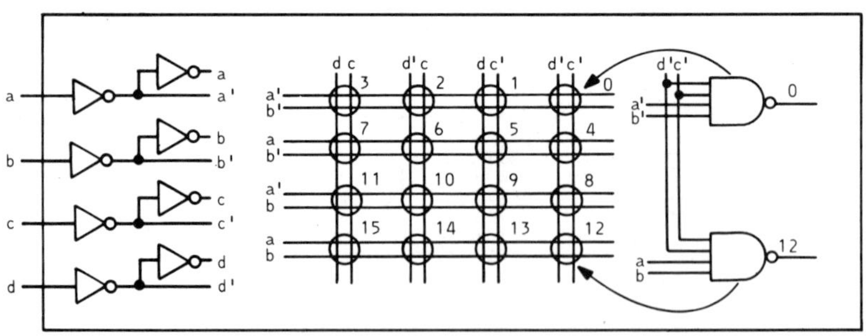

7-30 Binary decoders: with no pretranslator

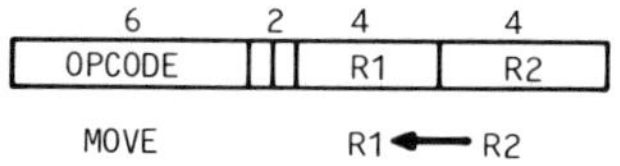

7-31 Simple move instruction format

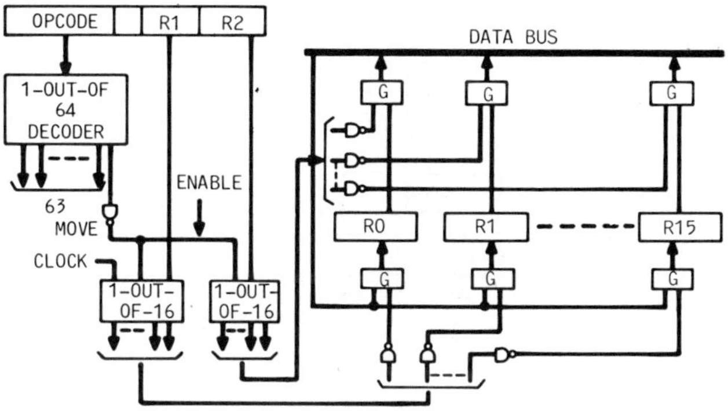

7-32 Multilevel decoders

If the opcode decoding is done at a centralized point, the resulting control signals require many leads that extend throughout the entire processor. It is desirable, in some instances, to reduce the number of interconnecting leads. This can be accomplished by distributing the coded control signals throughout the processor and performing the decoding at the destination of the data. This technique, commonly referred to as *distributed control*, is more frequently used in controlling peripheral equipment that is located remotely away from the processor.

7.3.13 Instruction Execution

The execution of the MOVE instruction only involves a single step. The decoder outputs implement the specified operation directly. More complicated instructions require a set of controls for each step (cycle) of operation. The number of controls may vary from cycle to cycle depending on the actions required to process a given operation. Figure 7-33 shows a possible structure for the instruction execution logic. The 6-bit opcode is divided into two 3-bit parts. Each 3-bit portion is decoded to produce a 1-out-of-8 control signal. The 64 opcodes are derived by combining the two groups of eight outputs (8 by 8). The opcode is represented by two control leads, one from each group. The decoder outputs combine with timing signals to generate cycle enables that occur sequentially one cycle at a time for a predetermined number of cycles. These signals in combination with the clock pulses produce the basic elementary control operations that occur within the cycle. In some instructions, certain operations are dictated by system conditions. Usually, they are specified by option bits. The logic for decision-type operations can be implemented at various levels of control.

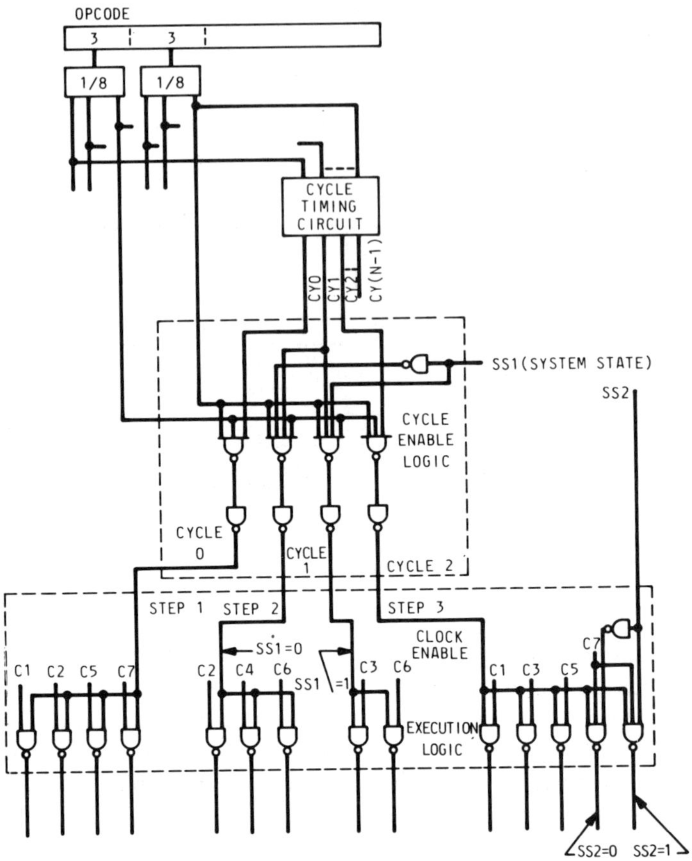

7-33 Instruction execution logic

If the action is completely different for a given cycle and is dependent on whether or not the condition was fulfilled, the conditional input is inserted at the cycle enable logic to select one of two alternative actions shown in Figure 7-33. However, if some of the final controls are the same for both actions, the conditional input is made part of the clock enable level. The cycle enable and clock enable logic can be combined and collapsed into a single level, depending on factors such as speed, fan-in, and fan-out. The choice may vary from instruction to instruction.

7.3.14 An Example Illustrating the Control Logic Design

The following examples illustrate a technique and procedure for designing the control portion of a CPU. The I/O portion has been omitted for simplicity. Only those parts that are directly involved are shown in the figures. A few assumptions have been made to simplify the design. These assumptions are:

1. A single NAND gate is used without regard to fan-in or fan-out parameters. Although these capabilities are not considered, they are important in calculating delays if additional logic stages are required to provide the needed fan-in or fan-out capability. Various functional integrated circuits (MSI or LSI) have not been included as a part of the execution logic design.
2. The CPU is operated synchronously with the main memory. Its instruction cycle is set equal to the memory cycle.
3. The CPU cycle is divided into eight intervals with clock pulses occurring as shown in Figure 7-34. This timing arrangement allows several data transfers within one cycle.
4. A single data bus is used to move data from any register to any other register internal to the CPU. Buffer registers A and B are provided in the ALU to store operands. The results of arithmetic or logic operations could be directed onto the bus directly and routed to any internal register. The execution of an instruction is, therefore, a series of data transfers.

Figure 7-35 gives a general block diagram of a processor that observes assumptions 1 through 4. A set of 16 hardware registers is included to provide short-term storage for information being used in transient data processing operations. They function as a flexible set of accumulators.

To make the block diagram more useful for implementation of the control logic, detailed gating paths and control points are indicated. These are shown either partially or completely so that timing analysis can be done directly from the information on the figure. Prior to the actual control logic design, the various functional units should have been detailed in block-diagram form. However, the controls to activate the various units from an instruction will normally not have been identified. For example, Figure 7-36 shows the detailed logic implementation of one general register, its associated gates, and the common data bus. The controls to gate the content of the register onto

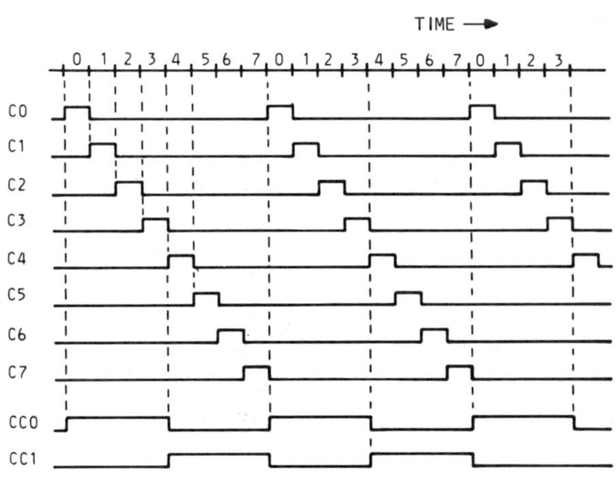

7-34 Clock pulses

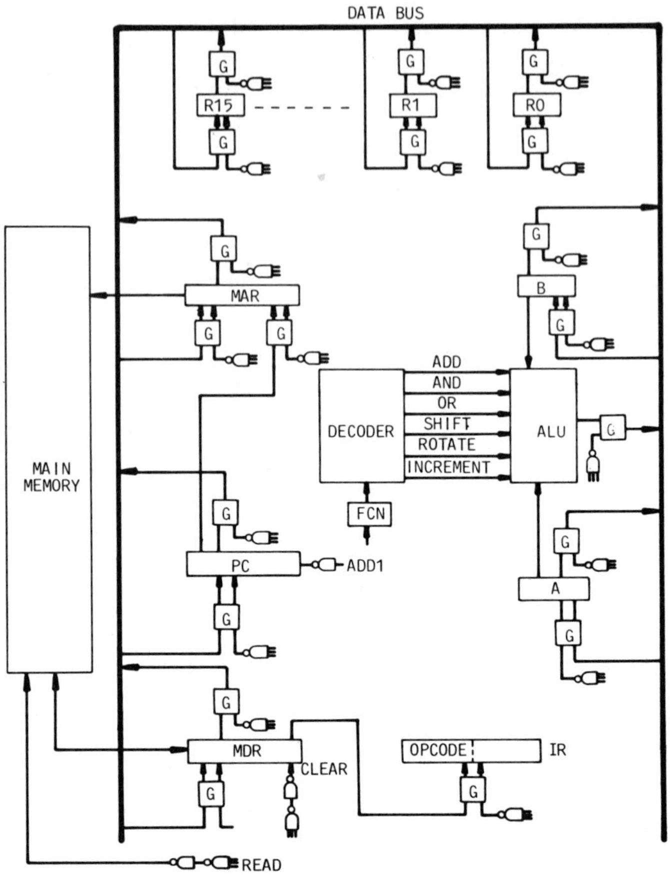

7-35 Functional processor block diagram

the bus or from the bus into the register are indicated, but for simplicity the actual interconnection of the control signals is not shown. It is assumed that the instruction execution logic will provide these controls. In order to keep the block diagram as simple as possible, functional blocks are used so that the information flow can be readily understood. At each output of the functional block in Figure 7-37, nG is used to denote that there are n gates in the logic path from the input signal to the output signal of that block. This notation is used if it is obvious how many gates the inputs go through before reaching the output. The data bus, drawn as a heavy line, is $1G$ (one gate), which represents the combining gates for all inputs to the bus. The exact number of gates involved with a given logic chain can then be established using this representation, and maximum or minimum delays can be evaluated for timing purposes. Also, the maximum and minimum delay through a functional block can be specified instead of the number of gates.

Because the execution logic is usually different for each instruction, a systematic approach of generating a proper set of diagrams is desirable. This not only allows the

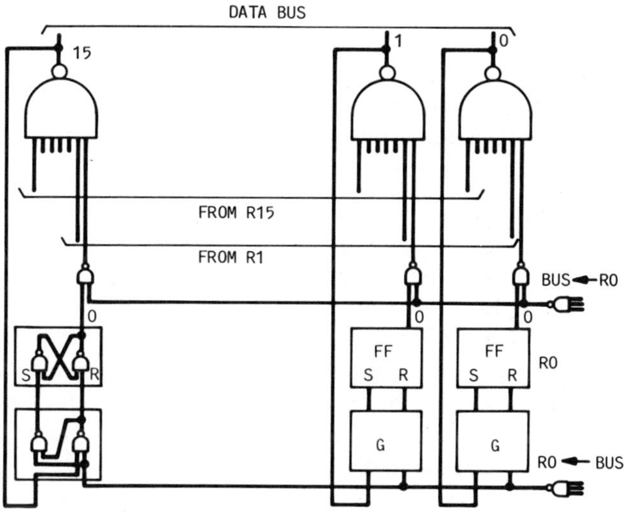

7-36 Logic diagram of a general register: logic diagram of R0 and bus

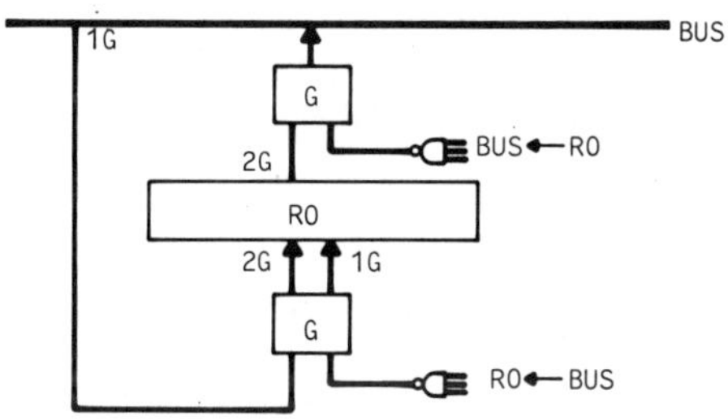

7-37 Logic diagram of a general register: functional diagram of R0 and bus

circuitry to be built, but also provides support documents to aid in debugging, training, and understanding the implementation. With these objectives in mind, the design procedure involves the development of the control logic for each instruction and the complete interconnection of the logical outputs with the various functional units. Consider how this can be done for a relatively simple instruction:

ADD X,R, I Add the content of the memory word that has its address stored in general register X to the content of general register R. I specifies indirect addressing. The sum is stored in R.

Although this function is very simple, it requires an intimate knowledge of the entire processor and the functional units. The design process consists of the following steps:

1. Generate a timing sequence chart for every control operation required to fully implement the instruction. This includes the fetching of the next instruction.
2. Translate the timing diagram into a logic implementation.
3. In order to obtain a partially detailed diagram of the instruction, merge the partially detailed functional blocks required to interconnect the logic outputs.
4. Analyze the resulting design for possible timing problems.

The timing sequence for the ADD instruction is shown in Figures 7-38 and 7-39. A solid line indicates that the control signal is active during that interval. The control could be either a high (1) or a low (0) signal, depending upon the control operation to be performed. For example, a low signal is required for setting an RS flip-flop, while a high signal is needed for gating data onto the bus. In the first cycle of the timing chart, the memory is accessed to obtain one of the two arguments for the addition. This is done by setting up the memory address, generating the command to read, and clearing the memory output register (MDR) so that it is ready to receive data from the memory. The control signal, BUS←X, enables the contents of general register X, which contains the memory address, to be gated onto the bus. These data are then strobed into the MAR during clock phase C2. The timing is arranged to avoid any conflict with the previous memory access. In this case, it is assumed that the previous memory cycle is about to be completed so that the address can be changed at C2.

At C3, immediately after the address has settled, the READ signal is generated to initiate the next memory operation, and the MDR is cleared to accept new data from the memory. The *function register* (*FCN*) in the ALU is set to perform the ADD

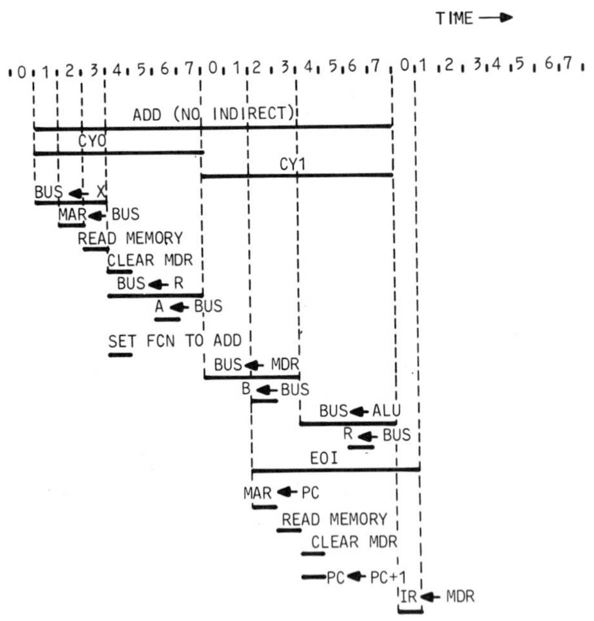

7-38 Timing diagram of ADD instruction: no indirect

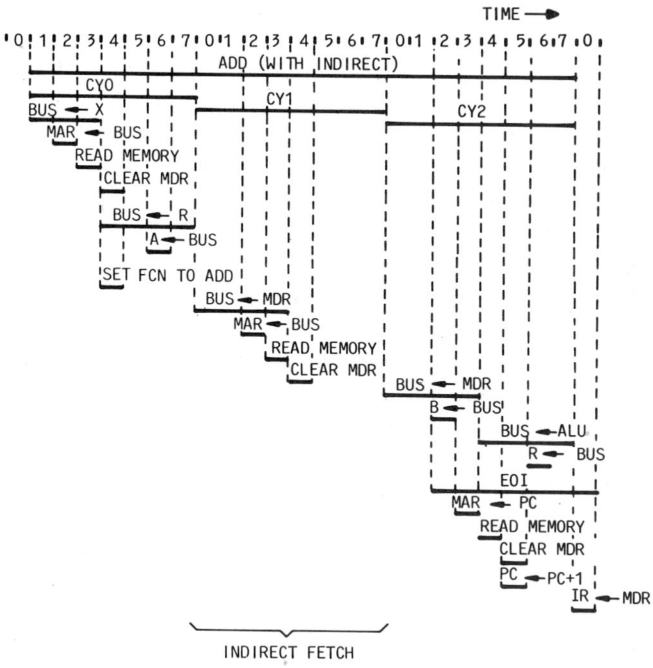

7-39 Timing diagram of ADD instruction: with indirect

operation. During the second half of the first cycle, while waiting for the memory output, the first operand is gated into buffer register A in the ALU by means of the data bus by signals BUS←R and A←BUS. This operand is stored in one of the 16 general registers specified by the R field of the instruction. When the memory outputs have settled in the MDR, the disposition of the contents depends on whether indirect addressing has been specified. If it has not (see Figure 7-38), the data in the MDR are transferred to buffer register B in the ALU as the second operation. This operation is performed by gating signals BUS←MDR and B←BUS during the first half of the second cycle. It is assumed that the result is settled in the ALU during the second half of the second cycle. The sum is then transferred to the destination, general register R, by the logic signals BUS←ALU and R←BUS.

Meanwhile, the cycle-timing circuit recognizes that the instruction is a two-cycle instruction in which indirect addressing is not specified. It then sets the EOI flip-flop near the beginning of the second cycle (C2) to initiate the fetching of the next instruction. This is done concurrently with the instruction execution. The next memory address from the PC is set up by a direct gating path (MAR←PC), and then a READ signal is sent to fetch the next instruction word from memory. The program counter is advanced by 1, which points it to the next program address. The current ADD instruction terminates when the contents of the MDR are gated into the IR. Then, the next instruction is decoded and the entire process is repeated.

If indirect addressing is specified, an additional memory cycle operation is required. The first instruction cycle remains the same whether or not indirect addressing is specified in the instruction. However, the memory data obtained in the first cycle must be used as an address to fetch the second operand. The second cycle is devoted to an indirect memory fetch operation (see Figure 7-39). The number of cycles allocated for the ADD instruction will be two or three, depending upon the indirect option bit in the instruction. The instruction fetch is automatically adjusted to take place during the last cycle of the instruction by the EOI flip-flop. This is a common control sequence used by all instructions.

Even though only the indirect option has been considered in the ADD instruction, there are other modes of addressing (such as indexing) that could also be part of the instruction. The number of execution sequences may vary with the number of available addressing options. For simplicity, only indirect addressing will be covered in this implementation. This should not reduce the effectiveness of the design procedure. The objective here is to show a technique of control logic implementation. The basic concepts can then be extended to include the various addressing options; otherwise, the added complexity might distract from the understanding of the design procedure.

The timing diagrams shown in Figures 7-38 and 7-39 represent the control sequences required to implement the ADD instruction with the option of indirect addressing. It is now possible to translate directly from these timing charts to logic gates that provide the control signals to carry out the desired function. Figure 7-40 shows the implementation of the execution logic. The opcode is subdivided into two 3-bit fields. Each field is decoded to a 1-out-of-8 output signal. A combination of two outputs, one from each group, decodes to a unique instruction. One of the two spare bits in the instruction defines the indirect option. This bit logically combines with the two decoder outputs representing the ADD instruction. The resulting logical output selects one of two possible actions: the operand is obtained either with the indirect option specified or without the use of indirect addressing. These two outputs determine the number of cycles allocated for processing the instruction. The cycle-timing signals, CY0 and CY1, are then automatically generated to provide the timing needed to step the instruction along one cycle at a time.

If indirect addressing is specified ($I = 1$), CY2 is also generated to extend the instruction to three cycles. These signals are needed to distinguish events occurring in the first, second, or third cycle of the instruction. The last cycle is recognized when the cycle-timing pulse has been shifted sequentially in the shift register to the active combining gate. The position of the 1 in the shift register indicates the number of cycles that have occurred. That is, there is a one-to-one correspondence between the bit position of the 1 in the shift register and the number of the currently active cycle. In this case, the last bit position depends on which one of the two combining gates is active—the two-cycle gate or the three-cycle gate. The EOI flip-flop is set during the last cycle to fetch the next instruction. At the end of the last cycle, the shift register is reinitialized with the 1 moved to bit 0 to begin a new instruction.

The resulting two outputs for the ADD instructions are combined with the cycle-timing signals to generate controls that are active only during a specific cycle. This is

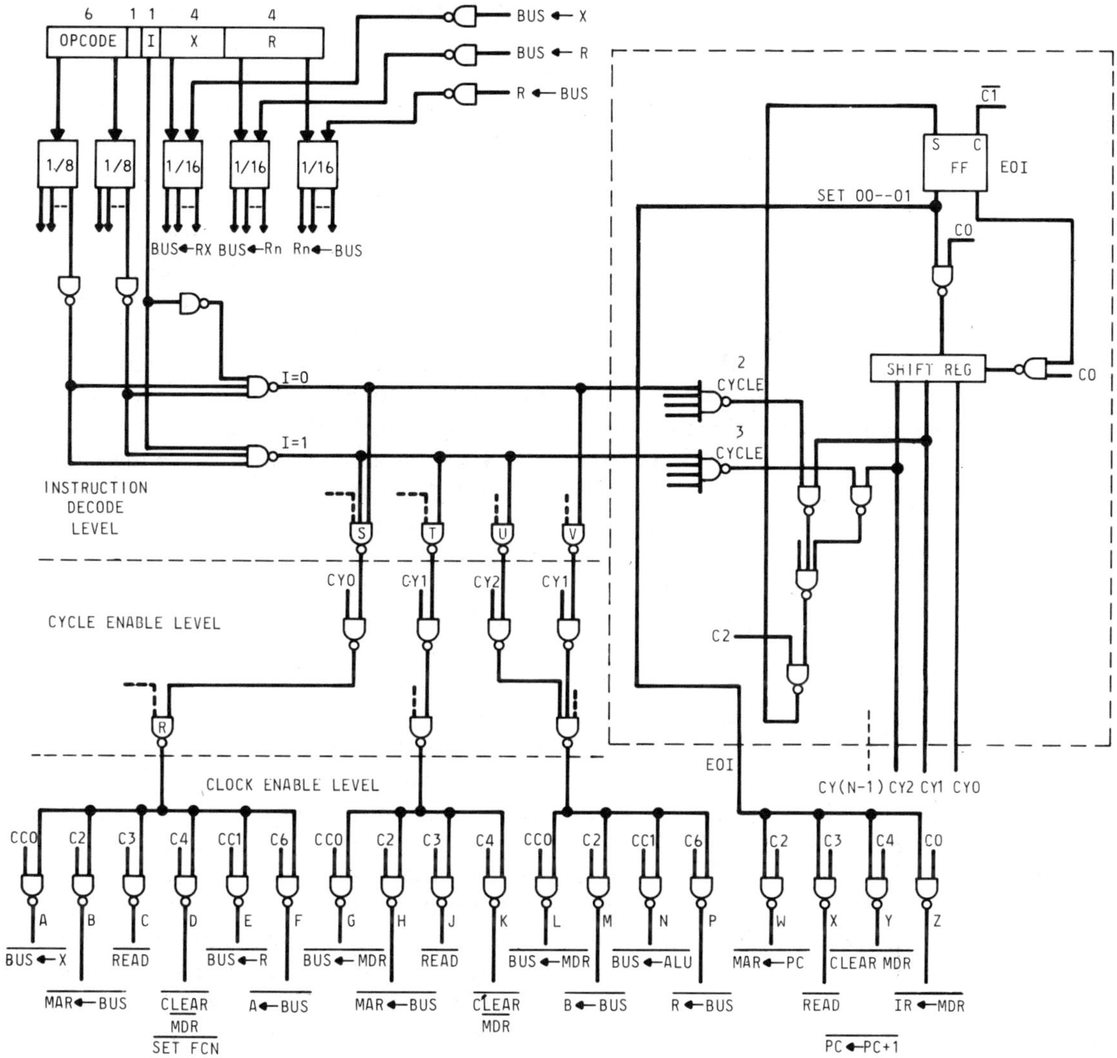

7-40 Instruction execution logic

done primarily to simplify and reduce the number of excution logic gates at the expense of additional gate delays in the logic chain. As indicated in the timing diagrams of Figures 7-38 and 7-39, the control sequence in the first cycle is the same for both conditions. The two ADD outputs are combined and timed with CY0 to give an active signal during the first cycle. This output is then combined with clock signals to produce individual control signals that represent part of the instruction execution logic (see Figure 7-40). When the control functions are the same for the entire cycle in two or more sequences, the combining of the control signals is done at the cycle-enabling level rather than replicating the execution logic. Figure 7-40 shows that the control signal for the second cycle (CY1) without indirect fetch and the control signal for the third cycle (CY2) *with* indirect fetch are logically combined to generate one set of common control signals. They are used for gating the second operand from memory into buffer B in the ALU and then transferring the sum by means of the bus to general register R. The third set of control signals is unique to the indirect fetch operation that occurs during the second cycle (CY1). As indicated in the diagram, the control signals can therefore be translated directly into logic gates with the appropriate timing signals. Simplification is achieved by consolidating common control sequences.

The logic implementation shown in Figure 7-40 is accomplished at the instruction-decode level, the cycle-enable level, and the clock-enable level. It allows a systematic and functional arrangement of the control logic. This arrangement may appear in some instances to be inefficient in terms of gates and logic delays. For example, the control signal occurring during the first cycle (CY0) has been derived by combining the two outputs representing the ADD instruction with and without indirect addressing specified. This combining gate, designated as S, is basically redundant since the same information can be obtained directly from the decoder outputs. If the decoder outputs are used directly with cycle timing pulse CY0, the same output would be generated, minus two gate delays. Gate S allows other controls to share the cycle enable and execution logic, as indicated by the dashed input. If the control sequence occurs in a different cycle, the entry point would be in the later stage, designated as gate R. It is reasonable to conclude that many logic arrangements may result in the same control function. Minimizing the number of logic gates is an important factor in generating a useful design. However, many other factors must also be considered, such as fan-in, fan-out, delay, interconnection, ease in understanding the logic flow, and ease in performing maintenance functions. The various trade-offs must be examined and balanced not only on the local control level, but also on the global control level. The criteria used vary considerably from system to system. In most cases, logic design that promotes ease of understanding will contribute to the ease of maintenance.

The dashed inputs shown in Figure 7-40 illustrate the need to be constantly aware of the interaction of other controls upon the design. It is very tempting to optimize the number of logic gates on the local control level without much regard for the consequences on the global control level. Another factor seldom considered in the design stages is the possibility of later changes. For example, gates T and U in Figure 7-40 have been provided in anticipation of additional inputs from other controls. If they are not used at the completion of the design, gate U can be eliminated with the output of T fan-out to the two gates shown following gates T and U. This would be a reasonable simplification. If the design is left as shown, it would provide some flexibility to make changes later. However, one must not go overboard in adding redundancy for this purpose. A good design should have flexibility without added cost. This can be accomplished if the designer is conscious of these factors at the beginning of the design process.

The detailed instruction execution logic (see Figure 7-40) can now be merged with the system functional blocks (see Figure 7-35) to obtain a complete diagram of all circuitry involved in the execution of the ADD instruction. This is shown in Figure 7-41, including the timing chart. A total picture is obtained by examining the various operations occurring at different intervals. Errors can be spotted more easily when a full picture of the functional organization is presented in one drawing rather than in many pages of extremely hard-to-follow schematics.

A timing study of all critical data or control paths can be performed using this detailed functional diagram. If necessary, the timing or the logic may have to be changed to correct any uncovered problems. For example, consider total delay from the time the second operand is gated into buffer register B in order to be summed in the ALU to when the final result is settled in destination register Rn. This delay is dependent on the logic chain indicated by the dashed line in Figure 7-41. This chain is also shown separately in Figure 7-42. The longest delay through this chain is given by

$$\begin{aligned} D_{\max} &= D_{\mathrm{B}}^{+} + D_{\mathrm{ALU}}^{+} + D_{\mathrm{BUS}}^{+} + D_{\mathrm{A}}^{+} \\ &= 2G_{\mathrm{ON}}^{+} + 2G_{\mathrm{OFF}}^{+} + D_{\mathrm{ALU}}^{+} + G_{\mathrm{ON}}^{+} + G_{\mathrm{OFF}}^{+} + 2G_{\mathrm{ON}}^{+} + G_{\mathrm{OFF}}^{+} \\ &= 5G_{\mathrm{ON}}^{+} + 4G_{\mathrm{OFF}}^{+} + D_{\mathrm{ALU}}^{+} \\ &= 50 + 80 + 400 \\ &= 530 \text{ nanoseconds (ns)} \end{aligned}$$

and assumes the following conditions:

1. $G_{\mathrm{ON}}^{+} = 10$ ns: maximum gate turn-on delay with the output going from plus to ground.
2. $G_{\mathrm{ON}}^{-} = 2$ ns: minimum gate turn-on delay with the output going from plus to ground.
3. $G_{\mathrm{OFF}}^{+} = 20$ ns: maximum gate turn-off delay with the output going from ground to plus.
4. $G_{\mathrm{OFF}}^{-} = 4$ ns: minimum gate turn-off delay with the output going from ground to plus.
5. $D_{\mathrm{ALU}}^{+} = 400$ ns: maximum delay through the ALU.
6. CYCLE = 800 ns: basic machine cycle; also memory cycle.
7. $D_{\mathrm{C}} = \pm 10\%$ or 10 ns: maximum variation of clock.
8. C = 100 ± 10 ns: clock interval.

The calculation of D(max), as shown in the previous calculations, results in D(max) being equal to 530 nanoseconds. This value plus the propagation delay of any long leads (approximately 2 nanoseconds per foot) and wiring capacitance delay must not exceed the allocated interval from the beginning of clock phase C2 to the end of clock phase C6. These two clock phases are used to initiate the beginning and the end of the data transfer operation. This interval, T_{AB}, represents a nominal period of 500 nanoseconds, assuming the delay of C6 to point B (as shown in Figure 7-42) is zero. When the variations of the clock pulses (10 nanoseconds each for C2 and C6) and the minimum logic delays for the four gates to point B are included, this interval

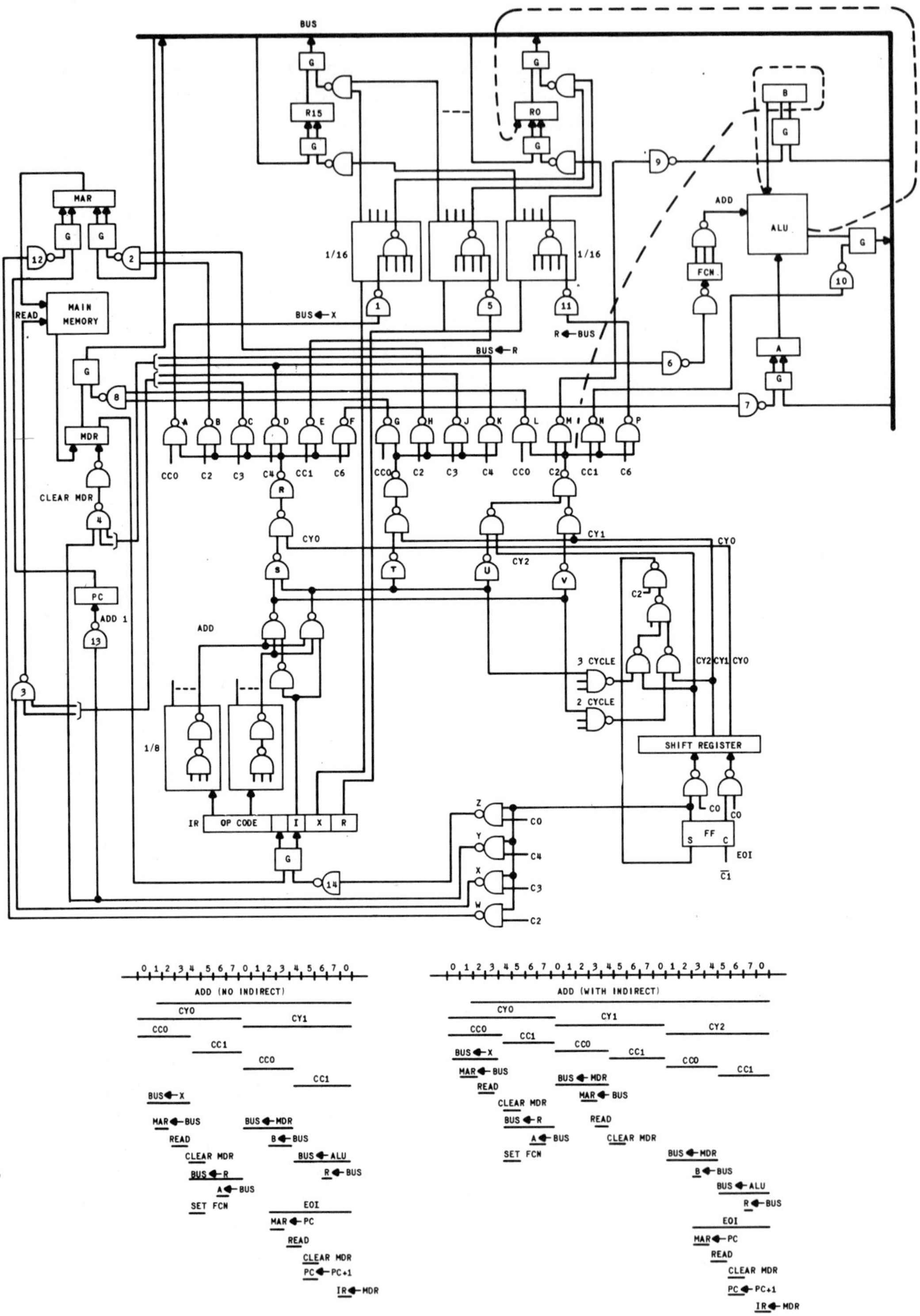

7-41 Detailed ADD execution logic

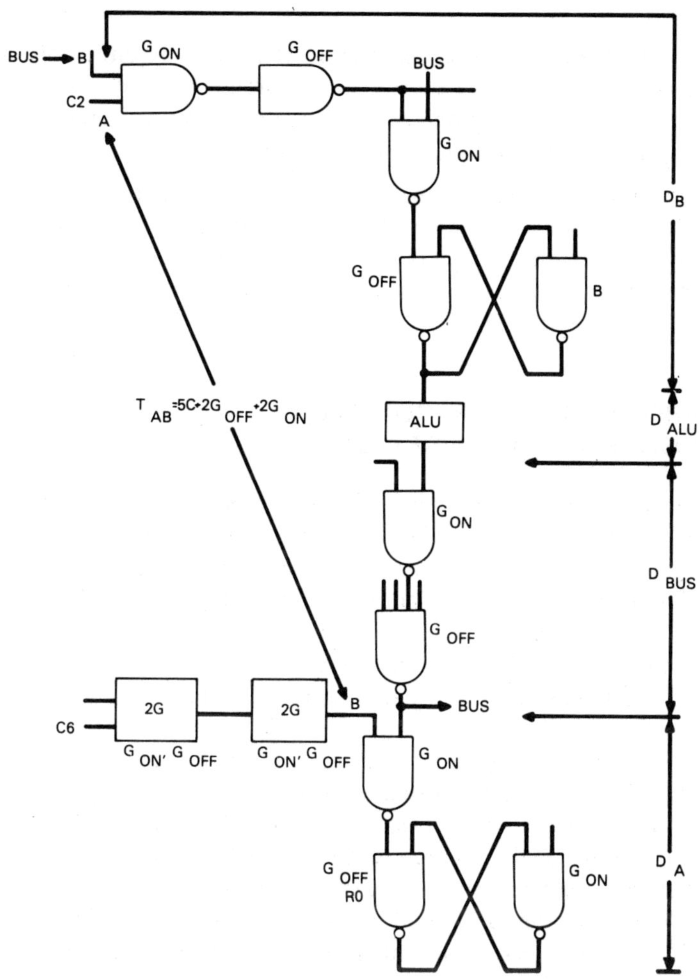

7-42 Timing analysis of ALU data transfer

($T_{\bar{A}B}$) is reduced to 492 nanoseconds and is given by

$$
\begin{aligned}
T_{\bar{A}B} &= 5C - 2D_C + 2G_{\bar{ON}} + 2G_{\bar{OFF}} \\
&= 500 - 20 + 4 + 8 \\
&= 492 \text{ nanoseconds}
\end{aligned}
$$

From the delay calculation, $D(\max)$ exceeds this value by at least 38 nanoseconds. To resolve this problem, there are two possible solutions:

1. Reduce the delay through the ALU by at least 38 nanoseconds. If this can be done easily, it would be a good solution, since most instructions involving arithmetic operations would be affected.

2. Delay the transfer of the result from the ALU by either one or more clock intervals to allow sufficient time for the circuitry to settle. If this can be accomplished without extending the instruction execution time from two to three cycles, the solution would be satisfactory.

Sufficient margins must also be provided to account for additional delays that may have been overlooked or underestimated in the design. For example, the bus gate did not include any additional delay in the calculation due to the high fan-in and fan-out of the bus. It is good practice to assign reasonable delays for any known factors that will affect the logic speed.

7.4 PROCEDURE FOR COMPLETE CONTROL LOGIC DESIGN

The execution logic for each instruction can generally be designed individually, as described in the previous sections. A complete self-sufficient diagram for each instruction may be obtained by repeating the functional units for each control sequence and exhibiting them on separate diagrams. Some relatively simple instructions can be consolidated and put on one diagram to minimize the number of drawings. This is particularly effective for those instructions which are similar in function and have common control sequences. The diagrams aid in understanding the logic flow and analysis.

The next step in the design is to obtain a complete logic diagram that specifies hardware. At this point, the functional units are generally straightforward and can be evaluated as units without further consolidation. However, in the case of control, a large collection of leads which compose the execution logic must be merged together. Figure 7-43 shows a general diagram of the various control signals used for instruction execution. Notice that the functional units include buffer registers, the ALU, general registers, PC, and so on. The combining gates collect the same control functions into single control points. These gates could be part of the functional units. They are removed and separated to show how the inputs are increased as instruction execution control signals are added. The execution logic is additive in the sense that most of the logic gates are unique for each instruction. However, some of the control sequences can be shared among several instructions. Such sharing requires interconnections between the various logic elements that form the execution logic of the machine (shown within the dashed line of Figure 7-43). The reduction in execution logic, as a result of sharing, tends to reduce the designer's flexibility in making hardware changes or providing for additions that may be needed later. The decoding logic and timing logic are intimately interrelated; they are not designed individually but with the total implementation of both in mind. Since the circuit is not a conglomeration of many smaller circuits, it is easier to manage. It can also be combined into a more compact arrangement.

Assembling the complete control logic from a set of detailed flow charts (similar

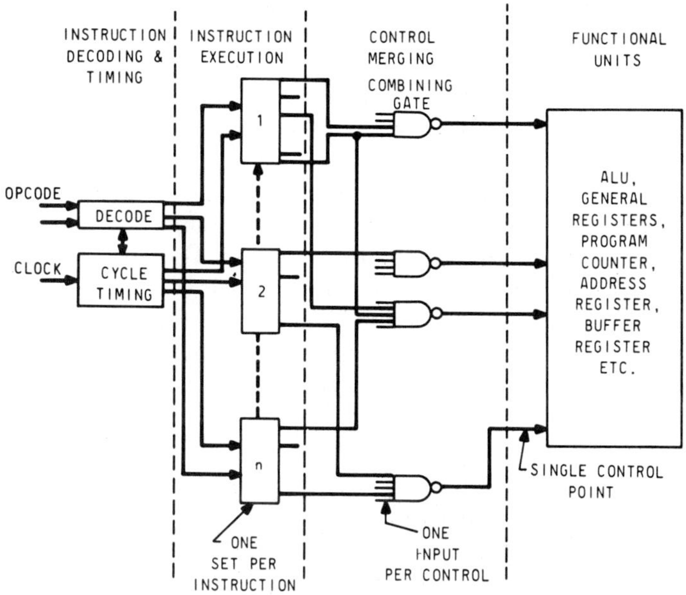

7-43 General diagram of collected instruction execution logic

to the one shown in Figure 7-41) becomes a relatively simple task. All the circuits that may be assigned to the control logic are collected at several logic gates as the control sequences are added. When the complete schematic of the execution control logic is complete, the circuit can be simulated, verified, and made ready for implementation. The equipment information, such as terminal numbers and module circuit assignments, can then be transferred back to the set of individual drawings that describe the instruction execution logic. These self-contained diagrams allow the designer to quickly trace the logical path of a control signal. This design eliminates the need to search through many unrelated pages of detailed schematics. Consequently, the diagrams have been found to be very useful aids in circuit debugging or system testing.

Although the execution logic for one instruction is relatively simple, a large collection of instructions merged together makes the logic complex and irregular. As a result, this systematic procedure is a desirable way to carry out a design from inception to physical reality. At the same time, documentation can be used for circuit debugging as well as an aid in training.

7.5 TWO-LEVEL CONTROL LOGIC

The implementation of the control logic, as described in the previous sections, was divided into two parts: designing the decoding circuitry and developing the execution logic. The parts were further divided into several levels, to minimize the fan-in of the execution logic. This, in turn, simplified the interconnection pattern and reduced the fan-out required for the outputs from the instruction register. Otherwise, the opcode outputs would have to be capable of driving most of the execution logic gates. The use of standard logic gates to perform the decoding and execution logic in one level is not economical because of the number and the complexity of the interconnections.

Consider the design of the decoding and execution logic in one level for the ADD instruction, as indicated in Figure 7-44. To reduce the number of leads, inverters are provided to generate both primed and unprimed inputs. The first level of logic selects the proper opcode (OP) in combination with clock signals (C0 and CC0), cycle-timing signals (CY0, CY1, CY2), an indirect option bit (I), and an EOI signal. The instruction control signals are realized as product terms, formed by logically ANDing the inputs to each gate. Gate A in Figure 7-44 is logically the same as gate A in Figure 7-41,

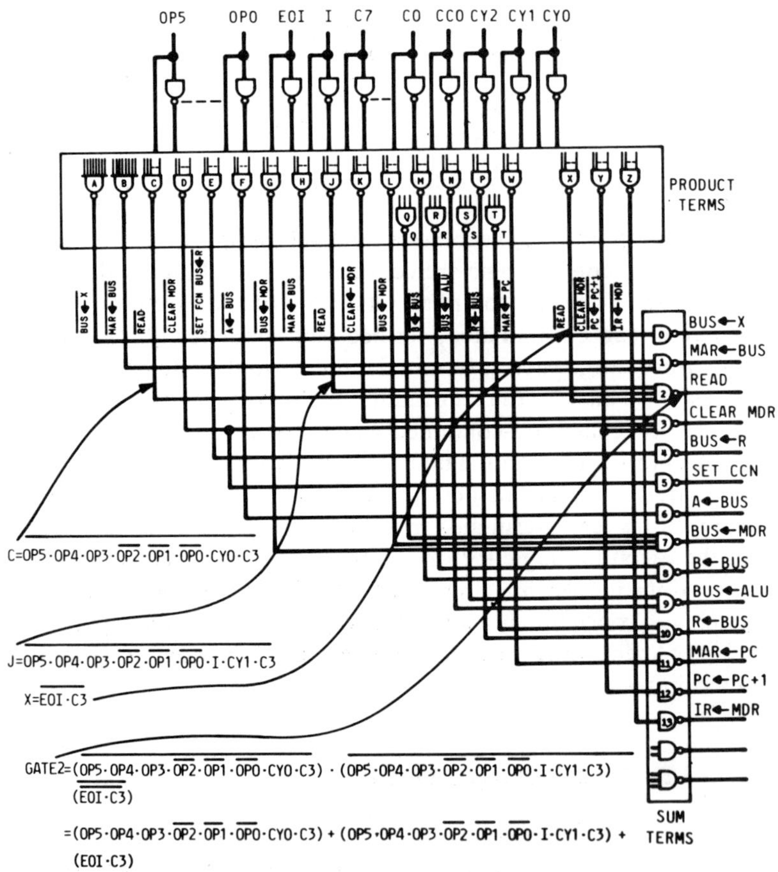

7-44 Single level ADD instruction

except that the inputs to the first gate are all applied on one level rather than on several. The inputs can be directly identified from the timing diagram of Figure 7-41. Assume that the opcode for the ADD instruction is 111000. The logic function for gates A and B would be

$$A = \overline{\text{OP5} \cdot \text{OP4} \cdot \text{OP3} \cdot \overline{\text{OP2}} \cdot \overline{\text{OP1}} \cdot \overline{\text{OP0}} \cdot \text{CY0} \cdot \text{CC0}}$$

$$B = \overline{\text{OP5} \cdot \text{OP4} \cdot \text{OP3} \cdot \overline{\text{OP2}} \cdot \overline{\text{OP1}} \cdot \overline{\text{OP0}} \cdot \text{CY0} \cdot \text{CC0} \cdot \text{C2}}$$

These functions represent the control signals shown as BUS←X and MAR←BUS, respectively. The timing chart given in Figure 7-39 shows the output signal MAR←BUS occurring in the middle of the BUS←X output signal. This means that both gates use the same inputs, with gate B using one more input (C2) for strobing. Control signals are often overlapped to provide concurrent operation. In this case, a pair of control signals is used to perform a coordinated data transfer from one of the general registers specified by the X field of the instruction to the MAR.

The second level of logic is represented by the combining gates that sum the product terms. Most of the gates shown in Figure 7-44 have only one input. This characteristic is true only for the realization of the ADD instruction. As other instructions are added, the inputs to the summing gates will increase. Gate 2 has three product terms—two from the ADD instruction and one from the common memory fetch operation. These inputs are taken from gates C, J, and X. Refer back to Figure 7-41. The logic expressions for the outputs from gates C, J, and X, which generate the READ memory control signal, are as follows:

$$C = \overline{\text{OP5} \cdot \text{OP4} \cdot \text{OP3} \cdot \overline{\text{OP2}} \cdot \overline{\text{OP1}} \cdot \overline{\text{OP0}} \cdot \text{CY0} \cdot \text{C3}}$$

$$J = \overline{\text{OP5} \cdot \text{OP4} \cdot \text{OP3} \cdot \overline{\text{OP2}} \cdot \overline{\text{OP1}} \cdot \overline{\text{OP0}} \cdot \text{I} \cdot \text{CY1} \cdot \text{C3}}$$

$$X = \overline{\text{EOI} \cdot \text{C3}}$$

The logic expression for gate 2 is

$$\begin{aligned}\text{Gate 2} &= \overline{\text{C} \cdot \text{J} \cdot \text{X}} \\ &= \overline{(\overline{\text{OP5} \cdot \text{OP4} \cdot \text{OP3} \cdot \text{OP2} \cdot \text{OP1} \cdot \text{OP0} \cdot \text{CY0} \cdot \text{C3}})} \\ &\quad \cdot \overline{(\overline{\text{OP5} \cdot \text{OP4} \cdot \text{OP3} \cdot \overline{\text{OP2}} \cdot \overline{\text{OP1}} \cdot \overline{\text{OP0}} \cdot \text{I} \cdot \text{CY1} \cdot \text{C3}})} \\ &\quad \cdot \overline{(\overline{\text{EOI} \cdot \text{C3}})}\end{aligned}$$

DeMorgan's theorem of Boolean algebra states that

$$\overline{A \cdot B} = \bar{A} + \bar{B}$$

or

$$\overline{\bar{A} \cdot \bar{B}} = A + B$$

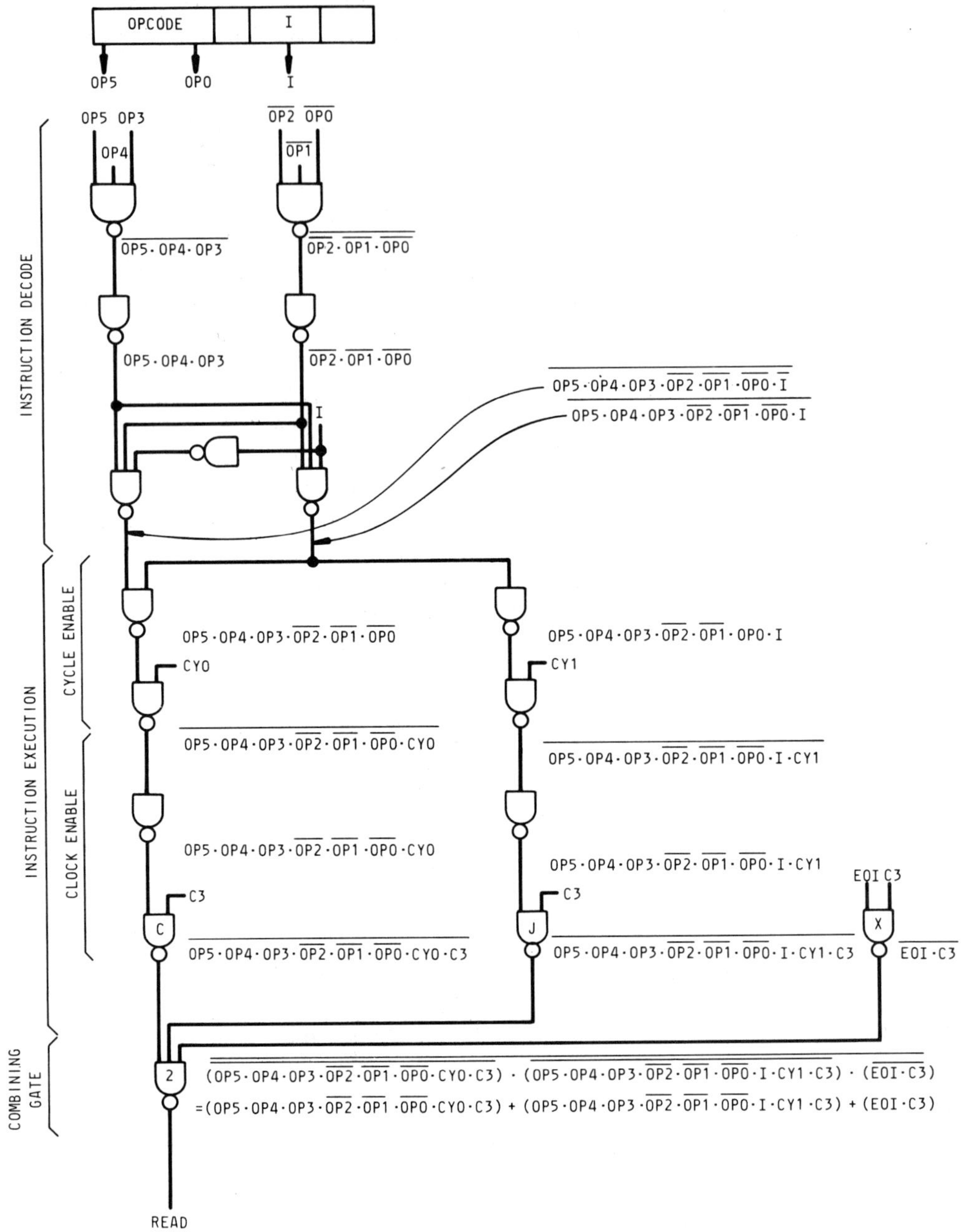

7-45 Logic flow of read control

Now applying this theorem, the output of gate 2 can be expressed as

$$\begin{aligned}\text{Gate } 2 = &(\text{OP5} \cdot \text{OP4} \cdot \text{OP3} \cdot \overline{\text{OP2}} \cdot \overline{\text{OP1}} \cdot \overline{\text{OP0}} \cdot \text{C3})\\ &+ (\text{OP5} \cdot \text{OP4} \cdot \text{OP3} \cdot \overline{\text{OP2}} \cdot \overline{\text{OP1}} \cdot \overline{\text{OP0}} \cdot \text{CY1} \cdot \text{C3} \cdot \text{I})\\ &+ (\text{EOI} \cdot \text{C3})\end{aligned}$$

which is a sum of three product terms. Each term generates the same control function, with the exception that each function occurs at a different time or condition. For this implementation, the ADD instruction requires two or three memory fetches and, hence, three terms for the READ operation.

Gate 2 of Figures 7-41 and 7-44 implements the same logic operation. Figure 7-45 shows the logic associated with gate 2, which was taken directly from Figure 7-41. The logic flow is traced all the way back to the original opcode. It gives the same logic expression for the output shown in Figure 7-44.

The product terms can be used to drive two or more gates in the second level that represent two or more actions. Figure 7-44 shows that the outputs of gates D and Y fan out to two gates in the second level. The logic structure is very regular, with high fan-in in both levels. The number of outputs from the second level is also fixed. As instructions are added, the product terms grow, even though they use the same inputs. The outputs are collected by the second-level logic. The interconnection between the two levels becomes more complex as product terms are added. The best feature of this arrangement is that the number of inputs and outputs of the two-level logic realization remains fixed as the product terms expand.

7.6 PROGRAMMABLE LOGIC ARRAY (PLA)

The regular structure and relatively small number of external leads required by the single-level ADD instruction make the logic circuitry feasible for LSI implementation. The integrated circuit chip designed for this type of application is commonly referred to as a programmable logic array (PLA). It consists of two matrices of crosspoints that usually contain transistors or diodes. At each crosspoint, a connection is either made or not made to the array. A mask is used in the last step of fabrication to implement the proper connection. For ease of understanding, Figure 7-46 shows a PLA arrangement that uses diodes as crosspoints. The two-diode arrays correspond to the two levels of logic shown in Figure 7-44. The first array implements the instruction decoding and execution logic, which is made up of the individual product terms. The inputs are the same as those shown in Figure 7-44, with the signals inverted to derive the complements of the inputs. Each vertical line represents one high fan-in NAND gate (shown in Figure 7-46), which corresponds to a product term. The number of product terms needed to implement a given instruction depends on the number of sequential operations that must be performed or the complexity of the instruction. The opcode inputs representing the ADD instruction are common to all control signals. The remaining control signals differ in terms of timing signals or how the option bit (I) is used. In this particular example, there are no inputs that represent the system state. The number of inputs is not the same for all terms, although with 17 inputs there exists the possibility of 2^{17} combinations of product terms. However, not all the terms will be used. Also, an output from one gate may overlap with another to provide the proper timing signals for both. For example, two control signals transfer the data from one register to another. The signal that controls the gating of the data onto the bus is longer in duration than the signal that controls the gating of data from the bus into the specified register. This latter signal is a strobed signal. It occurs during the middle of the clock interval in which the former data gating signal is active.

The second array sums the product terms. These terms are the inputs of the combining gates of the second-level execution logic shown in Figure 7-44. At each hori-

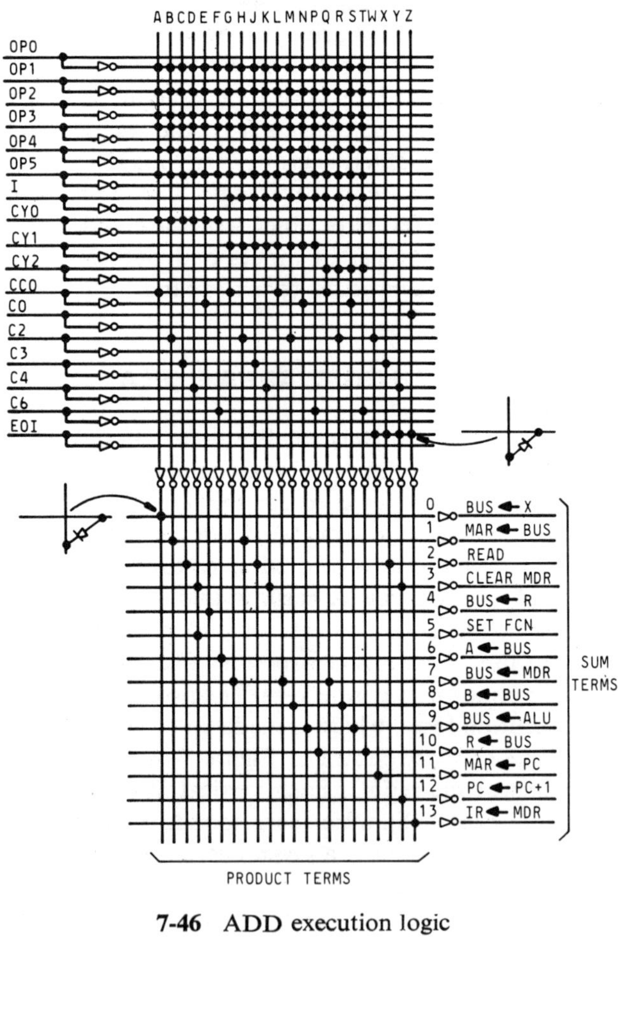

7-46 ADD execution logic

zontal line, a connection can be made to a diode crosspoint that connects to each vertical line. Whether or not a connection is made determines the presence or absence of the product term in the output. It is possible to have all product terms connected to a horizontal line. This situation will produce an exceedingly high fan-in into the output driver.

The two arrays provide a regular structure in which random logic can be implemented in a straightforward fashion. The regularity is realized by providing components at every crosspoint that may or may not be utilized. This is feasible because of the high packing density of LSI. All the complex interconnections required for the conventional design of control logic using standard logic gates can now be arranged in a grid array structure within a single LSI chip.

The external number of leads that can be brought out of a silicon integrated circuit (SIC) chip is determined largely by the size of the chip, the width of the conductor paths, and the spacing between the conductors. The 24-pin and 26-pin PLA's, commercially available on standard dual in-line packages (DIP's), have 14 or 16 inputs and 8 outputs; the additional pin is used as ground, and the remaining pin is used as the battery connection. Each output provides a sum of product terms. Each product term may contain any number of combinations of 14-input variables or their complements. The total number of product terms provided by both the 24-pin and 26-pin LSI DIP's is 96. For the 14-input PLA, the first array is arranged in a 28×96 matrix of crosspoints. This array supplies the inputs to the second array, which is arranged in a 96×8 matrix. The resulting logic structure provides 8 outputs. The two matrices represent 3456 bits of information. This PLA circuit features a typical delay of 50 to 100 nanoseconds.

7.6.1 PLA Output Option

The two-level logic realization (see Figure 7-47) uses NAND gates and provides a positive signal as the circuit's active output to indicate the *logical true* or *1's state.* In some instances, it is desirable to have a *logical 0* function as the *true output.* This would allow the outputs to be tied together in order to realize the wired negative OR function. If either a tri-state driver or an inverter stage with a passive pull-up resistor is added at the output, the output tie capability shown in Figure 7-47 may be obtained.

Commercial PLA chips provide the option of incorporating an inverter at the output. This allows the capability of selecting the PLA outputs so that either a logical 1 or a logical 0 can be used to represent the "true" state. Also, it eliminates the need of external inverters. Figure 7-48 shows the arrangement of the mask option that connects the inverter to the output. This two-level logic structure consists of an AND gate followed by a NOR gate to give a logical 0 as the true output. An inverter is inserted at the last stage if a logical 1 is desired as the active output. The faster *true 0 output* is desirable in that it compensates for any added delay if the outputs are connected together. The output mask option provides the flexibility of specifying either a *true 1 output* or a *true 0 output* to suit the need of the logic implementation.

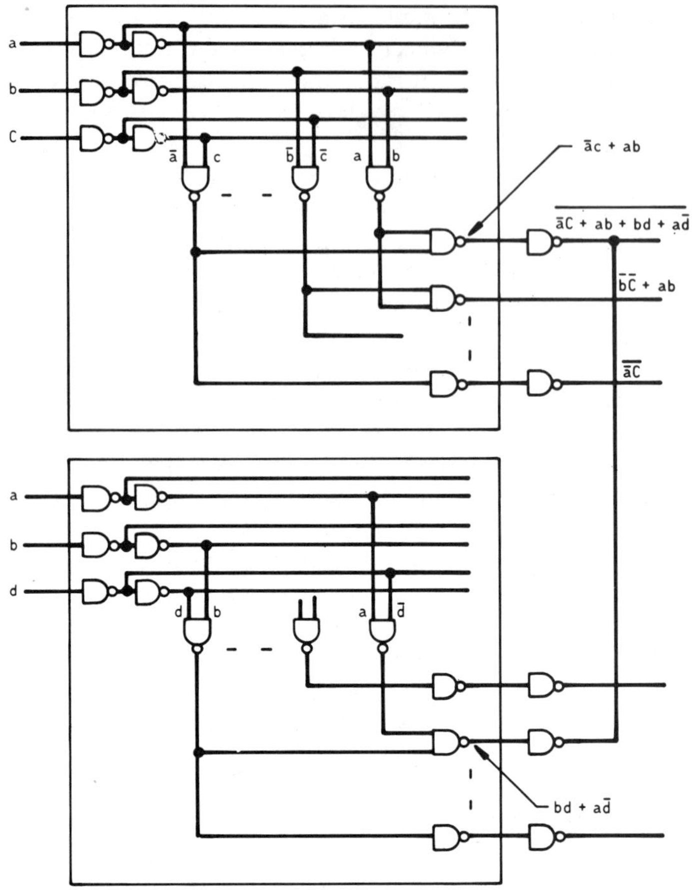

7-47 Output-tie capability

7.6.2 Use of PLA in Cycle Timing

The allocation of the number of cycles per instruction, as discussed previously, is derived from the opcode, option bits, and system states. This is done by sorting and grouping the decoder outputs according to the number of machine cycles required for instruction execution. The groupings vary according to the complexity of the instruction under consideration. In the case of instructions that take two, three, or four cycles, the decoder outputs will be combined with the appropriate conditions to generate one of several possible cycle groups. The control logic can then be implemented rather easily with a PLA to generate the required product terms and sum them to form a conventional logic realization. (This is shown functionally in Figure 7-49.) Most of the product terms are fed directly from the instruction decoder. The PLA logical realization permits a product term to be generated as it is needed. Consequently, this

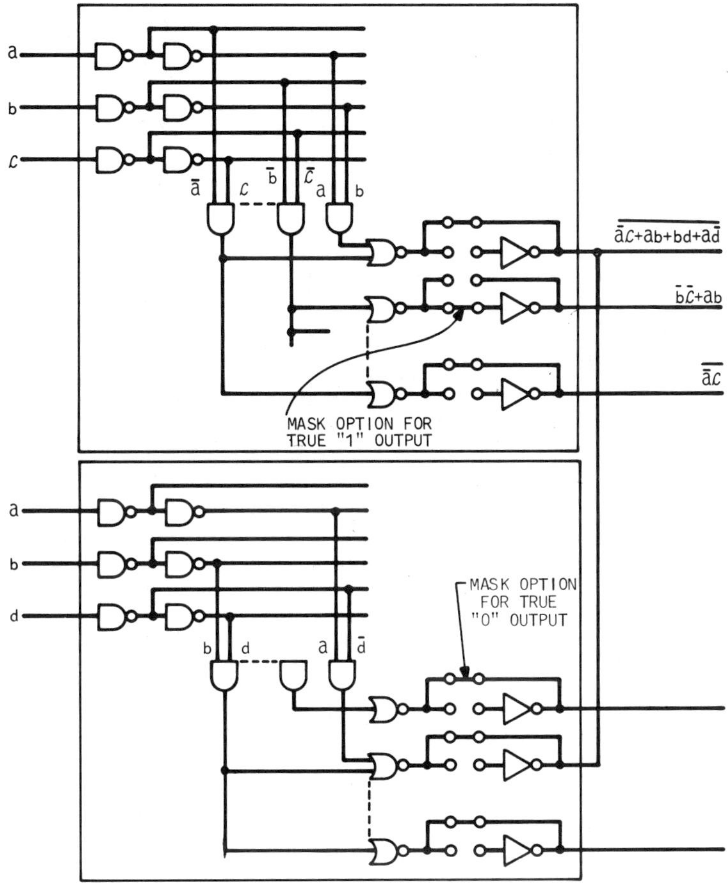

7-48 Mask option with true output either 1 or 0

capability makes the PLA control logic a regular structure that may be easily manufactured and used.

7.7 USE OF BASIC-SIZE PLA AS BUILDING BLOCKS

When designing a microprocessor on a chip, PLA's offer a systematic approach to control logic design. The size of the PLA can be tailored to the need of the design since it is incorporated as an integral part of the processor chip. At the minicomputer level, the design of the instruction and execution logic may be implemented with a standard-size PLA used as a building block (i.e., 14 inputs, 96 product terms, and 8 outputs). As in any design, these parameters may have to be expanded to meet the needs of the system. The number of product terms can be expanded by adding another PLA circuit with identical inputs and connecting corresponding outputs (see Figure

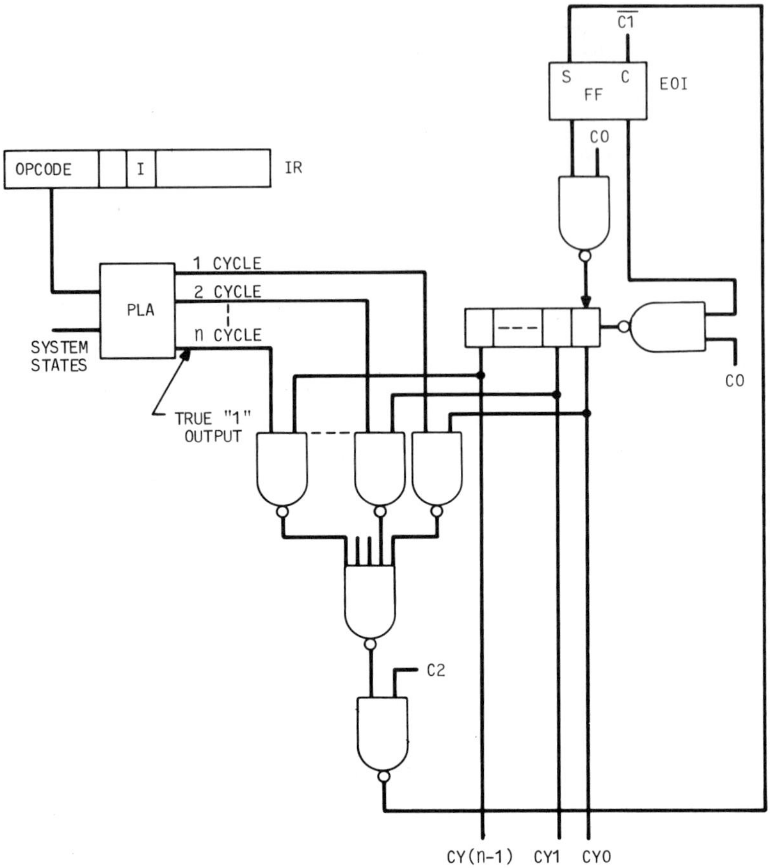

7-49 Use of PLA for cycle timing

7-50). The output connection must be made using either a tri-state device or an open-collector gate at the output. In addition, the proper polarity must be observed when the output connection is made. Commercially available PLA devices provide the option of connecting the outputs of separate PLA's together to generate a PLA with a larger capacity than either of the individual units.

If the number of input variables exceeds the number provided on the PLA chip, it is necessary to divide the product terms into groups that may be realized by two or more PLA devices. This can be done by dividing the mutually exclusive inputs into separate groups. Only those variables involved in generating the product terms will be included as inputs. For example, assume that there are 18 input variables and it is necessary to reduce this number to 14. Assume also that within these 18 variables there are eight clock timing signals. Some clock signals will be mutually exclusive in the sense that only one will be used at any given time in generating the product terms. Therefore, it is possible to separate the eight clock signals into two groups, with four signals in each group. The remaining 10 input variables plus one group of clock signals

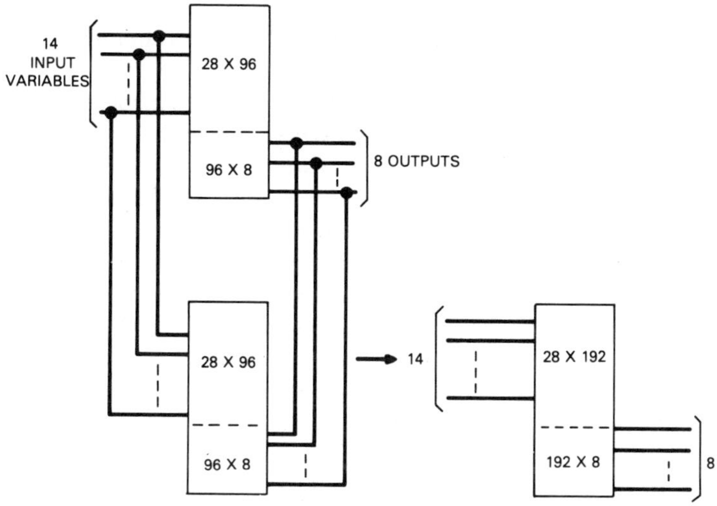

7-50 Expansion of product terms

will drive one PLA chip. At the same time, the second set of clock signals in combination with the same 10 input variables will drive a different PLA chip. Figure 7-51 illustrates this arrangement. Note that the input variables of two PLA chips differ only by four clock signals. This keeps the number of inputs within the physical boundary of 14, set by the size of the DIP. The outputs are wire-ORed to obtain the same set of control signals.

Alternatively, the opcode can be partially decoded to reduce the total number of input variables. For example, if the opcode is 6 bits, 3 of the 6 bits can be used to decode a 1-out-of-8 logical representation. Each of the eight outputs are mutually exclusive, and each can be used to select a particular PLA chip. The opcode inputs are reduced from six to four. This means that there must be eight PLA chips. If most of these PLA devices are not fully utilized, the technique results in an excessive waste

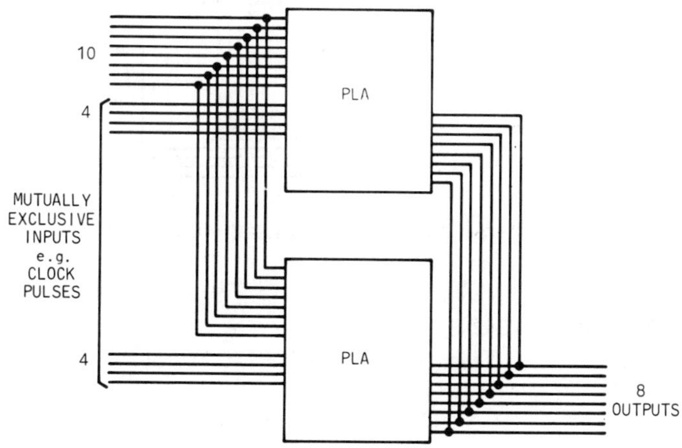

7-51 Expansion of input variables

of PLA chips. This consideration is in addition to the added circuitry that is required for decoding.

When more outputs are needed, they can be obtained by incorporating additional PLA chips. The optimum usage of the PLA chip is to divide the outputs into mutually exclusive groups, as shown in Figure 7-52. This means that all product terms fan out to outputs associated with one exclusive group, but not the other. If a product term is required for an output in the other group, the product term must be duplicated or generated as a logical signal for each PLA chip. This arrangement, shown in Figure 7-53, may be entirely satisfactory when the duplication does not become excessive. The nonexclusive outputs are connected jointly to both chips. Other output groupings are possible in which the amount of duplication of the product terms is reduced. The exact choice of the groupings is dictated by the system requirements.

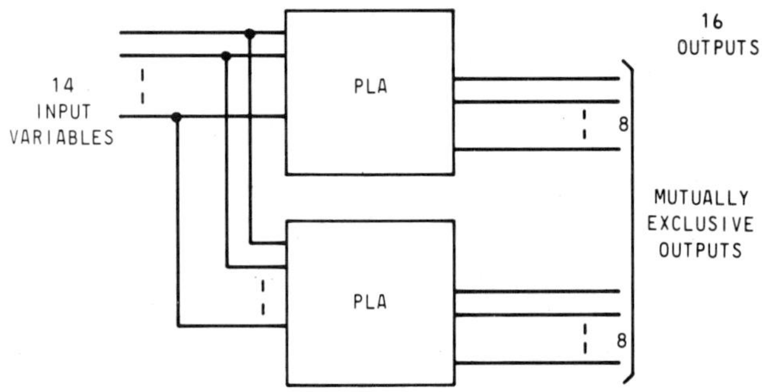

7-52 Expansion of outputs: mutually exclusive

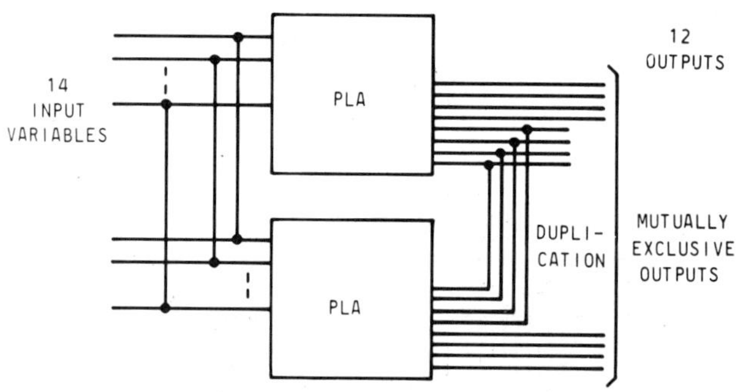

7-53 Expansion of outputs: partially exclusive

7.8 USE OF BASIC-SIZE PLA's TO IMPLEMENT THE ADD INSTRUCTION

The implementation of the ADD instruction, as shown in Figure 7-46, has been achieved without regard to the number of inputs or outputs required by the individual control gate. This, of course, is not a realistic requirement if the design is to use commercially available LSI components. The 24-pin DIP's (discussed in Section 7.6) will be used as building blocks to implement the ADD execution logic. The control implementation for the ADD instruction requires 17 inputs and 14 outputs. These numbers exceed the 14 input and 8 outputs provided by a 24-pin DIP realization of a PLA. In this case, both the inputs and the outputs must be expanded at the same time and grouped so that the resulting control logic may be realized on a standard commercial PLA unit.

The design procedure is to partition the inputs and outputs into mutually exclusive groups so that they can be separated and distributed to individual PLA chips. The objective is to keep the total number of inputs and outputs to 14 and 8, respectively, for each PLA. This means that a minimum of two PLA's will be required to accommodate the necessary signal leads. One possible technique would be to take the first array, as shown in Figure 7-46, and arrange the input variables according to their individual fan-out requirements or the number of times each variable is used in the product terms. The variable with the highest number of appearances should be placed at the top of the list. This is shown in Figure 7-54 with the input variables and their complements collapsed into a single horizontal line to reduce the total number of signal leads by one-half. Each vertical line represents a product term. If the input variable is used in the product term (either the variable or its complement), a dot is shown at the intersection of the appropriate horizontal and vertical lines. As indicated, the opcode input variables, OP0 to OP5, are used in every product term except the last four used in the instruction fetch sequence for all instructions. This sequence is initiated by the EOI input. The input variables with a large fan-out would have to be common to both PLA's, assuming that two such devices are adequate to handle the inputs and the outputs.

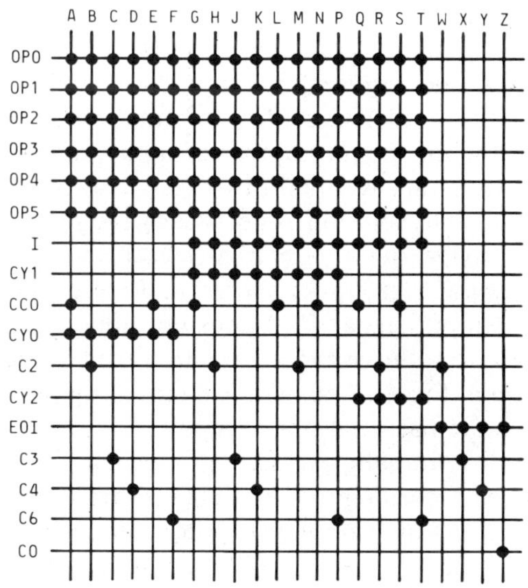

7-54 Product term array with input variables ordered by fan-out

The product terms in the diagram thus obtained may be rearranged to achieve a different PLA realization. The corresponding vertical lines may then be used to give two mutually exclusive groups of terms involving only low fan-out inputs (see Figure 7-55). Inputs CY2 and C6 appear in only the first group, while inputs EOI, C3, C4, and C0 appear in the second. Mutually exclusive, in this case, means that the input variables appear within their own group of product terms but do not appear in both.

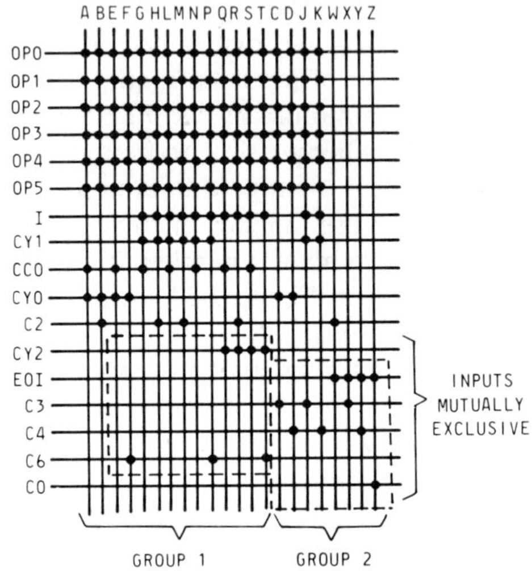

7-55 Product term partition

These inputs, therefore, can be separated and applied to different PLA chips. The remaining inputs are common and may be applied to both groups. There are 11 inputs belonging to the common set. The common set may be combined with the set of 2 inputs to drive a PLA chip that requires 13 inputs. The common set may also be combined with the set of 4 inputs to drive a PLA chip that requires 15 inputs. Since the 15-input device exceeds the maximum number of inputs available on a 24-pin DIP, another arrangement is necessary to obtain two PLA realizations that can make use of 24-pin DIP's. One possible solution is to reduce the common set to 10 inputs. Another solution is to divide the two mutually exclusive groups more evenly by assigning three inputs to each group as shown in Figure 7-55. However, a closer examination reveals that input signal CC0 does not appear in the second group of terms. It can be removed from the common set and placed in the first mutually exclusive group. This is shown in Figure 7-56, with C6 moved up to clearly display the two mutually exclusive and more balanced sets of inputs.

The outputs of the two mutually exclusive groups may be rearranged so that the product terms are grouped according to their first appearance by examining the product terms in a fixed sequence. For example, the product terms may be scanned from left to right starting with A (i.e., A, B, C, . . .). Product term A drives gate 0 (see Figure 7-46); hence, it is assigned to the top. As other terms are examined successively, the sum terms are assigned in the order shown in Figure 7-57. In this manner, the outputs are sorted into two groups.

The first group of outputs contains eight sum terms and satisfies the output requirement of the standard PLA chip. If more than eight product terms are required, another PLA chip could be added. This chip would accommodate the additional outputs (up to eight per PLA), but would use the identical set of inputs assigned to the first PLA chip. The product terms may also be regrouped in another arrangement to realize a better balance in the number of outputs per PLA.

The second set of outputs shown in Figure 7-57 is also mutually exclusive with the outputs of the first group. This is a coincidence. Usually, a product term from the

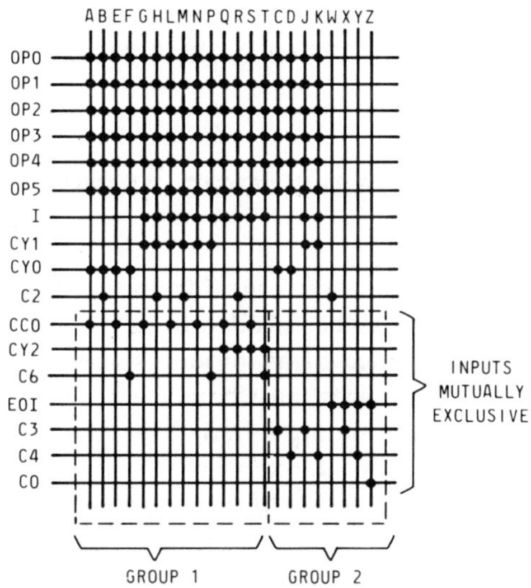

7-56 Product term partitioning with input rearranged

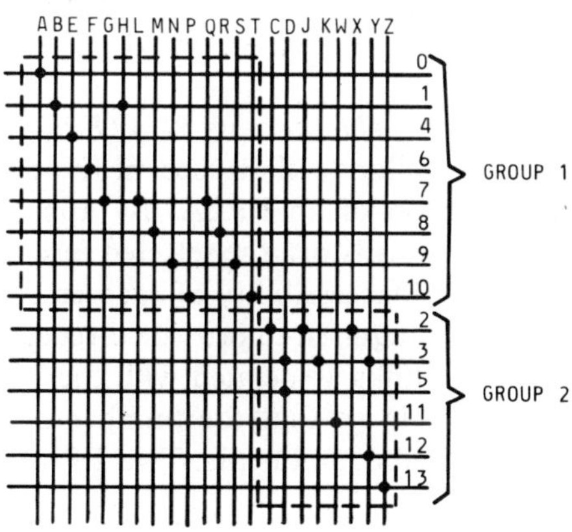

7-57 Output grouping of sum terms

second group will appear in the first group of the sum terms. In this situation, the sum term must be duplicated in the second group. In Figure 7-57, for example, if product term Z goes to output gate 1 and gate 13, gate 1 must also be assigned as a sum term in the second group. The two outputs, one from each PLA, must then be connected as a single output. The procedure of dividing the outputs is done for each group of product terms independently, which may result in duplicating several of the sum terms. They represent the common outputs among the PLA chips, but they may be realized using commercially available PLA devices.

The partition of the ADD execution logic fits into two basic PLA chips (see Figure 7-58), satisfying both the input and output requirements of a standard 24-pin DIP. Only 22 out of the 192 possible (96 per PLA) product terms have been used. The remaining 178 may, of course, be used to implement other instructions if the input variables and the output sum terms are adequate to handle the control steps required by the additional instructions.

7.9 FIELD-PROGRAMMABLE LOGIC ARRAY (FPLA)

The PLA is a mask-encoded device formed from two arrays of crosspoints. Each array requires that a separate mask be encoded to define the interconnection pattern to be used. The first mask-encoded array produces the product terms; the second generates the sum terms. Any changes must be made at the device level, which could delay work several weeks, since building a new PLA chip requires the manufacturer to set up new masks to obtain a new interconnection pattern. This is basically the same problem that a user encounters when ROM chips must be modified. However, in the case of a microprogram control implementation, it is customary to use either a *writable control store* (*WCS*) or a *programmable read-only memory* (*PROM*). Either of these devices permits the user to change the stored information easily and in a straightforward manner. Commercially available PROM's and ROM's are comparable in size and speed. They are normally available in pairs with identical pinouts to allow the direct replacement of a PROM DIP by a ROM DIP after the control sequence has been debugged and frozen.

To facilitate circuit changes, a *field-alterable PLA* (*FPLA*) can be used. Nichrome fuse-link technology, which is similar to that used in the manufacture of PROM's, is employed in the implementation of an FPLA. By applying high current to the appropriate crosspoint (diode or transistor), the selected fuse is "blown." The difficulty in using the FPLA is the relative inaccessibility of each crosspoint in the two arrays. Additional circuitry on the chip is required to provide direct access for each crosspoint and produce an FPLA. The fuse links associated with the FPLA take up a sufficient amount of silicon area on the chip so that the number of product terms must be reduced to accommodate the added components. Two FPLA sizes are available:

1. A 24-pin DIP with provisions for 14 inputs and 8 outputs.
2. A 26-pin DIP with provisions for 16 inputs and 8 outputs.

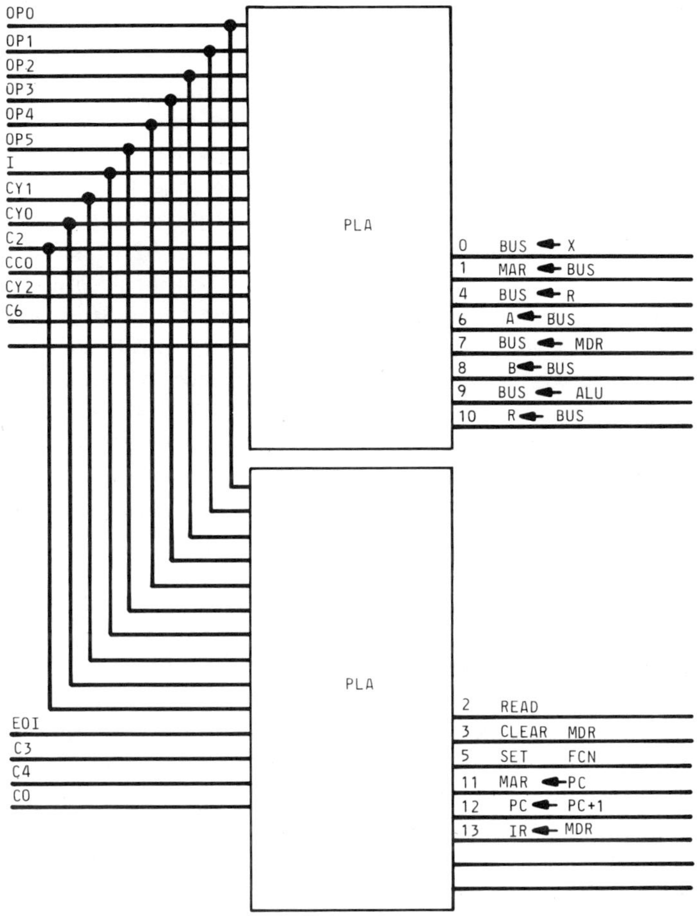

7-58 ADD execution logic using standard **PLA** chips

In both cases, the FPLA permits 48 product terms to be generated. This is one-half the number of product terms that may be generated if a standard-size PLA is used.

7.10 ASYNCHRONOUS MEMORY FETCH

Thus far, the control facility under study has been based upon the concept of a synchronous memory operation. The timing and machine cycle have been determined by the expected memory response time. The CPU and the memory are, therefore, closely interlocked. Any change in one would most likely affect the other. For example, if a slower memory were put into the system, the CPU would normally not operate properly without some extreme changes. On the other hand, if a faster memory were to be put into the system, the CPU would function properly but without fully realizing the speed capability of the faster memory. To achieve this realization, the CPU would have to be changed to match the response time of the memory.

It is not unlikely that the CPU will be required to work efficiently with memories of different speeds within one system. If a single semiconductor memory is used with a CPU, the characteristics of such a dynamic storage device require that the data stored in the memory elements be refreshed on a periodic basis. If this is done within the memory, the response time of the memory will be variable. When the memory fetch request occurs during an active refresh cycle, the response time is longer than that of a request that occurs during the nonrefresh interval. In this situation, the synchronous memory-to-CPU operation is no longer practical or desirable. This means that the machine cycle should be designed to perform the most basic elementary operation, such as a data transfer from one register to another rather than those operations that could be done within a memory cycle. A sequence of basic operations would then implement the more complex instructions. Several basic machine operations might be able to be performed within the period of a single memory cycle. Although the memory operates independently and asynchronously with respect to the CPU, the data transfer between the two must be synchronized. This is usually done using a handshaking or request-response convention which is established between the CPU and the memory controller. Whenever a read or write operation is requested, there is always a response to indicate that the data are ready to be used by the CPU. Since this can occur during any time within the machine cycle, the logic is arranged to examine the response-ready signal just prior to the time that the data are strobed into the memory data register at the beginning of a clock phase. If the response is not present, the data transfer is not performed and the operation is repeated for each successive cycle until a positive response is received. A flow diagram of a typical instruction requiring a memory data fetch is shown in Figure 7-59. For each memory-read operation, it may be necessary to wait one or more machine cycles for the data. Since the memory response is asynchronous with respect to the CPU, the average time required for synchronization is one-half of a machine cycle. In order to minimize the duration of this interval, the machine should be designed to have as small a machine cycle as possible.

A machine cycle is largely determined by the system structure used to carry out a specified operation. The operation may be complex, or it may be simple. Normally, clock phases are provided within the cycle to enable the proper actions to be carried out during the cycle. These clock pulses are repeated every cycle. When more than one machine cycle is required to perform a complex operation, external cycle-timing signals must be generated to distinguish the clock pulses from one cycle to the next.

The actual number of cycles for a given instruction may vary, depending on the wait period and the synchronization of the memory output. As indicated in Figure 7-59, the wait cycle may be repeated many times. In the actual hardware implementation of the execution control logic, the cycle timing is always fixed. However, the wait cycle experienced by individual instructions may vary extensively and cover several machine cycles. Figure 7-60 shows the modification required to provide the proper cycle-timing signals. In this example, the instruction has a memory with a variable

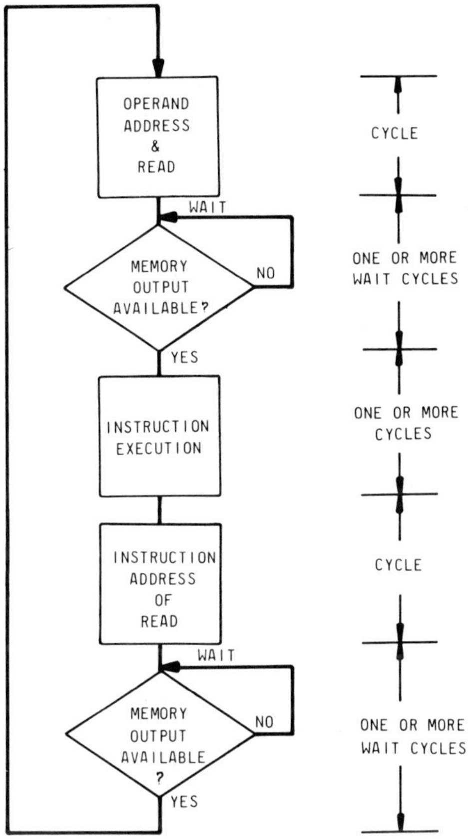

7-59 Flow diagram of instruction execution with asynchronous memory operation

response time and is dependent upon the instruction to be executed. The transfer of memory data into the MDR is performed by the instruction execution logic. If the data are not ready, a WAIT flip-flop (shown in Figure 7-60) is set to inhibit the advance of the cycle-timing counter (shift register). Immediately following this action, the WAIT flip-flop is cleared by a clock pulse, and then operation of gating memory into the MDR is again attempted. If it is successful, the WAIT flip-flop is not set, and the cycle-timing counter is then allowed to advance to the next cycle.

Instead of repeating the same cycle while waiting for the memory response to occur, the asynchronous operation may be arranged to stop the clock. When the completion signal is received, the clock timing is resumed. In this arrangement, the clock phase that is selected to halt the clock will be extended until it receives the memory-response signal. No additional time is lost in synchronizing the memory with the processor clock.

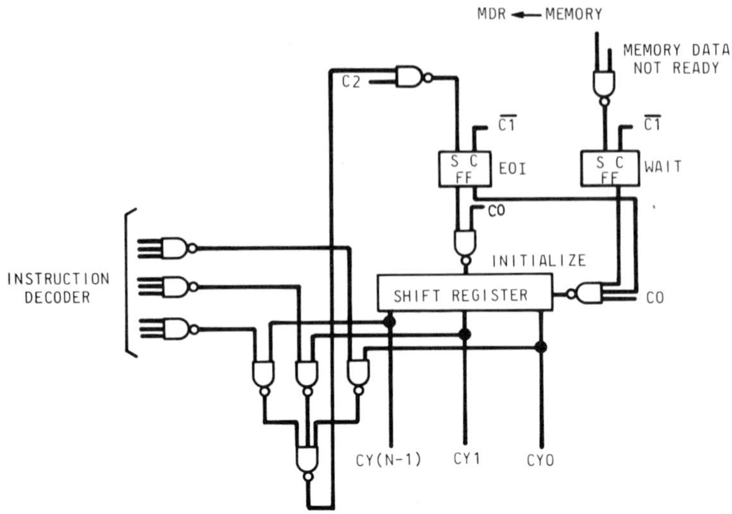

7-60 Cycle timing with variable memory response

7.11 SUMMARY

The various control functions associated with the instruction execution logic provide the necessary timing and control signals to direct all activities within the processor, including the execution of instructions. A continuous instruction stream is processed to realize the desired program function.

The control implementation requires an intimate association with the system structure and its overall organization. The control and the processor architecture are normally considered as a closely related whole. This also means that the interface structure of the processor and the external units (i.e., memory and I/O units) are taken into consideration.

An example was given to illustrate the detailed design of a typical portion of the instruction execution logic. The resultant diagram was shown to be self-contained in information flow and could therefore be used very conveniently for circuit debugging purposes. The procedure of designing the control logic on an instruction basis was shown to simplify the logic circuitry. A complete schematic of the entire control could then be obtained by systematically combining the execution logic for all instructions.

The random logic arrangement of implementing control logic was found to scatter circuitry throughout the machine. Through the use of PLA devices, it was shown that control logic can be consolidated and combined into a more regular structure. Some of the benefits of a PLA approach over random logic in the design of the control section are as follows:

1. *Design simplification.* The instruction decoding, execution logic, and combinational logic can all be implemented with a single circuit. Keeping track of the

fan-in, fan-out, and the interconnection pattern is no longer necessary, since these variables are implicit in the specification of the information content of the two arrays within the PLA chip.

2. *Physical size.* The LSI implementation of the PLA replaces many random logic circuits, reduces the physical size of the resulting logic configuration, and lowers the power consumption of the circuitry.
3. *Interconnection.* The irregular nature of the control logic is partially due to the complicated interconnection of the logic circuitry. Many of these complex wires can be removed from the circuit board or the backplane and placed on the PLA chip. This procedure also reduces long leads and potential noise problems.
4. *Maintenance.* It is much easier and simpler to maintain a regular circuit. Similarly, error detection can be incorporated as part of the PLA chip, using many of the coding techniques developed for checking memories.
5. *Cost.* If the circuit is a high-volume production item, cost can be reduced by replacing many random circuits (including terminals and interconnections) with one LSI circuit. This means that the initial cost of generating a unique mask for the device is small when spread over a large volume.

The PLA is an LSI solution to implementing the control logic of a computer system. Any random logic can be effectively implemented with PLA's. Also, PLA's provide the potential for a significant reduction in cost for high-volume production. In microprocessor design, the PLA control can be effectively employed in the microprocessor's internal structure. This technique is used in several microprocessors (e.g., Texas Instruments' TMS 1000 and SBP 0400A/401A, Fairchild's 9440, and Western Electric's MAC-8).

7.12 REFERENCES

1 Fleisher, H., and L. I. Maissel, "An Introduction to Array Logic." *IBM Journal of Research and Development*, Vol. 19, No. 2 (Mar. 1975), pp. 98–109.

2 Logue, J. C., N. F. Brickman, F. Hawley, J. W. Jones, and W. W. Wu, "Hardware Implementation of a Small System in Programmable Logic Arrays." *IBM Journal of Research and Development*, Vol. 19, No. 2 (Mar. 1975), pp. 110–119.

3 Toy, W. N., "Modular LSI Control Logic Design with Error Detection." *IEEE Transactions on Computers*, Vol. C-20, No. 2 (Feb. 1971), pp. 161–166.

4 Hill, F. J., and G. R. Peterson, *Digital Systems: Hardware Organization and Design.* New York: John Wiley & Sons, Inc., 1973.

5 Gorman, K., and P. Kaufman, "Low-Cost Minicomputer Opens Up Many System Opportunities." *Electronics*, Vol. 46, No. 12 (June 7, 1973), pp. 109–115.

6 Gorman, K., "The Programmable Logic Array: A New Approach to Microprogramming." *EDN*, Vol. 18, No. 22 (Nov. 20, 1973), pp. 68–75.

7 Mrazek, D., and M. Morris, "PLAs Replace ROMs for Logic Designs." *Electronic Design*, Vol. 21, No. 22 (Oct. 25, 1973), pp. 66–70.

8 PRIEL, U., AND P. HOLLAND, "Application of a High Speed Programmable Logic Array." *Computer Design*, Vol. 12, No. 12 (Dec. 1973), pp. 94–96.

7.13 PROBLEMS

1. The control logic consists of four basic functions: INSTRUCTION FETCH, INSTRUCTION DECODE, OPERAND FETCH, and INSTRUCTION EXECUTE. Which one of the four functions is most responsible for the irregular structure of the control circuitry? Explain why.
2. In early computers, the machine's memory cycle was also generally used as the basic machine cycle time. Why?
3. In core memories, the cycle time is divided in half: one half is for read, the other half is for write. INSTRUCTION FETCH and INSTRUCTION EXECUTE can be arranged to overlap, as was shown in Figure 7-5. For semiconductor memories, the information stored at a given location is not disturbed by the act of interrogating that location. Consequently, the entire memory cycle is devoted to the read operation since no restore function is required to regenerate the information formed at that location. In other words, the time required for a read access is nearly equal to the memory cycle time. Within these same parameters, design a timing sequence and functional block diagram that allow INSTRUCTION FETCH and INSTRUCTION EXECUTE to overlap (similar to Figures 7-6 and 7-7).
4. If, as a designer, you had to choose between using a conditional branch or a skip-on condition type of instruction, which would you choose? Why?
5. Provide the timing diagram and the instruction execution logic for the implementation of the ADD I instruction shown in Figure P7-5. Assume you are working with the processor whose block diagram is shown in Figure 7-35. (Use Figures 7-38 and 7-40 as examples to help you solve this problem.)

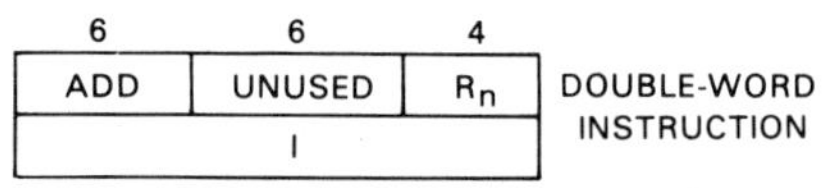

ADD I (IMMEDIATE DATA) TO THE CONTENTS OF R_n AND STORE THE RESULT IN R_n

P7-5

6. Implement the ADD I instruction-execution logic (see Problem 5) using PLA's. Assume that each PLA chip has 14 inputs, 96 product terms, and 8 outputs.
7. Provide the timing diagram and the instruction execution logic for the implementation of the branch-on-zero (BZ) instruction shown in Figure P7-7. (Use Figures 7-38 and 7-40 as examples.) Once again, you are working with the processor whose block diagram appears in Figure 7-35. For this exercise, assume that there is a signal lead (Z) going off from the ALU. This lead, which is *not* shown in the figure, represents the all-0's result. The BZ instruction checks this signal lead each time the processor executes this instruction. If the lead is in the 1 state, the program sequence will branch to the location

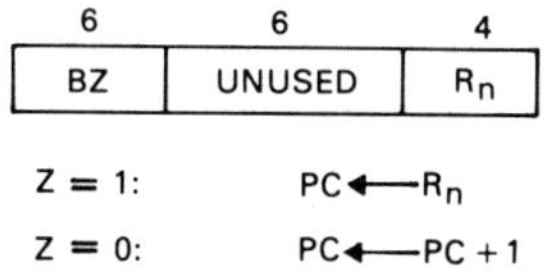

P7-7

specified in Register R_n. If the lead is the 0 state, the program will continue with the next sequential address.

8. Implement the BZ instruction execution logic (described in Problem 7) using PLA's. Assume that each PLA chip has 14 inputs, 96 product terms, and 8 outputs.
9. FPLA's and PLA's produced by the same manufacturer normally have the same pinouts, permitting a direct replacement of PLA's by FPLA's after the circuits have been "debugged." This direct replacement would *not* be done under a certain condition. What is that condition?
10. Work out a timing diagram similar to Figure 7-10 for the instruction fetch sequence which involves both indexing and indirection to generate the branch address. This fetch sequence is shown in Figure 7-11.

8

Program-Controlled Input/Output Operations

8.1 INTRODUCTION

The input/output (I/O) system provides the means for a CPU to interact with the external world as characterized by a peripheral device. Typically, the peripheral is administered by a *device controller*, which interacts with the CPU in a well-defined manner. Information may be communicated between a device controller and the CPU in either parallel or serial form. *Parallel I/O*, which transfers all bits in a data word at the same time, has been the most common form of information transfer used in minicomputer systems. The advent of the microprocessor, with its emphasis on low-cost computing hardware, stimulated the use of *serial I/O*. The emergence of computer networks has further encouraged the development of serial communications. In addition, for applications that require an ultra-reliable computing environment, serial I/O provides a facility for error-checking the data word at the transmission and reception sites.* Furthermore, a serial communication mechanism provides a particularly straightforward technique for interfacing a peripheral device with the CPU. For instance, the RS-232C EIA† data communications interface standard may be observed by both the CPU and the peripheral, or a private serial-communications convention may be used. In either case, the user simply inserts one end of a single coaxial cable

---

*See Chapter 9 for detailed elaboration of this concept.

†EIA Standard RS-232-C, "Interface Between Data Terminal Equipment and Data Communication Equipment Employing Serial Binary Data Interchange," August 1969, Electronic Industries Association, Engineering Department, 2001 Eye Street, N.W., Washington, D.C. 20006.

into the appropriate mainframe serial I/O port and the other end into the corresponding connector slot of the peripheral device controller.

The I/O operations of a reasonably sophisticated microcomputer are essentially the same as those of a conventional minicomputer. Both classes of machines may use the following three basic modes of I/O operations:

1. *Programmed data transfers*, including device polling, in which the CPU directs the entire I/O transaction by executing a sequence of I/O instructions.
2. *Interrupt-driven control*, in which the CPU interacts with its environment only when a hardware interrupt is directed to the CPU from its external system. The interrupt represents an immediate preemptive demand for service by an element in the system.
3. *Hardware-directed block transfers of data between an external device and main storage*, in which the transfers take place without the participation of the CPU. This technique is implemented via the *direct memory access (DMA) channel.*

Communication between the processor and its peripheral system is administered under control of either software or hardware I/O controllers. Typically, hardware controllers function independent of the CPU and interface with a specific external device. The advantage of using independent hardware controllers is that the system can perform I/O operations concurrently with CPU processing. Essentially, useful work can be done in parallel with the normal execution of a program sequence. Consequently, such hardware controllers offer the possibility of achieving a higher data transfer rate when operating on a large block of data. Figure 8-1 shows the two general data transfer techniques that may occur between the processor and the peripheral system.

Programmed I/O data transfers are directed toward a slow information exchange between the processor and its peripherals. In systems where the processor makes infrequent references to its peripheral devices and the throughput delay is of little importance, the simplest and most economical form of communication is I/O transfer that is completely under program control. For slow devices such as a teletypewriter, the data are usually available 1 byte at a time over an interval of many milliseconds. Effectively, the program works on only 1 byte of data for each I/O operation. This means that several instructions must be executed to process 1 byte of data.

For faster devices such as a 9-track magnetic tape unit, the program can transmit one word of data, wait until the device has processed the data, transmit another word, wait, and so on, until a block of words is transferred from the processor to the device. Unless the device is relatively fast, the wait interval is quite time-consuming. To eliminate this wait, buffer storage may be provided at the device controller to allow data transfers that are continuous and do not require the processor to wait until each individual transfer is complete. *LSI registers* or *first-in/first-out (FIFO) register stacks* are two examples of *buffer storage devices*. Block transfer is also called the *burst mode of operation*. Again, for many applications where the waiting period is tolerable, there is no need to complicate the controller by adding buffer storage to reduce the data transfer time.

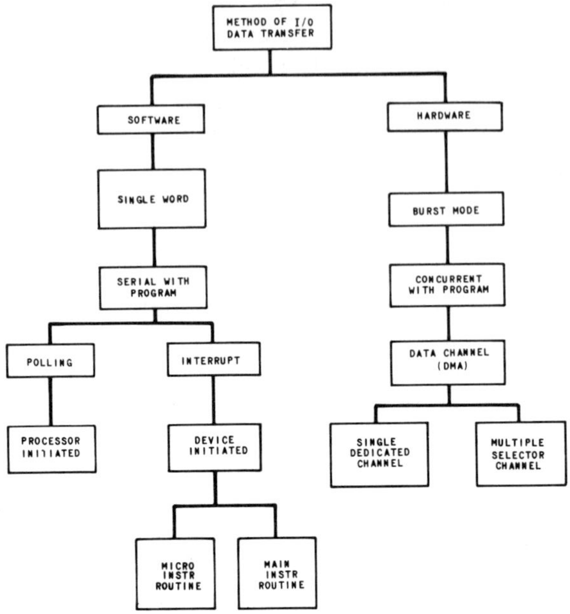

8-1 Method of I/O data transfer

Programmed I/O action can be initiated either internally or externally to service the peripheral devices. When the processor wants to communicate with the I/O, it simply issues the commands to perform the action it deems appropriate. The program sequence can be written to come back or wait if the device is busy. Once the program has control of the device, it can initiate the desired I/O function. The communication from the processor to the device is then straightforward. However, a problem arises if the device wants to communicate with the processor. The device can signal the processor to handle its request in one of two ways: *program polling* or *external interrupt*. In program polling, the program makes a periodic scan of all the attached devices and interrogates each one to determine whether it needs servicing. This procedure is time-consuming and must be done frequently enough to avoid missing a request. Depending upon the application, the polling technique may be entirely satisfactory for a low-performance or low-throughput system. Since no additional hardware is necessary, this technique is economical; however, it does sacrifice system time. With the external-interrupt technique, service is demanded from the processor at the time the device requests it. At the same time, this technique eliminates the need for the CPU to constantly poll each external device for service requests. This method does require, however, additional hardware cost. More details concerning the interrupt structure and implementation will be given in later sections.

The programmed I/O function has normally been a standard feature on all mini/microcomputers since the hardware cost is kept minimal (refer to Figure 8-1). In addition, programmed I/O has proved to be very flexible in handling a wide range of peripherals. However, for high-performance applications, the serial nature of programmed I/O, which requires that one instruction at a time be executed by the CPU, has often been inadequate to meet the high transfer rate of peripheral devices (e.g., a fixed-head disk, rotating drum memory, or a nine-track magnetic tape unit). An additional hardware facility has been devised to handle these devices without choking the system. Data can be transferred directly into main storage from such devices by a DMA facility. High-speed data transfer is controlled entirely by the DMA hardware and is performed without program intervention once the block-transfer process has been initiated. The operation involves time-sharing the main memory with the program sequence for the CPU on a cycle-stealing basis. Although the program sets up the initial conditions in the DMA channel, the data transfer is completely transparent to the main program sequence. At any given time, this concurrent operation allows a large block of data to be transferred at a maximum rate that corresponds to the cycle time of main storage.

8.2 INTERJECTION

8.2.1 Programmed I/O and the Interject Concept

Three I/O techniques may be used by a CPU to communicate with its external environment under program control. All three of these techniques may be employed by the same CPU. However, the form that is actually used for a given I/O transaction will be determined by the requirements of the application. The three forms of program-controlled I/O operation are:

1. *The use of a polling sequence.*
2. *The use of a program-interrupt facility.*
3. *The use of an interject mechanism.*

The first form makes use of a simple *inquiry-response* or *polling program.* In this case, the processor executes a sequence of instructions that test a peripheral device's availability to exchange information with the processor. The state of an external device may be characterized by a status flip-flop called the *device READY flag*. It, in turn, indicates whether the device is already engaged in an I/O operation (BUSY) or is available to dialogue with the processor.

Two separate situations must be handled by the device READY flag: (1) the peripheral acts as an input device *to* the processor, or (2) the peripheral acts as output device for data *from* the processor. Tables 8-1 and 8-2 summarize the interpretation of the READY flag when it is set or reset for each of these cases. The processor will test the device flag using one or more I/O-oriented instructions. If the flag is set, control is forced to branch to a service program that administers that specific external device. Typically, the service program will transfer one or more data words between the processor and the external device. If the device flag is not set, the processor may take one of three alternatives in terms of program execution:

TABLE 8-1 Peripheral Device Flag Interpretations

State of the Device Flag	Device Inputs Data to the CPU	Device Receives Data from the CPU
	Input Device Significance	Output Device Significance
READY Flag = 0	Information (i.e., a character) is not available for the computer in the device transmit (input) buffer	The device receive (output) buffer is unavailable to receive information (i.e., a character) from the computer
READY Flag = 1	Information is available in the device transmit buffer for access by the computer	The device receive buffer is available for the computer to transmit information into

TABLE 8-2 Standard Initialization Procedures for Device Flags

1. A peripheral device acting as an input source to the computer should always have its device flag cleared by an initialization program.
   (a) The loading of the device transmit buffer by an input stimulus should automatically set the READY flag.
   (b) The device service program executed by the small computer should always take the READY flag down.
2. A peripheral device acting as an output sink for information sent from the computer should always have its device flag set by an initialization program.
   (a) The device service program executed by the small computer should load the device receive buffer and take the device flag down.
   (b) The unloading of the device receive buffer by an output response should automatically set the device flag.

1. The processor may branch to a program segment totally unrelated to the I/O operation that it was attempting with the previous external device.
2. The processor may move on to test the availability of another peripheral in its external device set, provided that it wishes to enter into an I/O transaction with that device.
3. The processor may simply execute a tight loop over two or three instructions and continuously test the original device flag until it indicates that the peripheral unit is free.

A program that performs one or more device flag testing operations is called a *polling program*. Figure 8-2 illustrates a typical polling sequence for programmed I/O. Notice that the external device flags are polled by means of a flag-polling subroutine that is called during the execution of the main program. Consequently, the main program will branch to the polling subroutine only when it determines that conditions are appropriate to test the external device set for I/O availability (READY

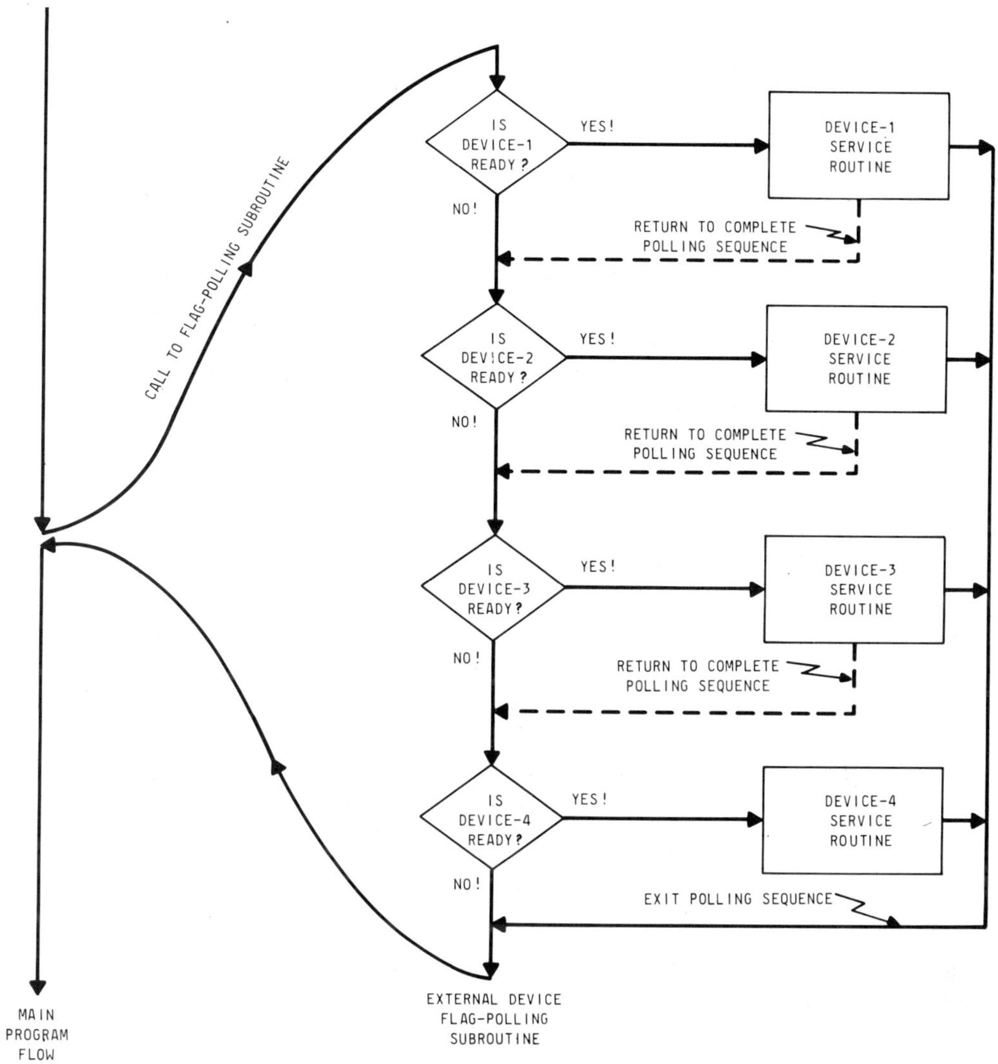

8-2 Typical polling sequence for programmed I/O operations

Flag = 1). In effect, this is a form of program-scheduled I/O. Once the polling subroutine is entered, the individual device flags are tested. The first device flag to be tested is normally the peripheral with the highest priority. Typically, that priority will be dictated by the response speed of the peripheral and how often the processor may have to service it. In the simple polling sequence of Figure 8-2, once a device is found to be available or requesting service, and control has been directed to its associated service routine, one of two actions must be taken by the program at the completion of the service routine:

1. Control may be returned to the calling program without any further device flags being examined. In this case, only those flags that occur early in the polling sequence will be tested frequently. The availability of a higher-priority device will inhibit the servicing of all lower-priority devices during the current pass through the polling subroutine. This feature may or may not be advantageous, depending on the speed of the individual peripheral devices attached to the processor.
2. Control may be returned to the polling sequence following the identification of the most recently available device. Each new device that becomes available or has requested service causes control to branch to the associated device service routine. When the service routine is completed, control is returned to the point in the polling subroutine where the next highest-priority device is tested for availability. In this way, the entire polling sequence is completed each time the polling subroutine is entered. Control is returned to the main program only after all devices have been polled. The advantage in this situation is that no device is denied attention indefinitely. Each device will be scanned as a natural consequence of execution being directed to the polling subroutine since execution will not be returned to the main program until all device flags have been checked.

The simplest example of how a polling environment is implemented in hardware is shown in Figure 8-3. Each external device is characterized by a device flag that is set if the device is available. The processor tests a specific device flag by broadcasting a

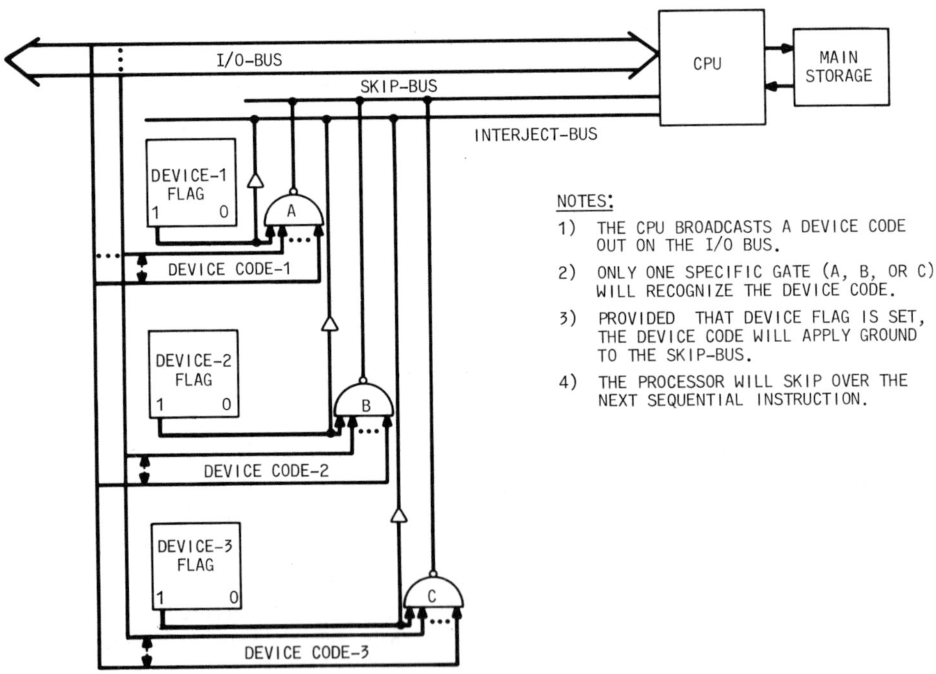

8-3 Use of a SKIP bus to poll the external device set

device code that is transmitted on the I/O bus to all external devices. Each device flag and a common set of address leads from the I/O bus are brought as inputs into logic gates A, B, and C. The address leads carry the device code sent by the processor and determine which specific logic gate will be enabled. For instance, if device code 2 is transmitted on the I/O address leads, logic gate B will be enabled. If device 2 is available, ground will be applied to the physical lead shown entering the processor. This lead, called the *SKIP bus*, signals the processor if a selected device is available. Since programmed I/O is being performed, ground on the SKIP bus causes the execution sequence to skip over the next instruction following the device flag-test command in the I/O program.

Typically, each operation that tests a device flag will be given a unique mnemonic. For instance, the command to test the flag for device 1 might be called *SKPDV1*. This would imply to the I/O programmer that if the device is available, the next instruction after the SKPDV1 command should be skipped over by the execution sequence. A group of devices may be individually polled in this manner to determine availability. Figure 8-4 illustrates a possible polling subroutine that could be used on the configuration shown in Figure 8-3. Note that each SKPDV1 command is followed by an

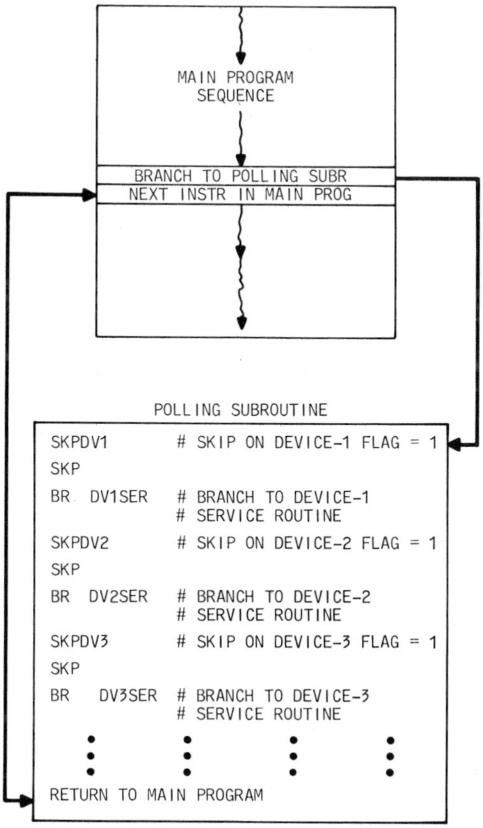

8-4 Example of the usage of a SKIP chain

unconditional SKIP command. This permits the polling sequence to continue by branching to code that tests the next device flag. For instance, if device 1 is available for an I/O transaction with the processor, the unconditional SKIP instruction is simply passed over by the program, and control is directed to branch to the service routine for device 1. However, if device 1 is unavailable, the processor is directed to execute the next instruction, which is the unconditional SKIP command. This causes execution to branch over the instruction that would transfer control to the service routine for device 1. Instead, the instruction to test the flag of device 2 is executed and the polling sequence continues. An instruction sequence of this kind, which uses conditional and unconditional SKIP commands to identify external devices in a polling sequence, is usually referred to as a *SKIP chain*. The PDP-8 popularized this term in the late 1960's, since its I/O programming was oriented toward this procedure. The basic advantage of the SKIP chain is that it may be extended indefinitely to service any number of devices. Its major disadvantage is its usage of real time to perform device identification. The highest-priority device will always be the first device tested in the SKIP chain. Priority is dictated exclusively by the placement in the SKIP chain of the command that tests the specific device flag. Obviously, high-speed devices must be checked close to the beginning of the SKIP chain so that no information is lost. Even then, the data transfer rate of some high-speed devices may be so high that a SKIP chain or polling sequence will not be able to service them effectively.

The disadvantage of using an environment that is exclusively polling-oriented is that each individual device flag must be tested to see if the associated device is available for access by the processor. This flag testing must even be done on those devices that do not need service. Each polling operation represents a series of I/O oriented instructions that must be executed by the CPU. If several devices are in the polling sequence, the number of I/O-related instructions that must be executed can quickly become quite large. This can represent a significant overhead for the processor in terms of the real time consumed. It can also slow down considerably the response of the CPU to its external devices. Because of this, a more attractive facility would include a machine feature that permitted the processor to respond only to those devices needing service and specifically requesting it. All devices not requesting service would be ignored. To optimize the real-time response for those devices requesting service, each external device would be handled on a preestablished priority basis. Consequently, if two or more devices should simultaneously request service from the processor, that device having the highest priority would be serviced first. The mechanism used to perform these operations has been termed the *hardware interrupt facility*.

The interrupt mechanism differs from the polling sequence philosophy of I/O operation in the following ways:

1. An interrupt is generated by a device; the CPU responds to the interrupt request but does not execute an I/O program to test for the presence of an interrupt request. It does, however, execute an I/O program to identify the interrupting device after the CPU has recognized the interrupt request.
2. The interrupt request permits the processor to complete execution of the current instruction. The CPU hardware control logic then saves the address of

the next instruction in a dedicated memory location and branches to an interrupt service routine. If any additional registers need to be saved before the interrupt is serviced, the service routine must execute an instruction sequence that saves the appropriate registers. The service routine must then attempt to identify the interrupting device.

The full details of interrupt operation are given in Section 8.3. The significance of mentioning the interrupt mechanism at this point is to contrast it with the concept of a polling sequence. Its basic advantage is real-time response. The interrupt permits a processor to be sensitive to events occurring in its external environment and demanding immediate attention. However, if the contents of various CPU registers must be saved each time an interrupt occurs and then restored each time execution is returned to the main program, real-time usage can quickly become critical. These save-and-restore operations represent a real-time overhead that can affect the response time of the CPU to individual interrupts. In particular, this overhead becomes increasingly significant as the number of devices attached to the processor and capable of generating an interrupt is steadily increased. It is possible for the system to reach a state of interrupt saturation in which, effectively, the CPU handles only interrupts because of the required save-and-restore overhead. At this point, the CPU is unable to carry out any foreground processing, and the interrupt facility has reached its limit in carrying out I/O transactions between the CPU and its peripheral device set.

The *interject mechanism* represents a compromise between the use of a polling sequence and a program interrupt facility. It attempts to combine the best features of both methods while minimizing any hardware or real-time overhead penalties that the system may have to pay. The interject mechanism makes use of a hardware flag that is set when any device requests attention from the CPU. Typically, all device flags are tied to an interject bus that is connected to the setting input of the INTERJECT flag. Figure 8-3 illustrates a simple interject environment. Any one of the three device flags will apply ground to the interject bus when it is in the set state. A ground signal, in turn, will set the INTERJECT flag. However, the processor does not respond immediately to the interject request. Instead, the INTERJECT flag is scanned on a scheduled basis by the system software. If the INTERJECT flag is set during any scan, the CPU will branch to a polling sequence to identify the interjecting device.

The polling process is identical to the procedure described earlier. The advantage of this scheme is that the computer does not have to go out and interrogate each peripheral device looking for work. It interacts with its environment only when an interject request has been made. Unlike the interrupt, no processor registers have to be saved or restored. Consequently, all the real-time overhead associated with these operations for an interrupt is made available to the system programs. These savings can be considerable in a heavy interrupt environment. On the other hand, the response to an interject is not normally immediate and, for the software-oriented interject, device polling must still take place to identify the interjecting device. This results in a loss in real-time efficiency by the CPU, which detracts from the savings in real-time overhead just mentioned. In addition, very high-speed devices may not be adequately serviced by a software-oriented interject because of the real-time response characteristics of such a mechanism. Trade-offs between the use of a program interrupt and a software-oriented interject need to be closely examined for any contemplated real-time environment.

The interject has not been used much by the commercial machine manufacturers largely because the interrupt mechanism has proven quite satisfactory over a broad range of applications.* Bell System designers of electronic switching systems (ESS) have been forced to evolve a sophisticated philosophy of interjection to accommodate the heavy real-time requirements of a telephone call processing environment. The No. 1 ESS uses a software-oriented interject mechanism that closely resembles the previous interject description. The No. 1A ESS combines many of the software response features of the interject in hardware which significantly quickens the real-time response of the processor to an interject request. In addition, interjection has been employed at the microprocessor level within the Bell System as an alternative to a hardware interrupt facility. The entire software-response sequence for the interject has been placed in microcode. When a microstore is employed with a cycle time on the order of 200 nanoseconds, the interject response of such a system can be faster than the response of a hardware interrupt facility that is handled by a macroinstruction service routine placed in a mainstore with a cycle time of 1 microsecond. This concept will be explored further in the following two sections.

8.2.2 The Software-Directed Interject Mechanism

A totally software-driven interject structure is illustrated in Figure 8-5. In such a facility, the programmer schedules the testing of the INTERJECT flag at strategic points in in-line code. The actual number of times the INTERJECT flag will be tested depends upon the number of devices attached to the mainframe and the individual data transfer rates of each external device. Typically, a special machine instruction will test the INTERJECT flag. If it is set, control will be forced to branch to a subroutine that identifies the interjecting device. Note that in Figure 8-5 program segments of different lengths conclude execution by testing for the presence of an interject. If the INTERJECT flag is not set, the next program segment of in-line code begins execution. If the INTERJECT flag *is* set, the interject service subroutine is called. Within this subroutine, the following operations take place sequentially as a function of in-line code execution:

1. The INTERJECT flag is cleared at the beginning of the interject service routine. This flag could just as easily be handled at the conclusion of the service routine. It is administered here to show that the actual clearing of the INTERJECT flag may be done at an arbitrary time after the service routine has been entered.

---

*As of the spring of 1978, no commercial minicomputer manufacturers had advertised usage of the interject concept. This seemed to indicate that their established market areas did not require the interject feature to sell their existing machines; the program interrupt apparently provided a perfectly adequate real-time response mechanism for the vast majority of commercial machine applications.

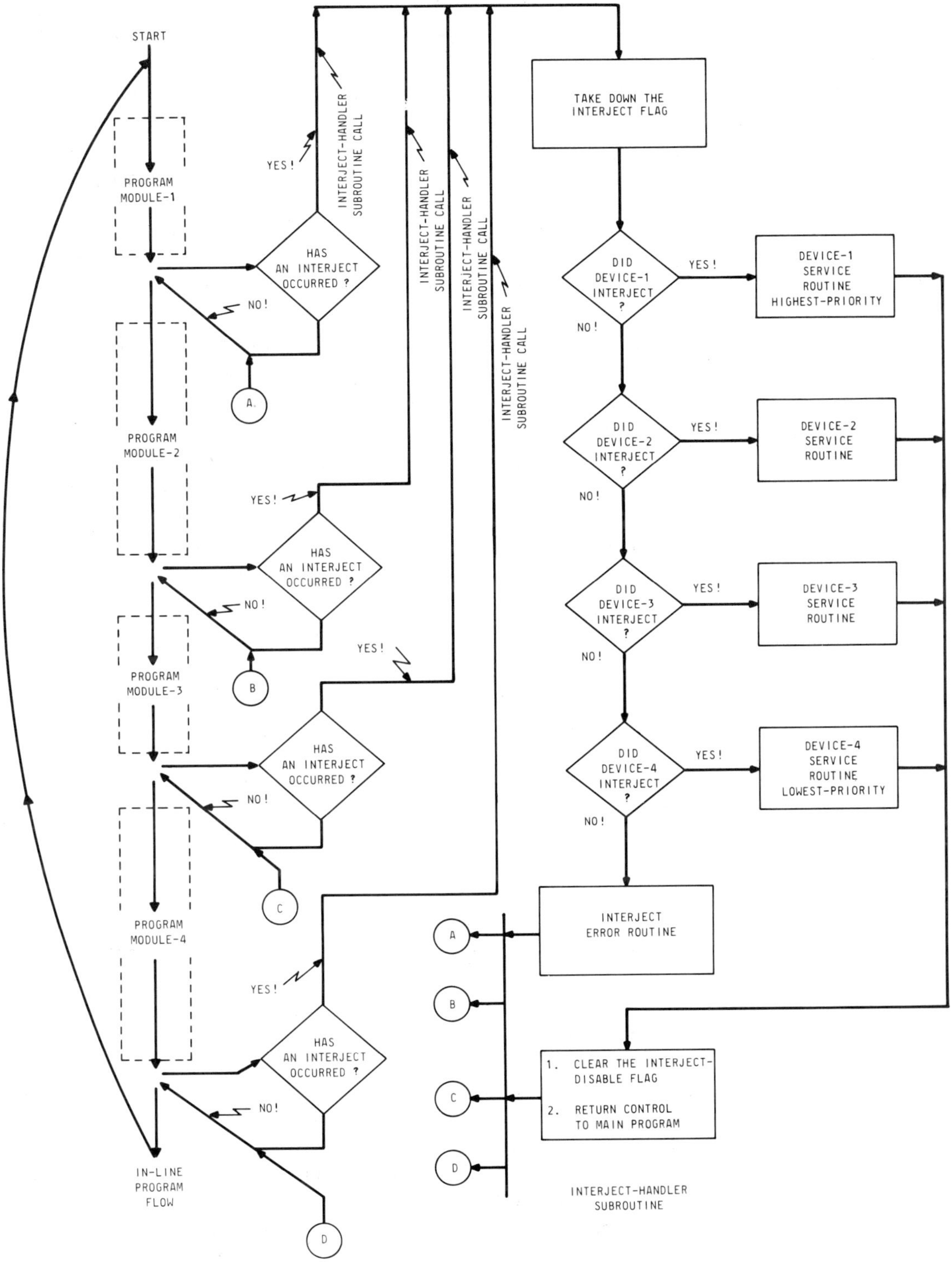

8-5 Typical software—driven interject structure

2. The priority of a device handled by a software-driven interject is determined by its placement in the polling sequence. Note that in the polling sequence shown in Figure 8-5, control is directed away from the sequence once the interjecting device is identified. Control does not return to the polling sequence after the interjecting device has been serviced. Instead, control is directed back to the next instruction in the main program that follows the test-interject instruction. This requires that each external device capable of interjecting must have the facility of continuously issuing interject requests until the processor actually services the device.
3. The possibility of the processor detecting an interject request, for which no peripheral device indicates responsibility, must be handled by the interject service routine. In this case, an interject error subroutine is provided to recognize this condition and set the appropriate system error flag.

Note that this entire process requires that one instruction after another be executed from in-line code. The number of instructions involved takes up space in main storage and uses up real time. The process is naturally slow because of the macroinstruction polling sequence used to identify the interjecting device. This obviously affects the response time of the system to its external environment. To further enhance the response-time characteristics of the interject mechanism, many of the polling and control functions may be placed in hardware and/or firmware.

8.2.3 The Firmware-Directed Interject Mechanism

The following two macroinstructions are needed to implement a microcoded interject facility:

1. *INJ*. This command places the address of the next sequential macroinstruction into a special storage register of the CPU and then forces execution to begin at a fixed address in the microstore. This is the starting address of the interject service routine that has been placed in ROM.
   (a) By scanning the device flags, the interject service routine attempts to identify which device requested service. This scanning function is achieved through use of a microcoded polling sequence which, typically, is many times faster than an equivalent macroinstruction routine.
   (b) The polling sequence allows the CPU to derive a fixed address in main storage (macroinstruction memory) where execution is then directed. These fixed addresses may be stored as a table of constants in microstore. The entry into the table is determined by the results of the polling sequence. The branch to the macroinstruction service routine for the interjecting device is very similar to a subroutine call at the macrostore level. However, the return address to the main program sequence was saved in a special register as the first operation performed by the INJ macroinstruction.

2 *RINJ*. This command is used when the service routine for the interjecting device completes its execution sequence. In this case, RINJ directs control back to the appropriate macroinstruction in the main program sequence. Typically, the following functions will be performed:
(a) The INTERJECT flag will be cleared.
(b) The return address in the main program is moved from the special storage register into the program counter (PC) and execution continues from this point.

Figure 8-6 presents a detailed operational sequence of such a microcontrolled interject facility. Note that both the INJ and RINJ macroinstructions are shown as microinterpretation modules in the control ROM. Control branches from macrostorage to microstorage and then back again. A speed advantage is gained in using a ROM routine to identify the interjecting device. A macroinstruction device handler makes it easier to modify programs. The greater the speed differential between the access times of the microstore and the main program memory, the more attractive such a microcontrolled interject facility is when compared with an interrupt mechanism that relies entirely on a macroinstruction service routine. In an entirely microcode driven machine, there may be no real advantage offered by the interject mechanism over a hardware interrupt facility. In such a case, the software overhead required to service an interrupt may be less than or, at best, no more than the overhead required to service an interject. Various methods, however, may enhance the speed of response to an interject. These methods may be classified according to the following categories:

1. Determining when to test for an interject request.
2. Expediting the identification of a high-priority device requesting interject.
3. Transferring control to the appropriate device service routine.

Two techniques have been considered within the Bell System for testing an interject. The first is the use of the INJ macroinstruction as previously described. The second technique is to specify the test of the INTERJECT flag as an option on a specific type of branching operation encountered during program execution. The functions performed by either technique would be identical if the INTERJECT flag were set. However, if the option on the branching instruction is used, the branching operation will be delayed until the interject has been serviced. The return from the interject service routine will then direct execution to begin at the location in the main program that is the target address of the branch instruction. Both techniques of testing the INTERJECT flag would make use of the RINJ macroinstruction to return control to the main program. However, in the resulting transfer operation associated with the branch instruction, the return-from-interject mechanism would have to recognize that the transfer operation must be completed in the main program before execution can continue.

The identification of the interjecting device may be handled by a microcoded polling routine, as mentioned earlier. In addition, the sources of an interject request may be broken up into two groups: hardware-initiated and software-initiated. Normally, the hardware-initiated group is always given priority over the software-

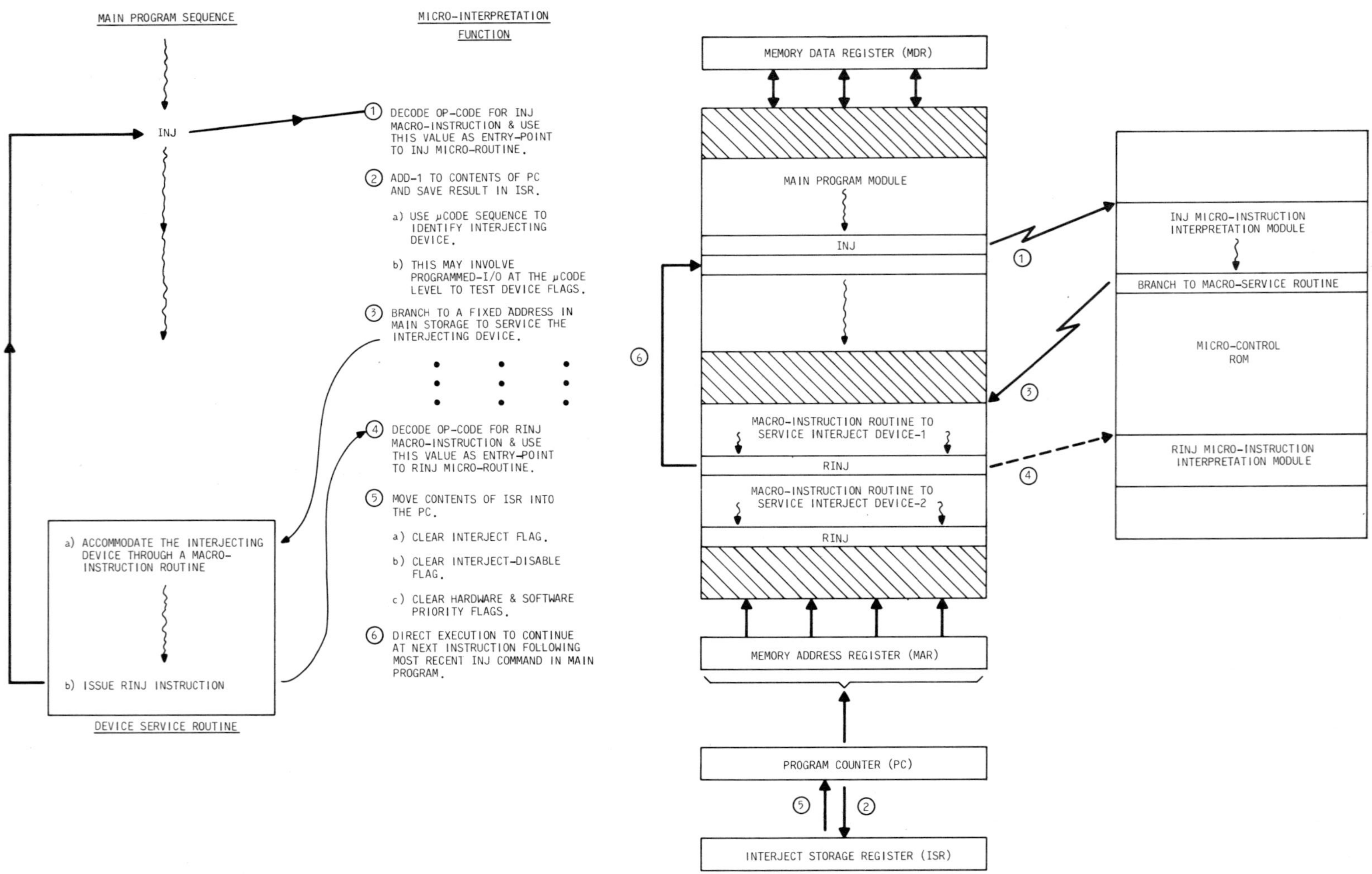

8-6 Basic operational sequence of a microcontrolled interject

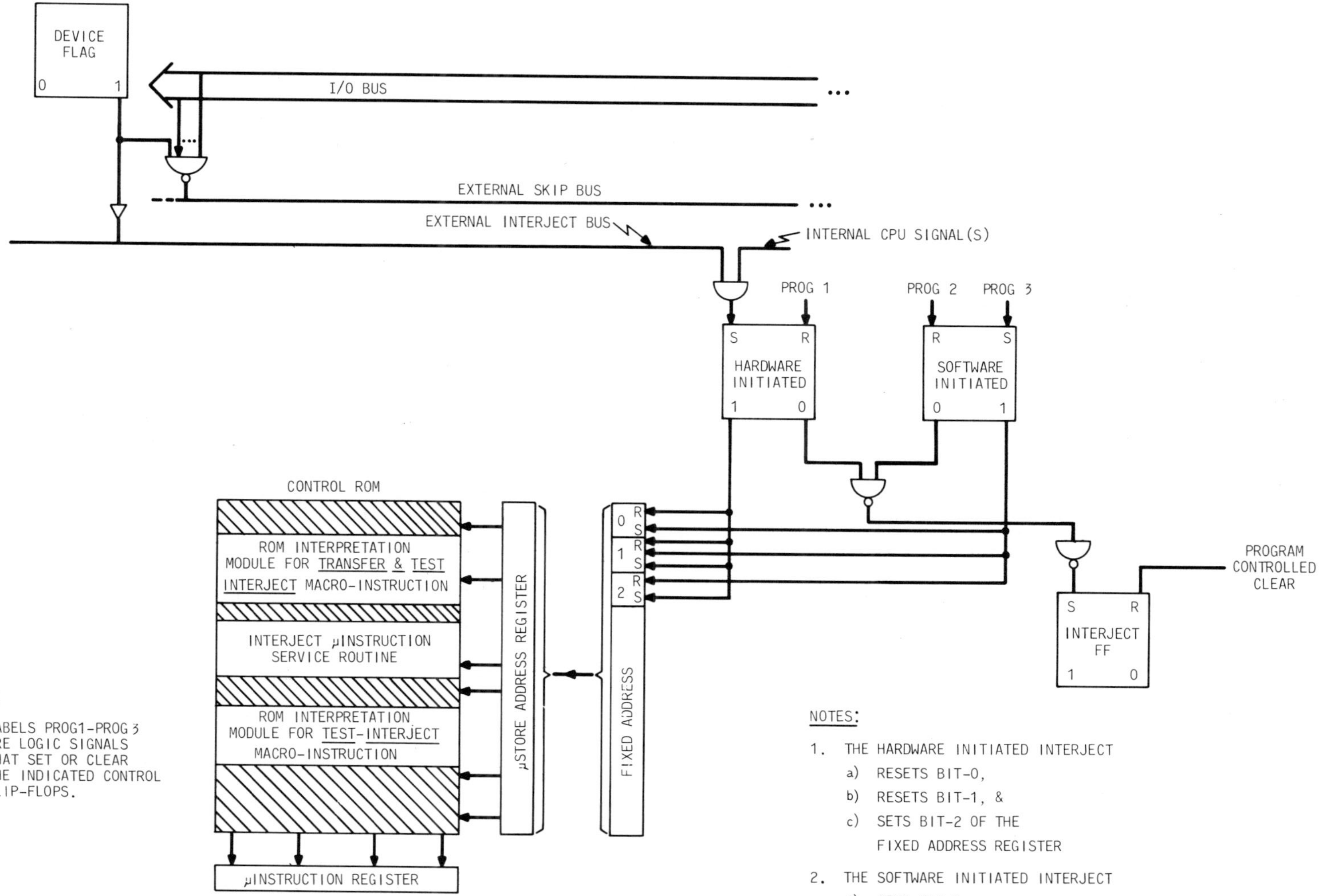

NOTES:

1. LABELS PROG1-PROG3 ARE LOGIC SIGNALS THAT SET OR CLEAR THE INDICATED CONTROL FLIP-FLOPS.

NOTES:

1. THE HARDWARE INITIATED INTERJECT
   a) RESETS BIT-0,
   b) RESETS BIT-1, &
   c) SETS BIT-2 OF THE FIXED ADDRESS REGISTER
2. THE SOFTWARE INITIATED INTERJECT
   a) SETS BIT-0,
   b) RESETS BIT-1, &
   c) RESETS BIT-2

8-7 Microcontrolled hardware/software interject mechanism

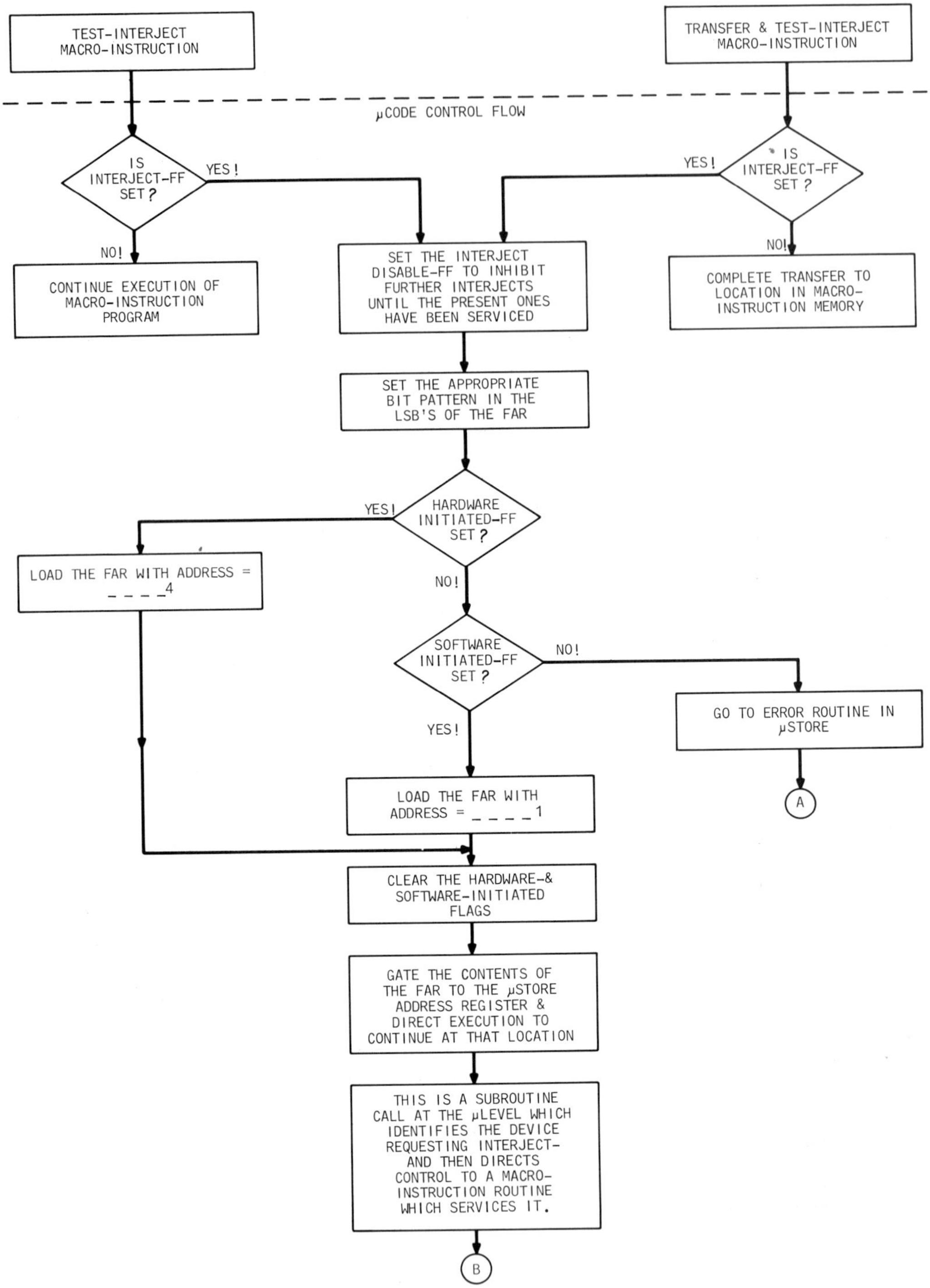

8-8 Flowchart of firmware—directed interject mechanism

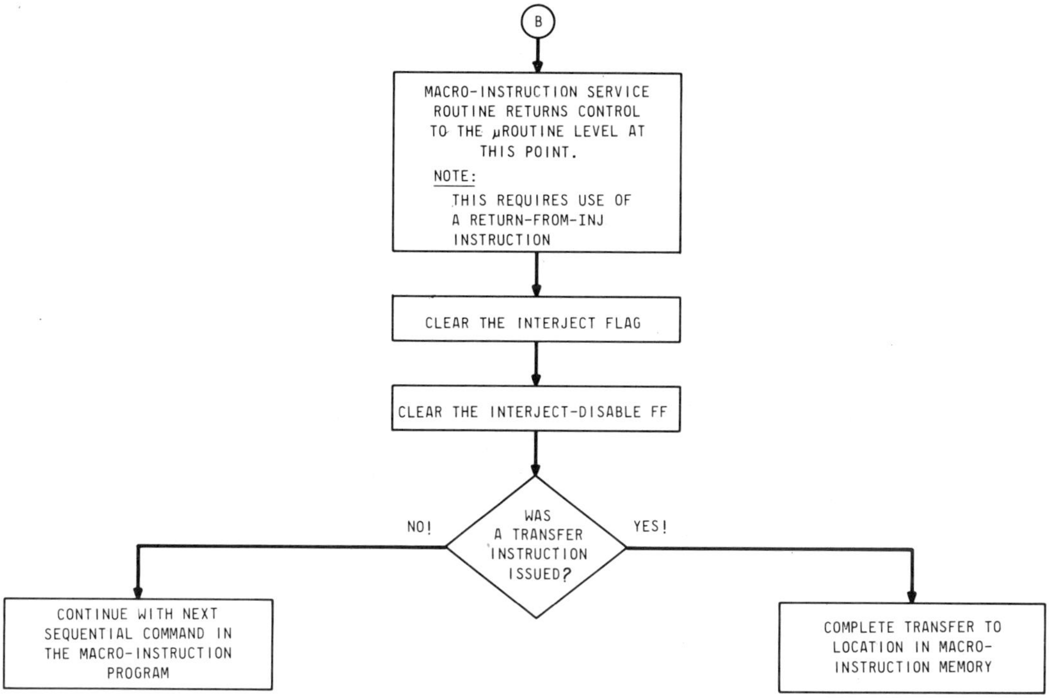

8-8 (*cont.*)

initiated group. In place of referencing one or more ROM locations, the lower-order bits in a hardware register will be set, depending on whether hardware or software has requested the interject. The address determined by this operation will transfer control to a location in microstore that handles the interject identification sequence and, once the interjecting device is established, this routine will transfer control to a macro-instruction device handler. This operation is very similar to that detailed in Figure 8-6. However, the additional hardware features allow a slightly faster transfer of control at the microcode level. Figure 8-7 gives a block diagram of such an interject arrangement, and Figure 8-8 presents the corresponding flow chart that describes the overall control mechanism. The Bell System No. 1A ESS interject mechanism is implemented in the manner just described. If a transfer is to be performed, the programmer can specify as an option on the branch command statement that the INTERJECT flag is to be sampled. If the INTERJECT flag is set and the transfer command specifies that it is to be tested, a branch will be taken to an interject service routine. The procedure is identical to that outlined previously. Using this procedure, the context or state of the system does not have to be saved when an interject request is recognized by the processor. Consequently, the contents of key registers within the machine do not have to be saved and then restored at a later time—which is the case in an interrupt-driven environment. The primary advantage of the interject in the heavy real-time environment of electronic switching is that the interrupt mechanism may be abandoned and replaced by direct polling of the device environment.

All these comments apply equally well at the microprocessor level. The primary consideration in the incorporation of an interject mechanism simply becomes real time. For non-switching-related applications, the program interrupt facility has proven cost-effective and of minimal complexity.

8.3 THE INTERRUPT MECHANISM

8.3.1 The Concept of Program Interruption

An organization of techniques has gradually emerged for performing programmed I/O. This organization is given in Table 8-3, which begins with the polling system and interject facility discussed in the previous section, and then proceeds from an *imprecise interrupt* through several intermediate levels of interruption to the *hard interrupt*. The table is organized by increasingly faster response rates. The polling sequence represents the slowest form of programmed I/O, while the hard interrupt represents the fastest

TABLE 8-3 Hierarchy of Programmed-I/O Behavior*

Polling system	The processor sequentially interrogates each peripheral device to determine if it is ready to engage in an I/O transaction. It does this by executing I/O instructions to test each device READY flag.
Interject system	This is a form of program-scheduled I/O. An external device sets the INTERJECT flag, which, in turn, is scanned periodically by the system software to see if an interject request has been made. If an interject request has been made, control is directed to a polling sequence that identifies the interjecting device and attempts to service it.
Imprecise interrupt	(Term coined by IBM.) When an interrupt request occurs, it is placed in a pushdown stack in memory. The stack is automatically administered by the system-executive and will ultimately empty out to the level of the interrupt request. The interrupt will then be identified and serviced at that time. Note that the exact point at which the interrupt will be serviced is indeterminate; it is a function of the load on the system and how rapidly items are popped off the stack.
Interwrite interrupt	Two or more machines share common memory. One machine wants to write in the memory area currently used by another machine. The first machine issues an interrupt to interleave data in the second machine's memory area.
Soft interrupt	(This term, used by the Burroughs Corporation, describes the B1700 interrupt facility.) A soft interrupt is an interrupt that is recognized by firmware; no specific rules are supplied for handling the interrupt. The precise response of the system is left to the programmer and the programmer's microcode.
Polite interrupt	The interrupt request permits the instruction to go to completion and then the processor is directed to service the interrupt. This includes long microcode sequences that interpret a specific macroinstruction.
Hard interrupt	A break in the instruction sequence is forced by the interrupt hardware; the current instruction is not permitted to complete execution, and the original control sequence cannot be reconstructed. This mechanism is used primarily for preemptive maintenance functions.

*This organization suggested by F. F. Taylor of Bell Labs.

form. In a sense, with the rapid advances in technology, each indicated form of programmed I/O has migrated downward from the large-scale machine structures and has been either implemented or considered for implementation on selected small-scale machines. In particular, the interrupt hierarchy found at the maxicomputer level has been found in a similar form in the sophisticated minicomputer structures marketed by several manufacturers.

What, then, is an interrupt? Its usage is almost universal, and many microprocessor structures employ an interrupt facility as a standard feature. An interrupt may be defined in the following manner:

1. It is a hardware-generated signal supplied to the CPU indicating that an event which is external to the currently executing program has occurred and requires immediate attention by the CPU.
2. The hardware signal occurs asynchronously with respect to the in-line execution sequence of the main program. The interrupt request may occur at any time, and its occurrence is not under control of the program sequence.
3. The interrupt hardware, provided that it is enabled, permits the CPU to complete the execution of the current instruction in the processor and then forces control to branch to a subroutine that services the interrupt.
4. A special return-from-interrupt instruction is normally employed to direct control back to the point in the main program sequence at which the interrupt occurred.

The difference between an interrupt and a *trap* is not always clear. For instance, traps have been defined by several manufacturers as stimuli that have been produced internally to the CPU, while interrupts are signals that originate externally to the processor. The real-time clock mechanism would be termed a *trap* by this definition, in contrast to a service request from an I/O device, which would be regarded as an interrupt. The system response to both is identical; that is, the CPU is directed to branch from its current program sequence and execute at least one instruction located in a fixed area of memory. This instruction could be a jump to a subroutine or a specialized instruction that is inserted in the normal program sequence. It is this latter interpretation that will form the definition of a trap in any discussions that follow. No distinction will be made between internally and externally generated interrupts. Consequently, a *trap* may be defined as a modification of the definition for the interrupt mechanism:

1. It is a request made to the CPU as a result of in-line code execution. A trap does not occur asynchronously with respect to the main program sequence. It is a direct result of executing a portion of that program sequence, and it will occur at the same point in that program sequence each time the main program is executed.
2. In all other respects, a trap is identical to an interrupt and is administered in the same way.
3. Some machines, such as those found in the PDP-11 family, employ a separate *return-from-trap* (*RTT*) *command* to return control to the main program.

The best example of a trap facility is found in the use of an operating system used to perform I/O operations. In such an environment, I/O is considered a privileged function that only the supervisory program may perform. A user program must make a request of the supervisory program to schedule an I/O transaction with an external device. The user program makes this request by executing an interrupt-producing machine instruction that is called a *supervisory call* or an *SVC*. An alternative expression often encountered is an *I/O trap operation* or, more simply, an *IOT*. The use of traps can provide a highly sophisticated programming environment for the user of a small-scale computer. For instance, the equivalent of a new instruction may be added to the processor repertoire by causing the processor to execute an opcode that is not implemented. The decoding logic is wired to detect this opcode and forces an interrupt to a service routine located in main storage. The function of the service routine is to interpret the "new" command using standard macroinstructions. When the interpretation is complete, the service routine executes an RTT instruction and returns control to the main program at the point following the new opcode. The process will be repeated each time the new opcode is encountered in a program sequence. It is a software-generated operation that is transparent to the user. Unless the user examines how the machine executes the new opcode, the new opcode cannot be distinguished from an opcode in the standard instruction set that has been realized in hardware.

An interrupt can be regarded simply as a subroutine call that has been invoked explicitly by a hardware condition. At the conclusion of the current machine instruction execution, control is forced to branch to a service routine that identifies the interrupting device and provides the proper response. To perform such a hardware-initiated subroutine branch, the CPU must save certain items of linkage information that will ultimately permit control to be returned to the interrupted program. The primary characteristic of an interrupt environment is the randomness of the interrupt requests that will normally occur. Since the processor cannot predict what state it will be in when an interrupt request is received, it must preserve the state of the CPU just prior to the recognition of the request by the hardware interrupt mechanism. This status information is also called the *context of the machine prior to interruption*. Saving this status information is called *context switching* and its goal is to preserve all the information relevant to an executing program so that an interrupt will appear transparent to the program. The response time between the occurrence of the interrupt signal and the start of the first useful instruction that handles that specific interrupt can be used as a measure of the effectiveness of the interrupt facility.

In an *automatic interrupt system*, the processor responds immediately to external or internal requests to handle unexpected conditions. When a system contains many peripheral devices, events may occur frequently that dictate the priority of the task that the processor must perform. When several interrupts present themselves at the same time, the processor must determine which request should be serviced first, based upon the importance of the event causing the interrupt. The decision-making and ordering facilities that perform this function are usually referred to as the *priority interrupt system*. Consequently, the automatic interrupt mechanism must perform the following functions in a manner that efficiently uses real time as it relates to the specific application of the machine.

1. The interrupt must be recognized by the CPU and execution suspended in the currently executing program.
2. The context of the machine must be saved so that control may be returned to the interrupted program.
3. The highest-priority device requesting an interrupt must be identified.
4. Control must be directed to begin execution at the starting address of the interrupt service routine associated with the device above.

In particular, the interrupt facility of a small computer may be classified by the number of these functions that have been placed in hardware and those relegated to software. The more that are implemented in hardware, the faster the response will be to an interrupt request.

8.3.2 The Single-Level Interrupt Facility

The basic structure from which all other hardware interrupt facilities are modeled is the *single-level interrupt* system. Normally, the single-level scheme assigns two dedicated consecutive locations in main storage to be administered by the interrupt hardware. The first location stores the address of the next instruction to be executed in the interrupted program, while the second location contains an instruction that branches control to an interrupt service routine. When an interrupt occurs, the hardware automatically stores the contents of the PC in the first location and directs execution to begin at the following location. This transfers control to the interrupt service routine. The PDP-8 interrupt facility uses locations 0 and 1 of field 0 in this manner. An alternative implementation of this single-level arrangement treats the contents of the second dedicated location as an indirect address. When an interrupt occurs, the hardware still saves the contents of the PC in the first location, but execution is forced by the interrupt hardware to branch to the address specified by the contents of the second storage location.

Typically, in such a single-level structure, all the interrupt signals from the various I/O devices are multipled together to form a single line that is physically brought into the processor (see Figure 8-9). Two bits are used by the interrupt hardware to control the operation of the single-level interrupt mechanism. The *interrupt request bit* registers the appearance of an interrupt. The *interrupt mask bit* disables the

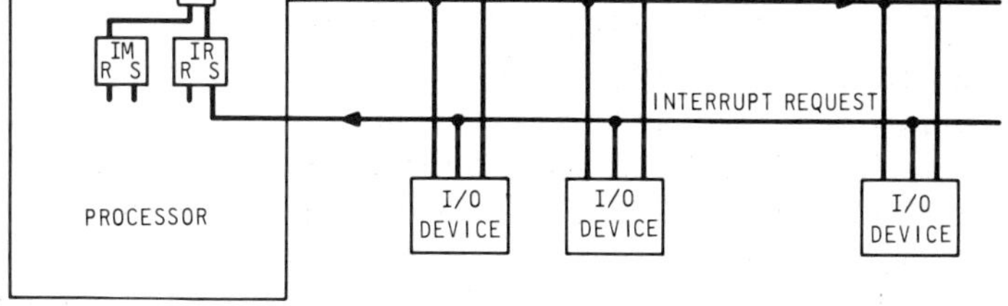

8-9 Single-level interrupt line facility with multisources

request bit from signaling the CPU that an interrupt request has been made. An interrupt request will be passed to the processor only if the request bit has been set *and* the mask bit is in the set state.

One or more of the devices shown in Figure 8-9 may be active simultaneously, but the processor will respond only to the highest-priority device that is requesting service. The mask bit blocks the effect of other interrupt requests once the CPU begins servicing an interrupt. If these additional interrupts are not blocked after the interrupt request is recognized, the service routine will be interrupted again. This process will overwrite the linkage information stored in the dedicated locations associated with the interrupt mechanism. Furthermore, if the internal registers of the processor are saved in the same area of main storage by the interrupt service routine for each interrupt that occurs, the previous values of those registers will also be overwritten when the interrupt subroutine is again invoked by a new interrupt. The simplest way to resolve this situation is by using two machine instructions. The first instruction would turn the interrupt mechanism off; the second instruction would enable the interrupt facility. The interrupt-off command would have to be the first executable instruction in the interrupt service routine since once execution has begun, the interrupt facility would be disabled until the system became ready to handle a new interrupt. At that point, the interrupt-on command would be executed by the processor and the interrupt mechanism reenabled. The fundamental drawback of this scheme is the assumption that the service routine will always be entered and the interrupt-off instruction encountered before another interrupt request is made. In an arbitrary real-time environment, the random nature of interrupts precludes this assumption. Consequently, it is always possible to configure a single-level interrupt environment so that a new interrupt request could be presented to the processor prior to the execution of the interrupt-off instruction associated with servicing the previous interrupt. In this case, the previous contents of the PC, stored in one of the dedicated locations associated with the interrupt, would be automatically overwritten with the current contents of the PC, destroying the linkage information required by the processor to return control to the previously interrupted program. This is the problem with repeated automatic interruption.

To circumvent this situation, the hardware-interrupt mechanism of most machines automatically disables the interrupt facility from further recognition of interrupt requests. The facility is disabled by the interrupt hardware immediately upon recognition of an interrupt request. The interrupt mechanism can only be reenabled by the execution of an interrupt-on instruction. For a typical single-level system, this instruction will not be encountered by the CPU until the interrupt service routine has completed its operations. Unfortunately, the restoration of control to the interrupted program cannot be guaranteed by simply executing the interrupt-on command. If this command is allowed to take effect immediately, any interrupt that has been queued by the interrupt-disable logic will automatically interrupt the service routine and overwrite the return information. Note that this situation may occur any time control is about to be directed back to the interrupted program. A pending interrupt will always overwrite the return information from the previous interrupt unless the effect of the interrupt-on command is deferred to permit control to be returned to the interrupted program.

The solution to this situation has been to delay the effect of the interrupt-on instruction until one additional command has been executed by the CPU. Typically, this command is a branch instruction that returns control to the interrupted program. This allows at least one additional instruction to be executed in the previously interrupted program before a new interrupt request is recognized by the CPU. Consequently, the linkage information from any interrupt is not destroyed by the immediate servicing of a second pending interrupt. Figure 8-10 illustrates this situation.

The interrupt-off instruction can play an important role in masking interrupts when that masking is done under program control. In various applications, situations may occur in which the processor cannot afford the real time to service interrupts. For such cases, the interrupt-off instruction disables the interrupt hardware until the program reenables the facility by executing an interrupt-on instruction. In effect, the interrupt-off instruction masks out all further interrupts until the system is able to administer them again. The interrupt-off instruction disables the entire interrupt facility but does not cancel any previously serviced requests generated by external devices. That is, once a device has requested an interrupt and has been serviced, it must be prevented from repeatedly interrupting the processor since the original request was never reset in the requesting device. This is the area of interrupt request cancellation that must be handled either automatically by the hardware or the interrupt service routine. Typically, for a single-level interrupt facility, separate I/O instructions are used to clear the INTERRUPT REQUEST flag in individual devices. If the appropriate instruction is not issued to cancel the proper device interrupt flag, that device will continue to interrupt the processor even though its interrupt request was serviced previously.

To achieve effective interrupt cancellation, each device capable of generating a processor interrupt makes use of two flags. The first is the device READY flag discussed in Section 8.2.1; the second is the INTERRUPT ENABLE flag. An interrupt can be generated by the device only if its device flag is set *and* its associated INTERRUPT ENABLE flag is also set. Interrupt cancellation is affected by the CPU executing an I/O instruction that resets the device flag. If the INTERRUPT ENABLE flag is reset by the CPU, the device will not interrupt the processor again until the ENABLE flag has been placed in the set state by another processor I/O instruction. The individual device INTERRUPT ENABLE flags are separate control flip-flops, external to the processor, that act independently of the processor INTERRUPT MASK flip-flop. The INTERRUPT MASK flag, as mentioned earlier, is internal to the CPU and is used by the processor to mask out the effect of all interrupts until the program can administer them properly in real time. The INTERRUPT MASK flag may be set or cleared under program control. Thus, not only must the device flag be cleared to cancel the effect of the immediate interrupt from the device, but the INTERRUPT ENABLE flag must be cleared if future interrupts are to be inhibited from the device (that is, if no further interrupts are to be recognized by the CPU from that specific device).

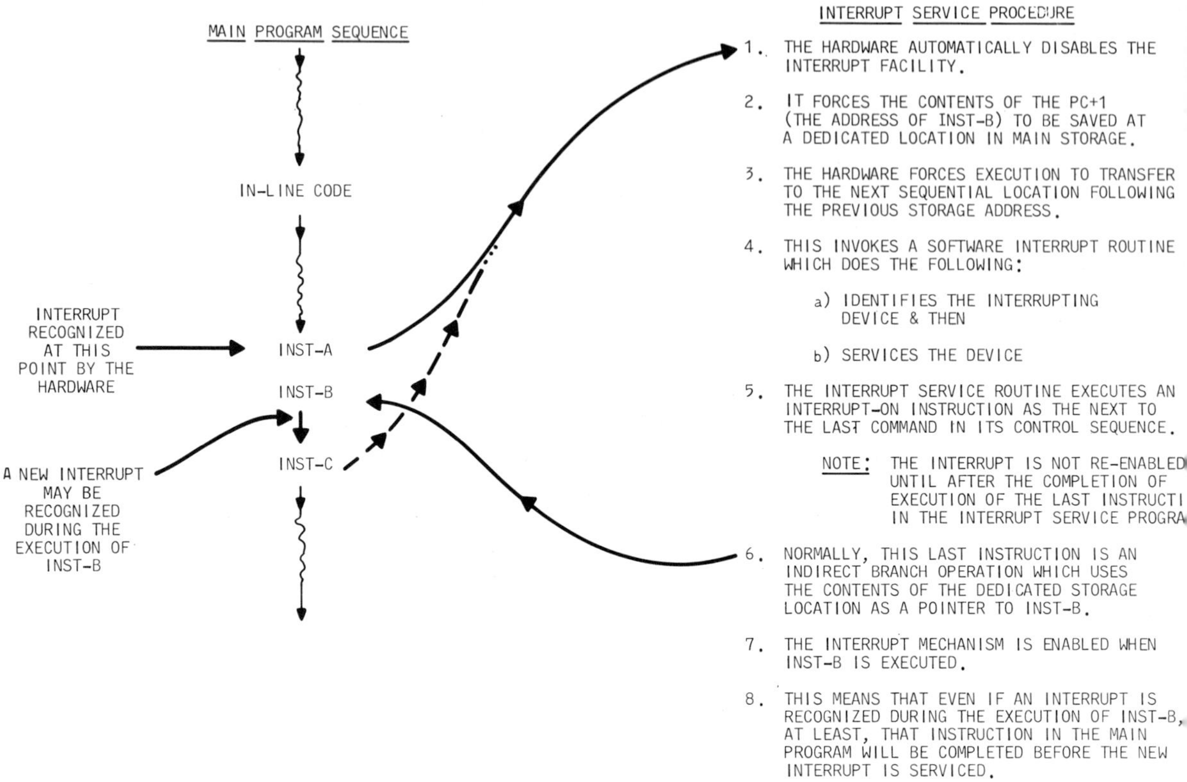

8-10 Automatic hardware control of the interrupt mechanism

The procedure to identify the device that has produced the interrupt is directly analogous to the polling method or SKIP chain described in Section 8.2.1 for use with an interject. The basic identification method is strictly software-oriented. In this case, as with the interject, the recognition of an interrupt request forces the processor to enter a subroutine that immediately begins polling the external devices to determine the highest-priority device requesting an interrupt. Placing the test of a given device flag in the polling sequence determines the priority of the device in the single-level interrupt system, exclusively. Typically, those devices requiring a high response speed by the CPU are located near the top of the polling sequence. If low-speed devices are intermixed with high-speed devices, they may be serviced later in the polling sequence. Normally, the interrupt system would be turned on immediately after the most recent interrupt was serviced. Assuming that this interrupt was generated by a high-speed device, the CPU will not have canceled any interrupt requests from lower-speed devices. Under most circumstances, any lower-speed device requesting attention will immediately interrupt the processor again and obtain service. However, reenabling the interrupt facility does not guarantee that the low-speed device with a request pending will be serviced. A device with a higher priority could interrupt the processor once the interrupt facility was again activated. Since a polling sequence is used to identify the interrupting device, the interrupt service routine would start at the top of the polling sequence and work its way down to the interrupting device, which would still not be the low-speed device. It is possible for service to be deferred to the low-speed device for an indefinite period of time under these circumstances, even to the point at which the service request made by the device is compromised because of the latency of the processor to respond to the request.

The alternative approach to handling this simple, single-level interrupt constraint is *not* to reenable the interrupt facility until the entire polling sequence has been negotiated by the processor. Thus, those devices that issue concurrent interrupt requests would be serviced as they are encountered in the polling sequence and would not be deferred to another cycle of interrupt operation. However, this means that high-speed devices would not be serviced immediately upon request. Instead, they would be deferred to the next cycle of interrupt operation if they did not generate an interrupt until the processor was past the point in the polling sequence where the CPU tested their respective device flags. In many applications, this delay could be intolerable. The exact philosophy to be used in the interrupt service routine, as to when the interrupt facility should be reenabled, is a function of the application requirements. Ultimately, it is the system designer who must examine the response requirements of the individual interrupting devices and determine what approach is most appropriate.

In general, the primary disadvantage of this method is the number of instructions that must be executed to identify the interrupting device and the corresponding real time required to proceed through the polling sequence. To eliminate this disadvantage, a hardware technique for identifying the interrupting device has been employed, which essentially provides an automatic polling sequence for device resolution.

8.3.3 Hardware Polling for Interrupt Identification

In hardware polling, the processor and its external set of devices are physically interconnected in such a manner that the CPU may interrogate the devices automatically in order to obtain the address of the interrupting unit. This is accomplished by the physical arrangement shown in Figure 8-11. When the processor is ready to honor the interrupt-request signal, the control sequence automatically sends an *acknowledge signal* (*ACK*) to the I/O devices on a wire that is *daisy-chained* from device to device. Each device interconnection is analogous to a link in a chain. As the signal moves down the chain, it interrogates each device to determine if the device is active (the device flag is set *and* the INTERRUPT ENABLE flag is set). If the device is not in the active state, the ACK signal is permitted to continue to the next device in the chain until the first active device is recognized. When this happens, the active device captures the ACK signal and prevents it from propagating farther down the chain. The active unit then gates a preassigned address onto the data bus, together with a timing pulse (SYN) that is used to inform the processor that the address associated with the

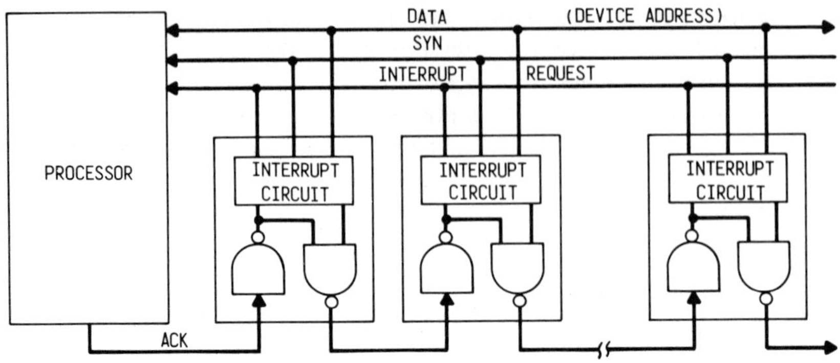

8-11 Hardware polling for interrupt identification

highest-priority device requesting an interrupt is on the bus. The SYN signal shown in Figure 8-12a functions as a synchronizing signal for the processor during an interrupt operation. Typically, this address is the first location in main storage of the service routine specifically associated with the interrupting device. Figure 8-12b illustrates the timing sequence involved in implementing the hardware polling feature.

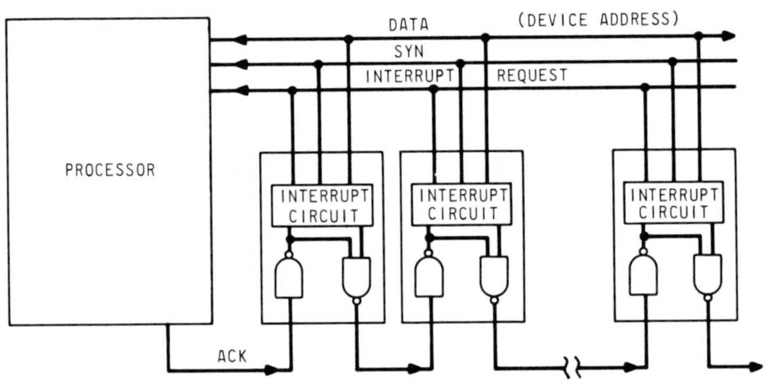

(a) HARDWARE POLLING FOR INTERRUPT

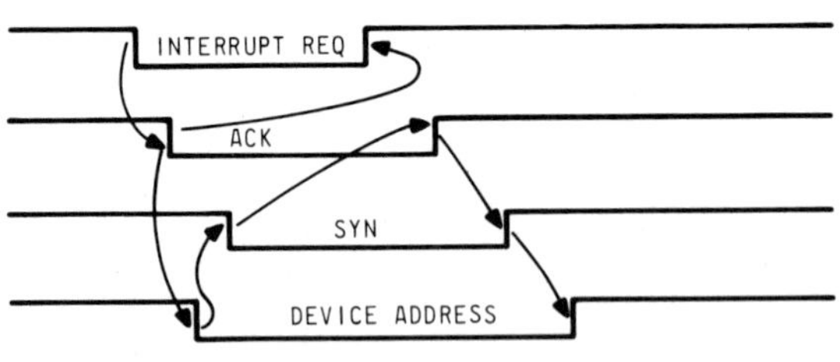

(b) HARDWARE POLLING TIMING DIAGRAM

8-12 Hardware polling timing diagram

On several machines, the address returned by this handshaking procedure is actually an index that is added to the contents of a preassigned processor register. The processor register acts as a base address, and the index points to a full memory word that is treated as an indirect address by the interrupt hardware. This permits a table of INTERRUPT VECTOR addresses to be located anywhere in main storage, as opposed to a fixed area of low core. Each device has a unique index into the table. The address found at the table location pointed to by the index vectors the processor to the appropriate device service routine. Changing the contents of the processor register simply relocates the table but does not change any of the indices into the INTERRUPT VECTOR address table. The Data General Nova uses this technique of automatic hardware polling for interrupt identification to obtain an index from the highest-priority device requesting an interrupt. In a daisy-chain structure, the highest-priority device will be the physical device that is electrically closest to the processor (i.e., the device that is physically connected first in the daisy chain). The Nova accepts the index and adds it to the contents of one of its preselected accumulators to obtain the necessary entry address into the interrupt vector table.

The address to be returned by an interrupting device may be hard-wired to the interface board associated with the device. It may be set using thumb switches placed on the board so that the address returned may be varied by the user, or the address may be determined by the physical slot into which the interface board is inserted in the mainframe. In the latter case, each connector slot is assigned a fixed address that will be used by whatever interrupting device is plugged into that slot. The slots are assigned in a fixed priority sequence. If the priority of an interrupting device is to be raised in this configuration, its interface card must be removed from its current connector assignment and physically relocated to a higher-priority connector location. This relocation involves interchanging both the interface board and cable associated with the device currently occupying the higher-priority connector slot. This scheme requires that there be no vacant slot between the start of the connector chain and the last device in the chain. However, the last device in the chain may occupy a connector slot that is located before the last physical I/O connector slot. In this case, the chain of connector-slot linkages is terminated with a stub to observe the proper transmission-line characteristics of the hardware priority chain. This technique has been used in implementing the interrupt facility on the HP 2100 minicomputer.

While there may be several active devices requesting an interrupt at the same time, the hardware polling scheme provides a rapid mechanism for identifying the highest-priority device demanding service. It does away with the time-consuming process of using a software polling sequence and permits a large number of devices to be connected to the CPU on the same interrupt line. The primary drawback associated with this technique is the logic delay experienced by the ACK signal as it proceeds down the daisy chain. As the number of devices attached to the interrupt line increases, the number of gate delays experienced by the ACK signal also increases. However, the total response of the system to identifying the interrupting device and obtaining the starting address of its service routine is still *much* less than the time required for an equivalent software polling sequence.

8.3.4 The Multilevel Priority Interrupt Facility

The multilevel priority interrupt mechanism makes use of two registers to service interrupts. They are called the *interrupt request (IR) register* and the *interrupt mask (IM) register*. For each bit in the IR, there is a corresponding bit in the IM. Each bit in the IR is dedicated to a specific device. This is the *basic distinction* between the single-level interrupt mechanism and a multilevel priority interrupt structure: the single-level interrupt facility has only *one* external interrupt request lead connecting the processor to its external environment while the multilevel arrangement has a separate external request lead dedicated to each I/O device. Consequently, there is no need for the processor to interrogate the individual I/O devices to identify the highest-priority device requesting service. Each bit in the IR has a preassigned priority level. Typically, the most significant bit represents the highest-priority device in the system, with decreasing priorities assigned to the intervening bit positions. The processor, starting from the most significant end, will scan the IR, looking for the highest-priority device requesting service. The processor begins this scan after an interrupt has occurred and control has been directed to the interrupt service routine by the hardware. The bit-scanning operation eliminates the execution of I/O instructions, which normally take longer than an internal machine operation. This removes the need for the CPU to poll its external devices to determine the interrupting device and, consequently, saves real time.

Figure 8-13 illustrates a multi-level priority interrupt facility. Note that there are separate set inputs on each of the IR bits that come from the external environment. A device will interrupt the processor only if its corresponding bit in the IR has been set and the associated bit in the IM is also reset. If the IM bit is in the set state, the effect of the interrupt request recorded in the IR will be masked out. In addition, Figure 8-13 shows an *interrupt-disable (INH) flip-flop* that will override the IM and block all interrupts from being recognized by the processor.

The complete operation of this multi-level priority structure uses two additional concepts to form a viable interrupt environment. The first concept is a dynamic hardware priority scheme that determines the priority assignment of each device capable of requesting an interrupt. This technique becomes significant when more than one bit is set in the IR (i.e., multiple interrupt requests have been generated concurrently). Once a particular device interrupt service routine has begun, all interrupts from lower-priority devices must be delayed while all interrupts originating from higher-priority devices must be allowed to interrupt the processor. This feature of having the CPU permit a higher-priority request to interrupt the service routine of a lower-priority device, but not vice versa, is called *nesting*.

The effect nesting has on a normal program sequence is shown in Figure 8-14. Note that the main program runs at the lowest priority level (priority = 5). The normal program sequence is interrupted at T1 by a level-4 priority interrupt request. The level-4 priority service routine continues until T3, at which time a level-3 request preempts further execution by the level-4 routine. Similarly, the level-3 priority service routine is preempted by a level-2 priority interrupt request at T4. However, in this

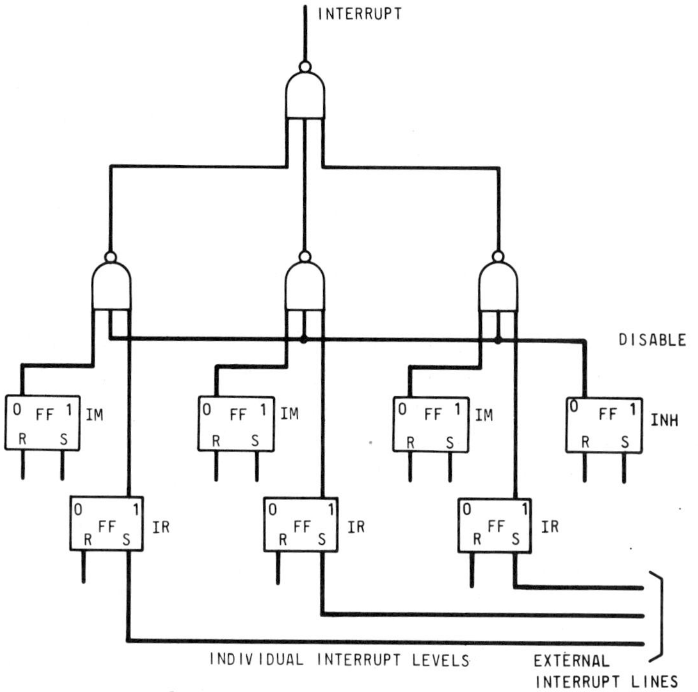

8-13 Multilevel priority interrupt facility

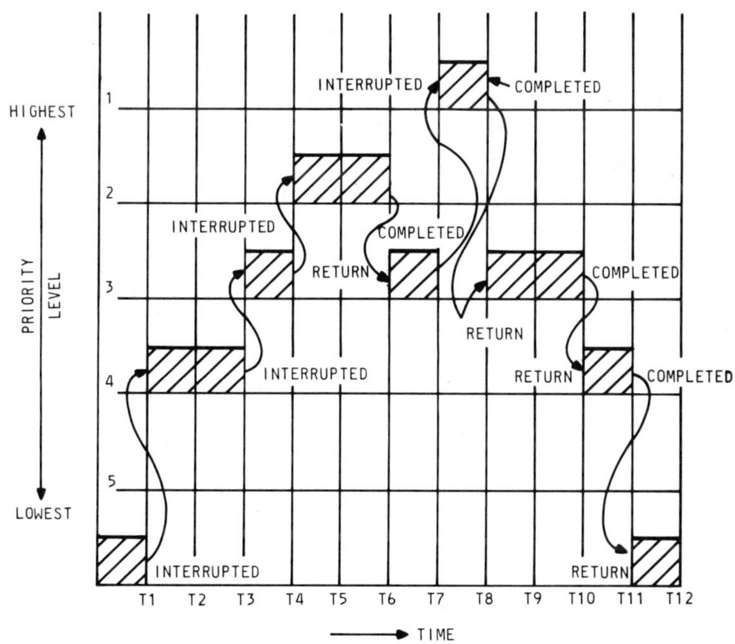

8-14 Interrupt nesting from a real-time viewpoint

interrupt routine, the level-2 service program is able to finish since no higher-priority interrupt requests are experienced by the CPU. Control is returned to the level-3 priority routine at T6, but the level-3 program is interrupted by a level-1 priority interrupt request at T7. The level-1 priority routine is allowed to execute to completion uninterrupted since it operates at the highest interrupt-priority level. When the level-1 priority routine has completed, it returns control to the level-3 service program at T8. After unwinding and completing all interrupts, control is returned to the main program.

Nesting higher-priority interrupts is done by setting or clearing the mask bits in the IM. As mentioned earlier, associated with each interrupt-request bit is a mask bit. When it is set, the corresponding interrupt is delayed until the mask bit is reset. If an interrupt is "masked," the CPU will not experience that interrupt request until the associated mask bit is cleared. In other words, an interrupt that is masked is not placed in the pending state by the processor. The request from the interrupting device continues to set the appropriate bit in the IR, but the CPU is unaware of the request from the masked device.

Consequently, there is a unique mask for each interrupt level, and each mask is stored in a separate, dedicated location in main storage. When the processor begins servicing an interrupt, the service routine identifies the interrupting device and pulls the interrupt mask associated with the device out of main storage. This quantity is loaded in the IM and has the following characteristics. It contains 0's for all higher-priority interrupts and 1's for all interrupts of priority equal to or less than the current interrupt level. As a result, only the higher-priority interrupts are allowed to affect the CPU while the lower-order interrupts are withheld from influencing the processor. A major requirement of a processor initialization routine is the preloading of the IM with an appropriate mask so that the interrupt facility will behave in a meaningful manner as program execution progresses on the system. Note that it is the responsibility of the interrupt service routine associated with each priority level to load the IM with the proper mask *before* the request for that level is serviced.

The second concept used to form a viable interrupt environment is the use of an *interrupt vector* in main storage to direct execution to the proper priority-level service routine when an interrupt is recognized by the CPU. Typically, an interrupt vector will consist of two dedicated locations in memory. One location will contain the starting address of the service routine for the current priority level. The other location will contain an interrupt mask which the service routine will use to provide the appropriate nesting capability for the current priority level. There will be a unique interrupt vector associated with each bit position of the IR. The service routine *must* save the previous contents of the IM before it inserts the new interrupt mask in the IM. The service routine will restore the old interrupt mask to the IM at the completion of the current priority service routine before it returns control to the interrupted program.

The technique of determining the highest-priority device requesting an interrupt is illustrated in Figure 8-15. The processor scans each bit in the IR, starting from the most significant end. The corresponding bit in the IM is simultaneously examined. If

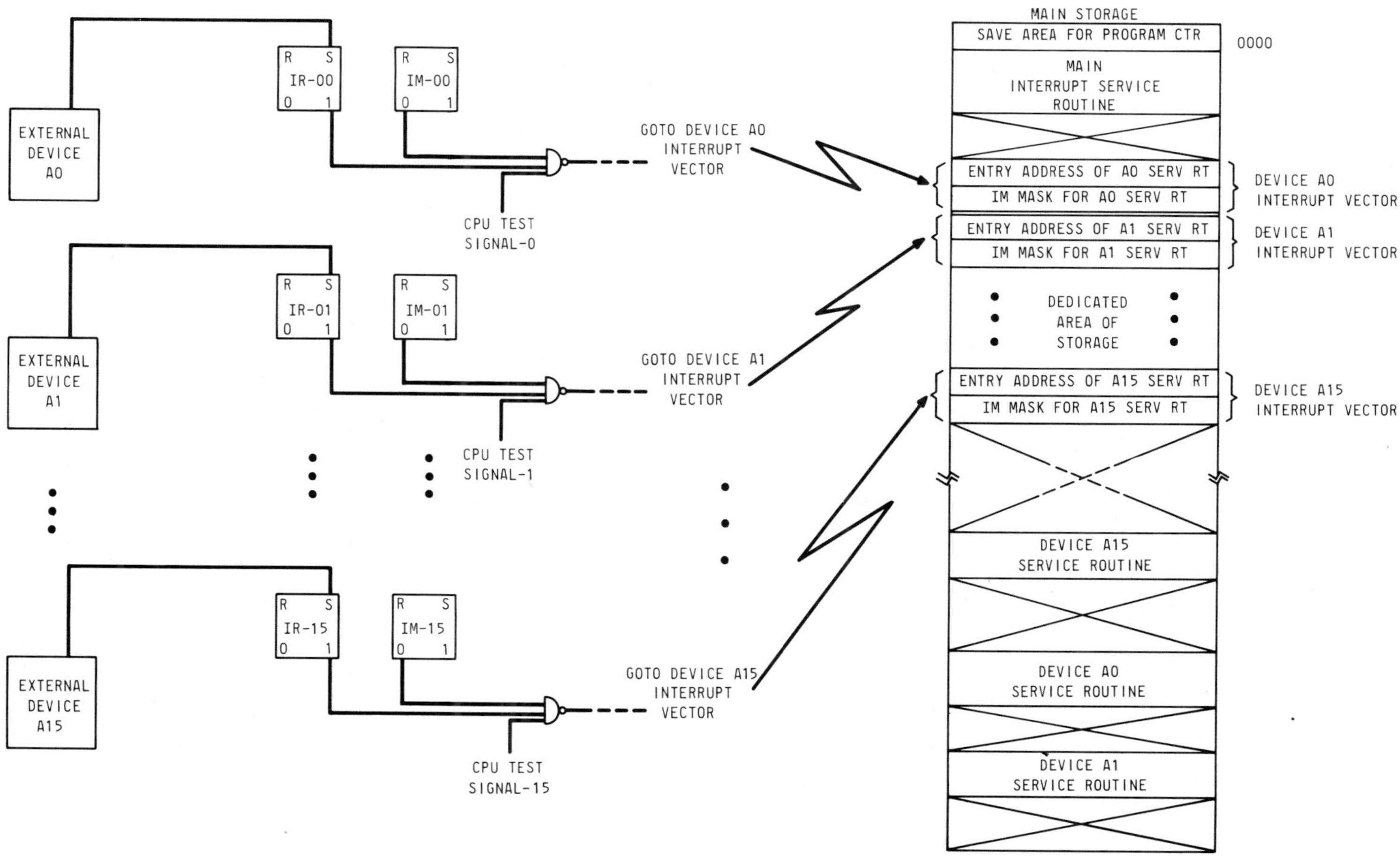

8-15 Derivation of multilevel priority interrupt vectors

the IM bit is in the 0 state *and* the associated IR bit is set, control is directed to branch through the appropriate interrupt vector to the proper priority service routine. This procedure is similar to program polling of the external devices except that no I/O instructions are executed. This reduces the real time needed to identify the interrupting device, since I/O instructions typically require more memory cycles for execution than an internal processor command.

The simplest form of the multilevel priority interrupt structure is a hardware mechanism in which an interrupt forces the processor to store the return address of the interrupted program in location 0000 of field 0. Figure 8-15 exhibits this scheme. Program execution will continue at location 0001 of field 0 after the return address has been saved in location 0000. Location 0001 represents the starting address of the interrupt service routine. The interrupt service routine scans the individual bits of the IR and IM to determine the interrupting device and uses this information to select the appropriate interrupt vector. Figure 8-15 shows the interrupt vectors stored as dedicated entries in a table found in the low address area of main storage. The interrupt service routine uses the selected interrupt vector to transfer control to the proper priority service routine.

The most severe disadvantage of this scheme is the time required to scan the individual bits of the IR and IM. If this scanning process could be automated so that the address of an interrupt vector could be generated automatically, the software complexity could be further reduced and the response of the processor to an interrupt request could be enhanced.

Instead of using individual instructions to scan the bits in the IR and IM, the priority identification and service routine address can be generated by hardware. This facility would direct execution to begin at the appropriate priority service routine almost immediately after an interrupt was recognized by the processor. Figure 8-16 illustrates a hardware priority structure for a multilevel interrupt facility. The highest priority is assigned to the rightmost bit position of the IR and is daisy-chained through all lower-priority logic gates that connect to the interrupt identifier mechanism. The

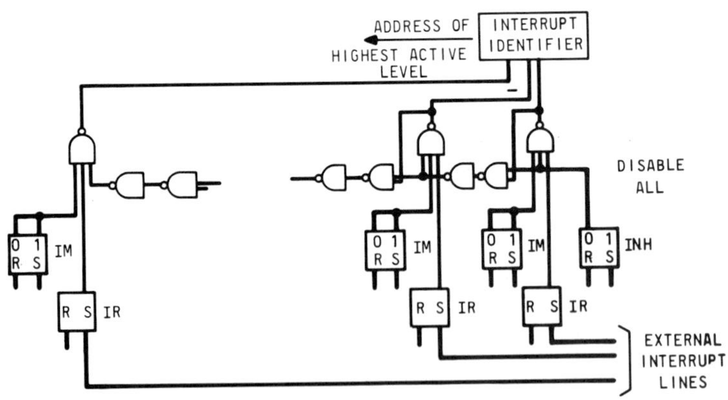

8-16 Hardware priority structure for a multilevel interrupt facility

most significant bit of the IR, which is in the set state (active), will disable all less significant bits from communicating with the interrupt identifier hardware. Consequently, only one output can be active at any given time after an interrupt has occurred, and the output in the set state farthest to the right in the IR will be selected as the highest-priority position requesting an interrupt. Each output is associated with an address that points directly to the priority service routine to be used for that device. Note that in this scheme, the IM is still scanned concurrently with the scan of the corresponding bits in the IR. Consequently, the IM remains in control of whatever devices will be permitted to interrupt the processor at a given point in time. The address vector supplied by the interrupt identifier logic is used by the processor to define the main storage location where the return address for the interrupted program will be saved. The following memory location will contain the first instruction of the priority service routine associated with the interrupting device. Figure 8-17 illustrates this situation. This convention forces execution to vector directly to the service routine for the identified priority interrupt. An alternative implementation is for the hardware to treat the contents of the location following the storage slot for the PC as an indirect address. This means that the priority service routine may be relocated anywhere in main memory; it is no longer required to follow the PC storage slot assigned to that priority level.

In general, the response time of a processor to an interrupt using a priority structure that employs hardware to generate the vector address of a priority service routine automatically is very quick. In addition, the software complexity of the interrupt service routine is kept to a minimum.

8.3.5 The Two-Dimensional Multilevel Priority Interrupt Facility

For many applications, a multilevel priority interrupt facility such as the one just described is entirely adequate. However, situations can be encountered in which the response time for a particular type of interrupt request can be sufficiently demanding that another level of hardware priority becomes necessary. That is, more than one I/O device may have to be connected to an external interrupt request level. An example of this situation occurs in large systems where many high-speed devices may be contending for interrupt service. Each of these devices, as well as certain important internal interrupts (i.e., the detection of power failure in the mainframe), requires an extremely rapid response time. In such cases, more than one I/O device or internal processor function may be assigned to a specific hardware interrupt level. The exact number of devices assigned to a given priority interrupt level would be determined by the peripheral devices that were being used. This arrangement, called a *two-dimensional multilevel priority interrupt facility*, is illustrated in Figure 8-18. It has been implemented on the modern small computer using the best features of the previous two interrupt schemes. In its simplest form, each interrupt level supplies an address when the level is queried by the processor. This address points to a location in main storage that contains the starting address of the priority-level service routine. The interrupt

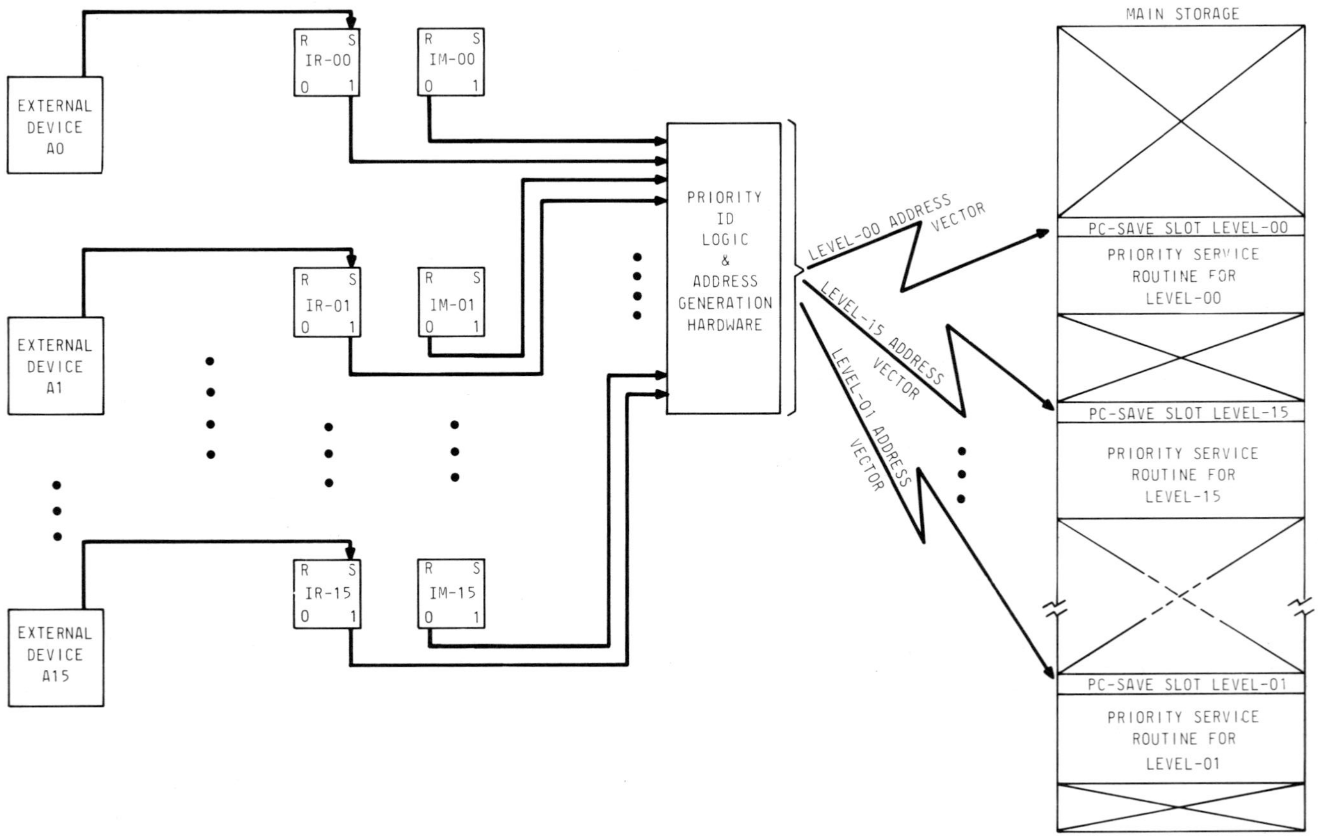

8-17 Multilevel interrupt structure with automatic vector address generation

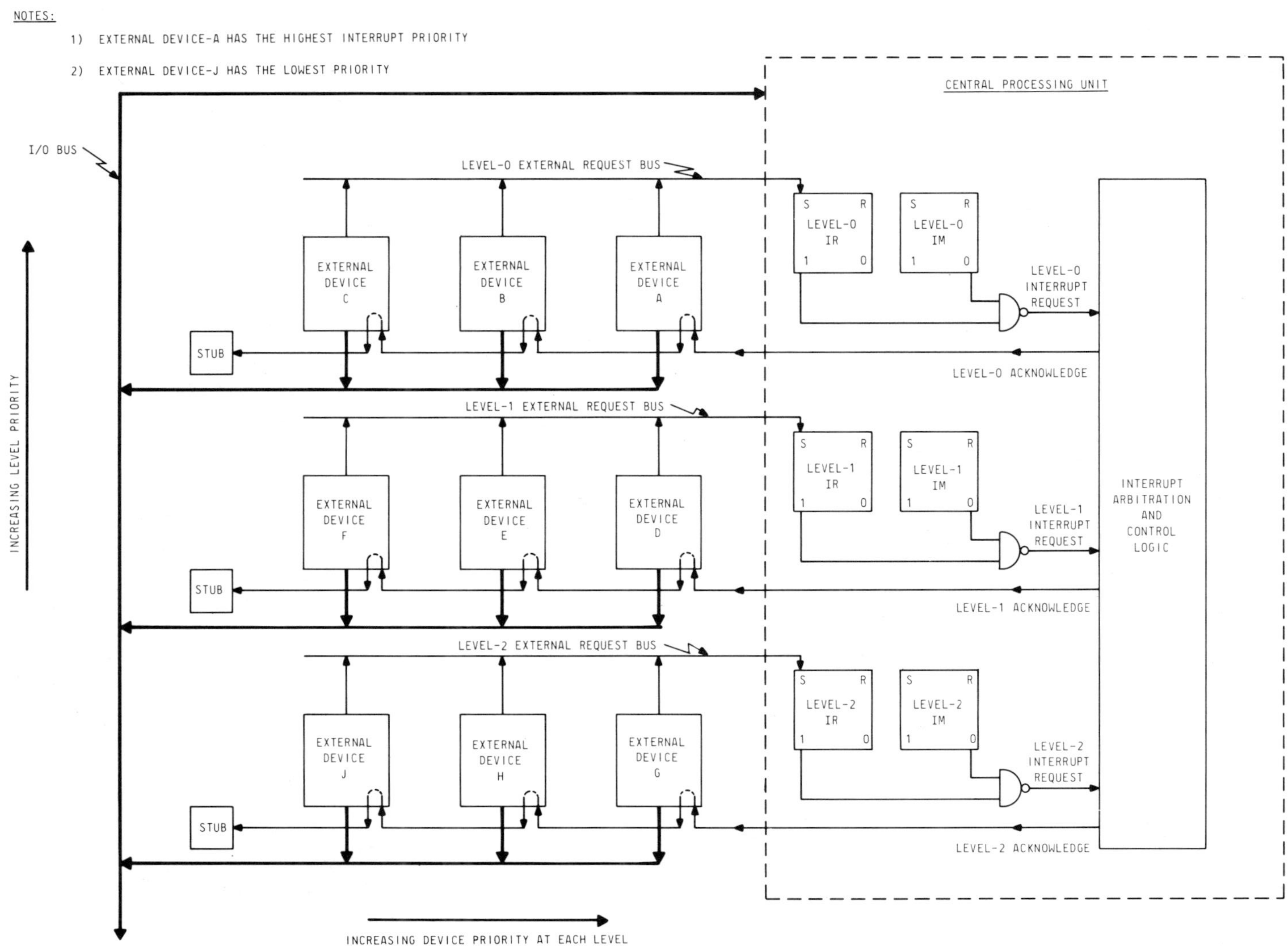

8-18 Two-dimensional multilevel priority interrupt configuration hardware uses the contents of the pointer address to transfer execution automatically to the priority service routine. It is the responsibility of this routine to poll the individual devices attached to this priority request level and identify the interrupting device. This is a software priority mechanism and is both slow and complicated.

Since the multilevel priority scheme is normally used to speed up the response time of the CPU to an interrupt request, the following two operations may be provided in hardware to obtain this goal:

1. Hardware polling of all devices connected to each interrupt level is automatically performed by the interrupt mechanism of the CPU. When the interrupt hardware recognizes an interrupt request, it responds by issuing an acknowledge ACK signal at that physical priority level. The ACK signal is daisy-chained through each device attached to that priority level. The highest-priority device requesting an interrupt at that priority level captures the ACK signal and blocks further propagation of the signal to lower-priority devices in the chain.

   Figure 8-18 illustrates this situation quite well. Note that there are three separate interrupt request leads (level 0, level 1, and level 2) that enter the interrupt arbitration and control logic. The interrupt-control hardware responds by issuing a single, physical interrupt ACK signal at the highest priority level requesting service. The ACK signal automatically forces the highest-priority device at that priority level to identify itself. The device does this by supplying an address to the CPU I/O bus and returning a handshaking signal to the processor to complete the device identification sequence.
2. The address provided by the highest-priority device requesting an interrupt automatically vectors execution to the device service routine; no software identification of devices is required. Typically, the first location in the device service routine will be used to store the return address of the interrupted program. The second location contains the first instruction of the service routine.

Note in Figure 8-18 that a mask bit is provided for each level of interrupt. However, individual devices at a given priority level may *not* be masked out. If the mask bit for a given level is set, interrupt requests from *all* devices connected to that level will be masked out. The only way to physically ignore requests from a single device at a given priority level is to clear the internal interrupt enable flip-flop of the device, which disables the device from issuing interrupt requests.

Interrupt administration using this two-dimensional multilevel priority scheme permits the automatic nesting of requests between priority levels. Servicing an interrupt at a given priority level will continue only until a higher-priority interrupt is experienced by the processor. The convention normally used to establish proper nesting on interrupts is to require that all interrupt levels of lower priority than the current interrupt level be masked out. In addition, the current level will also be masked out to permit only higher-priority interrupts to deflect the execution sequence. In such a situation, the main program is typically assigned the lowest priority in the system. It may be interrupted by all devices connected to the interrupt system. The highest-priority device, on the other hand, may *not* be interrupted by any other device.

Referring again to Figure 8-18, the hardware priority assigned to each physical interrupt level increases, as shown, from the bottom of the figure to the top. In turn, the physical priority of a device at a given interrupt level is determined by the placement of the device in the daisy chain. The closer a device is physically in the daisy chain to the processor, the higher the priority of the device at that interrupt level. Consequently, device priority increases from left to right, as shown. This makes external device A the highest-priority device (no other device may interrupt it). Device J is the lowest-priority device and may be interrupted by every other device but not the main program. This scheme forms a two-dimensional matrix with the placement of a device in the matrix determined by the interrupt-priority level to which the device is attached, and the relative priority of that device with respect to all other devices attached to its interrupt-priority level.

8.3.6 Dynamic Reallocation of Priority Assignments

In real-time applications, there may be a need to alter priorities to adapt to changing system constraints. Operations may be performed under normal operating conditions that consume real time but may be tolerated because the system interrupt load is low and the response time for the individual operations can still be met. However, as the interrupt load increases, the system will eventually reach a point of interrupt saturation, in which the system simply becomes incapable of responding to all interrupt requests. Interrupt saturation may be handled by the application engineer in one of three ways:

1. Ignore it, in which case the sanity of the system may be seriously compromised.
2. Obtain a new and more sophisticated interrupt facility. This must be installed in the host processor and can represent a sizable cash expenditure.
3. Ignore selected interrupts by having the system declare them noncritical during periods of interrupt saturation. Some information may be lost, but the basic sanity of the system will be preserved. The machine will still carry out its basic processing objective if this strategy is properly implemented.

The ability to dynamically change the priority of the interrupt levels is achieved through use of the IM register. When the system detects that interrupt saturation is being reached, the processor will simply load a new mask value into the IM. The new mask value will suppress all expendable interrupts during this period, but it will still allow critical interrupts to function. When the system detects that the saturation condition has passed, the processor will load a different mask into the IM. This new mask will permit both critical and noncritical interrupts to be active.

Another example of the dynamic reallocation of interrupt priorities occurs in a telephone electronic switching system (ESS). In an ESS, an error causes an interrupt request to be issued at the highest-priority maintenance level. *Maintenance*, in this context, refers to a structure of automatic analysis techniques that are invoked by the system to analyze any faults detected as call processing progresses. In this case, the interrupt request invokes a maintenance service program that attempts to diagnose the difficulty. All I/O interrupts are blocked while this diagnostic process is going on, since I/O interrupt requests occur at a lower-priority level than maintenance requests. It is possible for the system to miss critical I/O data, such as dialing information, if this situation persists. Consequently, after some initial processing, the maintenance program reassigns itself to an interrupt-priority level that is lower than that associated with I/O operations.

In this case, a dynamic allocation of priority is achieved by changing the IM. The maintenance program is physically permitted to accept interrupt requests at two separate levels. After processing is completed at the higher-priority level, the interrupt mask is changed to permit lower-priority requests to be active. The maintenance program does *not* have to terminate at the higher-priority level. It simply changes the contents of the IM to permit itself to execute at an interrupt-priority level below that of the I/O facility. Since, effectively, two levels of interrupt priority have been assigned to the same program, the program may dynamically select the priority level at which it wishes to continue operating. For example, one long interrupt program may be divided into two distinct segments. The first segment will execute at the higher-priority level until it elects to change its priority assignment, at which time it loads a new mask into the IM and continues processing. However, the new mask will permit lower-priority requests to interrupt it. Thus, the long interrupt program may still permit lower-priority routines to have a portion of the real time that it would normally use.

8.3.7 Interrupt Administration Using a Pushdown Stack

Each service routine that functions in either a single-level or multilevel priority interrupt environment is required to preserve all information that is essential to characterize the state of the machine at the time of interruption. If this information is not saved and then restored when execution is returned to the interrupted program, the program may be compromised. It is entirely possible that the data used by the interrupted program may be mutilated and the processing objective of the program destroyed. Normally, the information that needs to be saved when an interrupt occurs is as follows:

1. The return address at which execution should continue in the interrupted program.
2. The interrupt mask associated with the interrupted program (so that its priority assignment for nesting remains in effect).
3. The contents of processor registers that are used by the interrupted program as a workspace.

The nesting process used by a priority interrupt facility must be orderly. The same items are saved each time a higher-priority interrupt preempts a lower-priority interrupt. If, by convention, the same processor registers will always be saved each time an interrupt occurs, nesting results in stacking items 1 through 3 in main storage each time an interrupt service routine is itself interrupted. The appearance of this stack is shown in Figure 8-19a for a single interrupt. Figure 8-19b shows main storage for the first interrupt being preempted by a second. Similarly, Figure 8-19c shows main storage when a third interrupt has preempted the second. Nesting, consequently, builds a stack in main storage if the same area of memory is used to save the return information for each individual interrupt. For this particular example, three internal registers were assumed available for use by the processor. Each set of registers may clearly be seen in the memory stack used for nesting as well as the individual masks and return addresses needed by each interrupt level.

This memory arrangement is the LIFO buffer or hardware stack discussed in Section 4.3. It has several advantages when used with a priority interrupt facility. The advantages are as follows:

1. It can be built using very straightforward control logic. In its simplest form, processor instructions load each register in memory with the exception of the PC. All items are inserted or removed at the top of the stack (TOS).
2. A dedicated area of memory does not have to be assigned to each interrupt-priority level to preserve the state of the processor. The TOS is automatically used as the storage location of the next item of data to be saved on the stack.
3. If a hardware register is dedicated to act as a pointer to the TOS, an interrupt will automatically place the PC at the TOS and increment the register to point to the new location at the TOS.
4. When the interrupt service routine completes, it simply unloads the stack in the reverse order in which it was built. Just as each item that was added to the TOS automatically incremented the hardware stack pointer, each item removed from the stack automatically decrements it.

Typically, the register functioning as the TOS pointer will be a reversible up–down counter that is controlled by the interrupt hardware. Each time a new interrupt level is entered, the contents of the PC will automatically be placed in the location at the TOS and the counter will be incremented by 1. This allows the stack to build upward in main storage. Each new item, however, will require a separate instruction to place it on the stack. The details of this build procedure are discussed in Section 4.3. This process may be expedited if an instruction is provided to automatically load all the registers available to the user in consecutive locations at the TOS (see Section 8.3.9 for more details). Such an instruction will automatically increment the TOS pointer for each new register it places on the stack. Similarly, another instruction that automatically unloads the register set from consecutive locations at the TOS needs to be provided if the real-time overhead in this process is to be minimized. A *return-from-interrupt (RTI) instruction* will cause the TOS pointer to be decremented by 1 and the contents of the new TOS location placed in the program counter. Execution will then

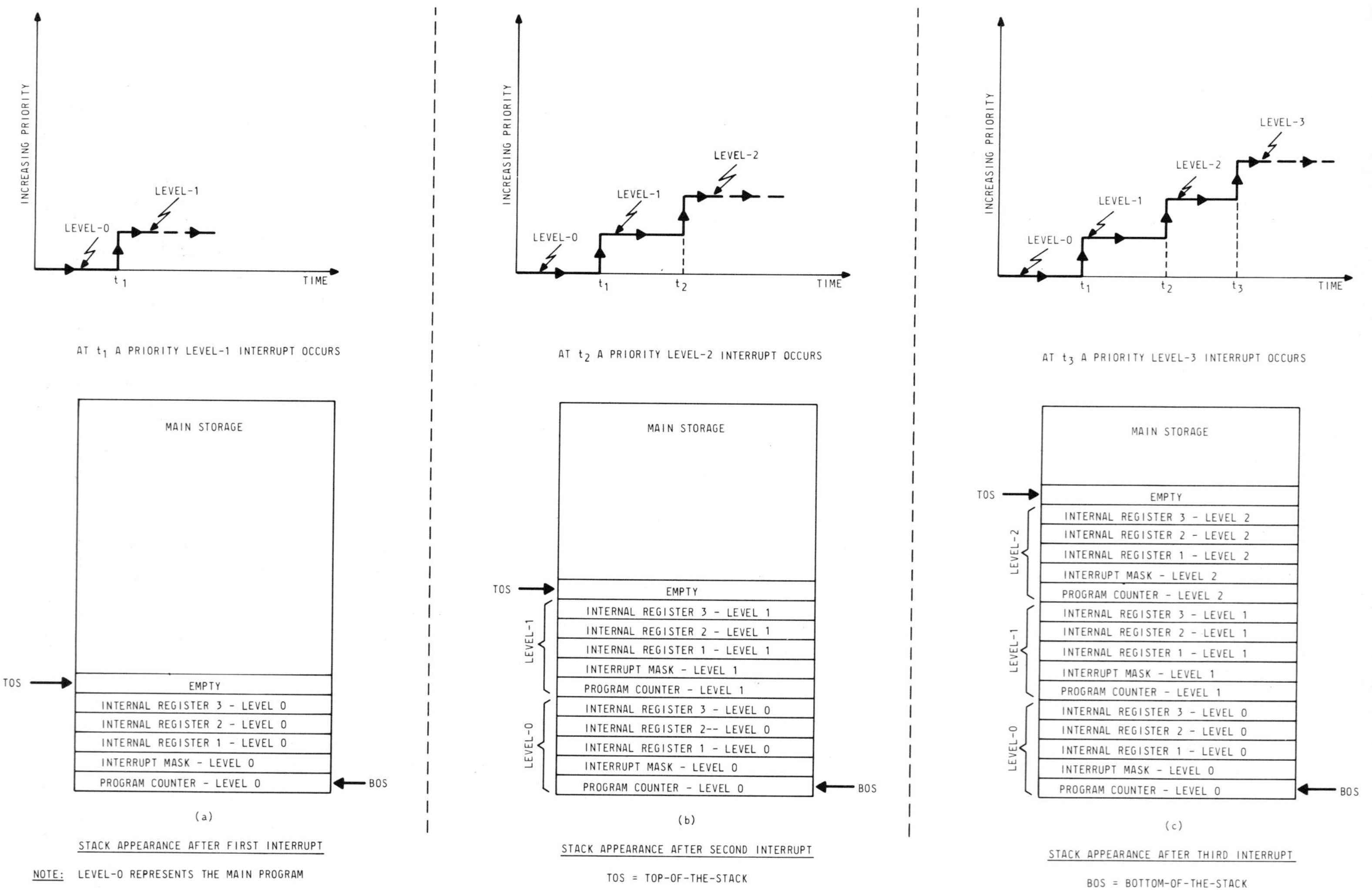

8-19 Stacking characteristic of nested interrupts

be directed to begin at the location in main storage pointed to by the PC. This procedure assumes that the interrupt stacking process used to nest priority service routines has been unstacked in the reverse order in which the nest was built.

It is possible to achieve a very fast response time to individual priority interrupt requests by associating a separate hardware register set with each interrupt level. Using this technique, there is no need to save the registers on the TOS each time a program is interrupted by a higher-priority request. The contents of the PC and the IM are still automatically placed in consecutive locations at the TOS, but the interrupt hardware simply switches from the register set associated with the interrupted program to the register set associated with the new priority level. The IBM System/7 uses this technique with four priority levels. Each level has a complete set of internal registers. There may be as many as 16 sublevels of priority assigned to each priority level. Current processing is interrupted only by requests on a higher-priority level. Saving registers is not necessary in processing from one sublevel to another sublevel within the same priority level. Each sublevel priority routine will execute to completion before another routine can cause an interrupt when both sublevel requests operate at the same physical interrupt level. This is an example of the nesting convention that permits physical higher-priority requests to interrupt the service routines of physical lower-priority levels, but not requests that occur at the same physical priority level as the current executing routine.

8.3.8 The Processor Status Word

More sophisticated small computers have been designed to optimally use the resources of the application system built around them. The philosophy of optimal usage is the same as that observed by the large computing machines and includes the administration of the following two major resources:

1. Usage of main storage by concurrently executing application programs. This encompasses the techniques used by the system to roll a program segment into memory. Such a facility provides a multiprogramming environment and reduces the possibility of the system spending a large portion of its time in moving programs from bulk storage into main memory. It optimizes the occupancy of main storage by concurrent programs.
2. Coordination of I/O operations with normal processing on the mainframe. This permits the machine to continue executing in-line code after it has initiated an I/O transaction. The machine does not have to wait for the I/O transaction to be completed before it continues with its control sequence.

To achieve these goals, the minicomputer is placed into one of two possible operating states by the system software:

1. *The executive mode.* A supervisory program assumes complete control of the machine. It coordinates the sequence in which concurrent programs may be executed. In addition, it assumes the responsibility for initiating and terminating all I/O operations. Any application program must issue a call to the

supervisory program if it wishes I/O to be performed. The supervisory program will schedule the I/O transaction and handle the details of communicating with the external world. The results of the I/O transaction will be reported to the application program by the supervisory program at the conclusion of the I/O operation. The supervisory program may execute all commands in the instruction repertoire of the machine. These commands include a group of special instructions that control the state of the machine.

2. *The user mode.* All processing instructions are valid; all I/O instructions and the previous group of special control instructions are invalid. If a user program attempts to execute one of the invalid instructions, the processor will generate an internal interrupt and vector to an illegal instruction service routine. Such illegal instructions are considered privileged and are reserved for the exclusive use of the supervisory program. Furthermore, since I/O commands are treated as part of the privileged class of instructions, the processor is denied direct access to the set of peripherals attached to the system when the minicomputer is functioning in the user mode.

A minicomputer running in the executive mode is sometimes said to be in the *kernel mode* (meaning that all features of the machine are accessible by the processor) or *supervisory state.* In contrast, a minicomputer running in the user mode is often said to be in the *problem state.* To implement this form of control in hardware, a *processor status word* (*PSW*) has been employed. The IBM System/360 series first popularized this concept with the acronym *PSW* used to stand for *program status word.* Interdata adopted the concept in their early machines, and it has continued to be widely used at the sophisticated minicomputer level.

Stated simply, the contents of the PSW define the state of the processor at any time. In large-scale computing machines such as the IBM System/360 line, the PSW contains both the PC and other status information about the internal state of the machine. However, the traditional short word length of the minicomputer (i.e., 12 to 16 bits) required that the small computer separate the PSW into two sections; one section contained the PC and the other section contained processor status information. This latter data segment is often referred to as the PSW of a small computer, with the PC specified separately. In any future discussion, a distinction will always be made between the PSW and the PC.

The *current PSW* is a separate hardware register that explicitly contains the status information that characterizes the state of the machine at any given time. Typically, the PSW will contain a *condition code field* that reflects the result of the last machine operation. The status information will enable or disable different levels of interrupts that may occur within the processor. Furthermore, the PSW will specify whether the machine is operating in the supervisory state or the problem state. Figure 8-20 illustrates the PSW used by the PDP-11/45. Since the PDP-11/45 employs two separate sets of general registers, the PSW uses bit 11 to indicate which register set is active. Information about both the current mode and the previous mode of system operation is retained in bits 12 through 15 of the PSW. The PC in conjunction with

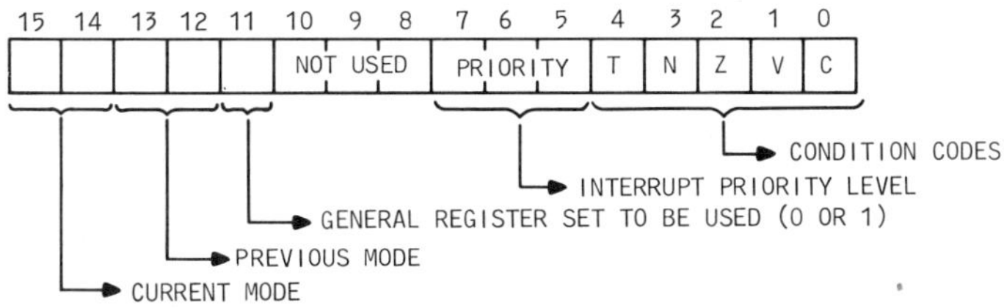

MODE BIT	COMBINATIONS
00	KERNEL
01	SUPERVISOR
11	USER

8-20 PDP-11/45 processor status word (PSW)

this PSW completely specifies the state of the processor at any time, including the time of an interrupt.

The current PSW controls instruction sequencing and maintains the status of the system in relation to the program currently being executed. A program may change the state of the machine by loading a new PSW. Typically, this will be accomplished by the user program issuing a *supervisory call* (*SVC*) to the executive program. The executive program then uses a privileged instruction to change the PSW. Since the SVC is an internal processor interrupt, the priority level at which it is issued by the user program indicates to the supervisory program what the new PSW should be. In this way, control is passed back and forth between user programs and the executive program.

This communication of control information is but one form of the more general use of the PSW in the administration of interrupts by the processor. Recall that for a generalized minicomputer, the PC and PSW are considered separate quantities. Consequently, each priority-interrupt level has a unique set of four consecutive locations in main storage assigned to it. These locations define an interrupt vector for a given priority level. The interrupt vector starting address is normally assigned at system generation time by the system designer and remains fixed thereafter. However, the operator can change this address by redoing the system generation process and physically reassigning the address returned by an external device when the interrupt request is acknowledged by the CPU. The four locations of a given interrupt vector contain the following:

1. A storage slot for the contents of the current PSW register when the interrupt is recognized by the processor.
2. A storage slot for the contents of the current PC, which is also saved when an interrupt is recognized.
3. The new PSW's value, which will be moved into the current PSW register after the former contents of the register have been saved.
4. The new PC's value, which will be used in conjunction with the new PSW to specify where execution is to branch. Normally, the contents of the new PC

are the starting address of the priority service routine for the interrupt level that has been recognized.

Figure 8-21 illustrates the procedure that is automatically initiated when the processor recognizes an interrupt request. The procedure is as follows:

1. The processor acknowledges a priority interrupt request. It then derives the starting address of the interrupt vector. The interrupt vectors are usually placed in the low address range of main storage. Typically, the interrupting device returns an address that forces the CPU to branch directly to the required interrupt vector.
2. The current PSW is copied into the storage location used for the old PSW.
3. The current value of the PC is copied into the storage location used for the old PC. The sole function of the old PSW and old PC is to retain the former value of the state of the processor so that the interrupted program may be successfully restored when control is returned to it from the priority service routine.
4. The contents of the new PSW location are used to overwrite the contents of the current PSW register. Typically, the new PSW will contain the masking information necessary to disable all interrupts that might occur at a priority level less than or equal to the current priority level.
5. The contents of the new PC location are used to replace the previous value of the PC. The new PC normally contains the starting address of the priority service routine assigned to that interrupt. This specific service routine will be invoked each time the processor recognizes an interrupt request at this priority level.
6. Execution is then directed to begin at the location specified by the PC.

All of these separate operations are performed automatically by the interrupt hardware mechanism once the processor has acknowledged a specific priority interrupt request. Processing continues until the CPU executes either an RTI or a *return-from-trap (RTT) instruction*. Either command causes the system to be restored to its state prior to the interrupt and allows the interrupted program to continue unmutilated. The return commands automatically perform the following functions:

1. The contents of the old PSW are returned to the current PSW register.
2. The contents of the old PC are placed back into the PC.
3. Execution is directed to begin at the location in main storage pointed to by the PC.

Figure 8-22 illustrates an allocation of main storage that exhibits a possible assignment of interrupt vectors in low memory. Note that three classes of interrupt vectors are shown:

1. Those due to internal machine interrupts.
2. Those due to SVC's.
3. Those due to interrupts from peripheral devices attached to the system.

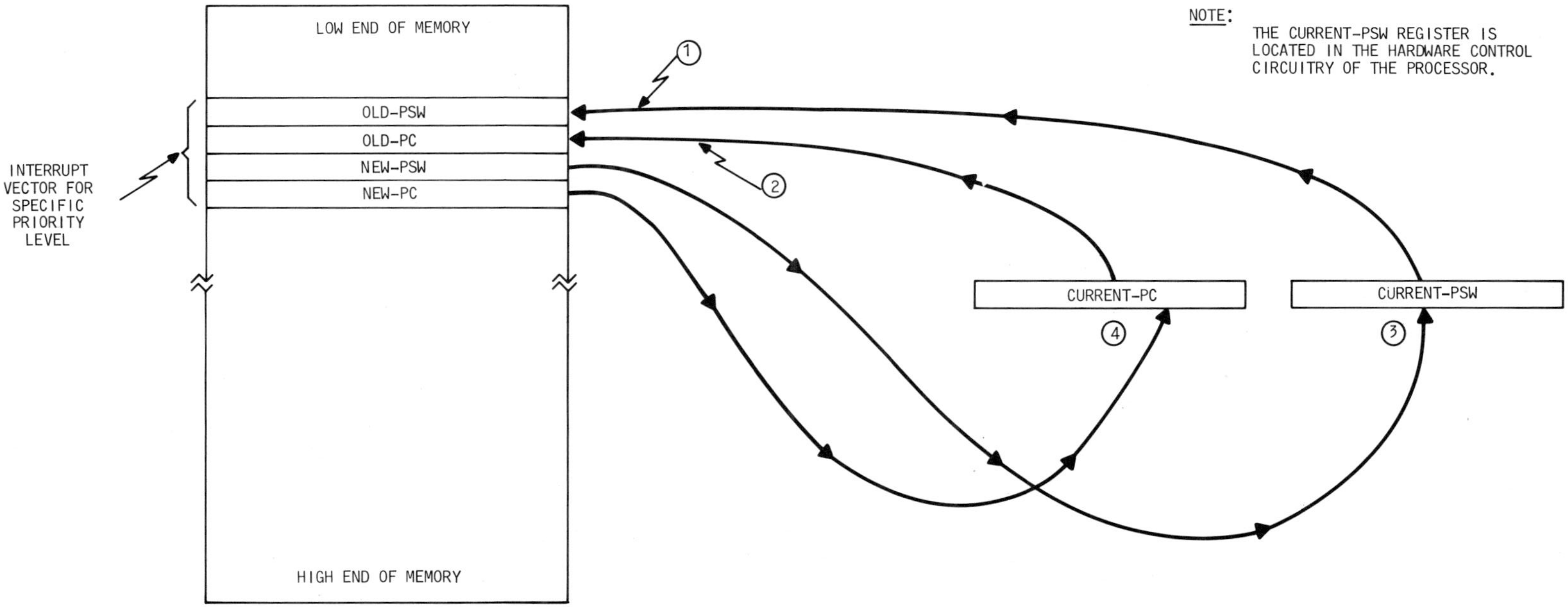

ON THE RECOGNITION OF AN INTERRUPT REQUEST AT THIS PRIORITY LEVEL, THE FOLLOWING SEQUENCE OF EVENTS OCCURS, AUTOMATICALLY:

(a) THE PROCESSOR DERIVES THE ENTRY ADDRESS OF THE INTERRUPT VECTOR ASSOCIATED WITH THIS PRIORITY LEVEL.

① THE CONTENTS OF THE CURRENT-PSW REGISTER IS SAVED IN THE OLD-PSW LOCATION.
② THE CONTENTS OF THE CURRENT-PC IS SAVED IN THE OLD-PC LOCATION.
③ THE CONTENTS OF THE NEW-PSW LOCATION IS FETCHED & INSERTED IN THE CURRENT-PSW REGISTER.
④ THE CONTENTS OF THE NEW-PC LOCATION IS FETCHED & INSERTED IN THE CURRENT-PC REGISTER.

(b) EXECUTION IS THEN DIRECTED TO BEGIN AT THE LOCATION IN MAIN STORAGE POINTED TO BY THE CURRENT-PC.

NOTE:
ALL THESE OPERATIONS ARE PERFORMED AUTOMATICALLY BY THE INTERRUPT HARDWARE MECHANISM

8-21 Interrupt program switching using a processor status word (PSW)

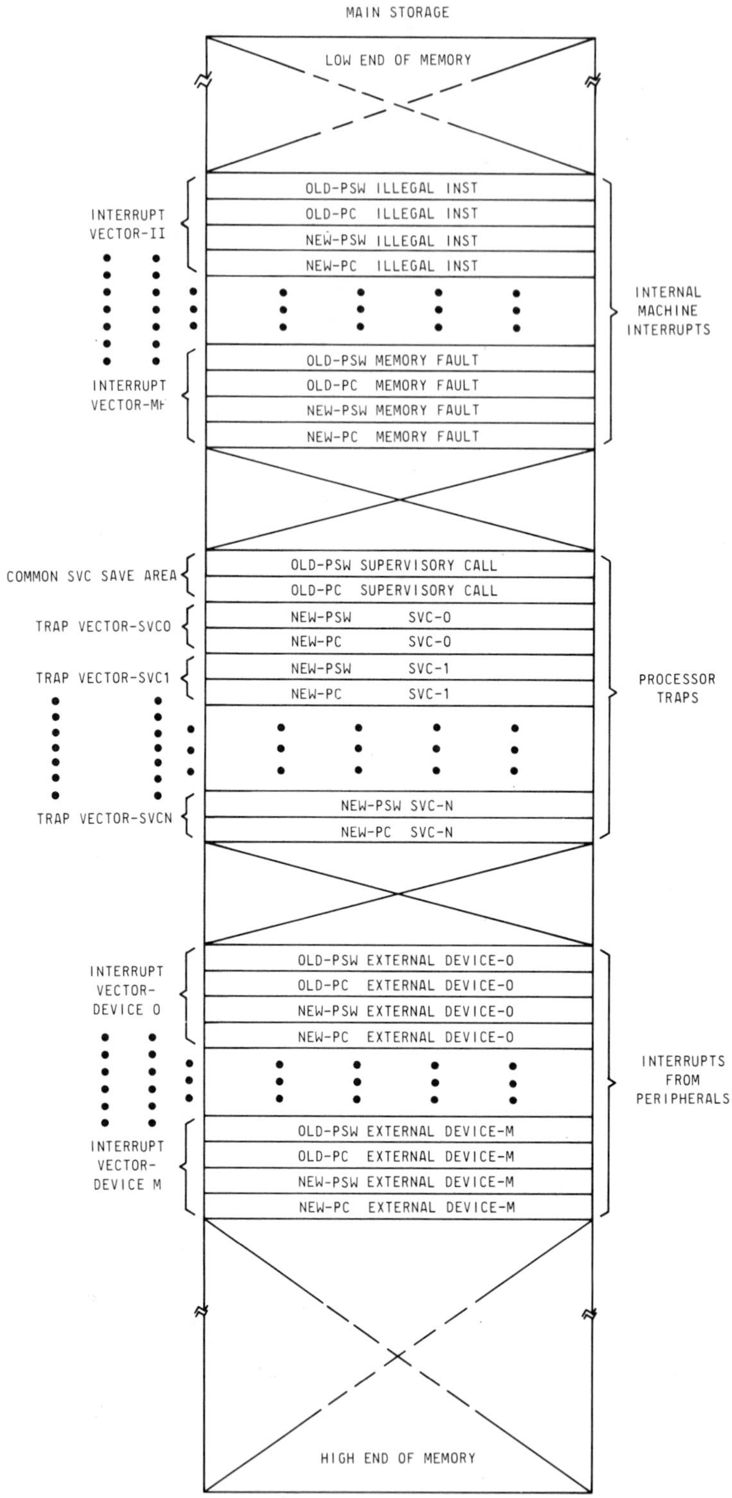

8-22 Main storage allocation showing possible interrupt vector assignments

All SVC's share the same two locations for storing the old PSW and old PC. This implies that SVC's may not be nested as in the case with priority interrupts. However, separate, new PSW and PC values are assigned to each of the SVC's. Aside from this convention, all interrupts are handled in the fashion just described.

The user normally assumes the responsibility for assigning the dedicated locations in main storage that are used as the interrupt vectors for each priority interrupt level. The user's manuals of many machines specify explicit core assignments for certain types of interrupts. The user must then ascertain that the proper starting address of the required interrupt vector has been either hard-wired or strapped in the control logic associated with each interrupting device.

In the most sophisticated minicomputers employing a PSW philosophy, no device polling is required to identify which service routine to execute. Each device capable of interrupting the processor is connected to a separate hardware interrupt level. Priority is established by the actual physical interconnection of these devices to the processor. After the processor has acknowledged an interrupt request at a specific priority level, the interrupting device transmits the address of its interrupt vector to the processor. If multiple devices are permitted to be daisy-chained at each priority level, the two-dimensional multilevel priority structure discussed in Section 8.3.5 is obtained.

In a stack-oriented processor such as the PDP-11, the old PSW and old PC are handled in a slightly different manner. The interrupt vector associated with each priority level consists of only two words instead of four. These two words are the new PSW and new PC. They are assigned by the user in exactly the same manner as for a non-stack-oriented processor. However, no formal storage locations are set aside to function as the old PSW and old PC. Instead, the current PSW and current PC are automatically pushed into consecutive locations on the top of the system stack in main memory. When the interrupt has been serviced, an RTI or RTT instruction is executed and the previous items are popped off the system stack. The RTI or RTT commands automatically place the saved items in the PC and PSW registers. As in the nonstack case, execution is directed to begin at the location pointed to by the PC and returns control to the interrupted program.

As an aside, both interrupts and subroutines may share the system stack. The only difference in their respective administration will be how control is returned to the interrupted program as opposed to the calling program. The RTI instructions are used to return from an interrupt: the *return-from-subroutine* (*RTS*) *command* is used to return to the program that called the subroutine.

8.3.9 Generalized Context Switching

Context switching is the procedure observed by the processor to save all information relevant to the state of the machine after control is transferred from one program to another when either an interrupt is recognized or an SVC is executed. Consequently, a context switch may be initiated by an event that has occurred external to the CPU or by a software process (program). Typically, an external event would be an interrupt from a peripheral device. However, the class of internal machine interrupts would be included in this category (i.e., a memory parity failure interrupt or an illegal instruction interrupt). "External," therefore, does not refer to software-generated interrupts or traps defined earlier in this chapter. An internal process relates directly to an event that is administered by the operating system or supervisory program. Such events would correspond to messages communicated between tasks that exist in the operating system, or the completion of specialized control functions performed by the supervisory program.

When the processor performs a context switch, *all* information needed to characterize the executing program is saved. Later, all this information will be restored to the proper registers in the CPU so that the interrupted program may continue its execution from the point at which the interrupt occurred. In the simplest machine structures, only one key register has to be saved—the PC. If an intermediate calculation is being processed, often a single accumulator will be saved. As discussed previously, the interrupt hardware will automatically save the PC, but the priority service routine will have to save the accumulator. If a PSW is employed, the interrupt hardware will automatically save both the PC and the current PSW. Any other register(s) that have to be saved will still be handled by the interrupt service routine. When general-purpose register (GPR) sets are employed, the problem of saving key registers is complicated. The interrupt hardware will still automatically save the PC and current PSW, but it is not always clear what other registers should be saved. The burden of placing some subset of the GPR's in main storage is still left to the interrupt service routine. The software overhead of writing the contents of selected GPR's into core storage quickly becomes expensive in terms of overall execution time. To facilitate the GPR save operation, a software stack may be used in which all the GPR's are placed in consecutive locations at the TOS in main storage. However, each load of the stack requires the execution of a separate PUSH instruction for each register in the GPR set.

To expedite this stack-save operation, several highly sophisticated machines, such as the Modular Computer Systems MODCOMP IV, have employed two additional instructions that automatically administer the system stack for the storage and retrieval of the GPR's during a context switch. When the processor executes either of these instructions, the GPR's are handled as a group; no further instructions are executed by the program to store or retrieve the entire register set. These two instructions take the following forms:

1. *PUSH N, Ri.* The contents of N GPR's are automatically saved at the top of the system stack stored in ascending sequence starting with i, where i is a whole integer representing R's location in the sequence of registers. For a machine with 16 GPR's, *N* may be less than or equal to 16. Consequently, only a portion of the GPR set may be saved on the system stack, or the entire 16 registers may be stored away. Note, however, that the registers are not automatically pushed onto the stack starting with R0. Rather, they are saved starting with Ri as the first element and ending with R(i − 1) as the top element. Consequently, the save of R15 will be followed by the save of R0; and so on. This is effectively a barrel storage operation in which R0 is treated as the next register in sequence after R15.

2. *PULL N, Ri.* The contents of the N locations at the top of the system stack are restored to the registers in the GPR set, beginning with R(i — 1) and terminating with Ri. This instruction, which is just the inverse of the PUSH command, assumes that the register set loops around on itself so that R0 follows R15. Thus, a particular GPR save sequence would look as follows:

R9, R10, . . . , R14, R15, R0, . . . , R7, R8

where R9 was the first register placed on the stack and R8 the last. The register set would be restored in exactly the reverse order: loading R8 first, then R7, then R6, and so on, then R10, and finally completing with R9.

A hardware arrangement of this type has been called a *register PUSH-PULL stack* or a *register HOLD-GET stack.*

In a less sophisticated structure, a machine such as the Bell System 3ACC automatically "HOLDs" all its GPR's on the stack, beginning with R0, when the processor encounters the equivalent of the PUSH command. No other ordering of the register sequence is permitted, and all 16 registers are saved each time a HOLD operation is specified. The GET command functions as a complementary operation to the HOLD instruction. It restores all 16 GPR's and starts by loading the contents of the TOS into R15, the next stack location into R14, and so on, terminating with a restore of R0. An additional feature of the 3ACC is that it permits nesting of GPR sets on the HOLD-GET stack to a depth of 32 sets, with each set containing 16 GPR's. Each GPR set is loaded at the top of the current stack with GPR-15 as the topmost element, followed by GPR-14, and so on, down to GPR-00. This is shown in Figure 8-23. The 3ACC administers its HOLD-GET stack entirely by microcode to obtain the fastest possible execution time. The only way to perform a faster context switch on an interrupt is to incorporate a separate GPR set for each interrupt level. An interrupt, then, would simply redirect control to a different *total* register set, including a new PC and current PSW. This technique has become quite viable with the appearance of low-cost LSI register chips.

An interesting variation of this technique has been employed by Texas Instruments in the implementation of the 990 computer family. Its general register set is placed in main storage and realized as a 16-word area of memory that is considered a workspace. This area is defined by a *workspace pointer* (*WP*) that is not fixed, but it may be changed dynamically under program control. If the WP is saved in main storage and a new value inserted into the WP register, a new workspace may be assigned according to system needs. Furthermore, the old workspace may be restored by inserting the previous value for the WP that was saved separately in main memory. Consequently, each interrupt level could be assigned a unique WP. If a higher-priority request interrupted the current service routine, the current WP would simply be saved in a preassigned memory location and a new WP fetched from another dedicated main storage location. The operation here is identical to that associated with the PSW procedure. The user must assign the locations in main storage where each priority interrupt request will cause control to vector. It is the user's responsibility to place the

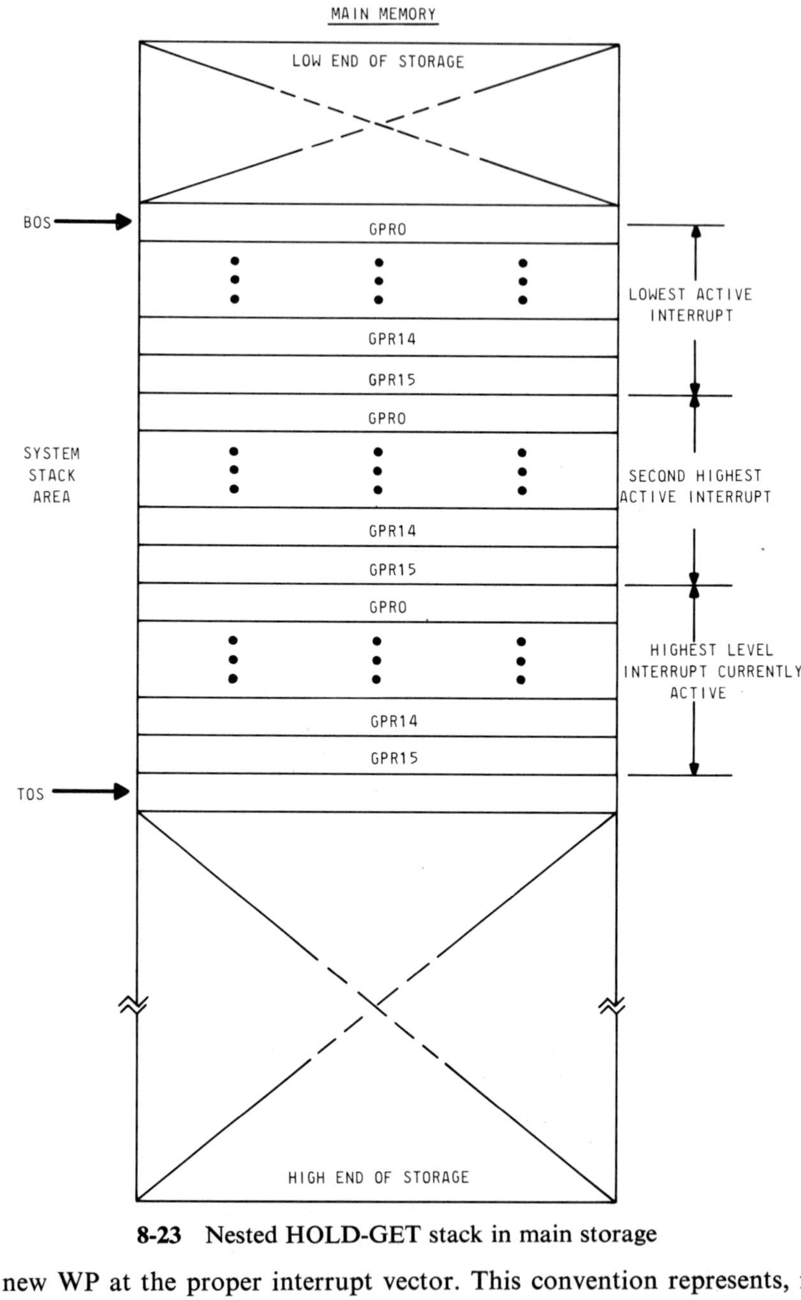

8-23 Nested HOLD-GET stack in main storage

correct new WP at the proper interrupt vector. This convention represents, next to separate hardware register sets, the fastest technique available for performing a context switch. Figure 8-24 illustrates the allocation of new WP and old WP slots in main storage.

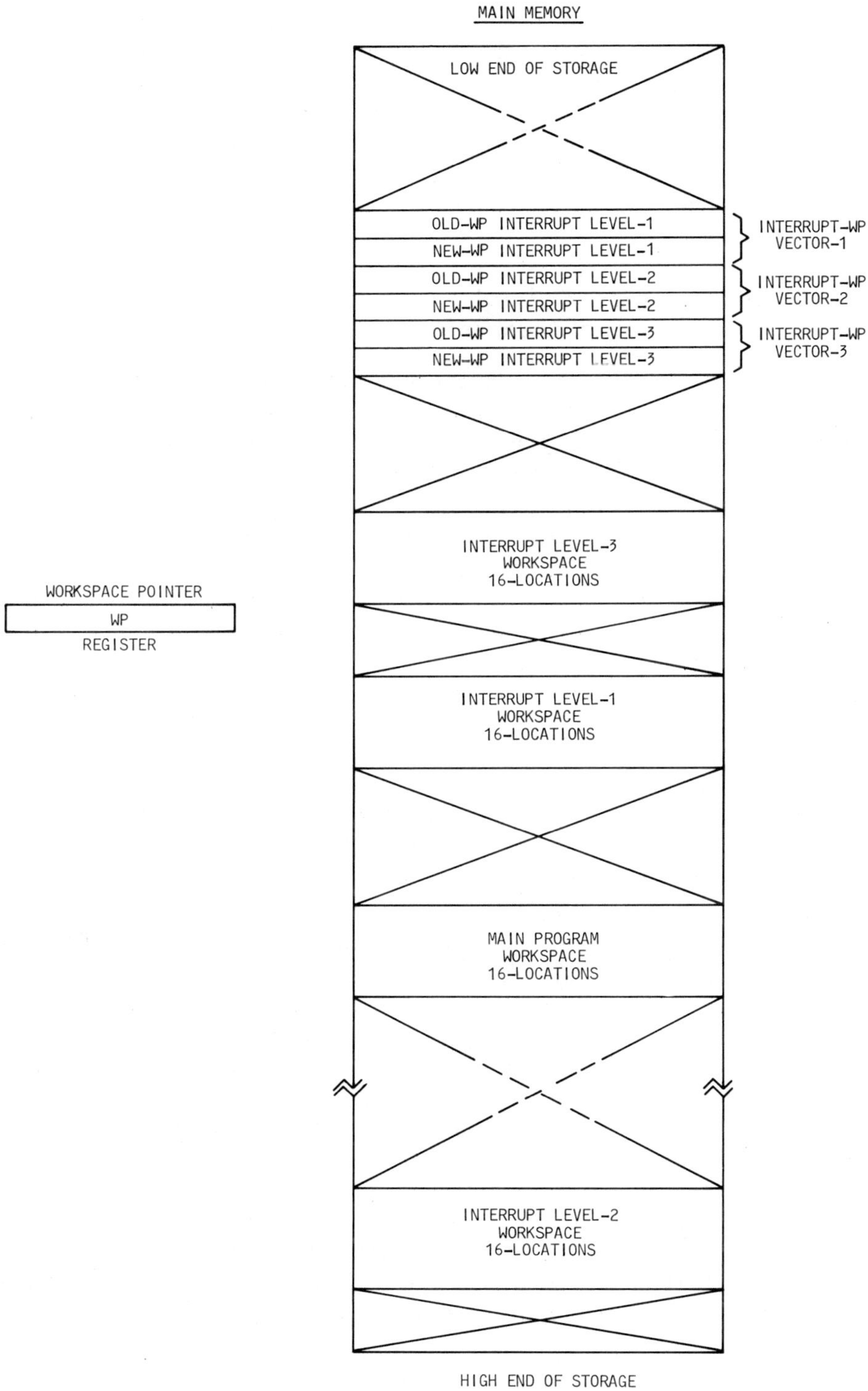

8-24 Interrupt workspace pointer allocation in main storage

The time required to save or restore all critical registers so that the state of the processor may be preserved is called the *context switching time*. It is distinct from the time required by a program to execute a control algorithm. The smaller the context switching time (relative to the execution time) required by individual programs, the more efficiently the CPU will be employed. This efficiency is a measure of the actual useful processing that may be performed per unit of machine time. The interrupt facilities of the modern mini/microcomputer structures have evolved toward the optimization of this goal.

8.3.10 Microprogram Control of the Interrupt Mechanism

It is worthwhile at this point to summarize the housekeeping chores that must be done before servicing the specific needs of the interrupt request. Prior to directing control to the interrupt service routine, the processor must disable the interrupt facility to prevent external interaction. The standard procedure observed by the overall interrupt mechanism from this point is to:

1. Save the contents of all internal registers in memory that will be changed during the execution of the interrupt program.
2. Set the mask bit for the current interrupt-priority level as well as the lower-priority mask bits. This prevents subsequent interrupts by the same or lower-priority signals when the interrupt facility is enabled.
3. Enable the interrupt system to allow higher-priority interrupt requests to be serviced.
4. Execute the interrupt-priority service program.
5. Restore all saved registers from memory.
6. Insert a new bit pattern in the mask register so that future requests at the current or lower-priority interrupt level(s) will be recognized.
7. Return control to the interrupted program.

All these items, with the exception of 4, may be implemented using microprogrammed control. And even item 4 may be executed at the microcode level if the user is willing to place each of the interrupt-level service routines in the microstore. This procedure, however, is normally not very efficient since the requirements of an interrupt service routine may change suddenly if the system is reconfigured. A substantial real-time benefit may be achieved by placing the other functions in microcode. In particular, context switching time may be improved.

The interrupt function normally begins at the end of a given instruction. For a microprogrammed machine, the last microinstruction in the sequence contains information to signify that it is the last instruction. This microinstruction sets up the hardware to gate the next microprogram address from the instruction register. However, if an interrupt is waiting, the microinstruction preempts the beginning of a new macroinstruction interpretation sequence. Instead, the logic presets the microprogram address to a prescribed location corresponding to the start of the interrupt sequence as shown in Figure 8-25.

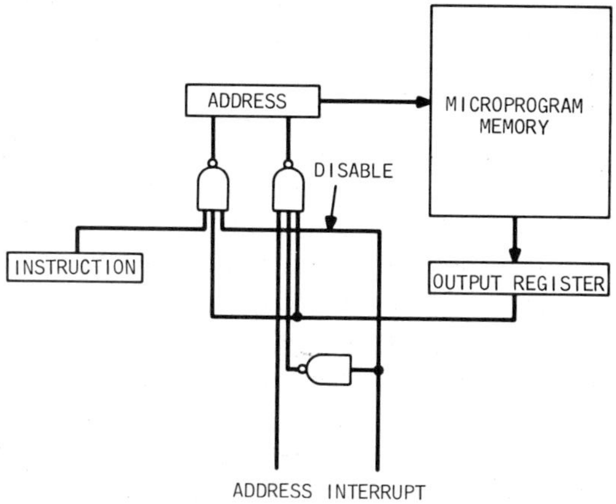

8-25 Microprogrammed interrupt access

The microprogram sequence may perform some of the control functions that would be accomplished by hardware in a regular machine. For example, if more than one interrupt is present, the microprogram sequence may determine the highest-priority request by examining the contents of the interrupt request register. It would then use this information to branch to the appropriate priority service routine. Much of the basic control philosophy of interrupt administration using firmware control is similar to that outlined in Section 8.3.3, where the operation of a microcode-controlled interject mechanism was discussed.

8.4 SUMMARY

Three different forms of program-controlled I/O that permit the processor to assess the needs of its external environment have been discussed. They are (1) the use of a polling sequence, (2) the use of an interrupt facility, and (3) the use of an interject mechanism. The polling sequence represents the slowest control procedure used to identify a device needing service by the CPU; the device flag of each peripheral must be interrogated using an I/O instruction. The position in the polling sequence of the interrogation routine used to test a particular device flag determines the priority of service given to that device by the CPU. The polling sequence consumes large blocks of real time, and devices are serviced *not* when they request service but when the polling sequence determines that they need service. In contrast, the hardware interrupt facility permits a device requesting an interrupt to be serviced by the CPU as soon as the interrupt is recognized by the processor.

Three distinct types of interrupt structures, which are employed at the small-computer level, were outlined. The simplest is the *single-level interrupt facility*, in which all interrupt requests are connected to a single internal processor request flip-flop. When the request flip-flop is set, the processor allows the current instruction being executed to complete and then attempts to identify the highest-priority device requesting an interrupt. This identification is performed by software and can be quite time-consuming. To expedite the identification process, the software procedure can be placed in hardware to generate a *multilevel priority-interrupt facility* in which all requesting devices are daisy-chained together at the same priority level. To obtain the maximum flexibility in an interrupt environment, the *two-dimensional multilevel priority-interrupt facility* is used. This is a two-dimensional arrangement of interrupt request leads in which various interrupt leads are assigned a priority in terms of their physical interconnection to the processor. Each priority level may have multiple devices daisychained together, with the highest-priority device at *each* level being the device which is physically closest to the processor. The greatest drawback in a heavy interrupt environment is the amount of real-time overhead required to save the current state of the machine each time an interrupt is recognized by the processor and then to restore the machine to that state after the interrupt is serviced. The interject facility is used to remove this real-time overhead. It uses the *best features* of both the polling scheme and the interrupt mechanism. The processor periodically samples the INTERJECT flag to determine if any external devices need service. If the flag is set, the processor enters a polling sequence to identify the device that made the interject request. The entire polling sequence could be placed in microcode for a microprogrammed machine to expedite the identification process. Since the interject is serviced during the normal course of program execution, the state of the machine does not have to be saved and restored each time an interject request is recognized. This can represent a significant real-time advantage over the interrupt procedure. The interrupt facility, in turn, represents a substantial real-time gain over the polling sequence.

8.5 REFERENCES

1 STRUBLE, G., *Assembler Language Programming: The IBM System/360*. Reading, Mass.: Addison-Wesley Publishing Company, Inc., 1971.

2 KATZAN, H., JR., *Computer Organization and the System/370*. New York: Van Nostrand Reinhold Company (a division of Litton Educational Publishing International), 1971.

3 CHU, YAOHAN, *Computer Organization and Microprogramming*. Englewood Cliffs, N.J.: Prentice-Hall, Inc., 1972.

4 STONE, Harold S., ed., *Introduction to Computer Architecture*. Chicago: Science Research Associates, Inc. (a subsidiary of IBM), 1975.

5 *Introduction to Programming* (PDP-8 Handbook Series). Digital Equipment Corporation, Maynard, Mass., 1973.

6 WEITZMAN, CAY, *Minicomputer Systems Structure, Implementation, and Applications*. Englewood Cliffs, N.J.: Prentice-Hall, Inc., 1974.

7 BLAKESLEE, THOMAS R., *Digital Design with Standard MSI and LSI*. New York: John Wiley & Sons, Inc., 1975.

8 KORN, GRANINO A., *Microprocessors and Small Computer Systems for Engineers and Scientists.* New York: McGraw-Hill Book Company, 1977.

9 VACROUX, ANDRE G., "Explore Microcomputer I/O Capabilities." *Electronic Design,* Vol. 23, No. 1 (May 10, 1975), pp. 114–119.

10 WYLAND, DAVID C., "Increase Microcomputer Efficiency." *Electronic Design,* Vol. 23, Nov. 23 (Nov. 8, 1975), pp 70–75.

11 MADNICK, STUART E., AND JOHN J. DONOVAN, *Operating Systems.* New York: McGraw-Hill Book Company, 1974.

12 HILBURN, JOHN L., AND PAUL M. JULICH, *Microcomputers/Microprocessors: Hardware, Software, and Applications.* Englewood Cliffs, N.J.: Prentice-Hall, Inc., 1976.

13 *MODCOMP IV Reference Manual.* Fort Lauderdale, Fla.: Modular Computer Systems, 1974.

8.6 PROBLEMS

1. A bus may be regarded as a *standardized interface* that interconnects the various components of a computing system. By employing this concept and observing the interfacing requirements that must be observed by a device to communicate on the bus, various peripheral devices may be added to the system at some future time, long after the machine has been designed.
   (a) What are the three basic functions performed by *all* busing structures?
   (b) What are the basic advantages—and disadvantages—of using a *radial* busing structure instead of a *party-line* bus arrangement? Is there any incompatibility between these two techniques, or can both structures *coexist* as parts of the same machine?
   (c) A peripheral device interface that links an external device to the processor/memory subsystem is called a *device controller.* What are the principal operational features required of a device controller to successfully interface with a digital machine?

2. Answer the following questions:
   (a) What does the term *standard peripheral set* mean for a given machine?
   (b) What is the difference between a standard peripheral set and a *nonstandard peripheral set*?
   (c) Can a microcomputer have a standard peripheral set associated with it?
   (d) How have the minicomputer manufacturers treated the situation in which a specific external device is to be controlled by the mini but no standard interface module is available? How have the microcomputer manufacturers handled the same situation? Is there any real difference between the two approxches?

3. Consider a small computer system in which a single-level interrupt facility is employed with the priority of service for an interrupting device determined by a software interrupt service routine. Develop the *flowchart* for the interrupt service routine such that a higher priority device can interrupt the service routine of a lower priority device without losing any information about the state of the lower priority service program.

   Assume that the processor uses memory banks or fields to extend the range of available main storage (i.e., the PDP-8/e).

(a) Consider the case of the main program and the service routines being required to execute in a field other than field 0. Specifically, the main program is to execute in field 2, and the interrupt service routines are to be located in field 5.
(b) How deep you would permit the nesting of interrupts in this software priority scheme?
(c) Assume each JMP I PSERV command in the polling sequence of the interrupt service routine skip-chain is replaced by a JMS I PSERV. How will this affect the service routine? How will it affect the overhead involved in servicing an interrupt?
(d) How would you modify the PDP-8/e structure to incorporate a multilevel, priority interrupt structure? Comment on any additional hardware needed and on new instructions that would make this feature easier to use. Also, draw a block diagram of how the "external world" would be connected to this system.

4. See Figure P8-4.

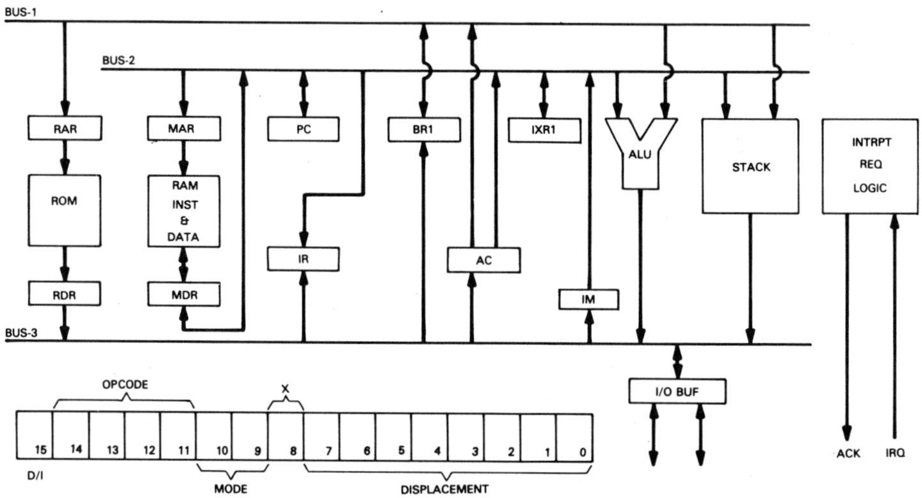

D/I DIRECT OR INDIRECT

MODE
0- ABSOLUTE
1- RELATIVE TO BASE REGISTER (BR1)
2- RELATIVE TO PROGRAM COUNTER
3- IMMEDIATE

X
0- NO INDEXING
1- RELATIVE TO INDEX REGISTER (IXR1)

NOTE: ALL REGISTERS ARE 16 BITS IN LENGTH

P 8-4

(a) What class of machine is represented by this architecture?
(b) If the hardware stack is used to service the interrupts, what information must be pushed onto the stack to preserve the state of the machine?
(c) Draw the timing diagram associated with the action of preserving the state of the machine upon the occurrence of an interrupt. *Note:* Assume each gating operation involving a bus requires 100 ns to complete. In addition, assume a BLOCK-PUSH instruction is executed so that the context-preserving operation takes place at the speed of the hardware control logic.
(d) What is the minimum hardware delay experienced by the system as measured from the time that an interrupt is first recognized by the CPU until the first instruction in

the service routine associated with the interrupting device is executed? *Note:* Assume that the interrupting device returns an index quantity which must be added to the contents of a fixed memory location to determine the starting address of the service routine for the interrupting device.

5. The interrupt mechanism for the system shown in Figure P8-5 uses a single-level arrangement that requires that the CPU service an interrupt request at the completion of the currently executing instruction. If an interrupt request is present at that time, the CPU transmits an acknowledge (ACK) pulse to the peripheral device set. To capture the ACK pulse, a device must issue an interrupt request. If *two or more* devices request an interrupt simultaneously, the device physically nearest the CPU will capture the ACK pulse.

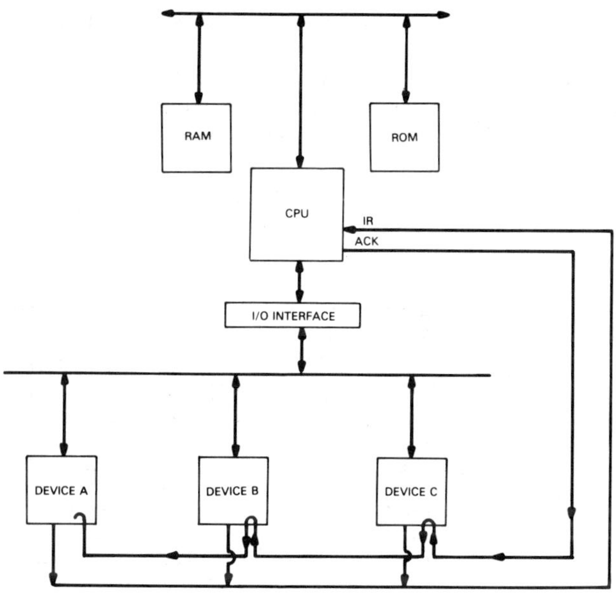

P 8-5

This capture prevents transmission of the ACK pulse to devices located further from the CPU in the ACK daisy chain. The interrupting device then places a vector address on the I/O bus and the CPU uses it to derive the service routine address for the device.

Assume the following:

T_{DC} The delay per device in the ACK daisy chain

T_A, T_B, T_C The respective execution times required of the service routines for devices A, B and C

T_S, T_R The time required to save and restore the context of the machine on an interrupt

(a) At what point would this system saturate in terms of the interrupt request environment? That is, what is the limiting frequency at which interrupts could occur without loss of information for all three devices acting concurrently? *Note:* The interrupt-on mechanism permits one instruction in the previously interrupted program to be executed before a new interrupt is recognized. Assume T_M represents the cycle time of main storage.

(b) Assume a multilevel priority interrupt structure is now employed. Device A is attached to the highest priority level, followed by Device B and then Device C. At what point would interrupt saturation occur for this structure?

6. Suppose it is desirable to replace a segment of code in a read-only memory (ROM) module in order to alter the associated control program of a microprocessor.
   (a) Develop the overall logic in block diagram form to perform this replacement function.
   (b) Could this hardware operate adequately using an interrupt? If so, what features must be included in the replacement logic to permit an interrupt to activate this operation?
   (c) Could a field programmable logic array (FPLA) be used to activate the replacement logic? If so, describe the details of the FPLA implementation?
   (d) Which approach offers the fastest system response time, and which is the simplest to implement in actual hardware?
7. See Figure P8-7. *Note:* After the CPU recognizes an interrupt, it responds with an acknowledge (ACK) pulse. The highest priority device requesting service captures the

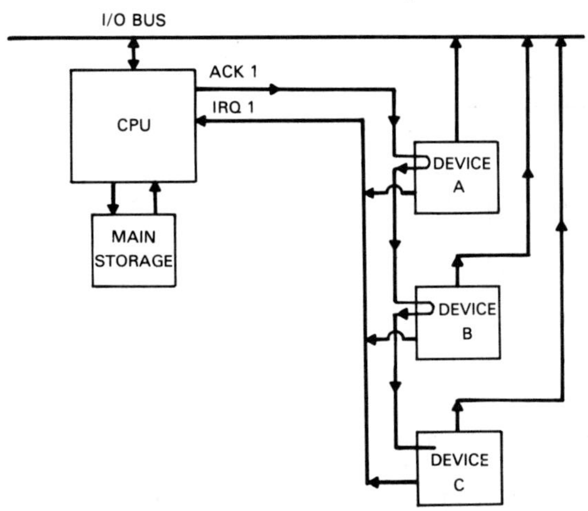

P 8-7

ACK pulse and returns the starting address of the interrupt service routine for that device.

(a) What type of interrupt scheme would this configuration be called?

(b) Suppose it is desirable to *nest* the interrupt requests from lower priority devices. What is the highest priority device in this arrangement? What are the values of the interrupt mask (IM) register for each device service routine so that interrupt nesting may occur?

(c) This interrupt configuration is to be replaced by an interject scheme. Describe how this would be done.

8. For the interrupt configuration shown in the Figure P8-8: (1) After the CPU recognizes an interrupt request at the highest priority level requesting service, the CPU responds

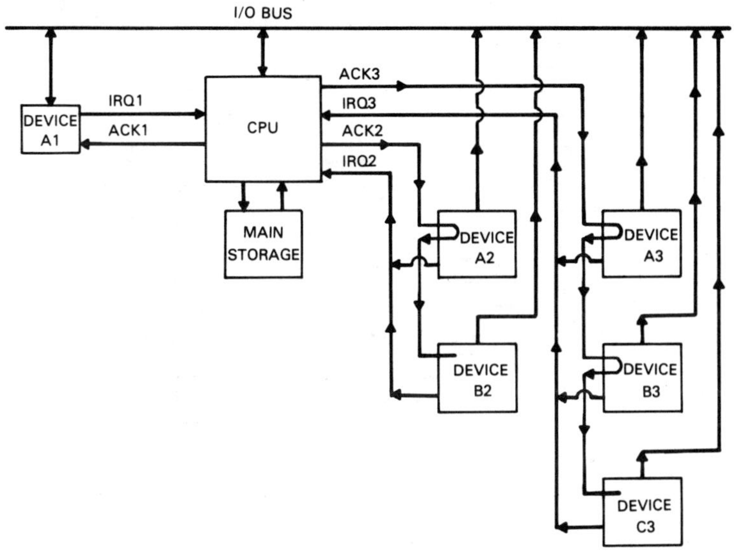

P 8-8

with an acknowledge (ACK) pulse *at that priority level.* (2) The highest priority device requesting an interrupt at that priority level captures the ACK pulse and returns a 16-bit address to the CPU. This is the starting address of the interrupt service routine for that device. (3) The *highest* priority interrupt request level is level 3, followed by level 2, and then level 1.

(a) Make a list, in order of decreasing priority, of the interrupting devices attached to the system. Where is the main program assigned in this priority scheme?

(b) The CPU contains an interrupt mask (IM) register. Define the interrupt masks associated with each priority level so that interrupt nesting may occur. Where should the values for these masks be placed and when is the IM loaded with a new value?

(c) Assume the service routine for device C3 is currently being executed by the CPU. Can device A3 interrupt the service routine for device C3?

(d) If it is *absolutely essential* that device A3 *always* be serviced if it issues an interrupt request, how should the devices be rearranged in the given interrupt configuration?

(e) What type of interrupt scheme would the given configuration be?

(f) What is the minimum amount of information about this system that must be saved each time an interrupt occurs?

(g) It has been proposed to *replace* this interrupt environment with an interject arrangement. Describe how this might be done and where any savings in real time might occur.

9. (a) When an interrupt is recognized by the processor structure shown in Figure P8-9a, what is the *minimum* amount of information needed to be saved by *both* the interrupt hardware and the associated interrupt service routine? *Note:* Assume a hardware-

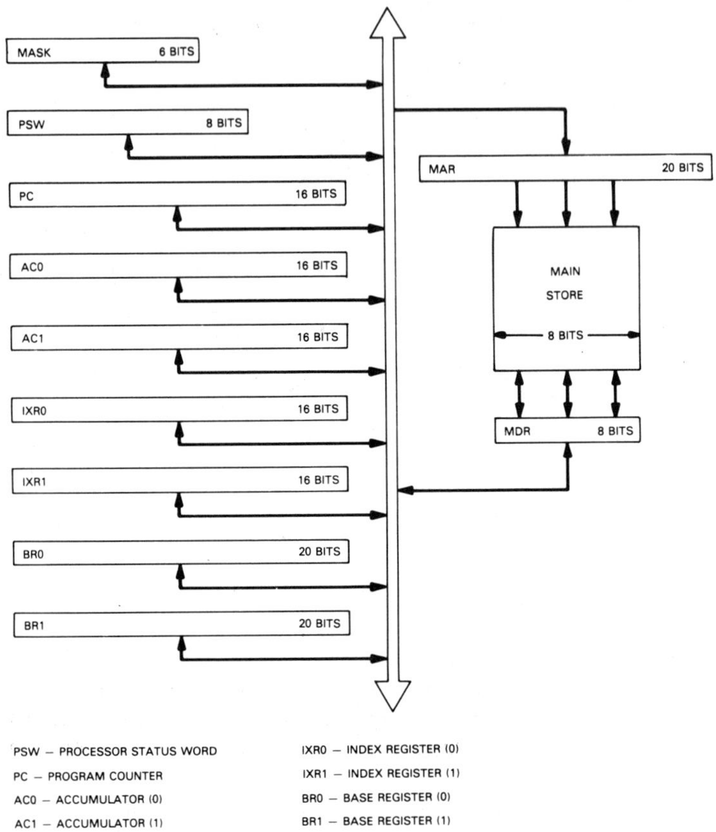

P 8-9a

vectored interrupt scheme is employed. The highest priority interrupting device returns a 16-bit address to the CPU when it has been recognized. This is the starting address of the interrupt service routine associated with the device.

(b) How many levels of interrupt may be nested by this processor?

(c) Let three peripheral devices be attached to the processor as shown in Figure P8-9b. When an interrupt is recognized, the CPU hardware automatically stores the MASK register, the PSW, and the PC in a dedicated area of main storage associated with the interrupting device. The CPU overhead to do this is 5 μs. In addition, it is the responsibility of the interrupt service routine to save any processor registers that might be significant. Assume that both accumulators and both index registers *must* be saved.

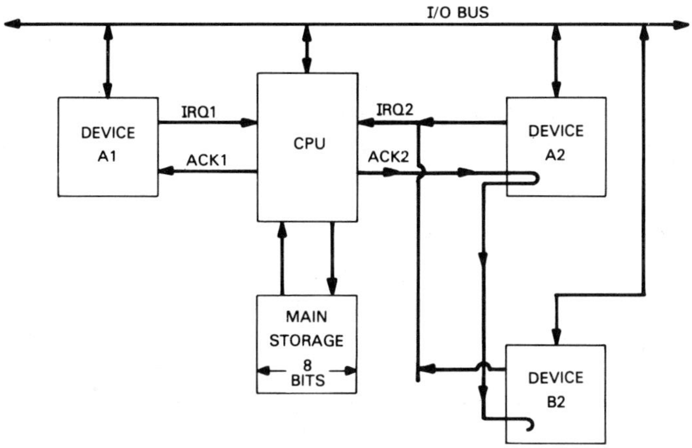

P 8-9b

The following instructions could be used by the interrupt service routine:

LDLB REG, MEM1 Load the 8 least significant bits of the specified register from the 8 bits of location MEM1.

Execution time of instruction = 1.2 μs

LDHB REG, MEM2 Load the 8 most significant bits of the specified register from the 8 bits of location MEM2.

Execution time of instruction = 1.2 μs

STLB REG, MEM3 Store the 8 least significant bits of the specified register in the 8 bits of location MEM3.

Execution time of instruction = 1.2 μs

STHB REG, MEM4 Store the 8 most significant bits of the specified register in the 8 bits of location MEM4.

Execution time of instruction = 1.2 μs

RET SUB1 The interrupt hardware automatically loads the MASK register, PSW, and PC from the appropriate storage locations. Execution then continues at the location specified by the new contents of the PC.

Execution time of instruction = 5 μs

What is the *context switching time* of the machine?

(d) What is the total *real-time overhead* experienced by the processor each time it services an interrupt *to completion*, i.e., until the interrupt service routine is exited?

(e) Lay out main storage so that the interrupting device (A1, A2, B2) will *vector* execution to the appropriate interrupt service routine.

(f) Specify the appropriate mask register contents so that nesting may be permitted for devices A1, A2, and B2.

(g) It is desired to replace this interrupt configuration with an *interject* arrangement. Calculate the time required to identify the lowest priority device requesting an interject using a SKIP chain approach. Assume the following: (1) Each machine instruction takes 1.2 μs to execute. (2) Each input/output (I/O) instruction takes 2 μs to execute.

(h) How does the amount of time calculated in part g of this problem compare with the context switching time associated with that device?

10. A processor has four hardware interrupt levels. Each level may have more than one device attached to it. The CPU replies to an interrupt with an ACK pulse that is daisy-chained through all devices attached to the priority interrupt level being serviced. The highest priority device requesting service replies to the ACK pulse with a 16-bit address which is the entry address of the service routine associated with the interrupting device.

    Four devices are to be attached to this system. These devices will use the hardware interrupt mechanism to transfer data between each of their I/O registers and the CPU. These devices are as follows: (1) A single-track cassette recorder that stores 800 bits per inch and operates at 37.5 inches per second. (2) Two teletype Model-37 ASR units that operate at 150 bits per second (or 15 characters per second). (3) A video terminal (with no refresh buffer) that operates at 2400 bits per second through a bit-serial interface with the CPU.

    At 10: 00 a.m. and 3: 30 p.m., *all* I/O processing has to come to a *halt*, and is not to be restarted until 10: 30 a.m. and 4: 00 p.m.

    (a) Show how each of these devices—and *any other unit(s)* you feel are needed by the processor—are attached to the hardware interrupt facility. Justify the priority assignments.

    (b) Describe exactly how this system works. (One flowchart, or perhaps more than one, would be appropriate.)

    (c) Draw an execution diagram and define the contents of the MASK register for all the critical event times handled by the system. What kind of control operation is this procedure called?

9

Channel-Oriented Input/Output Operations

9.1 THE CHANNEL CONCEPT

The early digital computers were configured so that each peripheral device was controlled directly by the CPU. This presented significant problems to the user since the CPU became "I/O bound"; that is, the CPU was locked into a communication loop with an external device until the required I/O transaction was completed. Invariably, this situation resulted in the high processing speed of the CPU being subordinated to the much slower information-handling capability of an external device. The mechanism developed to facilitate this situation was a hardware package that was a variation of the basic computer structure. This package has been called an *I/O processor*, a *channel mechanism*, or simply an *I/O channel*. The advantage of the channel mechanism was that I/O operations could be performed concurrently with CPU functions. A higher utilization of the CPU was achieved by using several channels to carry on multiple I/O transactions while the CPU processed high-speed calculations. Each channel unit was, effectively, a much less sophisticated computing structure that had the following characteristics:

1. Each I/O transaction was allowed to take place in a manner that was transparent to the CPU; the channel unit minimized the interference of each I/O operation with the CPU.
2. The hardware to implement each channel unit was much less expensive than the CPU and highly specialized in the control functions that it performed.

In its most general sense, a channel may be regarded as a communication pathway between the CPU and a peripheral device. Conceptually, the channel permits the CPU to interact with an external device through the exchange of control information and selected data words. A generalized channel unit may be implemented in either of two forms:

1. The CPU may directly control the transfer of each individual byte or word of information through the sequential execution of appropriate I/O instructions. The information exchange takes place between an internal processor register and the control logic located in the peripheral device. This implementation has been referred to as *a sequence of programmed data transfer (PDT) operations* or *direct program control of I/O*. The internal processor register used in such operations is often an *accumulator*. Because a separate I/O instruction must be executed for each data transfer, this technique has largely been confined to low-speed peripherals such as teletypewriters or incremental magnetic tape units.
2. The CPU may initiate the I/O transaction by loading certain control registers associated with the external device and then issuing an order to the peripheral to begin the I/O operation. The peripheral continues the I/O transaction from that point under control of the channel mechanism. The information exchange occurs concurrently with the operation of the CPU. Each data word is transferred between the channel hardware and designated locations in main storage. In effect, both the CPU and the activated channel contend for usage of main storage. A priority scheme is normally associated with the servicing of a request to access main storage. Typically, if both the CPU and the channel issue simultaneous storage access requests, the CPU will be denied access to main memory during the next memory cycle. Instead, the channel hardware is permitted to interact directly with the main store controller. If, during this cycle, another storage access request is issued by the channel, the CPU will again be deferred access to main memory for the following cycle. It is possible in this mode of operation for requests to access main memory to be issued at a sufficient rate that the channel environment seizes main storage and denies the CPU access until all such high-speed data transfers are completed. However, the majority of such high-speed channel transactions take place at rates that are slower than the cycle time of main storage. Consequently, such channel transactions are interleaved with the normal operations of the CPU and are transparent to the currently executing program.

The CPU, thus, does *not* participate directly in the transfer of each individual data word. Instead, an initialization program instructs the CPU to set up the channel mechanism. The peripheral device controller is also armed so that once it is told to proceed by the CPU, the channel mechanism will directly transfer each data word between the peripheral unit and preselected main storage locations. In this manner, the CPU informs the channel of the number of words that are to be exchanged between the peripheral device and main storage. The CPU then directs the channel unit to begin the data exchange when the channel determines that it is ready. Either one word or a large block of words may be involved in such an information exchange. The maximum rate of data transfer is normally limited by the cycle time of the memory. Programmed data transfer instructions are used by the initialization program to configure the channel; the individual transfers of each data word are interleaved with CPU accesses to main storage. The completion of the high-speed channel I/O transaction is normally signaled to the CPU by the channel returning an interrupt to the mainframe. An interrupt handler then identifies the actual cause of the interrupt and relates it to the completion of the channel operation.

Because the CPU is not directly involved in each data transfer, this high-speed channel arrangement has been called a *cycle-stealing* or *indirect program control mode*. This technique is also referred to as a *direct memory access* (*DMA*) *mode* and will be discussed in more detail in Section 9.2. The cycle-stealing arrangement characterizes the I/O transaction mode of the more recent computer structures.

Since the CPU does not participate in the transfer of each individual word in a block of data, it must supply the high-speed channel with enough information to perform the block transfer operation successfully. This information is supplied as part of the initialization program executed by the CPU before the block transfer operation is set off. It typically consists of the following data:

1. The starting address in main storage where the block of data words is or will be located. This memory block is also called the *data buffer area*.
2. The address in the peripheral device where the data block is or will be found.
3. The number of words in the data block.
4. The direction of the data transfer, that is, whether the data exchange is a write of main storage (a read of data from the peripheral device) or a read of main storage (a write of data onto the peripheral device).
5. The initial state of the device controller. This involves specifying the status of certain bits in the control logic of the peripheral.

The high-speed channel mechanism places virtually all its control in hardware to minimize the channel's interference with CPU operations. Obviously, the initialization data must be loaded into the channel control logic. However, after the initialization of the block transfer operation has been completed, a single START instruction directed to the peripheral device is all that is required to generate the transfer of a large block of data. Consequently, interfacing a peripheral device with a CPU that uses a high-speed channel mechanism requires a much more sophisticated design than the PDT mode and a correspondingly more expensive hardware configuration. In contrast, the basic advantage of the direct program control mode is the simplicity of the hardware required to interface an external device. This simplicity is reflected in the cost of the necessary hardware, which is lower than that required by the high-speed channel. However, the direct program control mode detracts from the overall system performance because a sequence of explicit machine instructions must be executed each time a data word is exchanged. As mentioned earlier, this feature keeps the processor from performing other useful tasks while each I/O transaction takes place. Figure 9-1 compares the characteristics of both the direct I/O mode of control and the channel-oriented mode.

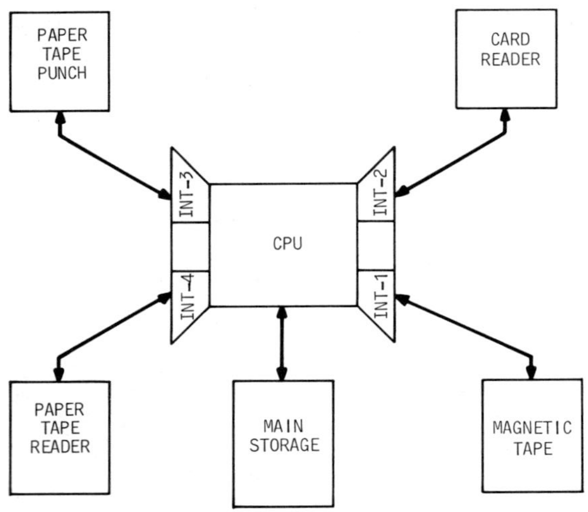

a) DIRECT-I/O (DIRECT PROGRAM CONTROL)

1. DATA TRANSFER TAKES PLACE BETWEEN EXTERNAL DEVICE AND A CPU REGISTER.
2. CPU CONTROLS EACH DATA TRANSFER.
3. CPU MUST FIRST COMPLETE THE PRESENT I/O - TRANSACTION BEFORE IT MAY CONTINUE WITH ITS INTERNAL HIGH-SPEED COMPUTATIONS.
4. THIS CONFIGURATION IS HIGHLY INEFFICIENT IN ITS UTILIZATION OF THE CPU DUE TO ITS CHARACTERISTIC OF BEING I/O BOUND.

NOTE: INT-1 THRU INT-4 REPRESENT INTERFACE UNITS BETWEEN THE INDICATED EXTERNAL DEVICE AND THE CPU.

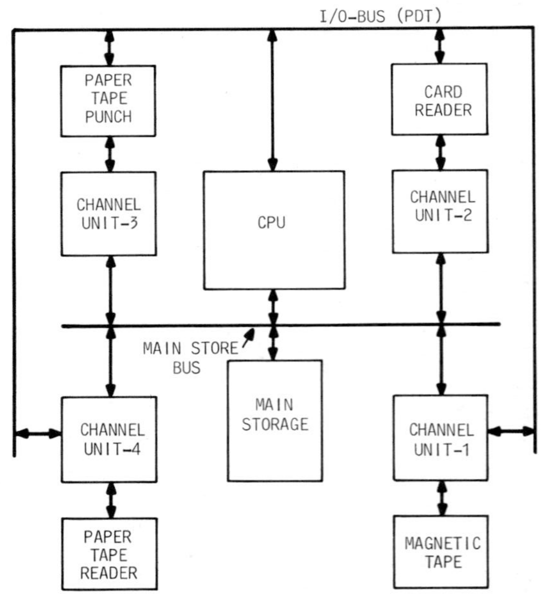

b) CHANNEL-ORIENTED I/O

1. DATA TRANSFER TAKES PLACE BETWEEN THE EXTERNAL DEVICE AND THE MAIN STORE BUS DIRECTLY INTO MEMORY.
2. THE CPU INITIALIZES EACH CHANNEL UNIT BUT DOES NOT DIRECTLY PARTICIPATE IN THE BLOCK TRANSFER OPERATION.
3. EACH CHANNEL UNIT CONTROLS ITS OWN I/O OPERATION AFTER IT HAS BEEN INITIALIZED & ACTIVATED.
4. THE CPU MAY PERFORM HIGH-SPEED CALCULATIONS CONCURRENTLY WITH THE I/O OPERATIONS.
5. THIS CONFIGURATION TENDS TO OPTIMIZE THE UTILIZATION OF THE CPU.

9-1 Direct-I/O versus channel-oriented I/O

The physical implementation of a channel may take either of the following forms:

1. The channel unit may be an entirely separate hardware unit that acts as an adjunct to both the CPU and main storage. Figures 9-2 and 9-3 illustrate the evolution of such a configuration. As more and more intelligence is placed in this structure, it can easily be represented by either a minicomputer or microcomputer interconnected to the host computer.

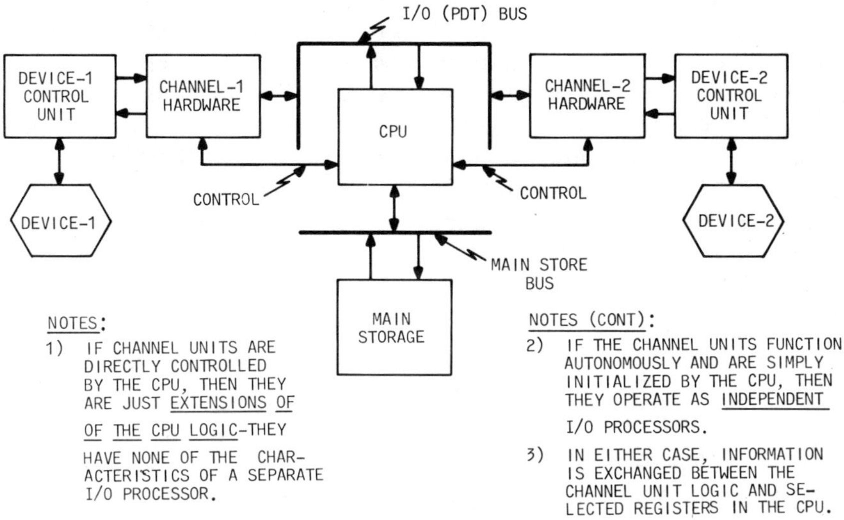

9-2 Low-to-intermediate-speed channel implementations

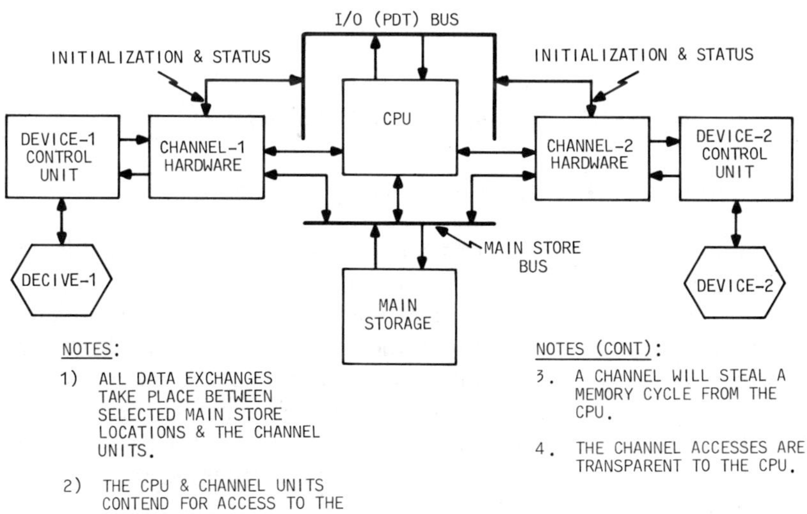

9-3 High-speed channel implementations

2. The channel may share some hardware with the mainframe. During the 1960's when high-speed channel operations were developed and refined, hardware was quite expensive. Main storage locations, however, were immediately available as part of the memory system associated with the CPU. It was a natural consequence that channel operations made use of main storage locations in some form to specify the initialization data for a block transfer operation.

The best example of this latter implementation is the channel structure that was developed for the IBM System/360 and carried over to the System/370 design. The IBM channel is constructed along the lines of a small computer, with the control section either hard-wired or implemented in firmware. The CPU and the channel function in a master–slave environment, with the CPU directing the channel as to what operation it should perform next. The channel, in turn, uses the hardware interrupt mechanism to alert the processor that attention should be directed toward the channel because of the completion of an I/O transaction or the occurrence of an extraordinary event in the channel (e.g., a device may have experienced a hard error that invalidates further I/O operations). The channel is told what to do by a channel program that resides in main storage. Each channel unit is controlled by its own channel program. The channel program may supply:

1. Initialization information to the channel so that it may begin an I/O transaction.
2. A termination command to the channel to halt a data exchange between a peripheral device and main storage.
3. A command to test the status of the channel.

IBM adopted a form of this high-speed channel implementation in the design of the model 1800 process control midicomputer and included a similar design in the System/7, which succeeded the 1800. Interdata used a similar channel structure in its family of minicomputers to pattern the programming features of its small machines after the IBM System/360 line.

9.2 DIRECT MEMORY ACCESS OPERATION

9.2.1 The Basic Features of DMA

As mentioned in Section 9.1, programmed I/O data manipulation is too awkward and time-consuming to transfer a large block of data between the processor and high-speed peripheral units such as disk or drum memories. In addition, such programmed I/O operations are grossly inefficient in the usage of CPU time. Minicomputer and microprocessor designers have adopted the high-speed cycle-stealing channel concept to minimize this CPU inefficiency. The high-speed channel has been implemented on virtually all minicomputers and most microprocessors by DMA hardware that allows data transfers to occur concurrently with normal program execution. The DMA hardware removes the burden of moving a block of data, one word at a time, between main storage and the selected peripheral device.

The DMA channel uses the cycle-stealing concept to share access to main storage with the CPU. Since a single, main store bus is normally encountered in most small computer structures, the access to main storage must be time-shared between the processor and the DMA hardware. When the DMA wants to make a memory access, it issues a DMA request. The priority logic associated with a main store access then examines the request. If both the processor and the DMA facility have tried to access main storage simultaneously, the latter is given a higher priority and the CPU is allowed to complete the current cycle of the instruction it is executing. The processor is then forced to pause for one cycle, and the DMA facility is given direct access to main storage. The CPU registers and the state of the processor are not disturbed during the memory cycle in which the DMA has control. If more memory cycles are needed by the DMA, it must request each new cycle in competition with the CPU. In this manner, DMA operations are interleaved with CPU functions and appear transparent to the program sequence. In effect, the CPU merely skips a cycle as each data word enters or leaves main storage. The individual data word transfers are under control of the DMA channel hardware. However, the initiation and termination of the DMA operation is program-controlled.

The basic elements in a DMA unit, in addition to the necessary control circuitry, are several key registers that coordinate the data transfer operation. These key registers address memory, count the number of words transferred, and receive or transmit data. Figure 9-4 shows the interrelationship between the processor and the DMA facility.

To move a block of data between an I/O device and memory, the initialization program sets up the device control registers to specify the following information:

1. Whether the operation is a READ from or a WRITE into main storage. This is usually implied by a direction-of-transfer signal that is passed from the I/O device to the cycle-stealing control logic of the CPU.
2. The starting address of the buffer area in main storage. This is the storage area that will be used by the I/O transaction.
3. The block size or number of words associated with the buffer area.

After the various device control registers have been loaded, the device initialization program turns on the DMA channel and continues with normal program execution. Once the DMA channel has been enabled, it uses the information loaded in its control registers to request a memory cycle every time the I/O device is ready to participate in a data word exchange with main storage. Typically, the DMA channel issues a DMA request to the processor to begin the DMA operation. The cycle-stealing logic of the CPU either accepts or declines the DMA request; the request would be denied if a higher-priority DMA device had made a DMA request. If the request were denied, the I/O device would have to wait a memory cycle before it could issue another request. The cycle-stealing logic of the CPU will ultimately acknowledge the DMA request. The acknowledgement is returned to the DMA channel, permitting the channel to steal a memory cycle from the CPU. As each word is transferred, the register containing the memory address is incremented by 1 and the register containing the word count is decremented by 1. When the word count reaches 0, it indicates to the channel

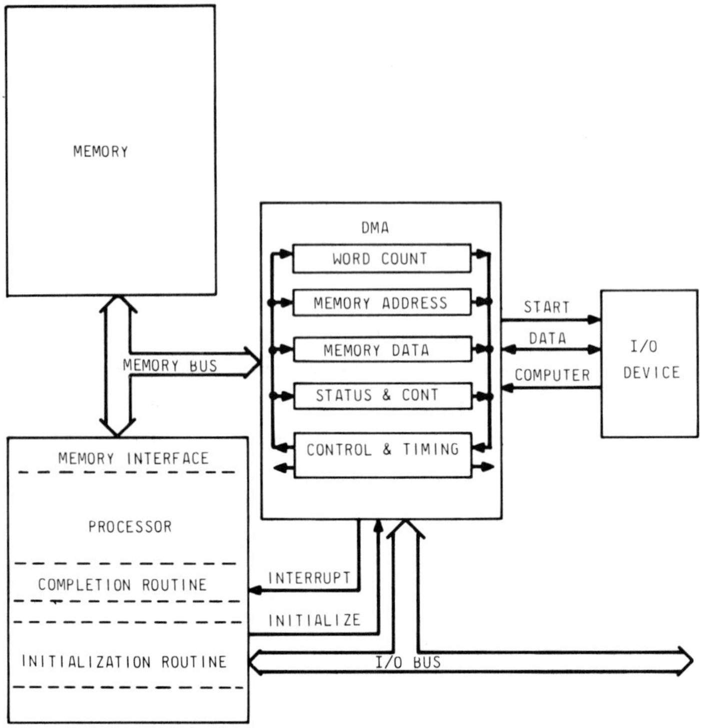

9-4 Basic small-computer DMA configuration

that the specified number of words has been transferred, and the DMA generates an interrupt to cause the processor to initiate a completion routine. In this manner, the applications program has complete control of the data transfer even though the data transfer itself is under the control of DMA hardware.

Keeping track of the word count may also be accomplished by other methods. A common technique has been to keep a 2's-complement count in the *word count* (*WC*) *register* and increment the register by 1 each time a data transfer takes place. When the last word has been transferred, a carry will be generated from the most-significant-bit position. This carry (also called an *overflow*) signifies to the DMA hardware that the block transfer operation has been completed. Another method has been to store the final address of the buffer in an *end address* (*EA*) *register*. After each data transfer, and before the *current address* (*CA*) *register* is incremented, the DMA hardware matches the contents of the CA against the contents of the EA. A match indicates that the last word in the data block has been transferred.

The most common DMA channel implementation at the mini/microcomputer level has been a single cycle-stealing operation that uses a 2's-complement count in its WC register. Figure 9-5 gives a detailed sequence chart for a single-cycle DMA operation. Note that the processor must acknowledge the I/O device's DMA request before a data exchange may take place. In addition, the WC register is incremented *after* the data word has been transferred. WC overflow is tested at that point, and the DMA operation is terminated if an overflow has occurred. Using this approach, the initial value of the WC and CA registers must be:

1. The exact number of words to be transferred (or the size of the buffer in main storage) expressed as a negative number in 2's-complement form.
2. The starting address of the buffer in main storage.

Another approach has been to have the DMA hardware manipulate the WC and CA registers *before* each data word is transferred. This technique modifies the requirements for the initial values of the WC and CA registers in the following ways:

1. The WC register must initially contain one less than the exact number of words to be transferred, again, expressed as a negative number in 2's-complement form.
2. The CA register must be preloaded with one less than the starting address of the buffer in main storage.

An overflow from the WC register, as in the other approach, signifies the completion of the block transfer operation to the DMA hardware, and it, in turn, interrupts the processor to notify the control program that DMA I/O transaction has been completed.

A priority DMA request mechanism allows several devices, each with a different data transfer rate, to be multiplexed to the store bus. These devices are able to perform independent DMA operations concurrently. The priority-request structure may be implemented in several ways. One way is to use independent store-bus request leads and store-bus grant leads (shown in Figure 9-6). Each DMA device is assigned to a separate store-bus request/store-bus grant signal couplet. Each couplet, in turn, is assigned a priority, with the CPU being given the lowest priority. A lower-priority DMA device may be stalled for a memory cycle by a higher-priority DMA device issuing a concurrent store-bus request. A store-bus grant will be sent to the highest-priority device requesting the bus. If there are no other bus requests pending, the CPU is given access to the store bus.

The DMA priority administration logic is virtually identical to the priority interrupt control facility observed in most small computers. As a means of design economy, many manufacturers supply circuit boards that may be used either for priority DMA control or for priority interrupt handling.

In general, the DMA requires (1) a direct path between the device and memory, (2) several registers to control the data transfer, and (3) a communication path to the processor in order to initiate and terminate the operation. There are various configurations designed to minimize hardware by sharing part of the circuitry either with the processor or among a group of peripheral devices. Again, as more hardware is provided, the DMA operation becomes faster. In some minicomputers, different options are incorporated into the machine to handle a variety of devices with different data transfer speeds.

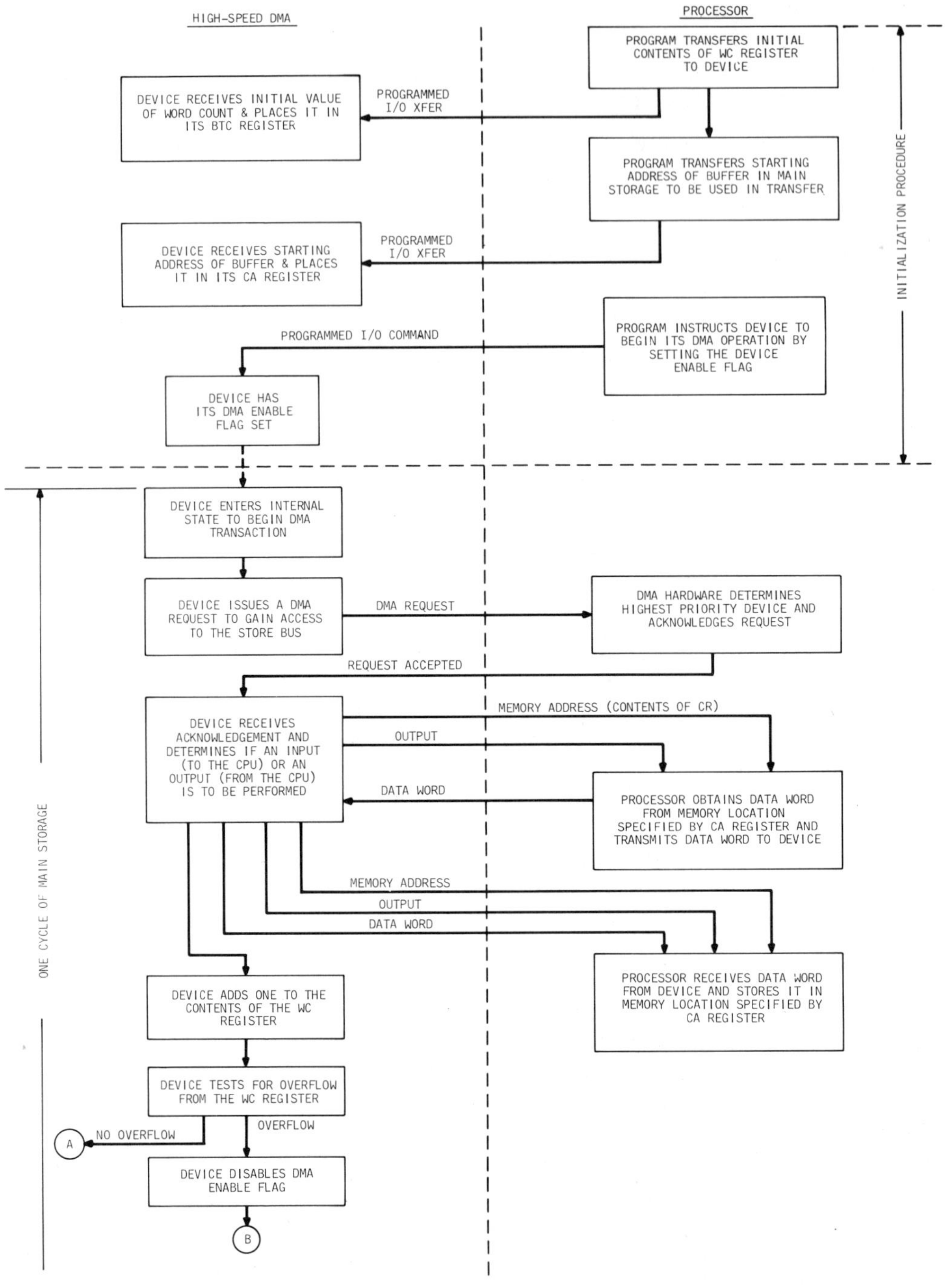

9-5 Sequence chart for single-cycle DMA operations

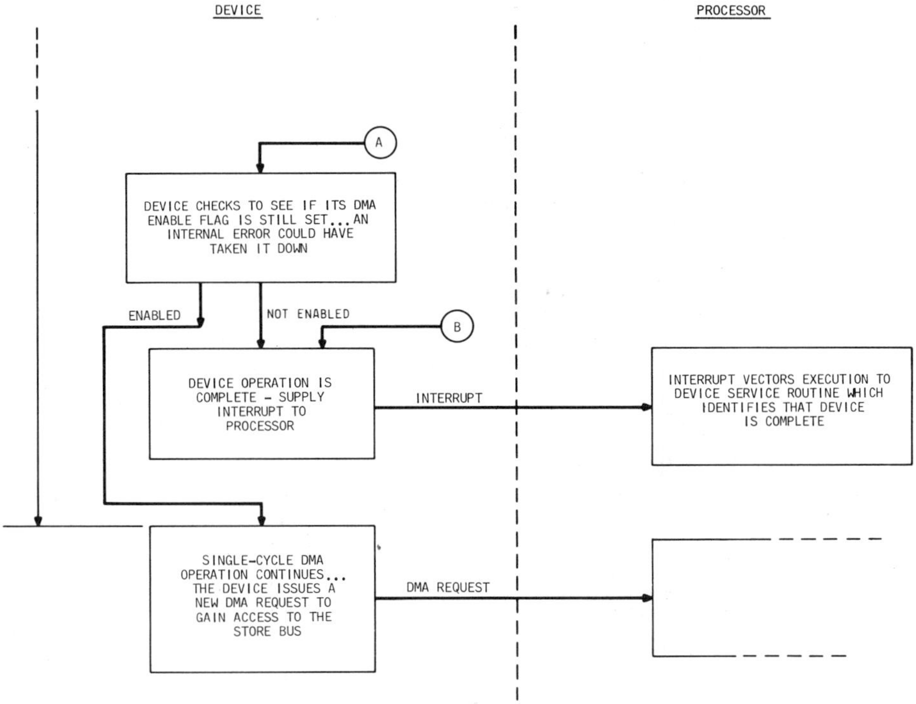

9-5 *(cont.)*

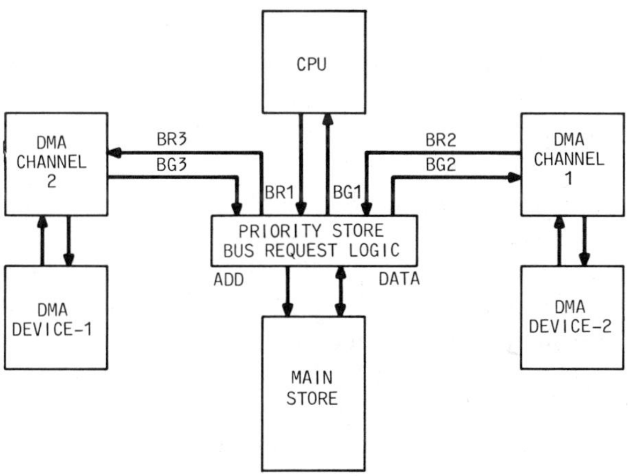

9-6 Use of separate store-bus request leads

9.2.2 Dedicated DMA

The most straightforward and expensive DMA method is the dedicated arrangement of one DMA channel per device (see Figure 9-7). The memory bus is time-shared with the processor to allow the DMA channel independent access between memory

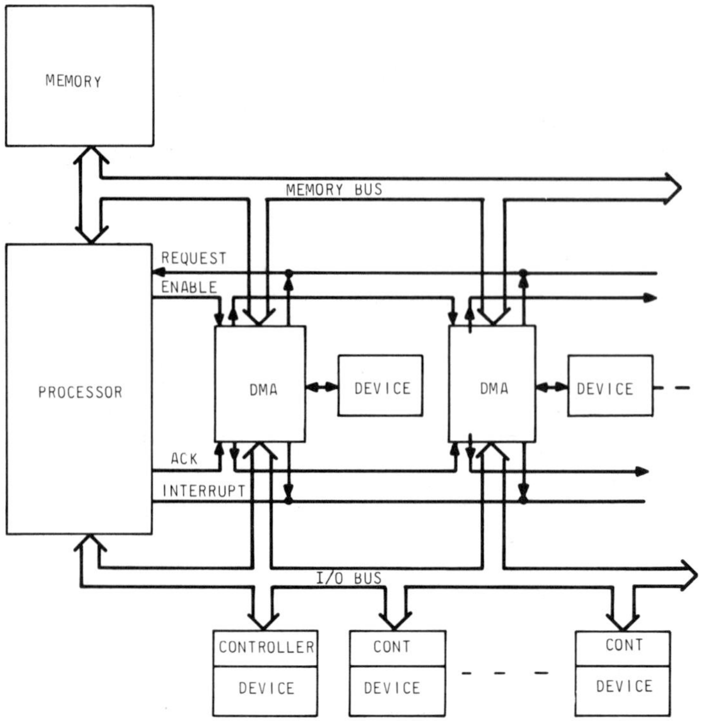

9-7 Dedicated DMA

and device. Any DMA channel may request memory access at any time. The processor scans the request line during every memory cycle. If the request line is active, the processor responds by generating an enable signal that is daisy-chained from unit to unit. The order in the chain determines the priority of the DMA channel in seizing the memory bus. If the enable signal is not "captured" by the highest-priority DMA channel, the signal is passed onto the next highest priority device, and so on, until the signal reaches the first active unit. The selected DMA channel must then be prepared to execute the memory operation. All channels may be active simultaneously, but only one unit, the highest-priority one, will gain access to the memory bus. Therefore, it is possible that the processor may be halted for a considerable length of time when several DMA channels are active simultaneously. The maximum memory transfer rate for the total system is still limited by the memory access time.

Each DMA channel is also connected to the normal I/O bus structure to allow program-directed I/O functions. This is the communication link that the processor uses to initialize the DMA channel by clearing the flags and loading the various registers within the DMA. Similarly, at the end of a DMA block transfer operation, the channel signals the processor over a high-priority interrupt line to indicate that the data transfer is complete. The processor will then enter a termination routine to update the memory allocation. The termination routine will release the block of memory locations used as a buffer for the DMA operation. In addition, it may perform other housekeeping functions involved with the memory transfer.

9.2.3 Selector DMA

The selector channel (see Figure 9-8) is functionally the same as the DMA channel described in the previous section except that the hardware is shared among a group of from 1 to 16 (or perhaps more) devices. Before the start of the DMA operation, the selector channel selects the I/O device with which it is to be associated. Once the device selection has been made and the DMA transaction initiated, the selector channel is completely dedicated to that device until the block transfer operation has been completed or the device terminates the process because it senses that an extraordinary condition has occurred. No other device may use the selector channel until the currently initiated DMA operation has been completed. Once initiated, the transfer is independent of the processor (the same as in the DMA channel). A more detailed block diagram of the information flow is shown in Figure 9-9. The data from the I/O bus can be directed to any internal register of the selector channel. In addition, the I/O bus can be connected directly to the selector bus, effectively putting all devices on the I/O bus. This allows programmed I/O functions on devices connected to the selector bus when it is not used for block transfer. In the selector operation, the program, by

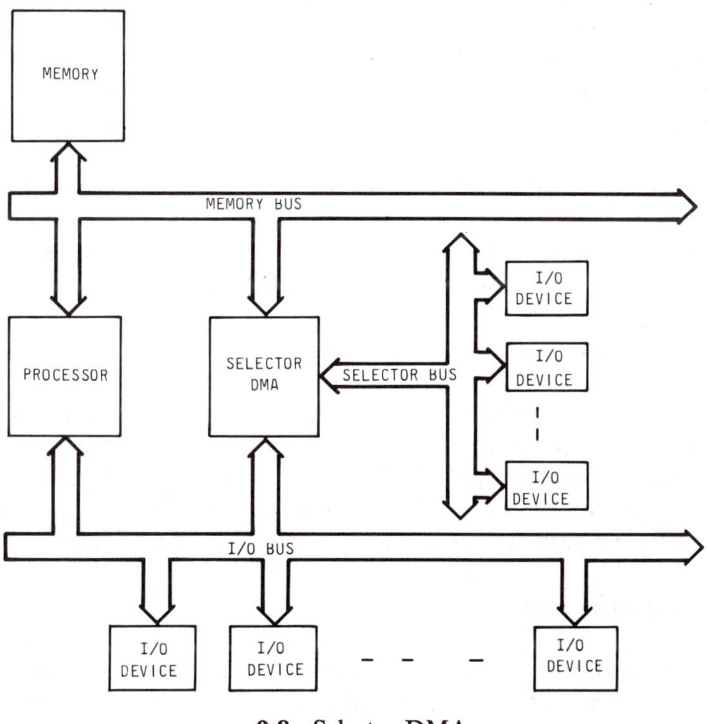

9-8 Selector DMA

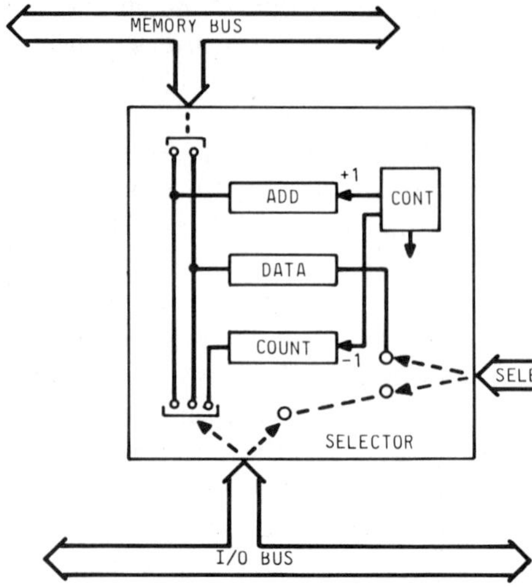

9-9 Functional diagram of selector DMA

means of the I/O bus, specifies the device address, the type of operation (read or write), the starting memory address, and the block size. Upon completion of the initialization procedure, the selector channel connects the selector bus directly to the memory bus and proceeds with the data transfer one word at a time, cycle-stealing from the processor, without further direction by the processor. As each word is transferred, the memory address and the word count are updated by the control circuitry overseeing the DMA operation. When the complete block has been transferred, the selector generates an interrupt signal to inform the processor of its termination. The selector arrangement permits many devices to share the direct memory path and the control circuitry for block transfers. Consequently, the selector channel facility permits the hardware cost for multiple DMA operations to be kept to a minimum without sacrificing the maximum data transfer rate that can be made available to a given burst-oriented device.

To reduce the hardware further, the selector bus can be eliminated entirely by having all devices connected to the I/O bus. This means that the direct memory transfer would be accomplished over the I/O bus rather than over a separate memory bus. With this scheme, there is contention not only with the memory bus but also with the I/O bus. Both memory accesses and I/O operations must be halted during data transfer between memory and an I/O device. In this situation, it may be easier to suspend the processor for a cycle rather than control the memory and the I/O buses.

9.2.4 Multiplex DMA

The selector arrangement allows only one device to access memory directly. The other units must wait until the complete block has been transferred before another can be permitted to gain access to the DMA channel. For high-speed devices, this serial operation is quite satisfactory, particularly if the transfer rate approaches the memory access speed. However, for many slower devices it is desirable to move blocks of data from several devices into memory on an interleaved basis without program intervention. Although this can be done by providing dedicated DMA channels for each device, it is costly to multiplex all the DMA's onto the memory bus.

IBM's multiplexer channel concept has been adopted by Interdata to handle several slower-speed devices that wish to concurrently access main storage rather than use individual dedicated DMA channels for each device. The multiplex channel, which contains register and control information for each device connected to it, may perform only one operation at a time. However, when operating in the multiplex mode, it breaks up these operations into short intervals. Each interval is dedicated to a specific I/O device, but every device is serviced, in turn, by the multiplexer channel during its major cycle. An I/O device is administered only during the time interval assigned to it. If it does not need service, the multiplexer channel proceeds to the next device in its scanning sequence until it locates a device requesting service. The scanning sequence determines the priority arrangement of each device.

When the recognized I/O device is ready to engage in a data word exchange with main storage, the multiplexer channel issues a DMA request. When the request is finally recognized, it steals a memory cycle from the CPU and executes the data word exchange. This technique still requires additional hardware to be concentrated in the multiplexer channel in the form of control logic and registers. An alternative approach in early machines, for instance the PDP8, is to place the control registers associated with each DMA device in main storage and allow the cycle-stealing hardware of the CPU to administer them.

When an I/O device wishes to perform a direct memory transfer using the *multiplex* DMA channel, it sends a request signal to the *direct memory control* (*DMC*) *unit*, as shown in Figure 9-10. The DMC responds with an acknowledge signal that is daisy-chained through all the DMA devices. The highest-priority device will capture the acknowledge signal and return the device address to the DMC. The DMC performs the DMA operation for the selected I/O device.

If the processor is halted during the DMA transfer, hardware simplification can be obtained by taking advantage of the processor's internal circuitry that is used to process the current instruction. This circuitry can be used for a DMA function without having to save and restore any data in memory. For example, the processor may contain a memory address register and a memory output register, which serve as temporary buffer registers for memory read and write operations. The registers do not store data to be used by the next instruction in the program sequence and, consequently, can be used between instruction fetches. By sharing these registers, the additional connection to the memory bus from the DMA circuitry may be eliminated. Furthermore, if the processor is a microprogrammed machine, the control sequence could easily be stored in the microprogram memory. Whenever a DMA operation is initiated from one of the devices connected to a special request (interrupt) line, a microprogram interrupt is generated between instructions to handle the direct memory transfer, using the common address and output registers. The operation

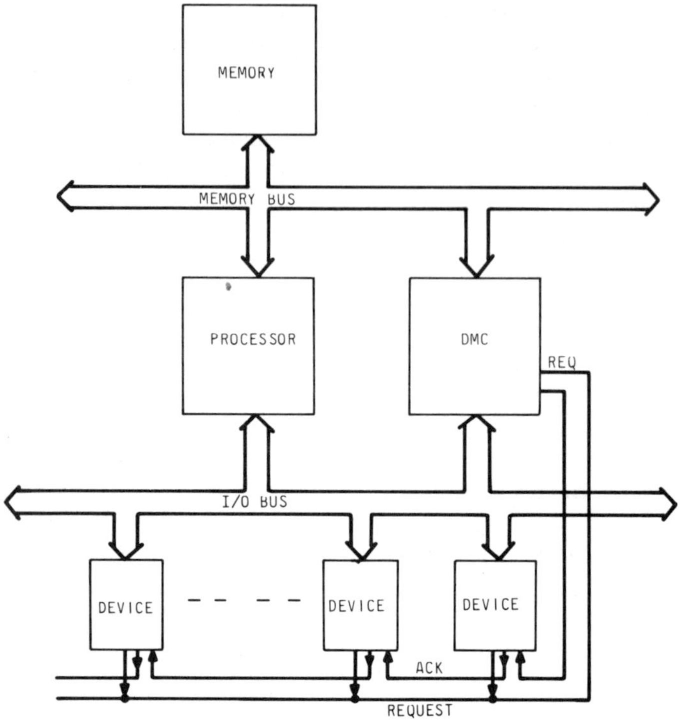

9-10 Multiplex DMA

steals an instruction cycle. This scheme of *interleaved-DMA* is almost the same as for programmed I/O except that the direct memory transfer is independent of the main program. The overhead of saving and restoring the PC and internal registers is not incurred by this technique, and the same microprogram sequence, rather than a separate routine for each device (see Figure 9-11), is used for the transfer.

9.2.5 The Usage of a DMA Scheduler

The DMA facility treats each machine cycle as a resource that must be shared by all devices that engage in an I/O transaction with main storage. Under normal operating conditions, a small computer system will have, at most, one or two DMA devices running concurrently. In special cases, three or more may be operational simultaneously. Two types of serious system operational problems can be encountered in a DMA environment in which multiple devices are active. The first type of problem is the *degradation of CPU utilization*, while the second is *seizure of store bus by a single DMA device* to the exclusion of all other DMA devices, as well as the CPU. In the first problem, one or more DMA devices may be active at a time so that the CPU is given

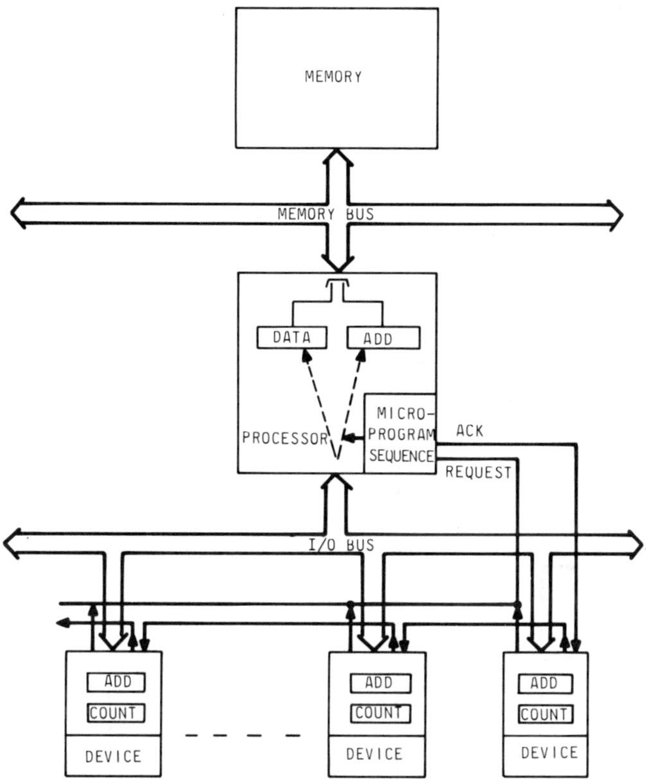

9-11 Interleaved DMA—instruction cycle-stealing

only occasional access to main storage by the store-bus arbitration unit. In the extreme case, the store bus is seized by the aggregate of DMA devices and the CPU is locked out from main storage until the critical DMA block transfers are completed. In this case, the CPU is given the lowest priority of any device attempting to access main storage. An alternative strategy is to permit the arbitration unit to concede a main store cycle to the CPU after a fixed number of store accesses by the concurrently running DMA devices. This strategy requires additional logic in the store-bus arbitration unit and is directly influenced by the second serious system problem which is outlined below.

Figure 9-12 illustrates the arbitration of main store usage for several concurrently operating DMA devices and the CPU. In this example, a fixed-head disk, a cartridge tape unit, and a high-speed printer are used. The interval between successive DMA requests for each device is given, assuming no store-bus contention. The allocation of each main store cycle is shown in the last illustration in the figure and represents a typical interleaved DMA operation. The interval between successive DMA requests for a device represents the assembly time for the next word required by the DMA device plus a store access interval. This is normally the maximum latency that a DMA

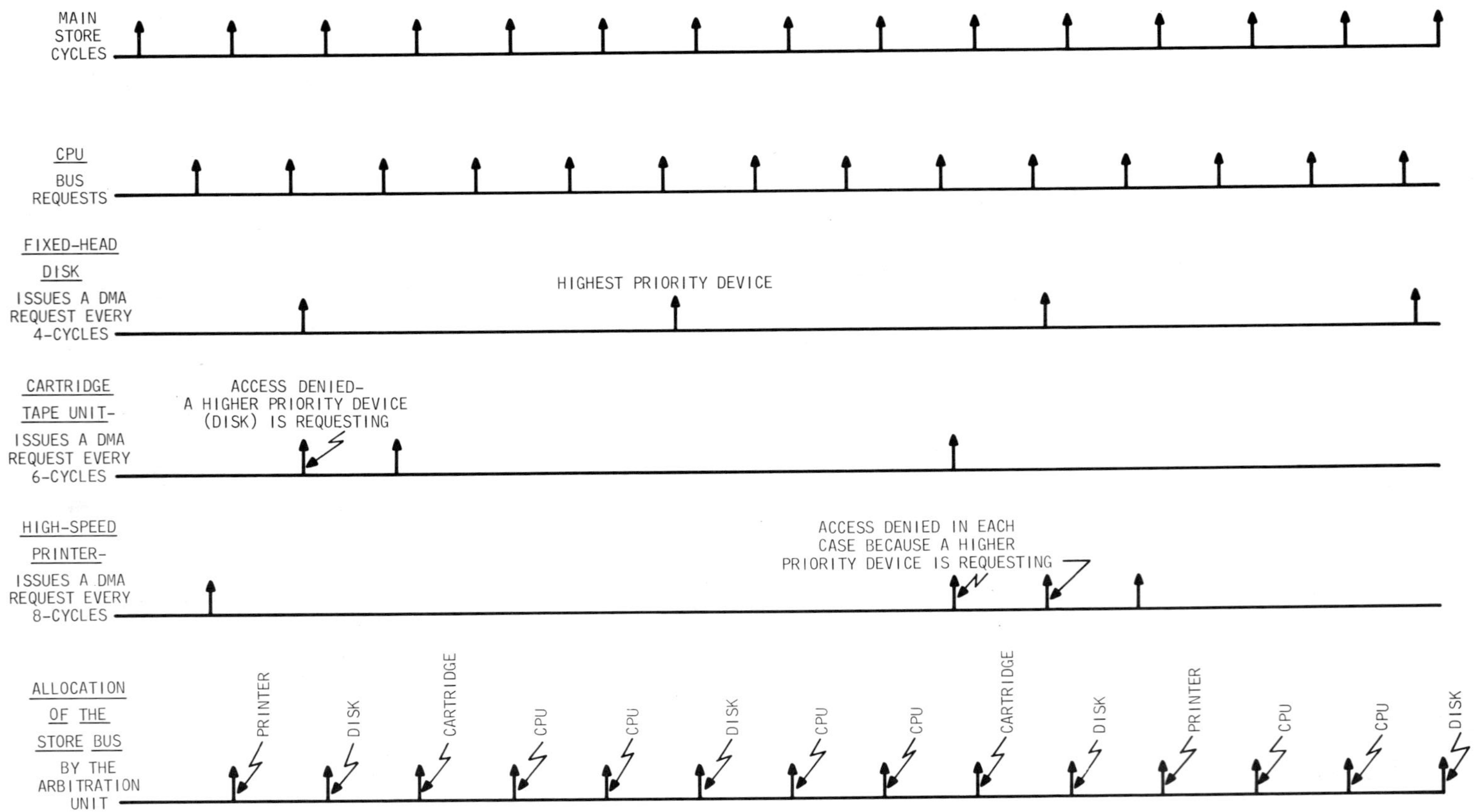

9-12 Store-bus arbitration for DMA requests

device can experience before the current word to be transferred will be mutilated by the next word to be transferred. That is, either the current word will be overwritten by the next word, or it will be stored in the wrong location on the DMA device. As the latency of a high-speed DMA device approaches the cycle time of main storage, not only will it lock out the CPU, but it can compromise the function of any other DMA unit running concurrently. The high-speed unit will "hog" the store bus and permit only an occasional access to main storage by any concurrently operational DMA unit. If the interval of occasional access is greater than the maximum time permitted by any DMA unit to transfer a data word, mutilation of information will occur. Since DMA operation at the small computer level proceeds to completion once a DMA device has been given the START command, this type of data mutilation cannot be prevented by the hardware-DMA facility. Instead, it can be prevented only by the judicious scheduling of DMA devices through software, so that two or more devices are not activated at the same time, with conflicting DMA information exchange rates.

This situation can be handled quite simply by a DMA scheduler that contains a record of all the DMA devices that are attached to the system. Included in this record is a table of the maximum delay that each DMA device may experience before the information being exchanged by the device with main storage is compromised. The fundamental characteristic of the DMA scheduler is that it is the only entity that may initiate a DMA operation. It determines those DMA devices that may be concurrently active by evaluating the associated waiting time of each device. A DMA scheduler would perform the following basic functions:

1. Evaluate any block transfer request by the system to determine if the requested DMA device may be activated under the current configuration of concurrently active DMA devices.
2. Keep a record of those DMA devices that are currently activated and dynamically update this record as a device completes its block transfer operation and/or a new DMA device is activated.
3. In its simplest form, use an algorithm based on the maximum waiting time that a device may experience to determine when that device may be activated to begin a block transfer operation. For instance, a DMA device that could wait no more then the cycle time of main storage would not be activated until all other DMA devices had been completed. Similarly, no other DMA devices would be permitted to start block transfer operations until the very high speed DMA device had completed. Obviously, the CPU would be stalled during the entire block transfer operation of the high-speed DMA unit. In this manner, a DMA scheduler would regulate the contention for the usage of main storage by enabling only selected DMA devices to operate concurrently. It would be possible to optimize CPU utilization if the DMA scheduler were made sufficiently intelligent. But, most importantly, such a DMA scheduler would minimize the possibility of information mutilation in an environment in which several different DMA devices would be simultaneously active.

9.2.6 DMA Operation at the Microprocessor Level

The facility for DMA did not appear in the first microprocessor structures. The Intel 4004 did not possess this feature nor did any other 4-bit microprocessor. The Intel 8008, however, possessed a DMA capability, as did several of the other early 8-bit devices. This trend continued with the appearance of second-generation devices; the 4-bit microprocessors were implemented without consideration for DMA operation. They functioned as serial calculator structures that performed highly prescribed internal algorithms. In contrast, by the spring of 1976 most 8-bit microprocessors were designed to permit some form of DMA operation.

One characteristic of microprocessor-oriented DMA is that each DMA device incorporates an interface that possesses the necessary control hardware to implement the DMA operation at the device. Typically, this control hardware consists of the same elements found in a minicomputer DMA interface but implemented as a special chip that mates directly with the microcomputer chip-set configuration. For example:

1. An address register is used to point to the main storage location at which the next data exchange is to take place. The address register is preloaded by the microprocessor to contain the starting address in memory at which the DMA transfer is to begin. This register is incremented by 1 by the DMA device control logic.
2. A data register receives or transmits information between main storage and the DMA device.
3. A counter determines when the block transfer operation has completed. It is preset to the number of words involved in the block transfer. The counter is decremented by 1 by the DMA device control logic after each data word exchange. When the counter reaches 0, it supplies an interrupt to the microprocessing unit, which signifies that the operation has concluded.

Figure 9-13 illustrates a microcomputer system that achieves multiplexed DMA operation through the use of a *direct memory access controller* (*DMAC*) *chip*. The DMAC permits up to eight I/O devices to simultaneously request separate DMA transactions. The requests are serviced on a hardware-priority basis determined by the input pin sequence. Normally, the input pin labeled *CH-1* has the highest DMA priority, while the input pin labeled *CH-8* has the lowest. Using this convention, an I/O device informs the DMAC that it wishes to engage in a DMA transaction. Each DMA unit enters the DMAC on a separate input path or channel. A DMA device issues a request to the DMAC over this path, and it, in turn, requests direct access to memory from the CPU. The DMAC arbitrates the priority of simultaneously requesting devices and enables the highest-priority DMA device to begin the I/O transaction after the DMAC has received an acknowledgement of the DMA request from the CPU. The DMAC acts as a hardware multiplexor for DMA operations and contains eight separate register sets, one for each channel. Figure 9-14 gives a possible logical organization for such a DMAC chip. Note that each DMA channel has its own address register and block counter. The DMAC determines which register set to use and

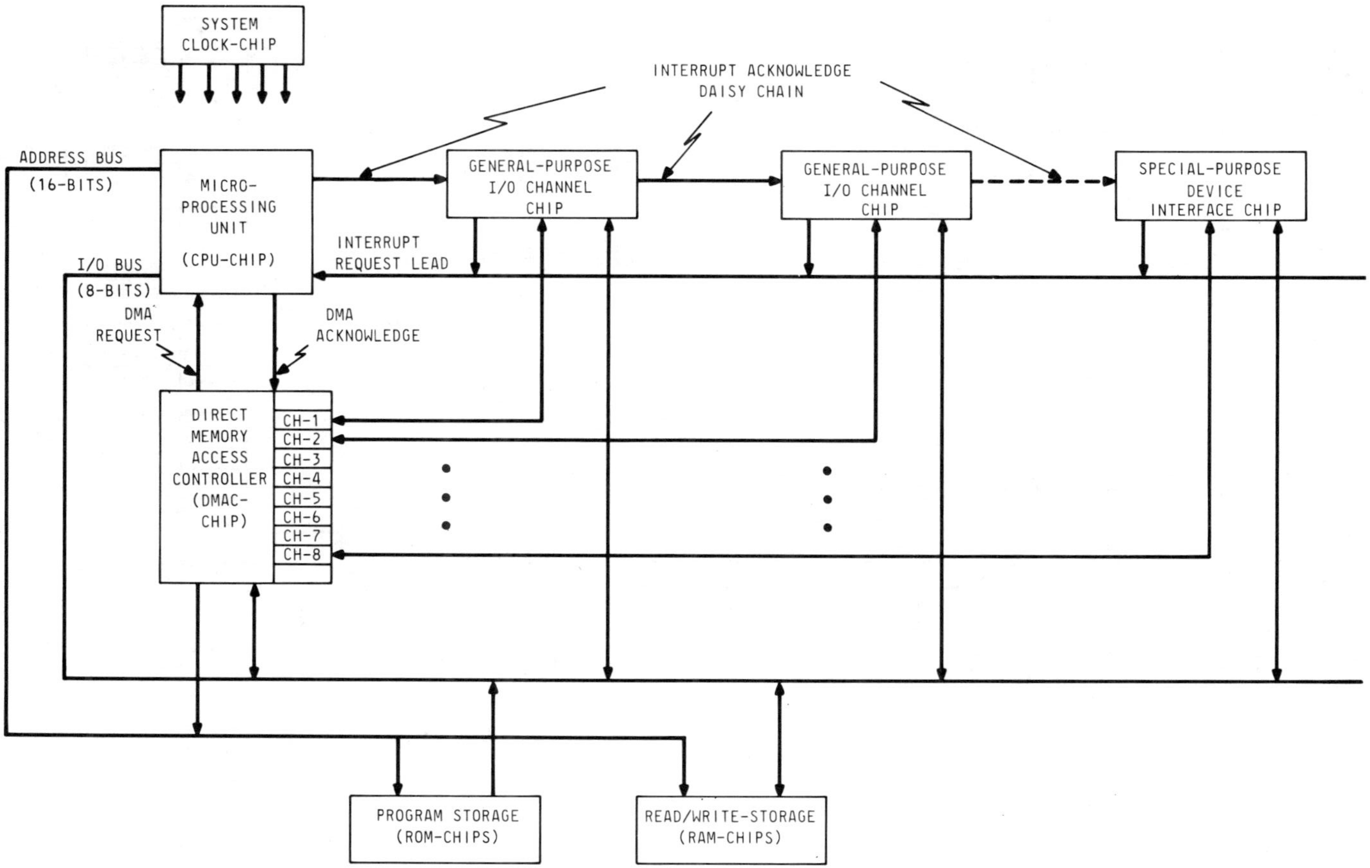

9-13 Possible microcomputer system exhibiting multiplexed DMA operation

then allows the block transfer operation associated with that channel to take place. Figure 9-14 also illustrates the types of signals that must be accounted for at the DMAC chip level. Since it is possible to use more than one DMAC chip, provision

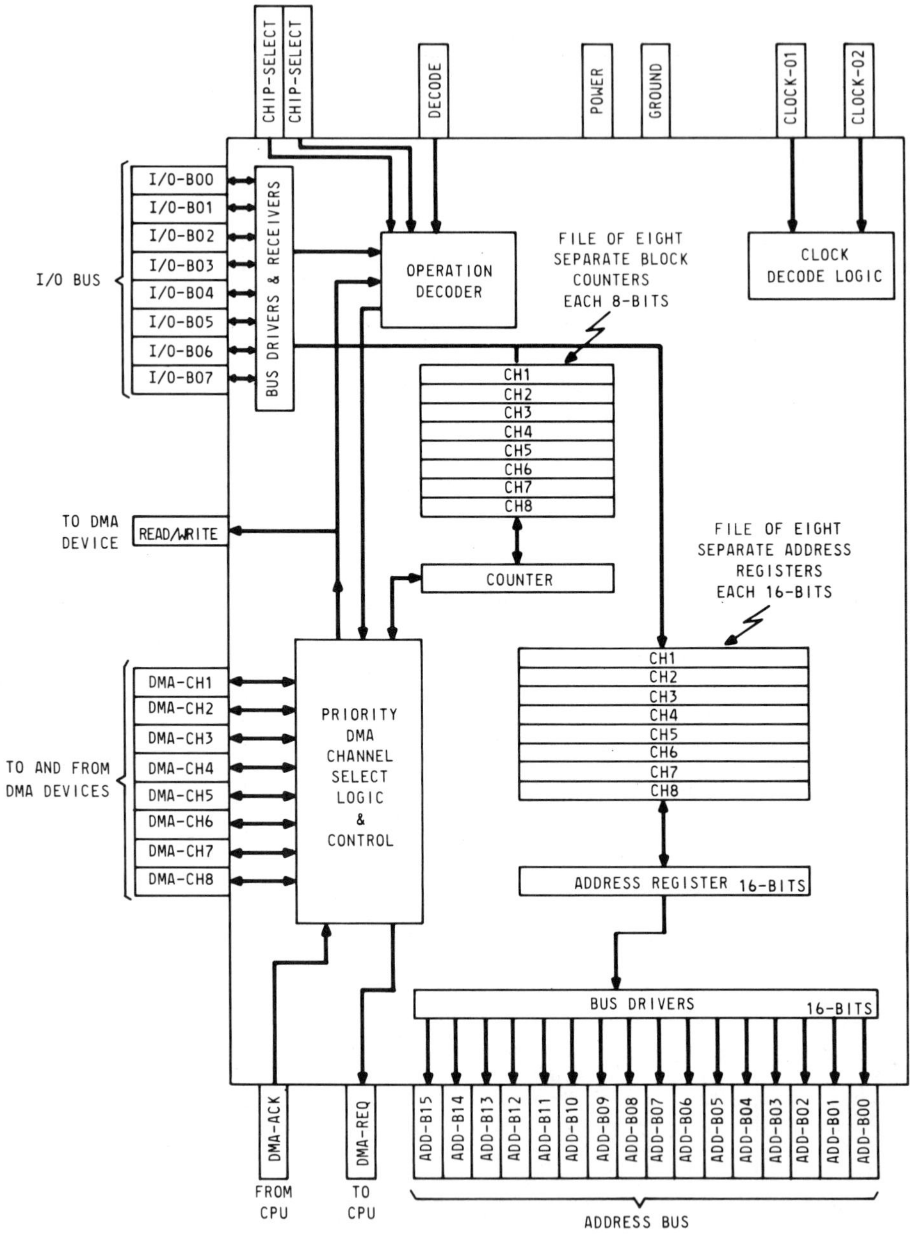

9-14 Possible logical organization for the DMA chip

must be made for a chip select code to enable the appropriate DMAC device. In addition, the width of the address word may be quite different from the width of the data word. Perhaps the most striking fact is the similarity of the DMAC chip to the T^2L boards used to perform the same functions on a conventional minicomputer.

For this particular microcomputer configuration, which is patterned after the Rockwell PPS-8 microprocessing system, the CPU will enter an internal hold state once the DMA operation has begun, and remain there until the block transfer has concluded. DMA completion is achieved by either the device relinquishing its DMA request signal to the DMAC or the block counter having been decremented to 0. This configuration permits only one form of DMA operation. There are other implementations, and it is worthwhile considering the main variations.

The expression "direct memory access" has been used to describe several different techniques for exchanging information between a peripheral device and main storage at the microprocessor level. In each technique, the DMA facility reads from or writes into main storage at a data transfer rate that exceeds the capability of the microprocessing unit to administer program-controlled I/O. In only one of these cases is the DMA implementation of the familiar cycle-stealing operation used on the conventional minicomputer. Three fundamental techniques have been used at the 8-bit microprocessor level:

1. The DMA transfer is achieved by placing the microprocessing unit in the HALT state. This is normally accomplished by the DMA device activating a halt request on the appropriate input pin of the microprocessor DIP. The result of this request is that the microprocessor is forced to enter an internal state in which the address and data buses are placed in their high-impedance states. Effectively, the microprocessing unit is divorced from its address and data buses. This technique permits a peripheral device to seize control of each bus and exchange data words directly with memory without any interaction from the microprocessor. The address and data buses appear to be physically ORed with the bus of the DMA device.

   A form of handshaking takes place between the microprocessor and the DMA device before a data word may be transferred. While the microprocessor must acknowledge the halt request, it will not respond with such an acknowledgement until it has finished executing the current instruction. When the execution of this instruction has completed, the microprocessor will enter the HALT or HOLD state and return a halt-acknowledge signal to the requesting DMA device. For instance, when the Intel 8080 enters the HOLD state, it sends a hold-acknowledge signal to the peripheral device and suspends operation of the CPU. When the Motorola MC6800 enters the HALT state, it replies with a *bus-available* (*BA*) *signal* to the requesting DMA device. The DMA device performs its data transfer, and when the block transfer is complete, it releases the halt request line; this action ends the DMA operation.

   The form of DMA operation just described permits data to be transferred between the DMA device and main storage at the maximum information exchange rate sustained by the memories used with the microprocessor. It definitely degrades the overall throughput of the system since the CPU is stalled at the start of each DMA transfer until the required number of data words have been transferred. No program execution may take place during this period.

2. The DMA transfer takes place on a cycle-stealing basis with the microprocessing unit. The microprocessor is allowed to run normally, with the DMA device gaining access to main storage on an interleaved basis with the CPU. The best example of this situation is Motorola's MC6800 microprocessor. The MC6800 provides an additional control signal as an input to the CPU. This signal is the *three-state control* (*TSC*) *input*, which may be used to implement short DMA transfer operations, as opposed to the halt line used for extended block transfer operations. The TSC-initiated DMA mode is used for operations in which control must be passed to the requesting DMA device within 500 nanoseconds of the first appearance of the DMA request. If the MC6800 clock is set to run at 1 megahertz, a TSC request will halt the microprocessing unit within 500 nanoseconds after receiving the request instead of at the end of the current instruction's execution phase. The MC6800 runs off two clock signals (the $\Phi 1$ clock phase and the $\Phi 2$ clock phase), both of which are stopped by the TSC signal for the period of the DMA transfer. The MC6800 has physical address and memory refresh requirements which dictate that the clocks must be reactivated within 5 microseconds or the microprocessing unit will lose the data it has stored internally. This requirement places a limitation on the length of time an individual block transfer may be active. However, 5-microsecond bursts of DMA operation may be interleaved with normal CPU processing to achieve a maximum DMA data transfer rate of 1 byte every 2.5 microseconds. In this case, the microprocessor's control program will be permitted to execute at a minimum rate of one cycle every 5 microseconds.

   The advantage offered by the TSC-initiated DMA is that it provides quick response to a DMA request. However, the major disadvantage of the TSC-initiated DMA is the limited length of time that an individual burst transfer may be active (5 microseconds as mentioned previously). In comparison, the halt-initiated DMA may take as many as 13 machine cycles before responding to a DMA request. Once the CPU operation has been suspended, the DMA transfer may continue indefinitely.

3. A third technique has been suggested for use with the MC6800 that makes the DMA operation completely transparent to the microprocessing unit. The MC6800 performs data transfers with memory only during the active portion of the $\Phi 2$ clock phase. Since the $\Phi 1$ and $\Phi 2$ clock phases function 180 degrees out of phase, individual DMA byte transfers can take place during the active phase of the $\Phi 1$ clock phase without ever halting or interfering with the operation of the microprocessing unit. This technique effectively multiplexes the DMA operation with the execution of the control program for the microprocessor. Compared to 1 and 2, this technique provides the highest program-execution rate and is most effective when used with very fast memories.

9.3 SERIAL COMMUNICATION METHODS

9.3.1 General Description of Serial Channels

Serial channel design has not been used extensively in peripheral communication, particularly in small systems where all modules are in relatively close proximity. The party-line bus structure, as previously described, is normally used. When the bus has to extend any appreciable distance, a repeater station is added to provide the necessary amplification. A serial channel removes the need for a parallel bus-repeater unit. One shortcoming of the serial technique is that it is slower than the parallel structure technique. However, for many applications, this is not a critical factor since (1) the response time of many peripheral devices is slow when compared with the execution time of the CPU, and (2) the throughput of the system is not limited by the use of serial communication methods. A more critical factor is the cost in converting a parallel data stream from the processor to a serial stream and then back to a parallel data word at the device. If the transmission distance is short, the double conversion is a bad trade-off for a few inches of wires.

When the transmission distance is long, the reduction of cable drivers, receivers, and cabling more than offsets the increase in complexity in digital electronics. In some instances, the simplification of connectors and cables allows the use of a patch panel so that expensive peripherals (e.g., a high-speed line printer or one-of-a-kind devices like a picture scanner) can be shared among several minicomputers. This flexibility enhances the total system in view of the fact that some peripherals cost many times that of the processor. Moreover, the interconnection of two or more minicomputers is easier if the ability to change or grow is a concern in an operational environment. Furthermore, checking and isolating trouble conditions is much simpler in a serial channel than it is in a parallel one.

In general, a serial channel can be arranged in a manner similar to the parallel channel. The two common structures are shown in Figure 9-15a. The first one is a dedicated configuration in which an individual device is assigned to a unique channel. As the system grows, channels can be added or removed without disturbing the rest of the system. Both simplex and duplex methods have been implemented; the choice depends on the distance and the cost of adding an additional pair of wires to allow simultaneous transmission in both directions. Simplex permits transmission of information in only one direction; it uses a single pair of wires. Duplex, on the other hand, permits transmission in both directions and involves two pairs of wires. One is used to send while the other is simultaneously being used to receive. The loose coupling of the dedicated serial channel arrangement allows a greater flexibility in organizing and positioning a variety of devices to meet the system's needs. The second structure is the closed-loop arrangement shown in Figure 9-15b. One channel is shared by all devices connected in a serial loop, permitting information initiated by the processor to be propagated from device to device and finally returned to the processor. The message normally contains a device address followed by data or a command. The selected device

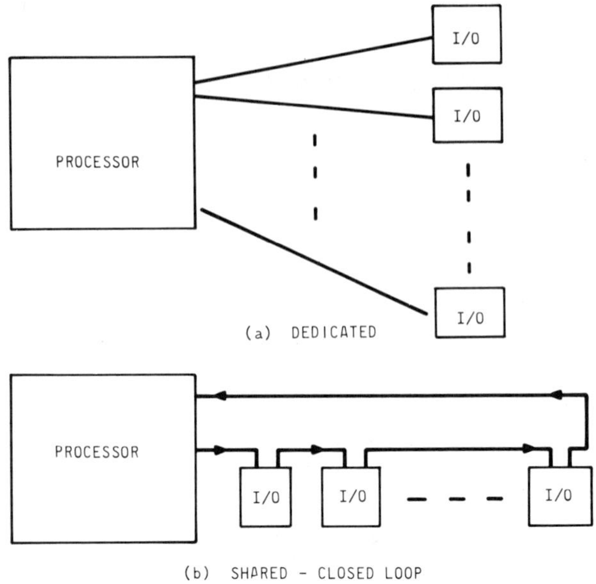

9-15 Two basic serial channel structures

will respond by accepting the data or inserting data at the end of the message to be routed back to the processor. The end result is that for each transmission, a response is obtained as a return message.

To communicate asynchronously with the devices, a handshaking protocol is used to perform data transfers in both types of serial channels. This is necessary to account for variations in the speed of different units and to provide the flexibility needed to handle new devices as technology advances. The shared serial channel is more tightly coupled as a system. Hence, it may be more difficult to change than the dedicated channel configuration.

9.3.2 Dedicated Local Serial Channel

The number of peripheral devices may vary from one I/O unit to many I/O units in the applications of small systems. In a party-line bus structure, the number of devices that can be connected to the same bus depends on the fan-out capability of the cable drivers and the length of the cables. Normally, the bus is capable of driving about 20 loads. If more loads need to be driven, the bus can be extended by adding a stage of amplification; no additional circuitry within the processor is needed. However, with the dedicated serial channel scheme, there is some circuitry associated on a per-channel basis. It may not be economical to partition and package one channel per circuit board and add channels as they are needed. On the other hand, if hardware *is* provided to achieve maximum processing capability, it penalizes the smaller systems that are usually very sensitive to cost considerations. A practical compromise is to partition and equip the channels functionally on a block basis (e.g., 16 at a time as shown in Figure 9-16). A system such as this could grow to a total of 16 blocks, giving a maximum of 256 serial channels. This approach also minimizes the number of internal interconnections within the processor.

Figure 9-16 shows the interrelationship between the I/O channels and the internal processor. A dedicated I/O buffer register transfers data between the processor and the channel. The I/O channel data bus is always directed to one of 16 channel blocks by the selector circuit. Transferring data from the processor to the I/O channel involves first loading the channel block number so that the bus is directed to the specified channel block. Next, the data are loaded, either from memory or from another general register, into the I/O buffer register. The last step involves gating the data into the I/O channel register. Although several steps have been indicated for the data transfer, they are normally combined as a single instruction that loads data into the specified I/O channel and then issues the necessary command to initiate the I/O operation.

Figure 9-17 shows a more detailed functional diagram of a block of I/O channels. Associated with each block is a common shift register that transmits or receives serial data to or from the device. A status and control register is also included to define one of 16 channels as the active channel and to keep track of the status of the channel. The control circuitry provides the autonomous timing and sequencing signals necessary to perform the shifting operations associated with sending or receiving the serial data. The system clock is the timing source for such functions. This is done

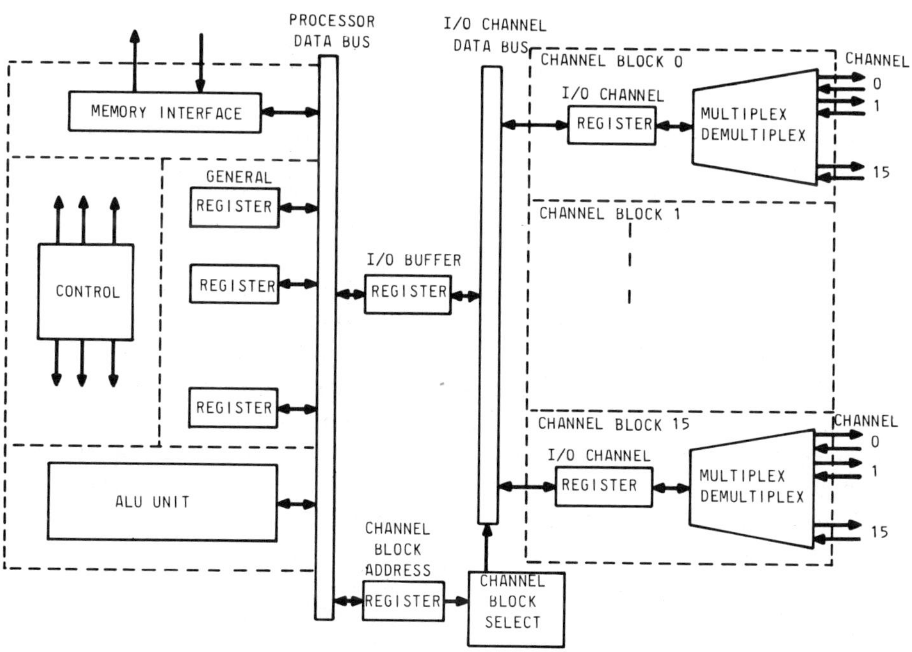

9-16 Interrelationship between I/O channels and the internal processor

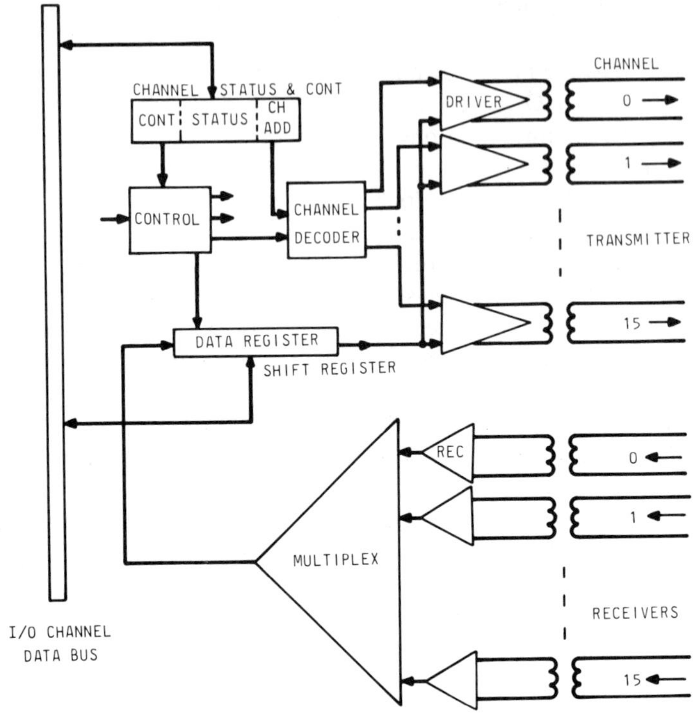

9-17 Functional diagram of an I/O channel block

automatically without intervention by the processor. In this specific application, the basic machine cycle is 125 nanoseconds, divided into four clock phases. They shift data at the rate of 8 megahertz. The operation of the I/O channel control and sequencing logic is independent of the processor. The program may continue to execute additional instructions and return at a later time to pick up the received message. This is particularly useful for a very slow peripheral unit. In addition, several serial channels may be activated concurrently without degrading the processor's performance.

To initiate an I/O command, the processor loads the I/O data register and the status and channel select register and then gives the go-ahead signal. As far as the processor is concerned, it has completed the I/O command. The I/O internal control logic, using the system clock, starts shifting out the contents of the data register. A 01 start code is added at the beginning of the 16-bit data message. The message is transmitted serially, 1 bit every 125 nanoseconds, into a twisted pair, or miniature coaxial cable, that may reach as far as 100 feet to the peripheral device. The maximum distance is largely determined by the transmission characteristics of the line, the electrical signal levels required by the drivers and receivers, and the size and frequency response of the cable. As the bits are shifted into the receiver at the peripheral device, the start code is used to detect the arrival of the data in the proper position in the device's shift register. The choice of 01 as a start code was dictated by the need for the hardware to check whether the device shift register was capable of shifting 1's and 0's correctly. A separate cable is used for each direction of transmission to simplify the circuitry.

The timing required to shift the message into the receiver is provided by the incoming bipolar pulses (a positive and negative pulse is used for a 1, and a negative and positive pulse is used for a 0). When the start code indicates that the message has been completed, the shifting is inhibited and the parity of the message is checked. The data link on which the message arrived continues to transmit clock pulses (all 0's) from the I/O channel to provide timing for the peripheral unit controller and a timing source for the shifting back of the return message. Thus, when the peripheral device completes its execution, it loads the response and the appropriate check bits into the buffer register and raises a flag. At that time, the message is shifted back to the data register in the I/O channel. The start code is added to this message, and then the end-of-shifting signal, indicated by the start code reaching the end of the shift register, results in the clock being inhibited from outpulsing additional 0's onto the channel. The I/O channel control then flags the processor by setting a status bit. The processor, upon interrogation of the flag, reads the contents of the return message in the data register (shift register), and the I/O command cycle is complete. The operation just described involves handshaking (request-response techniques to permit asynchronous communication). In addition to the 16 message bits, 2 parity check bits, and 2 start bits, an additional bit is used to indicate whether the 16 message bits are to be interpreted as data or command information. This allows considerable flexibility in interpreting the messages. For example, using a command message, an I/O controller may be set up to receive a continuous string of data words.

9.3.3 Dedicated External Serial Channel

In some industrial applications, small computers perform data acquisition, which requires data from many stations to be compiled, assembled, and processed in a larger central machine. For certain applications, a common data base with large resources is desirable to coordinate and furnish programs to be executed by the satellite stations. For example, in the production of IBM System/7 computers, another System/7 is used as a tester to check out the machines as they come off the assembly line. In order to meet the production volume, there are many stations operating concurrently. Each station is required to test extensively the System/7 being evaluated and log the results so that records can be kept. This, of course, requires a large program as well as constant changes and additions. An arrangement as shown in Figure 9-18 has been used for this purpose. The testers or satellite stations are scattered throughout the factory and may be several hundred feet away from the main computer. The computer-to-computer communication, as indicated in the figure, takes place by means of a serial channel operated in the simplex mode (i.e., there is only one coaxial cable connected between the main computer and each satellite station). Transmission cannot be carried out in both directions simultaneously. Since the distance is relatively long, the cost savings in sharing the same coaxial cable for data transfer in either direction outweighs the sacrifice of the small delay in turning the line around whenever reverse transmission is

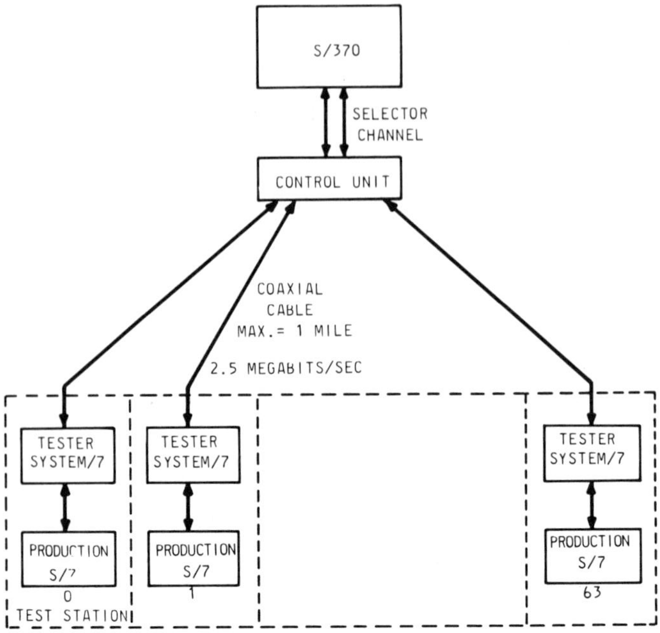

9-18 Main computer to satellite communication scheme

desired. At the main computer, a control unit is connected to the selector channel of an IBM System/370 to directly access main storage when entering or extracting data from the host machine. The control unit provides the interface for converting a parallel data word to a serial stream at 2.5 megabits per second. In addition, it coordinates the data transfers between the host machine and up to 64 satellite System/7 units. These units may be located as far away as 1 mile from the host processor. At each satellite, an adapter is required to receive the data and convert the serial bit stream to a parallel data word for the System/7.

The communication procedure that takes place between the host and each satellite is initiated by a sequential polling of any or all remote units. This is done by the control unit under control of the host program. This method determines whether a polled unit requires service. If the response is positive, the polled unit will send a block of 16 bytes of data to the host machine, indicating the desired action. The host system will interpret the data block sent by the satellite and then proceed to carry out the required operation. If the request is for a block of words in memory, the control unit will access and read the words one at a time through the selector channel. It will then transmit the data serially to the satellite unit until the specified block has been completely transferred. Similarly, if the data transfer is in the other direction, the information is obtained from the memory of the System/7 that is acting as a test station. The test station interface converts the test information into a bit stream and directs the serial data to the control unit of the host processor. The control unit uses the selector channel to access and write the test information into the host machine's memory.

One copy of the satellite program can be stored in the central memory of the host processor and called for by each of the satellite stations, facilitating changes and additions. The test results can be accumulated and processed automatically in one data bank on the host machine to obtain a quick, accurate, and economical summary of the overall testing process.

The serial channel technique used to connect satellite computers in a factory environment has many advantages. One advantage is that the cabling is simplified considerably, allowing the individual units to be moved easily. They can be added or removed from the system without many changes and without disrupting the other factory units. Since the separation between units can be quite long, it is much easier to protect against electrical noises when there are fewer interconnections. Also, the loose-coupling feature provides complete independence between satellite units. Therefore, it is much easier to maintain and isolate fault conditions.

9.3.4 Shared Serial Channel

Another serial channel configuration is the *single-loop arrangement*. In this configuration, information is transmitted in a serial stream that threads its way from device to device and then returns to the processor to form a loop. Information may be exchanged between stations as data move through the various I/O devices in a manner similar to the steam train that circles Disneyland. Passengers clamber aboard or disembark as the train passes through each station. The passengers represent information packets that are transported through each station until they arrive at their destination. Each station must be traversed sequentially with only those passengers bound for the current station actually leaving the train. This type of communication structure is ideally suited for linking many smaller devices that are scattered over a relatively long distance. For example, this technique is used as a means of providing a flexible plant communication and data collection system (a general block diagram is shown in Figure 9-19). Attached to the System/7 processor is a control module that coordinates the transfer of digital information from area stations at key locations in a plant to the host processor. Each area station may contain several data entry units (e.g., a printer, a badge scanner, a card reader, a display unit, or a key entry unit). The communication system is connected by a two-wire, high-speed loop, capable of operating at about 500,000 bits per second, with data represented by bipolar pulses. The area stations are attached to the transmission loop by inserting a 1-byte shift register in series with the line as shown in Figure 9-20. This shift register signals the area station if it is to examine the message and perhaps modify the data before passing them on to the next station in the loop. The maximum distance between two stations is 1000 feet, and the maximum number of stations that may be connected in the loop is 128. However, the limit depends largely on the program and storage available to process the data.

The data format of a message transmitted over the loop is shown in Figure 9-21. It consists of 5 information bytes and 25 synchronization bytes; the total is called an *active frame*. An *inactive frame* contains a start byte and 29 synchronization bytes.

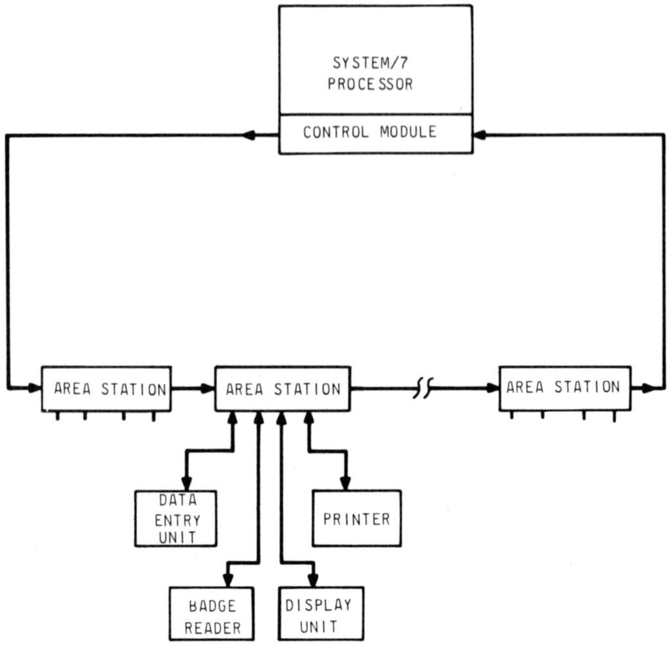

9-19 Serial closed-loop communication scheme

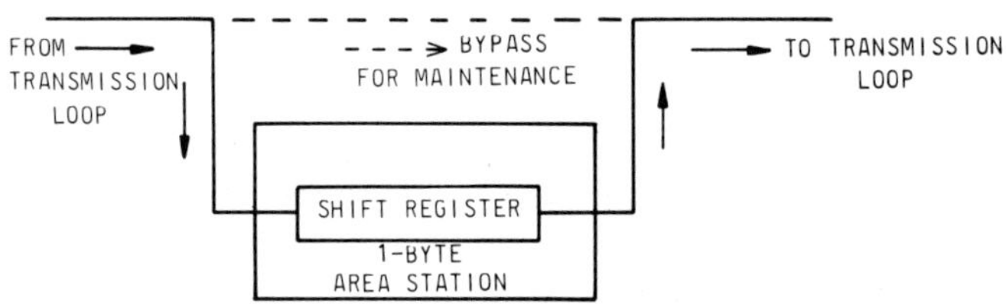

9-20 1-byte shift register

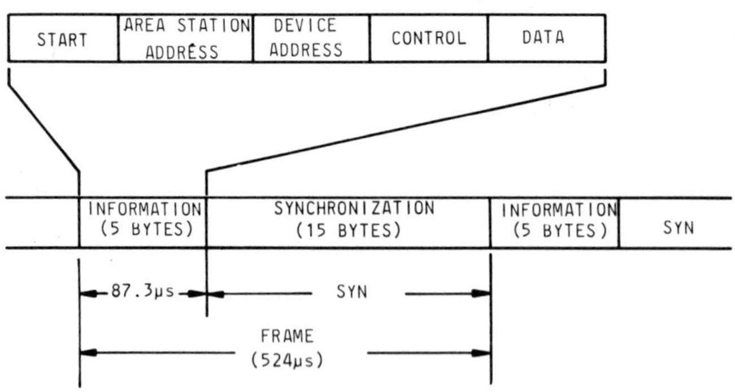

9-21 Data transmission format

The start byte and synchronization bytes are generated by the control module. The four information bytes (area station address, device address, control, and data) are generated by the program in the processor. Active frames can be separated by one or more inactive frames which serve as fillers to allow time for the program to process input frames and to prepare output frames. This procedure makes use of external devices that are oriented to slow-speed data-entry operations. Consequently, a large number of synchronization bytes are required to compensate for the slow device speed.

There are three specific addressing methods. The first method requires the selection of a unique device to which communication is directed by means of the circular bit stream. The second method requires the host processor to poll the individual units to determine which devices need service. This is done by using a preassigned area address code as a polling code. Whenever an area station needs service from the processor, it searches for a frame that has this special address code. Upon finding such a frame, the area station captures the frame and replaces the polling code with its own address. When the message returns to the processor, the program takes the appropriate action necessary to handle the request. The third type of addressing method is an *all-area-station address*. Another special code is designated for this operation. The message is directed to all area stations and every unit executes the instruction specified in the control byte. This is a broadcast mode that directs all units to perform the same operation.

The control byte is divided into two parts: *command* and *response*. An addressed station always responds to a command that is valid for that particular station with a return code in the second part of the control byte. This permits two-way communication for every step of operation in the handshaking arrangement. A data byte that is transmitted to an area station is always returned to allow checking by the processor. If the data received by the processor are the same as the data transmitted, the area station is then commanded to use the data in the form of a printout or to turn on a specified indicator light.

The serial channel, as used in the shared configuration, is particularly economical for communication when many slow devices are scattered over a relatively long distance. The loop provides two-way data transfer using a single pair of wires without having to turn the line around, and it does not require a separate pair of wires for communication in each direction. From a maintenance point of view, however, a single trouble in the loop can disable the entire communication system. The close coupling of the devices in this configuration makes it somewhat more difficult to implement changes if they become necessary.

9.4 SUMMARY

Two different types of channel-oriented I/O operations and their implementation on a small computer have been discussed. The direct memory access (DMA) facility is used to transfer a block of data words between main storage and a peripheral in a cycle-stealing mode of operation. Effectively, a word is exchanged between the peripheral and memory by the CPU yielding one or more memory cycles to the peripheral so that the I/O transaction may take place. This transaction occurs independent of the CPU and appears transparent to the executing program. A DMA transfer involves all bits in a data word being moved in parallel from/to main storage and to/from the peripheral associated with the I/O transaction. The three forms of DMA encountered at the small computer level were identified as (1) dedicated DMA, (2) selector DMA, and (3) multiplexed DMA. In contrast, the serial channel structure was shown to be extremely useful for communicating with peripherals that are not in close proximity to the CPU. A serial channel is slower than an equivalent DMA channel, but it does allow a considerable reduction in the electronics (cabling, cable drives, cable receivers, etc.) needed to interconnect a digital machine with a remote peripheral environment.

In general, I/O operations at the small computer level closely resemble I/O techniques developed for large-scale machines. The primary difference in the implementation of these features on a small machine is in the complexity of the hardware involved. Since cost is a major consideration for the small computer, features such as a DMA facility and serial channels are implemented with emphasis placed on packaging to reduce the board count and backplane interconnections.

9.5 REFERENCES

1 STONE, HAROLD S., ed., *Introduction to Computer Architecture.* Chicago: Science Research Associates, Inc. (a subsidiary of IBM), 1975.

2 KORN, GRANINO A., *Microprocessors and Small Computer Systems for Engineers and Scientists.* New York: McGraw-Hill Book Company, 1977.

3 WEITZMAN, CAY, *Minicomputer Systems Structure, Implementation, and Applications.* Englewood Cliffs, N.J.: Prentice-Hall, Inc., 1974.

4 FLORES, I., *Peripheral Devices.* Englewood Cliffs, N.J.: Prentice-Hall, Inc., 1974.

5 CLULEY, J. C., *Computer Interfacing and On-Line Operation.* New York: Crane, Russak & Co., Inc., 1975.

6 MOFFA, ROY, "Interfacing Peripherals in Mixed Systems." *Computer Design*, Vol. 14, No. 4 (Apr. 1975), pp. 77–84.

7 *Model 8/32 Processor User's Manual*, Publication Number 29–428. Interdata, Inc., Oceanport, N.J., 1975.

8 *M6800 Microprocessor Applications Manual.* Motorola Semiconductor Products, Inc., Phoenix, Ariz., 1975.

9 *TMS9900 Microprocessor Manual.* Texas Instruments, Inc., Houston, Tex., 1975.

10 *990 Computer Family Systems Handbook*, Manual Number 945250–9701. Texas Instruments, Inc., Houston, Tex., 1975.

11 *A Pocket Guide to Interfacing HP Computers*, Manual 5950–8718. Hewlett-Packard Co., Palo Alto, Calif., 1970.

12 HILBURN, JOHN L., AND PAUL M. JULICH, *Microcomputers/Microprocessors: Hardware, Software, and Applications*. Englewood Cliffs, N.J.: Prentice-Hall, Inc., 1976.

13 *IBM System/7 System Summary*, IBM Corp., Boca Raton, Fla., 1972.

14 *IBM System/7 Functional Characteristics*, IBM Corp., Boca Raton, Fla., 1972.

15 BRILEY, B. E., and W. N. TOY, "Telecommunication Processors." *Proceedings of the IEEE*, Vol. 65, No. 9 (September 1977), pp. 1305–1313.

9.6 PROBLEMS

1. (a) Describe the fundamental differences between *interrupt operation* and *direct memory access (DMA) operation.*
   (b) Carefully describe the features associated with each of the following DMA modes of operation. (If possible, illustrate your answers with appropriate figures.)
      i. Dedicated DMA
      ii. Selector channel DMA
      iii. Multiplexer DMA
   (c) Describe *interjection* and the application conditions under which it might be useful.
2. A 50 Kbps full-duplex line is connected to a large, centrally located data processing facility from a minicomputer functioning as a remote concentrator, as shown in Figure P9-2. Attached to the mini are the following devices: (1) a 300 character/second paper-tape reader; (2) an 800 bit/inch, single-track cassette tape recorder running at 125 inches/sec; (3) two model M37 TTY's that operate at 150 bits/sec (15 char/sec); (4) three model M33 TTY's that operate at 110 bits/sec (10 char/sec); (5) fifteen CRT terminals whose bit-serial transmission is to be established; (6) a card punch that punches at the rate of 100 card/minute, 80 columns/card, 8 bits/col; (7) a line printer that prints at the rate of 365 lines/min, 80 col/line, 8 bits/col. Assume no buffering is used for the CRT's and a character is represented by eight bits.

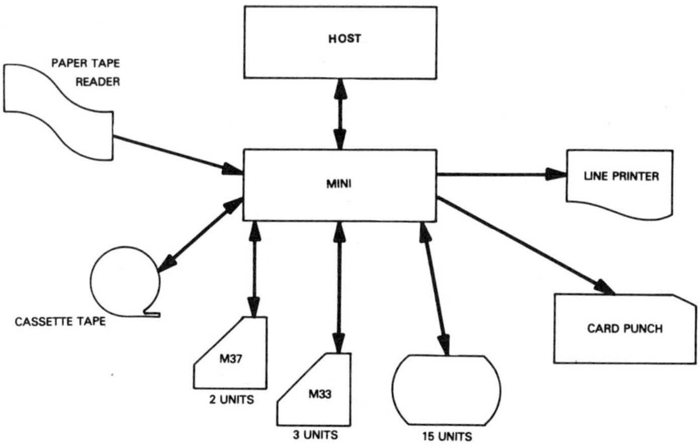

P9-2

(a) What is the *maximum transmission rate* permitted for each CRT if all peripheral units are considered to be transmitting concurrently?

(b) Let the single-track cassette be replaced by a nine-track magnetic tape transport which is to be run concurrently with the other system devices. The nine-track unit records 800 bits per inch and runs at 37.5 inches per second. What is the *maximum transmission rate* permitted for each CRT in this situation?

(c) Assume buffering is now used at each CRT. What is the *minimum buffer size* that must be used by each CRT so that the CRT transmission rate of part a of this question is obtained under the operating conditions of part b?

3. The processor shown in Figure P9-3 observes the following design conventions: (1) The cycle time of main memory is T_M μs. (2) The maximum rate at which device A will issue interrupt requests is T_A μs. (3) The maximum rate at which device B will issue interrupt request is T_B μs. (4) Device C is to operate in the *DMA mode* at a maximum rate of T_C μs. (5) The bus arbitration logic determines which device requesting use of the unified bus will be given control of the bus. (6) For a device to issue an interrupt request or a DMA request, it must first be designated the *current bus master.* (7) Each device issues a bus request (BR) and, if it is designated *bus master*, receives a bus grant (BG) signal. (8) In the event of a tie, in which two devices issue concurrent bus requests, the numerically *lowest* numbered request will be given priority—except if one of the devices is attempt-

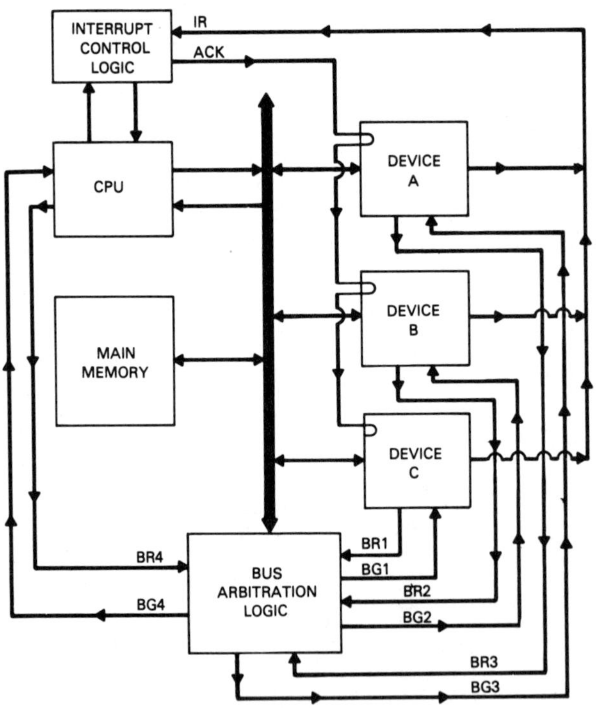

P9-3

ing to perform a DMA operation. In that case, the device requesting a DMA operation is the highest priority device.

(a) Draw a block diagram of the bus arbitration logic. *Note:* The interrupt control logic responds to an interrupt request by returning an ACK pulse which is daisy-chained through all devices that may issue an interrupt. The highest priority device in the chain will respond with an address that is the starting location of the device's associated service routine. Let the delay in the daisy chain be T_D for each device in the chain. Let the delay in the bus arbitration logic be T_L.

(b) What is the maximum rate at which device A may issue interrupts in this system with no other devices operational?

(c) What is the maximum rate at which device B may issue interrupts, assuming that device A is active and issuing interrupt requests at a rate of one every T_A seconds.

(d) If device C issues a DMA request at the same time that device A wants to issue an interrupt request, what will happen? Draw a timing diagram showing when device A will be serviced.

(e) What is the maximum rate at which device C may perform DMA transfers?

(f) Assume that the CPU *must* be given one bus cycle out of every four. Can the cycle time of the bus be different from the cycle time of main storage?

(g) Let the bus cycle time be the same as the cycle time of main storage. Under the assumption given in part f, above, what is the maximum rate at which device A may issue interrupt requests with no other devices operational? What is the maximum rate at which device C may perform DMA transfers?

(h) Is there any advantage to employing a DMA scheduler in this system?

4. The following functional building blocks are available to the system designer: (1) one or more central processing units (CPU's); (2) one or more parallel busing paths; (3) one or more direct memory access (DMA) channels; (4) independent memory modules; (5) one or more serial communication channels.

(a) Develop a high-reliability processing structure using the above building blocks and any other logic or devices that are appropriate.

(b) Compare this arrangement with the Tandem 16 *NonStop*™ System described in Appendix E as to *cost* and *reliability.*

(c) How would this system handle the separate problems of fault identification and fault recovery?

(d) How *essential* are diagnostic programs to the proper behavior of peripheral devices, and how *often* should these programs be run?

(e) What functions would *audit* programs perform in this environment and when should they be scheduled?

5. List the chief characteristics that a family of general-purpose small processors should have for use in high-reliability applications.

(a) How would reliability be introduced into DMA operations?

(b) Suppose an electronic bus switch was provided so that one or more peripherals associated with a particular processor could be logically switched over to another processor. What effect would this bus switch have on the reliability of the processor?

(c) If each peripheral associated with the family could be operated by *any* family member over high-speed half-duplex communication links, would the reliability of the family of machines be improved? In general, what techniques could be used to obtain high-reliability I/O operations using high-speed half-duplex links?

(d) What requirements must be placed on the software associated with such a family of high-reliability small processors?

6. Consider a uniprocessor arrangement that is administering a heavy data communications load, as depicted in Figure P9-6. The bulk storage devices are used to log history information on I/O transactions that take place on the communications network.

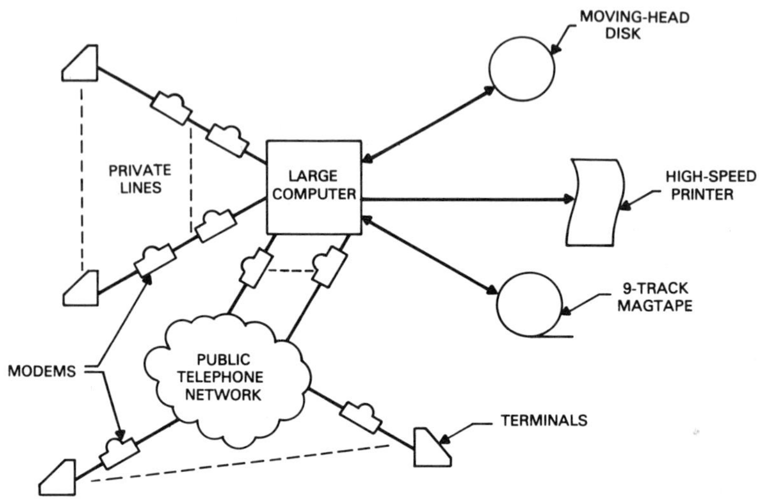

P9-6

(a) Functionally partition the facility shown into three processors: (1) a *front end* processor that handles communications requirements; (2) an *intermediate* processor that handles calculations and manages information; (3) a *back end* processor that handles administration of the data base. What specific functions may be associated with each of these machines?

(b) How should these three processors be interconnected? Show a block diagram of their interconnections.

(c) Assume that reliability is a main concern. How may high reliability be achieved with each of the three small processors? How may high reliability be achieved with their interconnections?

(d) Each of the private line connections has a reasonable probability for outage. What simple technique may be used to back up the private lines? How much *complexity* would this add to the system?

(e) Can any or all of the three small processors be functionally partitioned further into smaller machines? If so, what functions would these smaller machines perform? How would they be interconnected, and how would high reliability be introduced?

(f) Where would control reside in such a functionally partitioned structure?

(g) Is reconfiguration a *practical* approach with this functionally partitioned arrangement when a specific small processor experiences a total failure? Is there a *simple* solution to this situation?

7. Suppose it is desirable to interconnect a large computer and a small computer to a com-

mon hardware frame. The large machine is to control the hardware frame while the small computer is to be used to diagnose the hardware frame and validate its operational sanity The small computer is to report the results of its diagnosis to the large machine through two 16-bit words located in the hardware frame. The first word consists of a set of status bits that are read and/or written by both processors. The second word is strictly communication from the small machine to the large machine.

(a) Define the *minimum* set of status bits that must be used to permit communication between both machines. Assume the small computer will scan the status bits every 10 ms from its side while the large machine will scan the status bits every 5 ms from its side. The scanning rates are *independent* of each other and no interrupts are to be used.

(b) Draw a flowchart for the control seen from either side. How should the problem of *status bit contention* (i.e., one machine is trying to read the status bits while the other machine is writing into them) be handled?

(c) A simple block diagram of this interconnection arrangement is shown in Figure P9-7a. Suppose that a *second* hardware frame were to be controlled by the large machine as shown in Figure P9-7b. How does this change the control scheme for the large machine? Does this change the control philosophy of the small computer?

(d) The large machine is now permitted to communicate with the small computer using

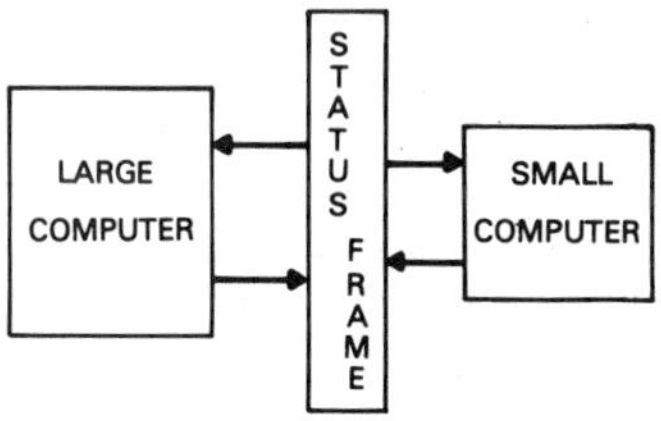

P9-7a

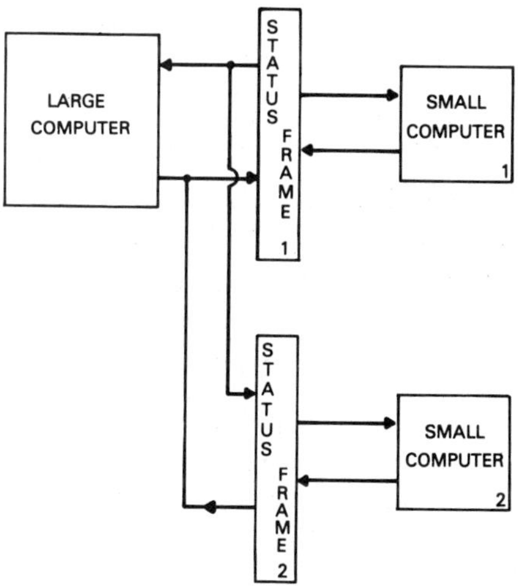

P9-7b

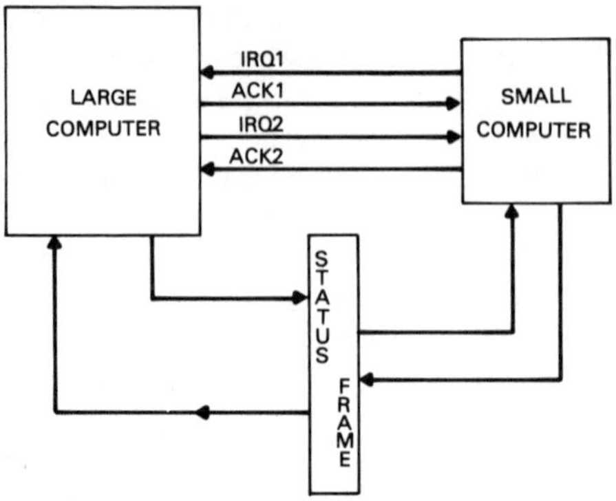

P9-7c

interrupts as shown in Figure P9-7c. *Note:* (1) IRQ1 represents an interrupt request issued by the small computer to the large machine; ACK1 is the associated acknowledgment. (2) IRQ2 represents an interrupt request issued by the large computer to the small computer; ACK2 is the associated acknowledgment. Describe the control mechanism used by the two machines to communicate information between them.

(e) Which implementation—the scan arrangement or the interrupt facility—offers the *fastest response* to changes in the status frame? Which makes the *best use* of real time? Which is the *most reliable*? Which is the *simplest* to implement?

8. Figure P9-8 shows a multimicrocomputer arrangement that uses a *decentralized bus control* structure with a *fixed* hardware priority-bus-request assignment.
   (a) Logically design the bus control logic used by each processor.
   (b) Since all peripherals communicate with a common peripheral bus, how does one processor interact with another?

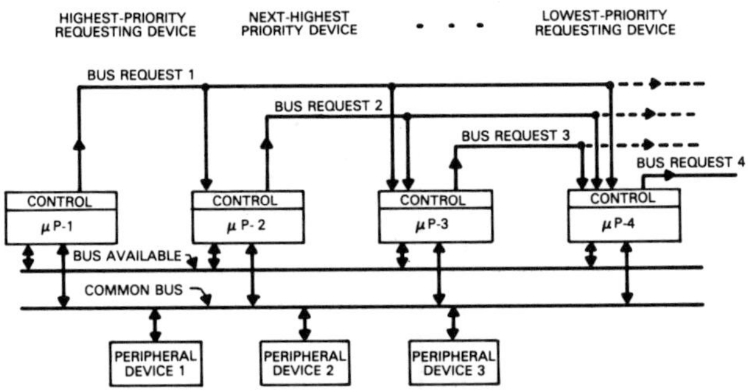

P9-8

(c) A multicomputer system is to be built using microprocessors as controllers for the following devices: (1) a high-speed line printer; (2) a floppy disk; (3) a video terminal with a local, refresh buffer; (4) a paper-tape reader/punch. Draw a block diagram of a functionally partitioned multiprocessor system that will administer the above peripherals and also perform internal calculations that may or may not be used by the peripherals. Address the problems of communication between processors, bus arbitration, and reliability.

9. Describe the control philosophy for each of the following interconnection schemes for multiple computers. In each case, outline where the overall executive or decision-making functions reside.
   (a) *A DMA-Mailbox Configuration* as in Figure P9-9a. What mechanism(s) may be used to determine when a processor's mailbox is read?
   (b) *A Ring Structure or High-speed Circulating Serial Link* as in Figure P9-9b. Specify the logical structure of the RIU.
   (c) *A DMA-RING Structure* as in Figure P9-9c. What are the advantages of the DMA-RING over the SERIAL-RING arrangement? What are the disadvantages?

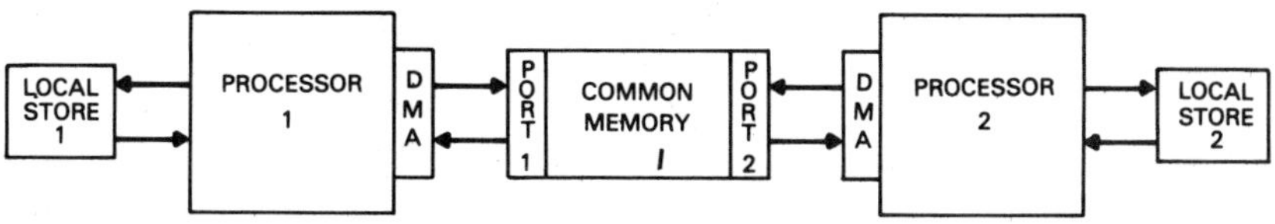

P9-9a

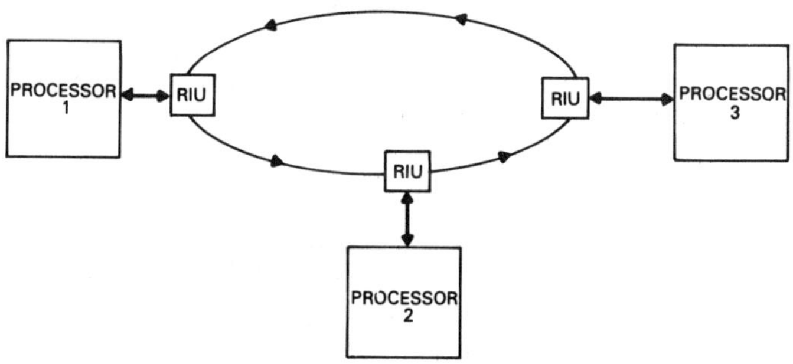

P9-9b

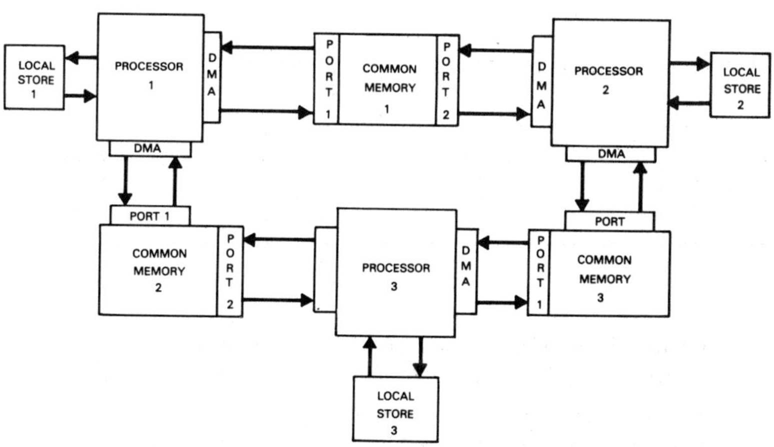

P9-9c

10. For the following multiple-computer arrangements, discuss the possible *recovery philosophy* to be used if one machine takes a catastrophic fault and is rendered inoperative.
    (a) *A Star or Exhaustive Structure* (*Serial Interconnections*) as in Figure P9-10a.

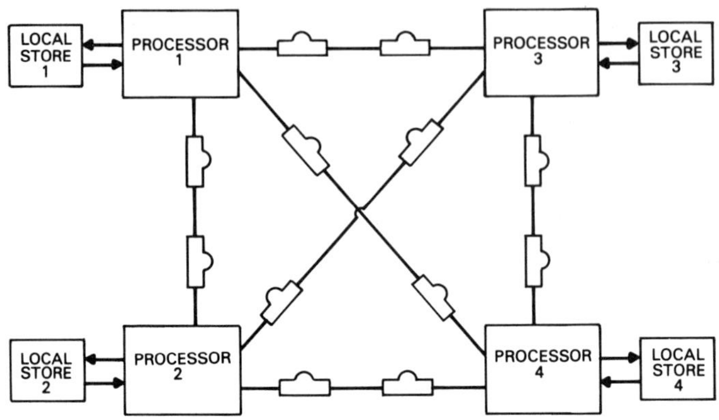

P9-10a

(b) *A Tree or Hierarchical Structure* (*Serial Interconnections*) as in Figure P9-10b. Is this a "true" tree structure? If not, redraw the interconnection arrangement so that it is.

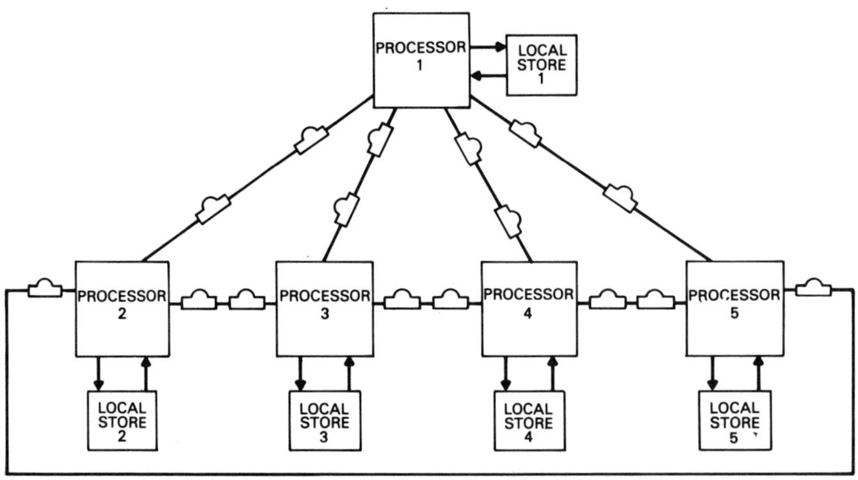

P9-10b

(c) What modifications—if any—must be made in the recovery philosophy if the serial links are replaced by DMA paths to dual-ported common memories?

11. Consider the floor plan for a home shown in Figure P9-11.
    (a) What functions could be performed by a computer based in the home?

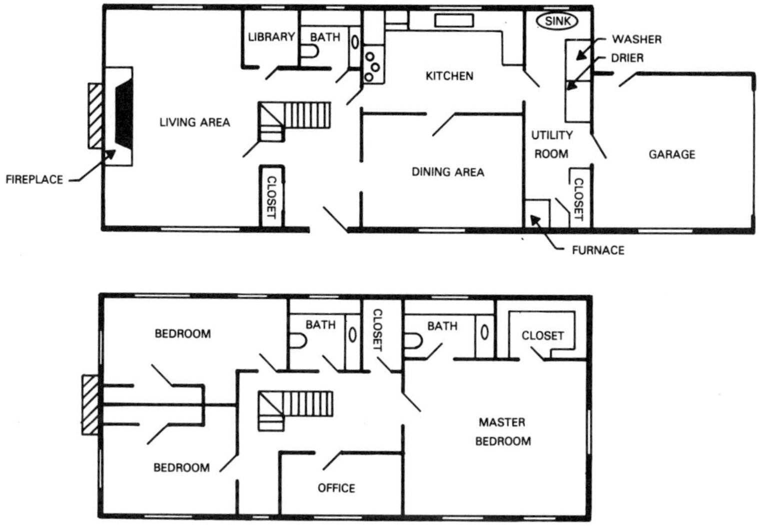

P9-11

(b) What kind of sensors, controls, and displays would be needed? Where would they be located in this house?

(c) Could you distribute microcomputers in this house? How would multiple microcomputers affect reliability? How would they affect control?

(d) How could they be maintained and serviced economically?

(e) What operations could be performed in conjunction with the home telephone?

Appendix A MOS Technology

A.1 PMOS

Improvements in semiconductor processing techniques have made commercial *metal-oxide semiconductor* (*MOS*) devices a reality. While simple MOS integrated circuits were being produced as early as 1964, not until 1967 did process control cease to be a major problem in MOS fabrication. A better understanding of solid-state surface conditions and the improvement and refinement of MOS processing led to better yields of MOS circuits with stable performance characteristics.

P-channel MOS became the early standard of LSI designs. The first P-channel process was used in the original, single-chip, hand-held calculators. The use of a low-threshold, P-channel process led to higher-speed logic devices and the appearance of the initial 4-bit microprocessor structure. The choice of the P channel over the N channel (discussed below) was based upon the ease with which the surface properties of oxidized silicon could be controlled in the P-channel process. A cross section of a P-channel MOS transistor is shown in Figure A-1. The *supporting body*, or *substrate* of the transistor, is a thin slice of lightly doped N-type silicon material. The source and the drain are formed by the selective diffusion of P+ material. A thin layer of silicon dioxide covers the area between the source and the drain, and a thin layer of metal is deposited on top of the silicon oxide. This metallic layer, usually aluminum, is called the *gate*. The silicon oxide provides the electrical insulation between the substrate and the gate. The conductive path between the source and the drain is controlled by adjusting the gate bias. This action turns the transistor on or off like a switch. The input resistance for the P-MOS transistor is extremely high because the gate is electri-

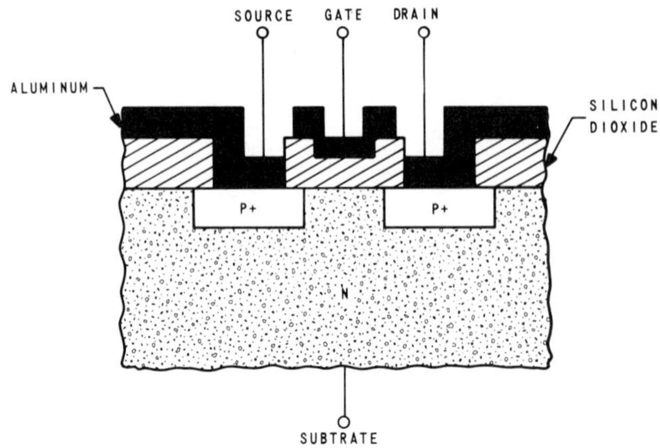

(a) CROSS SECTION

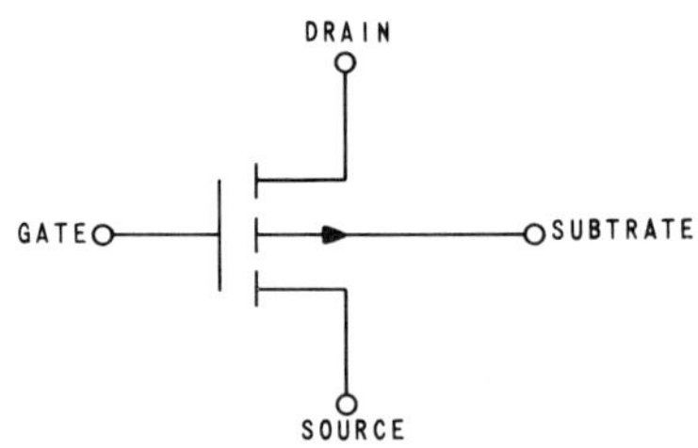

(b) SYMBOL (P-CHANNEL)

A-1 P-channel MOS

cally insulated from the substrate, the drain, and the source region. This characteristic is similar to the high impedance of a vacuum-tube circuit. When the PMOS transistor functions as a switch, the drain is normally connected to plus potential, while the substrate and the source are connected to ground.

A.2 NMOS

The relatively slow speed of P-channel circuits and their inability to work with lower voltages encouraged the rapid development of N-channel technology. Electron carriers in N-channel devices have mobility values that are two to three times higher than those of the hole carriers in P-channel devices. Consequently, the performance of N-channel devices is better, theoretically, than the performance of P-channel devices. Because of processing difficulties, however, the development of MOS technology was forced to concentrate on producing P-channel devices.

The N-channel process led to structures that included the first 8-bit microprocessors and the original 4096-bit RAM chips. A cross section of an N-channel MOS transistor is shown in Figure A-2. The substrate is made up of lightly doped P-type (instead of N-type) silicon material. The source and the drain are composed of N+ regions. The continued development of new fabricating techniques solved the earlier manufacturing difficulties associated with N-channel devices.

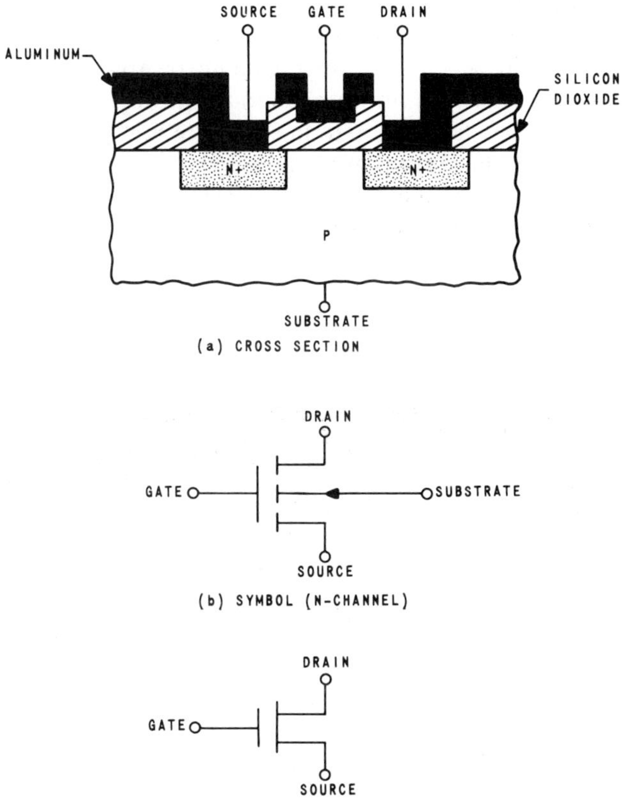

A-2 N-channel MOS

The utility of ion implantation made the manufacture of N-channel devices a practical process. It enabled the manufacturers to overcome the low breakdown voltages and the troublesome body effect of N-channel structures. The precise control of the fabrication process offered by ion implantation lowered the threshold voltage of the devices. This meant faster operation of NMOS devices over PMOS designs. In addition, the NMOS devices operated at lower voltage levels and required less power than their PMOS counterparts. Consequently, N-channel technology may be regarded as the second generation of MOS development.

A.3 CMOS

Complementary MOS (*CMOS*) technology combines both P-channel and N-channel technology on the same substrate. In Figure A-3, both transistors are connected in tandem in a "push-pull" arrangement. The N-channel transistor functions as the driver; the P-channel transistor functions as the load. Normally, only one transistor is ON except during the switching interval. The great advantage of this structure is that it requires extremely low standby power and operates at high speed. When the input voltage is at near-ground level, the source-to-drain voltage of the P-channel transistor approaches the supply voltage (V_D), and the P-channel transistor is turned ON. A low-impedance path is created between the output and the power supply while the N-channel transistor is in the OFF state, maintaining the high impedance between the same output and ground. When the input is at a positive value near V_D, the P-channel transistor turns OFF and the N-channel transistor turns ON. The output voltage in this situation approaches near-ground voltage.

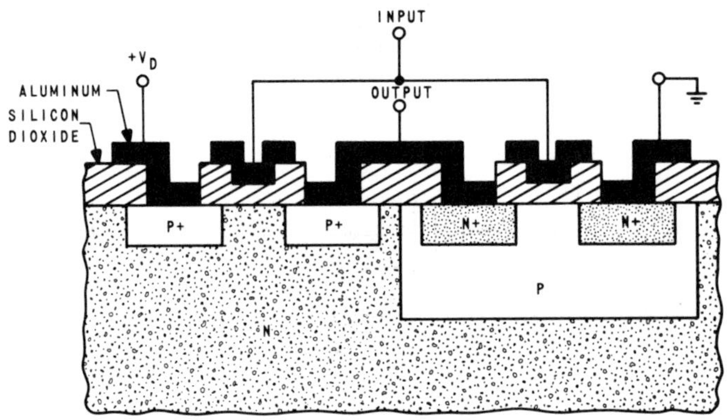

(a) CROSS SECTION

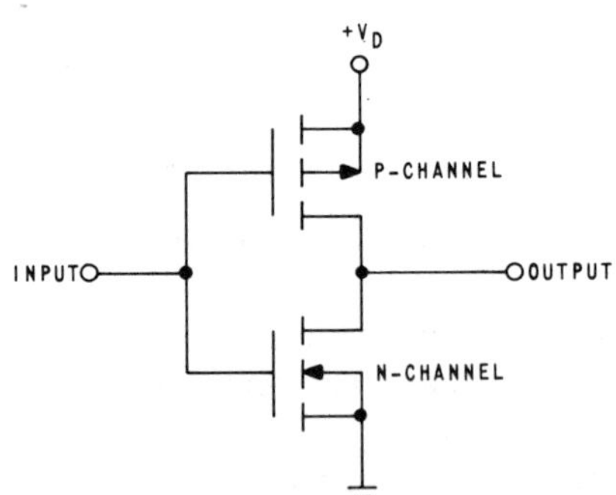

(b) SYMBOL

A-3 CMOS

In addition to low operating power, a single supply voltage with a wide range of voltages (3 to 15 volts) can be used without disturbing the circuit. A low-cost, unregulated supply is, therefore, sufficient to operate most CMOS devices. Also, CMOS circuits have high noise immunity, with a guaranteed noise margin of approximately 1.5 volts.

CMOS devices are more complex than either NMOS or PMOS designs, since both N-channel and P-channel transistors are required. There are more processing steps involved in the manufacturing operation (two additional diffusions and two additional photomasking steps). In addition, more silicon real estate is required to accommodate what are basically two separate MOS transistors.

The speed capability of CMOS can be extended into the lower range of *transistor-transistor logic* (*TTL*) by the use of *silicon-on-sapphire* (*SOS*). The starting silicon layer is epitaxially grown on a single crystalline wafer of sapphire. By a repeated process of growing silicon dioxide, etching, and diffusing, the configuration shown in Figure A-4 is obtained. Any unused silicon is removed from the substrate, leaving totally isolated islands of silicon that form individual N-channel and P-channel transistors. This structure virtually eliminates the parasitic capacitance associated with bulk silicon MOS circuits and doubles or triples the logic speed of the resulting device. In addition, the logic packing density of such SOS devices is increased by a factor of two or three over bulk silicon MOS circuits. The major technical problem with SOS technology is the substantial cost required to manufacture high-quality sapphire substrates.

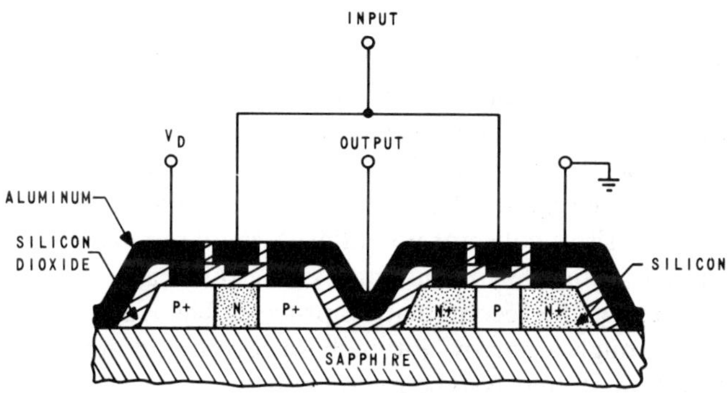

A-4 SOS CMOS

Appendix B Bipolar Technology

B.1 BIPOLAR TRANSISTOR

A simple cross section of a bipolar transistor is shown in Figure B-1. It is made up of two closely spaced P-N junctions. If the first junction, the *emitter*, is forward-biased and the second junction, the *collector*, is reverse-biased, the N-type emitter will inject electrons into the P-type base. These electrons will become minority carriers and diffuse across the base region. They are pulled across the collector junction by the field produced by the positive collector potential. A small number of injected electrons are lost to recombination as they diffuse across the thin base. A small base current flows to provide holes for the recombination process. The transfer of electrons from the N-type emitter through a narrow P-type base region and across a reverse-biased collector junction into a second N-type region constitutes *transistor action*. The electron current flow to the collector is only slightly less than the initial electron current flow from the emitter. By applying the appropriate base voltage, the collector current can be controlled in one of two conditions: high (saturated) or no (small leakage) collector current, corresponding to the ON and OFF states of a switch.

When the transistor is operated as a switch, there is a delay between the applied input signal and the output signal. This delay is due to two factors: the time required to charge and discharge capacitors (Figure B-2a) and the time required to sweep out excessive carriers in the base due to the saturation current. This delay is also called the *storage time* of the transistor. The input and output voltage relationship is shown in

Figure B-2b. When the input voltage changes from near ground to a positive voltage, a finite time is required to charge up the capacitance associated with the base-emitter junction. The input voltage must rise beyond the inherent biased voltage of the base-emitter junction before any base current starts to flow. This delay is called the *turn-on delay* (t_d) of the transistor. The *output signal rise time* (t_r) and/or *fall time* (t_f) is required to change from the 10 percent to the 90 percent points of the final value of the output signal. The delays (t_r and t_f) depend on the time constants associated with charging and discharging the capacitance at the collector node. The *storage time* (t_s) is defined as the time it takes to reduce the stored charge in the base from its full saturation value to the value at which the transistor is at the edge of saturation.

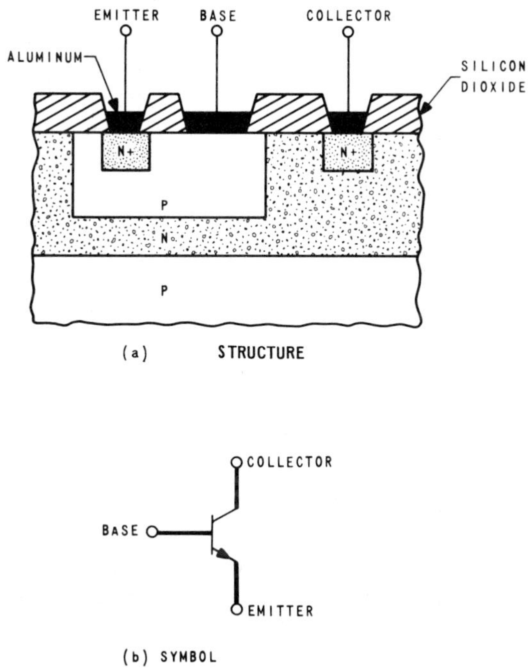

B-1 Bipolar transistor

In measuring propagation delay through a transistor or gate (which consists of several transistors), it is useful to define the propagation delay from one transistor or one gate to another at the 50 percent point of the input to the 50 percent point of the output. As indicated in Figure B-2b, the time required to propagate from high to low voltage at the 50 percent points is defined as T_{PHL}; from low to high voltage it is defined as T_{PLH}.

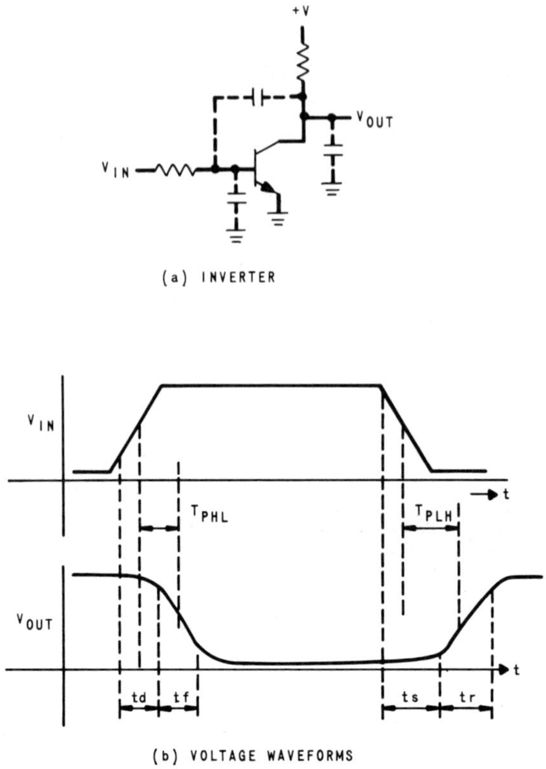

B-2 Signal delay

B.2 SCHOTTKY DIODE CLAMP TRANSISTOR

The storage time is a major factor in slowing down the operation of a transistor. Depending on the technology, it can contribute to more than half of the delay in the turn-off of a saturated transistor. A possible range of values for t would be between 5 and 50 nanoseconds. The total turn-off time (t_{off}) will normally be several times longer than the turn-on time (t_{on}). If the storage time can be reduced, the transistor action of a device can be immediately speeded up. One of the most effective techniques for reducing the storage time is to prevent the transistor from going into saturation by using a special form of diode called the *Schottky diode.*

The Schottky diode is incorporated between the base and collector of a transistor junction as shown in Figure B-3. The voltage drop across the Schottky diode is much less than that of a collector junction drop for the same forward current. A voltage drop of about 0.3 volt is typical for the Schottky drop (compared to 0.5 volt for a typical collector junction). If an attempt is made to saturate this transistor by increasing the base current, the collector voltage will drop, causing the diode to conduct, thereby limiting the base-to-collector voltage to approximately 0.3 volt. Since the collector junction is below its saturation voltage, the transistor does not enter saturation. Any excess base current will be shunted to the collector by way of the Schottky diode, preventing saturation.

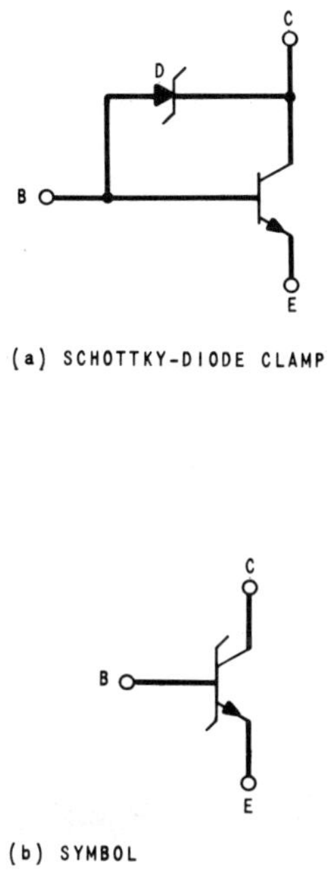

B-3 Schottky transistor

A cross section of a Schottky diode is shown in Figure B-4. The aluminum and the lightly doped N region form a rectifying junction. The aluminum acts as a P-type impurity when in contact with silicon, forming an equivalent P-N structure. This results in an excellent metal semiconductor diode. On the other hand, if N+ is diffused into the N region near the surface where the aluminum is deposited, the contact is ohmic (nonrectifying). Consequently, formation of a Schottky diode is extremely simple on an integrated circuit. Figure B-5 shows the cross section of a Schottky-clamped transistor.

The Schottky diode is formed by allowing the aluminum contact to be made in both the P-type base and N-type collector regions. Notice that the metal is in contact with the lightly doped N-collector region in order to form the diode junction. The emitter and collector ohmic contacts are made to N+ regions.

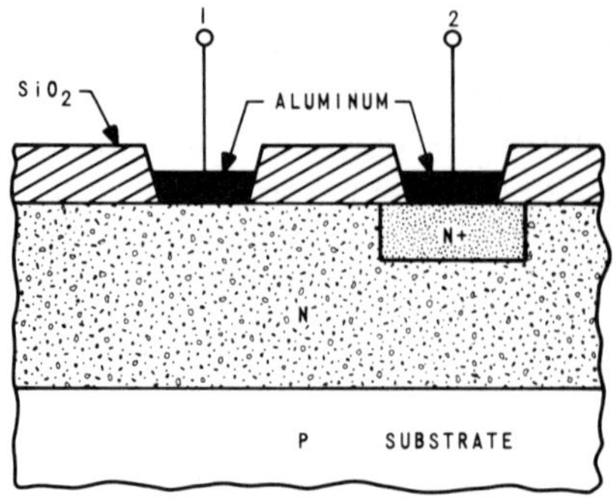

(a) CROSS-SECTION

(b) SYMBOL

B-4 Schottky diode

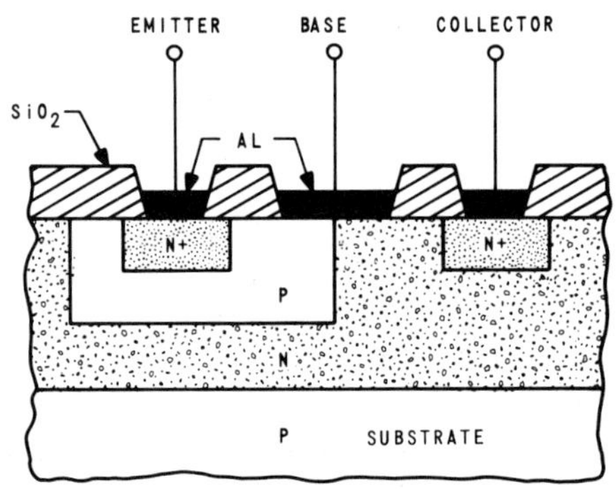

B-5 Schottky clamped transistor

B.3 INTEGRATED INJECTION LOGIC (I^2L)

The conventional form of a bipolar structure, which is rather complex, does not easily lend itself to an LSI implementation. Almost every bipolar circuit element on the chip has to be isolated in all directions. Such isolations require chip real estate that might be used for additional active devices. Similarly, the interconnections between the circuit elements on the chip reduce the available space. The end result is that the density of devices on a conventional bipolar chip is highly limited. Another equally important constraint on the density of a bipolar chip is the power requirement. The approximate total power dissipation must not exceed 1 watt. If this rule is not observed, external cooling must be provided. To limit the current flowing through the various gates, resistors are used as loads. Higher-value resistors lower the power dissipation but require large areas of silicon on a chip. This is in direct conflict with the philosophy of LSI implementation, since larger resistors reduce the density of active elements on the chip. However, if the power dissipation is lowered, it has the adverse effect of reducing the operating speed of the bipolar device. In general, higher speed requires greater power dissipation, and greater power dissipation reduces the number of circuits on the chip.

Injection logic eliminates the need for resistive components in the gate structure. This can readily be seen from the generalized form of an inverter circuit shown in Figure B-6. The load resistor is required for charging and discharging the output capacitances when the transistor is turned on and off. In addition, it provides base current to the next stage. An equivalent inverter circuit with an active load is shown in Figure B-6b. The load resistor and voltage supply have been replaced with a generalized current source, I_0. When I_0 is attached to the base of the transistor instead of to its collector, the same current source can serve the collector of the preceding stage as well as its own base circuit. By using an active load, power is not dissipated needlessly through the resistor. In addition, the current supplied to any transistor is determined by the supply voltage across the device. The supply voltage, in turn, may be easily adjusted to any desired value. The charging and discharging times of the transistor

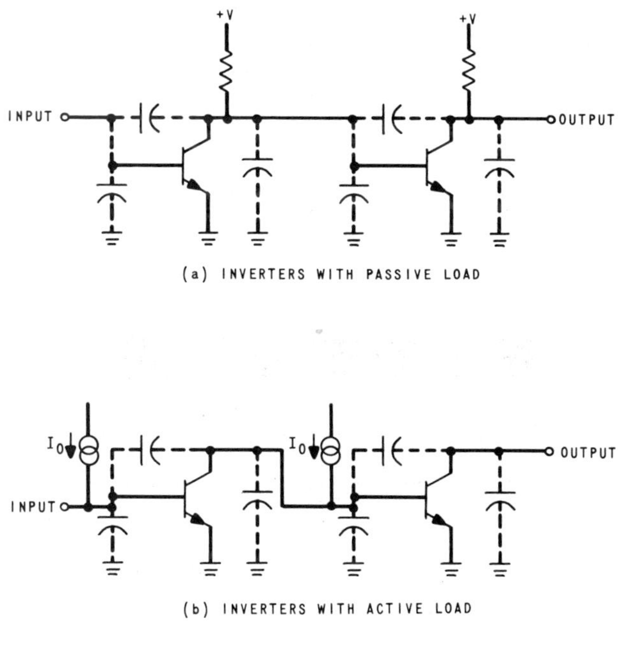

B-6 Inverter circuits

capacitors are determined by the magnitude of the current source, I_0. This, in turn, dictates the switching speed of the device.

A higher supply current will produce a faster switching time. Similarly, a lower supply current will extend the switching time of the device. By adjusting the voltage level, the logic speed of the I²L device can be tailored to a particular application.

The current source can be obtained easily with a PNP transistor in the common base configuration shown in Figure B-7a. A single PNP transistor can supply current to several NPN transistor collectors. The inefficient resistors are replaced with small PNP's. This results in a high packing density for on-chip circuit elements and a much lower power dissipation. In most LSI designs, many NPN transistor emitters are connected to a common point (e.g., ground) as shown in Figure B-7a. These designs may be greatly simplified by operating the transistor upside down in the inverted mode. This allows all common emitters to share a single N layer. Using this approach, the cross section of the PNP current injector and the NPN transistor for an I²L gate is shown in Figure B-7b. A single emitter contact will suffice for many transistors. Since there is no need to isolate the transistors, valuable real estate is saved for more active devices. Because the current-injector PNP transistors share a common N bed with the NPN transistors, the number of metal interconnections is also reduced. Although Figure B-7b shows only one pair of complementary transistors, additional pairs exist

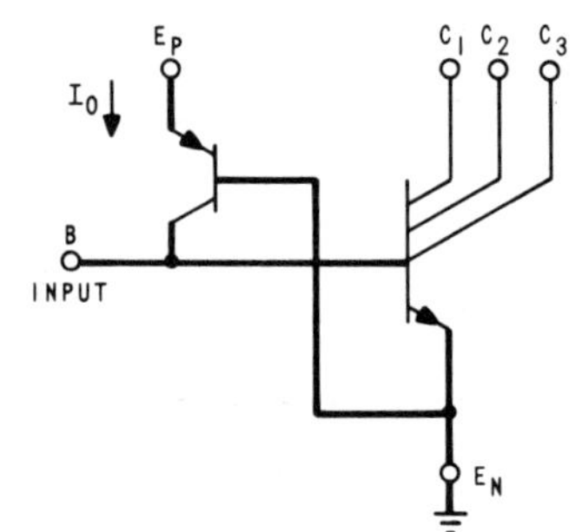

(a) INJECTION LOGIC GATE

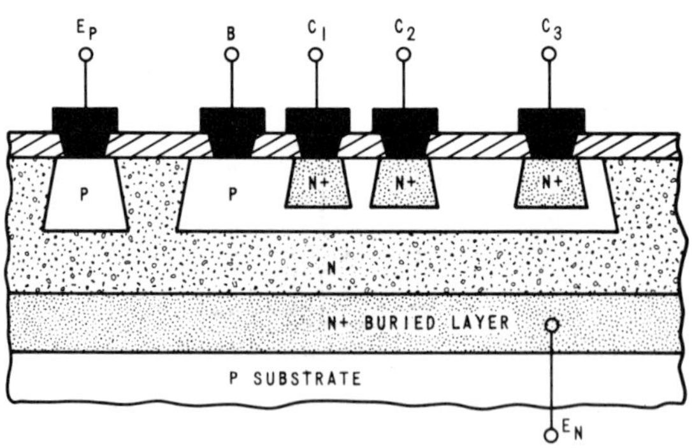

(b) CROSS-SECTION OF INJECTION LOGIC GATE

B-7 I²L gate

in the dimension that extends into the page. As a result, the P regions for the collectors of the PNP transistors and the corresponding bases of the NPN transistors can all be merged and fit into an area of a single transistor. Consequently, I²L is also known as *merged transistor logic* (*MTL*). In constrast with the typical six to eight transistors and several resistors required to produce a TTL gate, a pair of I²L transistors will function as a compact logic gate. This further reduces not only the device area required by the chip but also the number of metal interconnections needed on the chip.

B.4 SCHOTTKY I²L

An increase in the overall performance of an I²L device may be obtained by inserting Schottky junctions into the basic I²L gate. In one scheme, a multiple array of Schottky diodes simply decouples the signals on the collector output of the gate as shown in Figure B-8. The diodes perform a level shifting function that results in a better power-delay efficiency. In a typical I²L circuit, the logic swing will be given by the difference of two voltage levels that correspond to the logic values for 0 and 1. This voltage differential for a regular I²L circuit is approximately 0.75 volt. In the

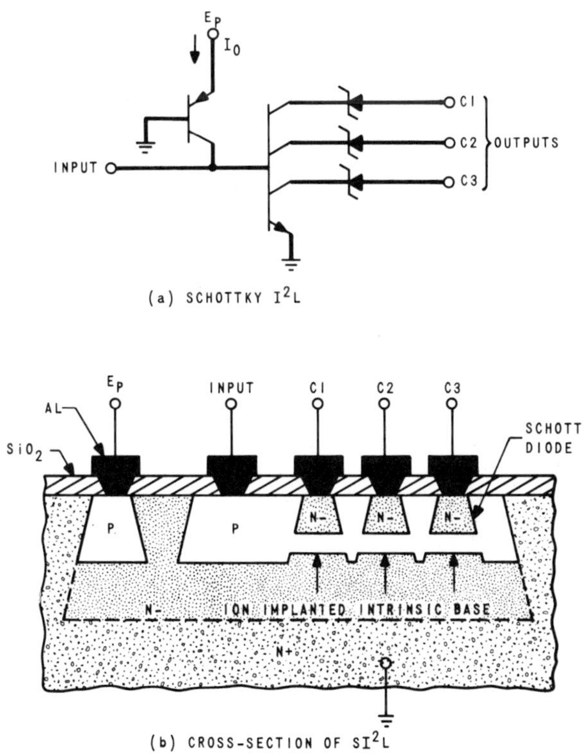

B-8 Schottky I²L circuit

Schottky I^2L circuit (*SI^2L*), the logic swing is reduced by the drop across the diode. This diode voltage drop will typically range between 0.3 and 0.45 volt.

The cross section of an SI^2L unit is shown in Figure B-8b. The Schottky diode is formed by the metal (aluminum) contact on the lightly doped N collector regions. Since the collectors are N− rather than N+ as in the conventional I^2L circuit, the collector base capacitances are reduced. This reduction in base capacitance improves the circuit delay of the device. The circuit delay is further reduced by the reduction in the signal switch of the output voltage. A practical circuit delay between 10 and 15 nanoseconds is realizable with SI^2L. This may be compared with the 20- to 30-nanosecond delay experienced by a basic I^2L circuit.

Appendix C
The Characteristics of Software

C.1 A DEFINITION

The stored program concept places all instructions in the program memory of the computer along with any data processed by the instruction sequence. All items placed in storage take the same form; they are expressed as strings of binary 1's and 0's. The term *machine code* has been used to describe such binary strings. Programs are made up of sequences of machine code that can be executed by the computer. Because of the many difficulties encountered in writing programs directly in machine code, some form of intermediate language is normally employed by the programmer to simplify the process. Programs written in an intermediate language must have their instruction sequences translated into the machine code of a particular computer. Such translators have been called *assemblers*, *compilers*, or *interpreters*.

Software may be defined as a general category that includes all programs associated with a computer. Items that do not directly relate to the machine hardware are often considered to be software as well. Consequently, software includes not only the programs that run on the system, but also the documentation describing the structure and use of each program. Software also encompasses all programming languages used on the target computing system (i.e., each language for which a translator exists to generate executable code for the target computer). The translator, which may run on a different computer, will generate machine code for the target machine. A translator run on an IBM System/370 to generate executable code for a DEC PDP-11/40 from a text source written in assembly language would be called a *cross assembler*. The IBM System/370 would be referred to as the *host computer* for the cross assembler; the PDP-

11/40 would be identified as the *target computer* (i.e., the computer that receives the executable object program module generated by the cross assembler). Thus, while the result of a translation process must be transportable to the target computer as an executable program, the source module and the programs that operate on it do not have to execute directly on the target machine to be considered part of the overall software associated with the target computer system.

This definition of software includes programs written in assembly language or programs written in a higher-level language. It does not include any control sequences that are implemented as a hard-wired sequencer(s). Considerable attention has been given to the placement of microcoded programs in the hardware/software dichotomy. Because such microprograms have been placed in read-only memory (ROM), they have been dubbed *firmware* (i.e., software modules that are "firmly protected" from being transiently changed). Traditionally, such microprograms have been supplied by the commercial small-computer manufacturers as hardware ROM modules that plug directly into the memory bus. The programs have already been debugged and function as an integral part of the control hardware. For this reason, firmware has been considered separate and distinct from software. However, many users have attempted to place macroinstruction subroutines in microcode to enhance the execution rate of these routines. The user, therefore, has had to write and debug a microprogram. Often, this can only be done in conjunction with the commercial machine manufacturer. The microprocessor revolution has further complicated this situation, since many microprocessors can only be programmed at the microcode level.

The techniques for producing good microcode require programming facilities that are very similar, if not identical, to the software support facilities required to write useful macroinstruction code. For this reason, programs written in microcode, while still referred to as firmware, will be considered software. Consequently, the T^2L implementation of a floating-point arithmetic processor would be strictly regarded as hardware, whereas a microcoded version of the same facility would represent a user package with most software features. The microcoded program for the floating-point processor would have had to be written and debugged either on a simulator or on the equivalent of the target machine before the microprogram was ever placed in ROM.

C.2 GENERAL CATEGORIES OF SOFTWARE

Three distinct software categories have emerged. These categories characterize the program modules that can execute on an arbitrary computing system.

1. *Systems software* is software that is oriented toward the efficient use of the computing system resources. Normally, this software will be independent of any application. It is designed to administer functions that recur in the normal operation of the computing system (i.e., file manipulation, operator interaction with the main console, system generation procedures, etc.). Systems software provides a standard interface to the operating environment of the machine and permits the application programmer to concentrate on application code. Systems software may be subdivided into the following categories:

(a) *Operating systems or monitors* that administer I/O operations, schedule functions or tasks which must be performed by the computing system, and handle the details of coordinating application programs for execution on the system.
(b) *Utility systems* that allow the software programmer to operate on the program's textual structure with an on-line editor, access library routines that may be stored by a variety of programs, and debug application software in real time by using an on-line debugging processor.
(c) *Language processors* such as FORTRAN, ALGOL, or COBOL compilers which provide the programmer with a graceful and precise way to generate application-oriented code. Programming is done in English-language-type statements that eliminate the need for the programmer to be concerned with the intimate details of machine operation. Such higher-level languages make the computer largely transparent to the user.

2. *Application software* is software developed by or for the user and relates directly to the requirements of the application. For a commercially obtained machine, the user typically assumes responsibility for the development of the application programs; the manufacturer supplies the systems software. If the user obtains a "turnkey" system, the manufacturer may supply the systems software and the application software. Examples of such software are turnkey business systems that perform specialized accounting functions and the firmware that controls hand-held calculators.
3. *Diagnostic software* is software that relates to the maintenance and proper operation of the CPU, the standard peripherals attached to the CPU, and those external devices interfaced to the CPU which have been supplied by the application. Consequently, diagnostic software will normally consist of vendor-supplied programs that test the manufacturer's equipment and user-supplied programs that test the application-related equipment. This category has become increasingly significant as more and more emphasis has been placed on implementing highly reliable computing systems that may be easily diagnosed and maintained.

Software, in general, requires an environment in which it may be written and debugged. Such a programming development facility consists of systems software packages that may be further classified as:

1. *Program composition software* that makes use of the language processors, text editing, and file administration capabilities of the utility system to perform program creation or program modification.
2. *Program execution software* that provides a real-time development environment for application-oriented or systems-oriented programs. In particular, this type of software includes such packages as device drivers, supervisory control programs, and on-line debugging modules that permit the programmer to debug code interactively in the actual environment in which it would normally execute.

Note that these general categories of software apply across the spectrum of computing machines. The major difference between software for the microcomputer and software for the larger machines is where program development takes place. Typically, for the microcomputer, software development will be done on a larger facility such as a mini; the debugged, executable object code would then be transferred to the small-scale machine for final evaluation.

It is a basic characteristic of software for the small machine, however, that no programming techniques are really indigenous to the mini/microcomputer. Rather, the software facilities of the small machine have been adopted from the larger computing structures. As new architectural features have made a small computer look like a large computer, the software techniques for the larger machine have been modified to run on the smaller machine. In a sense, the categories of software for the small machine computer are simply the same categories associated with the large computer.

C.3 LANGUAGE TRANSLATORS

In developing an instruction sequence for a specific computer, the programmer may write the entire coding sequence in the actual code executed by the machine (i.e., its machine language). Machine-language programming requires the programmer to use strings of binary 1's and 0's. Even very short program segments can be difficult to implement since the ordinary programmer does not think comfortably in binary. In addition, hand-coded, machine-language programs are virtually impossible to read since comments are nonexistent. The difficulties in trying to mentally translate each string of binary 1's and 0's into user-recognizable commands prevents the separate lines of machine code from being self-documenting. In short, machine-language coding is complicated and uneconomical since the programmer must devote large segments of time to interpreting exactly what each instruction will cause the machine to do.

Assembly-language programming evolved so that a programmer could have a more graceful method of writing programs. Each machine operation is given a mnemonic representation, usually consisting of three or four alphanumeric characters that convey a specific function to the programmer. For instance, the "add" operation might be denoted by ADD, while placing a word in main storage might be represented by STORE. In each operation, however, additional information is needed to complete the instruction. This information is the location of the operand to be referenced by the instruction. This underscores the main advantage of using an assembly language in writing a program; it allows the programmer to reference locations in main storage *symbolically* rather than using absolute binary addresses. The assembler accepts the symbolic name and calculates the necessary information so that the symbolic location will be properly referenced by the resulting machine-language instruction. The process of assembling executable machine code from alphanumeric text strings expressed in assembly language is called *translation*.

In general, a programmer may communicate with a specific computer using several different language levels. The most fundamental level is machine-language programming. All coding is written as strings of binary 1's and 0's; the translation is performed in the mind of the programmer. The next level up is the assembly-language programming just discussed. The programmer may be removed from the intimate details of a specific machine by employing a "higher-level language." A higher-level language allows machine operations to be expressed in statements which more closely resemble the language spoken by the programmer. Typical higher-level languages encountered at the minicomputer level are FORTRAN, ALGOL and BASIC.

Whether the programmer is coding in assembly language or a higher-level language, the instruction sequence supplied to the computer forms the source program that is to be executed on the machine. The translation process may occur in one of two ways:

1. A *self-translation system* employs the target computer itself. The appropriate translator program is loaded into the main storage of the target machine. The translator program reads the source program into the machine and translates it into an executable binary object program. The *object program module* (*OPM*) will be made up of machine-language instructions and binary data words. The translator program will then either punch the resulting object program on paper tape or save it on some bulk-storage medium. Typically, the bulk-storage medium will be on a nine-track magnetic tape or a moving-head disk.
2. A *cross-translation system* employs a host computer for the translation process instead of the target computer itself. A translator program, written to run on the host machine and produce executable machine code for the target computer, is loaded on the host. It, in turn, reads the source program and performs the required translation. The resultant object program is stored on paper tape or on a nine-track magnetic tape supplied for later use on the target machine. In some instances, the magnetic tape may be replaced by a magnetic tape cartridge.

There are three fundamental types of translators for generating object programs from source programs written in languages other than machine language. Figure C-1 illustrates general language translation and the forms in which the source program may be expressed. The three types of translators are:

1. An *assembler* translates a source program written in the assembly language of a specific machine into executable object code for that machine. Each assembly-language statement is translated into an equivalent machine-language statement on a one-for-one basis.
2. A *compiler* translates a source program written in a higher-level (compiler) language into executable object code for a specific machine. Each language statement is written to closely resemble the native language of the user (i.e., BASIC, FORTRAN, and ALGOL). One higher-level language statement may expand into many machine-language instructions to implement the desired operation. Strictly speaking, a true compiler will not generate an intermediate program composed of assembly-language statements, but it will expand directly into the machine-language object program. Certain specialized compilers, how-

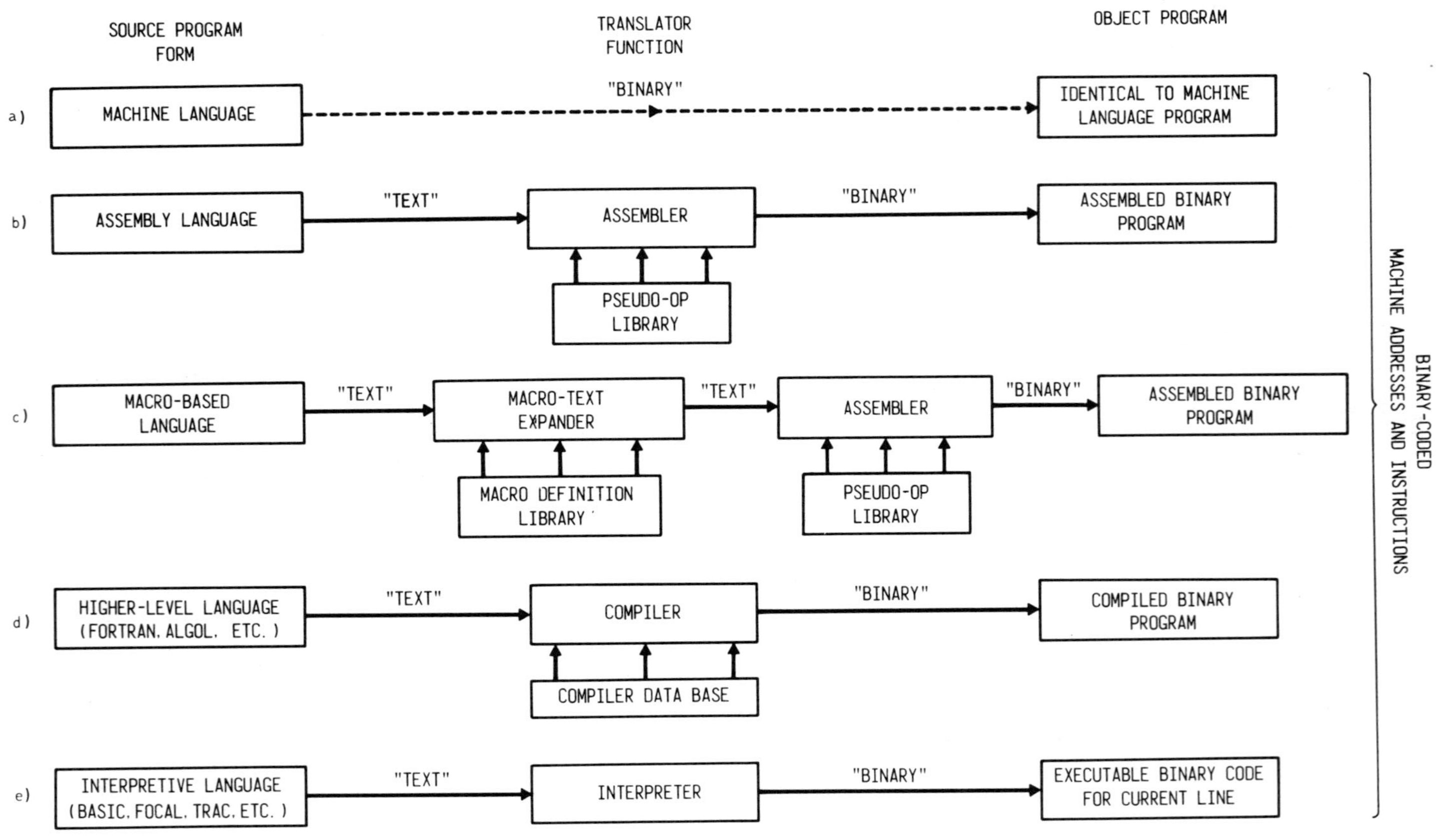

C-1 Language translation process

ever, do employ this feature. Usually, they closely resemble the macro-based language translation shown in Figure C-1.

This process employs a macro-text expander as a front end to the assembler program for the target computer on which the source program executes. The source program is read into the macro-expander as a text string. The macro-expander echoes each character in its output text string except those character strings that represent macros which have been previously defined and entered in the macro-definition library. Each defined macro expands into one or more assembly-language statements (with the proper parameters inserted), which are, in turn, inserted in the output text string from the macro-text expander. This text stream is then translated into the resultant executable object program for the target computer. More than one level of macro-expansion can be used: the output of the first macro-expander can act as the input text stream to a second, but different, macro-expander, and so on. The details of a specialized language's software implementation can be concealed in this manner. The language elements and assembler may be supplied by the developer but not the intervening stages of macro-expansion.

One can regard the macro-based language as a form of compiler language. However, the translation process has several characteristics that are markedly different from those of a compiler:

(a) A macro-assembler has none of the data-structure defining capabilities inherent in a good compiler. No elaborate data arrangements can be defined by the user unless some elaborate, special-purpose macros are defined.

(b) Each macro-call must be expanded before the assembly process can be started. Macro-expansions take time. A macro-based language can take excessive translation time since an intermediate text stream of assembly-language statements must be produced before the executable machine-language program can be assembled. For large programs (those containing a great number of source-code statements), the assembly process may require a night run on a batch operating facility.

(c) A macro-based language still allows the user to reference specific hardware registers. The language expansion will normally require the user to make register assignments and keep track of certain architectural details such as the administration of condition code bits. A true compiler language will handle such details automatically and completely remove the programmer from the structure of the machine. Two different machine times are associated with an object program. The first is the *assembly time* or *compilation time* of the translation process. The second is the time required to execute the object program. These two times are normally unrelated. Both an assembler and a compiler generate complete object-program modules for execution on the target machine. Execution begins only when the object program is loaded and control is directed to its starting address. Consequently, the execution time of the object program and the time required to generate the object program are completely divorced.

In certain applications, execution time is much less important than providing the user with the ability to interact directly with the system. For example, in the process control industry, the computer operator must interactively change set points using some form of a higher-level language. The language statements are entered directly into the system and are translated, one statement at a time, into executable machine instructions.

3. An *interpreter* translates a source program written in a higher-level language into executable object code for a specific machine. The translation process takes place on the target machine, one source-language statement at a time. The statement being translated is expanded into one or more machine-language instructions. When the expansion for that source statement is complete, the resulting machine-language instructions are immediately executed. When that instruction sequence has been completed, the interpreter fetches the next source-language statement and begins translating it.

When the interpretive language is used, execution immediately follows the translation of a source-language statement. Typically, an interpretive language will be used in an environment where on-line conversational computing would be considered attractive. Interpreters are very slow when compared to the execution time of object programs generated from either an assembler or compiler. This is due to the time required to translate each individual statement in the source program. Consequently, interpretive languages would normally not be used in applications requiring repetitive execution of a source program several times a second. BASIC is the most common interpretive language for small and large computers.

Both an assembler and compiler must supply additional information to the loader program so that all external variable references, as well as the required areas of main storage, are properly assigned.

Perhaps the prime objective of the translation process as it relates to the generation of an object program for a small computer is that the translator allows the object program and those programs with which it interacts to use main storage in an optimal manner.

Appendix D MAC-8: A Microprocessor for Telecommunication Applications*†

Abstract: Microprocessor technology will be used in the Bell System for reducing costs and providing product and process features that were not realizable in the past because of cost or size restrictions. A single-chip, byte-oriented, bus-structured microprocessor called "MAC-8" has been developed by Bell Laboratories as a significant step in this direction. MAC-8's instruction set emphasizes Boolean logical and integer arithmetic operations on 8-bit quantities supplemented by 16-bit instructions used to accomplish address arithmetic. Tools for software and hardware development are being provided for use with the incorporating of this microprocessor within products, production control and testing. With these tools the MAC-8 may be programmed and debugged entirely in a high-level language.

The microprocessor technology that has gained wide acceptance in the commercial world over the past few years will have significant effects within the Bell System. At Bell Laboratories, a microprocessor whose architecture is ideally suited for communication applications has been developed to provide the designer with device and development tools required for an effective job. With the microprocessor architecture that has

---

*With an architecture that represents considerably more than the optimization of silicon usage, a new microprocessor developed by Bell Laboratories is programmable in a high-level language. Its utilization in Western Electric manufacture can be facilitated by the extensive software and prototyping tools provided.

†The author of this article is Herbert H. Winfield. It is reprinted, with permission, from *The Western Electric Engineer*, Vol. XXI, No. 3 (July 1977).

D-1 The Bell Laboratories—Western Electric MAC-8 microprocessor packaged in a 40-pin dual-in-line package. The top has been removed to show the processor chip together with the bonded wires connecting it to the terminal pins. Photograph is actual size.

resulted, minimum hardware configuration will not penalize the small user (see Figures D-1 and D-2).

A programmer's efficiency increases with the availability of a high-level language, and for a microprocessor to be used effectively by a designer, it must be programmable in a high-level language. One way to accomplish this has been to offer many accumulators (or data registers) and address registers. To make the larger number of registers available, they are placed off the cpu (central processing unit) chip in Random Access Memory (RAM). Because of the large number of accumulators, single instructions accomplish processing functions that would otherwise require multiple instructions. The adoption of this many-register architecture for the MAC-8 microprocessor developed by Bell Laboratories has facilitated the programming of this microprocessor in a high-level language. The architecture enables the development of a high-level language compiler that produces machine-level code as efficiently as well-designed assembler-level coding.

The MAC-8 microprocessor is presently available in sample quantities. It has been designed for broad usage in Bell System equipment. Though it is not designed for "number crunching" (numerical calculations) operations as found in mini- and maxicomputers, like other microprocessors the MAC-8 is well suited to do control functions in an efficient manner. In this regard, microprocessors are finding use in test set control and production monitoring by increasing the use and function of the equipment into which they are incorporated. Microprocessor technology will be used in the Bell System for cost reduction and to provide features that in the past were not realizable because of cost or size restrictions.

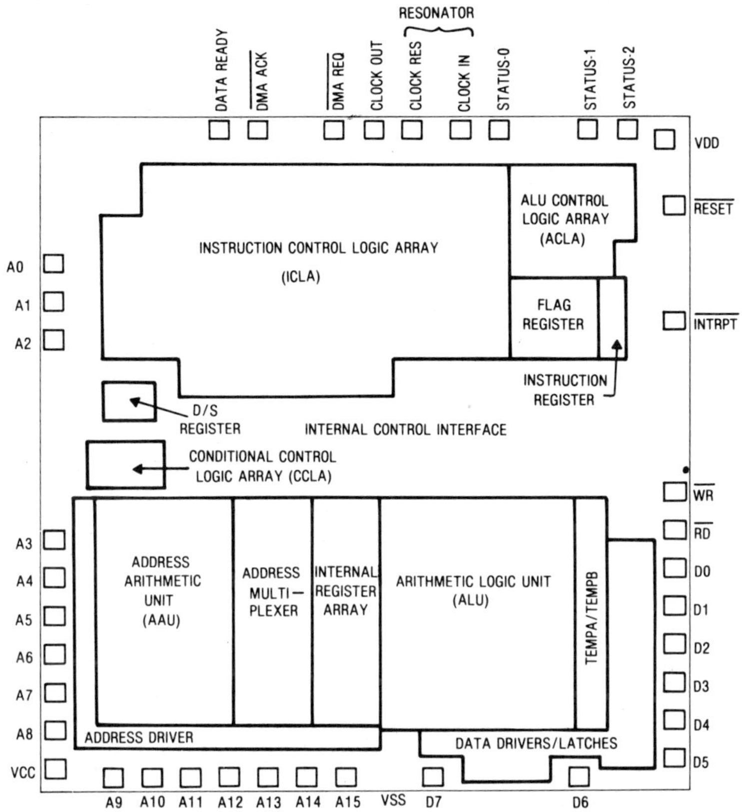

D-2 Function diagram of the MAC-8 microprocessor. Pin assignments are noted outside the periphery of the chip.

Architecture Description

It was recognized, as mentioned above, that to facilitate the product development procedure the MAC-8 architecture must be attractive for use with a high-level language. To be attractive, the architecture would have to offer multiple accumulator, or data, and index (address) registers. However, the size of the chip was limited by current technology and process yield objectives. This presented a problem. On the one hand, the cpu needed more registers that required more chip area, but on the other hand, that chip area was limited. To overcome this problem, BTL designers decided to move the user registers off the cpu chip and put them in Random Access Memory (RAM). An apparent speed penalty had to be paid because the cpu had to go off chip for its registers, but because of the fact that the off-chip registers can be accumulators, a function on the MAC-8 takes effectively less time to execute. The accumulators do not have to be loaded and unloaded when the execution is complete, nor do intermediate results have to be saved to free the accumulator.

The MAC-8 is a single-chip, byte-oriented, bus structured microprocessor. The instruction set emphasizes Boolean logical and integer arithmetic operations on 8-bit quantities. These are supplemented by 16-bit instructions used to accomplish address arithmetic. The MAC-8 cpu block diagram is presented in Figure D-3.

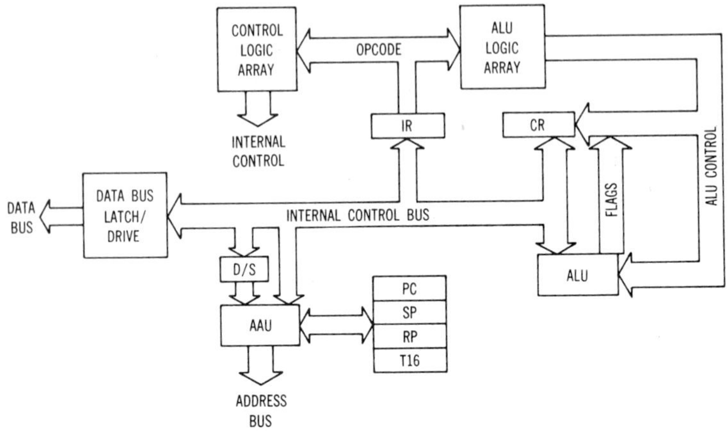

D-3 Block diagram of the MAC-8 central processing unit

Five major blocks plus three user programmable internal registers constitute the MAC-8 cpu. The Instruction Control Logic Array is the heart of the microprocessor. It is a large Programmed Logic Array (PLA) that directs the cpu circuitry through the sequence of states or steps necessary to execute instructions. A smaller PLA called the ALU Control Logic Array, controls the operation of the Arithmetic Logic Unit (ALU) if called upon to do so. The ALU performs both arithmetic calculations such as addition or subtraction and logical calculations such as "ANDing" and "ORing". The ALU Control Logic Array also directs the operation of the condition register by latching flags generated by the ALU. The Address Arithmetic Unit (AAU) is a new feature that is incorporated on the chip. The AAU calculates addresses independent of the data calculations in the ALU. The last major block is an internal register array that consists of four 16-bit registers. The Program Counter (PC) contains a pointer to the address of the next instruction to be executed. The Stack Pointer (SP) points to the address that represents the top of a "pushdown" stack that is used to save and restore the PC and Condition Register (CR). The Register Pointer (RP) points to the address of the beginning of a 32-byte segment of memory allocated for user registers. Finally, T16 is a temporary storage register used for intermediate results.

The remaining registers on the block diagram are the Instruction Register (IR), Condition Register (CR), and Destination/Source (D/S) register. The IR contains the operation code and addressing mode of the next instruction to be executed. The CR describes the result of the most recent arithmetic and logical operation. In addition, it provides user flag and interrupt enable bits. The D/S register is divided into two 4-bit nibbles that are used with the RP to specify the location in memory of individual working registers.

The advantage of having off-chip registers is the potentially large number of working registers available for use. In the case of MAC-8, at any one time sixteen registers are available. These registers can be either 8-bit accumulators or 16-bit index registers. The RP can be changed under program control, permitting the working registers to be located almost anywhere throughout RAM. By changing the RP, all sixteen working registers can be relocated saving all the information in the original locations simultaneously while making new register space available. Passing parameters between subroutines is accomplished by relocating the RP so that the new register set partially overlaps the old set, thereby saving some registers, making new register space available, and making it possible to pass parameters through the overlapped registers. Subroutines can therefore be nested with relative ease.

Pin Assignments

MAC-8 is packaged in a 40-pin Dual In-Line Package (DIP). Pin assignments are presented in Figure D-2. Sixteen pins are allocated to the address bus providing an address space of 65,536 (65K) bytes. However, address location 65,536 is not usable because it is reserved for the interrupt acknowledge function. The MAC-8 does not have a separate I/O bus, instead, I/O ports are assigned address locations and accessed as memory. This approach permits the designer to assign addresses to program memory, random access memory or I/O ports as required by the implementation. Eight pins are assigned to the data bus and provide for the handling of data in 8-bit quantities. Two pins are assigned for Direct Memory Access (DMA). DMA is useful when blocks of data are to be transferred directly between a high-speed peripheral, such as a floppy disk, and memory. The cpu examines the DMA request at the beginning of each machine cycle and provides access to the bus. The DMA acknowledge is generated when the bus is free for use by the requesting device.

The interrupt and reset inputs are checked at the start of the last machine cycle of an instruction or function. The interrupt stops program execution in such a way that the program can be resumed, while the reset returns the cpu to its initial state.

Three pins are allocated for status indications. The status bus indicates what the cpu is performing. The indicators show the internal status of the cpu. Such status indications are a valuable and unusual feature of the MAC-8. Because these status indications are available, errors can be readily detected and therefore provide for reliable operation. Table D-1 indicates the available status indications.

TABLE D-1 Available Status Indications

Function	(S_1 S_2 S_3)
PC change	0 0 0
IR fetch, no CR	0 0 1
RP change	0 1 0
IR fetch, with CR	0 1 1
No reportable status	1 0 0
Halt	1 0 1
SP change	1 1 0
Trap or trouble	1 1 1

A data ready pin is provided to permit the cpu to interface with slow memory or I/O. Two pins are assigned for clock inputs. The cpu has its own internal clock circuitry that is designed to operate from DC to over 2MHz. The clock input requires a resonator in the form of a crystal. The clock output pin provides a clock signal for use with peripheral hardware. Power supply requirements will be discussed later.

Addressing Modes

The MAC-8 architectural decision made space available on the cpu chip that would otherwise have been required for registers. This space was profitably used to implement the Address Arithmetic Unit (AAU). The AAU calculates addresses independent of data calculations in the ALU giving an inherent speed advantage. More flexible addressing modes are made available by the AAU. These are shown in Table D-2.

TABLE D-2 Addressing Modes for the MAC-8

Basic			Special	
Mode	Destination	Source	Destination = 15	Source = 15
0	Register	Register	Register	Immediate
1	Register	Indirect	Direct	Immediate
2	Offset memory	Register	Offset stack	Immediate
3	Auto increment	Register	Auto increment	Immediate
4	Offset memory	Offset memory	Offset stack	Offset stack
5	Register	Indirect	Register	Direct
6	Register	Offset memory	Register	Offset stack
7	Register	Auto increment	Register	Auto increment

The eight basic modes represent a means of determining a source operand address and destination operand address. Source and destination fields that equal fifteen have special interpretation and extend the addressing capability of the cpu. Counting the submodes within each addressing mode brings the total number of usable modes to 21. The modes determine how the effective addresses of the operands of an instruction are formed. For the basic addressing modes, the possibilities include register, indirect, offset memory and auto-increment. Special modes add direct, immediate and offset stack possibilities. The register operand contains data in 8- or 16-bit quantities for 8- or 16-bit instructions respectively. The indirect operand contains a pointer to an address in memory where the data can be found. The offset memory operand contains a memory pointer to which an 8-bit signed displacement is added. The new address points to the location in memory where the data can be found. The auto-increment operand points to an address location where the data is located. The address is then incremented after the memory location is accessed.

In the direct operand, the address pointing to the data in memory is included as two additional bytes of the instruction. Because the address is written into the program, it is always a constant. The offset stack operand is similar to the offset memory operand, except that the memory pointer is now the SP and the 8-bit signed displacement is added to it. The offset stack operand permits easy interrogation of the contents of the stack.

Instruction Set

Three types of instructions are executed by the MAC-8: Arithmetic and Logical (A/L), Control Transfer, and Special. Arithmetic and Logical instructions perform an operation on one or two operands. Operands can either be the contents of a register or a memory location. A/L instructions are either dyadic or monadic. Dyadic instructions operate on two operands called the destination and source. Add, subtract and compare are examples of A/L dyadic instructions. The result of the operation is generally returned to the destination. Monadic instructions operate on one operand. The single operand serves both as source and destination. Increment, decrement and negate are examples of A/L monadic instructions.

Instructions are usually executed in sequential order. Control transfer instructions alter the sequential order by setting the PC to another value. Control transfer instructions take two forms. The short form, which includes branch, call, and return from subroutine, is unconditional and uses abbreviated addressing modes. The call conditional form, which includes jump on condition, call on condition and return from subroutine on condition, executes the instruction depending on a condition being set or cleared.

Special instructions operate on internal processor registers (RP, SP) and significantly change the state of the program. BUMP and DEBUMP instructions are used to manipulate the RP, while PUSH and POP instructions are used to manipulate the SP.

MAC-8 instructions require one to six bytes depending on the addressing mode and D/S designation. Figure D-4 represents the encoding for a basic A/L instruction and jump on condition instruction. The basic A/L instruction contains two bytes. The first byte contains a 5-bit operation code and 3-bit mode field. The second byte contains two 4-bit nibbles used for the source and destination pointers. Control transfer instructions require only a destination field. The source field can be used to specify which of sixteen possible conditions is to be evaluated. The example in Figure D-4 indicates that because two modes are allowed for this instruction, one mode bit is all that is needed. The operation code, therefore, occupies seven bits Special encodings (for example, "Halt") do not require the second byte and consist only of a one-byte opcode.

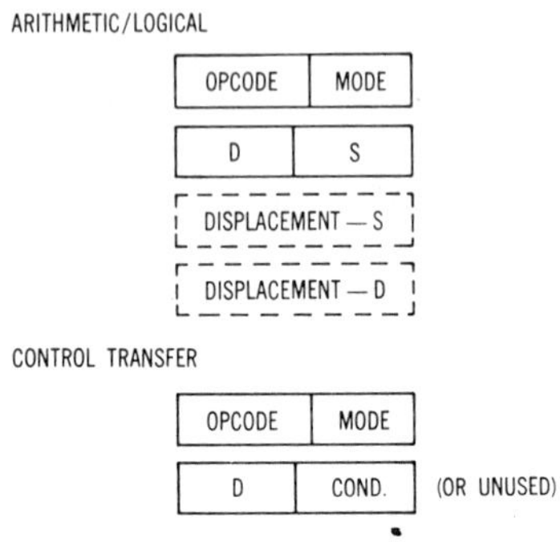

D-4 Instruction formats

Considering the addressing modes, the instruction formats, and the ability to define memory locations as accumulators or indexing registers provides for a rich instruction set that has over 400 instructions. Because the MAC-8 registers can function as accumulators, programs require less instructions and, therefore, less program memory. Studies have indicated that a memory savings as much as 30 percent can be accomplished compared to a hypothetical machine with a single accumulator. Furthermore, because a program requires less instruction to perform a task, the throughput of the cpu is greater than the hypothetical machine mentioned above.

Device Implementation

CMOS technology was chosen because of the flexibility of having both n-channel and p-channel transistors on the same chip. In addition, CMOS technology offers low power dissipation compared to NMOS technology, while meeting other objectives.

CMOS also permitted the mixing of different kinds of technology on the chip. Full CMOS was used for most of the random logic and control portions of the chip. CMOS technology requires an n-channel transistor for each p-channel transistor and, therefore, is not as efficient for complex circuits because of a penalty in chip area that must be paid. To save chip area, pseudo-NMOS circuits were used. These circuits are NMOS with a shared p-channel load transistor. Dynamic pseudo-NMOS circuits were used for the control PLAs. The ALU circuitry was not suited for CMOS because of its complexity. CMOS would use almost twice the area over that required for pseudo-

NMOS. Because the ALU is typically used only 20 percent of the time for an instruction, it is switched off when not in use. This approach contributed to reducing the power consumption of the chip. The end result being a device having a gate density approaching NMOS with power consumption typical of CMOS.

The MAC-8 cpu chip measures 220 × 230 mils and uses in excess of 7000 transistors. Figure D-2 indicates the functional blocks. The cpu was designed for 2-MHz operation at 12 volts. Running at 2 MHz, the power consumed is less than 200 milliwatts. Supply voltages can be varied from 4.5 to 13 volts, while the internal clock can operate from DC to 2 MHz. A second 5-volt supply is required for the Transistor-Transistor Logic (TTL) interface circuitry. Single 5-volt operation is possible if the clock frequency is reduced to approximately 600 KHz and the 12-v supply reduced to 5 v. All inputs and outputs of the cpu are directly TTL compatible. On-chip TTL circuitry can drive one standard load at 100 picofarads.

Software Development Tools

The MAC-8 architecture was adopted to provide the programmer with the tools necessary to permit efficient microprocessor developments. Because of this architecture, tools exist that permit the MAC-8 to be programmed and debugged entirely in a high-level language. Without the availability of these features, the programmer is obliged to debug at the assembly language level.

Software development tools include a compiler, assembler, linker/loader, simulator, and various library and utility routines. Figure D-5 shows the interrelationships among the major components of the software development tools for the MAC-8.

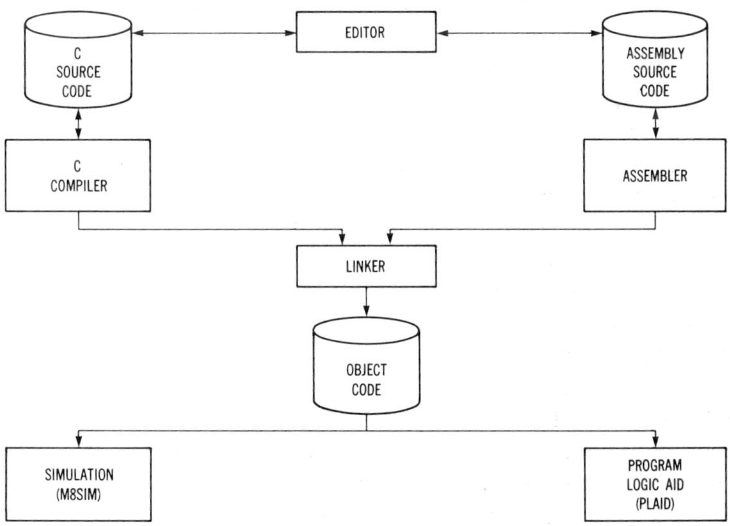

D-5 MAC-8 software development support system

The software development tools to support the MAC-8 are executable on the UNIX operating system in a time-shared environment. UNIX is a BTL developed operating system running on various PDP 11 series computers. UNIX is generally available to the Bell System community. The MAC-8 software development tools will be centrally supported in BTL by the UNIX Support Group.

Studies have indicated that programmer productivity can be increased with the use of a high-level language. MAC-8 programs can be generated using C-language, a BTL developed compiler language. Because a programmer can work more efficiently in a high-level language, it is possible to try several approaches to a development algorithm in the time it takes to program one at the assembly language level. C-language provides for increased control over the machine resources by permitting the specification of character variables to allow for the manipulation of memory; the assignment of pointer variables to allow address manipulation; and the assignment of register variables to allow register manipulation. The compiler produces relocatable object code. It is anticipated that C-language will be the primary language of MAC-8 because the compiler produces efficient code generation in a systematic way.

MAC-8 Microprocessor

When compared to a high-level language, the use of an assembly-level language is less desirable. Assembly-language programming will be required, however, for some applications. MAC-8 assembly language gives control over the instruction set while offering C-type constructs. This assembly language has purposely been structured in the image of C-language. The structured assembly language benefits the programmer because only one syntax convention must be learned. Even though the assembly language resembles C-language, it is nonetheless a true assembly language. There is a one-to-one correspondence between the assembly instructions and machine instructions. The assembly language can specify every machine instruction and every addressing mode for each instruction. For cases where every memory byte and machine cycle is precious, assembly language is available.

Both compiler and assembler produce relocatable object modules. The MAC-8 linker/loader provides the capability to join together specified relocatable object modules and assign absolute addresses. It is possible to link relocatable C-language routines and assembly language derived routines into absolute modules ready for execution. Therefore, assembly language programming can be limited to critical routines and the balance programmed in C-language for development productivity's sake.

The ability to generate programs in an efficient manner is important to the designer. Equally important is the ability to simulate programs in software without the requirement for an investment in hardware. A software simulator called M8SIM has been designed to run under UNIX. M8SIM is a low-cost method of testing, debugging and correcting MAC-8 programs. The simulator uses a UNIX/C command language and avoids the need to learn a new command language. The programmer can converse in symbolic and absolute terms with the simulator. It is possible to display values of symbols, registers and expressions. Other simulator functions include memory management, simulation/execution control, breakpoint capability and user-controlled timers. Because M8SIM is a software package there can be no real-time execution. The simulator is typically the first step in the program debugging process.

Various library and utility routines complete the software development offering. A review of the MAC-8 instruction set reveals that multiply, divide and floating point operations do not exist. However, these functions have been implemented in software and are available as system calls. A memory management routine provides for the assignment of RAM addresses, program memory addresses, and the addresses assigned for input/output ports. Several utility programs are available to the user. They include: a disassembler routine that generates assembler code from object code, provides a symbol table and cross reference information; a routine that converts object format to hex format used to write PROMS; a routine that tells the size in bytes of all program segments; and a routine that prints the symbol table.

The software development tools for MAC-8 ensure that the developer has the tools required to be as efficient as possible.

Hardware Development Tools

After the software has been specified, written and debugged using the simulator, the next step is to execute the program on some form of development hardware. The Program Logic AID (PLAID) has been designed to provide a high-level development capability to MAC-8 users. It will enable the designer to code, debug and simulate a MAC-8-based implementation from a single console. PLAID provides an interface to the UNIX-based software development tools and also provides a hardware system to simulate the MAC-8-based design. PLAID will allow the user to test an implementation in real-time with real I/O operations.

The use of microprocessor technology is relatively new in the Bell System. It is important, therefore, that designers have educational facilities available to ease the transition from digital logic to microprocessor technology. The MAC-TUTOR is being designed to enable a designer to learn MAC-8 fundamentals, either through formal instruction or self-instruction using a programmed text. In both cases the MAC-TUTOR will function as an electronic textbook. Figure D-6 is a photograph of MAC-TUTOR. The MAC-TUTOR will be a single-board computer complete with I/O. It will function as a stand-alone desk top unit. Programs can be coded, compiled, simulated, debugged on UNIX, and down-loaded into MAC-TUTOR. In addition to being an educational tool, MAC-TUTOR could be used for low-end design work, where the sophistication of PLAID is not needed.

A MAC-8-based cpu card for the PROETEL system has been designed. PROETEL is a general-purpose microcomputer that performs a common control function for E-telemetry terminals. In addition to the cpu cards, I/O cards,RAM cards, PROM cards and a card cage are available. Use of the MAC-8-based replacement card and the PROETEL card set precludes the requirement to design printed circuit cards for applications such as test sets and process controllers.

D-6 The MAC-TUTOR, an "electronic textbook," will enable a designer to learn MAC-8 fundamentals, making the transition from digital logic to microprocessor technology.

Development Scenario

A development scenario of a hypothetical design is presented to show how the tools of the MAC-8 system come together. It is assumed that the designer has access to UNIX, a MAC-TUTOR, a teletypewriter terminal, a PROETEL card set and frame.

In the conceptual stage, the designer determines the requirements of the proposed system. These requirements are reflected as block diagrams of both the hardware system and the software programs to drive the system. Using the software block diagram, the designer implements the logic from the diagram in C-language code. The UNIX text editor is used to create a source file. If the implementation calls for a time critical routine, it will be programmed in MAC-8 assembler language, using the UNIX text editor to create the source file. The C-language source file is compiled by the C-compiler. The assembly source file is assembled by the MAC-8 assembler. The output of both compiler and assembler are relocatable object modules. These modules can be linked together by the linker/loader, the result being an object module having absolute addresses. At this time, program, data, and I/O addresses are assigned by the designer.

The next step is to begin the software debugging process. The MAC-8 simulator allows non-real-time simulation of the program to check logical operation and execution. Input/output is simulated through use of UNIX files located at the addresses assigned to I/O. When bugs are found and corrected, the designer returns to the UNIX text editor and makes corrections in the appropriate source file. The program is then reassembled or compiled, and linked as above. The debugging process continues until the program executes on the simulator to the satisfaction of the designer. Until this point, no new investment in hardware has been necessary.

Work on the hardware design could have been going on in parallel with the software design. It is now time to estimate and specify the hardware required to support the system, and estimates can now be exact. The exact size of the program in bytes is available using the MAC-8 utility called M8SIZE. The size of the program indicates the quantity of program memory required for this application. Program storage and working storage requirements can be determined to segregate read-only from RAM portions of memory if both are employed. The hardware configuration of the PROETEL card set (using the MAC-8 card) and frame can now be determined. The PROETEL system will be the controller of the equipment under design.

The program is then put into hexadecimal (hex) format using the MAC-8 utility called M8HEX. The program in hex format is down loaded into MAC-TUTOR to encode the PROMs for use in the equipment under design. Assuming the program is less than 3K bytes, the PROMs can be plugged into sockets on MAC-TUTOR and the program verified. After the PROMs have been verified, they can be used to populate the PROM boards for the equipment under design. This is the point where the software to run the system is joined to the rest of the hardware required for the system. The final step in this development scenario is the verification of the integrated system. Oscilloscopes, logic analyzers, and the like can further assist the designer to verify system operation. Development of a system using MAC-TUTOR represents a "brute force" approach. A more sophisticated approach would require the PLAID development system. PLAID enables complete verification of the hardware using the slave MAC-8. Once the cards are assembled in the frame, MAC-CABLE can be used to verify the final equipment design. However, it must be noted that this additional sophistication requires a significantly larger capital outlay than for the MAC-TUTOR.

Conclusions

The MAC-8 is a microprocessor that has all the tools to enable a designer to do a design in an efficient and cost effective manner. Its architecture goes beyond the optimization of silicon usage. It reflects the efforts of systems, software and integrated circuit designers working together to design a microprocessor well suited for telecommunication applications. MAC-8 is not merely a microprocessor device. The extensive software and prototyping tools are key items. It is these tools that permit efficient and cost effective designs. The availability of MAC-8 will benefit the Bell System by enabling the design of features into Western Electric products that could not have been implemented otherwise because of size or cost restrictions.

Appendix E Tandem 16 NonStop™ Computer System*

[The Tandem 16 system represents one of the first commercially available small computer systems expressly oriented toward applications that have a high reliability requirement. The architecture of the Tandem 16 system is highly innovative, and its description is included here so that the interested reader may relate the system's implementation to concepts discussed in the text.]

The Tandem 16 system, described in this document, represents a major departure from existing mini/midi computer architecture. For the first time, a complete system has been designed to meet the growing demand for on-line, transaction processing systems with "fail-safe" capability. Using standard Tandem 16 hardware and software modules, the user may build a system to match necessary requirements exactly, both in throughput and in system reliability. No special or custom designed hardware or software is necessary. Equally important, the Tandem 16 can grow to meet increasing throughput demands with no change in operating system or applications software and without loss of the system during expansion.

One Tandem 16 processor module is a powerful computer. Two or more Tandem 16 processor modules connected together by Tandem's high-speed interprocessor bus structure (DYNABUS) provide an extremely powerful multiprocessor system. (See Figure E-1.) This capability coupled with the Tandem 16's unique *NonStop* or "fail-safe" features make it the ideal choice for systems requiring economy today plus assured power to meet tomorrow's increased demands.

---

*This material is reprinted, with permission, from *Tandem 16 NonStop Systems Introduction* (Cupertino, Calif.: Tandem Computers, Inc., 1975).

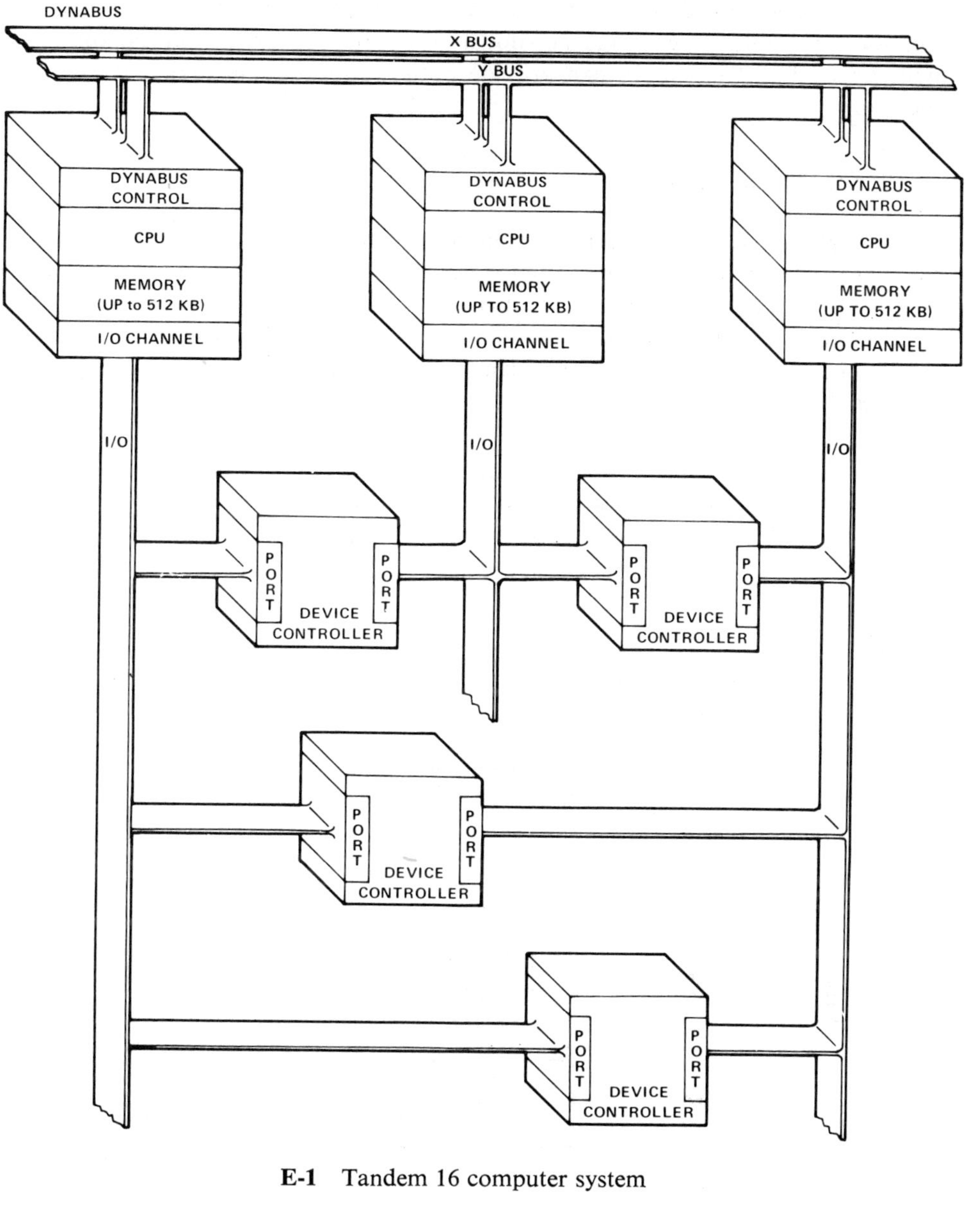

E-1 Tandem 16 computer system

The Tandem 16 computer system fills three important and interrelated needs: it is a computer system where applications run *NonStop* regardless of a module failure, it provides a computer system that can support high transaction rates to large on-line data bases, and it provides a system that is easily adaptable to any application.

The basic design philosophy of the Tandem 16 computer system is that no single module failure will stop or contaminate the system. This assurance of *NonStop* operation is sometimes called "fail-safe" when no loss of throughput occurs as a result of a failure or "fail-soft" when some slowdown occurs but full processing capabilities are maintained. The Tandem 16 can provide both "fail-safe" and "fail-soft" modes of operation.

Processor Modules

A single Tandem 16 computer system may contain from two to sixteen processor modules; each module contains a micro-programmed central processing unit, its own memory (up to 512k bytes), and its own micro-programmed input/output channel. (See Figure E-2.) Each processor module is fully capable of operating independently of all other processor modules yet can be configured to back up other processor modules.

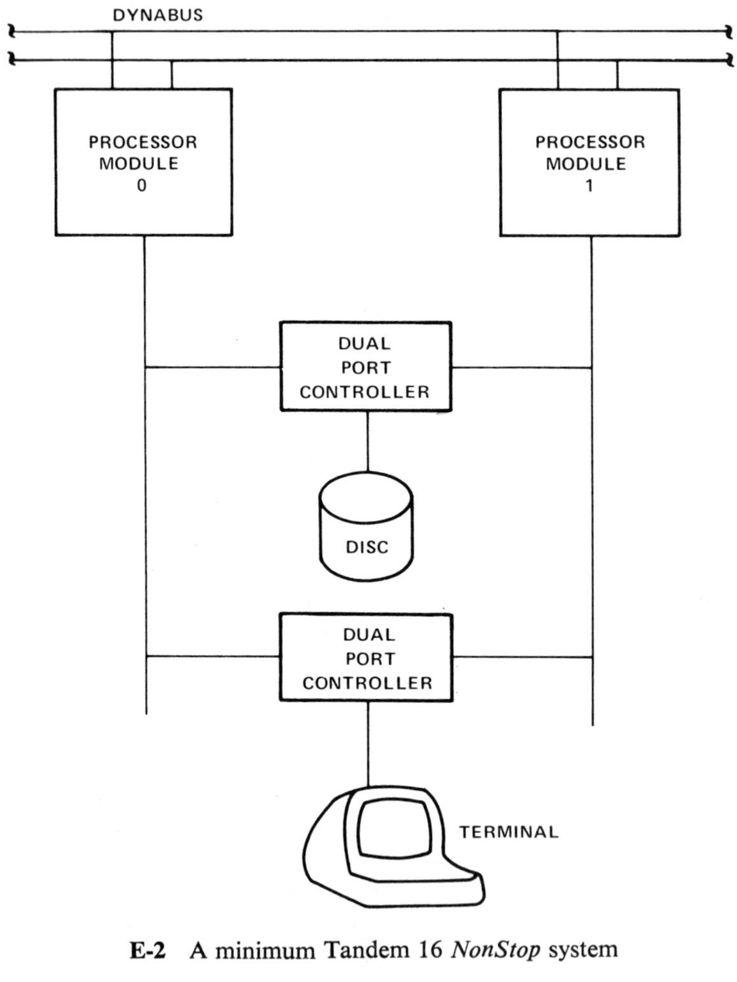

E-2 A minimum Tandem 16 *NonStop* system

Interprocessor Buses (Dynabus)

Each processor module is connected to all other processor modules via redundant high speed interprocessor buses. Programs running in one processor module communicate with programs running in other processor modules by means of these buses. Each interprocessor bus if fully autonomous, operating independently of (but simultaneously with) the other bus. The use of two buses assures that two paths exist between all processor modules in the system.

Input/Output Channel

Input/output devices (i.e., magnetic tape units, disc drives, terminals, etc.) are interfaced to the computer system via dual-port I/O controllers. Dual-port means that each i/o controller is connected to the input/output channels of two processor modules. This provides two paths of communication to each input/output device. A dual-port controller is "owned" by (i.e., will accept commands from) only one processor module. But in case of a failure, the other processor module can take control programmatically. The dual-port controllers are designed so that the number of components common to both paths are at a minimum.

Tandem 16/Transaction Operating System (T/TOS)

Overseeing system operation is the Tandem 16 operating system. The operating system provides the multiprocessing (parallel processing in separate processor modules), multiprogramming (interleaved processing in one processor module), and *NonStop* capabilities of the Tandem 16 computer system. A copy of T/TOS resides in each processor module.

The operating system automatically schedules application programs for execution according to an application-assigned priority, provides memory management functions (automatic overlaying, swapping to disc, etc.), and gives application programs the capability to start programs executing in any processor module from any processor module.

File System

As part of the operating system, the Tandem 16 file system provides a single interface between programs and the outside world. The file system, which handles all data transfers, provides the capability for any program running in the system to communicate with any other program running in the system as well as any input/output device connected to the system; programmers need not be aware of the physical location of the device/program. Up to 4094 bytes can be transferred in one file system operation.

Index